# Communication for Business and the Professions

**Seventh Edition**

## Patricia Hayes Andrews
Indiana University at Bloomington

## John E. Baird, Jr.
Baird/Melnick Associates

Boston   Burr Ridge, IL   Dubuque, IA   Madison, WI   New York   San Francisco   St. Louis
Bangkok   Bogotá   Caracas   Lisbon   London   Madrid
Mexico City   Milan   New Delhi   Seoul   Singapore   Sydney   Taipei   Toronto

# McGraw-Hill Higher Education

*A Division of The **McGraw-Hill** Companies*

COMMUNICATION FOR BUSINESS AND THE PROFESSIONS

This book is printed on acid-free paper.

1 2 3 4 5 6 7 8 9 0 DOW/DOW 9 0 9 8 7 6 5 4 3 2 1 0 9

ISBN 0–697–32727–2

Editorial director: *Phillip A. Butcher*
Sponsoring editor: *Marjorie Byers*
Editorial assistant: *Suzanne Driscoll*
Marketing manager: *Kelly M. May*
Project manager: *Kimberly Moranda*
Production supervisor: *Debra R. Benson*
Freelance design coordinator: *Pam Verros*
Photo research coordinator: *Sharon Miller*
Photo researcher: *Inge King*
Supplement coordinator: *Marc Mattson*
Compositor: *Shepherd Incorporated*
Typeface: *10/12 New Aster*
Printer: *R. R. Donnelley & Sons Company*

**Library of Congress Cataloging-in Publication Data**
Andrews, Patricia Hayes.
    Communication for business and the professions / Patricia Hayes Andrews, John E. Baird, Jr. – 7th ed.
        p.   cm.
    Includes bibliographical references and index.
    ISBN 0-697-32727-2 (softcover)
    1. Business communication. 2. Public speaking. I. Baird, John E. II Title.
HF5718.A745 2000
658.4'5–DC21                                    99-31252

http://www.mhhe.com

**To our parents**

Arthur L. Hayes
and Helen D. Hayes;
John E. Baird and Eleanor B. Baird

# Brief Contents

# Contents

## PART two
# Public Communication

PART three
# Dyadic Communication

# Preface

## THE BOOK'S UNDERLYING PHILOSOPHY

Without question, communication is important to any organization. Thousands of books, articles, and speeches have arrived at the same conclusion: Without communication, organizations could not exist. At present, however, a trend that is sweeping U.S. business and industry is changing the role of communication in organizations. "Participative management" in its various forms is increasingly replacing other styles of management as the preferred method of decision making and governance in organizations. For example:

"Self-managed work teams" in many businesses allow employees to set their own work methods, select new employees and discipline current ones, monitor quality and productivity, and perform other functions traditionally assigned to "supervision" or "management."

"Shared governance" systems in hospitals provide nurses with opportunities to establish their own work schedules and systems of rotation between units and shifts, to set and monitor standards of patient care, and to develop methods for improved staff education.

Employee advisory groups provide top-level company executives with important feedback concerning pending decisions and actions, and with important advice about the perceptions and problems of employees.

Problem-solving groups composed of nonsupervisory staff identify and solve work-related problems in organizations of all types, resulting in improved efficiency and millions of dollars in savings.

As this trend continues, managers and supervisors increasingly are playing the role of "facilitators" rather than "order givers," and nonsupervisory employees are contributing their minds (as well as their hands) to the achievement of organizational goals.

Such fundamental changes in the way organizations are managed has placed the burden of communication effectiveness on all levels of the organization, not just on members of management. For example, an employee in a typical company can expect to:

- Participate in one or more group problem-solving projects.

- Be asked to contribute his or her ideas for improving work.

- Deliver to management all or part of a presentation outlining ideas or proposals.

- Work informally with peers and superiors in making decisions previously reserved for management alone.

All these activities require communication skills and sound judgment by organizational members at all levels. Knowing this, forward-thinking organizations are currently training their staffs in communication skills and recruiting people who are skilled communicators and whose values and principles are consistent with those of the organization. Now more than ever, getting and keeping a job requires excellent communication skills.

## EMPHASIS

The structures and functions of communication in organizations are virtually limitless. As in the past, we have selected some of the more general types of situations students will encounter as part of organizational life, and then described communication strategies and skills that are widely applicable across diverse contexts. After establishing foundational principles of communication, organizational culture, perspectives on management, and ethics, we devote considerable attention to public speaking, interpersonal communication (with a special emphasis on interviewing), group communication, teamwork, and conflict management. Our purpose throughout is to analyze the demands placed upon people in each situation and to present strategies and techniques by which students might meet those demands and learn to communicate effectively.

Like the previous six editions, the seventh edition emphasizes skills acquisition in the context of organizational communication theory and research. This edition, however, contains several new features, significant content reorganization, and several new sections.

We have continued our practice of including many real-world illustrations throughout the text, based on the testimony and experience of successful managers whom we have known. As in earlier editions, we emphasize business and industry and the professions. We do this with the belief that the students who read this text are preparing for diversified careers in education, law, agriculture, and the health sciences, as well as in business and other professions.

The seventh edition, like previous editions, is peppered with Business Briefs that depict contemporary illustrations of theories, research, or principles. Each attempts to highlight or illustrate important concepts elaborated in the text. More than half of the Business Briefs are new to this edition.

## NEW FEATURES

Among the seventh edition's new features are special boxes:

Highlighting Technology

Highlighting Diversity

Highlighting Ethics

At the end of each chapter, questions for discussion and exercises are followed by new:

Case Applications

These case applications can be used for in-class discussions, for homework assignments, or for group work.

To assist students in reading and remembering chapter content, we have added:

Objectives
Previews
Key Concepts (section summaries)

Finally, the seventh edition includes new material on such subjects as:

- Technological challenges—recruitment and hiring, knowledge management, and privacy issues.

- Management philosophies—values-driven, information-driven, customer-driven, the learning organization, the commercial school, and others.

- The creation and use of computer-generated graphics.

- Using the computer to do research.

- Globalization and ethics.

- The legal environment of the employment interview.

- Self-assessment exercises for the job applicant.

- The scannable résumé.

- Group agenda setting.

- Using technology to conduct meetings.

- Collective action.

- Labor-management conflict.

## ORGANIZATION OF THE SEVENTH EDITION

In the current edition, we begin the book (Part I, Chapter 1) by examining foundational principles of organizational communication, including the meaning of communication, the nature of organizations, and fundamental communication channels people use to communicate, both formally and informally. Chapter 2 examines the organization's cultural environment, looking at various aspects of corporate culture, considering various perspectives on management, and examining the basic issues that confront managers as we approach the twenty-first century. Chapter 3 offers a careful consideration of the ethical environment in which communicative interaction occurs, looks at diverse ethical perspectives for making judgments, and introduces several issues that offer ethical challenges for all organizational members.

In Part II, we turn our attention to public speaking. Chapter 4 considers topic selection, audience analysis, and diverse speaking purposes (to interest, to inform, and to persuade), as well as the formulation of purpose and thesis statements, the discovery of evidence to support and develop ideas, and ways of testing evidence to determine its quality and likely effectiveness. The chapter concludes with an examination of inductive and deductive reasoning, together with reasoning fallacies to be avoided. Chapter 5 examines the organization of the speech (the introduction, the body, the conclusion, and transitions), as well as different kinds of outlines (formative, formal, and key word). A new full-sentence outline is provided as a model for students to follow. The fifth chapter also discusses modes and principles of delivery and the use of presentational aids. This part concludes with Chapter 6, which is devoted to special persuasive speaking applications. After examining principles of persuasion (emotional and logical appeals, as well as credibility), we move to a detailed consideration of proposal presentations and sales presentations.

Part III is devoted to interpersonal communication. In Chapter 7, we look at interpersonal relationships, considering the dimensions of such relationships, stages of perception, and how communication impacts the development of human relationships in organizations. A special section is devoted to the role of listening in relationship development. Chapter 8 takes up the principles of sending messages, both verbally and nonverbally. The first segment of the chapter is devoted to semantics, and both negative (defensive) communication and positive (supportive) communication. The last segment focuses on nonverbal communication—including proxemics, kinesics, artifacts and environment, and vocalics. The relative impact of verbal and nonverbal communication are discussed. The last two chapters in Part III are devoted to interviewing—a common form of interpersonal communication in organizational contexts. Chapter 9 considers fundamental interviewing principles, and then looks at special interviewing applications, including the corrective, the appraisal, and the complaint-resolution interviews. In Chapter 10, we offer a detailed consideration of the employment interview, including the roles of interviewer and interviewee. Interviewing is presented in a legal context, and guidance is offered on preparation, performance, and evaluation. Applicants are given special advice on constructing résumés and cover letters.

Finally, Part IV turns to communication in the context of groups or teams. Chapter 11 considers the socioemotional dimensions of group work, including group role structure, status and power, group pressure and groupthink, and group cohesiveness. Chapter 12 examines the process of group decision making, considering the advantages and disadvantages of group work, diverse ways of organizing a discussion and planning an agenda, and the ways that technology can assist group interaction. Chapter 13 focuses on group meeting management. After considering diverse styles of leadership, the chapter looks at how to handle problem participants and different ways of getting all members involved. The book's final chapter (Chapter 14) turns to a consideration of conflict and its management. After examining the nature and sources of conflict, we look at how conflicts develop and at individual styles of conflict management. We conclude by offering a model of collaborative conflict management.

# OUR APPRECIATION

Many people have contributed to our personal communication effectiveness. We think it appropriate to acknowledge their contribution to our still-developing skills. Professors J. Jeffrey Auer, James R. Andrews, the late Raymond G. Smith, Richard L. Johannesen, the late Robert G. Gunderson, Paul Batty, and Dennis S. Gouran and colleague Herbert G. Melnick taught us by word and example the techniques of effective communication. Our friends and colleagues at Indiana University and Baird/Melnick Associates have shown us the pleasures and successes that good communication can bring. We would also like to thank the reviewers of this edition for their suggestions and comments. They are: David Roach from Texas Tech University, Tom Endres from the University of St. Thomas, Kevin Merritt from Louisiana Tech, Bill Henderson from the University of Northern Iowa, Hazel Blackmore from Alaska Pacific University, and Julie Albers from Montgomery College.

Finally, we are indebted to our parents, whose encouragement, support, and love have been sustaining forces in our lives. To them, we again dedicate this book.

**Patricia Hayes Andrews**
**John E. Baird, Jr.**

# PART one

# Communication in Organizations

**THE UNQUESTIONED AUTHORITY** of managers in the corporation has been replaced by . . . the need for managers to persuade rather than to order, and by the need to acknowledge the expertise of those below.

—*Rosabeth Moss Kanter,* **The Changemasters**

# CHAPTER one

# An Introduction to Communication in Organizations

Think for a moment about success. What does success mean to you? What do you want for yourself, on both a short-term and a long-term basis? Short term, your goals may be relatively specific: obtaining an entry-level job with some organization, being promoted to some higher-level position, getting a raise, achieving a particular grade in a certain class, or graduating at a certain time. Long term, your goals may be less well defined, but definite nevertheless: financial security, happiness, status, love, the chance to make a lasting contribution, and so on. Whatever your goals—whatever success means to you, both short-term and long-term—two important facts hold true:

**1.** Much of your professional success will be achieved through your participation in some organization or group of organizations.
**2.** Your professional success will be determined to a significant extent by your skills as a communicator.

Let us examine each of these facts one at a time. First, the success you achieve will probably come through some organization. The reason for this is simple: our society is composed almost entirely of organizational entities. Indeed, whenever human beings gather together for the purpose of accomplishing some goal, organizations are born. Some are informal and loosely structured; most are characterized by deliberate structuring and formal divisions of power, labor, and authority. Whatever their nature and scope, however, we seldom escape their influence. We are born in organizations, are educated by organizations, work for organizations, and spend much of our leisure time in organized activities.

Second, your ability to succeed will be determined largely by your skills as a communicator. This is true in a number of respects. Your ability to enter an organization in the first place depends heavily upon your communication skills. For example, several years ago Hafer and Hoth surveyed 37 companies, representing a broad range of industries, from manufacturing to public service.[1] They asked employment officers in those companies to rate a list of job applicants' characteristics according to how important those characteristics are in their selection decisions. These characteristics, listed in order of their importance, are:

**1.** Oral communication skills
**2.** Motivation
**3.** Initiative
**4.** Assertiveness
**5.** Loyalty
**6.** Leadership
**7.** Maturity
**8.** Enthusiasm
**9.** Punctuality
**10.** Appearance
**11.** Written communication skills

While oral communication is listed first, it is important to note that many of the other characteristics are also types of communication skills: appearance is an element of nonverbal communication, for example, just as enthusiasm, assertiveness, loyalty, maturity, leadership, and initiative are typically shown most clearly through communication behavior. And as we shall see very clearly in Chapter 10, the employment process itself is an exercise in oral and written communication. Perform well in that setting, and you have made the first step toward success.

Once you have joined an organization, your ability to perform successfully in your current job and to move to jobs with greater responsibility and status will be determined by two important elements: your technical skills and your communication skills. You perform your job well by skillfully completing your assignments and, in today's increasingly team-oriented environment, working well with others. As others learn of your accomplishments, however, you gain prominence and begin to move up within the organization. Written memoranda, for example, are important "advertisements" of your identity, your achievements, and your skills as a communicator. Meetings, everyone's favorite target for criticism, also provide opportunities for you to demonstrate your knowledge and communication skills. Presentations of project proposals and progress reports give you the opportunity to make a positive impression in the minds of people holding influential positions within the organization. Certainly, doing your job tasks well is important, but communicating effectively may be even more important.

The higher you move in an organization, the more important communication becomes to your overall job performance. Indeed, some believe that communication style becomes more important than technical skill. Andrew Sherwood, president and chief executive officer (CEO) of Goodrich & Sherwood Company, the human resources firm, says that "meeting goals and objectives are quantitative measures of 'what' you do on the job—'what' you're being paid for. When you begin your career, and until about age 35, 'what' criteria are generally used to judge work performance. After age 35, however, when most people move into middle management or beyond, performance criteria begin to shift and style becomes more important." After this point in your career, "how" you do your job becomes most important. The "how" criteria include such things as "how you relate to your superiors, how you interact with your peers, how you handle and motivate people, and how you communicate," Sherwood explains. "The higher you rise in your company, the more visibility you have, the more you become a public figure—the more important 'how' you do your job becomes," he says.[2]

Sherwood's conclusions are based on interviews with over 100 company executives. When he asked them to rank performance criteria, middle managers said good performance is composed equally of "how" and "what" factors, vice presidents felt performance is 70 percent "how" and 30 percent "what," and corporate presidents said the value of "how" to "what" is 90:10.

When one reaches the top of an organization, communication activities occupy virtually all one's time. Several years ago, for example, the administrator of a large hospital kept a detailed record of his activities for 10 consecutive workdays. Of his 5,186 minutes, approximately 70 percent was spent in oral communication, about 17 percent in writing, and less than 13 percent in activities involving no form of communication.[3] To get to the top requires communication skills; to perform effectively once you get there requires even greater skill.

Of course, as we move into the new millennium, organizations are changing, sometimes at an unprecedented pace. Some changes have been brought about by advances in modern technology, others by developments in the economy, and still others by the increasingly global environment. The world marketplace has many participants, of which the United States is only one. Over 100,000 American companies are doing business abroad; about one-sixth of our nation's jobs come from international business. American-made products are increasingly rare. At the same time, jobs are changing. Cetron, Rocha, and Luchins predict, for example, that 5 of the 10 fastest-growing careers in the next few years will be computer-related.[4] The typical large business will be information-based, composed of specialists who guide themselves based on information from colleagues, customers, and top managers. Even now, one out of every two Americans works in some aspect of information processing. The new technologies offer change as well as opportunity.

Recognizing these changes, the purpose of this book is to help you develop the communication skills you will need to be successful in whatever career and organization you choose. We begin, then, by defining and examining organizations and organizational communication.

## PREVIEW

In this chapter, we will consider several key concepts related to communication within organizations. After defining both "organization" and "communication," we will review common communication functions and failures within organizations. Then we will consider the primary "types" of communication within organizations—upward, downward, horizontal and informal—and cite examples and shortcomings of each. Finally, we will consider the impact of new information technologies on organizational communication and note some difficulties those technologies pose.

## DEFINITIONS

Communication theorists have defined *organization* in various ways:

"a stable system of individuals who work together to achieve, through a hierarchy of ranks and divisions of labor, common goals"[5]

"an information and decision system"[6]

"the complex pattern of communication and other relations between human beings"[7]

"social relationships . . . interlocked behavior centered on specialized task and maintenance activities"[8]

In these definitions are common threads: goal-directed behavior, coordinated actions, information sharing, decision making, and human relationships.

These elements in turn emphasize the importance of communication in organizations. Communication is a process involving the transmission and reception of symbols having meaning in the minds of the participants. Communication is not merely an important activity in organizations; rather, it is the lifeblood that allows organizations to exist. No human relationship could be maintained, no organizational objective achieved, no activities coordinated, and no decisions reached without communication. Perhaps Bavelas and Barrett expressed it best in their classic article on organizational communication, where they noted, "It is entirely possible to view an organization as an elaborate system for gathering, evaluating, recombining, and disseminating information. It is not surprising in these terms that the effectiveness of an organization with respect to the achievement of its goals should be so closely related to its effectiveness in handling information." In other words, organizational success is directly tied to communication effectiveness, in their view. They conclude, "Communication is not a secondary or derived aspect of organization—a "helper" of the other presumably more basic functions. It is rather the essence of organized activity and is the basic process out of which all other functions derive."[9]

Not surprisingly, when Peters and Waterman had concluded their "search for excellence," they said: "What does it add up to? Lots of communication. All of Hewlett-Packard's golden rules have to do with communicating more. . . . The name of the successful game is rich, informal communication. The astonishing by-product is the ability to have your cake and eat it, too; that is, rich, informal communication leads to more action, more experiments, more learning, and simultaneously to the ability to stay better in touch and on top of things."[10] In short, the effectiveness of communication in an organization usually determines how successful that organization will be.

## THE COMMUNICATION PROCESS

To acknowledge the importance of communication is crucial. Equally critical, however, is to understand it as an interesting and complex process. Early models of communication failed to do this. They conceptualized communication as *linear*, largely a one-way process involving the flow of information from a source to a receiver. These models also focused on channels, so that communication was viewed as a conduit through which individuals attempted to accomplish their goals. Barriers to effective communication were viewed as noise, or anything that interfered with or distorted the message's movement through the channel. Noise might involve anything from crackling telephone wires to garbage on a computer screen to the receiver's attitudes—any one of which might affect message reception and interpretation.

More contemporary models of communication are *transactional*, emphasizing communication as a two-way, reciprocal process of mutual message exchange. Gerald Miller, for example, argues that communication is a process and "should not be thought of as discrete events with identifiable beginnings and ends, but rather as parts of a dynamic, on-going whole which has no clearly defined temporal boundaries. In particular, process stresses the *transactional* nature of . . . communication, rather than conceptualizing it as a unidirectional, linear act.[11] The transactional view is also described by communication scholars Wenburg and Wilmot, who note that during communication, "All persons are engaged in sending (encoding) and receiving (decoding) messages simultaneously. Each person is constantly sharing in the encoding and decoding process and each person is affecting the other."[12]

The transactional perspective declines to make a sharp distinction between the roles of source and receiver since one person plays both, and often does it at the same time. In this perspective, unlike the linear view, verbal and nonverbal feedback is considered central to the transactional model. How meaning is constructed is another concern. The linear view posits the notion that the meaning of a particular message resides with the sender, whose challenge is to use a message channel effectively. By contrast, the transactional view is more oriented toward the receiver and toward the construction of a message's meaning in her or his mind.[13] In short, people grow to share meanings through mutual experiences and by negotiating shared interpretations.

As human beings work together in organizations, they often share information and experiences. Over time, they grow to embrace similar goals and values. When they do this, negotiating common interpretations of events, persons, and messages may come easily. Under less harmonious circumstances (involving, for instance, interpersonal conflict), negotiating common interpretations of reality may be more demanding. The transactional model of communication is quite compatible with several contemporary views of organizing and managing (to be discussed in the next chapter).

Within the framework of the transactional model, then, *organizational communication* is that process wherein mutually interdependent human beings create and exchange messages, and interpret and negotiate meanings, while striving to articulate and realize mutually held visions, purposes, and goals. Organizational communication is influenced by the reality of hierarchies. However, as organizations have become flatter with hierarchical layers reduced, the communication challenges begin to change. Managers exchange some measure of control in return for shared responsibility for outcomes. Now motivation is as much a question for peers who work together in teams as for their formally appointed leaders. Even so, in organizations, the tensions remain—between the desire to cooperate for the good of all and the need to compete so as to promote oneself, between one's professional demands and one's private life, between those formally called "labor" and those formally labeled "management." Each organization is unique, and it is only by studying the organization's communication practices, patterns, and processes, that we will come to understand the organization itself.

| KEY CONCEPTS 1.1 | The Nature of Communication in Organizations |
|---|---|

Key communication concepts include:

**Transaction** Communication is a two-way reciprocal process.
**Process** Communication reflects what preceded it and influences what follows; it has neither a clear beginning nor a definite end.
**Meaning** Messages are interpreted and meaning formed by the receiver; the sender's intent is secondary.
**Sharing** Communication occurs via sharing of common

*Continued*

## A DAY IN THE LIFE

Debbie works for a large insurance firm located in downtown Chicago. At 26, she has been employed in the sales department for three years, ever since she graduated from college. Her job is to take information about newly sold policies that comes in from field sales agents; to open the new account on the company's computer system; and, as necessary, to obtain any missing information from either the field agent or the person to whom the new policy has been sold.

Thursday was a typical day in Debbie's work life. She arrived at the office at 8:15, dropped her briefcase off in her cubicle, and headed for the office kitchen where—good luck!—the coffee had already been made by some early bird. Three of her co-workers were already there, and they sat around a table and chatted about the momentous events of the day: the latest Washington scandal, the special 12-hour sale happening today at Nieman-Marcus, and the likelihood that the Bears once again would take a thrashing this coming Sunday. At 8:29, everyone left the kitchen to start work.

At 8:45, Debbie headed for the conference room to participate in her daily 8:30 team meeting. Experience had taught her that these meetings never started on time, and what's the point in wasting 15 minutes waiting for everyone else to arrive? Besides, everyone dreaded these meetings. By 8:50, all 15 employees in the department had gathered. At 8:55, mumbling, "Sorry I'm late," the director of sales rushed into the room to start the meeting.

"I've got a conference call at oh nine hundred hours, so we don't have much time," he said. "Here are a couple of announcements: sales are down, so we really need to pick up the pace. Customers are complaining, so you all need to get off your dead ends and show a little customer service. Any questions?"

As usual, there were none.

"Meeting dismissed," he concluded.

Debbie returned to her cubicle, logged onto her computer, and checked her e-mail. She found 173 messages that had accumulated since she left work at 5:00 the day before. Rather than wade through all of them, thereby blowing an entire morning, she simply deleted them all, reasoning, "If it's really important, they'll send it again." Then she sent an e-mail to her friend Marsha describing the play she had attended the night before; asking Marsha how her love life was; and "flaming" the director of sales, describing him as "that slimy moronic little Nazi"—an accurate if unflattering description. With all this out of the way, she began processing the new accounts at 9:30.

Several of the new accounts had incomplete information, so Debbie was forced to call three field sales agents to request additional data about the people who had purchased the policies.

"You sales guys are all alike," she told one. "All you care about is getting the sale, and you leave us in the office to clean up the mess. We're really sick of your cavalier attitudes."

The sales agent was unimpressed, since all he cared about was getting the sale. Also, since one of the agents had not collected information from the new customer, Debbie was forced to call that customer directly.

"I really apologize for having to bother you like this," she said, "but our sales guys are total idiots when it comes to getting the information we need."

The customer was very understanding.

During lunch, Debbie and her small circle of friends ate in the cafeteria and engaged in their favorite pastime: complaining about the company. As a group, they agreed that the pay stinks; the cafeteria food is too expensive and probably unhealthy as well; parking for employees should be free; and the director of sales is, indeed, a Nazi. These decisions were very similar to the decisions they had reached every day for the past three years. At 1:00 PM, everyone returned to work.

After lunch, Debbie went on-line to do a little research. She called up a Web site that offers tips to people wishing to have a successful career in sales; she called up another Web site listing job openings nationwide for sales personnel; she went to a third that serves as a "chat room" for employees disgruntled with their work lives. All this research took her to her 15-minute break at three o'clock.

When she returned to work at 3:40, Debbie noticed she had received a voice mail message. It was the "slimy moronic little Nazi," summoning her to his office. She took a deep breath and walked down the hall to the corner office of the director of sales. He motioned her in.

During the next 30 minutes, Debbie learned some amazing things. First, e-mails are not confidential: They can be and are monitored by company executives, some of whom, apparently, dislike being called "slimy moronic little Nazis." Second, telephone calls also are not confidential: They too are monitored as a measure of employees' job performance, and some company executives take a dim view of office sales staff insulting field sales people either directly or behind their backs to customers. Third, security cameras have been placed in the company cafeteria, kitchen and break areas to "reduce theft," and the cameras had recorded some interesting employee opinions. Fourth and last, the company has rules against "insubordination" and a "progressive discipline" policy, whereby employees receive warnings and progressive levels of punishment for violating company rules. Debbie was given a written warning and told that another offense would result in her being suspended without pay for three days.

Believing she had been treated unfairly, Debbie slunk back to her cubicle and placed a call to the Human Resources Department to ask about procedures for filing a grievance. Using the company intranet, Human Resources sent

Debbie a grievance form she could call up and complete on-line, sending it back immediately to Human Resources for processing. When she completed and sent back the form at 4:45, Debbie decided she might as well go home. It was too late to get started with another project, she decided, since she had only 15 minutes left before quitting time anyway.

# COMMON COMMUNICATION SHORTCOMINGS

During the past 20 years, the authors have consulted with nearly 1,000 different organizations and, believe it or not, seen hundreds of "Debbies." Our experiences and observations have consistently borne out Professor Drucker's observation: Communication is not done very well in most organizations, despite the flurry of communication activity. Generally, we have found five basic causes of communication failure:

**1.** *Communication in most organizations is activity-oriented, not results-oriented.*   When consulting with hospitals, for example, it is our practice to ask the hospital administrator to show us the hospital's employee handbook. Then we ask, "Do you feel this is a good employee handbook?" Typically, the answer will be yes, followed by such reasons as it has won national awards for design and layout; it costs us a lot of money to produce; my picture is on the inside cover; and consultants helped us to develop it. We then ask, "But does it do what it is supposed to do?" Typically we receive a puzzled look and a long silence in response. Communication is a tool designed to produce some effect upon its receiver. Too many organizations, however, view communication as something that "ought to be done," losing sight of the impact their communications should have. Debbie's daily department team meetings, for example, typify the kinds of communication events that eat up time and serve no purpose, except that "We've always done these."

**2.** *Communication often is one-way.*   Managers frequently assume that, as long as they are sending messages regularly to the rest of the organization, they are communicating. They therefore engage exclusively in downward communication, receiving little or no feedback from lower levels of the organization. As a result, they often do not know whether their downward messages were received, understood, believed, or approved of by employees, and they cannot adjust future messages to employees' needs or characteristics. To be effective, communication in organizations must flow not only downward but upward and laterally. The "communication" that occurred during Debbie's team meeting typifies the kind of downward communication too often seen in organizations. Yet when a consultant asked the director of sales about his management style, he reported, "It's very participative—I always ask for their input, even though they choose not to give it to me."

**3.** *The impact of communication is not measured.*   This problem is related to the preceding one. In many organizations, management receives informal feedback. However, no systematic attempt is made to measure the impact of communication in terms of the objectives or results the communication was supposed to achieve. If, for example, the employee handbook is designed to inform employees about company benefit programs, actual measures should be taken to determine how much information employees get and retain about benefit plans by reading that handbook. In effect, management must clearly define the results they want their communication systems to achieve and then regularly measure the extent to which those results have been produced. A truly participative director of sales, for example, would allow adequate time for employee questions and feedback rather than assuming that his staff was "fired up" by his brief pep talk.

**4.** *Communication is not responsive to employee needs.* When defining the objectives of their communication systems, managers should first ask employees what information they want or need. Then they can tailor downward messages to meet those needs. Rarely, for example, do companies ask new employees what information they would like to receive in their orientation meetings; rather, they assume that the information they are providing is exactly what the employees need. When we interview incoming employees about their concerns and desires, we find an entire body of information is needed that company orientation programs do not provide. Certainly, Debbie's director of sales had no clue to what she and her colleagues needed.

**5.** *The people who implement communication systems lack the necessary communication skills.* Department meetings cannot be effective if the department heads conducting them lack meeting leadership skills—as probably was the case with Debbie's director of sales. Customer service and sales representatives cannot be expected to maintain good relations with customers if they never have been taught customer communication skills—as was the case with Debbie herself. Communication systems and opportunities are not enough; the people who use those systems must have skills as communicators.

As the preceding discussion indicates, communication in organizations has two basic elements: *communication systems* (the meetings, electronic systems, publications, conversations, and so on in which messages are transmitted) and the *communication skills* of the people participating in those communication systems. In the remainder of this chapter, we will focus on the systems through which people in organizations communicate. In later chapters, we will discuss the skills you need to communicate effectively.

| KEY CONCEPTS 1.2 | Fundamental Concepts of Organizational Communication |
|---|---|

Communication within organizations often is ineffective because:

- • *it is activity-oriented rather than results-oriented,*

- • *it is one-way rather than multidirectional,*

- • *its effectiveness is not measured,*

- • *it is not responsive to the needs of others,*

- • *people using that tool lack the necessary skills.*

# FORMAL COMMUNICATION CHANNELS

As we have already implied, communication in organizations takes two forms: formal and informal. Formal communication is that which follows prescribed channels of communication throughout the organization—typically, the chain-of-command, although team-oriented communications among peers are increasingly being emphasized by companies that encourage lateral problem solving and decision making. Often depicted on official organizational charts, formal channels provide for the structured flow of upward communication; downward communication; and, occasionally, horizontal communication. Hierarchy, chain-of-command, specialization, and other traditional organizational principles are incorporated into this structuring of communication behavior. On the other hand, informal communication generally is considered to be any interaction that does not follow official channels of communication or the chain-of-command. Traditionally, many companies have viewed such communication as a "time waster" and an activity to be discouraged. Now, however, many more enlightened organizations recognize that, among motivated, goal-directed employees, casual communications can do even more than formal communication channels to build organizational success.

# DOWNWARD COMMUNICATION

Messages flowing from upper to lower levels of an organization's hierarchy constitute *downward communication*. Through downward communication, organizations direct the activities of employees, instruct them in proper behaviors and work methods, persuade them to adopt certain attitudes and ideas, evaluate their performance on the job, solicit upward communication, and provide entertainment—all typical functions of communication in organizational settings.

In modern organizations, downward communication takes a variety of specific forms. In describing some methods used by companies to communicate their benefits plans to employees, for example, Hourihan discusses three "generations" of benefits communication: the printed materials provided by insurance companies themselves (which are written from the insurer's viewpoint using highly technical language), written communications from the employer (such as an annual computerized benefits statement for each employee), and a large meeting presentation using dual-projector slide shows and professional speakers, with a social event afterward (cocktails and dinner) in which the questions about benefit programs can be discussed and answered.[14] Through this description, he also illustrates a current change in emphasis in downward communication, with companies moving from a traditional reliance on written messages to greater face-to-face interaction.

## Types of Downward Communication

Communication from higher to lower levels of an organization occurs through a variety of written, face-to-face, and electronic channels, several of which were illustrated by our "day in the life" of Debbie.

Written forms of downward communication often include:

*Employee handbooks,* which are given to employees when they first join an organization and summarize the mission, values, policies, and pay and benefits practices of the organization. Had Debbie read her handbook, she

## CREATING AN ORGANIZATIONAL CULTURE THAT WORKS

One of America's most innovative organizations is 3M (Minnesota Mining & Manufacturing). Here are some simple rules that guide leaders' communication behavior:

- **Tolerate failure.**   By encouraging experimentation and risk-taking, chances are greater for a new product hit. Divisions must derive 25% of sales from products introduced in the past five years.

- **Motivate the champions**.   When a 3M employee comes up with a product idea, he or she recruits an action team to develop it. Salaries and promotions are tied to the product's progress. The champion has the chance to someday run her own product or division.
- **Don't kill a project.**   If an idea can't find a home in one of 3M's divisions, a staff member can devote 15% of his time to prove it is workable.

Source: Russell Mitchell, "Masters of Innovation," *Business Week* (April 10, 1989): 58–63.

would have known that e-mails and telephone calls are routinely monitored and that "trashing" the boss through either mechanism constitutes "insubordination."

*Job descriptions and work procedures and protocols,* which typically are given to supervisors and managers to help them govern employees' day-to-day behaviors, and in turn are shared with employees as expectations for their performance are clarified. When employees become focused exclusively on their own jobs and lose sight of the larger goals, however, the sorts of divisive behaviors Debbie exhibited tend to crop up: she actually damaged the company's overriding goal of increasing customer satisfaction by telling customers how foul-ups were the fault of the field sales representatives, while she was doing her own job as required.

*Newsletters and publications,* which carry information ranging from social activities to important organizational decisions and events.

*Bulletin boards,* on which are posted important notices (particularly those required by various governmental agencies), but which frequently are ignored by passersby. Some companies use electronic bulletin boards that provide constantly changing messages and thus attract more interest.

*Letters and memoranda,* which may be sent to employees' homes, distributed in paycheck envelopes, or handed out by supervisors and managers to facilitate conversation with staff. In all likelihood, Debbie received a formal letter summarizing her disciplinary discussion with the director of sales, and a copy of that letter was put into her personnel file.

*Electronic mail* (e-mail) is a computer-based system whereby messages are sent from one personal computer (PC) user to another. Many companies routinely use e-mail to communicate information to management and staff, often replacing written letters and memoranda with these electronic messages. Debbie obviously is a skilled (if injudicious) e-mail user.

*Intranets* are internal company networks, similar to the World Wide Web, whereby individual employees can log on, check their personal e-mail and access any information of interest to them. For example, Certified Grocers of California has an intranet for its employees on which announcements, stories about the company appearing in the media, detailed messages about current activities or future plans, job openings throughout the organization, and so on are listed, and an employee can peruse any or all of these messages.

Written downward messages offer the advantages of being relatively permanent, easily distributed, and time-efficient for the receivers, who can read them whenever it is most convenient. In addition, these messages can serve as legal documentation of a company's philosophies and practices, thereby helping to defend the company (or convict it, if the messages are inappropriate) in court proceedings. However, written messages do not allow discussion between sender and receiver, thereby hindering clarification or debate of unclear or controversial information.

Face-to-face interaction also provides opportunities for downward communication:

*Employment interviews* often are one of the first instances of downward communication employees encounter and are useful for transmitting information about an organization.

*Performance evaluations* tell employees how effectively they have performed over the last six months or year (in the view of their supervisor) and offer suggestions for improving performance in the future.

*Disciplinary interviews,* often used after corrective interviews have failed to improve behavior, mete out some form of punishment in addition to advice for behavioral improvement. Debbie's disciplinary interview with her director is a common example in that the interview identifies what the employee did wrong, states what will happen if the problem is repeated, and documents the discussions that took place.

*Department or unit meetings* involve groups of employees and their supervisors or managers. As channels for downward communication, such meetings often discuss what one author calls the "4 P's": progress (how we are doing), people (who are changing jobs), policy (what is unclear or changing), and points (anything that arises during the meeting).[15] Debbie's director conducts meetings that can probably be characterized by another "P": pitiful.

*Mass meetings* often are used by top-level executives to communicate important information to large groups of employees. Often taking the form of town hall meetings, these forums are used to make important announcements, explain significant events, initiate companywide programs or processes, and keep employees up to date on the organization's progress.

*Educational and orientation programs* can be used to indoctrinate and educate new employees about companywide practices, benefits, pay procedures, and so on, or to teach employees new information and skills related to their jobs.

Recently, a variety of electronic media has been developed to facilitate face-to-face (or voice-to-voice) downward communication:

*Video conferencing and presentations* often are used during large group, or department or unit, meetings to present important information. In large organizations where personal visits by senior executives are impractical, for example, video-conferenced presentations can be used to communicate information to all employees at the same time. Certified Grocers of California, for example, announced their new "cultural change initiative" by setting up huge video screens in their warehouses throughout California and using satellite technology to transmit a presentation by their chief executive officer and other key executives to all employees at the same moment. For less immediate (or dramatic) messages, many companies place video monitors in high-traffic areas (such as near cafeteria entrances or in break rooms) and replay videotaped messages constantly for viewing by passersby.

*Voice messaging* (or voice mail, or V-mail) is a telephone-based system whereby callers leave brief recorded messages for the receiver. Such systems can range from relatively simple telephone answering machines to extremely sophisticated organizationwide networks. The receiver can decide when to listen to the recorded messages, although those messages typically must be listened to in the order in which they were received.

*Telephones* have been in use for years, of course, and remain one of the most frequently used channels for downward communication in organizations.

## Problems with Downward Communication

In most organizations, a variety of problems commonly afflict downward communication. Frequently, for example, *messages are not received*. Announcements or letters often are not read, meetings are poorly attended, needed corrective interviews are not conducted, and so on. But just as frequently, *information overload* occurs. Too many messages are sent by management, so that employees are bombarded with letters, memos, bulletin board announcements, meetings, and the like. As a result, the impact of any one message becomes diluted. During Debbie's day, a surprisingly common event occurred: rather than wade through a bog of e-mails, she simply dumped them all. *Organizational bypassing* often can occur as well, with top management communicating information directly to lower levels and, in the process, omitting one or more members of middle management who then must obtain the information from their staff. *Distortion or filtering* can also occur as one person passes a message on to another, who in turn communicates that message to a third, and so on. At each link in the communication chain, the message is changed and filtered slightly so that, by the time it reaches its final destination, it may bear little resemblance to the original form.

In addition, some organizations provide downward communications carrying information employees don't particularly want to know while withholding information employees would like to hear. What types of information should be communicated downward? Employees surveyed by Allstate Insurance said they want to know what will help them understand the business, what will help them serve customers better, and the "whys" behind the information they receive, and they also want to receive integrated, coordinated, and reinforced messages. When asked to suggest ideas to make communication more effective, they said it should be straightforward and timely, should use supervisors and peers as key communicators, should be organized and delivered in a simple style, and should use face-to-face interactive approaches.[16]

## EFFECTIVE COMMUNICATION: CENTRAL TO PARTICIPATIVE MANAGEMENT

Many leaders like to think of themselves as fostering an open, supportive communication climate, where employees feel free to tell them what they really think. But what should manages actually *do* to foster such a climate? Based on the University of Michigan's research on effective management, the participative manager is someone who:

- gives subordinates a share in important decision making
- keeps subordinates informed of the true situation, good or bad, in all circumstances

- is easily approachable
- trains, counsels, and develops subordinates
- shows thoughtfulness and consideration of others
- is willing to make changes in the way things are done
- is willing to support subordinates, even when they make mistakes

Source: See Patricia Hayes Andrews and Richard T. Herschel, *Organizational Communication: Empowerment in a Technological Society* (Boston: Houghton Mifflin, 1996), p. 74.

Failure to use communication as a motivational tool is one final shortcoming typically seen with regard to downward communication. *Communication Briefings* suggests formally acknowledging employees' sacrifices and reminding them frequently of how much they are valued by the company, as well as involving them deeply in making decisions, offering them opportunities to learn new skills, giving them new titles or greater visibility, having lunches or coffee breaks involving upper management and employees, and providing inexpensive tangible rewards symbolic of the company's appreciation (such as pens or plaques). Such efforts can be extremely useful in organizations that simply do not have the funds to provide pay increases to all employees.[17]

Effective downward communication most often is achieved through a thoughtful and strategic *combination* of oral, written, and electronic messages. Written messages are easily distributed and consistent in form, but do not allow feedback or further discussion. Oral messages allow interaction, but may be transmitted inconsistently (or not at all) from person to person or group to group. Electronic messages often limit interaction as well and may require a certain level of skill and technological sophistication that not all organizations or employees possess. Thus, the most effective downward communication process might be written or electronically communicated announcements, followed by individual or group discussions that are then summarized in writing for permanence. For particularly important messages, this approach to combining written, face-to-face, and electronic media is usually most effective.

## UPWARD COMMUNICATION

Communication sent from lower to higher levels of an organization constitutes *upward communication*. Like downward communication, messages flowing upward are vital to an organization's success. Employees' ideas, concerns, reactions, and recommendations are extremely valuable resources that are tapped only when upward communication works effectively.

**Types of Upward Communi-cation**

Like downward communication, upward messages can be sent in writing, orally, or via electronic media. Some commonly used written channels include:

*Employee opinion surveys,* which ask employees to report anonymously their perceptions, attitudes, and values so that management can determine what actions, if any, are needed to improve employees' feelings toward the organization.

*The leader who calls regular meetings in which employees can share ideas and interact face-to-face, creates an organizational climate where communication channels are likely to function effectively.*

*"Write to know" or "gripevine" systems,* which typically allow employees to write messages, often anonymously, to management and to see their answers published in an employee newsletter or posted on a bulletin board designated for that purpose.

*Suggestion boxes or suggestion systems,* which are often effective in obtaining employee input, although their effectiveness tends to wane over time. Typically, these systems provide some recognition and reward to employees whose suggestions save money or improve operations in the organization. Interestingly, the concept of soliciting employee suggestions has been in use for a very long time. During the 1800s, an English shipbuilder realized that the people who worked for him were experienced and knowledgeable in their crafts, so he let them know that if anyone had an idea that would help build better ships, he wanted to hear about it. While he did not operate a formal suggestion system, his was the first recorded instance of employee suggestions being solicited. A few years later, the Yale and Towne Manufacturing Company hung a suggestion box in its plant. The first formal suggestion system was put into operation by the National Cash Register Company in 1896; two years later, Eastman Kodak Company implemented a program that continues today—the oldest continuous suggestion program in the United States. At present, there are estimated to be as many as 6,000 formal suggestion systems in operation, and probably even more semiformal systems.[18]

*Letters and memoranda,* which are frequent channels for upward as well as downward communication.

*Complaint or grievance procedures,* through which employees express in formal terms dissatisfaction with some decision that impacts their work lives. At the end of her day, Debbie used an electronic form of her company's grievance procedure to express her dissatisfaction with and request a review of her director's disciplinary action.

Upward communication also occurs frequently via face-to-face interaction:

*Open door policies* tell employees that they are welcome to enter any manager's office with a question or concern whenever they wish. However, managers' doors too often literally are not open, and employees too often are afraid to walk through those doors even when they are open. Thus, a more effective policy is the "open floor" approach, whereby managers leave their offices and "manage by walking around," having informal conversations with employees in their workplaces.[19]

*Formal grievance procedures* give employees some recourse when they have a complaint or feel they have been treated unfairly. While initiated in writing (as Debbie did), grievances then are processed in formal interviews and hearings. In unionized companies, shop stewards or union business agents assist employees with their grievances, which typically are presented to successive levels of management until a solution is reached or taken to outside arbitration if a solution cannot be agreed upon. Nonunion companies occasionally have trained ombudspersons to assist grievants and may use employee committees to hear and resolve grievances.

*Performance evaluation* traditionally has been used as a tool for downward communication, but some companies are instituting upward appraisal systems as well. In 1992, AT&T developed a 40-question survey asking subordinates to evaluate the effectiveness with which their supervisors show respect, emphasize helping customers, promote teamwork and innovation, and maintain high standards. MassMutual Insurance instituted a similar system of written surveys in 1987, asking employees to evaluate the effectiveness of their supervisors and managers. Employees at AMOCO Corporation requested opportunities for upward appraisals, and a 135-question feedback instrument was developed as a part of the week-long mandatory training session for middle-level managers. Each of these systems is based on the realization that a manager's "customers" are the people who work for him or her (and thereby are the recipients of that manager's communication skills) and that an assessment of "customer satisfaction" is an important element of improving managerial performance.[20]

*Department or unit meetings* should serve as effective channels for upward and downward communication, with announcements being made and employee input sought by the manager conducting the meeting.

*Individual interviews* similarly should promote both upward and downward communication. During corrective or disciplinary interviews, for example, the employee's reactions should be solicited and heard, and his or her ideas for behavioral improvement should be sought and integrated into a plan of action.

*Advisory committees* are formal bodies of employees who provide management with information about employee concerns, perceptions, and reactions. For example, Purdue University uses its Clerical and Service Staff

Advisory Council to obtain advice from employees and hear their concerns, and Cedars-Sinai Medical Center in Los Angeles makes similar use of its Employee-Management Advisory Committee.

*Task forces and problem-solving groups* often are formed to empower employees to identify, analyze, and resolve work-related problems. Quality circles and other participative problem-solving groups typically are used within individual departments, while task forces frequently involve people from a variety of areas throughout an organization.

Electronic media also may be used to communicate messages upward:

*Telephone hot lines* may be used to encourage employees to express their feelings or report problems anonymously. For example, at one division of General Electric, more than 100,000 calls were processed during a single year, with topics ranging from questions about rumored salary increases to complaints about sexual harassment.[21]

*Electronic mail* and *voice messaging* often are used for upward as well as downward communication. Indeed, since many executives spend most of their time in meetings, these systems often are the only way in which these people can be reached by others in the organization.

*Intranets* are also used by some companies to gather employee suggestions and feedback. After reading an announcement, for example, an employee can send his or her response to the originator of the announcement. Indeed, some companies include a brief questionnaire at the end of each story posted on the intranet to assess employees' interest in and understanding of the information provided.

Problems with Upward Communication

Upward communication has its share of problems in organizations. First, *upward communication is subject to substantial distortion.* Specifically, as subordinates we are especially reluctant to communicate negative information to our superiors. Instead, we make every attempt to send messages aimed to please management and not without good reason. Tompkins has noted that negative ("bad news") feedback is discouraged by superiors, who tend to reward *positive* feedback rather than *accurate* feedback.[22] As a result, in most organizations, monthly reports present a positively exaggerated account of performance and productivity. Attempts to improve the climate of the organization as well as the utilization of human resources have led to the encouragement of open, honest communication in all directions. Studies have demonstrated that when fear of punishment is reduced and trust runs high between employees and management, the accuracy of upward communication is greatly facilitated.[23] Accurate upward communication is also more likely to occur when the supervisor is perceived as friendly, approachable, and considerate.[24]

Second, *some members of the organization actively discourage upward communication.* Weak supervisors, for example, will perform the organizational ritual called "CYA" (cover your posterior) by attempting to block communication between their employees and other members of management. They discourage employees from participating in opinion surveys, fail to conduct departmental meetings, falsify their monthly reports, and sharply criticize employees who "go around them" by talking to management or "hang out our dirty laundry" by taking problems to the personnel department. Naturally, it is imperative that top management discover and deal with these situations as quickly as possible.

Third, *upward communication can be intimidating* to some employees. Many find it difficult to talk to their superiors, choosing instead to smile and answer "everything's fine" when asked how things are going. Entering a manager's office via the open door policy is virtually impossible for them, and writing a letter to the editor of the newsletter is too challenging. In many organizations, there is a "silent majority" of employees who simply are nervous about talking to the people over them.

Fourth, *upward communication also can be intimidating to management.* As Zaremba notes, "People, no matter who they are and how confident they might appear to be, are reluctant to solicit rejection." Since upward channels allow criticism or negative feedback from employees, he concludes, "a simple reason upward communication networks are not used effectively is because few people want to invite such criticism."[25]

Last, *employees simply may not know that management wants them to communicate upward.* While employees may want to contribute their ideas, express their thoughts, or voice their concerns to management, they often believe (with some justification) that reprisals might be taken against them if they complain or that management simply is not interested in their input. For that reason, as Jablin points out, most organizations must provide systems designed specifically to promote upward communication.[26]

## HORIZONTAL COMMUNICATION

The final formal communication channel involves exchanges of messages among individuals on the same organizational level, or *horizontal communication.* Traditional organizations discouraged horizontal exchanges between individuals in different divisions because messages were supposed to be passed vertically throughout the organizational hierarchy. The assumption was that, by following vertical flows, each message would touch all appropriate points of authority. Rank-and-file workers were neither expected nor trusted to work out their own problems without the assistance of their superiors. Today, however, emphasis on teamwork, participative decision making and "empowerment" of everyone throughout an organization makes horizontal communication among peers vital to organizational success.

Types of Horizontal Communication

Progressive organizations have implemented a variety of programs designed to improve horizontal communication and teamwork. Most of the written, face-to-face, and electronic channels listed above are used frequently for lateral communication as well, but some other channels may also be utilized:

*Team-building seminars* often are conducted by trained specialists to improve relations among individuals or groups that interact with one another in the workplace. Top-level executives, for example, may by taken on team-building retreats lasting several days, while nonsupervisory employees may simply meet in break areas to discuss ways of working together more effectively.

## BUILDING TEAMWORK

Several methods can be used to build a sense of teamwork among organizational members. In its simplest form, team building is the guided discussion of several questions, through which the team members examine themselves and decide how their teamwork might be improved. Questions commonly considered in team building meetings include:

- What would we be like if we were an ideal team?
- What are we like now as compared to that ideal?
- How do we need to change?
- How can we change?
- How, specifically, will we change?

- What things can each of us do to help other team members more?
- What things can each of us do to support and encourage other team members to adhere to the commitments we have made?

The decisions made by the group are written down and distributed to each member, as well as to any person to whom the team reports. When done well, the team building meeting (or series of team building meetings) will improve the relationships among team members and, in so doing, improve communication and cooperation among them.

Source: Based on William I. Gordon and Roger J. Howe, *Team Dynamics* (Dubuque, IA. Kendall/Hunt, 1977); and William G. Dyer, *Team Building: Issues and Alternatives* (Reading, Mass.: Addison-Wesley, 1977).

*Cross-departmental visitation* is a simple but effective method for improving lateral communication. One department manager, for example, may invite the manager of another department to visit her or his work area, talk with employees, and discuss more effective and efficient ways in which the two departments might work together.

*Committee meetings* occur when representatives from different departments or units meet to hear announcements or discuss problems of mutual concern. Most organizations, for example, conduct department head or management meetings designed to build horizontal communication. Too often, however, these meetings are dominated by the leader and serve only as a channel for downward messages.

*Work teams* are being used with greater frequency to manage the operation of individual units in an organization. Semiautonomous or autonomous groups of employees often meet to plan their work schedules, assign duties, review their own performance and progress, and even hire or dismiss team members. For example, Epson, a leading maker of printers for personal computers, has instituted a bizarre-sounding method of developing new products. It's called "scrum and scramble." This method, also known to company insiders as the "rugby-team" approach to product development, is vastly different from the traditional "relay-team" approach. Under the "scrum-and-scramble" approach, a hand-picked, multidisciplinary team, with its members working from start to finish of the development process, "goes the distance as a unit, passing the ball back and forth," according to Professor Hirotaka Takeuchi of Japan's Hitotsubashi University. The team usually has a high degree of autonomy and often includes representatives of key suppliers.[27]

*Virtual work teams* are formed through the use of electronic media—videoconferences, intranets, conference calls—that allow horizontal communications among groups of people who never meet one another face to face. Teamwork among employees spread across the globe is an important outgrowth of this emerging technology.

Naturally, other communication channels already described, such as e-mail, voice mail, telephone calls, memos, and letters, can carry communications between peers. The growing importance of horizontal communication is illustrated by a feature article in *Business Week*, which lists seven steps needed to gain "quantum leaps" in performance: (1) organize around process, not task; (2) flatten hierarchy; (3) use teams to manage everything; (4) let customers drive performance; (5) reward team performance; (6) maximize supplier and customer contact; and (7) inform and train all employees.[28] As organizations eliminate unneeded levels of middle management, horizontal communication will continue to take on greater importance.

Problems with Horizontal Communication

Kanter, in her book *The Change Masters: Innovation for Productivity in the American Corporation*, describes the thinking that typifies too many organizations today:

> In the traditional mechanistic bureaucracy, the isolation of departments and levels means that people will see only local manifestations of problems, and they will perhaps appear puzzling or idiosyncratic. Furthermore, the message to the troops is clear: keep the lid on; the messenger with bad news will be shot. Because each segment is expected to do its work without troubling any other segment, communicating primarily in pre-specified ways and mostly to transfer good news (results or output), then identification of a problem is a sign of failure likely to get the identifier in trouble.[29]

As Kanter indicates, horizontal communication should serve to solve problems, promote cooperation, and improve the overall effectiveness and efficiency of the organization. Unfortunately, *most organizations do little to encourage horizontal communication.* In fact, highly competitive organizations may even discourage it. The employee who is eager to obtain some reward for his or her work may not be willing to share bright ideas or coveted data with peers who are after the same, usually limited, rewards. By the same token, managers may believe that their workers will, in fact, be more productive in an atmosphere that encourages *competition* and rewards selectively. When this is true, horizontal communication usually decreases or becomes routine.

Even when organizations want colleagues to communicate freely and frequently, such a goal is not readily accomplished because of *specialization.* The highly skilled machinist uses a specialized vocabulary, as does the neurosurgeon, the corporate lawyer, the engineer, the chemist, and the accountant. Yet many large organizations bring all these specialists together under the same professional roof. While informal social chitchat may be manageable, serious exchanges of task-relevant information are far more difficult. One way of dealing with this problem is to hire employees who have a good general background of education and experience, with their specialization representing only one aspect of their interest and skill. In addition, many organizations hold regular meetings that bring together individuals from different divisions. These people take turns talking about their work, skills, and frustrations in jargon-free language that can be understood by those not familiar with their areas of specialization. Through efforts such as these, many companies are achieving noteworthy improvements in their lateral communications and teamwork.

# EXTERNAL COMMUNICATION

Increasingly, organizations are realizing that effective communication with external audiences is crucial. Certainly, communication to potential customers (in the form of advertising or public relations) long has been an important element of organizational communication. Now, however, companies have come to realize that effective communication with suppliers, customers, consumers, governmental agencies, and the general public all are vital to organizational success.

## Types of External Communication

Communication between an organization and its environment can involve many of the same types of written, face-to-face, and electronic channels used for internal organizational communication. For example, some commonly used written channels include:

*Newspaper and magazine press releases* distributed by an organization to communicate its message to readers.

*Newspaper and magazine stories* written about an organization that may carry information the organization would just as soon not have communicated (such as an unfavorable review of the organization's products or some internal scandal the organization wished to suppress).

*Brochures and publications* that describe the products and services of the organization to prospective customers, summarize the financial achievements of the organization for shareholders and the public (in the form of quarterly or annual reports, for example), or recruit new organizational members.

Face-to-face communication also can be used by organizations to communicate with their environment:

*Tours* of company facilities, conducted for members of the general public or for the media, can be useful in acquainting the public with company operations.

*Large group meetings* may be conducted for shareholders or for the public at large. For example, when two Massachusetts hospitals—Leonard Morse Hospital in Natick and Framingham Union Hospital in Framingham— merged to form MetroWest Medical Center, the chief executive officer of the new organization used large town meetings effectively to respond to and defuse community concerns about losing their community hospitals.

*Using modern technologies can save time and money. Through videoconferencing, for example, individuals who are in different locations can hold meetings through closed-circuit TV, enabling realistic interaction.*

*Seminars and workshops* may be provided by organizations either as the core of their customer services (such as by consulting firms specializing in supervisory and management training) or to augment their services and products (as when technicians from IBM teach customers how to use their newly purchased hardware).

*Customer or supplier meetings* increasingly are being used to improve service, either by having customers communicate their preferences and expectations directly to groups of employees or by having suppliers meet with employees (their customers, in effect) to hear concerns and preferences regarding the supplier's services or products.

*Employment interviews* are an often-overlooked channel of communication with the environment. For every position filled, there may be several candidates rejected. Yet those candidates' perceptions of the organization are strongly shaped by their interview experiences, making this an important channel of external communication as well.

Electronic media also play a key role in external communication:

### INTERNET TECHNOLOGY AND MEDICINE

Joan Barber is a doctor in Santa Cruz, California, who starts her day in an unusual way: by reading her e-mail. On this particular day, the first message she reads is a critical blood test, red-flagged by a lab's computer when it was sent the night before. Dr. Barber sends a copy of the results to the referring doctor and suggests immediate follow-up. Over the next 30 minutes, she reads and sends more than a dozen messages. She approves an experimental treatment, forwards a prescription request to her assistant and consults on-line with two colleagues concerning whether surgery is warranted for a patient they share.

Dr. Barber is using a messaging system that uses the Internet to link 150 doctors throughout Santa Cruz with two hospitals, a dozen labs, an independent practice association, and insurance companies. More than 160,000 patients are also registered to use the system. Unlike ordinary e-mail, all communications are coded to ensure confidentiality. "It has freed me to spend more time with my patients," Dr.

Barber claims, estimating that the system saves her office hundreds of hours in paperwork and telephone calls. She even credits the system with saving the life of an 11-year-old patient suffering from acute kidney disease by getting approvals to see a specialist in just days—a process that normally can take weeks for an HMO patient. Her biggest gripe: trying to reach colleagues who aren't on-line. "They might as well be on the moon," she complains.

The growth of on-line communication among members of the medical community is growing with incredible speed. Still, there are issues that eventually will have to be resolved. Can doctors be held legally responsible if they fail to answer an e-mail? What about privacy issues for patients using e-mail at work? Despite concerns such as these, the future is clear: Graduates from medical school will need skills in using this communication technology, as well as an effective "bedside manner."

Source: Michael Meduno, "Prognosis: Wired," *Hospitals & Health Networks* 72 (November 5, 1998): 28–35.

*Radio and television* serve as channels both for advertising and for public service announcements by organizations and news about those organizations.

*Telephone* communication is key for most organizations; many companies provide in-depth training for employees in telephone courtesy and monitor employees' communication performance in telephone conversations with customers.

*Electronic mail and voice messaging* are important for communication with the environment as well. Some companies use e-mail extensively to get information from or communicate it to their environment, and many use V-mail to record messages for people who were unavailable when the call arrived.

*Teleconferencing* via satellite is used by many organizations to conduct news conferences or to provide information to external audiences. A few organizations use this channel for internal communication as well, although it tends to be too expensive for frequent internal use.

*Video* communications often are prepared and released to news services, customers, and other organizations in the environment as a means of communicating the organization's message in an interesting, compelling manner.

Electronic media also make useful information available to members of today's organizations. For example, to support sales professionals' self-development efforts, Virginia-based MaxPitch Media, Inc., launched a Web site called www.Justsell.com. The web site's founders, two former salesmen, envision it as a sort of college of sales knowledge. "We want to create a community where people can hang out and exchange ideas about selling," said Jim Gould, cofounder along with his partner Sam Parker. The site is written with a particular bent toward the needs of small business. Recently, for example, the commentary section of the site offered a three-part, step-by-step series on how to hire a company's first sales representative, including writing a recruitment ad, structuring an interview, asking the right questions, and sifting through candidates. Other articles deal with how to target a market, size up the competition, and discover the real reasons customers choose not to buy from you. The "Sales Mine" section links readers to top stories about selling from a range of magazines and filters the best sales-related information from on-line sources, describing it in a one-paragraph summary.[30] Indeed, the research and self-development efforts historically undertaken by employees in libraries and college night courses now are being enhanced by on-line information resources done in the convenience of one's home (or, as in the case of Debbie in her "day in the life," during working hours using her company's computer system).

## Problems with External Communication

Communication to external audiences suffers from many of the same problems that afflict upward, downward, and lateral communication within organizations, such as information overload, unreceived messages, and filtering and distortion. Indeed, organizations have far less control over the distribution of messages sent to external audiences than they do over internally communicated messages, making these problems even more likely to occur.

Regardless of the external channel or channels chosen, several principles should be observed to minimize the impact of potential communication breakdowns. Communication consultant Frank Corrado claims that a formal plan for managing issues should be developed by every organization and that communication with external audiences should be carefully coordinated with internal communications.[31] In addition, the impact of external communication should be carefully and continually evaluated to ensure that the desired effects are being achieved. In this manner, then, relationships between organizations and their environment can be more effectively managed.

# THE COMMUNICATION SYSTEM: INFORMAL DIMENSIONS

Within every formal organization there also exists an informal organization in which a great deal of communication behavior occurs. Much communication in large organizations is informal, springing up whenever an individual feels a need to communicate with someone with whom he or she is not connected by a formal organization channel.[32] Whereas formal communication

Some companies have put the concept of communication networks to formal use. For example, New York City–based Avon Products, Inc., set up three networks for its employees: the Avon Asian Network, the Avon Hispanic Network, and the Black Professional Association. These groups originated in the 1970s as the Concerned Women of Avon, which then became the Women and Minorities Committee. In the mid-1980s, committee members branched out and began networks to address their specific needs.

Each network holds quarterly meetings, has a budget and a clear mission statement, and has at least one member who is a senior officer in the company. These senior officers help keep management apprised of employees' reactions to their policies, particularly with regard to diversity issues.

Source: Charlene Marmer Solomon, "Networks Empower Employees," *Personnel Journal* 70 (October 1991): 51–54.

consists of messages the organization recognizes as official, informal messages do not follow official lines. According to Tompkins, informal networks often develop through accidents of spatial arrangement, similarity of personalities, or compatibilities of personal skills.[33] For example, employees may end up talking simply because they have adjacent offices, enjoy NCAA basketball, or feel similarly about various issues. Of course, what they share at an informal level will affect their ability to communicate about their jobs. Most employees are involved in several networks at the same time: some grow from political ties, others from technical interests, and still others from social preferences.[34]

As you might expect, informal communication is by far the dominant form of oral interaction in organizations. Indeed, Deal and Kennedy suggest that 90 percent of what goes on in an organization has nothing to do with formal events.[35] Rather, the informal network, the "hidden hierarchy," is in reality how an organization operates. And the operation of informal networks is not necessarily bad. Peters and Waterman noted in *In Search of Excellence* that "the excellent companies are a vast network of informal, open communications. The patterns and intensity cultivate the right people's getting into contact with each other, regularly, and the chaotic/anarchic properties of the system are kept well under control simply because of the regularity of contact and its nature (for example peer versus peer in quasi-competitive situations)."[36]

It is important to note that top-level management also benefits from informal communication. "After closely observing 15 better-than-average general managers in action, professor John Kotter of the Harvard Business School concluded that his subjects got work done not by giving orders or churning out reports, but mostly by talking to people—asking questions, making requests, maybe prodding a bit. These conversations often consisted of nothing more than a two-minute encounter in the hallway or on the phone."[37]

It is not uncommon to find writers referring to informal message behavior as "grapevine" communication. Information introduced into the grapevine travels quickly because it is not inhibited by structural constraints. Although we tend to publicly discredit information we receive through the grapevine, research has shown that it is amazingly accurate. Scholars have consistently reported 78 to 90 percent accuracy figures in their extensive studies of grapevine communication in organizational settings.[38] When errors do occur, however, they are often of a critical or dramatic nature.

Probably the most negative attribute of the grapevine is that it serves as a network through which *rumors* travel. Unlike much grapevine activity, which consists of verifiable informal communication, rumors are unconfirmed; that is, they are devoid of supporting evidence or cited sources. Rumors develop in part because employees perceive the formal communication system as inadequate. Whenever there are organizational policies that foster secrecy or superiors and subordinates who regard each other suspiciously, rumors are likely to flourish. For some, participation in rumor transmission may serve as an emotional safety valve to relieve frustrations and worries.

In their classic study of rumor transmission, Allport and Postman noted that rumors spread both as a function of their *importance* and their *ambiguity*.[39] If you are up for promotion and you hear through the grapevine that a promotion decision has been made, you are quite likely to discuss this rumor with others, especially your friends. The issue is vital to you and the message is ambiguous. Who was promoted? When did it happen? Why haven't you been officially informed? Myth has it that certain people function as specialists in rumor transmission, but research does not confirm this notion. Whether or not an individual will pass on a rumor usually depends on the individual's degree of interest in the rumor, perception of others' interest in the rumor, access to others, and personal goals. Relatively few people who receive rumors actually transmit them. Those who do often tell a cluster of others, only a few of whom will send the message further.[40] Figure 1.1 depicts a typical rumor cluster chain. Like other grapevine information, rumors spread quickly. One journalist described rumors this way: "With the rapidity of a burning powder trail, information flows like magic out of the woodwork, past the water fountain, past the managers' doors and the janitor's mop closet. As elusive as a summer zephyr, it filters through steel walls, bulkheads, or construction glass partitions, from office boy to executive."[41]

The grapevine is a part of organizational reality—a natural outgrowth of humans being together. Managers who do not admit to the grapevine's existence usually have trouble. Managers who try to stamp out the grapevine with such policies as "Employees must not discuss their salaries with each other" also have trouble. Policies to that effect simply tend to drive the discussions underground.

Davis, who has studied grapevine communication for more than 20 years, believes that management should accept the grapevine as an inevitable fact of organizational life. He points out that "if properly guided, it can help build teamwork, company loyalty, and the kind of motivation that makes people want to do their best. It may weld the group together more effectively than company policy and other formal tools of the organization."[42] It is vital that managers be in touch with informal networks, participate in them, learn from them, and use them carefully to disseminate information.

Esposito and Rosnow suggest that managers do several things to defend against destructive rumors: keep employees informed (so that rumors do

FIGURE 1.1     Typical rumor transmission pattern: the cluster chain

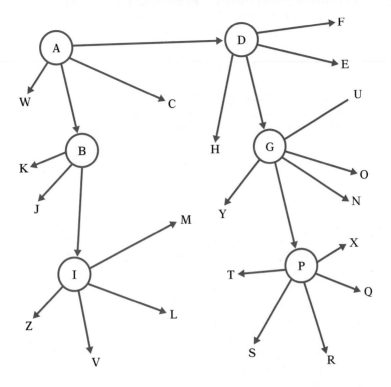

*Note:* Only circled letters represent active rumor transmitters.

not occur to fill an information void), heed rumors (to identify employee concerns), act promptly (before rumors spread and attitudes harden), and enlighten personnel (teaching them about the potential destructiveness of rumors).[43]

Informal communication in an organization's environment can be extremely important. On September 1, 1993, Snapple Beverage Corporation began an advertising campaign to rebut rumors in the San Francisco Bay–area black community that the company supported the Ku Klux Klan. One rumor suggested that a small letter K printed on Snapple labels stands for the KKK. But the symbol means that Snapple, like Coca-Cola and other famous products, meets kosher dietary standards. Another rumor contended that the illustration on the label of Snapple iced tea portrays ships bringing black slaves to America. But the illustration, from the Bettmann Archive, is a famous drawing of the Boston Tea Party.

In other situations, underground rumors have been devastating to companies. Procter & Gamble (P&G) battled a rumor for nearly 10 years that its 140-year-old logo, showing a man-in-the-moon face and a cluster of 13 stars, was a symbol of the devil. Despite lawsuits and an intense public relations campaign, P&G could not dispel the myth and in 1991 was forced to redesign the logo. McDonald's spent a year and a small fortune trying to dispel the 1978 rumor that it was using red worms in its hamburgers to boost their volume and protein content. Reports at the time said hamburger sales dropped sharply at about 20 percent of McDonald's stores.

In Snapple's case, the company fought back by advertising in local newspapers and on radio stations. Eventually, the rumors were quelled, but sales of Snapple's iced tea and other beverages suffered.[44]

---

| **KEY CONCEPTS 1.3** | **Downward, Upward, Horizontal, Informal, and External Communications** |
|---|---|

*Downward communication is composed of messages flowing from higher to lower levels of an organization and often suffers from:*

Messages not being received.
Information overload.
Organizational bypassing.
Distortion or filtering.
Providing the wrong information.
Not using communication as a motivational tool.

*Upward communication is composed of messages flowing from lower to higher levels of an organization and often suffers from:*

Substantial distortion emphasizing positiveness instead of accuracy.
Discouragement by management.
Intimidation of employees and management.
Lack of apparent management interest.

*Horizontal communication is composed of messages exchanged between peers within organizations and often suffers from:*

Lack of encouragement by management.
Specialization among peers.

*External communication is composed of messages exchanged between organizations and their environment and often suffers from the same problems that afflict other forms of communication:*

Information overload, unreceived messages, and filtering and distortion.

*Informal communication is composed of messages exchanged among organizational members in ways other than official communication channels and often damages formal communications by communicating inaccurate or distorted information.*

---

## THE COMMUNICATION SYSTEM: TECHNOLOGICAL CHALLENGES

As John Naisbitt and the other trend forecasters foresaw, information technology is booming in organizations today.[45] Voice mail, e-mail, teleconferencing, the World Wide Web, company intranets, cellular telephones, and

A glossary of some useful Internet and Intranet terms:

- *Domain.* The name of a computer or a service on the Internet—referred to by the characters following "@" in an on-line address.
- *Download.* Receive a file from another computer.
- *Firewall.* Hardware or software that protects a private network from an unsecured or public network.
- *FTP (file transfer protocol).* An Internet protocol for transferring files to and from another server over a network.
- *Groupware.* An application that enables users to collaborate over a network.
- *Home page.* The first page of a Web site or a group of HTML documents.
- *HTML (hypertext markup language).* The language in which World Wide Web documents are formatted.
- *Hyperlink.* A linking mechanism that allows a user to jump from one Web page, graphic, or document to another.
- *Internet.* The world's largest computer network, which enables users to send e-mail, transfer files, participate in newsgroups, and access the World Wide Web.

- *Intranet.* A private network that uses Internet software and standards.
- *Java.* An object-oriented language, developed by Sun Microsystems, that creates distributed Web applications.
- *Newsgroup.* An electronic bulletin board on which users can post and exchange messages.
- *SSL (secure sockets layer).* A method of authentication and data encryption between a Web server and a Web browser.
- *Upload.* The process of transmitting a file to another computer.
- *URL (uniform resource locator).* A standardized character string that identifies the location of an Internet document. Also known as a Web address.
- *Web browser.* Software that requests and displays HTML documents and other Internet or intranet data.
- *World Wide Web.* Part of the Internet; a worldwide, HTML-based, hypertext-linked information system.

Source: Samuel Greengard, "Internet/Intranet Glossary of Useful Terms," *Workforce* 76: 3 (March 1997): 82.

laptop computers all have helped to link organizational members wherever they happen to be, whenever they wish.

Greengard reports, for example, that nearly every Fortune 200 corporation has instituted an *intranet*.[46] In turn, these electronic systems have proved extremely effective in improving efficiency and saving time. Employees at Ostram-Sylvania in Danvers, Massachusetts, now can handle their own records updates without any assistance from the Human Resources Department, and benefits information and job postings all are handled automatically on-line. If a manager wants a job posting to expire on a particular date, she simply enters the data into a field and the event will take place. Not only has this eliminated paper and work, it also has reduced hiring time from weeks to days. In addition, the system has saved the company nearly $150,000 per year in data collection and reporting costs, and recent employee surveys show employees are pleased with the new system.

Now, companies are beginning to take yet another step forward. This is what James Barksdale, president and chief executive officer (CEO) of Mountain View, California–based Netscape Communications Corp., refers to as "the beginning of a whole new attitude in business about how to communicate—within the business, among employees and managers, as well as between the business and its external constituents: partners, customers and vendors." This new development, which has been called the "*extranet*," involves designing private networks so that data can flow freely between companies. A growing number of organizations have realized the value of linked databases. For example, Oracle Corp. of Redwood City, California, now conducts open benefits enrollment for more than 8,500 employees in only three weeks. Here's how it works: Oracle's intranet contains a link to pages on Aetna's Web site that have been specially designed for Oracle employees. Using a variety of electronic forms and hyperlinks, employees can step through the entire enrollment process on-line—even choosing a doctor directly from insurance provider Aetna. Employees of Houston-based Compaq Computer Corp. can access their 401(k) accounts by linking directly to a financial institution's, or mutual fund provider's, computer to make investment decisions or reallocate their assets.

## Technology Applications: Recruitment and Hiring

An important technological tool, the World Wide Web, has allowed corporations to improve their recruitment efforts by marketing themselves directly to college students and professionals, 24 hours a day. As résumés come in, they are automatically routed into databases. When a manager needs to fill a position, he or she can search on keywords and find top prospects. Then, using videoconferencing software over the Internet, it's even possible to conduct a preliminary interview.

Many prominent companies are using the Web for recruitment. Since Silicon Graphics, a Mountain View, California manufacturer of computer workstations, went live with its Internet site (http://www.sgi/com), it has collected 4,000 to 12,000 résumés each month. More than one-quarter of new hires now come to the organization through cyberspace. IBM's CyberBlue site (http://www.cybrblu.ibm.com) offers searchable job postings, job fair information for college students, benefits information, a résumés builder, and a page that links to some of the most entertaining sites on the Web, including "Calvin and Hobbes" and "The Dilbert Zone." Other companies have found that services such as E-Span (http://www.espan.com), Career Mosaic (http://www.careermosaic.com), IntelliMatch (http://www.intellimatch.com), JobTrak (http://www.jobtrak.com), JobWeb (http://www.jobweb.organization), and the Monster Board (http://www.monster.com) provide quick ways to get job postings on the Web without establishing their own sites.

Technology now is playing an important role in employment interviews, too. A *Chicago Tribune* article described one person's experience. After New Yorker Laura McCormick did well in a phone interview with an executive at Kinko's, Inc.'s headquarters in Ventura, California, she was invited for a second interview—at Kinko's video conference center in Manhattan. "It was very exciting," McCormick recalled. "I could see the person I was speaking to on one video monitor and could see my own face on another, so I knew how I was coming across. The interview was at least an hour and a half, and I developed a personal rapport with the person, much more than over the phone." "When doing a search, interviewing by video is often an expedient way of narrowing the prospect list to the best two or three, who you would then arrange to interview personally," said Paul Ray, president of Ray &

Berndtson, a New York–based executive search firm. "At the senior levels, it's still face-to-face," Ray said, "but it won't be long before everybody has a laptop on their desk with videoconferencing capability."[47]

Technology Applications: "Knowledge Management"

A relatively recent development within organizations is "knowledge management," termed by Greengard "the hottest idea spiraling through the corporate universe right now."[48] Collecting, culling, and trading information throughout organizations is nothing new, but companies now are using "knowledge management" in a thorough, systematic fashion to promote organizationwide communication. Buckman Laboratories in Memphis, Tennessee, established a series of "forums" on CompuServe so employees could share wisdom throughout the 1,200-person company. Using on-line forums, connected knowledge bases, electronic bulletin boards, libraries, and virtual conference rooms, employees began exchanging proposals, presentations, spreadsheets, technical specs, and more. The payoff was quick. When a Buckman sales representative approached the management of an Indonesian paper mill with a potential business deal, the plant's senior executives asked to see a detailed proposal within two weeks—a deadline that seemed impossible to meet. The sales rep went into the on-line forum and mentioned that he had a potential $6 million deal, but needed sample proposals and information. Within two days, he had responses from other Buckman employees scattered across the globe, and he was able to go back to the customer with the proposal and make the sale.

Knowledge management uses technology to create the "learning organization" described in the next chapter and can give organizations a major competitive advantage. Thomas Koulopoulos, president of the Delphi Group, a Boston-based consulting firm, argues that "An organization's ability to quickly tap into wisdom gives it a competitive edge in the marketplace. Today, the challenge is to capture all the data, information and interactions that occur so an organization can collectively benefit. Within many organizations, valuable knowledge too often disappears into a black hole."[49]

Knowledge management can be categorized in three ways. First, "competency management" tracks skills and competencies throughout an organization by developing and maintaining a data bank of all employees' knowledge and skill areas. This information is used by the company to identify skill gaps and training needs that could endanger future performance, to guide decisions concerning recruitment and hiring and to assemble cross-disciplinary teams of employees holding the knowledge and skills required by a particular project. "Knowledge sharing" is a form of knowledge management that uses intranets and on-line forums to spread knowledge throughout an organization, much as Buckman Laboratories uses technology to interconnect its employees worldwide. Finally, "competitive knowledge management" blends competency management and knowledge sharing. Arthur Andersen's Atlanta-based business consulting division established an intranet in 1996 where consultant firms post information—work plans, methodologies, research, proposals, and résumés—so that others can tap into high-level expertise on an as-needed basis. A consultant at Arthur Andersen can log onto Arthur Andersen's intranet, fill in a search form and instantly view the results. She can request information from specific functional areas, such as human resources, finance, or marketing, but can also mine for information outside the realm of individual departments.

During her memorable "day," Debbie discovered that technology that feels private when used often is not. Employers have both the ability and the inclination to monitor employees' e-mails, voice mails, telephone calls, and other informal communication activities. As an article published not long ago in *Workforce* magazine noted, many employees probably do not realize that e-mail is permanent—that it really can't be deleted in the traditional sense. Several copies of each e-mail are usually stored or archived within the system and may be found if needed or looked for.

Recent legal actions and court cases have made clear several important realities[50]:

**1.** Legally archived or deleted messages can be acquired by a court of law or a government agency in regard to antitrust, discrimination, termination or copyright infringement investigations.
**2.** E-mail is not the place for discussing sensitive issues, such as suspicions, employee performance, hiring, or firing. Anyone using this venue for such issues should always consider it a formal and permanent form of communication.
**3.** Stating a negative opinion or feeling about an employee while using e-mail lends merit in a legal proceeding related to discrimination or termination.
**4.** Prosecuting attorneys count on the fact that e-mail archives will be ripe with incriminating information. They want employees to be careless with their e-mail—and usually, they are not disappointed.
**5.** Certain comments, suggestions, and even graphics delivered by e-mail to others can give merit to a harassment claim.

In view of these issues, some advice seems in order with regard to the use of electronic communications[51]:

• Be careful what you write about others. You can't control who will read your documents. E-mail should always be considered public, not private. Don't ever write anything you wouldn't want everyone in your office to see.

• When replying to someone's message, check the list of recipients before you respond. Often, e-mail is automatically copied to a preprogrammed distribution list. Your messages can be forwarded without your knowledge.

• If a message you've received is personal or even informal, let the sender know you'll be forwarding his or her message before you pass it along to someone else.

• Downloading and viewing graphics that are personal in nature is not an appropriate activity at work.

Common sense will usually tell you what you should or should not do. If you even wonder whether something is inappropriate, don't do it.

## Technology Issues

The emergence of electronic technology has not been without problems. The *Chicago Tribune* reports, "Now that we have instant communication, thanks to the new technology, some workers find it so daunting they call it 'information

There is a troubling side to the growth of technology in business. Today's electronic systems also provide the tools to collect data and monitor the workplace with amazing efficiency. "At the touch of a button, it's possible to view e-mail messages employees send to one another, listen to voicemail or telephone conversations, and actually see what's on their monitors while they're sitting at their computer terminals," says the director of DePaul University's Institute for Business and Professional Ethics. "It's also possible to view a dressing room or break area using a hidden video camera, and use surveillance devices to hear what's going on in various parts of an office or building." In addition, vast databases provide information about employees: their driving records, credit history, medical records, and more. An entire industry has sprung up to conduct background checks on applicants and dig into existing employees' histories. And now, companies are developing badges with electronic sensors that let a manager know where a worker is at any given minute of the workday.

Source: "Privacy: Entitlement or Illusion?" *Personnel Journal,* 75: 5 (May 1996), 74.

overload.'"[52] "Between e-mails, voice mails and faxes, each day employees are exposed to more messages than ever before," observed Jeannie Glick, an employee communication consultant who cited a study by Pitney Bowes Inc. showing that 71 percent of employees at the nation's top 1,000 firms "feel overwhelmed by the number of messages they receive." Another finding: 84 percent of respondents are interrupted by messages three or more times an hour. Glick concludes that "the reality is our technological ability to share information is more advanced than our human ability to process it, much less act on it."

In addition, some organizations have applied technology inappropriately to situations that still require the human touch. Serb reports that, "According to a new Towers Perrin/Care Trac survey, Medicare HMO members truly appreciate plans that reach out to them via strong customer service. 'If I were a Medicare HMO, I would retune my approach to the marketplace,' says Stephen P. Wood, Towers Perrin's national practice leader for health plan consulting. 'I would steer away from high-cost electronic media—the 'Have Betty White pitch your plan on TV' approach—and I'd get down to the physical approach, reaching out to people through visits and phone calls.'"[53]

Research demonstrates that Medicare health maintenance organizations (HMOs) need to stay in touch with their members to gain a competitive advantage. But many fail to do that. Of seniors living in high-penetration managed care markets, just over a quarter received follow-up phone calls from health plans once they signed up. Yet seniors place a premium on that type of contact: 87 percent view those calls very favorably. In addition, only 36 percent of seniors in HMOs say they have received a visit from HMO sales reps, while at the same time 93 percent credit visits from a sales rep with helping them to choose their health plan. The upshot, according to the survey, is that the personal touch leads to loyalty. Phone calls, sales rep visits, and knowledgeable support staffs can give a company a competitive advantage over other health plans and traditional Medicare. But too often, companies rely on the media and other impersonal media technologies to maintain contact with their clientele.

Proper usage of technology also is important within an organization. Some common errors that are made in day-to-day use of e-mail, for example, include:

**1.** *Hiding behind the terminal.* Don't use e-mail for performance reviews, disciplinary actions, resolving personal conflicts, or other touchy matters. It's worse than breaking up over the phone; some things you have to do in person.

**2.** *Forgetting it's in writing.* The informality of e-mail is part of its convenience. But it is a permanent record of a written communication—often much more easily retrieved than an ancient memo. Just because you've forgotten about it doesn't mean you won't see it again.

**3.** *Flaming.* Spontaneity is another benefit of e-mail, but you should watch the tone of an e-mail message as closely as you would a memo written on paper. Anything you say via e-mail can (and probably will) be used against you.

Clearly, knowledge of how to use today's burgeoning communications technology is important. But so too is knowing when to use it.

---

**KEY CONCEPTS 1.4    Technological Issues**

- • Computer technology is growing rapidly as a communication tool; most large organizations now have intranets for use by their people.

- • Recruitment and hiring practices particularly are being affected by new technology.

- • "Knowledge management" is an approach whereby all members of an organization are linked together electronically, achieving the "learning organization" that will be described in Chapter 2.

- • The primary problem with technology seems to be information overload.

- • Electronic communications are not private and must therefore be used very carefully.

---

## SUMMARY

At the beginning of this chapter, we made two assertions: first, much of your professional success will come through participation in some organization (or groups of organiza-tions), and second, your professional success will be determined to a significant extent by your skills as a communicator. Learning to function effectively in an organizational setting requires considerable understanding of organizations, how they are structured, and the underlying principles that have influenced their traditions and contributed to their culture. Developing communication skills that will contribute to your professional success is equally important. Many employees understand their organizations rather well. They accurately perceive the management philosophies and practices that affect their daily lives. But because of their own lack of experience with or knowledge of effective communication practices, they cannot influence others in the organization. Nor can they do much to enhance their own upward mobility.

The inability to communicate effectively in organizations can result in feelings of powerlessness and anonymity, and in the experience of being passed over when important committee assignments are made or promotion opportunities arise. It is not enough simply to know your stuff. You must also be able to communicate with others about your knowledge, ideas, and suggestions for change. To be able to inform others, to ask good questions, to listen carefully, and to persuade others—these are the basic elements of effective communication.

In this chapter, we have demonstrated the importance and diversity of communication within and between organizations. In writing, in face-to-face conversation, and through electronic media, we continually exchange information, convey our ideas and attitudes, render judgments, and assist in making decisions. Your future organizational experiences may take you into a business firm, a hospital, a school, or an industrial organization. You may function as a marketing analyst, an accountant, a teacher, a chef, or an executive. Whatever the organization or the specific function you fulfill, your daily activities, productivity, and pleasure will be greatly influenced by the quality of your communication interactions.[54]

## QUESTIONS FOR DISCUSSION

1. Why is communication so important to success in an organization?

2. Since people already know how to talk to one another, why would formal training in communication skills be helpful for organizational success?

3. How is communication a "process" in an organization?

4. How might communication serve to translate workers' abilities into job performance?

5. In your opinion, why has the amount of communication in organizations increased but the quality of communication not improved?

6. What might cause an organization to take an "activities" approach to communication rather than a "results" approach?

7. Why might management be more comfortable with one-way communication?

## EXERCISES

1. Consider an organization with which you are very familiar. List the systems of upward communication that organization uses, the systems of downward communication, and the systems of horizontal communication.

2. Consider an organization you know well. List instances within that organization in which you have observed each of the functions communication plays in an organization.

# CASE application 1.1

*Communicating Difficult Information*

Michael Johnston is a top supervisor in a large food manufacturing corporation. He must communicate some bad news to a number of the organization's employees (all of whom are under him in the organizational hierarchy). New, more stringent health regulations will require them to wear special caps to cover their hair, to wash their hands frequently with a special antibacterial soap, and to have two checkups per year with the company physician (instead of just one as is the present practice).

## Questions

1. Given your knowledge of downward communication, how should Johnston approach the communication of this information?
2. Should he utilize both formal and informal channels and both oral and written modes of communication? Why or why not?
3. What problems might he encounter, and what strategy might he use for overcoming them?

# CASE application 1.2

*Communicating Difficult Information*

You are administrative assistant to the vice president for sales in a moderate-sized business firm. While your boss is extremely bright and superbly competent in her area, marketing, sales, and public relations, she tends to run a fairly authoritarian operation with minimal desire to let others assist her in decision making. She neither seeks nor is particularly receptive to feedback from anyone. While many lower-level employees are reluctant to discuss problems with *her,* they often come to *you* to complain about both task-related problems and the fact that they are frustrated with the managerial style of the vice president. You have known this woman for many years—first as a friend and only recently (for six months) as a boss. You have high regard for her as a person, but you are appalled at the lack of congruence between her general humanitarian philosophies and her conservative, rigid style of leadership.

## Questions

1. Using your knowledge of communication behavior, how would you approach this situation?
2. How might your upward mobility aspirations figure into this?
3. Consider your probable feelings with regard to trust and status.

# CHAPTER two

*After reading this chapter, you should be able to:*

**1** Explain the concept of "corporate culture" and how it is reflected in organizational communication practices and behaviors.

**2** List and explain at least five organizational philosophies and their implications for communication practices and behaviors

**3** Identify at least five critical communication practices that differentiate one philosophy from another.

**4** List and explain at least four key issues facing organizations today.

**5** Identify which organizational philosophies seem best suited to meeting the key issues organizations face today, and explain why.

# Communication in Organizations: The "Cultural" Environment

## TRANSFORMING THE ORGANIZATION'S CULTURE: THE POWER OF LEADERSHIP

In recent years, dramatic changes in the cultures of several major corporations have been brought about almost entirely through the efforts of the individual in charge of those organizations. For example, Yutaka Kume almost single-handedly changed the culture of Nissan from a lumbering, bureaucracy-ridden organization into a fast-moving, highly successful company by taking such actions as subdividing the organization into three market-oriented groups, putting a complaint desk in every dealership, changing the procedures by which new cars are engineered, rotating managers through assignments in all areas of the company, changing the basis of personnel decisions from seniority to performance, and minimizing organizational rank by banning the practice of putting titles on employees' name badges.

Similarly, Sir John Harvey-Jones changed the culture of Britain's Imperial Chemical Industries in only five years by reorganizing the top management team and the divisions of the company, developing and communicating a new vision and strategy for the company, and becoming personally visible throughout the organization.

In both instances, actions taken by the chief executive officer transformed the organization by creating new sets of values and priorities and discarding old, outmoded assumptions and practices.

Source: From John P. Kotter and James L. Heskett, *Corporate Culture and Performance* (New York: Free Press, 1992).

In every organization, communication is of vital importance. Indeed, without it, the organization by definition could not exist. But the forms, functions, and frequencies of communication vary from one organization to the next. In some organizations, employees are involved in making meaningful decisions and solving important problems. In others, their communication experiences are confined to receiving orders from management and complaining to one another during break times. Indeed, your experience with any organization will be a largely communication-driven experience, and the nature of those communications in turn will be shaped by the organization's "culture" or underlying philosophies and practices.

Deal and Kennedy, in their book *Corporate Cultures*, provide an in-depth analysis of the cultures that typify today's organizations, and identify four key attributes of organizational cultures.[1] First are *values*—the shared views, philosophies, and beliefs of organizational members. An organization's values establish the tone, set the direction and the pace, and suggest appropriate attitudes and courses of action. One can often glean some insight into an organization's values by listening to the way its members communicate among themselves. In large research-oriented universities, for example, professors commonly speak of their teaching *loads* while referring to their research *opportunities*. In this way, they suggest that teaching is a burden and research a pleasure, a view quite consistent with the values of the university as revealed in hiring and promotion practices and other forms of rewards.

Those organizational members who personify and illuminate the organization's values are *heroes*, the second cultural attribute identified by Deal and

CEO Herb Kelleher of Southwest Airlines has inspired a unique organizational culture. Employees are encouraged to be creative, to work with a spirit of playfulness, and to cheer one another's accomplishments.

Kennedy. Often, these heroes occupy the top position in their organizations. Such chief executive officers (CEOs) as Herb Kelleher at Southwest Airlines, Jan Carlzon at SAS, Lee Iacocca at Chrysler, and Ted Turner at Turner Broadcasting articulated and reflected their organizations' visions and values. Their actions showed by example the way others should think, behave, and talk. Their language was quoted often, and their way of discussing the world was imitated by others throughout their organizations. Thus, they influenced their organizations' sense of social reality. It is the hero who defines the allies and the enemies, who writes or sanctions the slogans, and who regularly participates in the third cultural attribute, *rituals and rites*.

Through rituals, organizational members celebrate and reinforce their beliefs, applaud their heroes, and share their visions of the future. In Christian religious organizations, for example, rituals abound, as people marry, celebrate communion, baptize their children, and bury their dead. While these sorts of rituals are shared by many different denominations, each church develops distinctly different traditions regarding how each ritual is enacted. Within two churches of the same denomination in a single community, for example, one church celebrates Holy Communion by passing a basket of tiny wafers down the pews. No one kneels, and individual glasses are used for drinking the wine. On the other side of town, however, the congregation comes forward, kneeling together around a large altar. The minister breaks a loaf of bread in half and passes it from person to person, each of whom breaks off a small piece to dip in a communal wine cup. Although these rituals are quite different in method and detail, they celebrate common beliefs, and the recited liturgies are virtually identical. Although rituals are of obvious importance in religious organizations, they are also evident in other kinds of organizations when members are initiated, promoted, honored, and retired. Whatever the organization's values, members who attend or participate in rituals will be reminded of them and often urged to believe in and live up to them.

The final cultural attribute discussed by Deal and Kennedy is the *communication network*. While rites and rituals represent the ultimate form of formal organizational communication, communication networks are *informal* channels of interaction, typically used for influencing members' perceptions of reality and indoctrinating them to hold the right attitudes and behave in appropriate ways. Networking begins even before the individual formally joins an organization. The job candidate may be taken out to lunch by a group of his or her future peers who tell stories about the organization, gossip about its heroes and villains, and enlighten the candidate as to the ways of upward mobility. Later, networking continues over coffee breaks, lunches, dinners, parties, and other social events. One can learn a great deal from these informal interactions since, in such contexts, people often feel free to raise issues and offer comments that they would never share in more formal settings. Are women really taken seriously here? What about minorities? How ethical are our leaders? Although these kinds of questions may never be posed directly, answers to them can be gleaned by listening to the stories told by those who already belong.

Every organization has a culture, and that culture shapes the work-life experiences of employees within the organization. Some are enjoyable and supportive, and they encourage personal and professional achievement. Others are repressive, fear-ridden, and detrimental to personal and professional health. But all shape and are shaped by organizational communication, and all begin with the organization's leadership philosophy.

## PREVIEW

This chapter takes a macroscopic view of organizations that ultimately translates into the microscopic, day-to-day work experiences everyone in an organization enjoys or endures. By reviewing various philosophies of organizational leadership and culture, and the ways in which those philosophies shape organizational communication, we hope to enable you both to select the right kinds of organizations in which to participate and to develop some skills in shaping organizational cultures yourself should the opportunity arise.

# LEADERSHIP PHILOSOPHIES

Organizations are shaped by their leaders, and organizational cultures ultimately begin with the philosophies held by the people who control rewards, punishments, information, and other organizational resources. In this section, we will review some of the most prominent leadership philosophies and their implications for communication in organizations.

## The Classical Philosophy

In the late nineteenth and early twentieth centuries, the Industrial Revolution had taken hold. Factories were in wide use, and the assembly-line technique of production was about to be implemented in the Ford automobile plants. Because so much of the technology of manufacturing was new then and because the techniques for large-scale production were just being developed, management theorists of that age focused largely on work methods as the source of performance improvement. The view that developed at that time is now called the *classical school* of organization theory, or the school of *scientific management.*

One leader of this school of thought was Frederick Taylor.[2] Taylor's approach to organizations was highly structured and mechanistic. His famed time-and-motion studies attempted to break down each minute aspect of a given job, and to match each worker with the task he could most efficiently perform. Taylor believed in instigating a competitive spirit in organizations by rewarding workers on the basis of their individual output. Praising workers or encouraging creativity never crossed Taylor's mind as being potentially motivating. Rather, he believed that real rewards would invariably be of a monetary nature. Taylor saw no particular clash between the interests of the organization and the welfare of the workers. Rather, he assumed that if individuals could increase their own prosperity while contributing to the organization's efficiency, then everyone would be satisfied. Such a view proved unrealistic. With the growing strength of labor unions in the 1930s, both workers and labor leaders bitterly opposed Taylor's views. They witnessed jobs being eliminated because of Taylor's efficiency-training techniques. This resulted in rises in unemployment. They argued further that those workers who learned to produce with dazzling efficiency were seldom fairly compensated for their extraordinary productivity.

In organizations managed by people who adopted the classical philosophy, communication took on certain characteristics. As a rule, communication was almost exclusively downward. Executives issued general orders and plans to their managers, who in turn issued the same orders (perhaps with more specific instructions) to their employees. Upward communication was virtually nonexistent. Employee suggestions were rarely solicited. Employee complaints were rarely expressed, and those employees who did express them were often encouraged to leave. Conflicts were handled through the chain-of-command and usually were resolved through decisions made by the chief executive officer. In effect, a very rigid, militaristic hierarchy was maintained, with work-related communication flowing downward through the chain of command.

Classical organization theory provided the impetus for Douglas McGregor's first theory of managing human behavior.[3] McGregor labeled this

### WHEN CLASSICAL LEADERS FAIL

The thinking embodied in the classical school still can be found in many organizations today. For example, the ways in which some large corporations select new chief executive officers frequently reflect an emphasis on such Classical factors as moving up through the ranks, understanding the company bureaucracy, and demonstrating technical competence.

In recent years, some celebrated instances of chief executive officer removal have occurred. For example, Robert C. Stempel resigned his position as chairman of General Motors Corporation in October 1992, under considerable pressure from his board of directors. Similar situations were seen recently when Tom H. Barrett resigned as chairman and chief executive of Goodyear Tire & Rubber Company and Kenneth H. Olsen resigned the presidency of Digital Equipment Corporation. Both had been long-time company men— Barrett had spent thirty-eight years with Goodyear, and Olsen had founded and spent thirty-five years with Digital—and both had been under intense pressure from their boards of directors. Like General Motors, both Goodyear and Digital had faced significant changes in market demands and competition.

Some management experts claim that the chief executive officers of most big companies are the products of ponderous, deliberate, and often very highly structured management-succession systems. Particularly in old-line industrial organizations, these individuals often joined their companies right out of school and worked their way up through the ranks, assuming greater and greater management responsibility along the way. Like Stempel, they exhibited a high level of competence in the lower-level jobs they held and were well-respected inside their companies, but they were perhaps unable to respond to the complexities and rapidly changing environment business leaders face today.

Leaders groomed in one business environment would thus wind up ill-prepared for another. In short, many executives who have moved up in the Classical tradition risk being the right leaders, but for the wrong times.

Source: From Amanda Bennett, "Many of Today's Top Corporate Officers Are the Right People for the Wrong Time," *Wall Street Journal* (October 27, 1992): B1–B3.

approach *Theory X.* In the spirit of scientific management, its central principle is one of direction and control through the exercise of authority. The Theory X manager makes most decisions alone, issues many orders and commands that flow downward through appropriate formal channels, displays little interest in acquiring suggestions and information from those near the bottom of the organizational hierarchy, and generally treats workers as economic beings who are most readily motivated through wage incentive plans and other monetary management methods.

Unfortunately, as McGregor pointed out, supervisors who manage their workers in accordance with the principles of Theory X often create climates of distrust, fear, and misunderstanding. Because so little information flows upward through the hierarchy (and the information actually reaching the top is usually filtered and considerably distorted), decision making is based on only partial and often inaccurate data.

As an alternative to this authoritarian approach to management, McGregor advocated a second management philosophy, *Theory Y,* which emphasizes the social nature of workers. It contends that human beings can be meaningfully motivated to work productively only when organizations fulfill their higher-level needs for belonging, esteem, and self-actualization. Theory Y further argues that workers prefer self-control and self-direction over being directed and controlled by executive commands. Managers practicing the principles of Theory Y encourage the flow of messages up, down, and across the organization. They are sensitive to employee feedback and facilitate frequent, honest interaction in an atmosphere of confidence and trust.

Significantly, McGregor's Theory X and Theory Y are more theories about people than they are theories of leadership or management. Theory X leaders assume that people are untrustworthy and unmotivated, and thus must be carefully watched and controlled. Theory Y leaders assume that people are self-motivated and want to achieve company goals, and thus can be trusted to participate in problem solving and decision making and allowed to manage their own efforts to some extent. And both sets of leaders are right. Certainly, there are some people who are untrustworthy and unmotivated, and there are others who are self-starters and who do not need any supervision whatsoever. But more importantly, Theory X leaders tend to produce Theory X employees (thereby proving in the Theory X leader's mind that his or her assumptions were right all along), while Theory Y leaders tend to develop Theory Y employees. For instance, a leader who shares information with employees, asks their opinions, and tries to ensure that their noneconomic needs are met soon will have a group that has high morale, works well without supervision, and is self-motivated—just as the leader assumed they would. In short, Theory X and Theory Y tend to be self-fulfilling prophesies in which the leader's own behavior (stemming from her assumptions about people) ultimately causes those people to become what she expected all along.

One should not assume, however, that Theory X leaders are automatically doomed to fail. Benevolent autocrats still abound, and many have achieved noteworthy success. One example featured recently in a national publication was Jack Hartnett, president of D. L. Rogers Corp., a company based in Bedford, Texas, whose primary business consists of owning 54 franchises of Sonic Corp., the drive-in restaurants that dot the South.[4] At a time when management experts preach the importance of companywide learning and flat hierarchies, Hartnett instructs his employees to "do it the way we tell you to do it." Here are some of his management principles:

1. *Show them the money.* Hartnett believes the best way to motivate people is to give them what he covets most: cash, and lots of it. "We're all money motivated," he says. "If someone tells you they're not, they've just committed one of the eight sins of this company." Those who have memorized his list of commandments know he is referring to the fourth: "You don't lie to me."
2. *Share their secrets.* Hartnett believes the more he knows about his workers, the more he can help them stay focused at work and happy at home. No subject is too delicate for his ears. "There are no secrets here," he says.
3. *Make them part owners.* Executives are required to buy equity stakes in the stores they run, while most fast food chains give managers and supervisors little more than an occasional free meal.
4. *Motivate through fear.* Hartnett rarely yells or screams at his managers or supervisors. He doesn't have to: So frightened are they of provoking him that they go out of their way to please him. "If you're really nice and you occasionally get upset, you'll get their attention," he says.

**5.** *Be a commanding presence.*   Hartnett tells people exactly what he expects and how to get there. "I want people to want to do what I want them to do."
**6.** *Sweat the small(est) stuff.*   In Hartnett's world, to delegate is to shirk responsibility. He's the master of minutiae. Nothing escapes his attention. He'll even rummage through a trash bin to see what customers are not eating. "If they're throwing away fries, maybe we're not cooking them right," he says.

His eight commandments include "I don't steal from you" as the first and "You don't steal from me" as the second. "I will only tell you one time" is the last.

## Likert's Philosophy

An approach to management theory that provides a wider range of leadership philosophies is the one offered by Likert and his colleagues.[5] Likert's research suggests that most management styles can be classified as belonging to one of four possible systems. System 1 parallels McGregor's Theory X. It focuses on centralized decision making, conflicting organizational and individual goals, a preponderance of downward communication (to the exclusion of adequate upward communication), and a general atmosphere of distrust.

Next on the continuum are Systems 2 and 3. System 2 involves greater interaction between managers and subordinates, but the confidence demonstrated by superiors is often condescending. Decision making is somewhat more diffuse, but significant decisions continue to be made at the top of the organization. System 3 moves in the direction of integration and is characterized by increased interaction throughout the organization, with communication occurring within an atmosphere of general trust and confidence. Specific decisions are made by more members of the organizational family, although policy making continues to be carried out at the top.

The final Likert system approximates McGregor's Theory Y. System 4 focuses on complete manager and subordinate trust and confidence; the unrestricted flow of messages up, down, and across the organization; and shared participation in decision making, goal setting, and evaluation. The central concept of Likert's fourth system is "participative decision making." According to this notion, organizations should permit employees to participate in making decisions that directly affect them, particularly if they must execute them.

Likert's research in the early 1960s found that System 4 organizations had the highest level of productivity and System 1 the lowest. He also noted that managers' personal preferences leaned toward the System 4 approach and that the most successful managers worked to develop a "supportive" climate within their organizations. Subordinates usually perceived these supportive (System 4, Theory Y) managers as friendly and helpful, genuinely interested in the well-being of each employee, and trusting in the ability and integrity of all workers. Unfortunately, Likert also found that most managers worked in organizations that adhered to classical notions and thus followed the System 1 approach.

Many U.S. companies today are moving toward the more participative, System 4 approach Likert advocated. A study by the U.S. Department of Labor, for example, noted that nearly half of some 500 U.S. businesses or business units of major corporations that had been surveyed had instituted some form of employee involvement program. Xerox, Dayton Power and

Light, Preston Trucking Company, and A & P stores were but a few examples cited in the study.

**Blake and Mouton's Philosophy**

A third approach to the study of management is based on the findings of small group research on leadership. Two types of leadership behavior predominate in this research: that which concerns itself with the *task* before the group or organization, and that which focuses on the *socioemotional* maintenance of the group itself.

Basing their approach on these two basic leadership dimensions, concern for employees and concern for production, Blake and Mouton have developed a leadership grid for the scrutiny of managerial behavior.[6] According to their theory, there are five possible managerial styles. The first, the *impoverished style*, is illustrated by the manager who cares neither for people nor for productivity. He or she provides no guidance for employees, avoids involvement in any conflict, delegates decision-making responsibilities to others, and prefers to leave others alone and to be left alone. Actually, this person is a manager in name only and a leader in no sense of the word.

Another style Blake and Mouton identify is the *task-oriented style*. As the name implies, this kind of manager demonstrates a low concern for people and a high concern for production and is a direct parallel to McGregor's Theory X and Likert's System 1 managers. Thus, the task-oriented manager issues commands, cares little for employee feedback, and bases his or her reward system on concepts of lower-level need satisfaction.

A third style represents the opposite of the managerial approach just described. It is totally *people-oriented*. These managers are entirely interested in interpersonal relationships, to the exclusion of any concern for organizational productivity. They smooth over conflict, reward extravagantly, and promote good fellowship and harmony—at the expense of the organization.

The fourth style is the *middle-of-the-road* approach, emphasizing moderate concern for both people and production. Managers espousing this philosophy probably fall somewhere near Likert's System 3. They generally support participation in decision making, and encourage teamwork and employer-employee interaction, but they are not totally committed to the concept of integration.

Finally, Blake and Mouton point to the fifth style, the *team manager*. This person has high concern for both people and production; thus, he or she parallels the Theory Y, System 4 managers already discussed. The team manager strives to maintain the group while accomplishing the organizational task. He or she confronts and resolves conflict, encourages consensus in decision making, and seeks candid and spontaneous employee feedback in an atmosphere of trust and mutual respect.

Probably the greatest advantage of Blake and Mouton's approach to management is the fact that their grid may be applied to each manager within the organization. Thus, it allows for individual analysis and assumes that different philosophies of management are often operative within the same organizational setting. As with McGregor and Likert, however, each manager is classified with regard to his or her basic approach, allowing little room for the adoption of different managerial styles with varying tasks and personnel.

Like Blake and Mouton, Hersey and Blanchard focus on two elements of leadership: managing work and managing people.[7] However, unlike other management theorists, Hersey and Blanchard do not make static assumptions about both managers and workers. In their examination of leadership styles and employee needs, they acknowledge the inevitability of some change, as well as the potential for growth. Their theory of leadership affirms the need for a dynamic leadership approach in which the manager's effectiveness is determined by the ability to assess the needs and abilities of employees accurately and adjust his or her leadership strategy accordingly.

According to Hersey and Blanchard, an effective manager should begin by assessing a subordinate's maturity, which they define as the "willingness and ability of a person to take responsibility for directing his or her own behavior." Actually, there are two dimensions to maturity in any work environment: (1) *psychological maturity*—the willingness or motivation to do something, the belief that responsibility is important, and the confidence to complete tasks without extensive encouragement, and (2) *job maturity*—the ability or competence to do something, the knowledge, experience, and skill needed to carry out work without the direction of others.

Hersey and Blanchard recognize that a number of important situational factors exist in any organizational environment. They remain convinced, however, that the behavior of the manager in relation to individual employees in the work group is the most crucial. Consequently, these researchers describe four leadership behavior categories, any one of which might be appropriate, depending upon the maturity level of the employees concerned.

Hersey and Blanchard's situational approach to management has been labeled the *life cycle theory of leadership* in that it examines leader-subordinate interactions over an extended period of time and assumes that changes, adjustments, and growth will occur. A manager who is dealing with an individual or a group of employees whose psychological and job maturity are low begins by emphasizing task-oriented leadership. As the employees' maturity level increases, the manager decreases task behavior and increases relationship behavior until a moderate level of maturity is attained. Ultimately, with increases in maturity, the manager begins to decrease both task and relationship behavior. At this point, employees possess both job and psychological maturity and are capable of providing their own reinforcement. Hersey and Blanchard believe that when high levels of maturity are reached, employees accept the reduction in close supervision and attention as an indication of the manager's confidence and trust.

Perhaps the greatest contribution of Hersey and Blanchard's approach is its recognition of employee differences and changes in maturation over time. While managers hope for highly mature employees, most work with at least some individuals who are less talented and motivated. Hersey and Blanchard's theory accepts the fact that some workers may never reach high levels of maturity. In those instances, these writers contend that the manager's task is to provide highly task-oriented leadership.

A different approach to organizations, leadership and communication grew out of an already established theoretical framework called *general systems theory*. At the time this theory was applied to organizations, it had already influenced several areas of scientific thought, including economics, biology, logic, and sociology. The central principle of general systems theory rests on the idea that the whole is more than the sum of its parts; each part must be considered as it interacts with, changes, and is changed by every other part within the system. The parts, or subsystems, of any given system are assumed to be interdependent, and it is primarily through *communication* that this interdependence is facilitated. Indeed, the main contribution of the systems philosophy is its definition of communication as an essential element of organizations.

Although a number of organization theorists have discussed the systems approach to organizations, perhaps the work with the greatest initial impact was Daniel Katz and Robert Kahn's *The Social Psychology of Organizations*. Katz and Kahn conceive of organizations as open systems; in fact, they believe that "social organizations are flagrantly open systems in that the input of energies and the conversion of output into further energy input consist of transactions between the organization and its environment."[8] Thus, the distinction is drawn between open and closed systems. The former are dynamic, everchanging, and particularly responsive to environmental concerns. The latter are static, predictable, and devoid of environmental interaction. Boundaries defining the closed system are fixed, but those associated with the open one are necessarily flexible and ever permeable. In fact, the precise line or boundary between the organization (open system) and its external constituency (environment) is forever variable. Figure 2.1 represents our model for viewing an organization from an open systems perspective.

This model presents several key components necessary to our understanding of organizations as open systems. To begin with, organizations are always involved in some process of *transformation*. Organizations usually develop in response to the felt needs of the societies, cultures, and environments in which they operate. When we create organizations, we believe that we can fill a void; produce a new or superior product; or create a better, safer society. But no organization can begin without resources: raw materials, buildings, people—in short, energy. The energy the organization draws from its environment is called *input*. Clothing manufacturers require inputs of wool, cotton, machinery, and laborers to produce garments. Colleges must have administrators, buildings, faculty, students, and libraries to contribute to a knowledgeable society. Churches need ministers, laypersons, places of worship, and religious literature to spread the doctrine of their faith. In all these examples organizational goals are implicit. Whatever the *reasons* for the organization's existence, whatever its goals are construed to be, the organization's *output* should reflect those goals.

When organizations fail to produce output reflecting their goals, we say they lack *accountability*. For an organization to be accountable (to actually do or produce what it claims to be doing or producing), some process of *transformation* must occur within the organizational structure. Automobiles exist because steel, rubber, and plastic have been changed by workers and machinery into a completed automotive product. The automobile represents design and purpose, and it reflects one reason for the existence of Ford or General Motors.

Figure 2.1 shows a broken line depicting the boundary between the organization and its *environment*. This demonstrates the fact that in one sense both organization and environment are part of the same continuous process.

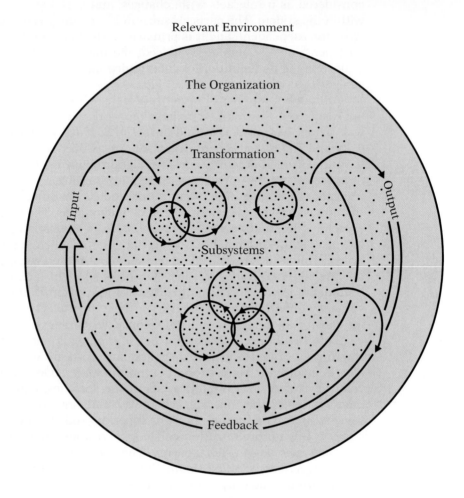

*Dotted area:* presence of formal and informal communication.

The actual boundary separating a given organization from its environment is open to interpretation. An organization's environment does not include everything in the world beyond its immediate scope. Rather, the environment is more profitably viewed as those physical and social factors outside the system's boundary that are directly considered in the decision making of individuals in the system. Our primary concern is with the *relevant environment,* which is useful for understanding organizational behavior. No organization can be viewed in isolation, for each is as much a product of its environment as it is a contributor to it.

    Within each organization are a number of parts or *subsystems,* each serving definite and often interdependent functions. Our model depicts this interdependence with overlapping subsystems—each affecting and being influenced by the others. Different subsystems within the same organization may be aimed at different, or even conflicting, subgoals. In the long run, however, they ought to move in the same general direction, furthering the purposes of the organization of which they are integral parts.

The final factors depicted in our model are *communication* and *feedback*. Clearly, communication dominates the systems approach to organizations. Communication is everywhere. It passes up and down formal channels in the organizational hierarchy; it moves quickly within and among small informal work groups; and it passes through organizational boundaries and into the environment, often to be recycled as feedback. Indeed, communication between organizational systems and their environments has become an increasingly important priority for many organizations.

The influence of the systems philosophy can clearly be seen in one of the hottest trends in business today: the *360-degree performance review*. Simply put, it is a process by which everyone who has contact with the person being reviewed gives input into the appraisal. This means that an employee is reviewed by his or her boss, his or her direct reports, if any, and his or her co-workers. Some companies also ask vendors, customers, or clients to give input for the review.

This system offers the advantage of providing a variety of perspectives concerning the employee's performance. By asking people at different levels and in different roles about the person, the reviewer gains a much more complete picture of the kind of employee the person is and what his or her strengths and weaknesses are. However, this system also can become a popularity contest, particularly among co-workers who give good reviews to people they like and poor reviews to those they dislike. In addition, many are afraid to provide information that is critical of their boss, regardless of how anonymous they are told their comments will be. Nevertheless, this rapidly spreading practice is a clear indication of the importance of interrelationships throughout today's organization.

## The Japanese Philosophy

During the 1970s and 1980s, American managers invested much time and money studying Japanese approaches to management because of the fine quality of Japanese products and the general productivity of their organizations. While the American and Japanese cultures differ significantly in many ways, it is still possible to examine Japanese management and discover several relevant principles.

In his widely acclaimed book *Theory Z*, William Ouchi describes the predominance of work teams throughout Japanese industry and argues that this approach to productivity is one of the reasons the Japanese have been so successful over the past several decades. He notes that the "Type Z company is characterized by many cohesive and semi-autonomous work groups even though a Z company seldom undertakes any explicit attempts at teambuilding."[9]

Extensive studies of Japanese organizations have demonstrated that Japanese managers stress the following:

**1.** *Bottom-up initiative.* Japanese managers believe that change and initiative within an organization *should* come from those closest to the problem. So they elicit change from below. Top-level Japanese managers see their task as creating an atmosphere in which subordinates are motivated to seek better solutions.

**2.** *Top management as facilitator.* Japanese managers do not view themselves as having all the answers. When a subordinate brings in a proposal, the manager neither accepts nor rejects it. Rather, he tactfully, politely asks questions, makes suggestions, and provides encouragement.

**3.** *Middle management as impetus for and shaper of solutions.* In the Japanese system, junior (middle) managers are initiators who perceive problems and formulate tentative solutions in coordination with others; they are not functional specialists who carry out their boss's directives. Because so much emphasis is placed on coordination and integration, solutions to problems evolve more slowly, but they are known and understood by all those who have been a part of the solution-generation process. Horizontal communication is stressed as essential to the coordination of problem-solving efforts.

**4.** *Consensus as a way of making decisions.* The Japanese are less inclined to think in terms of absolutes, that is, the solution (which is right) versus the alternatives (which are wrong). Rather, they recognize a range of alternatives, several of which might work and all of which possess advantages and disadvantages. When a group makes a decision, all members become committed to the chosen solution. From a Japanese perspective, that commitment, and the ensuing dedication to working to make the solution successful, is probably more important than the objective quality of the decision. The Japanese have an interesting concept of consensus. Those who consent to a decision are not necessarily endorsing it. Rather, consent means that each person is satisfied that his or her point of view has been fairly heard, and although he or she may not wholly agree that the decision is the best one, he or she is willing to go along with it and even support it.

**5.** *Concern for employees' personal well-being.* Japanese managers have a kind of paternalistic attitude toward their employees. Traditionally, Japanese organizations have offered their workers housing, extensive recreational facilities, and lifetime employment. The Japanese believe that it is impossible to divorce a worker's personal and professional lives. Good managers express concern for workers as persons with homes and families as well as for the quality of the products the workers produce. Managers typically work alongside their subordinates, counsel them regarding their personal lives, and encourage much peer interaction.

It is interesting that principles that are considered by many to be advantages of the Japanese system can also be viewed as problems, at least from an American perspective. There is a fine line between encouraging consensus and forcing it. When groups place too much emphasis on being agreeable and conforming to organizational expectations, poor-quality decision making is a likely outcome. Moreover, the Japanese notion of taking care of employees can extend into an extreme form of paternalism with which few well-educated Americans would be comfortable. It is appropriate to protect children or others who cannot think for or look after themselves. But professionals hardly fall into these categories. Most Americans would prefer an organizational system that makes it possible for them to function as mature, intelligent human beings, responsible for their own security and well-being.

Finally, the realities of today's work environment in America make irrelevant some of the assumptions underlying Japanese-style leadership. For example, job security is virtually a thing of the past: every year, literally hundreds of thousands of U.S. workers lose their jobs as a part of corporate "downsizings" or "restructurings" intended to increase their organization's profitability and returns to shareholders. Concern for employees' well-being too often has been replaced by concern solely for the bottom line. As a result, employees' loyalty to their organizations has diminished significantly, and many theorists are advising employees to be loyal not to their companies, but to their professions, the projects in which they are involved, and their own careers. In turn, savvy companies are recognizing the "new deal" in employment relationships and trying to retain employees not by relying on blind loyalty, but by customizing the work environment to meet their work and personal life needs.[10]

## The Teamwork Philosophy

Increasingly, theorists have been adopting the position (long held by the Japanese) that productivity in an organization is the result of communication in all directions: upward, downward, and lateral. Such communication fosters the development of work teams. The "teamwork" and "team work" (that is, the sense of team identity and the tasks performed by this work team) achieved by these groups determines how successful the organization is.

Edward E. Lawler, in his book *High-Involvement Management,* takes the perspective that entire organizations should act as teams, with every level participating to some degree in decision making and problem solving. "No more fundamental change could occur than that involved in moving power, knowledge, information, and rewards to lower levels," he claims. "It changes the very nature of what work is and means to everyone who works in an organization. Because it profoundly affects the jobs of everyone, it can impact on the effectiveness of all work organizations."[11]

Bradford and Cohen similarly call for a "post-heroic" conception of workplace leadership, one based on "shared responsibility" to replace the "outdated and inadequate" model that had held sway for so long—the idea that "Lone Ranger rides to the rescue."[12] They portray the post-heroic manager as someone who sees everyone as a leader, who views her primary function as the building of a strong team with a common vision and mutual influence, who invites other employees to share the responsibilities of managing—thereby producing better decisions and ideas, more learning, and higher morale.

Lawler points out, however, that teams are not appropriate in every organizational context. Most agree that teamwork is most effective when a task entails a high level of interdependency among three or more people. For instance, complex manufacturing processes common in the auto, chemical, paper, and high-technology industries can benefit from teams, as can complicated service tasks in insurance, banking, and telecommunications. In most cases, simple assembly-line activities are less amenable to teamwork. As Lawler points out, the more complex the task, the better suited it is for teams. Presumably, when the right kind of task is matched with the team approach, the result will be greater problem-solving speed and effectiveness. Dumaine contrasts this with the traditional approach to problem solving in a hierarchical organization: "A person with a problem in one function might have to shoot it up two or three layers by memo to a vice-president who tosses it laterally to a vice-president of another function who then kicks it down to the person in his area who knows the answer. Then it's back up and down the ladder again."[13] The rewards of teamwork come in the form of enhanced responsibility. Nevertheless, with fewer middle management positions, opportunities for advancement are diminished. And managers must recognize that organizing teams is a long, difficult process. All members of the team must learn to think differently about themselves and how they approach their work and one another. Advocates of teamwork, however, are convinced that the results are worth the time and effort.

Many American organizations already have instituted various team approaches to managing and communicating. Nearly all of Motorola's 57,000 U.S. employees are involved in some stage of its "Participative Management Program." Honeywell, Xerox, General Motors, and Westinghouse, among others, have publicly committed themselves to using a more participative approach to organizing and managing people. Hundreds of companies are using quality circles or some other form of group problem solving to involve employees in identifying and resolving work-related problems. Clearly, as Lawler claims, "participative management is an idea whose time has come."

Still, not every organization has seen the team philosophy succeed. As Stewart reported in her article "Teams Don't Always Work," companies from Motorola to the Ritz-Carlton hotel chain have successfully used work teams as they try to achieve optimum productivity, but others have seen productivity actually decline because of infighting and a lack of direction.[14] A particularly striking example of the difficulties involved in the team approach took place at Levi's, the jeans manufacturer. In 1992, the company directed its U.S. plants to abandon the old piecework system, under which a worker repeatedly performed a single, specialized task (like sewing zippers or attaching belt loops) and was paid according to the amount of work he or she completed. In the new system, groups of 10 to 35 workers would share the tasks and would be paid according to the total number of trousers the group completed. Levi's figured that this would cut down on the monotony of the old system and that it would enable stitchers to do different tasks, thus reducing repetitive-stress injuries. Instead, it led to a quagmire in which skilled workers found themselves pitted against slower colleagues, damaging morale and triggering corrosive infighting. Threats and insults became more common. Longtime friendships dissolved as faster workers tried to banish slower ones. "You hear so much shouting, lots of times you don't even look up from your work," recalls Knoxville seamstress Mary Farmer.[15]

Levi's vows to persevere with the team strategy at its remaining U.S. plants. But unofficially, much of the approach is being scrapped as individual managers seek ways to improve productivity. Perhaps this situation proves Lawler's point: some tasks and processes may not be suited to the team approach.

The teamwork philosophy thus contains elements of the Japanese philosophy, "Theory Y," Likert's fourth "system" and the Systems philosophy; yet it also has characteristics of its own. Communication in this sort of organization moves in all directions, including laterally in informal meetings between peers. Spontaneous problem solving is encouraged, and conflict is resolved at the lowest level possible. Opportunities are created for employees in different departments to meet and talk with one another, and formal task teams are created whenever appropriate. Above all, communication cuts across formal organizational boundaries, occurring between people directly involved in getting the work done.

## The Self-Management Philosophy

The teamwork philosophy has begun to emphasize informal leadership in place of formal management. In an article titled "Who Needs a Boss?" *Fortune* describes self-managed "superteams" that typically consist of between 3 and 30 workers, "sometimes blue collar, sometimes white collar, sometimes both."[16] For example, teams in a General Mills cereal plant in Lodi, California, schedule, operate, and maintain machinery so effectively that no managers are present on the night shift. Similarly, after organizing its home office operations into teams, Aetna Life & Casualty reduced the ratio of middle managers to workers from 1:7 down to 1:30 (and at the same time improved customer service).

*Employees who work at home should be self-motivated and be able to manage their own work. They must set goals, be self-reliant, and act independently and responsibly.*

Responsibilities often undertaken by self-managing teams include such traditional management functions as preparing an annual budget, timekeeping, recording quality control statistics, monitoring inventory, assigning jobs within groups, training other team members, adjusting production schedules, modifying production processes, setting team goals, resolving internal conflicts, and evaluating team performance.

Leadership within self-managed teams usually emerges informally. Once company managers have trained team members in basic problem-solving and group-dynamic skills, and defined for them their scope of responsibility and authority, they allow the team to develop their own procedures and relationships. Team members most skilled in group communication techniques are most likely to emerge as the informal leaders.

Self-managed teams have proved extremely effective in many organizations. During their weekly meeting, a team of Federal Express clerks identified a billing problem that had been costing the company $2.1 million a year (and eventually they resolved the problem). In 3M, cross-functional teams tripled the number of new products produced by one division. Teams of blue-collar workers at Johnsonville Foods of Sheboygan, Wisconsin, helped increase production by more than 50 percent over four years.

Despite such successes, the spread of self-managed teams has been relatively slow for several reasons. First, it requires a great deal of mutual trust between top management and employees—trust that may take years to build (and only a moment to undo). Second, middle managers often feel highly threatened by the concept because they believe it will reduce their power and influence. Thus, they may openly or covertly oppose the process. In addition, implementation of self-managing teams often takes a long time (18 months to two years is common), and training employees in self-management skills can be time-consuming and expensive. Nevertheless, the benefits of self-management have been dramatic enough to convince many organizations to commit to this new management style.

## The Values-Driven Philosophy

Recently, theorists have begun to argue that the most effective organization is one that lives according to a clear, widely supported set of values. Their thinking is based on the principle that the key to an organization's success is the culture that exists in that organization. Briefly, an organization's culture consists of "a system of shared values (what is important) and beliefs (how things work) that interacts with a company's people, organizational structures, and control systems to produce behavioral norms (the way we do things around here)." Culture is not simply a component of the organization. Rather, as Pacanowsky and O'Donnell-Trujillo note, "a culture is something an organization *is*."[17]

One of the most influential theorists taking the values-driven philosophy is Stephen R. Covey, whose book *The 7 Habits of Highly Effective People* propelled him to national prominence and provided him with the funding to establish the Covey Leadership Center and the Institute for Principle-Centered Leadership. Shopping malls everywhere now are dotted with retail outlets for Covey paraphernalia, such as desktop decorations, personal planners, pictures and posters, and other accoutrements apparently vital to an effective person's work life.

In his original book, Covey noted that highly effective people are proactive, begin with the end in mind, put first things first, think win/win, seek first to understand and then to be understood, synergize and sharpen the saw.[18] Covey then turned his attention to organizations in *Principle-Centered Leadership,* arguing that organizational leaders should apply his seven habits on four different levels: organizational (to achieve alignment between individual and organizational objectives), managerial (to achieve empowerment of others), interpersonal (to build trust with others), and personal (to achieve trustworthiness in the eyes of others).[19] All these things are achieved through such communication behaviors as listening before explaining; involving others to produce win/win solutions; refraining from saying unkind or negative things; and admitting mistakes, apologizing, and asking for forgiveness. As such, Covey's approach to leadership and organizational communication theory is much more behavioral and interpersonally based than the philosophies outlined above.

Kenneth Blanchard, advocate of the situational leadership philosophy, also has adopted the values-driven philosophy. In *Managing by Values,* he and coauthor Michael O'Connor argue that leaders should clarify their organization's values, communicate them thoroughly and consistently, and then build alignment toward those values through a participative "gap" identification and problem-solving process.[20] Labovitz and Rosansky apply the systems approach to values-driven leadership, discussing the need for both "vertical" and "horizontal" alignment with organizational goals and values, and incorporate the self-management philosophy in their discussion of "self-aligning" organizations.[21] Others similarly have argued that the most effective organizations are ones in which every individual's efforts and behaviors are guided by a common set of values and a shared vision for the future.[22]

The values-driven philosophy takes into account both how an organization communicates and what it communicates. Initially, communication is downward as the organization's leadership states clearly what the vision for the future is and what values are to guide employees' behaviors. In turn, the values may dictate that superiors talk with their subordinates in certain ways or that employees participate actively in making decisions that affect their work lives.

## The Information-Driven Philosophy

An interesting combination of the classical school of organizational thought (which heavily emphasizes measurement as a guide to employee behavior) and the values-driven philosophy is "open book" leadership, which holds that employees' efforts should be guided and motivated by information. For example, Kaplan and Norton argue that organizations should use a "balanced scorecard" that measures four categories—financial performance, customer knowledge, internal business processes, and learning and growth—to align individual, organizational, and cross-departmental activities and to motivate better performance.[23] Using this principle, a large health care system in upstate New York every three months provides its management and employees with a single page that shows charts tracking patient satisfaction, employee satisfaction, financial performance, and costs involved in delivering patient care. They assume that managers and employees will be motivated to achieve improvements in these measures (a key Theory Y assumption), and to date their experience has proved this assumption correct.

*Open book* management is a similar philosophy intended to encourage all the people in an organization to "think and act like business partners."[24] Based on the assumption that employees want to know about the industry in which they work and will act responsibly if they are given enough information, the open book management philosophy suggests that organizational leaders should do four things: (1) make full information about the organization's performance available (create the open book); (2) build "business literacy" among all employees so they understand what the information means; (3) empower all employees within the organization so they can act on the information they are given; (4) create reward structures that give employees a stake in their organization's success.[25]

Like the values-driven leadership philosophy, the information-driven philosophy is heavily communication-oriented. Upward, downward and lateral communication all are emphasized, as Theory Y assumptions are followed in allowing employees to do whatever is necessary to improve measures of organizational performance. Reward systems are put in place to encourage employee support of organizational goals—an important divergence from the Japanese philosophy, where loyalty to company goals is a given. But the morality of organizational goals is not an important consideration, apparently, within this body of thought.

## The Customer-Driven Philosophy

The values-driven and information-driven philosophies are combined in the *customer-driven* philosophy, whereby everything an organization and its members do should be guided by the goal of satisfying the organization's customers. For example, Whiteley argues that a customer-driven company is based on several communication practices, including:

The impact of constituents' concerns—in this case, the concerns of stockholders—upon leaders' decision making was illustrated by the recent decision of a chief executive officer to give up not only his position, but his company. Richard C. Notebaert, chairman and chief executive officer of Ameritech, was interviewed concerning his feelings about an impending deal whereby SBC Communications Inc. would acquire Ameritech. The move would mean that Mr. Notebaert would no longer call the shots at Ameritech, but would answer to corporate headquarters in San Antonio. The interviewer asked, "The consensus among industry people is that the SBC offer was so good for Ameritech's shareholders, you really had no choice. That if you turned it down, your shareholders could come back and say, `Dick, where's your fiduciary responsibility?'"

Notebaert answered, "Well, the shareholder would never have known. There are many things that occur, conversations like that between companies, that never get into the public eye. The most important thing is we would've been hypocrites . . . you say to yourself, it is necessary to put aside your own driver or to ask yourself are they the same drivers you've been espousing all these years. In my case, I had been espousing consistently: right opportunity, right proposition, right folks. Bam. So there was no way I could look our board in the eye and say to our board this is inconsistent. You have to remember why you are here. I represent the shareowners. That's my job. I work for them. If you don't put the shareowner first, I think you've got a problem."

The interviewer then asked, "Dick Notebaert is just about synonymous with Ameritech. For you, this deal must seem more akin to a divorce than a business deal."

Notebaert answered, "It was worse than that. I've never been through a divorce, but it has to have been worse than that. . . . I didn't sleep for six weeks while this was going on. Every night, toss and turn. But I think you have to be that way. The one thing I think Ameritech has the reputation for is being a straight shooter. I think that reputation has served us very well with our customers and with our shareholders. But it wasn't an easy thing."

Source: Jon Van, "Putting Company First, Even if You're Not," *Chicago Tribune* (October 29, 1998): sec. 3, p. 1.

1. Creating a customer-keeping vision through top-down communication of the organization's values.
2. Saturating the company with the voice of the customer by using a wide variety of communication tools to listen to customer opinions: surveys, group discussions, informal customer-employee contacts, and so on.
3. Liberating "customer champions" by giving all employees freedom to make decisions and solve problems related to customer service.
4. Following the rule "Measure, measure, measure," so that customer satisfaction information can be used to assess individual, team, and organizational performance and to motivate and guide performance improvements.
5. "Walking the talk," so that the values and customer focus are exhibited by everyone in the organization—particularly top management.[26]

Wiersema similarly argues that communication and relationships with customers should guide communication and relationships within organization, such that every organization achieves true "intimacy" with its customers.[27] In his view, organizations should be characterized by *judgment* (where everyone is sensitive and responsive to customer needs), *cooperation* (where positive teamwork among coworkers and with customers are maintained), and *learning* (whereby everyone is helped formally and informally continuously to build understanding of what it takes to achieve customer satisfaction).

The customer-driven philosophy is also heavily communication-oriented, emphasizing upward, downward, and lateral communications, all pointed toward a single goal: achieving customer satisfaction. However, many advocates of a customer-driven culture do not deal with some particularly ticklish issues (for example, what if the customer wants something that is immoral or unethical?) and they tend to take an overly altruistic view of organizational life, not recognizing that employee satisfaction must be achieved to some extent before they will be eager to please their customers.

## The "Learning Organization" Philosophy

A relatively recent philosophy of organizational communication and leadership that combines elements of the systems, vision and values-based teamwork, and information-driven philosophies initially was expressed in Peter Senge's influential *The Fifth Discipline*. Senge argued that, in order to survive, organizations must become "learning" entities characterized by five "disciplines":

1. *Systems thinking.*  Recognizing the interrelationships among all elements of an organization.
2. *Personal mastery.*  Continually "clarifying and deepening our personal vision, focusing our energies, developing patience and seeing reality objectively" to develop individual mastery of skills and the organization's values.
3. *Mental models.*  Building "assumptions, generalizations, or even pictures or images that influence how we understand the world and how we take action" in a manner that builds organizational success.
4. *Building shared vision.*  Creating a shared picture of the future the company seeks to create.
5. *Team learning.*  Using "dialogue" to create teams whose intelligence exceeds the intelligence of the individuals in the teams and teams that "develop extraordinary capacities for coordinated action."[28]

Gifford and Elizabeth Pinchot extended Senge's thinking, claiming that in today's complex and intelligence-intensive world economy, organizations can no longer rely solely on the thinking and intelligence of those few at the top of the bureaucracy.[29] The amount of clear thinking required to deal with the multitude of customer demands, ethnic cultures, technological advances, and diverse workforce needs makes it necessary to involve everyone within the organization. Organizations therefore must develop and engage the intelligence, business judgment, and systemwide responsibility of all members in order to respond to customers, partners, and competitors. Successful organizations will be characterized by "voluntary learning networks" composed of informal contacts among organizational members, "democratic self-rule" whereby decision making is delegated to the lowest levels of the organization, and "limited corporate government" such that centralized control is minimized in favor of decentralized thinking and action.

Signicast Corp., an investment castings manufacturer based in Milwau-kee, provides an excellent example of the evolution from a traditional "plant" culture into a team-based "learning organization" culture.[30] In 1992, the com-pany recognized the need for a new, larger facility—one that could be any-thing they wanted it to be. Management initially talked with customers, ask-ing how Signicast could improve its service. Customers' principal concerns were long lead times, unreliable delivery dates, and cost. Accordingly, the new plant would be designed to attack those concerns by creating automated continuous-flow processing that ensured reliable on-time shipment and mini-mized personnel needs (and thus labor costs).

A core group of five executives started planning the new facility, with input from everyone else. The core group would develop an idea and then put it out for evaluation, soliciting reactions. Then they asked for volunteers to assist with problem solving. Each group of volunteers would meet with the executives and explain to them how a piece of equipment or a cell was going to work. Then came time for employee suggestions, provided in meet-ings that could last for hours. Employees even had the final word on whether the new plant project would go forward at all; 98.8 percent voted in favor of proceeding.

Employees for the new plant were hired according to several important competencies: a team orientation, good communication skills, and a willing-ness to do a variety of jobs. The new hires (and employees transferring from the old facility) worked with equipment vendors to plan the building and in-stallation of new machinery, and even went to vendors' training facilities to learn to use the equipment before it had been installed. Employees were cross-trained so that virtually everyone could operate every machine.

When production began, teams were created in which each subunit had a master technician to provide technical expertise, but in which team members were expected to do a variety of jobs and to decide many of their own work rules and procedures. Training of new team members was overseen by the master technicians and assisted by more senior employees. The company set up a pay structure that allowed employees to get more money by learning more jobs, thus providing rewards for teamwork as well. Finally, employees unable to work effectively in a team environment were identified by their peers and, if corrective actions did not produce behavioral improvement, asked to leave the organization.

Central to the learning organization is communication. Downward com-munication and participative discussions are used to create shared visions and values; classroom training and individual mentoring are used to build skills and knowledge; lateral networks among all components of the organi-zation share information quickly. Indeed, the ultimate learning organization might be the one featured on the television series *Star Trek: The Next Genera-tion:* the "Borg." A population of cyberbeings, the Borg are completely and in-stantly connected, so that the thoughts of one are shared by all and the learn-ing of one contributes to the knowledge of all. Their ability to acquire and share information instantly and to make quick adjustments to their environ-ment make the Borg a threat to the universe; the ability to learn and adjust quickly makes a more mundane organization a threat to its competitors.

In sharp contrast to the thinking of most management experts is what some are calling the *S.O.B. school of leadership*—an approach that views people as something to be sacrificed in the interests of corporate profitability. In his book *Confessions of an S.O.B.*, Al Neuharth, founder of *USA Today* and former chairman of Gannett publishing, attributed his success to the principle that "cream and S.O.B.s rise to the top."[31] Through such principles as "Promote thyself," "Build molehills into mountains," and "Best the boss," he transformed himself from a "poor country kid from South Dakota" to a multimillionaire media mogul. However, careful reading of his book indicates that he achieved his success by using more Theory Y principles than Theory X.

The same cannot be said for other executives who have achieved recent prominence—the true S.O.B.s. In his article "The Hit Men," Sloan reports, "Once upon a time, it was a mark of shame to fire your workers en masse. It meant you had messed up your business. Today, the more people a company fires, the more Wall Street loves it, and the higher its stock price goes."[32] To improve profits, massive layoffs have been implemented by executives in such companies as AT&T (40,000 layoffs), Chemical–Chase Manhattan (12,000), GTE (17,000), Boeing (28,000), IBM (60,000), Delta Air Lines (15,000), General Motors (74,000), Digital Equipment (20,000), Sears, Roebuck & Co. (50,000), and McDonnell Douglas (17,000). Employees at AT&T reportedly quip that chairman Robert Allen will soon fire everyone but himself, and AT&T will stand for "Allen & Two Temps."[33]

Perhaps the most prominent proponent of the S.O.B. philosophy was "Chainsaw" Al Dunlap, the former chief executive officer (CEO) of Sunbeam who preferred the nickname "Rambo in pinstripes." In a picture of Mr. Dunlap that was published in *USA Today*, he was holding an automatic pistol in each hand and wearing a black headband and bullet-laden bandoleers that criss-crossed his chest. Dunlap was a throwback to the iron-fisted school of management—a West Point graduate with a gruff demeanor and an air of blunt outspokenness. Employees found him abrasive and unforgiving if they didn't meet results. In his first year at Sunbeam, Dunlap cut 6,000 jobs, or half the workforce, and closed 18 of 26 factories.[34] Interestingly, when *Newsweek* asked more than 50 CEOs of large American companies to discuss corporate restructuring, only Dunlap was willing to talk. His comments: "When journalists and politicians spout off about corporate downsizing, it's the Al Dunlaps of the world who tend to get the blame. We're painted as villains; but we're not. We're more like doctors. We know it's painful to operate, but it's the only way to keep the patient from dying."[35] Ultimately, Dunlap was fired from Sunbeam, and shortly after his departure it was revealed that he had overstated the company's losses when he first took over, and then overstated their profits after he had been in office for a time, thereby artificially inflating the "turnaround" he had achieved.

Not all companies that have been forced to lay off employees have adopted the S.O.B. philosophy, however. United Technologies (UT), which had cut 33,000 jobs since 1990, unveiled a new, expensive plan to help workers get reeducated, giving them time off to attend classes, paying for tuition and books, and giving employees who completed their studies 50 shares of UT stock. But for decency, it's hard to top Malden Mills, which became

## PROTECTING YOURSELF FROM AN S.O.B.

Bosses who treat their employees like punching bags rather than assets are not uncommon in the workplace, and you should take steps to protect yourself should you find yourself working for a proponent of the S.O.B. philosophy. Katherine Sopranos suggests, "From the beginning of your employment, keep dated records of conversations, comments and scenarios that occurred between you and your boss. Detailed documentation is evidence of your tumultuous working conditions, and it allows you leverage if you decide to sue for emotional distress or physical harm, such as stomach conditions." Having collected this documentation, you should discuss it individually or with a group of colleagues with Human Resources or a higher-level executive in the company, including your boss' boss. And," Sopranos concludes, "mention that you spoke with an attorney."

Source: Katherine Sopranos, "Who's Afraid of the Big Bad Boss," *Chicago Tribune* (June 21, 1998): sec. 6, p. 1

---

famous when it kept 1,400 workers on the payroll after its plant in Lawrence, Massachusetts, burned down.

## The Commercial School of Organizational Philosophy

In her book *Fad Surfing in the Boardroom,* Eileen C. Shapiro decries the "endless array of prepackaged programs and management mantras purported to launch companies to 'world class' status."[36] In her view, too many organizational leaders take a management "fad-of-the-month" approach and create mission statements no one believes, organizational structures that don't work (but sound good in books), empowerment that no one wants, corporate cultures that serve more as excuses than descriptors, or open books that no one reads. In effect, they do what philosophers (such as consultants, authors, or professors) preach, not what makes the most sense for their own organization. And too often, those philosophers have a goal unrelated to the well-being of today's organizations: selling books, going on the lecture circuit, and making a lot of money.

The beginning of the "commercial" school can be traced to *In Search of Excellence,* the best-seller that made millionaires of its authors, Tom Peters and Robert Waterman.[37] When the Japanese began competing effectively against American business, U.S. managers' confidence began to wane and the belief emerged that "somebody, somewhere, knows how to do business—but it isn't us." This sense of insecurity led to a desire to find experts who could tell American managers how better companies do it—and helped Peters and Waterman sell over one million copies of *In Search of Excellence* within the first 11 months of its release.

While the book gave some insight into the practices of organizations Peters and Waterman deemed "excellent," its commercial success also caused consultants to realize that they could increase their income and build their consulting practice by writing books on "management theory." Book titles such as *The Wisdom of Wolves: Nature's Way to Organizational Success, Make It So: Leadership Lessons from Star Trek: The Next Generation,* and *Leadership Secrets of the Rogue Warrior: A Commando's Guide to Success* litter bookshelves and

## DIVERSITY AND THE "COMMERCIAL" PHILOSOPHY

Ethnically diverse viewpoints are finding their way into the commercial school of management thinking. Rainbow Hawk and Wind Eagle, a married Native American couple, have created a tepee-strewn training facility at the Ehama Institute, in California's Santa Cruz mountains, overlooking the Pacific to the west and Gilroy, world garlic capital, to the East. At Ehama, visitors from institutions as diverse as the U.S. Air Force and Mattel (which paid $14,500 for each of 17 employees they sent for a weekend) can learn, among other things, an ancient tribal approach to problem solving called a "council ceremony."

The sessions are conducted out-of-doors, on the perimeter of a 60-foot circle with a fire pit at the center. Each participant adopts one of eight perspectives or attitudes. One executive, for example, might speak only of the danger that could come from a proposed course of action; another, only the creative possibilities it offers; a third, the present condition of the company; a fourth, future strategy. Clothed in special robes, the participants approach the fire pit, in which a central fire and bunches of sage and other herbs are burning. Hours later, the correct solution often emerges.

According to Rainbow Hawk, the reason this approach is effective is that inherent in all of us is a body of ancient wisdom. The ceremony awakens and invokes our wisdom, and the approach ensures that all viewpoints are represented. Rainbow Hawk and Wind Eagle recently toured Europe, exposing Finns and Scotsmen to their approach. They also offered a "corporate intensive" on decision making at a New York hunting lodge.

Source: Alan Farnham, "In Search of Suckers," *Fortune* 134: 7 (October 14, 1996): 119–126.

best-seller lists, but make questionable contributions to the body of management and communication.

Such "gurus" apparently fill an important need. "The public's hunger for guidance (as measured by sales of how-to books) is running at an all-time high," reports Alan Farnham in his *Fortune* article "In Search of Suckers." "So open has the national mind become to new ideas that it might as well be porous. Eager to shovel in still more stands a guru army." But in addition to guidance, these "management theorists" provide another important service: entertainment for the many conferences and conventions held almost daily in the business world. Twyman Towery, author of *The Wisdom of Wolves*, reported in an interview, "I do four speeches a month at $4,500 a speech—about all I have time to do." "The best gurus never forget they are headliners," Farnham notes, "often sharing a bill with other acts a client has retained." After his speech, "a guru finds himself poolside enjoying cocktails with others on the program—a ventriloquist, say, or a cocker spaniel that can howl 'La Marseillaise.'"

Harriet Rubin, business editor for Doubleday, noted that "many people write books just to get onto the circuit." However, the reverse also is true: lecturers send her 20 or more tapes a week, hoping she will take them on as authors (thereby increasing their visibility and, ultimately, their lecture fees). She tried recently to enlist Las Vegas lion tamers Siegfried & Roy to author a book on management, explaining "If one can control wild beasts, one can run a business. The word 'manage,' after all, comes from "managgiare"—to tame the wild horses."[38]

Whatever the motives of its authors, the commercial philosophy has influenced the thinking and actions of today's organizational leaders. As Micklethwait and Wooldridge point out in their book *The Witch Doctors: Making Sense of the Management Gurus,* "Management theory . . . is propelled by two primal human instincts: fear and greed. . . . However, it also is clear that management theory is bound up with three revolutions that directly or indirectly affect all of us: the reinvention of companies, the reinvention of careers and the reinvention of government."[39] And not every current management book is without value, of course. The difficulty is separating those that have something to offer from those that find new ways to express old ideas. Belasco and Stayer's *Flight of the Buffalo,* for example, provides extremely useful advice for directing organizational change.[40] Lynch and Kordis's *Strategy of the Dolphin* is less helpful.[41] More and more, "Buyer beware" is the watchword for assessing theories of leadership. As media mogul Rupert Murdoch observed, "You go to Doubleday's business section, and you see all these wonderful titles, and you spend $300, and then you throw them all away."[42]

The "Cool" Organizational Culture

In her excellent summary of the ways in which organizational philosophies have been applied on a day-to-day basis, Coudron observes that today's most successful companies have an organizational culture that might best be described as "cool," "ku," "clutch," "tasty," "far out" or "groovy," depending on one's age group.[43] She reports that the "coolest" organizations possess several key dimensions:

1. *Respect for work/life balance.* These companies recognize employees have pressures outside the office and work to ease those pressures by providing such benefits as flexible work schedules, part-time jobs, job sharing, telecommuting, sabbaticals, on-site day care, dry cleaning, and banking. Among the leaders in this area are Deloitte & Touche LLP, Eddie Bauer, and the city of Phoenix. But some companies go even further, allowing employees to bring life into their work by casual dress and personalized office decor, or even by allowing them to play while at work. OddzOn Products, a toy manufacturer, closed the office and took all 100 employees to a movie in the middle of a workday.

2. *A sense of purpose.* Cool companies are those in which employees feel connected to the product, to the corporate mission, or to the overall vision of the industry. In such companies, employees are energized by the sense that they are making a meaningful contribution. Employees at Harley-Davidson, based in Milwaukee, Wisconsin, apparently are so excited about their product that many of them have tattooed the company's name on their bodies.

3. *Diversity.* An increasingly important dimension of coolness is diversity. Cool companies are ones where employees feel it's safe to express their differences, whatever those differences may be, including gender, race, sexual orientation, work style, temperament, and opinion. Allstate Insurance, headquartered in Northbrook, Illinois, takes diversity seriously and has received extensive recognition for its work to provide opportunities to women, Hispanics, and disabled individuals. But true commitment to diversity, according to Jerry Hirschberg, president of Nissan Design

International Inc. in San Diego, California, can best be illustrated by two kinds of parties: "An uncool party is one where people are invited for the sole reason of having a proper and impressive guest list. A cool party, on the other hand, is one where people are invited because they provide a stimulating and enjoyable mix, regardless of whether or not they have the right credentials."[44] Cool companies operate the same way.

**4.** *Integrity.* Integrity refers to the ability of a company to communicate the truth to employees—whatever that truth may be. But it also refers to an organization's ability to care about the quality of its products and services. Companies with integrity want employees to do a great job, and not just get the job done. Companies also want employees to stand up for what they believe in.

**5.** *Participatory management.* Cool companies have realized that employees on the front lines often have the best ideas, and that it is often counterproductive to tell them what to do. In such companies, collaboration is the norm but it is also possible for individual employees to have an impact.

**6.** *Learning environment.* In cool companies, employees leave at the end of the day knowing more than they did when the day started. Companies such as Motorola, based in Schaumburg, Illinois, offer massive amounts of training and education to their people.

Research demonstrates that companies that have established a cool corporate culture, like the ones named above, show significantly lower rates of employee turnover and higher levels of employee morale than do noncool organizations.

## MANAGEMENT THEORY IN PERSPECTIVE

We have all had experiences with undesirable corporate cultures created by ineffective organizational leaders. They can be found in schools, churches, hospitals, small private firms, and large corporations. In the clever film *Nine to Five*, we are delighted to observe the authoritarian, abusive boss who is bound, gagged, and kept captive in his own home for six weeks while three female employees, including his own secretary, try to prove him a crook. While he is "tied up," these three women also take the liberty of initiating several changes in the office. They have the place redecorated, institute flexible work hours, start a day care center and an alcoholism rehabilitation program, begin to hire the disabled, and remove the time clock. When, at last, the boss returns, at first he is horrified but later he is stunned to discover that productivity is up by 20 percent!

The movie is a comedy, but the point it makes is provocative. These three women, who had never been allowed to make decisions before, demonstrated their ability to take risks, make tough decisions, and deal with their fellow employees in compassionate and creative ways. The effectiveness of their leadership could not be questioned.

It is possible for nearly any employee to provide leadership. We concur with Tannenbaum, Weschler, and Massarik, who define leadership as "interpersonal influence, exercised in a situation and directed, through the communication process, toward the attainment of specialized goal or goals."[45] But the manner in which that leadership is exerted through the communication process typically will reflect the philosophy of the individual, which in turn is shaped by his or her understanding of the organization's culture.

## ISSUES FACING CONTEMPORARY ORGANIZATIONS

In his 1982 best-seller *Megatrends: Ten Directions Transforming Our Lives,* John Naisbitt described ten trends that, he felt, would shape the lives of everyone in our society.[46] In his view, we were moving from an industrial to an information society, from "forced technology" to an emphasis on both "high tech" and "high touch," from a national to a world economy, from a short-term perspective to one emphasizing long-term consequences, from centralized to decentralized decision-making practices, from a reliance on institutions to an emphasis on self-help, from a representative democracy to one emphasizing active participation, from hierarchies to networking, from a North to a South concentration of economic power and from a focus on "either/or" to an understanding of multiple options. His thinking (and possibly his economic success) spawned subsequent efforts to project future trends. Morrison and Schmid noted that new business realities include the older and wiser American worker, a general sense of insecurity, a global marketplace, failing social institutions, a desire for shared authority, and burgeoning information technologies.[47] More recently, Celente discussed the implications of such trends as longer life spans, increasing technology, revivals of community spirit and family values, and changes in the delivery of medical and educational services.[48]

These and other authors provide this important realization: organizations and everyone within them face an ever-increasing rate of change and a set of issues that have critical implications for organizational communications. In this section, we will review some of the issues that are most closely related to organizational cultures and communication practices.

## Empowerment

To what extent should power be shared? How are the sharing of power and effective leadership related? In an attempt to answer these questions, Bennis sought to identify the defining characteristics of excellent leaders by interviewing 90 individuals who had been nominated by their peers as the most influential leaders in all walks of life.[49] Bennis found that these individuals all shared one significant characteristic: they made others feel powerful. Together with others, these leaders were able to accomplish exceptional organizational goals.

Bennis concluded that empowering others consistently produced several important benefits. First, those who felt empowered reported feeling important and valued by their fellow workers. They also developed a conviction that learning and competence really matter, and sought to behave in ways consistent with those convictions. They perceived themselves as part of a team or as embedded within a community. Finally, they came to view their work as more engaging and challenging than ever before.

Bennis's research suggests many positive outcomes associated with empowering workers. You may be wondering, however, *how* managers might approach empowerment in terms of their attitudes, behaviors, and communication practices. Several researchers have pursued these issues, attempting to describe the culture, practices, and behaviors that might typify an empowering organization and its leaders. Conger, for instance, describes several specific managerial techniques and strategies[50]:

*Involve Subordinates in the Assignment of Work*  Normally, it is the manager who makes work assignments. Thus, when subordinates are permitted to make decisions about which tasks they choose to tackle, they are sharing some of the manager's authority.

*Provide a Positive, Collaborative Work Environment*  Whenever individuals are able to set aside formal role relationships and focus on common problems while seeking mutually acceptable solutions, they move in the direction of empowerment.

*Reward and Encourage Others in Visible and Personal Ways*  For most individuals, the value of a reward is increased when it is awarded in public and when it is very personal (in the context of professional good taste). Acknowledging the excellent performance of someone during a public speech or reading aloud a letter praising someone's fine work during a staff meeting might serve as such visible recognition.

*Express Confidence*  The manager who shares a difficult task with others, who actually involves others in demanding, challenging problem solving, communicates the message that she is confident that others are up to the challenge. While sentiments of confidence can be expressed verbally, taking actions that demonstrate confidence and trust may communicate an even more powerful message.

*Foster Initiative and Responsibility*   One especially effective manager encouraged his subordinates to identify problems within the organization and come to him with ideas for how to solve them. He consistently expressed tremendous enthusiasm whenever a subordinate identified a legitimate problem and offered a sound, promising, or innovative solution. This manager prodded subordinates into being problem detectors and problem solvers—thus encouraging energetic, intelligent, and responsible employee behavior.

*Build on Success*   The wisest managers are those who applaud and celebrate others' accomplishments. Rather than being threatened by those beneath them, these managers point to others' successes with genuine enthusiasm, reward them generously, and challenge them to excel even more.

Another approach to describing empowering organizational cultures has grown from Pacanowsky's long-term study of W. L. Gore & Associates.[51] Pacanowsky offers several "operating rules of the empowering organization" and suggests that they might serve as a model for other organizations. His rules include:

*Distribute Power and Opportunity Widely*   This focuses on letting people own the problems they are interested in, decentralizing the process by which important decisions are made, and emphasizing the power to accomplish (rather than the power to dominate).

*Maintain a Full, Open, and Decentralized Communication System*   Information in this sort of organization flows freely, with fewer distortions and less attention to impression management. Mistakes are tolerated as people learn, grow, take risks, and keep on working.

*Use Integrative Problem Solving*   This approach distributes problem- solving responsibilities among functional work units. Power, information, and opportunity are genuinely and widely distributed. Task forces are used abundantly. With new configurations of people coming together to solve problems, innovation and creativity are encouraged in a climate that fosters visibility for many and nurtures a "we" attitude among everyone.

*Practice Challenge in an Environment of Trust*   Individuals will be better problem solvers when they participate in debate and lively conversations about the relative strengths and weaknesses of competing courses of action. Ideas are to be challenged and concerns expressed—but criticism and challenge must be offered in a spirit of support rather than in a spirit of one-upmanship. Ultimately, after issues have been thoroughly discussed, people must be given the chance to act according to their best information and judgment.

*Reward and Recognize People so as to Encourage a High-Performance Ethic and Responsibility*   The best rewards grow from giving others increased power and opportunity, rather than from instituting "employee of the month" awards. Thus, the emphasis is upon internal rather than external incentives. As individuals are given greater responsibilities, their credibility is also enhanced.

*Become Wise by Living Through, and Learning From, Organizational Ambiguity, Inconsistency, Contradiction, and Paradox* Most organizations exist in complex, ambiguous environments where information is equivocal and decision making is shrouded in uncertainty. Organizational values are often characterized by inconsistencies. People are encouraged to excel as individuals, while, simultaneously, cooperative teamwork is praised and rewarded. Learning to live with these apparently conflicting realities is critical to empowerment and growth.

Finally, some scholars have offered a more theoretical approach to defining empowerment. Based on the notion of empowerment as a process of creating intrinsic task motivation by providing an environment and tasks that increase feelings of self-efficacy and energy, Thomas and Velthouse have developed a conceptual model that specifies four dimensions of empowerment: impact, choice, competence, and meaningfulness.[52] *Impact* is related to whether accomplishing a particular task or job will make a difference in the scheme of things. In theory, the greater the impact employees believe they have, the more internally motivated they will be. The second dimension, *choice*, means the degree to which personal behavior is self-determined. According to this model, the more individuals are given the opportunity to select tasks, to decide how they should be accomplished, and to elect to take responsibility for their outcome, the more empowered they should feel. The third dimension is *competence*. For empowerment to be possible, those to whom tasks are assigned must possess the necessary skills, knowledge, experience, and other qualifications to enable them to move forward with confidence and competence. Finally, *meaningfulness* is crucial. This dimension points to the value of a task or job in relation to the individual's own beliefs, ideals, and standards. The more closely a task is consistent with someone's value system, the more conviction he or she brings to its accomplishment. Without perceived meaningfulness, a sense of empowerment is unlikely.

Taken together, the empowerment model and practical guidelines provide a broad vision of what empowerment might actually mean on a day-to-day basis. Even so, several questions remain. Can an empowering organizational profile ever be identified, or must each manager define empowerment in terms of her or his specific organization? Is empowerment possible in all kinds of organizations? Does empowerment grow from the relationship between the manager and the employee, or is it rooted in the employee's own intrinsic need for self-efficacy? To what extent are there individual differences; that is, does every employee want to be empowered?

## Globalization

As technology and transportation continue to shrink our world, members of organizations increasingly will be confronted with the challenges inherent in dealing with people from other cultures. While barriers of language and custom pose many difficulties for communicators, even more fundamental are differences in values and ethics. In parts of Africa, for example, a celebration at the conclusion of a business deal (a party for which you might be asked to pay) would be considered a sign of friendship and lasting business relationships, not a payoff by you in exchange for cooperation from your customers. Similarly, in many parts of the world, custom, law, and religion all support the denial of women's personal and professional rights of equality, much to the frustration of American female business executives. Yet each of these practices is part of some culture's ethical standards and value systems.

Hodgson argues that the key steps to overcoming the hurdles posed by cultural differences are these[53]:

**1.** Become sensitive to the customs, values, and practices of other peoples—the things they view as moral, traditional, practical, and effective.
**2.** Do not judge customs different from your own as being immoral, corrupt, or inappropriate; assume they are legitimate until proven otherwise.
**3.** Find legitimate ways to operate from others' ethical and commercial points of view; do not demand that they operate by your customs or ground rules.
**4.** Conduct relationships and negotiations as openly and aboveboard as possible.
**5.** Avoid rationalizing borderline actions, and refuse to do business when suggested actions violate or seriously compromise laws or fundamental organizational values.

Consider, for example, bribery. Most governments and organizations have statutes against most forms of private payoff. Yet in some African countries, ancient traditions take precedence over laws or company policies. Payoffs have become the norm and are rooted in such traditional practices as the Nigerian "dash" (private pay for private service), which are an expected part of business transactions.

Some companies have sought to promote globalization through the development of strong organizational cultures designed to facilitate adaptation to different environments. Asea Brown Boveri, Inc., an electrical engineering giant, has 213,000 employees worldwide and lives by the motto "Think globally, act locally." The company is tightly focused on making money, and is managed in a hands-on, action-oriented style. Yet members of management are strongly encouraged to be sensitive and adjust to the cultures of the countries in which they work. Indeed, one culture difficult for the senior management team (most of whom are Europeans) to understand is that of the United States: most seem puzzled when told, for example, that they cannot ask a person's age or marital status during an employment interview. Nevertheless, these executives work to adapt to this "strange" set of cultural practices.[54]

Another instance of cultures being merged occurred in 1993, when London-based British Airways formed an alliance with Virginia-based USAir. To begin blending the two organizations' corporate and national cultures, the companies initiated an exchange program in which management personnel from one company "shadowed" their counterparts at the other to learn how they did business, made decisions, and managed employees. For example, an individual from British Airways worked side by side in Washington, D.C., with USAir's director of employee relations, learning how the company makes key personnel decisions. In turn, the USAir executive then went to London to spend several weeks at British Airway's headquarters, observing its personnel management processes.

The two airlines also initiated a series of training programs to help employees recognize and deal with cultural differences. In addition, they formed working committees within major departments (composed of representatives

## A REPORT ON GLOBALIZATION

A survey of globalization practices by major U.S. companies conducted by Runzheimer International revealed that:

1. The companies have an office or operation in an average of twenty different countries.
2. The companies employ an average of 6,331 employees in countries outside their home location.

3. Fifty-seven percent of the companies provided no formal training to brief their employees on the countries to which they were assigned; 30 percent did provide such training.
4. Sixty-seven percent of the companies that did provide formal training included training for nonemployee family members.

Source: Survey results presented in "HR from a Global Perspective," *Personnel Journal* 72 (October 1993): 87.

from both organizations) to work out programs and procedures by which the two companies could work as partners. Through these sorts of efforts, the organizations helped their people to develop greater sensitivity to and appreciation of their cultural differences.

While sensitivity to cultural norms and avoidance of judgmentalism about unfamiliar practices are important, more specific advice concerning communication behaviors also can be provided. DeVries suggests that when corresponding with people outside the United States, we ought to make sure that the words and phrases we use do not confuse, frustrate, or offend others.[55] For example, we should try to avoid the use of slang (such as "two-bit," "blackball," "off-the-wall"), jargon and buzzwords ("ballpark figure," "across the board"), and clichés ("back to the drawing board," "dog-eat-dog world") that might be difficult to interpret. Similarly, Huber recommends that we speak slowly and enunciate well when addressing those for whom English is not their first language, avoid idioms and sarcasm, be careful in our use of humor (which often does not translate well), and realize that people from other cultures may be reluctant to ask questions or provide feedback.[56]

As the "global village" continues to shrink and more companies establish a presence in countries other than their home base, the ability to interact with and adapt to other cultures will take on increasing importance. Many companies are attempting to help their employees develop skills in cross-cultural communication, but the most successful people are likely to be those who, on their own, prepare for increasing globalization.

Reengineering

Related to the quality imperative is the effort under way in many organizations to reengineer the ways in which work is done. Many organizations have developed layer upon layer of management, creating bureaucracies that significantly slow work processes and decision making, and hamper organizational achievement. In an effort to regain the efficiencies they enjoyed as smaller firms, many companies are attempting to recreate themselves.

Teleconferencing is a useful way to conduct meetings and build teams involving participants across the globe. To make the best use of teleconference meetings, Solomon suggests:

- Use the best equipment possible; the quality of sound varies tremendously.
- Allow individual participants ample time to learn to use their technology.
- The group should choose a conference leader and rotate that leadership.
- Written agendas should be distributed to everyone in advance, perhaps via e-mail.
- The group should decide in advance how long the conference will last.
- The conference leader should state the goals of the discussion at the beginning and review any updates since the previous teleconference.
- The leader should encourage everyone to participate, calling on particularly quiet individuals or encouraging them later with a phone call or an e-mail.
- The group should be sensitive to time zone differences; since someone will always be inconvenienced, it may be best to rotate the times meetings are held.
- Someone should write and e-mail to the others a brief summary of the main points covered during the conference.

Source: Charlene Marmer Solomon, "Make the Most of Teleconferencing," *Global Workforce* 3:6 (November 1998): 14.

Briefly, reengineering involves radically changing and reinventing the way work is done in an organization. According to a *Business Week* cover story, this typically involves seven key elements[57]:

**1.** *Organizing around processes, not tasks.* Just as some automobile manufacturers have abandoned traditional production-line approaches in favor of having work teams build entire cars from the ground up, so too are many companies attempting to change how they organize themselves and their work. Rather than creating a structure around functions or departments, some companies are attempting to build themselves around three to five core processes with specific performance goals.

**2.** *Flattening the hierarchy.* Organizations that are reengineering are attempting to "de-layer" themselves by eliminating entire categories of middle-level managers, doing away with work that does not add value to the company's key products or services, and cutting the activities within each core process to a minimum.

**3.** *Using teams to manage everything.* Work teams are being made the building blocks of the organization. Indeed, more and more employee teams are being taught to manage themselves, without supervision, and to achieve clear goals and objectives for which they are held directly accountable.

**4.** *Letting customers drive performance.* In some companies, customer satisfaction has replaced profitability or stock appreciation as the primary driver and measure of performance. These organizations realize that profits and higher stock prices come only as a result of satisfying customers.

**5.** *Rewarding team performance.* Most organizations use performance evaluation and pay systems that reward individual achievement, not teamwork. Since the management principle "what gets rewarded gets done" can either support or hamper team performance, many companies are developing some form of team-based awards (augmenting or, in some cases, entirely replacing individual pay increases).

**6.** *Maximizing supplier and customer contact.* Reengineering frequently seeks to bring employees into direct, regular contact with suppliers and customers. Indeed, some organizations have added supplier or customer representatives as full working members of employee problem-solving teams as a means of facilitating organization-environment communication.

**7.** *Informing and training all employees.* Management of companies that are reengineering must communicate information fully and frequently, not just on a need-to-know basis. Financial data traditionally withheld from employees must be communicated so everyone can monitor and feel a part of the organization's progress.

To create a "horizontal corporation," McKinsey and Company recommend, senior management must identify clearly their strategic objectives; analyze key competitive advantages to fulfill those objectives; define core processes and focus on what is essential to achieve the goals; reorganize around those processes rather than by traditional function; eliminate all activities that do not contribute to achievement of the key objectives, cut function and staff departments to a minimum; appoint a manager or team as the "owner" of each core process; create multidisciplinary teams to run each process; set specific performance objectives for each process; empower employees with authority and information to achieve goals; and revamp training; appraisal, pay, and budgeting systems to support the new structure and link it to customer satisfaction.[58]

The "reengineering revolution" has spawned a consulting firm—CSC Index—whose principals have generated several books.[59] These books deal with all aspects of positioning organizations within marketplaces, building effective customer relations, and organizing work flow efficiently; they also offer some useful hints concerning communication practices. For example, in the *Reengineering Revelation,* Hammer and Stanton offer their list of "the ten principles of reengineering communications":

**1.** "Segment the audience," so that your message can be tailored to the interests and needs of each specific constituency.

**2.** "Use multiple channels of communication," so that the audience is reached in as many ways as possible.

**3.** "Use multiple voices" to increase the chances the audience will hear from someone with whom they can "connect" and identify.

**4.** "Communicate clearly" to improve comprehension, particularly concerning "why" things are being done as they are.

**5.** "Communicate, communicate, communicate," since the sheer volume of messages serves both to promote retention and signal the seriousness of the effort.

**6.** "Honesty is the only policy," since lying is unethical and counterproductive, and "the truth is almost always less terrible than the fears that people build up."

**7.** "Use emotions, not just logic," since both are important in building support for organizational initiatives.

**8.** "Communicate to heal," so that the stress and trauma caused by reengineering can be minimized and overcome.

**9.** "Communicate tangibly," using such symbols as pens, posters, flyers or participative games to convey important issues.

**10.** "Listen, listen, listen" to assess the audience's reactions and identify needs for future communications.[60]

Reengineering places heavy emphasis on the communication and problem-solving skills of organizational members, even though it often results in there being fewer members within the organization to communicate. A study of the impact of reengineering on hospitals, for example, showed that relatively few made significant changes in their administrative structures, but 81 percent reduced staff either by attrition (not replacing workers who left voluntary) or involuntary layoff.[61] The "bottom line" impact of reengineering varied widely, improving the operating margins for some but actually worsening the financial well-being of an equal number of others.

## Managing Diversity

During a period of rapid growth in the late 1980s, GE Silicones in Waterford, New York, hired several chemical engineers and other professionals in several key initiatives, including formation of a total quality management department, expansion of its research and development function, and reorganization of its manufacturing operation. Nearly 30 percent of the new hires were women or minorities, some of whom objected to several of the company's current practices, including:

- The presence of pinup-style calendars in work areas.

- The lack of women's rest rooms in the plant.

- Managers' condescending attitudes toward women.

- Managers' reluctance to give women work assignments that were considered to be difficult and therefore more suitable for men.

- Lack of advancement opportunities for minorities and of minority representation in management ranks.

Company managers quickly realized they were not in tune with today's diverse workforce and took steps to manage the diversity of their employees more effectively. Initially, they formed a steering committee of volunteering employees to oversee the development of programs to improve the management of a culturally diverse employee population. Using that committee's recommendations, they then embarked on two major efforts: teamwork and diversity training.

The teamwork initiative consisted of forming teams of volunteers representing a cross-section of the organization to investigate a variety of cultural diversity issues raised by employees. These issues included family leave, flexible hours, working couples, minority recruitment, personal and professional development of employees, and mentoring. The teams worked to find ways to manage those issues and ultimately produced new company policies on family leave, child care services, job sharing and flextime, mentoring, and relocation.

## WOMEN REPORT ON LEADERSHIP

A survey conducted by *Working Woman* magazine found some unique perceptions and expectations of female bosses. Among the findings were:

61 percent of the 2,250 women who responded to the poll said they did not prefer male bosses—a reversal of the findings of previous surveys.

69 percent of the respondents who were top-level female executives reported feeling a special sense of duty to mentor women at lower levels in their organization.

83 percent of all respondents felt the best way for women to help other women is to mentor them and set a good example.

Women who have experienced sex discrimination were much more likely to mentor other women than were those who had not been discriminated against.

The larger the company, the greater the dissatisfaction with the treatment of women.

Source: From Pamela Kruger, "What Women Think of Women Bosses," *Working Woman* (June, 1993): 40–43.

The diversity training initiative began with top management, who attended a three-day workshop on attitudes and stereotypes that impair communication with a diverse workforce. Through role-playing, group exercises, and written inventories, workshop participants were helped to understand themselves and their assumptions and biases more thoroughly, and to develop skills for overcoming those stereotypes to communicate effectively with others.

Ultimately, diversity training was provided to all levels of the organization. The training program included a videotaped instructional presentation, question-and-answer sessions, reviews of organizational policies, and, occasionally, role playing.[62]

The experience of GE Silicones typifies those of many organizations. Starting with a realization that the composition of today's workforce has changed dramatically (so that white males, in fact, are now a minority of the employee population), companies have worked to involve employees in developing ways to manage more effectively. Indeed, a recent survey found that 74 percent of corporations say they have or are planning to start a diversity program.[63]

The Prudential Insurance Company, for example, surveyed its African-American workers in 1988 to determine why so many were leaving the company and discovered that these individuals felt management was insensitive to diversity issues—a feeling shared by the company's female, Asian, and other minority employees, the firm later discovered. In response, the company initiated an organizationwide diversity training program, instituted a policy of holding all managers accountable for improving diversity, formed diversity councils to monitor the effectiveness of diversity efforts, and required all senior-level managers to submit plans telling how they would address bottom-line diversity issues.

Diversity can have a positive bottom-line impact for a company. For example, when Avon realized that women of color weren't buying its products,

# HIGHLIGHTING DIVERSITY

Capowski distinguished between two "paradigms" of attitudes toward diversity found within today's organizations: the "traditional paradigm" found in less progressive companies, and the "Valuing Diversity Paradigm" found in organizations that truly value the diversity of their workforces:

## Traditional Paradigm

- Expectations, standards, and explicit and implicit rules are shaped by the needs of those at the top.
- Success is linked to assimilation.
- Limited range of appropriate communication, work, and leadership styles.
- No strategic business linkage.
- Diversity equals a potential liability.
- No human resources systems alignment.
- No linkage to compensation and rewards.
- Token gender and/or racial diversity at middle management level.

- Uncommitted and uninformed leadership.
- Underlying assumption: Change the people and preserve the culture.

## Valuing Diversity Paradigm

- Expectations, standards, and explicit and implicit rules are shaped by diverse customers and employees.
- Success is linked to unique contribution.
- Expanded range of styles.
- Diversity is a competitive business strategy.
- Diversity equals a unique asset.
- Human resources systems in alignment.
- Strong linkage to compensation and rewards.
- Visible diversity at all organizational levels.
- Aware and committed leadership.
- Underlying assumption: Modify the culture to support the people.

Source: Genevieve Capowski, "Managing Diversity," *Management Review* 85:6 (June 1996): 13–19.

management started talking to female African-American and Latino employees. Avon wasn't making cosmetics that complemented darker skin tones, the women said; because the company wasn't marketing directly to minority communities, there was little awareness of Avon's products. As a result of input from their diverse employees, Avon diversified its product line and marketing efforts as well, and improved its sales success as a result.[64]

While increased emphasis on effectively managing workforce diversity generally has produced positive results, not every experience has been a good one. For example, in 1988, Lucky Stores Inc., a California-based grocery store chain, conducted workshops to increase sensitivity among its store managers. During those workshops, the participants were asked to mention stereotypes they had heard about women and minority-group members. Though the intent of the exercise was to expose potential prejudice and deal with it, to the company's horror, notes from this session later turned up as evidence in a sex-discrimination lawsuit arguing that female employees were not being promoted equitably. The company lost the suit in part because the court decided that some of the stereotypes mentioned during the workshop amounted to management bias.[65]

Ultimately, the key to managing diversity effectively is valuing rather than suppressing differences and developing skills in listening and adapting to others. Realizing, for example, that some cultures (such as Asian, Hispanic, Native American, or African-American) place great value on body language and other nonverbal cues, while others (such as Northern European, Swiss, or Anglo-American males) focus more on verbal behavior can help one to adapt his or her behavior more effectively to others.[66] As the workforce becomes increasingly diverse, such communication skills will take on added importance.

---

| KEY CONCEPTS 2.2 | Critical Issues Facing Organizations at the End of the 20th Century |
|---|---|

Issues facing contemporary organizations are largely communication-related and pose several important challenges:

1. Finding ways to provide "empowerment" by involving people in meaningful communication and decision making.
2. Adapting to differences across countries and cultures in an effort to deal with the "globalization" of the nation's business and economy.
3. Implementing organizational "reengineering" that probably will cut jobs and reduce the job security of those who remain while maintaining employee satisfaction and motivation.
4. Meeting the needs and maximizing the abilities and contributions offered by increasing workforce "diversity."
5. Keeping up with and effectively using the booming information "technology" available to business and individuals today.

## SUMMARY

It is our view that in almost any organization, the preferable organizational philosophy, and the corresponding leadership style, is one that encourages others to participate, respects a diversity of perspectives, values listening as much as talking, and encourages everyone to exert leadership appropriately. Every organization needs employees who are capable of influencing others, completing tasks without close supervision, suggesting constructive changes, and thinking in independent and creative ways. Each of these is a form of leadership behavior that should be widely distributed across the organization rather than concentrated at the very top. Thus, the most effective leaders share leadership roles with others while remaining role models themselves. They demonstrate high expectations and goodwill toward their fellow employees, a willingness to listen and tolerate dissent, and high personal and professional integrity. In short, they create the cool culture described in this chapter.

# QUESTIONS FOR DISCUSSION

1. What is leadership?
2. Which of the organizational philosophies and cultures do you prefer? Why?
3. Which philosophy or culture is most likely to produce a successful organization? Why?
4. How would you describe an empowering organizational culture? Have you ever been a part of such an organization? Briefly, describe your experience.
5. If you were asked to construct a profile of an effective leader, what characteristics would you include? Why?
6. How does the concept of money as a motivator of employee performance fit into each of the organizational philosophies/cultures?

# EXERCISES

1. Think of an organization for which you have worked or with which you are very familiar. Which organizational theory seems to prevail in this organization? Cite specific examples to support your views.
2. From the business section of a newspaper, clip articles referring to any organizational practices that illustrate principles of one of the organizational schools of thought.
3. Arrange to interview an individual who currently serves in a leadership position. Ask this person to describe her or his philosophy of or approach to leadership and management. How does this leader make decisions or solve problems? After the interview, write a brief essay in which you describe the theory (or theories) of management that best characterizes the leader you interviewed.
4. Find an organization that is culturally diverse. Talk to a member of that organization regarding how that diversity is managed. Share your findings with the class.
5. Talk to at least three people who have held several jobs. Ask them to describe organizational situations in which they have felt especially empowered—or, by contrast, not at all empowered. What factors contributed to these situations?

# CASE application 2.1

Adam Smith, author of *Wealth of Nations,* is generally credited with the development of the principles that are the basis for current industrial production techniques, such as specialization and division of labor. Unfortunately, his book (written in the mid-1700s, at the beginning of the Industrial Revolution) also developed something else—a philosophy of management.

Smith's experience as a business owner convinced him that employees have certain characteristics. They do not want to work very hard. They cannot be trusted: If a supervisor stops monitoring them for even a second, they probably will stop working and begin fooling around. They are not dependable: They come in late for work, complain a lot, want to leave early, and generally seem disinterested in the success of the company. They have nothing meaningful to contribute to problem solving or decision making, since they are far less experienced, motivated, and interested than the supervisors who watch over them. Therefore, Smith concluded, supervisors needed to watch employees at all times, communicate with them only in the form of demands and orders (primarily "Get back to work!"), use rewards and punishments to control their behaviors, and throw them out if they became unruly.

The management theory Smith developed probably was desirable in governing his workforce: boys aged 12 and under. However, some important questions should be considered:

## Questions

1. Does Smith's management and communication philosophy have any application today? Are there situations in which people should be led in that manner?
2. Are there elements in Smith's philosophy that appear in the philosophies reviewed in this chapter?
3. Are there ways the values-driven, customer-driven, or information-driven philosophies could be applied (by accident) in a manner consistent with Smith's leadership style?

# CASE application 2.2

*Complaining on the Net*

An interesting use for the Internet has developed recently—complaining. As Guynn reports, the traditional labor movement may have lost some of its vigor, but there is a growing worker rebellion on the Web. Hundreds of sites have popped up—serving as public forums where disgruntled workers "kvetch" and moan about their companies, jobs, and bosses. Workers say they are overworked, underpaid, mistreated, or fired for no good reason. Some sites, such as "Working for the Man," offer subversive advice, such as frown while "fake-working," randomly delete files or documents, or skimp on personal hygiene.

With the power and reach of the Web, this kind of job misery has found a lot of company. But some companies contend that people are taking their rage to extremes. And they're fighting back. The Adobe Systems legal team is working to shut down the Adobe Trouble site. And the *Orange County Register* made headlines of its own when it took legal action against a Web site, called the Orange County Unregistered Press, operated by a former newspaper employee.

Source: Jessica Guynn, "Rankled Workers Go On-line," *The Valley Times* (July 24, 1998): sec. 1, p. 1.

## Questions

1. From the perspective of an employee, what is your view of the appropriateness of the Web being used in this fashion?

2. From the perspective of a business owner, what do you think about the appropriateness of using the Web in this fashion?

3. If you were a business owner, how might you use such Web sites to your own advantage?

## CHAPTER three

*After reading this chapter, you should be able to:*

1   Explain the importance of ethics for organizations.

2   Explain how communication both shapes and reflects an organization's ethical standards.

3   Describe ethical issues involved with "service" versus "profit," social responsibility, and employee rights.

4   Explain the impact of "globalization" on the development of ethical standards.

5   Explain ethical perspectives on what is "right."

6   List and explain the methods organizations are using to improve ethical behavior.

# Communication in Organizations: The "Ethical" Environment

Throughout your life you will face decisions about what is "right," "proper," and "fair." You may decide, for example, how to rear your children, what life occupation you want, and how you should use your material possessions. On the job, you may have to consider how to communicate bad news to your superiors, how to promote your product or service (and indeed, yourself), how carefully to report your business expenses to your employer and/or the Internal Revenue Service, or how to use your power responsibly in dealing with subordinates. All of these decisions about what is "right," "proper," and "fair" are *ethical* decisions.

Similarly, the organizations in which you work will struggle with ethical concerns: how employees should be treated, how products or services should be priced, how the environment should be protected, how they should fulfill their social responsibilities, and so on. As a member of those organizations, you will need to decide how you feel about their ethical decisions and, if you disagree with them, what you should do about it.

## PREVIEW

In this chapter, we will consider the nature of ethics in organizations and some key ethical issues organizations today are facing. After exploring the importance of behaving ethically, we will examine several different perspectives for making ethical judgments. One or more of these perspectives might guide the actions and underlie the judgments you make as an individual; they also influence the behavior and worldview of every organization with which you are or will be associated. Finally, we will consider some ways in which organizations today are trying to promote ethical behavior.

## DEFINING "ETHICS"

At the outset, it might be useful to attempt to define "ethics" in the context of the modern organization. Perhaps Bowen H. McCoy, managing director of Morgan Stanley & Company, Inc., investment bankers, put it best when he said:

> Ethics involves the art of integration and compromise, not blind obedience and conformity. Ethics calls for tolerance of ambiguity; yet, it is an action-oriented, interpersonal process. [It] signifies a heightened ability to seek truth that stems from core beliefs and to decide consciously on one's action in a business context. Ethics deals with free choice among alternatives. In a practical sense . . . ethics is wrapped up with the integrity and authenticity of the businessman and the business enterprise.[1]

Ethics goes far beyond simple questions of legality or illegality—of bribery, theft, or collusion. Ethics considers what our relationships are and ought to be with our employers, co-workers, subordinates, customers, stockholders, suppliers, distributors, neighbors, and all other members of the communities in which we operate. As Solomon and Hanson note, ethics is "a way of life," not a set of absolute principles divorced from day-to-day life. "It is the awareness that one is an intrinsic part of a social order, in which the interests of others and one's own interests are inevitably intertwined."[2]

## ETHICAL ISSUES CONCERNING ORGANIZATIONAL COMMUNICATION

The issue of ethics within organizations has received a great deal of attention recently. In recent years, news reports have chronicled the questionable actions of companies like Sears, General Dynamics, Archer-Daniels-Midland Co., NYNEX, and Columbia/HCA Healthcare Corp. Certainly, the impact of these reports can be devastating, costing a company tens of millions of dollars in legal fees and lost sales, demoralizing the workforce, and diminishing productivity. Yet evidence of continuing unethical behavior within organizations continues to mount[3]:

- A 1994 Gallup Poll found that only the government ranks lower than corporations in perceived trustworthiness.

- A 1996 Tulane University study found that two of every five controllers and nearly half of all top executives were willing to commit fraud in role-playing exercises. In fact, 87 percent made at least one fraudulent decision during simulated work situations.

- A 1997 study by the American Society of Chartered Life Underwriters and Chartered Financial Consultants and the Ethics Officers Association found that 56 percent of all workers feel some pressure to act unethically or illegally, and 48 percent admitted they had engaged in one or more unethical and/or illegal actions during the past year. Their transgressions included cutting corners on quality, abusing or lying about sick days, covering up safety-related incidents, lying to supervisors or subordinates, deceiving customers, and taking credit for others' ideas.

Ironically, all this is happening despite increasing efforts among American corporations to improve ethical behaviors. The Ethics Resource Center, a Washington, D.C.–based organization that helped start many corporate ethics programs in the 1980s, found the number of firms with ethics training programs has increased from 7 percent to 40 percent and the number of companies with codes of ethics has increased from 13 percent to 73 percent since 1994. In addition, companies have created ombudsperson positions, confidential hot lines, and other mechanisms whereby employees can safely report unethical behaviors. Yet the problem persists, and is growing worse.

Experts argue that several pressures are bringing about increases in unethical behavior. Increasing competition and razor-thin profit margins are driving organizations to cut costs, often by reducing staff and demanding

## FINDING AN ETHICAL ORGANIZATION

As you look for employment, one factor you should consider is the ethical standards of any organization you might join. Before you accept a position at a company, you might use these strategies to find out what its values are:

- Throw out what you hear in interviews. The interviewers are selling you on the company. You'll hear that the organization is "family friendly" and "committed to open communication." The gap between buzzwords and reality is often huge.
- Ask clever questions to get at the truth. Rather than asking vague questions about values, ask questions that elicit anecdotes. Ask how the company handled the latest downsizing; ask about senior management turnover; ask if there has ever been a problem with an employee who had a conflict with the company's values. Get the interviewer telling stories rather than reciting stock phrases, and you'll learn a lot more.
- Find and interview a "superstar." Ask the interviewer to tell you about one or two superstars in the department or organization—people who have had great success. Ask these superstars if they've had to compromise their principles to succeed, or if they've had to put family and personal values on the back burner. Stress that the conversation will remain in confidence so they'll speak freely.
- Do research in the field. You'll never learn about a company in an interview. Ask to sit in on a team meeting. Listen carefully to how employees talk to and treat each other. See if they feel comfortable speaking freely to managers and leaders.

Source: "Pinpoint a Company's Values," *Positive Leadership* (July 1998): 11.

that remaining employees "do more with less." The temptation to "do whatever it takes" to be successful, whether what it takes is deceiving customers or cutting corners on quality, can be irresistible under such circumstances. In turn, employees' trust in and loyalty toward organizational leadership has declined, increasing the likelihood that they will take action against their own companies through any or all of the actions listed earlier: abusing sick time, lying to supervisors, stealing company time or property, and so on. Michael Hoffman, executive director of the Center for Business Ethics at Bentley College in Waltham, Massachusetts, argues, "When a company sets unrealistic sales targets or implementation schedules, the pressure to meet goals gets pushed down through the organizational structure. All of a sudden, you wind up with people who begin to say, 'I don't want to mislead my customers, and I don't want to cut corners. But if I don't go along with things, I'm afraid I'll lose my job or wind up falling behind when it comes to income and promotions.' That's when employees begin to do things they wouldn't ordinarily do."[4]

As you might infer from the previous chapter, an organization's culture can be extremely influential in shaping the ethical—or unethical—behavior of its members. Sears, Roebuck & Company provides an example of how culture can influence individual actions. In the early 1990s, the attorneys general in 43 states charged Sears with overselling parts and services to nearly 1 million customers. Among the actions Sears employees allegedly committed were making false and misleading statements, fraud, failure to state clearly what parts and labor were on repair invoices, and false advertising, as mechanics allegedly charged customers for parts and services that were never received. By the time Sears admitted responsibility and settled the issue (at a cost of more than $40 million), it had been devastated by bad press and negative public opinion.

The Sears situation arose from several key elements of its corporate culture. It had few safeguards against poor workmanship or unnecessary repairs, and employees earned commissions by both selling parts and making repairs. There were few customer satisfaction checks. In effect, then, the Sears pay system rewarded unethical behavior and there were few checks in place to discourage employees from increasing their pay by taking advantage of Sears customers. Employees adapted to the culture in which they worked—to the detriment of those who came to Sears for their auto repairs.

---

**KEY CONCEPTS 3.1**     **The Nature of Ethics in Organizations**

1. Ethics considers what our relationships are and ought to be with our employers, co-workers, subordinates, customers, stockholders, suppliers, distributors, and neighbors, and with all other members of the communities in which we operate.

2. Despite their efforts to increase ethical behavior among their employees, many companies are confronting difficult ethical challenges.

3. Unethical behavior may be encouraged by increasing pressure in the workplace and by practices adopted by employers that encourage unethical conduct.

---

The concept of ethics has important implications for several topics related to organizational communication, and in the following sections we will review several.

Service versus Profit

Most business theorists argue that good service means better profits—that maximizing the services provided to customers ultimately improves an organization's bottom line. In health care, however, that principle does not necessarily hold true.

In the mid-1980s, the federal government became increasingly concerned about rapidly rising health care costs. As a result, in 1983, Congress enacted the Medicare prospective payment system, which established fixed amounts that would be paid to hospitals for each of 468 different types of treatments (Medicare would pay a certain amount for appendectomies, a certain amount for tonsillectomies, and so on). Prior to that time, Medicare and Medicaid had paid hospital charges regardless of the amount. Under the new plan (which uses changes based on diagnosis-related groups), hospitals whose actual costs fell below the fixed levels could keep the difference, while hospitals whose costs were above the established levels suffered losses. Since 40 percent of all hospital patients on the average are covered by Medicare, this represented a significant change in health care funding. Soon after, other private insurers implemented similar plans of their own.

More recently, the concept of "managed care" has become prominent. Many health care organizations now sign contracts with payers (such as insurance companies) that provide a yearly payment for each of the payer's subscribers. Those subscribers are strongly encouraged to use the hospital's facilities for all of their health needs, and if the hospital can meet those needs for less than the insurance company pays, it makes money. Conversely, if providing that care costs more than the insurance company pays, the hospital loses money. In short, it is in the hospital's best interests financially to provide as little care as possible, thus maximizing the difference between what it costs to provide care and what the insurance companies pay per person.

Health care organizations have responded to these financial pressures in several ways, most of which involve cutting the cost of providing care.[5] Reducing patients' length of stay was a key element of cost reduction: for example, by reducing from five days to three the amount of time an appendectomy patient spent in the hospital, hospital administrators could reduce the cost of delivering care to that person. "Get 'em out quicker and sicker" became the motto for many hospitals.

Many health care organizations also began marketing their services more aggressively, with ethical implications. One such situation involved a Chicago-based hospice (hospice programs are designed to provide care at home for terminally ill patients believed to have six months or less to live). In two memos sent to employees, hospice management offered to pay cash bonuses to nurses who recruited patients and directed them immediately to hospitalize all patients admitted during the weekend as well as all patients who were at home when they first signed up (despite federal guidelines requiring that no more than 20 percent of hospice care is to be in a hospital). One memo from an administrator stated that "the low census in both inpatient units cannot continue to occur. Quite frankly, it is strangling us financially."[6] More than a dozen employees quit their jobs in the organization, saying they were disturbed by what they viewed as unethical practices.

Finally, many health care organizations have begun to take other steps to reduce costs and improve their financial strength: reducing the number of staff (including the number of people who provide care directly to patients), replacing registered nurses with lower-paid (and lesser skilled) nonlicensed staff, reducing or eliminating services and treatments that have proved unprofitable, conducting fewer routine tests, and attempting to control equipment and supply costs. Still, over 100 hospitals have been forced to close each year, and continued financial pressures are expected.[7]

Health care administrators and managers thus face a variety of ethical choices: What level of care is good enough? Should services offered be based on community needs, financial realities, or some compromise of the two? How far should a health care organization go in trying to increase its business volume? How much work can reasonably be demanded of hospital employees? The answers to ethical questions like these will determine the quality and type of health care we receive in the future.

## Social Responsibility

In response to the question "Do corporations have social responsibilities over and above their obligations to their stockholders?" most would answer "Of course!" But the scope of that responsibility remains an area of some controversy.

One interesting example is provided by Control Data Corporation and its founder, Chairman and Chief Executive Officer William C. Norris. During 1967, when riots erupted in a depressed area of Minneapolis not far from Control Data's headquarters, Norris responded in a manner that should serve as a model of social responsibility. "You can't do business with the town on fire," he said. "So you stop and think why this has happened. It happened because of inequities. The people felt so damn frustrated that this was their way of expressing themselves."[8] Thus, in 1968, Norris and Control Data opened a new plant in the riot-torn area of Minneapolis and provided their new employees with a child care center and intensive job training (including basic courses in computer skills). In 1970, they opened a second plant in St. Paul. The company went on to launch programs to revitalize urban and rural areas, create jobs through small business development, provide training to prison populations, and meet other social needs.

More recently, a major shoemaker was accused of shirking its social responsibilities. Operation PUSH, a Chicago-based civil rights group founded by, among others, Reverend Jesse Jackson, demanded that the Nike shoe company change the composition of its management and board of directors. Their reasoning: Since African-Americans compose a significant portion of Nike's athletic footwear market, African-Americans should hold prominent positions in the company as well. When Nike refused Operation PUSH's demands for detailed financial information about the company and changes in the organization's structure (and indeed, countered with similar demands for detailed information about Operation PUSH), leaders of Operation PUSH declared economic war and attempted to organize a boycott of Nike products.[9] That boycott generally has proven unsuccessful.

Concerns about manufacturing plants abroad also have caused pressure to be put on various company spokespersons. For example, Kathy Lee Gifford found herself under criticism because a line of clothing she endorsed was made in Asian sweatshops. Similarly, Michael Jordan, formerly of the Chicago Bulls, was criticized for endorsing Nike shoes made in horrendous working conditions by poorly paid Asian workers. Both were given assurances by the companies they represented that conditions in those manufacturing settings would be improved, and both in turn conveyed those assurances to the general public.

The impact of organizations on the environment is yet another area of ethical concern. Some companies have made a genuine effort to minimize any harmful effects they or their products have on the environment; others have been less thoughtful. For example, British Petroleum pledged in 1998 to reduce by 10 percent its greenhouse gas emissions that contribute to global warming. The London-based giant intends in the future to eliminate 4 million of the 40 million tons of carbon dioxide and greenhouse gasses it emitted in 1990, its baseline year. Its progressive stance is in contrast to that of a Chicago-based company with which British Petroleum is merging: Amoco. Along with other U.S. refiners, Amoco consistently has fought tougher environmental rules. Some analysts believe that merging the two organizational cultures will prove very difficult, in part because of their differing philosophies concerning environmental impact.[10]

Again, questions arise: Do corporations have an ethical responsibility to support their communities and assist in the resolution of social problems? Do company spokespersons have any accountability for the conditions in which the products they endorse are made? Do organizations have an ethical responsibility to preserve the environment? Does any group have the ethical right to declare itself the spokesperson for some segment of society and make demands on manufacturers who sell their products to that segment? Relations between organizational systems and their environment will continue to raise ethical questions in the future.

## Employee Rights

The treatment of employees by their superiors involves a myriad of ethical issues. Most theorists imply that employees have certain basic rights and that the ethics of management's treatment of employees can be judged, at least in part, by the extent to which those rights are upheld. We will consider just a few of those rights here.

### The Right to Fair and Equitable Treatment

In recent years, government regulations, often in the form of affirmative action policies, have required equitable procedures in screening, hiring, promoting, and terminating employees.[11] Discrimination on the basis of race, religion, national origin, disability, or sex is strictly forbidden, according to the law.[12]

Discrimination on the basis of age is becoming a particular concern. The Bureau of National Affairs reports that "age discrimination actions challenging employer decisions represent the hottest area of employment discrimination litigation today." In its view, the aging of the American workforce, combined with employees' increased awareness of their rights under the Age Discrimination in Employment Act of 1967, should lead employers "to expect to be sued whenever they make an employment decision—especially a termination decision—that is perceived to be adverse to the interests of an older worker."[13]

Another issue of concern is sexual harassment. As more women have entered the workforce, problems with sexual harassment have grown. Cornell University conducted one of the first studies of sexual harassment and reported that 92 percent of 155 respondents viewed sexual harassment as a serious problem and 70 percent had personally experienced some form of harassment.[14] However, the question of what exactly constitutes harassment has remained complex. In its most obvious form, sexual harassment occurs when a person's supervisor requests sexual favors under the threat of denying promotion, pay increase, or even termination. But this is a narrow definition, describing only the most stereotypic cases.

In 1980, the U.S. Equal Employment Opportunity Commission (EEOC) issued guidelines stating that sexual harassment is a violation of Title VII of the 1964 Civil Rights Act. It defined harassment as occurring when:

**1.** Submission to the sexual conduct is made either implicitly or explicitly a term or condition of employment.
**2.** Employment decisions affecting the recipient are made on the basis of the recipient's acceptance or rejection of the sexual conduct.
**3.** The conduct has the purpose or effect of reasonably interfering with an individual's work performance or creating an intimidating, hostile, or offensive working environment.[15]

*Sexual harassment has been recognized as a growing problem in many organizations. Although perceived harassment can be an issue in any relationship, when men supervise women, special vigilance is needed.*

Clearly, according to this broad definition, much sexual harassment is fairly subtle. It could be viewed as including leering, staring, or verbal harassment, such as sexual joking or referring to women as "girls," or even making sexist comments such as "Women are just too emotional to take the pressure."

Apart from legal definitions of harassment, some researchers have concerned themselves with the ways that women themselves define harassment. One study, for instance, found that while close to 80 percent of women considered sexual propositions, touching, grabbing, and brushing as harassment, only 50 percent thought that sexual remarks and suggestive gestures were sexually harassing. Although most believed that staring and flirting were perhaps the most frequent form of female-directed attention, most did not view such behaviors as harassment.[16] It is also important to note here that even though the majority of cases of sexual harassment involve *women* as victims, the EEOC guidelines apply equally to *men*. A different United Nations survey, conducted in 1975, found that 50 percent of females and 31 percent of males had experienced some form of sexual harassment.[17] The *Wall Street Journal* notes that sexual harassment can involve gay workers harassing others, women harassing men, subordinates harassing managers, and outside vendors harassing customers.[18]

Three more recent court cases have served to illustrate the breadth of sexual harassment definitions[19]:

- In the case of *Oncale* vs. *Sundowner Offshore Services,* the U.S. Supreme Court ruled that a male roustabout working in an eight-man crew on a Chevron USA oil platform had been sexually harassed through threats, name-calling, and physical assault, even though the people involved were of the same sex. In short, they ruled, what matters is the conduct at issue, not the sex of the people involved.

- In the case of *Burlington Industries, Inc.* vs. *Ellerth,* the U.S. Supreme Court ruled that comments made by a male supervisor to a female employee constituted sexual harassment, even though the employee did not report her supervisor's misconduct to management and did not suffer any tangible job detriment.

- In the case of *Faragher* vs. *City of Boca Raton, Florida,* the U.S. Supreme Court ruled that eight female lifeguards had been sexually harassed by two supervisors, despite the city's argument that it had a clear policy against sexual harassment and was not aware of the supervisors' behaviors. The court stated that an employer is liable for a pervasive, hostile atmosphere of harassment and for its supervisors' misconduct, whether or not the employer is aware of the harassment.

The financial and human costs of sexual harassment can be immense. The financial costs include fines and other legal settlements, which can be substantial. In 1998, for example, an Iowa jury awarded $80.7 million to a former United Parcel Service employee who had sued for sexual harassment.[20] Moreover, if the employer is a contractor with the federal government, it may lose its federal contracts. The human costs of sexual harassment are equally great. Victims suffer embarrassment, intimidation, helplessness, and anger.[21] In many cases, the victims live with these feelings rather than confront the offender, for fear of retaliation. Several studies report that some victims eventually suffer from serious psychological problems requiring medical attention because of the harassment.[22] More frequently, however, these emotional problems lead to increased absenteeism, reduced efficiency, and even resignations.[23] Thus, even in small businesses (with fewer than 15 employees) where EEOC guidelines are not binding, employers should still be concerned about lowered morale and productivity. In most instances of harassment, both the victim and the perpetrator ultimately suffer.

Many companies have taken steps to avoid incidences of sexual harassment. One study revealed that over 27 percent of *Fortune* 500 respondents said they hold EEOC or affirmative action training programs and seminars for employees; 20 percent provide continuing education through company magazines or journals, films, and training sessions of various kinds. Slightly more than 9 percent said they included sexual harassment topics as part of supervisory training.[24] Some companies have made major advances in addressing the problem. DuPont, for example, invested $500,000 to develop a program designed to teach employees how to avert sexual harassment, rape, and other safety risks.[25]

**The Right to Privacy**   Most would agree that employee offices or lockers, files, telephone conversations, personnel data, outside activities, and so on should not be invaded by their employers—that people have a right to privacy at work. Yet the limits of employee privacy are being pushed back almost daily. For example, as Chapter 10 will describe in some detail, employees now are being tested in a variety of ways by their employers: for drugs and alcohol usage, for AIDS, for honesty, and for job skills.[26] Employees subjected to such tests often object, saying, "What I do on my own time is my own business" (including, supposedly, taking drugs). Yet three Northwest Airlines pilots were convicted of flying under the influence of alcohol as the result of participating in a party on their own time the night before the flight. Employees at a meat-packing company in Monmouth, Illinois, objected to random drug and alcohol testing conducted by their employer, despite the fact that their jobs required them to use extremely sharp knives to butcher hogs and the testing was designed to improve safety. As one company foreman said to this consultant and author, "We try to protect those who are too dumb to protect themselves."

Electronic monitoring of employee performance also has increased. An estimated 10 million workers in the United States have their work output measured electronically or their phone conversations listened to during the workday. Employees who often are monitored include telephone operators; airline, auto rental, and hotel reservation clerks; telemarketing sales and order clerks; insurance claims processors; and newspaper classified ad and circulation workers. "Not only are their keystrokes, customer contacts and unproductive time measured by computers, but their conversations also are often secretly monitored by supervisors checking on employees' efficiency and effectiveness."[27] Critics raise concerns that such monitoring increases work stress (bringing about "electronic sweatshops") and may lead to a loss of freedom. However, Alan Westin, professor of public law and government at Columbia, disagrees: "The premise that a conversation between an employee and a customer on the employer's premises in the name of the employer's business is somehow a private chat is 180 degrees wrong. Monitoring in principle is essential to assuring the quality of customer service work."[28] Nevertheless, legislation to limit employer monitoring of employees is pending.

Another area of growing controversy concerning employees' rights to privacy involves the use of electronic and voice mail. In 1993, for example, *Macworld* magazine published a survey showing widespread eavesdropping by employers. Based on responses from 301 businesses employing over 1 million workers, *Macworld* estimated that as many as 20 million Americans may be subject to electronic monitoring on the job.

The *Macworld* survey found that more than 21 percent of the respondents have searched employees' computer files, electronic mail, voice mail, or other networking communications. Of those who admitted to snooping, 74 percent had searched computer work files, 42 percent had searched electronic mail, and 15 percent had searched voice mail.[29] A 1998 study by the American Management Association found 35 percent of employers use surveillance tactics that may include reading e-mail.[30]

The courts have upheld employers' rights to conduct such snooping. For example, a sales manager at Pillsbury and his boss exchanged e-mails in which an executive was described as "a back-stabbing bastard." Someone in the company read this and fired both of them. The sales manager sued to get his job back on the grounds that his privacy had been invaded. Too bad, said the federal district judge who heard the case: Pillsbury owns the system and hence everything on it, and they can browse with impunity. Generally, one author concluded, a good rule of thumb is to think of an e-mail message not as a sealed letter but as a postcard—one that might be read and copied in every post office it passed through, then kept on file for years afterward. In other words, don't say anything via e-mail that you wouldn't want announced over the company loudspeaker.[31]

Why do companies conduct these searches? To monitor work flow, investigate thefts, or prevent industrial espionage, some say. But whatever the purpose, there are no legal limits placed on employers spying on their employees in the workplace. They are free to view employees on closed-circuit television, tap their telephones, search their e-mail and network communications, and rummage through their computer files with or without employee knowledge or consent, 24 hours a day.

On the other hand, not every company takes this approach to employee privacy. Amtel Corp., a San Jose, California–based company that manufactures specialized semiconductors, takes great pains to protect the privacy of its employees.[32] Employee files, still kept in paper-based folders, are locked away in file cabinets and can't be viewed by anyone other than an approved Human Resources Department clerk. Medical records are kept in a separate file that cannot be viewed by anyone outside the Human Resources Department. In addition, Amtel avoids using Social Security numbers and instead generates a unique employee number for each employee—a practice that eliminates many of the concerns employees have over privacy and makes it more difficult for someone to misuse, or commit fraud with, another employee's Social Security number. Employees receive a handbook that spells out the company's privacy policies and are given training on privacy issues. Last, the company has a strict policy covering the kinds of information employees can have on their computers and how they use electronic media, such as e-mail and voice mail. Telephones, e-mail, and voice mail are not monitored unless the company has concrete cause to believe that an individual is misusing the system or stealing. The company's Human Resources director is an attorney, which makes it likely that legal trends and rulings will be monitored and followed, and that the rights of employees and the company alike will be protected.

Just as employees' rights to privacy can be jeopardized by new electronic technology, so too can technology threaten the rights of citizens who may not be organizational members or of entire organizations themselves. Consider some recent examples:

- In June 1993, executives of Procter & Gamble in Cincinnati complained to police that company information was being illegally leaked to the press. To identify the source of the leak, Cincinnati Bell Telephone Company, acting in response to a subpoena from a grand jury, searched the phone records of every one of its 655,000 customers in the 513 and 606 area codes. Procter & Gamble executives later admitted that this might have been an error in judgment.

- Lotus Development, a software manufacturer, and Equifax, a company that compiles financial information about individuals, developed a plan to sell a database that would have allowed anyone with a personal computer to purchase a list of names, buying habits, and income levels of selected households. Small businesses, such as pharmacies, pizza parlors, and dry

## TECHNOLOGICAL INVASIONS OF PRIVACY

A telephone poll of 500 Americans taken by Yankelovich Clancy Shulman for *Time* magazine showed a high level of concern about technological invasions of privacy:

76 percent said they are very concerned about the amount of computerized information businesses and government have collected about them.

78 percent said they are concerned about the amount of information the federal government, credit organizations, and insurance companies, specifically, have about them.

90 percent felt companies should not be allowed to sell information about their household income, 86 percent felt they should not be able to sell information about their bill-paying history, and 83 percent felt companies should not be able to sell information about their medical history.

93 percent felt companies should be required by law to get permission from individuals before selling information about them.

95 percent felt employers should not be allowed to listen in on employee phone conversations.

Source: Richard Lacayo, "Nowhere to Hide," *Time* (November 11, 1991): 34–40.

---

cleaners, would have been able to get all such information on potential local customers. Public uproar forced the companies to scrap their plan.

- The Employer's Information Service, based in Gretna, Louisiana, is creating a massive data bank on workers who have reported on-the-job injuries. For a fee, employers can request a report on prospective employees, including a history of prior job injuries and a record of worker's compensation claims and lawsuits. To keep from being added to other data banks, workers in Idaho are suing that state's industrial commission to prevent it from releasing such records.[33]

- Playboy Enterprises created a stir when they announced that they are considering gathering information about who buys what from their catalogs, combining it with other personal data and sharing it with marketers. Joining forces with First Data Solutions, a division of database marketing specialist First Data Corp., Playboy could identify which customers buy its "Complete Guide to Sex Toys & Devices" video, First Data could identify which of those customers own luxury cars, and using this shared knowledge Playboy could target other products to this consumer group. "If you're running for the church board of directors, would you want it known that you bought something from the Playboy catalog?" asked Evan Hendricks of *Privacy Times*.[34]

Increasingly, organizations are developing or acquiring technology to spy on their employees, the public, or other organizations. But the biggest threat to privacy is not video surveillance cameras, listening devices, or telephone answering machines—it is the computer.

To obtain a credit card, mortgage, driver's license, or admission to a hospital, people typically must complete forms that ask for a variety of information

*Communication in Organizations: The Ethical Environment*    **93**

about their financial, medical, and family histories, their buying habits, and so on. In turn, these data are often sold to other organizations (as when a state government sells lists of driver's license holders to advertisers) that use the information for their own purposes. Such information routinely is made available to government agencies, mortgage lenders, retailers, small businesses, marketers, and insurers. Credit reports, for example, are used by banks to determine whether they will give someone a mortgage, and medical records are used by insurance companies (and sometimes by potential employers) to determine whether someone will be covered (or hired). And marketers use information about income and buying habits to target recipients of their mail-order and telephone solicitations.

Three huge organizations—TRW, Equifax, and Trans Union—dominate the consumer-data industry. Every month, these companies purchase computer records, usually from banks and retailers, that detail the financial activities of almost every adult in the United States. While these organizations have argued that their databases do not disclose truly confidential details, Equifax used credit card use patterns and census data to develop projections of each card user's estimated annual income—information it then sold to its customers. Only when this practice proved too controversial did Equifax discontinue selling this information, in the summer of 1993.

Other forms of technology are also becoming more sophisticated. A number of catalog retailers and financial companies now make use of an updated version of *caller ID*, which in its simplest form displays the telephone number from which an incoming call has been placed. The more sophisticated version displays the caller's name, telephone number, and credit history almost as quickly as the call is answered.

Certainly, concern is rising about the use of technology to invade the public's privacy. Yet privacy cannot be taken as having inherent value. For example, with U.S. banks being used as conduits for drug money, law enforcement officials have pressed banks to report any suspicious movement of cash. Although such reports may conflict with traditional concepts of bank clients' confidentiality, most banks have been willing to comply. In addition, some business groups argue that controlling their sale of data about their customers violates their property rights; the information is theirs, they claim, and they should have the right to sell it to whomever they choose.

Ultimately, some of these issues may be resolved via legislation. For example, Congress is expected soon to review the appropriateness of the automated dialing machines used by telemarketers to call every number in a telephone exchange, one after another, to make a recorded sales pitch. Some also have proposed that the 1974 Federal Privacy Act, which defends citizens from government misuse of data, should be extended to cover private industry as well and should be enforced more stringently. But important questions remain. Do the rights of organizations take precedence over the rights of individuals? To what extent should government be involved in regulating the actions of private organizations? And when does an organization's use of personal data about individuals become unethical?

**The Right to a Safe and Healthful Work Environment**   The Occupational Safety and Health Administration (OSHA) was established to ensure that employers provide safe working conditions for their people. Yet abuses occur. Scientists from Argonne's Center for Human Radiobiology, for example, found nine breast cancer deaths in a group of 463 women who had worked in a Luminous Processes plant in Ottawa, Illinois, painting clock and watch dials with radium. These women reported that safety precautions were almost nonexistent and that workers were constantly contaminated with the radioactive material. In fact, they stated that company officials told them that radium was safe to handle. Women at the plant sometimes painted their fingernails with radium paint; others took pots of radium paint home to paint light switches that would glow in the dark. Workers routinely contaminated their hair, arms, legs, and feet with the radioactive material accidentally while they worked, and they wiped paint-covered hands on the front of their work smocks.[35] The plant closed in 1978.

While the need to protect workers in the workplace would seem incontrovertible, many important issues remain. For example, many major U.S. corporations (including American Cyanamid, Olin, General Motors, Gulf Oil, Dow Chemical, Du Pont, Union Carbide, and Monsanto) have policies concerning fetal protection that prohibit women from working in areas that might endanger pregnancies. "I can't go anywhere," said Patricia Briner, who fills batteries with acid for Milwaukee-based Johnson Controls, Inc. "The good jobs are in departments where lead is used—and women aren't allowed to work in them. The company says it's too dangerous. That includes women who aren't pregnant and who don't ever intend to become pregnant."[36] A spokesman for the company said that, according to company research, lead exposure "has a minor impact on men, but an overwhelming amount of evidence indicates risk to fetuses. It would be unconscionable to expose women to it. We're trying to do the right thing."[37] The Supreme Court in 1991 determined that Title VII of the U.S. Civil Rights Act, which prohibits discrimination in job assignments, took precedence in this instance over OSHA regulations, which require companies to take steps to protect third parties (such as fetuses) from workplace dangers, and ruled that Johnson Controls's policy discriminated against women.

## GLOBALIZATION AND ETHICS

Maintaining ethical behavior becomes particularly challenging for companies with a global presence. U.S. corporations encounter countless obstacles as they walk the fine line between the requirements of the Foreign Corrupt Practices Act—passed by Congress in the 1970s to restrict unethical business practices of U.S. companies internationally—and the realities of local business culture. Corporate ethics statements often deal with gift giving and receiving, proprietary information, bribes, nepotism in hiring practices, conflict of interest, sexual harassment, treatment of racial and ethnic minority employees, and use of convict or child labor by suppliers. All these areas are viewed differently depending on the cultural perspective. Therefore, some important issues must be considered as ethical rules are exported by U.S. businesses.[38]

- *Rules definitions:* Are rules supposed to be obeyed without question or exception, as generally they are in Switzerland and Germany? Or are they merely ideals meant to be honored in the abstract but not feasible in many situations, as in some Latin American countries?

- *Exempt status people:* In companies with rigid social hierarchies and great differences in economic status, members of the elite class assume they have privileges and prerogatives others don't. Therefore, they feel exempt from the rules and standards that apply to other people—and accepting this behavior is common in the Philippines, India, and Latin America.

- *Public service norms:* The main purpose of bloated government bureaucracies in some countries is to provide jobs—mostly low-paying ones. The bureaucrats, in turn, aren't required to be very productive. Therefore, receiving gratuities for doing a task with extra speed or efficiency is considered appropriate. Such payoffs are so common in India that a local newspaper recently published a "bribe index" cataloging the bribery cost of various government services.

- *Gifts and bribes:* In Asia, gift giving has been used for thousands of years as a means of gaining access to, and favorable consideration from, important business contacts and government officials. The gifts are not viewed as bribes unless they are paid in cash to the recipient for doing something blatantly illegal or immoral.

- *Confidentiality and group identity:* In Japan and other countries where group bonds are strong, people function as parts of entities rather than as autonomous individuals. Confidentiality and shared information are essential within the group. The outsider's right to confidentiality is valued less than group loyalty.

- *Office gender roles:* Touching between female and male employees isn't seen as sexual harassment in Latin America. Slightly flirtatious behavior and somewhat provocative dress for women aren't considered out of place in many business environments. Rules to the contrary would seem unnecessarily punitive and stifling.

These are only a few of the myriad of cultural factors that complicate a corporation's attempt to create a global ethics standard. Worldly wise organizations take into consideration the cultural values of the countries in which their ethics standards are to be applied. They do not assume their standards automatically will be understood the same way in all locations.

---

**KEY CONCEPTS 3.2**     **Ethical Issues in Organizations**

Organizations face important ethical issues in several areas, including:

- • *Service versus profit.*

- • *Social responsibility.*

- • *Employee rights, including the right to fair and equitable treatment, the right to privacy, and the right to a safe and healthful work environment.*

- • *Globalization.*

In recent years, an alarming number of "unethical" situations have arisen in American business. For example, Ivan Boesky was found to have engaged in "insider trading," an unethical and potentially illegal practice for investment counselors. Chrysler was found to have disconnected the odometers in "new" cars that had been driven by its executives. Barry Minkow, founder of ZZZZ Best, was accused of money laundering, fraudulent credit card usages, phony business contracts, and connections to organized crime. Health care giant Columbia/HCA was found to have billed Medicare for medical services that were not delivered. Directors of savings and loan associations were found to have defrauded depositors, in many cases depriving people of their life savings. And of course, the president's private behavior in the White House, followed by public denials that the behavior occurred, cast doubt on the ethics of our nation's highest leadership. In these and many other situations, prominent organizations or individuals have behaved in ways that seem not to have been ethical.

But why should we be concerned about ethics in the first place? Why is it important to behave ethically if unethical behavior might provide us with some advantage in the competitive business world? Although each of us must answer these questions to his or her own satisfaction, recent events suggest the following:

First, unethical behavior can have seriously damaging consequences. These consequences can affect both the person committing the practice and the people that practice touches. In some of the cases noted above, for example, innocent investors lost large amounts of money, and some of the perpetrators were sentenced to jail. But beyond that, the people and organizations (and indeed, entire industries) who were involved lost credibility. And once your image is so tarnished that people no longer are willing to believe or put their faith in you and your business, failure is almost certain.

Second, ethical behavior usually has important positive consequences. Honesty in business dealings allows others to trust you and your organization, and makes you far more effective in your dealings with them. Indeed, business in general depends on the acceptance of rules and expectations, and on mutual trust and fairness. Simply put, ethical behavior is good business.

Third, your behavior serves as a model, both to yourself and to others. If you behave ethically and discover the effectiveness of such behavior, you are more likely to behave ethically in the future. Similarly, the people with whom you work (particularly your subordinates) will be more likely to engage in ethical behaviors. Conversely, if you behave unethically and get away with it (or even gain some short-term profit from it), you become more likely to continue your unethical behaviors and to promote such behavior by others.

Fourth, our own observations indicate that ethical errors end careers more quickly and with more finality than any other mistakes in judgment. Lying, stealing, cheating, reneging on contracts, and so on undermine the very foundation upon which the business world is built and thus are not readily forgiven or forgotten. For every newspaper headline discussing major breaches of ethics, there may be hundreds of "minor" situations where an

Of the 24 percent of 4,000 American workers who responded to a recent survey on technology and ethics in the workplace, the following percentages do *not* believe the following actions are unethical:

- Playing computer games on company equipment during office hours: 49 percent.

- Using office equipment to help children/spouse do schoolwork: 37 percent.
- Using company e-mail for personal reasons: 34 percent.
- Using office equipment for personal reasons: 29 percent.

Source: "Ethical Actions," *HR Fact Finder* 12: 3 (July 1998).

individual is fired (or "asked to resign") for unethical behavior, or where an executive or manager is put in a dead-end career track by a company wishing to avoid a public relations scandal.

Finally, ethical behavior is intrinsically valuable. Knowing that you are honest, that you behave humanely in your dealings with your fellow employees, that you are fair in your evaluations of others, and that you are concerned for the welfare of the whole organization and the society it serves—these are important self-perceptions, ones that carry no price tag.

Ultimately, the need for ethical behavior might best be expressed by the old maxim, "What goes around comes around." When we have unimpeachable integrity in our dealings with other people, we earn their trust and make them more willing to support us and our organization. Conversely, when we lack integrity, we promote mistrust on the part of those with whom we deal and, as managers, create employees who are ashamed of their organization and the products or services they provide. Since they feel their work is not worthy, they cease to care.

## DECIDING WHAT'S "RIGHT": SOME ETHICAL PERSPECTIVES

We have already stated that ethical concerns are involved in much organizational activity. Every day, employees must decide how to conduct themselves ethically. Ethics can be viewed from several perspectives, each of which provides a different basis for making judgments. Depending on the specific perspective employed, the answer to any given ethical dilemma will vary.

Hosmer describes three general approaches to ethical decision making in business.[39] *Economic analysis* bases ethical judgments on impersonal market forces. This school of thought holds that managers always should act to maximize revenues and minimize costs, and that this strategy itself will ensure that society gains the greatest benefit over the long term. This approach, however, does not take into consideration the well-being of some segments of society (for example, the poor and minorities, who do not or cannot participate in corporate ownership), nor does it exclude the use of questionable practices (bribes, environmental pollution, hazardous working conditions, or unequal treatment) that might improve an organization's bottom line. Indeed, this line of reasoning suggests that hospitals should provide the minimum amount of patient care—regardless of those patients' needs—in order to maximize hospital profits. In effect, it is an impersonal approach that considers people a means to an end and that takes no account of the nature of those people themselves.

*Legal analysis* reduces ethical judgments to a matter of law. Anything that is illegal is unethical. If a given behavior falls within legal limits, no ethical question can be raised. This approach has the advantage of ensuring simple ethical decisions: one has only to investigate the law, the rule, or the regulation covering a particular behavior. Thus, if a specific managerial practice is within the legal limits of an organization, the practice is considered ethical. While some may take great comfort in guiding their decisions and behavior by legal standards, this perspective often leads to oversimplification and superficiality. For example, the law does not prohibit lying except under oath in a court or in some formal contracts. Moreover, the law tends to forbid negative actions but does not encourage positive ones (for example, no law requires someone to go to the aid of a drowning child). Finally, some laws in and of themselves are morally objectionable to some people: Until the early 1960s, some areas of the United States legally required racial discrimination, and even now, laws concerning abortion, homosexuality, or religious observances in schools are repugnant to many.

*Philosophical analysis* seems more likely than the first two to provide useful guidance in making ethical decisions. However, a wide variety of such philosophical perspectives is available, including the following.

## Religious Perspective

Within the framework of every world religion, there are crucial moral and spiritual injunctions that might be used to measure the ethics of a given behavior. Most religions teach that behavior such as lying, committing adultery, slandering, and murdering are wrong. From a Judeo-Christian perspective, for instance, Christians are taught to love their neighbors as themselves, discouraging any remark or behavior of harmful intent directed toward another person. The Taoist religion stresses empathy and insight as roads to truth, deemphasizing reason and logic.

Some writers have attempted to apply these standards to certain facets of organizational behavior. McMillan discusses the concept of "multiple neighbors"—of organizational accountability extending to owners, employees, clients, customers, and the general public.[40] Although some contend that business persons are dishonest and deceitful, others suggest there is a trend toward more positive Christian values. Alderson believes that a good deal of business conduct is controlled by rules of morality, many of which have the force of law. He contends that most businesspersons keep their word when they make a promise, devote many hours to civic institutions and social concerns, and try to influence others to give their best, not only for the sake of the firm but also for the sake of themselves and their families.[41] The religious perspective thus provides some ethical guidelines, but leaves one with the problem of deciding which set of religious teachings to follow.

## Utilitarian Perspective

From a utilitarian perspective, usefulness and expediency are the criteria used to make ethical judgments. Taking this approach, one would conclude that a behavior is ethical if it provides the greatest benefits to the greatest number of people. A utilitarian critic judging the effectiveness of a public speech would be mainly concerned with whether or not the speech actually got the vote, changed the belief, or positively stimulated the audience. Techniques used to achieve the speech's purpose would be judged in terms of practical results. One might evaluate the worth of an advertising campaign, an incentive plan, or a public relations program from the same perspective.

While it is probably safe to say that the utilitarian view has less intrinsic appeal as an ethical perspective, it still has great practical significance. There would be no persuasive appeals, marketing strategies, or incentive plans without some pragmatic goal in mind. Organizations must be concerned with the ultimate effects of their plans, policies, and procedures, and laudable means that fail to promote important organizational goals should be subject to criticism, just as questionable goals themselves should be scrutinized. However, ends do not always justify means, and the rights of the minority must not be sacrificed for the "good" of the majority. Thus, this perspective, too, has its limitations.

## Universalist Perspective

While the utilitarian perspective considers the outcomes of an action, the universalist perspective holds that because outcomes are too difficult to predict or control, we should focus on intent. In effect, the morality of an action depends on the intentions of the person making the decision or performing the act. If that person wishes the best for others, his or her actions are ethical even if, due to the person's clumsiness or ineptitude, those actions end up hurting someone. This approach holds that there are certain universal duties people have in dealing with one another (hence the "universalist" perspective), such as telling the truth, not taking another's property, and adhering to agreements, and that if our intent is to uphold those duties, we are behaving ethically.

Under this approach, people are seen as ends rather than means. They are worthy of dignity and respect, not tools to be used by us for our own purposes. Perhaps that is the greatest lesson the universalist approach teaches. On the other hand, it is difficult to determine what "intent" is (even our own motives for performing various actions may be unclear to us), and in business, people at times *do* serve as a means to an end: For example, customers are a means of making money and earning a living, and employees are a means of getting work done.

## Humanist Perspective

Some writers attempt to make ethical judgments philosophically by isolating certain unique characteristics of human nature that should be enhanced. They then look at a particular technique, rule, policy, strategy, or behavior and attempt to determine the extent to which it either furthers or hampers these uniquely human attributes. Aristotle believed, for example, that truly human acts were performed by rational persons, individuals who recognized what they were doing and chose freely to do it.[42] In the case of a persuasive speaker, for example, his or her persuasive appeals and strategy should be judged in terms of their tendencies to enhance or reduce the listeners' rationality and decision-making ability.

Contemporary writers have identified such uniquely human attributes as the individual's symbol-using capacity; the need for mutual understanding; the motivation to serve both self and others; and the necessity for rational, reflective thought. Burke talks of the human need to transcend individual differences and to communicate cooperatively.[43] In her book *The Worth Ethic*, Kate Ludeman argues that "the Worth Ethic is a belief in your indelible self-worth and the fundamental and potential worth of others. . . . Worth Ethic managers commit themselves to help employees develop and use their skills and talents."[44]

One might infer from these statements that the ethical organization would encourage its members to communicate fully, freely, and cooperatively. Thus, organizational incentives aimed at encouraging cooperative deliberation should be encouraged, whereas competitively oriented programs should be deemphasized.

## Political and Cultural Perspective

Political systems and specific cultures provide another perspective from which to view ethical behavior. Within any given cultural or political context, there exist certain values or processes that seem basic to the well-being and growth of society. Values govern the way we behave as well as the kinds of goals we seek throughout our lives. Rokeach defines a value as "a type of belief, centrally located within one's total belief system, about how one ought or ought not to behave, or about some end-state of existence worth or not worth attaining."[45] Thus, values provide standards for judging behavior.

Of course, cultural perspectives are widely diversified. Haiman believes that the development of the human capacity to reason is a goal to which our American society is inherently committed and labels as unethical any behavior or technique that attempts to circumvent or demean the individual's ability to reason.[46] Wallace further asserts that the essential values of democracy are belief in the dignity and worth of the individual, faith in equality of opportunity, belief in freedom, and belief in each person's ability to understand the nature of democracy.[47] Finally, John Gunther wrote in *Inside USA*, "Ours is the only country deliberately founded on a good idea."[48] This idea combines a commitment to each person's inalienable rights with the belief in an ultimate moral law.

## Dialogic Perspective

An interesting viewpoint for making ethical judgments has emerged from scholarship on the nature of ethical human communication as dialogue rather than monologue. According to this perspective, the attitudes that individuals in any communication transaction have toward one another are an index of the ethical level of that communication. Some attitudes are believed to be more fully human, facilitative of self-actualization, and humane than other attitudes. According to Johannesen, for example, when people communicate from a dialogic perspective, their attitudes are characterized by honesty, trust, concern for others, open-mindedness, empathy, humility, sincerity, and directness. They are nonmanipulative, encourage free expression in others, and accept others as persons of intrinsic worth, regardless of differences of opinion or belief. Communication as monologue, on the other hand, is characterized by such qualities as deception, superiority, exploitation, domination, insincerity, distrust, and so forth. Freedom of expression is stifled, and others are viewed as objects to be manipulated.[49]

In using this perspective, you would observe any behavior, advertisement, speech, managerial practice, or organizational policy and determine the degree to which it reveals an ethical dialogic attitude or an unethical monologic attitude toward its intended audience. For the dialogic critic, any communication act or attitude that promotes deception, exploitation, or domination is unethical, regardless of the situation.

Some writers are less universal in their approach to ethics, believing it impossible to set definite ethical guidelines apart from the specific situation. They believe ethical criteria vary as factors in the communication situation vary, as the needs of the listeners vary, and even as role relationships change. According to this view, receiver expectations and knowledge levels are especially critical determinants. For example, we often expect hyperbole in political speeches and filter our responses accordingly. We do not, on the other hand, anticipate exaggerations from a college professor giving a lecture or from a doctor explaining the nature of an illness.[50] Thus, in the political context, hyperbole might be acceptable; but in the educational or medical setting, it would be taken literally and therefore should be considered unethical.

In his controversial book *Humbuggery and Manipulation: The Art of Leadership*, F. G. Bailey argues that political leadership is a special situation requiring special ethical judgments. He claims that leaders are "inescapably polluted by what they do, and, since leadership is by its very nature defiling, it follows that moral judgments are as appropriate in this regard as they are about foul weather." He continues by asserting that "no leader can survive as a leader without deceiving others (followers no less than opponents) and without deliberately doing to others what he would prefer not to have done to himself." Bailey concludes that "leaders everywhere must set themselves above the morality of their own society."[51] Unfortunately, it is all too easy to list political leaders, past and present, who have followed this school of thought.

Clearly, there are a variety of approaches to making ethical judgments, and each approach has its advantages and limitations. Perhaps the best thing to do in any given situation is to ask oneself a series of questions designed to test an action in terms of almost all these approaches. The questions might include the following:

- Would I want this action to be broadcast on the six o'clock news?

- Would I want my boss and top management to know I did this?

- Would I want my parents to know I did this?

- Would I want my spouse or family to know I did this?

- Would I want my customers to know I did this?

- Would I want my subordinates to know I did this?

- Would I want this action to be announced to my church congregation, with me present, during next Sunday's service?

- Would I do this if a police officer were standing or sitting next to me?

- Is doing this "good business"?

- Will doing this promote trust in me by others?

- Will I be able to sleep at night knowing I've done this?

- Would I want others to do this to me?

Even these questions provide an incomplete guide. For example, a professional football player who also happens to be homosexual might well answer no to most of these questions, not because he feels his lifestyle is unethical but because he fears the reactions of teammates, coaches, other players, his family, the public, and so on—people who have a different set of ethics. Nevertheless, if as you contemplate some action you find the answer to many of these questions to be no, you should consider carefully whether this action is truly ethical.

| KEY CONCEPTS 3.3 | Perspectives on Ethics in Organizations |
|---|---|

Some perspectives for deciding what's "right" in an organization include:

| Perspective | Ethical Guidelines |
|---|---|
| Economic analysis | Striving to maximize revenues and minimize costs automatically leads to long-term ethical behaviors. |
| Legal analysis | Stay within the boundaries of the law. |
| Philosophical analysis: | Adhere to principles embodied by one or more philosophical perspectives, such as: |
| *Religious* | Follow moral and spiritual injunctions taught by a particular religion; love your neighbor as you do yourself. |
| *Utilitarian* | Do what achieves the greatest good for the greatest number. |
| *Universalist* | Have the best of intentions; do what maintains the dignity and worth of others. |
| *Humanistic* | Enhance the unique human characteristics: reasoning, reflective thought, motivation to serve self and others. |
| *Political and cultural* | Follow society's values and norms. |
| *Dialogic* | Promote and show trust, concern for others, open-mindedness, empathy, humility, sincerity, and directness. |
| *Situational* | Take into account receiver expectations and knowledge levels when making judgments. |

# BUILDING ORGANIZATIONAL ETHICS

As organizations have come to realize the importance of ethical behavior, they have attempted to develop a sense of organizational ethics in a variety of ways. Each of these involves communication.

Corporate
Mission
Statements

Increasingly, organizations are seeking to establish a system of ethics by developing a statement of mission that tells employees what the organization is about and where it is going, builds a set of values with which everyone can identify, and supports cohesiveness and productivity. According to Jerome Want, a mission statement should separate a company from its competition and provide it with a sense of identity, legitimacy, and direction.[52] Its primary components are the following:

- *Purpose* of the organization. The mission statement should clearly outline the reasons for the organization's existence, the primary businesses in which it engages, and the products and services it provides (and the manner in which they should be provided).

## SAMPLE MISSION STATEMENT

Presented below is the mission statement developed by a small Chicago-based company.

### Mission Statement

Our mission is to manufacture wire, cable, and related products which enhance the day-to-day lives of the people who work and live in the buildings, use the computers and appliances, and enjoy the parks and golf courses of which our products become an integral part. We will achieve success by working together to make XXXXX a profitable, quality company:

**Committed to Manufacturing Quality Products:**   Our first commitment is to provide our customers with quality products that are innovative and technologically responsive to their needs, at competitive prices.

**Committed to Providing Quality Service:**   We likewise are committed to providing our customers with service that is responsive, flexible, dependable, and tailored to their unique problems and demands.

**Committed to Pursuing Quality Work Life:**   We commit to establishing and maintaining the kind of environment in which our employees want to work—one that encourages each person to achieve his or her highest potential, provides equal opportunities to all, and gives all employees a chance to make a meaningful contribution to the fulfillment of our mission and to be recognized for their accomplishments. A safe work environment also is critical, and every employee must be committed to his or her own safety and that of fellow workers.

**Committed to Developing Quality Relationships:**   We commit to establishing and maintaining high-quality relationships among all XXXXX personnel. This means that everyone strives to understand and follow the company's objectives and policies, communicates with co-workers, acts in a professional manner, and tries at all times to treat co-workers with respect, dignity, and cooperation. It also means that every XXXXX employee has the opportunity to speak with any other person in the company, so that all managers maintain an "open door" policy for all employees.

**Committed to Contributing to Quality Community Service:**   We are committed to serving the communities from which our people come. We strive to improve quality of life in those communities through our support of community organizations and projects, through encouraging service to the community by employees, and by promoting participation in community services.

### Reaching Quality in Individual Performance

We pledge to make our time at work "quality time"; to work with a sense of urgency, dependability, accuracy, and consistency; and to make each working minute count toward the achievement of our mission.

- *Principal business aims,* such as market share, profitability, or size; strategies for achieving growth or optimizing productivity; and impact on the competition.

- *Corporate identity,* or how the company wants to be perceived by its customers, its competitors, the business community in general, and its employees.

- *Policies* concerning the philosophy and style of leadership managers should use; the relationships among senior management, owners, shareholders and the board of directors; and the overall decision-making structure of the organization.

- *Values,* or a clear set of business standards against which the company and its members' actions should be judged. Typically, statements of values allow the company to be judged from several different perspectives: those of customers, competitors, employees, regulatory agencies, and the general public. As Weiss notes, these values should be simple and easy to articulate, should apply to internal as well as external operations, and should be communicated early and often even during the recruitment and selection process.[53]

However, mission statements are by no means an ethical panacea. In his article "Sex, Lies and Mission Statements," Christopher Bart argues that the mission statement, "the most popular management tool deployed in recent decades," represents an "organization's sex drive" and should fulfill two fundamental purposes: motivating "organizational members to exceptional performance" and guiding "the resource allocation process in a manner that produces consistency and focus." So much for the sex part; now for the lies: Bart's survey of 88 leading North American corporations revealed that, despite all the time, money, and effort that goes into crafting mission statements, "the vast majority are not worth the paper they are written on and should not be taken with any degree of seriousness." Bart concludes that a statement's ability to affect organizational behavior improves "the more the various stakeholders are involved in its development," "the more organizational arrangements are aligned with the mission," and "the greater the satisfaction with the statement."[54]

## Codes of Ethics

Many companies have attempted to ensure ethical behavior by their members by establishing a code of ethics. Indeed, Davis reports that more than 200 of the *Fortune* 500 now have their own codes of ethics.[55] While these codes vary somewhat, they have some common characteristics:

- They speak to activities that often cannot be closely supervised by company management (such as honesty with customers or mutual respect among employees). Thus, motivators such as fear or coercion cannot be applied to these activities, making the individual employee's ethics all the more important.

- They ask more than might otherwise be expected (such as avoiding criticisms of competitors during sales calls or taking pains to help customers).

- They contribute to the long-term success of the organization only to the extent that they are upheld by members of the organization. That is, they depend on voluntary cooperation by management and employees alike to ensure ethical behavior.

Baxter International, a worldwide producer of medical products, distributes to its people a booklet titled "Baxter Ethics" that deals with several key ethical policies:

- *Business conduct:* "Display good judgment and high ethical standards in your business dealings."

- *Legal obligations:* "Do not break the law."

- *Financial records:* "Keep honest and accurate financial records."

- *Company property:* "Use company property for business only."

- *Conflict of interest:* "Conduct personal business to avoid conflicts of interest."

- *Payments to government officials:* "Do not use funds for improper or illegal activities."

- *Confidential information:* "Do not use confidential information for personal gain."

- *Securities trading:* "Avoid writing options on Baxter stock."

- *Customer gifts:* "Use good sense when giving gifts to customers."

- *Advertising:* "Sell Baxter's products fairly and honestly, stressing their value and capabilities."

- *Government requests:* "Requests from national, state and municipal government agencies should be forwarded to the corporate Law Department."

- *Antitrust:* "Comply with the company's antitrust policies."

Each of these policies is explained in detail and illustrated with a series of commonly asked questions and answers.

Simply announcing a code of conduct to all staff, posting the code on bulletin boards throughout the company, or having new employees sign a copy of the code as a part of their orientation will not ensure cooperation. Individual managers must serve as role models of the code, and organizational rewards and punishments must be applied to encourage following the code's provisions.

Corporate Mottos

Corporate mottos are a little-used means of communicating an organization's guiding principles, sentiments, or philosophies. Research conducted by Hershey found that most *Fortune* 100 companies have never thought of a motto as a vehicle for transmitting corporate values to employees, but many use slogans to exhort workers or impress customers.[56] The mottos Hershey found included *Semper fidelis,*[56] or "Always faithful" (the U.S. Marine Corps); "We always get our man" (Royal Canadian Mounted Police); "Neither snow, nor rain, nor heat, nor gloom of night stays these couriers from the swift completion of their appointed rounds" (U.S. Postal Service); "The difficult we do immediately; the impossible takes a little longer" (U.S. Army Corps of Engineers); and "To keep it, you have to give it away" (Alcoholics Anonymous). A Cleveland-based health organization took the saying "Sometimes you eat the bear, and sometimes the bear eats you" and made it into its motto of the year: "Eat More Bear." Ford Motors claims that for them, "Quality is job one." Hershey claims that the ideal corporate motto would convey and promote a core philosophy of an organization, have an emotional appeal, and be somewhat of a mystery to the general public (thus reinforcing cohesiveness among organizational members). He found no corporate motto that meets all these criteria.

## Work Rules

Most companies try to ensure ethical behavior by developing and enforcing work rules. Typically, rules prohibit such actions as gambling, assaulting others, destroying property, theft, and trying to sell things to other employees at work. Yet these rules also tend to be somewhat loosely enforced: office pools gamble on the outcome of football games or buy state lottery tickets, employees conduct Tupperware parties, and so on.

The way in which a company develops and enforces its rules may reveal more about its ethics than the rules themselves. Steelcase, the nation's largest manufacturer of office furnishings, developed a form of participative management to enforce adherence to its values and policies. As a first step, a committee representing a cross-section of the entire company classified rules violations into three categories: Class I offenses (failing to punch in, gambling, unauthorized use of company telephones), which call for penalties of 1 to 60 points; Class II offenses (careless workmanship, destruction of company property, theft up to $10), which call for assessments of 60 to 120 points; Class III offenses (being under the influence of alcohol or drugs, assaulting a supervisor, drinking on company time), which call for 80 to 110 points. Employees accumulating 160 points are dismissed. Whenever an employee reaches 80 points, the Employee Performance Improvement Committee (comprising the plant manager, the area superintendent, the employee's foreman, an employee relations representative, and a professional from the company's counseling center) meets with the employee to encourage performance improvement. If the employee goes on to reach 100 points, the committee meets again. And even those employees who reach 160 points may not be through with the company: Many are rehired; and of those given a second chance, 80 percent succeed.[57]

## Ethics Training

Many companies are taking action to ensure ethical behavior among all of their employees. In fact, 95 percent of "Fortune 50" firms now teach ethics codes to their employees. At Texas Instruments, Lockheed Martin, and United Technologies, for example, efforts are under way to transform ethics policies and value statements into action. Texas Instruments has written and distributed a code of ethics since 1961, and the company introduced a formal ethics training program in 1986. The company communicates with its 60,000 employees by a weekly, electronic newsletter over the corporate intranet, and at least one article about ethics is always included. A toll-free hot line handles about 100 calls every month, and employees can report ethical issues anonymously for investigation by the vice president of ethics and his five-person field staff.

Lockheed Martin Corp. takes an unusually comprehensive approach to strengthening corporate ethics, offering employee training, a hot line, and a variety of written materials. Every employee receives a booklet titled "Our Values," which lists the company's ethics standards and discusses why honesty, integrity, and quality are crucial. Another booklet, "Ethics in our Workplace," provides detailed discussion of a variety of topics, including ethics in cyberspace, conflicts of interest, cultural differences, and excuses for misconduct. A separate newsletter, "Corporate Legal Times," provides self-assessments and information. In addition, every year all 200,000 employees attend a one-hour ethics awareness seminar conducted by their own supervisors, and the company provides a three-inch-thick binder that discusses the role of the company's ethics officers and gives realistic scenarios dealing with sexual harassment; interpersonal communication; and gifts, gratuities, and other business courtesies. A board game, called "The Ethics Challenge," reviews ethical issues in a humorous way (featuring characters from the "Dilbert" comic strip), and employees play the game during ethics training to spur discussion. Finally, there is a toll-free hot line that brings in more than 4,000 calls a year, and ethics officers are located at all 70 business units worldwide.[58]

Not every ethics training effort has been this successful—or this ethical— however. Labich reports that, for several years, the U.S. Department of Transportation (DOT) provided perhaps the most egregious example of how not to conduct ethics and diversity training.[59] In the name of exposing racial and sexual prejudices, DOT trainers continually subjected employees to what amounted to psychological abuse. The sessions, finally suspended in 1993 after outraged complaints from employees, included a gauntlet where men were ogled and fondled by women. Blacks and whites were encouraged to exchange racial epithets, people were tied up together for hours, and some were forced to strip down to their underwear in front of co-workers. Trainers also verbally abused participants, referring to one obese employee as "muffin queen." Not surprisingly, this training did not produce an increase in ethical behavior among DOT personnel.

Ultimately, improved ethics "doesn't come about as a result of pounding workers over the head and telling them they have to be ethical or else," according to Michael Hoffman, executive director of the Center for Business Ethics at Bentley College in Waltham, Mass.[60] It comes from understanding that business ethics involves individual and institutional values and that the two are inexorably intertwined. It also comes from recognizing that problems in the corporate world are often systemic and not the result of a few bad apples in the corporate barrel. A company that finds a way to change the system so people can be influenced to act ethically and responsibly is far more likely to succeed.

## Collective Action

In some organizations, employees have taken ethical matters into their own hands, acting in concert to fight, and ultimately to change, organizational practices. One of many such instances occurred in the mid-1980's and made labor relations history. Female reservationists working for Trans World Airlines were fed up with being electronically monitored and decided to stand up for their rights—literally. One morning, at the stroke of 11:00, about 50 reservationists, who were separated from management by a glass wall, stood up. A few days later, they did it again. And again a few days after that. "It really freaked them out," said Harriette Topitzes, then a TWA reservationist and now a committee chairwoman for the International Association of Machinists and Aerospace Workers. "We were pretty weak until we started standing up for ourselves. By standing up, we were sending a message."[61]

The results of these actions ultimately were an employee union, an in-house monitoring policy, and a federal law regulating employee monitoring. In addition, an organization called "9to5" was formed to support workers in their fight against sexual harassment, discrimination, and workplace abuse.

*Labor unions strive to protect employees and to encourage organizations to treat everyone ethically. Here, health care workers from across New York rally at the state capitol in support of Universal Health Care.*

Of particular concern to the group are low-wage, low-income working women. "We're the only group focusing on this constituency," says Ellen Bravo, Executive Director of 9to5. "Other groups focus on changing the situation at the top. We focus on the sticky floor instead of the glass ceiling, things that keep women stuck at low-wage, dead-end jobs."[62]

Labor unions often work to ensure ethical treatment for employees in the workplace, and to encourage organizations to behave ethically in general. For example, the American Nurses Association, along with many state nurse associations, has worked to combat hospital efforts to cut costs by cutting licensed staffing and quality of patient care. The Service Employees International Union similarly has tried to provide employees with protection from executives seeking to maximize profits by taking away employee benefits or job security. In these and other instances, collective action by employees, often with the assistance of union representatives, has helped to encourage ethical behaviors by employers.

## Management Behaviors

One key to developing organizational ethics seems to be the behaviors of individual supervisors and managers. Dolecheck advises four approaches a manager or supervisor should take to improving ethics.[63] First, a manager should *emphasize and discuss ethics continually*. A code of ethics becomes real only when a manager talks about it by encouraging subordinates to raise

Before his ouster in May 1993 as chairman of New York's Empire Blue Cross and Blue Shield, Albert Cardone took home $600,000 a year in his chauffeur-driven Lincoln Town Car. Both the salary and the transportation were paid for by the nation's largest *nonprofit* health insurer at a time when it was trying to stave off insolvency by drastically raising the premiums on the elderly, the poor, and the chronically sick.

Other problems surfaced in the form of numerous helicopter trips, accounts at Tiffany and Cartier for Empire employees and directors, a fleet of 123 cars, $130,000 in art and sculpture, $62,832 in tacky silk plants, $48,000 for computer and security systems in Cardone's home, and a $20,000 Chippendale desk that was purchased as part of an aborted office redesign—then placed in storage and never used. Under Cardone's management, Empire had racked up $255 million in losses since 1990.

In hearings before the Senate's Permanent Subcommittee on Investigations, Cardone defended his management of Empire. He had no convincing response, however, to the damning testimony of Empire's chief auditor, Maroa Velez. She told of being "stonewalled" by superiors when she tried to investigate discrepancies between internal books and the financial reports Empire sent to regulators. The company allegedly overstated losses incurred in providing insurance to poor customers.

The Empire story is not isolated. Some $70 billion flows annually through the U.S. system of 70 not-for-profit Blue Cross and Blue Shield companies, which control more than 30 percent of the private health insurance market. While the majority of "Blues" are financially sound, others, like Empire, have been walloped by spiraling health costs and "cherry picking"—the loss of the best customers to for-profit rivals. In 1989, for instance, New Hampshire regulators had to intervene when the state's Blue Cross and Blue Shield exhausted its cash reserves. West Virginia's Blue ran out of money three years ago, leaving 51,000 individuals with unpaid claims. Investigators discovered that, among other unethical management practices, executives had funneled Blue Cross money to businesses in which they had a financial interest.

Source: Richard Behar, "Singing the Blue Cross Blues," *Time* (July 12, 1993): 48.

ethics-related issues, doubts, or concerns; by referring to it when answering questions or making decisions concerning quality, safety, work methods, and so on; and by keeping others' attention focused on it. Second, it is important that the manager *develop realistic goals.* People faced with goals they cannot achieve are tempted to cut corners, sacrificing ethics for achievement. Third, by *identifying areas that are vulnerable to unethical practices,* a manager might avoid ethical problems by discussing with employees the sorts of temptations that might arise. Finally, *encouraging reporting of unethical activities* lets everyone know that the manager has a role in enforcing ethical standards and indicates serious intent to ensure ethical behavior.

As members of organizations, we must promote ethical behaviors by serving as role models. As Weiss notes, "values cannot be taught, they must be lived." People emulate what they see, not what they are told. If they see unethical behaviors or tolerance for improper practices, they will cease to believe any written codes of ethics. Richard Zimmerman, Chairman and CEO of Hershey Foods Corporation, refers to his company's value system as an "anchor" for the organization and asserts that "each manager must have a grip on those clearly defined values and be able to demonstrate them through their own behavior to employee groups." President and Chief Operating Officer Kenneth Wolfe agrees: "There is no grey area on ethics at Hershey. Here, you will never bend the ethical standards of doing business."[64]

| KEY CONCEPTS 3.4 | Approaches to Improving Ethics in Organizations |
|---|---|
| Organizations try a number of strategies to encourage ethical behavior, including:<br><br>• • *Corporate mission statements*<br><br>• • *Codes of ethics*<br><br>• • *Corporate mottos* | • • *Work rules*<br><br>• • *Ethics training*<br><br>• • *Collective action*<br><br>• • *Management behaviors*<br><br>• • *Emphasizing values* |

Emphasizing Values

What then, are the most important values an organization can stress? Surveys reveal that managers at all levels seem to place the highest value on *integrity* and *competence* in their superiors, peers, and subordinates.[65] Moreover, American managers thrive in companies that stand for values they can embrace in their personal lives. Excellent companies have clear values that make sense to their employees—and they reinforce these values through everything they do. In his American Management Association *Memos for Management: Leadership*, James L. Hayes points out that ethical issues are just as much a part of everyday business practices as they are embedded in broad corporate philosophy. Hayes reports that managers lack credibility on the big issues if they have demonstrated a lack of moral fiber when it comes to handling the smaller, everyday ethical issues. He goes on to define "moral fiber" as "respect for the customers and employees and sensitivity to the concerns of society in general."[66]

Similarly, in *Thriving on Chaos*, Tom Peters argues that "without doubt, honesty has always been the best policy. The best firms on this score have long had the best track records overall—Johnson & Johnson, IBM, S. C. Johnson (Johnson Wax), Hewlett-Packard, Merck, Digital Equipment."[67] Thus, managers should "demand total integrity" from themselves and their people: "if a promise (even a minor one) is not kept, if ethics are compromised, and if management behaves inconsistently, then the strategies necessary to survival today simply can't be executed."

Most people prefer to work for an organization they believe to be guided by ethical principles. In the Schmidt and Posner survey, 80 percent of the respondents agreed that the organizations for which they worked were guided by highly ethical standards. The strongest vote of confidence came from top management, however, while younger respondents and those of lower rank provided answers that implied more cynical views. All respondents, regardless of rank or experience, agreed that their bosses had the greatest influence on their own professional ethical conduct. And those bosses generally prefer ethical behaviors themselves: Schmidt and Posner concluded their report by noting that the profit motive and ambition, for example, do not receive the highest rating on most managers' lists of most admired qualities. In fact, both rank "well below responsibility, honesty, and imagination."[68]

In his 1998 editorial, *Chicago Tribune* writer Dale Dauten provides a final overview:

> I received from a reader in Florida a newspaper clipping on a business ethics speech by the compliance officer for Pratt & Whitney. She said, "our message is, we don't lie, we don't steal. The consequences just aren't worth it." Is this the best we can hope for? What happened to honor, dignity and the dream for a better life? All that these endless ethics debates offer us is mere practicality. Once practicality becomes the issue, then all behavior is just a matter of interpretation. . . . Don't you long to hear someone say, "We don't lie or steal because it's wrong." But no, there's always a need to consult the Book of Profits. Try to picture Winston Churchill pronouncing, "The consequences just aren't worth it." Or Martin Luther King, Jr., standing up and telling America, "I have a compliance." Maybe we should start by throwing out the compliance officers and instead promote real leaders who do what's right, period. The kind of person Fred Allen described in one simple sentence: "he was so honest, you could play craps with him over the phone."[69]

# SUMMARY

At the beginning of this chapter, we noted that ethical issues within organizations are important and involve relationships among all members of an organization and other organizations with which they have contact. Despite efforts to increase ethical behaviors, however, there seems to be a rise in unethical acts, driven in part by increasing pressures in the workplace and various organizational practices. The areas of service versus profit, social responsibility, and employee rights seem particularly relevant to ethical concerns, and we reviewed some important issues related to each.

Next, we considered some perspectives for determining what's "right," evaluating both organizational and communication ethics from various philosophical perspectives, including religious, political, utilitarian, universalist, dialogic, and situational. Sometimes more than one perspective can be used, and often, they function interdependently.

Despite these difficulties, the contemporary thrust of organizational leadership and behavior embraces a compelling appeal for a sense of ethics within the context of social responsibility. Thus, we reviewed some efforts organizations are making to improve ethical behavior, including mission statements, codes of ethics, corporate mottos, company work rules, ethics training for management and employees, collective action among employees in support of ethical behavior, changes in the behaviors of individual supervisors and managers, and emphasizing values.

# QUESTIONS FOR DISCUSSION

1. Discuss the assertion that the end justifies the means. Are there any particular kinds of situations in which this position might be defensible? Elaborate with at least one example.

2. It is not uncommon for individuals to vary their ethical perspectives, depending on the precise nature of the situation in which they find themselves. Can you justify this point of view?

3. What are some of the best ways for organizations to create a climate in which sexual harassment is unlikely to occur?

4. How has technology affected employees' rights to privacy?

5. What should an employee do when he or she feels an immediate supervisor is doing something unethical? Outline a series of actions that the employee might take.

6. How would you define the ethics of an organization with which you are presently affiliated? What do the ethical standards of the organization seem to be? How are standards communicated? How are they enforced?

# EXERCISES

1. Choose any prominent person (such as an educator, a religious leader, a politician, a lawyer, or an executive) and discuss her or his behavior from an ethical perspective. What is the apparent value system of this individual? On what is it based? From your own view, is this person's behavior ethical? Be specific.

2. Select any three advertisements. Consider their bases of appeal, operating assumptions, and general taste. To what extent is each a reasonably accurate representation of reality? How would you rate each in terms of *your* ethical perspective?

3. Choose an executive of a moderate-sized to large organization, and arrange for an interview. During the interview, ask the executive to discuss his or her philosophies of management, relating them to his or her own values and those of the organization.

4. Contact several major organizations that have branches near your community. Ask them whether or not they have written procedures for dealing with discrimination and/or sexual harassment. If they do, obtain copies. Do the procedures seem adequate? If not, how could they be improved?

5. You are the manager of a newly established realty company in a medium-sized town in the Midwest. While the organization has nationwide branches, your office is new, and you are relatively free to run it as you prefer—so long as you operate in the black. Your 15 years of experience in the real estate business has taught you that it is a competitive, exciting, and in some senses treacherous business. Yet one of its major purposes is to serve the public.
   a. What values would influence you most in building your organization? Why?
   b. How would these values be reflected in your hiring and handling of employees, especially fellow real estate agents?
   c. How would your values relate to your handling of the public?
   d. What is the ethical basis for your particular values? Elaborate.

6. Imagine yourself as a fairly new employee in a rapidly growing firm. You have high hopes for rapid promotion, but your boss is a person who presents certain problems. His ideas of how to manage are very command-oriented, whereas yours are

much more democratic. His political views are conservative (far to the right of George Bush); yours are just left of Ted Kennedy. He loves sports; you loathe sports. Unfortunately, he often asks for your views on all of the above and on other painful issues as well. What do you do? Do you articulate your true opinions? Do you pretend to agree? Do you downplay your views or simply attempt to change the subject? Is it possible to distort your position in some areas but not in others? *What is the relationship here between the ethical and the political thing to do?* What ethical perspective would you use to resolve this dilemma? Why?

*Hospitals and Health Networks* magazine created an ethically challenging scenario and asked a panel of five hospital chief executive officers to respond to it. The scenario was as follows:

Robin Wood Medical Center has posted large losses for three years in a row. It is located in a decaying neighborhood on the fringes of a large city with plenty of—perhaps too many—hospital beds available. The hospital is the largest employer in its area and serves pockets of elderly and poor residents, many of whom do not own or drive cars. The community leans heavily on the hospital, which operates an adult day care center, a busy emergency room, and other key services. However, the number of patients using the hospital has been declining steadily.

Longtime hospital president Joan Morgan has the confidence and trust of her Board of Directors, who have asked her to investigate affiliations with other hospitals. MetroCare, a large health system that owns two hospitals in the area, has offered to buy Robin Wood Medical Center, but for a very low price. MetroCare has also made promises to Joan Morgan, offering her a generous severance package and consulting agreement if she persuades the Board to accept their offer. MetroCare has also made clear to Joan its plan to close the hospital and transfer only a fraction of its employees to other sites. It has given no assurances that the hospital's services will be continued near its present location.

Two other city hospitals also have approached Joan Morgan, but they have recently entered into their own merger talks. Executives from the two facilities have told Morgan that they cannot consider deals with Robin Wood Medical Center until those discussions come to a conclusion. Morgan worries that MetroCare's offer may be the only affiliation possible.

Source: From "Ethics and the CEO," *Hospitals and Health Networks* 72: 2 (January 20, 1998): 28–34.

## Questions

1. How should Morgan weigh the ethical issues concerning the hospital's survival versus the survival of its vital services?
2. What are the ethical implications of MetroCare's offer for the hospital versus its financial promises to Morgan? What should she do?

# PART two

# Public Communication

**PUBLIC SPEAKING, WHICH IS THE** best way to motivate a large group, is entirely different from private conversation. A speaker may be well informed, but if he hasn't thought out exactly what he wants to say *today, to this audience,* he has no business taking up other people's valuable time.

—*Lee Iacocca,* **Iacocca: An Autobiography**

# CHAPTER four

*After reading this chapter,
you should be ready to:*

1  Select an appropriate speech
   topic, based on your own
   interests, the interests of
   your audience, the demands
   of the situation, and your
   organizational affiliation.

2  Decide on your speech's
   purpose, in broad terms, as
   well as in terms of the
   specific audience response
   you are seeking.

3  Conduct research,
   investigating your topic by
   visiting the library,
   exploring the Internet,
   interviewing for
   information, and reflecting
   on your own resources.

4  Choose effective evidence to
   support your ideas.

5  Draw sound conclusions from
   the evidence you have
   found.

# Preparing for and
# Supporting Your Speech

Speaking in public is an increasingly common organizational communication activity. While administrators, board directors, and other executives have always made speeches, today professional men and women of varied occupations are called upon to speak with increasing regularity. Consider these examples: (1) a lawyer talks to an organization of concerned parents about the legality of textbook censorship; (2) an obstetrician informs a group of expectant mothers about alternative methods of childbirth; (3) an accountant speaks to a local Rotary Club, giving members some tips on how to file their income tax returns; (4) an educator addresses a group of fellow teachers in an effort to get them to unionize; and (5) a social worker speaks to a group of junior high school students about the use of illegal drugs. Clearly, regardless of your occupation—whether you are an educator, a social worker, a realtor, or a salesperson—you are likely to be asked to make some speeches throughout your professional life.

Many believe that the most critical skills any prospective organizational employee can possess may be the ability to speak effectively and write clearly. Economist Peter Drucker exemplifies this view when he notes that colleges teach the one thing that is most valuable for the future employee to know: the ability to organize and express ideas in writing and in speaking.[1] Unfortunately, many bright young men and women graduate from college every year without having mastered these vital skills. In fact, it is often only when they are confronted with the realities of their first jobs that they recognize how frequently they must write reports and letters, and must inform and persuade varied audiences in public speaking situations.

## PREVIEW

In this chapter we will address the first steps in preparing to speak. The speaker's first challenge is choosing an appropriate topic and deciding on the speech's purpose (in both general and specific terms). The speaker then begins to investigate the topic, doing research to find information and to form and develop his or her ideas. As information is discovered, the speaker must choose sound and effective supporting evidence to use in the speech and, through judicious reasoning, must draw sound conclusions based on that evidence.

## SELECTING THE SPEECH TOPIC

Whenever you are asked to make a speech, you are faced with one of two basic situations: (1) the topic is suggested, or (2) you are told to speak about anything of your choice (occasionally, within some rather broad parameters). Often a topic is suggested that is related to your job. Automotive executives are asked to speak about the impact of the nation's economic woes on their industry; journalists are invited to discuss media coverage of controversial trials; and teachers are asked to talk about pedagogical innovations.

For many speakers, having to choose the subject presents a problem. Though the possible topics appear endless, no *one* topic may seem quite appropriate. In fact, many speakers spend an inordinate amount of time on topic selection and are left with inadequate time for researching, organizing, and practicing. Yet, topic selection can be approached rather systematically if potential topics are examined in relationship to four major perspectives: (1) *personal,* (2) *audience,* (3) *situational,* and (4) *organizational.*

## Personal Perspective

Certainly the richest source of speech ideas resides within you as an individual. Begin, then, with some assessment of your personal knowledge, experiences, attitudes, and beliefs. Speeches vary in purpose; yet each is essentially a personal statement from you as a speaker to others who choose or are asked to listen. You may want to select a topic about which you already know a good deal but would like to learn more. Building upon your initial interest, you may need to conduct research. After you have worked within your chosen field for some time, you will develop considerable expertise and insights into accounting, teaching, marketing, or public relations. When this happens, you only need to reflect on what you know and organize your thinking into some effective, appealing strategy. More often, both self-reflection and research will be needed.

Your personal interest in a subject may evolve from intellectual enthusiasm and curiosity as well as from firsthand experiences. Not every speaker has traveled extensively, worked for 20 years in a hospital, or written speeches for a prominent political candidate. What is important, however, is that, as a student, you have had certain kinds of secondary experiences. You have read books, seen movies, and listened to lectures and speeches. You have read newspapers and news magazines, and you may have explored the Internet. You have listened to your professors and exchanged ideas with your peers.

Sometimes conducting a *self-inventory* of your interests and experiences can be helpful. Table 4.1 presents some factors to consider as you go through a thorough, thoughtful self-assessment.

**TABLE 4.1**
**Self-Inventory for Public Speakers**

1. Educational background (including anything interesting or unusual)
2. Jobs held (and skills developed through jobs)
3. Memorable childhood experiences
4. Traveling (familiar or interesting places visited)
5. Special training
6. Organizational affiliations
7. Hobbies and leisure activities
8. Books or authors you have especially enjoyed
9. People who have influenced your thinking and values (friends, writers, family members, political figures, teachers, leaders)

## The Perspective of the Audience

The second major perspective from which any potential topic should be considered is the audience. Select a subject about which the audience has some information but would enjoy learning more. You will need to find ways to connect your interests with your listeners. No speaker can succeed without the cooperation, goodwill, and interest of his or her listeners. Choosing the speech topic is the first step in establishing that connection.

*Every topic, then, should be selected with an equal concern for speaker and audience needs, values, and interests.* Both you and your listeners must be "turned on" if the communication exchange is to be meaningful. Successful communication can only occur when the speaker is audience-centered and when reciprocal exchange occurs.

In choosing a subject, there are a number of audience-related dimensions to be considered. At the most basic level, contemplate potential subjects with regard to the *demographic characteristics of the audience*, including age, gender, socioeconomic status, and educational level. This kind of information helps you select a topic, and it also provides clues to *how* to handle a given topic tastefully and persuasively. The topic "Health Care Options" is relevant to everyone. Yet your approach to this topic if you were addressing a group of young married couples would differ considerably from the way you would discuss it for a group of elderly citizens.

Also, seek information about the social, economic, political, and religious beliefs of the audience. Such knowledge may provide insights into the needs and values of the audience. With persuasive speaking, in particular, an assessment of such values is crucial. As soon as you accept an invitation to speak, it is appropriate to question the individual who contacted you about his or her perceptions of the audience's interests and values. It is important to avoid making stereotypic assumptions about an audience based on minimal information.

Finally, in selecting a topic, you might consider the audience's immediate background. Some people share concerns and have common interests in problems simply because of the context or setting in which they find themselves. As a student enrolled in a basic business and professional communication course, you will often address your classmates. Your audience in this instance represents a diversity of religions, political views, abilities, and socioeconomic levels. But because your classmates share the bond of attending college, they have common interests. Such topics as grade inflation, the job market, the university's grading system, graduation requirements, faculty evaluation, and the university's reputation would all be potentially relevant to them.

As we move into the twenty-first century, keep in mind that audiences are increasingly diverse. No longer can we assume, for example, that a management group will be mostly male. Nor can we assume that most listeners will share the same religious or political beliefs. Pointing your listeners toward the features of your topic, proposal, or action plan that they all can connect with, regardless of their diversity, is a critical first step to your effectiveness as a public speaker.

## The Situational Perspective

Every public speech is given in some context. Right now, your speaking context is your business and professional communication classroom. Your instructor may suggest topics that are more or less appropriate to the classroom setting. In the future, you will speak in contexts as diverse as workshops, meetings, award ceremonies, conventions, weddings, and funerals. Sometimes topics will grow directly from the occasion.

In every speaking context, there will be time constraints. In fact, most public speeches are delivered in 20 to 30 minutes. If you are pursuing a substantive topic, it is imperative that the audience have some initial information so that your remarks are understood. Let us say, for example, that a representative of General Motors (GM) is speaking to an audience of business and professional women, on the topic of some of the company's automotive innovations in response to the projected fuel shortage. Although the speaker may assume that the members of his audience are not extremely knowledgeable about automotive technology, he can be reasonably sure that they are well aware of the nation's overall economic condition, that they know of the predicted energy shortage, and that they are aware of the basic responses of automobile designers and manufacturers to fuel consumption problems. As a result, the speaker can spend most of his time discussing specific features of particular models and plans for future innovations. Notice that this topic is a good, manageable choice for this context because of the assumed level of audience knowledge and interest in the subject.

Regardless of the particular speech situation you are facing, *you should ask yourself how the context should be taken into consideration in choosing your topic.* Sometimes the occasion may point you in a specific direction. For instance, if you are presenting an award to someone, you will clearly talk largely about the honoree. If you are speaking at a conference with an overarching theme, such as "Technology and Communication" or "Education and Our Children's Future," your speech topic should be relevant to the theme. In addition, speaking situations vary in formality; fitting the topic and your treatment of it to the formality of the occasion is also a must.

## The Organizational Perspective

The final perspective from which you might consider topic selection is that of the organization you are representing. When you are called upon to make a public speech, it is often because of your affiliation with a specific organization. You are the president of your sorority, the head of student government, a long-standing member of 4-H, or a member of the basketball team. In the future, you may be asked to represent your law firm, the business you work for, or the church to which you belong.

In those situations, you may wonder whether you are speaking for yourself or largely as an organizational representative. In many instances, the distinction is irrelevant. On some occasions, however, you may hold views that differ in important ways from those of your organization. For instance, your church may have taken a formal stand against the ordination of women. While you agree with your church's views on *most* controversial social issues, you take strong exception to the church's stance on this one. Now, you have been asked to speak about your church's position on recent social issues, and you are almost certain that the ordination of women will come up. What should you do?

The process of public speaking involves choice making from beginning to end. One choice you might make in this situation is to ask those who asked you to speak to find another speaker—one who is more strongly committed to each of the church's positions. Or, you might choose to direct your speech toward two or three other issues and hope that you can guide listeners in the

**TABLE 4.2**

**Speech Topics from the Perspective of the Organization**

1. Is this topic of any concern to my organization?
2. What is my organization's stand on the issue?
3. Is its position public knowledge?
4. To what extent does my opinion differ from that of the organization?
5. Am I being asked to speak for myself, for the organization, or for both?
6. Might I deal with the topic by sharing information but not articulating a specific point of view?
7. How important is this issue to me and to my organization?

direction of your choice. Or, you might approach the social issues in an informative way—simply explaining the church's stance and outlining some of the complexities and controversies associated with each. Each of these options has practical and ethical implications.

Clearly, you need to consider the organization you are representing as you go about the task of selecting a speech topic. This does not mean that you are simply an outlet through which your organization communicates its views to the public. But the organization does create some potential constraints that ought to be reflected upon. As you begin to think about possible speech topics, consider the questions raised in Table 4.2.

Just as the topic you choose should reflect a consideration of your interests, those of the audience, the nature of the situation, and the organization you represent, the way in which the topic is *narrowed and focused* should also reveal a sensitivity to these factors. If the general topic is pollution, for example, you might focus on the issue of noise pollution for a group of teenagers, on the practical concerns of how pollution affects our daily lives at the university for a classroom audience, and on how the automotive industry is attempting to cope with air pollution for an audience of business people. Once the topic has been selected with these considerations in mind, you are ready to think about the basic goal or purpose of your speech.

---

**KEY CONCEPTS 4.1     Choosing the Speech Topic**

When selecting your speech topic, consider:

• • *Your own interests, knowledge, attitudes, and experiences:*

Firsthand experiences
Secondary learning
Self-inventory

• • *The audience's needs, interests, values, and beliefs:*

Audience demographics—age, gender, beliefs, etc.
The audience's immediate background
Audience diversity
Balanced concern for self and audience

*Continued*

| 4.1 CONTINUED | Choosing the Speech Topic |
|---|---|

**Concluded**

• • *The situation in which the speech is presented:*
    Specific occasions
    Time constraints
    Other contextual factors, such as speaking in the classroom

• • *The organization you are representing:*
    Speaking for the organization versus speaking for yourself
    Considering options; making choices

• • *Narrow and focus the topic, with the above considerations in mind.*

## CHOOSING THE SPEECH'S PURPOSE

In many instances, the speech purpose is virtually assigned or, at best, tactfully implied. Not long ago we were asked to make a speech as part of the opening session for a weekend-long leadership retreat. The contact person suggested to us, "Now these kids [college juniors and seniors] really want something interesting. I mean, they've been studying and listening to lectures all week; they've got finals coming up in two or three weeks. So . . . use a little humor, make them laugh! I mean, I know you're both professors, but frankly the last thing we want is a lecture."

Aside from our amazement that he had bothered to seek out such dull, lifeless "professor types" to reduce this audience to giggling hysteria, we were perplexed by what he asked us to achieve. Specifically, he wanted us to introduce the audience to all of leadership theory, cite supporting research for each theory, give them practical guidelines for their own leadership behavior, and uplift them in such a way that they would feel moved to go forth with great pride in their positions and faith in themselves. Thus, we were to interest and entertain, inform and instruct, persuade and inspire—be a combination of comedian, master teacher, and evangelist! Although this example presents a rather dramatic set of public speaking demands, it is not all that different from the situations in which many speakers find themselves. In fact, most successful speeches *do* interest, inform, and persuade in varying proportions. Yet, as you choose your topic and begin the task of narrowing and focusing your speech, you should do so with some overarching purpose in mind.

**To Interest** Some public speeches do little more than entertain. Often the speaker has no serious intention of being either informative or persuasive. Comedians and after-dinner speakers often speak to entertain. Sometimes the speech is built around a kind of theme, frequently involving recounting a series of personal experiences, each with a humorous point. Comedian Bill Cosby does a great deal of this kind of speaking, focusing on such themes as going to the dentist, paying one's bills, and having a baby.

Most of us seldom speak publicly for the single purpose of entertainment. Even so, the general notion of entertainment in the sense of listening to something for intrinsic enjoyment or interest does have a critical place in effective public speaking. All too often we overlook the importance of interest. We assume that if a speech is packed full of good, factual information and well-reasoned appeals, it is sure to be a success. We fail to consider the fact that information, statistics, ideas, and visual aids must all be related to the interests and needs of the audience. Without interest, listeners cannot learn; neither can they be moved, uplifted, inspired, or incited to action. Thus, *every speech must interest.*

It is not always easy to determine what subjects audiences will find interesting, but most audiences will respond with interest to information they perceive to be:

- *Relevant.* An audience of single parents struggling with child discipline problems, financial woes, and loneliness would be interested in hearing a family therapist discuss strategies for dealing with these problems. For an audience of happily married couples whose children are grown, however, this subject would not be particularly relevant.

- *Useful.* A group of graduating college seniors is motivated to learn about the job market in a way that a group of retiring executives is not. For the seniors, the subject is useful.

- *Startling, unusual, or new.* Novelty sustains attention. The speaker who presents new insights into the economic woes of Russia, the home as the office of the future, or the ethics of cloning is more likely to interest the audience than one who presents a standard treatment of legalizing marijuana, the dangers of smoking, or abortion.

- *Worth knowing or repeating.* Not everyone would agree on what is worth knowing. However, speeches dealing with such topics as religion, the economy, or education are likely to be perceived as substantive and worthy of invested listening time.

- *Amusing or entertaining.* Some speakers' primary goal is to make the audience laugh and enjoy themselves. While this goal may sound frivolous, it is one of the most difficult public speaking goals to accomplish. Speeches to entertain must be virtually perfectly attuned to the particular interests, tastes, and values of the audience.

## To Inform

For most public speakers, interest is only the beginning. Much public discourse is primarily informative. Its purpose is to teach, to impart information. On occasion, you will actually present the audience with new information; at other times, you may take familiar data, information, or ideas and present some different perspective or interpretation.

*Whenever you choose to give an informative speech, your major purpose is to gain audience understanding.* Informative speeches should meet several criteria: (1) *accuracy*—the result of careful observation, study, and research; (2) *completeness*—the inclusion of information essential to a proper understanding of the subject; (3) *unity*—adherence to a central theme and clarity of thought progression; and (4) *meaningfulness*—related to the audience's needs, interests, and levels of understanding.[2]

Often in organizational settings informative speaking takes the form of oral technical reports. Here are some examples: (1) a floor supervisor explains to assembly-line workers the reason for a new job rotation schedule; (2) an attorney enlightens a group of citizens about the laws governing child abuse cases; (3) an electrical engineer explains to a school board the plans for wiring a new school complex; and (4) a salesperson presents figures to her department depicting the successful marketing of a new fluoride mouthwash. Informative speeches usually require the use of visual aids to increase clarity and enhance understanding. Because achieving audience understanding is so important, informative speeches should be followed by a question-and-answer period.

Finally, it is important to remember that not all informative speeches are purely informative. Many speakers transmit information to build a common ground of understanding before urging the audience to support a given point of view or to act in a specified way. In this manner, then, information dissemination creates a foundation for persuasion.

## To Persuade

Persuasion is the final goal or purpose of public speaking. Some would argue that all communication is inherently persuasive, for even the speaker who provides factual information about specific subjects, such as how legislation is passed, how to take excellent pictures, or what the federal regulations are regarding advertising, does so with some persuasive intent of getting the audience to understand and accept the speaker's presentation of the facts. However, *speeches that are explicitly persuasive fall into three basic categories: those whose purpose is to stimulate, to convince, or to move to action.*

Often you will be asked to address an audience whose interests, values, feelings, and beliefs are virtually identical with your own. In this case, your strategy may be to reinforce already existing beliefs. Thus, the speech to stimulate does not attempt to effect change except in the sense of changing the degree of listener commitment, that is, intensifying and enhancing an already existing belief or attitude. Speeches that stimulate are quite common in political and religious settings.

Most of the time as a public speaker you will not find yourself in the position of addressing large groups of totally supportive listeners. Instead, you usually face a mixed group: some members supportive, some negative, and many undecided. On occasion, you may encounter a totally hostile audience, but these instances are also relatively rare. Changing people's beliefs is difficult, particularly those beliefs that are rooted in deep clusters of attitudes and values, and that have developed in response to personal experiences and observations.

It is not uncommon for listeners to respond positively to a speech, demonstrating appreciation for its language and delivery, and yet remain unmoved by its appeals. This is especially true when the speaker is advocating a behavioral commitment on the part of the audience. Many persuasive speeches go beyond the realm of idea acceptance and attempt to move the audience to action. As public speakers, we are often in positions of soliciting votes and money, of requesting commitments of time and talent, of asking people to give, to share, to show their involvement in their beliefs in some measurable way. These tasks are immensely challenging. Moving listeners to believe is difficult; inspiring them to act is even more demanding. In Chapter 6, we will examine persuasive strategies for changing audience attitudes and moving them to action.

## Specific Purposes

Once you have some basic notion of your speech's general purpose, you are ready to consider your specific purpose. It is not adequate to say that you want to persuade the audience regarding sound investment practices. Rather, be specific about the kind of response you are seeking; have a precise goal. With that goal in mind, choose evidence, draw conclusions, organize your arguments, and select a fitting delivery style.

*The specific purpose of your speech should be phrased in terms of the audience response you are seeking.* It is a good practice to write out a precise purpose statement specifying what you intend to accomplish. Some examples follow:

I want my audience to enjoy my account of my study-abroad semester in the Netherlands.

I want my audience to invest their savings in money market CDs.

I want my audience to recall and recognize the seven warning signs of cancer.

I want my audience to reexamine their views on child custody.

I want my audience to attend the next school board meeting and vote against closing any elementary schools.

I want my audience to understand the implications of recent court cases that affect disabled employees and their rights.

Writing a specific purpose statement encourages you to think concretely about what you are trying to achieve, with the desired audience response as your particular focus. With a clearly articulated purpose, you are better able to make sound judgments about how to develop your speech. Moreover, after you have delivered your speech, thinking about the purpose you set forth to achieve can help you judge your success.

In formulating your purpose statement, check it against these guidelines:

**1.** *What is the basic purpose of the speech?* To interest, inform, stimulate, convince, or move to action? How do you hope to be interesting? What kind of audience understanding do you hope to gain? For what kind of persuasion are you aiming?

**2.** *What is the specific audience response you are seeking?* As examples: "I want my audience to enjoy my discussion of the Japanese tea ceremony"; "I want my audience to understand the differences in eastern and western values that cause workers to view their jobs differently"; or "I want my audience to sign up for a weekend seminar on time management."

**3.** *Is your purpose realistic?* Can the purpose be achieved within the time limits? Is it a reasonable topic, given your knowledge of the audience's needs, interests, values, and demographic characteristics?

**4.** *Is your purpose clear?* If your purpose is vague, both you and your audience may experience a good deal of confusion. If you say, for example, "I want my audience to understand about the problems with women's competitive gymnastics," that is about the same as saying that you are going

FIGURE 4.1          Public speaking purposes

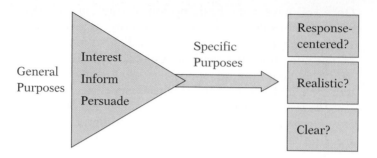

to talk about problems with women's competitive gymnastics. By contrast, the statement, "I want my audience to be convinced that the U.S. Gymnastics Association should revise its rules to enhance the safety of women's competitive gymnastics" is clear about the specific kind of audience response the speaker is seeking.

Figure 4.1 summarizes general speech purposes and criteria for assessing specific purposes

## The Speech's Thesis

Every speech should have a central idea to which every piece of information, every bit of supporting material, and every main idea is related. While the specific purpose focuses on the desired audience response, the thesis articulates the speech's underlying central idea, assertion, or argument.

Let us say, for instance, that a speaker lists as his specific purpose: *I want my audience to buy an IBM computer for their next personal computer.* With the specific purpose clearly stated, the speaker now knows what he is looking for and how he will judge his own effectiveness. He can then move to stating his thesis, which might be: *The IBM computer is the best personal computer on the market.* When the speaker is gathering information and organizing his ideas, he will want to ask himself if what he is saying *both* supports his thesis *and* advances his specific purpose.

Here are some additional examples of how the specific purpose and the thesis work in tandem:

*Specific Purpose 1:*    I want my audience to become familiar with diverse options for allocating their retirement funds.

*Thesis 1:*    Diverse options exist for allocating retirement funds, each possessing different risks and benefits.

*Specific Purpose 2:*    I want my audience to become convinced that our company needs a new recreational facility.

*Thesis 2:*    Having a new recreational facility offers advantages to employees and managers by enhancing productivity, reducing stress, and contributing to a healthy work environment.

*Specific Purpose 3:*    I want my audience to become more committed to unionization.

*Thesis 3:*    Unions have made our workplaces safer and our salaries higher, and have ensured our rights to participate, to debate, and to vote.

The specific purpose is a guide for the speaker which is rarely spoken to the audience. The thesis, however, is usually mentioned in the speech's introduction and may be reiterated during the conclusion.

In examining your thesis, ask yourself:

**1.** Is my thesis consistent with my specific purpose? Does it grow logically from it?
**2.** Does my thesis incorporate all of the main points, key ideas, and arguments I hope to address?
**3.** Is my thesis clearly stated, so that listeners will understand it?
**4.** Do I have a reasonable chance of getting my audience to be open to my thesis, possibly accepting it, given what I know of their attitudes, needs, and values?

Once you have selected a topic and articulated its specific purpose and thesis, you are ready to begin investigating the topic—discovering ideas, evidence, and information that will develop and substantiate your thesis and advance your purpose.

---

**KEY CONCEPTS 4.2**    **Choosing the Speech's Purpose**

• • *Choose the speech's overarching purpose:*

To interest
To inform
To persuade—stimulate, convince, actuate

• • *Test the interest value of information against the criteria of:*

Relevance
Usefulness
Novelty
Significance
Entertainment

• • *Examine information used according to its:*

Accuracy
Completeness

Unity
Meaningfulness

• • *Articulate the speech's specific purpose:*

To identify the audience response you are seeking
To test the specific purpose for its realism and clarity

• • *Develop the speech's thesis:*

To articulate the speech's underlying idea
To grow from or be consistent with the specific purpose
To incorporate the speech's main points
To have a reasonable chance of audience acceptance

---

# INVESTIGATING THE SPEECH TOPIC

## Taking a Personal Inventory

Before you head off to the library to start doing research or begin to surf the Net, it's wise to take stock of what you already know. Chances are that you already know quite a bit about your topic, since one of the key reasons you selected it was your interest in, experience with and/or knowledge of the subject. Return to Table 4.1, the self-inventory for public speakers that you used to guide your topic selection. Again using the self-inventory as a guide, make a list of courses you've taken, relevant work experiences you've had, books you've read, your special training or skill, and so forth that led you to your topic. One student, for example, selected the topic: "Disabled Students and the Challenges of Getting a College Education." As she began to consider her topic, she knew that she wanted to talk about her own experiences following a serious automobile accident after which she spent several months in a wheelchair. Because of some of the problems she had encountered, she started reading widely on the subject, she took a business law class that familiarized her with the laws affecting the disabled students and employees, and she even took a part-time job in the Office for Student Disabilities at her college. Her personal reflection and knowledge growing from these experiences made a substantial foundation upon which she could begin to build her speech.

Of course, not everyone will have such extensive preexisting knowledge pertinent to the topic, but nearly everyone will have some knowledge and initial ideas upon which to build. Taking the time to reflect on those impressions, experiences, and knowledge is the first step in investigating the topic.

## Conducting Research

After conducting a personal inventory, gathering information through research is the next step. Doing research will allow you to expand your information base, discover fresh perspectives and ideas, and find evidence to support your views. Every speaker can benefit from doing research—even a speaker with years of topic-relevant experience. Speakers with less direct experience will find much of their information in sources located through research.

### Field Research: Surveys and Interviews

One way of gathering information is to conduct *field research*, either by interviewing or by doing a survey. The major advantage of the *survey* is the breadth of response it provides. If you decide to conduct your own survey, you should recognize that, to be valid, the survey must be conducted on a sample representative of the population to which you want to generalize the responses. So, if you want to know what the members of your fraternity think of recently adopted antihazing legislation, you will want to make sure that you sample broadly, surveying pledges, officers, and established members who are freshmen through seniors.

Most of us are not expert pollsters or statisticians. Even so, the appropriate strategy to follow in conducting surveys is to select respondents at random and to gather relatively large samples. For an ideal survey, you would draw several samples independently from the same population to check the validity of your results. Then, if you obtained consistent results across all samples, you could reasonably assume that your data accurately reflected the general population of interest to you.

The construction of valid survey questions is a task that should be undertaken with particular care. This matter is also relevant for anyone who wants to collect information by means of interviews. In either case, one of the most common problems encountered by inexperienced researchers is the tendency to ask leading or loaded questions. These are questions that, intentionally or unintentionally, reveal your opinions or feelings. Often, they elicit a response that reinforces the questioner's prejudices rather than measuring the actual attitudes of the respondents. To be avoided, then, are such leading questions as: "Why do you think this company has adopted such an inequitable approach to dealing with male and female employees?" "Doesn't it seem to you that the new antihazing laws are rather harsh?" or "Why would anyone want to work for a government-funded institution these days, anyway?"

While the survey taps the views of a large number of individuals, through the *interview* it is possible to acquire greater depth of information. Whenever you want to know the reasons behind specific positions (rather than construct a profile of the views of the general population) or wish to explore the ideas of experts on a particular topic, you will probably find the interview a useful research tool.

Before seeking an interview with an expert, you need to be well prepared. In fact, it is probably wise to do some reading on your topic before approaching anyone with questions. Your questions should be designed to fill in gaps in your information and understanding of the topic. To prepare for an interview, here are some steps to follow:

- Do some preliminary research so that you can ask intelligent questions and make efficient use of the interview time.

- Prepare a list of questions to use in the interview. Make sure they are open, unbiased, and geared toward gathering insights you cannot gain through reading.

- Come prepared to take notes and to listen actively, probing and asking follow-up questions as needed.

- Begin the interview by greeting the interviewee by name and thanking him or her for taking the time to talk with you. Explain why you are interested in interviewing him or her.

- Find out how much time is available for the interview and stay within those limits.

- Give the interviewee a sense of the sources you have already consulted and ask if he or she could recommend other articles to read or others whom you should interview.

- At the close of the interview, thank the interviewee again and ask if you can get in touch, via e-mail or phone, if other questions occur to you.

If you are dealing with a controversial topic, it is usually wise to interview individuals representing a variety of points of view or perspectives. Suppose you were going to give a persuasive speech, advocating that your college move to a pass-fail grading system. You might want to interview (or survey) administrators, students, parents, professors, and prospective employers to gain a broad, diverse, and balanced sense of different points of view.

**Doing Research through the Library**   Reading carefully and thoroughly on your speech topic is a vital way of gaining the information you need. The library is the place to start, and librarians are among the most helpful resources the library offers. Professional librarians are schooled in the latest information and communication technologies and systems, and they use this knowledge and skill daily. Never hesitate to ask a librarian for help.

Even though libraries and the information web with which they are connected are vast, they are increasingly user-friendly. For example, the library's catalogue of holdings is likely available in electronic form, accessible from computer terminals located throughout the library. You can search the holdings file for a particular subject, topic, or title. Information searches can be conducted from the library or from home via modem. Promising sources can be printed out for further exploration.

The same server that contains the catalogue may also feature various reference materials, such as encyclopedias and databases, including indexes to periodicals. There are a number of standard sources for locating reference works, such as *Basic Reference Sources, Guide to Reference Books,* and *The Guide to the Use of Libraries.* Because the sources of specific bibliographies are seemingly endless, anyone doing research should become familiar with such indexes as the *Bibliographic Index: A Cumulative Bibliography of Bibliographies and of Bibliographical Catalogues, Calendars, Abstracts, Digests, Indexes. The Reader's Guide to Periodical Literature* is a familiar index whose citations are largely from popular magazines. Other guides to articles published in professional journals include *Applied Science and Technology Index, Psychological Abstracts, The Education Index,* the *International Index: Guide to Periodical Literature in the Social Sciences and Humanities,* and *Business Periodicals Index.*

If you wish to acquire information on a news event, you should begin by exploring *The New York Times Index.* On occasion, you will need materials that pertain to official government records. *The Catalogue of the Public Documents of Congress and of All Departments of the Government of the United States* is the major comprehensive index of government documents from 1893 to the present. A helpful source of information for recently published books is *Books in Print.* A less complete reference is the *Book Review Digest,* but its advantage is that it contains summaries of works cited so that you can glean some notion of the book's relevance to your particular needs. Finally, many research projects are never actually published, but much of the material they contain is indexed in *Dissertation Abstracts.*

If you are uncertain about where to go for information, and especially if no librarian is available to assist you, you might want to consult the *Guide to Information Access: A Complete Research Handbook and Directory,* published by the American Library Association.[3] This guide presents over 3,000 of the best standard and electronic sources in the most widely researched subject categories and tells you where you can find them. It also offers guidance on research methods.

**Using the Computer to Conduct Research**   Whenever you use the computer to explore your library's holdings, you are exploring the local information network. But, you may wish to go beyond local sources, and the computer opens the door to virtually limitless information. At the most basic

**Evaluating Internet Information: Some Guidelines**

- Your source should contain this information:
  Names and titles or positions of the authors
  Organizational affiliations of the authors
  Date the page was created or updated
  How to contact the authors
- Ask yourself these questions about the information you're thinking of using in your speech:

Is the source credible?
Is the source affiliated with a credible organization?
Does the source provide links to other relevant credible sites?
Is the information up to date?
Do the claims reflect balanced, well-reasoned arguments?

level, you can use *e-mail* to learn more about your topic. For instance, you can arrange an interview with an expert via e-mail, or you can request information from experts whom you cannot interview due to distance constraints.

You might also want to use the *Internet* to explore your topic. The Internet can connect you with people and information from around the world. All kinds of organizations, corporations, schools, agencies, universities, libraries, and interest and political groups have rushed to establish Internet presences. When you explore the Internet, you can find information and opinions on almost any topic imaginable—not only in textual form, but also in images, sound, and video.

Through the *World Wide Web*, you can explore speech topics and retrieve information about them. The Web is a popular network resource because Web browsing software features a graphical interface and operates like the MacIntosh or Windows operating systems. To locate information for your speech topic, you can proceed in various ways: by conducting a keyword search, by exploring various links between pages and sites, or by going directly to a page for which you know the address.

Let's say, for example, that you plan to give an informative speech about Procter & Gamble's (P&G's) much advertised fat substitute, Olestra. Let's further assume that you have no leads on where to go for information. You'll begin with a search, choosing from among several popular Web databases, such as Infoseek, Excite, Lycos, Yahoo, and Magellan. These databases can connect you to on-line newspapers and magazines, agencies, and organizations. To begin your search, you might enter "Olestra" or "fat substitutes." The search engine will scan an index of sites that have titles or abundant information that matches the keywords you have supplied. In a matter of seconds, you will receive a listing of Web pages. You can scroll through it and click on any that appears promising. Once you've explored a given entry, you can return to the list and choose another entry to explore. As you investigate new sources, you will occasionally encounter links that will give you the option of collecting with other related sources that may prove relevant.

On occasion, you may want to explore the Web site of a particular organization. If you wanted to see what Procter & Gamble had done to promote its Wow chips containing Olestra, you might go directly to the P&G Web site. Or, if you wanted to do research on the causes of colon cancer, you could go directly to the American Cancer Society's Web site (www.cancer.org). The last three letters designate the kind of Internet membership, such as "edu" for educational institutions, "org" for nonprofit organizations, and "com" for commercial companies. Most organizations try to keep their sites labeled in predictable and easy-to-guess ways. Like other information sources, Internet sources should be checked for their quality. See the guidelines for evaluating Internet information listed in the Highlighting Technology box.

## SUPPORTING THE SPEECH WITH EVIDENCE

The information you discover through your research will be used to support your ideas. Regardless of your speech's specific purpose, you will articulate several ideas, contentions, and propositions that will need to be supported with evidence. *Evidence is the body of fact and opinion pertaining to a subject.*

In most of your speeches, you will use varied kinds of evidence. Some kinds of speeches, such as technical reports, rely heavily on statistical evidence, often presented with the assistance of visual aids. But even technical presentations can be enhanced by the use of examples, comparisons, and the opinions of experts. In general, varied evidence is an asset. Figure 4.2 illustrates the different types of evidence that may be used to support your main ideas, or *contentions*.

**Facts as Evidence**

Much of the evidence you collect will be factual; that is, it will involve relatively objective descriptions without interpretation or judgment. It is important to recognize that *facts* are not absolute truths. We make assertions about what we view as reality. If our view of reality is accurate and verifiable, then

| FIGURE 4.2 | The different types of evidence that may be used to support contentions |

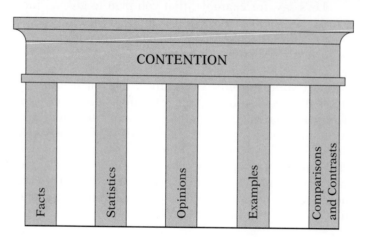

it is factual. In collecting factual information, it is important to seek reliable sources and to look through different sources to make sure you are finding consistent factual information. You ought to be able to look in more than one place and find a consistent account of how many people voted for Bill Clinton in the 1996 presidential election, what the unemployment rate was for the first six months of 1999, and what major factors accounted for the decline in the stock market in 1998. Whenever you discover inconsistencies, carefully examine your sources for bias. You may conclude that there are different approaches to explaining a particular phenomenon. In the latter case, avoid representing such information as factual, relabeling it instead as perspectives, approaches, or theories.

Statistics as Evidence

Most public speakers use statistics as one form of factual evidence. In the business and professional world, statistical support is usually anticipated by listeners. *Statistics* provide a numerical method of handling large numbers of instances. When statistics are used appropriately, they provide the most precise information about factual matters available to any public speaker.

Notice how Sheila Wellington, president of Catalyst, uses statistics effectively to portray "the abundant talent" of women in the U.S. workforce:

> Many of you know that our nation's workforce is now over 46% women. Many of you know that women now earn more than half of the BA degrees in this country. Virtually half of new business, law, and doctoral degrees

*In organizational settings, most speakers use statistics as a way of supporting their ideas and making their arguments more compelling. Often, they use presentational aids to clarify and reinforce their statistical evidence.*

decorate the office walls of women. More and more engineering degrees are going to women: in 1994, women earned 17% of BS degrees, 16% of Masters, and 11% of doctorates in engineering. This is a bounty of brains to harvest.

Yet did you know that women fill only 2.4 percent of the top corporate jobs in America—those jobs in Fortune 500 companies with the titles of chairman, vice chairman, CEO, president, COO, and executive vice president? What to do about it is the pressing matter I will address today.[4]

By using these descriptive statistics, Wellington is able to set the stage for the problem she wants to address: the underrepresentation of women in key corporate leadership positions.

*Statistics fall into two general categories: descriptive (such as those used by Wellington) and inferential.* A descriptive statistic states a population fact; for example, 30 percent of all Americans smoke cigarettes. Frequently, however, it is inconvenient or impossible to obtain descriptive data. In this instance, you can turn to inferential statistics. The collection of inferential statistics involves gathering a sample and, on the basis of that sample, reaching a conclusion about the population of interest. When Louis Harris samples a few thousand Americans and predicts the election day behavior of all the American people, he is using inferential statistics. For past elections, he and other professional pollsters have done this with impressive accuracy.

It is important to remember that *each inferential statistic has a confidence interval or margin of error.* Since inferential statistics are always probabilistic in nature, you can never be certain that you have accurately described the population in question. For example, if you were to report on the basis of a survey of 1,000 assembly-line workers that 50 percent of all such workers are dissatisfied with their health insurance plans, it would be important to recognize that this particular percentage is only one of a number of different figures that might represent the workers in question.

Another important statistical issue is sample size and representativeness. In general, *as the size of the sample approaches the size of the population, the more confidence you can have in the accuracy of the statistic.* Thus, if you want to know how workers in an organization of 3,000 employees are responding to a new incentive plan, you are more likely to reach valid conclusions if you sample the views of 300 than if you sample only 30. Moreover, *your sample should be diverse,* tapping the views of all kinds of workers, male and female, experienced and inexperienced, supervisors and subordinates. If you examine the views of only managerial personnel, or only those in a couple of departments, you may well obtain a distorted view of employees' attitudes.

When using statistics, a few practical concerns should be kept in mind. Speeches should never be padded with statistics. *Statistics should be used only when they are needed* and when they represent the most precise way of demonstrating a point. They should never be used simply because they sound impressive. Moreover, every attempt should be made to *make the statistics as clear and personally meaningful to your listeners as possible.* To say that a bond issue will cost the city $89 million sounds overwhelming, but the same figure presented as approximately $5 per taxpayer clearly makes the proposal appear manageable. Finally, *seek statistics that are as recent as possible.* Nothing is more useless than an outdated statistic. Figure 4.3 summarizes tests for statistical evidence.

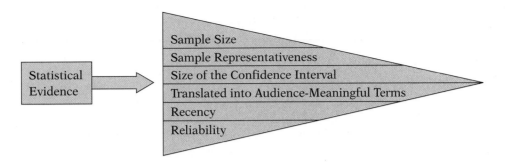

FIGURE 4.3 Tests for statistical evidence

Statistical Evidence →

Sample Size
Sample Representativeness
Size of the Confidence Interval
Translated into Audience-Meaningful Terms
Recency
Reliability

## Opinions as Evidence

While evidence of fact is rooted in the notion of objectivity and suspended judgment, *evidence of opinion is the application of interpretation and judgment to the known facts.* There are three different types of opinion evidence you might use: personal testimony, lay testimony, and expert testimony.

It is probably safe to say that all speakers support their presentations with personal views from time to time. Your success in using *personal testimony* for support will largely depend on your credibility with the audience in question. If you are perceived as intelligent, accomplished in your area of endeavor, sincere and trustworthy in your motives, and fair-minded, you might rely extensively on personal testimony. This is especially true if you are speaking about a problem with which you have had years of experience.

In his commencement address to the graduating seniors of Cal Tech, Dr. David Ho, who has devoted his life to the study of AIDS, shares some of his personal experiences:

> I feel extremely privileged to work on AIDS. As a young physician in Los Angeles in 1981, I witnessed the beginning of the visible part of the AIDS epidemic. Over the course of a year, young men, one after another, were presented to the hospital with a multitude of opportunistic infections, leading to death within days to weeks. It was evident that their immune system was damaged. But, by what? [He then describes the spread of the HIV virus and his work with colleagues, structural biologists, and medicinal chemists, as they tested various chemicals to fight the virus for more than a decade.]
>
> Three years later [in 1994], we again had the privilege of being the first to administer one of these chemicals to infected patients. Unmatched were the joy and amazement as we watched the level of HIV fall, ever so dramatically. . . . Little did we know that we were sitting on top of a fundamental discovery in AIDS research.[5]

Regardless of high credibility, seldom will any public speaker rely on his or her own views without additional reference to other support, such as statistics or examples.

Another kind of opinion evidence is *lay testimony.* Suppose you wanted to argue that most employees in your department were dissatisfied with the food being served in the company cafeteria. To support this argument you might cite the results of a poll you have taken that indicate 85 percent of all employees in your department found the food to be "extremely poor." In this case, lay opinion is good evidence because the matter being judged does not require the testimony of an expert; nor would your personal views suffice. Thus, *lay testimony is useful when you want to describe the habits, attitudes, and behaviors of ordinary people.* Normally, you would collect information about lay opinion by conducting a survey or by interviewing.

A third kind of opinion evidence is *expert testimony*. Most of us are not such renowned experts in our own fields that we could not profit from quoting others of greater renown who happen to support our views. Whenever you decide to use expert testimony to support your views, you need to observe a few guidelines. First, you must be concerned with the issue of actual expertise. That is, *the person must be a recognized authority in the area in which he or she is being quoted.* You should also *be concerned with the expert's objectivity or fair-mindedness.* It is entirely possible for an expert to be competent in a given area and yet be a poor source of testimony because of some known bias in his or her views. It is far better, for example, to know the views of laypersons concerning the quality of a particular brand of television set than to quote the opinion of the president of the company that manufactures them. While the president may well be an expert in electronics and quite knowledgeable about television sets in general, his views in this instance are probably influenced by self-interest. Thus, his credibility as a source is questionable.

Once you have collected some highly credible expert testimony to support your presentation, the task that still remains is to *identify the expert for the audience.* It is critical that the quoted expert be known and acceptable to the listeners; if he or she is not, then it is up to you to provide the necessary information. Assume that you are addressing a topic related to medicine; an appropriate identifying phrase might be stated as follows: "Dr. William Johnson, chief of neurosurgery at Johns Hopkins University Medical Center, has pointed out that . . . ." This kind of identification is specific, precise, concise, and adequately informative.

## Examples as Evidence

One of the most difficult problems public speakers face is trying to make general principles or abstract notions interesting and meaningful to the audience. One of the best ways of doing this is through examples. *Examples provide concrete frames of reference and by doing so interject life and meaning into the ideas you are communicating.*

Examples can be either actual or hypothetical. They can be elaborate or brief. *Actual examples* point to real events or people. In the example that follows, Cesar Chavez, late activist and founder of the United Farm Workers of America, used actual examples to dramatize the danger of pesticides:

> A few months ago, the parents of a brave little girl in the agricultural community of Earlimart came to the United Farm Workers to ask for help. Their four year old daughter, Natalie Ramirez, has lost one kidney to cancer and is threatened with the loss of another. The Ramirez family knew about our protests in nearby McFarland and thought there might be a similar problem in their home town. Our union members went door to door in Earlimart and found that the Ramirez family's worst fears were true. There are at least *four* other children suffering from cancer and similar diseases which the experts believe were caused by pesticides in the little town of

Earlimart, a rate *1200 percent* above normal. In Earlimart, little Jimmy
Caudillo died recently from leukemia at the age of three.

The grape vineyards of California have become America's Killing Fields.[6]

The other kind of example you might want to use is hypothetical. *Hypo-thetical examples* are ones that might reasonably or plausibly take place, but in using them you are not referring to an actual event or person. Although hypothetical examples are concocted, they should not be unrealistic or dis-torted. In a classroom speech, a student used hypothetical examples to help her audience understand the experience of being disabled:

Suppose you used a wheelchair, and you were shopping for groceries one day. Your chair is partially blocking one of the aisles and a shopper comes up behind you and pushes you out of the way, much as she would an abandoned grocery cart. Later that day, another woman asks you what happened to you. You tell her that you were in a very serious automobile accident and she proceeds to lecture you on why you should have worn your seat belt.

Are you having a hard time imagining that people could be so rude and unkind? If you are, you might want to give some thought to how people usually treat the disabled: like they are little children, or are stupid, or simply don't exist. I know all about these reactions from first-hand experience. Five years ago, I was in a serious automobile accident. I broke over 50 bones and spent months in rehabilitation, in casts, on crutches, and in a wheelchair. All too often, people's reactions to my disability stunned, disappointed, and angered me.[7]

You will notice how this student firmly establishes the plausibility of her hypo-thetical examples. She also combines such examples with personal testimony. Speakers often use multiple kinds of evidence to reinforce their arguments.

Because examples are so easy to identify with, they can be a powerful way of supporting your ideas. Even so, they must be used with care. Most of the time when we use examples we are arguing that the example represents the general principle we are discussing. Thus, *one test of a good example is its typicality.* If you are talking about the reading habits of children, you might, during your research, run across an example of a nine-year-old who regularly reads *Penthouse*, "trashy" comic books, and other questionable materials. Of course, you would not use this example to illustrate the point that children's reading habits were impoverished these days, unless you had reasons to be-lieve that this child was typical.

## Comparisons and Contrasts as Evidence

One of the primary ways we learn is through *comparison*. We compare the known with the unknown, the more familiar with the less familiar. Whenever we encounter a new problem, we compare it with similar problems we have experienced in the past. New jobs, friends, and concepts are compared with old ones. Thus, a good way to help an audience understand what you are talking about is to compare your idea with something with which they are quite familiar or experienced. You might compare the job of managing a company with the job of managing a family. You might discuss the architec-tural design you had in mind for a new municipal complex by comparing it to one in a neighboring town with which you know the audience is familiar. Or you might compare a new book with one you know they have read. By using these comparisons, you hope to enlighten, to make the unknown more familiar, perhaps to make your audience less afraid of something you are advocating, more comfortable, and more at ease.

In his speech to the Conference Board in New York, A. Thomas Young, president and CEO of the Martin Marietta Corporation, used the following compelling comparison in discussing ethics and breaking the law:

> Whether in Washington, New York or Peoria, most people seldom set out with the deliberate intent of breaking the law. They are drawn into it, almost as a boa constrictor defeats its prey.
>
> Most of us probably think a boa crushes its target in the powerful folds of its body. Actually, this snake places two or three coils of its body around its prey. Each time the victim exhales its breath, the boa simply takes up the slack. After three or four breaths, there is no more slack. The prey quickly suffocates.
>
> This deadly phenomenon of a victim becoming the unwitting accomplice of its own destruction is not confined to the world of reptiles. It exists in the human behavior that characterizes all walks of life anywhere on the globe. The boa we have to face—and sometimes fail to face—is following our ethical values: each lapse is another coil of the snake.[8]

Young's comparison emphasizes his argument that if we go too far with ethical breaches, we may find ourselves unable to recover.

On occasion, you may want to inform an audience about a concept or principle by showing them its opposite. By *using contrast rather than comparison, you are highlighting differences.* This can be a compelling form of evidence when your goal is to stress the value of your advocated approach or plan in comparison to the approaches of others.

In 1984, then-governor of New York Mario Cuomo delivered the keynote address to the National Democratic Convention. Throughout his speech, Cuomo sought to contrast the Democratic Party with the Republican Party. He used the metaphor of a wagon train to portray this contrast:

> It's an old story. It's as old as our history. The difference between Democrats and Republicans has always been measured in courage and confidence. . . . The Republicans believe that the wagon train will not make it to the frontier unless some of the old, some of the young, some of the weak are left behind by the side of the trail. The strong, the strong they tell us will inherit the land!
>
> We Democrats believe in something else. We Democrats believe that we can make it all the way with the whole family intact. And we have more than once. Ever since Franklin Roosevelt lifted himself from his wheelchair to lift this nation from its knees. Wagon train after wagon train, to new frontiers of education, housing, peace; the whole family aboard![9]

Cuomo goes on to point out that, as voters approach the election, they must focus on the contrast between the two parties.

Regardless of the kind of supporting materials you select as evidence, you must be concerned about quality. *In using comparisons and contrasts as evidence, remember that they are only useful or enlightening when they are justified*—that is, when the events, people, or phenomena you are comparing are similar enough to warrant the comparison.

## CONSTRUCTING A SOUND ARGUMENT

When you have investigated your topic and identified the evidence you want to use in supporting your ideas, you will want to concern yourself with *how* you will develop your arguments. When you make an argument, you advance a claim supported by evidence; and you hope that the evidence will be judged by your listeners as relevant, sufficient, and compelling.

The Persuasive Argument

A *persuasive argument* consists of a claim supported by evidence grounded in a premise. A good persuasive argument must be audience-centered—judged by both speaker and listeners to be sound and appealing. A persuasive argument does not prove anything absolutely, but it does make a case that seems to ring true, that seems reasonable and sensible.

Premises

In considering an argument you are about to advance, you must be aware of the *premise*, or accepted generalization, upon which your argument is built. *The first test of a premise is whether it is accepted as true by the audience.* What can you assume about the premises your audience would be likely to accept? Perhaps you can assume that your audience believes in fairness and justice for all, individual integrity, and respect for the individual. Yet, how do those generally accepted premises affect your speech? Perhaps you want to convince your audience that athletes are being given preferential treatment by the university. In making this argument, you would hope that your classmates accept the premise that all students should be held to the same academic standards (a fairness premise). A different audience, however, such as the Athletic Boosters, might reject that premise in favor of the premise that the university needs to support all policies that maximize its teams' chances of winning. Clearly, premises are audience-specific. Identifying premises that are widely accepted by the audience is a crucial step in making ideas and arguments understandable and believable.

Premises often go unarticulated. Yet, there exists a premise beneath every argument, which may or may not be acknowledged or understood. When a speaker argues that the company will save money by pursuing a particular course of action, he is assuming that the audience accepts the premise that saving money is desirable. But suppose the speaker is arguing that the company can no longer afford to operate its day care center. In this case, the premise that frugality is a good thing would have to be weighed against other possible premises, such as the value of supporting employees in diverse ways. Depending upon which premises are most salient, the speaker may or may not succeed.

Sometimes speakers will need to make the audience aware of a premise from which they may be operating. Suppose a speaker is trying to convince a student audience to vote in favor of a newly proposed campus safety fee, to be assessed from each student annually. In this case, the speaker will understand that students feel they are poor, that there are already too many exorbitant fees, and that the campus is reasonably safe. Being aware of these premises, the speaker might argue that this fee is reasonable (the lowest of any other currently assessed), that it will lead to very little sacrifice (the equivalent of two cokes each week), and that the campus has become less safe over the past two years (with statistics to demonstrate the decline).

**Claims and Evidence**   Once the premises have been examined and deemed valid, we can turn our attention to the claims being made. *Claims* are assertions put forward by a speaker as true and are supported by evidence that attests to their accuracy. In short, the strength of the claim is judged by the strength of the supporting material. There are three basic standards we can apply to help us assess the evidence for a claim.

- *The quality of the evidence should justify the audience's acceptance.* Consider the tests for evidence discussed above. Are the examples compelling, yet realistic? Are the statistics representative? Is the testimony from a respected authority?

- *The evidence presented should be relevant to the claim.*   Evidence can be accurate and truthful and still not be related to the claim being advanced.

- *The evidence must be sufficient to support the claim.*   Many tests of evidence focus on quality, but there is also the matter of quantity. Is there enough evidence to persuade us? Has the argument been explored in sufficient detail? Are additional examples or statistics needed?

Inductive and Deductive Reasoning

Whenever you stand before an audience and propose a particular solution as the best response to a problem, your proposal is based on some conclusion you have reached on the basis of supporting materials you have discovered. The cognitive process by which you do this is *reasoning*, the process of drawing conclusions from evidence.

Sound reasoning is not automatic. Not everyone examining the same evidence would draw the same conclusions from it. Sometimes we draw different conclusions from evidence because we are operating from different premises. Other times we are looking at different evidence, different specific examples that may lead to different perceptions. These two ways in which we reason—from particular instances to generalizable conclusions or from a general premise to specific cases—represent inductive and deductive reasoning.

### Inductive Reasoning

When we use *inductive reasoning*, we examine a set of specific instances or make a series of observations and proceed to draw from them a general conclusion. An example follows:

*Observation 1:*  Jim is good at math and is majoring in business.

*Observation 2:*  Suzanne is good at math and is majoring in business.

*Observation 3:*  Jennifer is good at math and is majoring in business.

*Conclusion:*  All business majors are good at math.

As you can see, we reason inductively every day, often without thinking about it. We observe a number of women, young children, doctors, accountants, and college professors, and we draw general conclusions about others who fall into these categories but whom we have not observed. This process of generalizing through inductive reasoning is one way we learn, although we must guard against stereotyping (where we completely disregard individuality, allowing our generalizations to grow into rigid categories).

Speakers who draw conclusions and advance arguments based on inductive reasoning are relying on probabilities. How sound our conclusions are will depend on how good our observations have been, whether they have been sufficient, and whether they represent a good sample of the general population. Suppose a speaker argues that when organizations offer diversity training, the result is a more respectful, inclusive organizational climate. Probably she is right. But, it could be that the organizations she happened to study already had a healthy climate prior to diversity training. With inductive reasoning, we can never be absolutely certain. The best the speaker can do is convince the audience, through the weight of evidence, that the outcome is likely.

### Deductive Reasoning

When we begin with a generally accepted premise and apply that premise to a specific situation, instance, or person, we are reasoning deductively. The classic example of *deductive reasoning* is the *syllogism*, which might look like this:

A. People with college educations get good jobs.
B. Peter has a college education.
C. Therefore, Peter will get a good job.

Is this a good argument? Much depends upon our view of the validity of the general premise. If we can think of a number of examples of people with college degrees who have failed to gain good jobs, we may begin to counterargue. We may say, "Well, it depends on whether it's a good college." Or we might point out, "But a lot depends on what students major in." And so the premise is modified to read, "People who graduate from reputable colleges and major in business, computer science, engineering, or one of the health professions get good jobs."

The syllogism may seem a bit formal, and often, when we argue deductively, we rely on the listeners to fill in unspoken premises. This "rhetorical syllogism"—a syllogism adapted to persuasive argument—is called an *enthymeme*. We construct many arguments in our daily lives using enthymemes. For instance, "She's lazy. She never works more than is absolutely required." Here, the missing premise is "Those who are not lazy often work more than the bare minimum."

Once again, whether this argument is persuasive to the audience will depend on whether they accept the missing premise. Some listeners might ask, "Why should anyone have to work more than the minimum?" That is, there may be some disagreement about the meaning of laziness in relation to the quantity of work. In general, however, if the premises are perceived as true by the audience, then the speaker can move forward with the deductive argument.

It's important to remember that the conclusions that grow from arguments are not absolute. The audience will judge whether the case that has been made is a good one. However, when flaws in reasoning occur, arguments become unsound.

## Fallacies in Reasoning

Any claim is only as good as the evidence that supports it. Many things can go wrong during the reasoning process, leading one to draw a faulty conclusion. Following are some *fallacies* in reasoning that ought to be avoided.

- The *glittering generality* jumps to a hasty conclusion on the basis of inadequate and unrepresentative observations. This is perhaps the most common inductive fallacy. We observe a limited number of Democrats, Jews, teenagers, or salespeople and draw sweeping generalizations about others who fall into the same category.

- A *faulty analogy* compares two things, persons, events, or phenomena that are not similar enough to warrant the comparison. A college administrator once stated, "The notion of restoring student direction and control of intercollegiate athletics is silly. You might just as well talk about giving horse racing back to the horses." The inference that students and horses are equally inept at directing their own "athletic" activities is absurd. There might be a number of reasons why students should not be given this sort of control. On the basis of this analogy, however, it is impossible to discern what those reasons are.

- *Faulty causal reasoning* confuses a chronological relationship with a causal relationship. The simple fact that one event follows another in time does not necessarily mean that the first caused the second. There are often other less obvious factors that contributed to the second event. An undergraduate history student once made a study of European war for a final term paper. He noticed that during the years immediately preceding the outbreak of recent wars, there occurred an increase of armaments among the aggressive nations. On the basis of this observation, he concluded that "Increased armaments are one of the major causes of European wars." It is probably far more likely that increased armaments were the *reaction* to other causative factors, such as political upheaval or international tensions. Thus, increased armaments could reasonably be viewed as an effect rather than a cause.

- *Circular reasoning* uses arguments that go in circles, with no proof for the assertions advanced. Not long ago, one of our students informed us that a mutual acquaintance had abandoned high school teaching to go into professional theater. The remainder of our conversation went something like this: Friend: "She's really a gifted actress, you know." Us: "Oh, you've seen her act?" Friend: "No, but she is currently acting on Broadway!" The circularity in this reasoning results from accepting a questionable assumption: namely, that anyone who acts on Broadway is gifted in acting. If one were to accept this peculiar premise, then the conclusion could be viewed as logical. The difficulty here is not rooted in the deductive thought process but in an erroneous assumption affecting that process.

- *Guilt by association* judges the quality of an idea or the worth of a person or a program solely on the basis of other ideas, persons, or programs with which it is associated. An idea may be demeaned or rejected simply because it is attributed to a particular source. Research on source credibility has demonstrated that speeches, poems, or pieces of art are consistently judged to be of high quality when attributed to persons held in high esteem and of poor quality when attributed to low-credibility individuals.[10] Real-life examples of the guilt-by-association fallacy abound. During the 1960 presidential campaign, for example, John F. Kennedy attempted to associate Richard M. Nixon with Republican candidates of the previous half-century or more by saying: "I stand tonight where Woodrow Wilson stood, and Franklin Roosevelt stood, and Harry Truman stood. Dick Nixon stands where McKinley stood and Taft—listen to those candidates—Harding, Coolidge, Landon, Dewey . . . Where do they get those candidates?" Kennedy made no attempt to establish the common ideas, programs, and principles of Nixon and the other candidates. He simply associated their names with his. The assumption operating here is that there are no substantial differences among any of a party's presidential candidates, even over a considerable historical span. Certainly this premise is open to argument.

- The *bandwagon effect* is the endorsement of ideas primarily because many other people are supporting them. When you are asked to make some judgment about a matter of physical reality, such as determining whether or not a stove is hot, it is relatively easy to decide without knowing the views of others. For matters involving social reality, however, it is often comforting to know that others support our views. Children learn how to employ this fallacy early in life when they beg their parents to be allowed to play outside after dark, go swimming for the afternoon, or wear blue jeans to church, on the grounds that all their friends are allowed to do it. The assumption is that those children's parents simply couldn't all be wrong! Bandwagon appeals continue to haunt us as we are asked to drink, smoke, eat, and enjoy because others are doing it. Knowing that other people support an idea or a product is one piece of information we might want to be aware of, but is not terribly persuasive by itself.

- The *red herring argument* attempts to throw the audience off track when a speaker does not want the quality of the argument examined. The red herring raises emotional, often irrelevant, issues aimed at gaining listeners' hasty support. A speaker once argued in favor of book censorship in the schools by asserting, "The real issue here is whether we are going to allow irresponsible and immoral administrators to expose our children to trash and filth!" Yet, perhaps those administrators who opposed censorship were deeply committed to the education of young people, but were equally committed to freedom of speech and freedom of the press. When viewed this way, the issue is not about irresponsibility or immorality, but about weighing the potentially adverse affects of such books against fundamental rights of American citizens.

The fallacies discussed above are not the only problems with reasoning you may encounter, but they are some of the more common ones.

---

**KEY CONCEPTS 4.4**     **The Sound Argument: Guiding Principles**

- • *A good persuasive argument must be audience-centered.*

  *Premises:*
  Arguments are based on premises.
  The audience must accept the premises as true.
  Sometimes premises go unarticulated.
  *Claims and evidence:*
  Claims are assertions supported by evidence.
  The evidence must be judged by its:
  - Quality
  - Relevance to the claim
  - Sufficiency

- • *Reasoning: the process of drawing conclusions from evidence.*

  *Inductive reasoning* moves from specific instances to a general conclusion.
  *Deductive reasoning* applies a generally accepted premise to a specific situation.

- • *Fallacies in reasoning are to be avoided, including:*

  *Glittering generality* (jumping to a hasty conclusion)
  *Faulty analogy* (an unjustified comparison)
  *Faulty causal reasoning* (confusing a chronological with a causal relationship)
  *Circular reasoning* (repeating assertions without offering proof)
  *Guilt by association* (judging the quality of an idea, plan, etc. by the quality of its source)
  *Bandwagon effect* (endorsing ideas because others have endorsed them)
  *Red herring argument* (raising emotional, irrelevant issues to urge the audience to make a hasty decision)

# SUMMARY

Early in their careers, many people believe that they will never have to make a speech. They do not initially see why a doctor or an accountant or a police officer would need to acquire public speaking skills. After several years on the job, they have a different view. They have found themselves being asked to present their ideas or areas of expertise to others, often in a public situation. They have learned that it is not enough to be a competent professional. One must also be able to communicate effectively with others—to present ideas for change persuasively, to brief new employees, and to convince others to act.

In this chapter, we have introduced you to some of the fundamentals of public speaking: selecting an appropriate topic, choosing a purpose, framing a specific purpose in terms of the audience response you are seeking, articulating your speech's thesis, doing research, and discovering and testing evidence to support your ideas. We have also discussed the nature of argument and effective ways of reasoning, so that you avoid reasoning fallacies and make sound and persuasive arguments.

Many speakers fail—not because they are stupid, not because they lack presentational skills or experience on the job, but because they have not taken the time to connect their ideas with the needs and interests of the audience, or have not spoken with a clear sense of purpose so that the audience understands what they are expected to do, believe, or think. If audience members leave a speech scratching their heads and asking, "What does she want me to do about it?" the speaker has not been clear about her purpose, and that creates problems for everyone.

Speakers who know what they are talking about, who have gathered sound and sufficient evidence, and who have reached logical conclusions in advancing their arguments are well on the road to effective public communication.

# QUESTIONS FOR DISCUSSION

1. To what extent should a public speaker consider his or her responsibilities as an organizational representative when speaking to an audience beyond the organization's boundary?

2. We mentioned four perspectives to be considered in selecting a topic for a public speech: personal, audience, situational, and organizational. Which of these (or which combinations of these) do you feel is generally most important? Why? What kinds of contextual factors might influence your decision?

3. What are some of the basic purposes or goals of public speaking? Provide at least one example of a topic that would work well with each basic purpose you name. Then phrase a specific purpose and a thesis statement for each topic.

4. Suppose you were making a speech on a recent tuition hike on your campus. In investigating this topic, where would you likely go to get information? How would your approach to doing research differ if you were going to talk about censorship on the Internet? Explain.

5. How will you assess the quality of information you find on the Internet?

6. What are some of the hazards of using statistics as evidence? How can these hazards be avoided?

7. Compare and contrast personal, expert, and lay testimony. What are some important considerations in using each kind of testimony as evidence?

8. How important are examples in developing persuasive arguments? Which kind of examples do you feel are generally most

effective? Why? What are some ways of testing examples as evidence?

9. Is there anything wrong with any of the following:
   a. Quoting the president of General Motors regarding the superiority of the Oldsmobile?
   b. Using only statistical evidence to support a point of view?
   c. Relying exclusively on your own opinion to support a proposal?
   d. Comparing a managerial approach at a small private business with that at IBM?

10. What is meant by a "persuasive argument"?

11. How will you determine whether your premises are good ones?

12. What is the relationship between claims and evidence?

13. Contrast inductive with deductive reasoning, defining and giving an example of each.

14. What are some of the main fallacies in reasoning that should be avoided?

## EXERCISES

1. Find a recent (1999) issue of *Vital Speeches of the Day*. Select a speech that you find interesting and compelling. Read it through two or three times. Then, in a short essay, respond to these questions:
   a. What is the speaker's specific purpose and thesis? Given his or her audience, do they seem clear, reasonable, and achievable?
   b. What types of evidence does the speaker use? Which are most and least effective? Explain the basis of your assessment.
   c. To what extent do the conclusions reached by the speaker seem sound and reasonable? Is there any evidence of reasoning fallacies?

2. Choose a topic you might want to use for a classroom speech. Begin to explore the topic by doing some research. Read at least three articles on the subject. Based on your reading, respond to the following in a short essay:
   a. What is your tentatively selected topic?
   b. What are three pieces of evidence you found that you think you might like to use with this topic? Why did you choose these pieces of evidence?
   c. Before you could consider moving forward with this topic, what other kinds of sources would you need to consult? What kinds of evidence do you think you still need?

# CASE application 4.1

You have just been chosen to represent your college or university as a public speaker. Your audience is to be the powerful finance committee of the state legislature. You have been told to speak on any topic related to your interests and/or to higher education (so, the options are many). You are one of five students who are there to give the legislators some idea of what is on the minds of young people who attend your college. You have been asked to speak for about 8–10 minutes.

## Questions

1. What topic would you choose? Why?

2. To what extent would you consider yourself a representative of the university and to what extent are you speaking just for yourself? How would your view of your role affect your communication behavior?
3. What are some of the values, demographic characteristics, and other salient factors of this audience (assuming that their profile is similar to that of your own state's legislature)?
4. Given the audience, topic, and situation, what would be your specific purpose?
5. What would be your thesis?

# CASE application 4.2

*Candor or Punt?*

Steve Johnson is a senior scientist in the research laboratory of a prominent pharmaceutical company. For several months, the members of the executive board (of which Steve is a part) have argued fiercely about whether the firm is ready to move forward and request Food and Drug Administration (FDA) approval of a new drug to treat Alzheimer's disease. Steve has conducted a number of studies, with mixed results. In most studies, patients improved significantly (becoming more alert and showing signs of improved memory), but Steve's research also spotted some potential problems or possible side effects. Two patients developed colon cancer, and three others nearly died of high blood pressure after taking the drug for a few weeks. While the numbers were not large (since over 200 patients were tested), Steve felt that the health problems were sufficiently life-threatening to justify further investigation before going to the FDA.

After vigorous debate, the executive committee voted. Steve's views were considered with care but ultimately rejected—with a narrow majority voting to move forward with FDA approval. Almost immediately, news of the decision reached the press, precipitating considerable public interest. As an outgrowth of this interest, Steve has been asked to speak to a local service club (of which he is a lifelong member) regarding the firm's decision to take the drug to the FDA.

## Questions

1. Should Steve agree to speak on this topic? Why or why not?
2. If he does speak how should he approach the speech in terms of his personal views versus the position of the organization? What strategy might he use?
3. What should be his specific purpose and thesis?
4. How might his dual allegiance to both his audience and his firm affect his presentation?

# Organizing and Delivering the Public Speech

Many speakers carefully select and focus their topics, judiciously choose a specific purpose, seek out good supporting materials, and still never really experience success in their speaking endeavors. Part of their failure may be attributed to bad luck, but more commonly, a good measure of it is related to some significant problem with the way they have organized their ideas or delivered their speeches.

## PREVIEW

In this chapter, we will examine elements of effective public speaking we have not yet considered. First, we will look at speech organization, considering diverse patterns from which speakers may choose. We will also examine the steps that should be taken in introducing and concluding a speech, as well as how transitions can be used to help listeners follow the main ideas and understand their progression. Finally, we will turn our attention to the presentation of the speech, including the use of effective delivery (usually extemporaneous), the appropriate use of language (following the principles of good oral style), and the creation and use of effective presentational aids.

## ORGANIZING THE SPEECH

Rhetorical theorists have long observed that speeches must be well structured if they are to be effective. Among the earliest to comment on the importance of organization was the Greek philosopher Plato, who wrote, "Every discourse ought to be a living creature, having a body of its own and a head and feet; there should be a middle, beginning, and end, adapted to one another and to the whole."[1] In keeping with Plato's metaphor, we will next examine the three basic parts of speeches: the introduction, the body, and the conclusion.

### The Introduction

If you have ever had the experience of rising to confront a room filled with chattering high school students, excited, noisy convention folks, or even a group of contented and disinterested Rotarians following a luncheon, you are well aware of the first problem encountered by every public speaker: *gaining the attention and interest of the audience.* Every speech introduction should do this, although the manner in which it is done will vary greatly. Sometimes with serious topics about which there is great common interest, you may assume that the topic itself has captured the audience's attention. As a result, the best approach is to move directly into its discussion. This was the approach President Jimmy Carter used in his speech to the nation on October 1,

1979. He began his remarks concerning U.S. response to Soviet military force in Cuba by moving directly to the subject: "Tonight I want to talk with you about the subject that is my highest concern, as it has been for every President. That subject is peace and the security of the United States."[2]

It is more common, however, for public speakers to address audiences with mixed interest levels; thus, it is important to make an early attempt to gain their attention.

**Common Attention-Getting Devices**   Experienced speakers have found a number of introductory devices helpful in gaining the attention of the audience. These include: (1) establishing common ground with the audience, (2) paying the audience a deserved compliment, (3) asking a rhetorical question, (4) using humor, (5) using a narrative or illustration that leads into the subject, and (6) using an appropriate combination of these techniques. This list is not intended to be exhaustive; it merely suggests approaches that have been used successfully in the past.

Sometimes as a speaker you are separated from your audience in some significant way. You may hold a position of high status or influence, or you may have vastly different experiences or knowledge. When this is the case, you may feel it necessary to establish an early bond with the audience through the introduction. Notice how Neal W. O'Connor, chairman of the board of N. W. Ayer ABH International, *establishes common ground* with his audience, the Syracuse Press Club:

> Thanks for the warmth of your welcome, a welcome back to Syracuse. One does feel old when he comes back to a place where he's been young. . . .
>
> I owe a lot to Syracuse. My father and mother both graduated from the University. Two of my father's brothers made their careers in this city. One was even president of this very hotel. I met a certain Nancy Turner, class of 1950, here. She is now Mrs. O'Connor. One of our oldest and most valued clients, the Carrier Corporation, has made this its headquarters city. I have many good friends here whom I see all too seldom. . . . I have a great respect for Syracuse, for the city and its people.[3]

In Chapter 4, we discussed the potential significance of the speech occasion. Often the introduction is the most appropriate place to *make direct reference to either the occasion or the efforts of the audience* when praise or recognition is deserved. Eric Rubenstein, president of the Single Room Operators Association, paid the audience an honest compliment when he spoke to a group representing Job Resources, Inc. in Chicago:

> I am delighted to be here. Let me compliment your fine organization, Job Resources, on having counseled and job-trained more than 7,000 individuals, and having also obtained permanent employment for over 2,000 men and women since 1979. Clearly, much of your success is due to the hard work and dedication of your founder and Executive Director, Ms. Michal Rooney.
>
> Job Resources' track record is especially impressive because you only assist disabled individuals, economically disadvantaged people, and displaced workers. Your non-profit agency truly helps needy people train for and obtain jobs, and this is appreciated.[4]

The third attention-getting device is the *rhetorical question*. Unlike ordinary questions, rhetorical ones do not seek an outward verbal or behavioral response; rather, they are meant to stimulate thought and perhaps pique curiosity. In the following speech introduction, John D. Garwood, dean of instruction at Fort Hays State University, describes a hypothetical situation involving value judgments and then poses a thought-provoking rhetorical question:

> O'Hare Airport in Chicago was about one hour away from being fogged in for the night. One plane would be leaving for New York in thirty minutes. Five seats were left; six people bought tickets. No other planes would leave that night.
>
> John Jones, laborer, had won a trip to Europe and the boat left that evening.
>
> Mark Johnson, serviceman, back from two years overseas, is returning to his wife and baby in New York.
>
> Marie Wilson is hurrying to the bedside of her father, a heart attack victim, who is dying.
>
> Thomas Roberts is scheduled to attend a father-son banquet in New York with his son, who has been having some problems.
>
> Sam Brown, rock star, is on stage at Madison Square Garden that evening before 15,000 fans.
>
> Barbara Wright, retired schoolteacher, is being honored that evening at a class reunion.
>
> Which of the six would you leave behind?[5]

The fourth introductory device is *humor*. Several words of caution are necessary here. Humor should be used only as an introductory device when it is appropriate and tasteful. Some speakers seem to believe that every speech should begin with a joke—all too often of the standard, canned variety. Some humor can be planned in advance, but often the best kind of humor grows naturally from the speech situation and includes some references to persons present or preceding events. Moreover, some individuals are more skilled with humor than others. As a public speaker, you must honestly assess yourself with regard to this issue. There is probably no worse way to begin a speech than by telling a joke that flops. When tastefully employed, however, humor that is relevant to the topic and the occasion can serve as an extremely effective attention-getting device. In the following introduction, Richard Lamm, representing the University of Denver's Center for Public Policy and Contemporary Issues, begins his speech to the 1998 World Future Society with this humorous anecdote:

> A priest was riding in a subway when a man staggered toward him, smelling like a brewery, with lipstick on his collar. He sat in the seat right next to the priest and started reading the newspaper. After a few minutes, the man turned to the priest and asked. "Excuse me, Father, what causes arthritis?"
>
> The priest, tired of smelling the liquor and saddened by the lifestyle, said roughly, "Loose living, drink, dissipation, contempt for your fellow man and being with cheap and wicked women!"
>
> "That's amazing," said the drunk and returned to his newspaper. A while later, the priest, feeling a bit guilty, turned to the man and asked nicely, "How long have you had arthritis?"
>
> "Oh," said the man, "I don't have arthritis. I was just reading that the Pope did."

The parable, of course, is a lesson on assumptions.[6]

Another attention-getting device is a *narrative* or *illustration* leading into the topic. Sometimes these devices focus on a personal experience; on other occasions, they simply recount an example or event read or remembered. They may be true to life or hypothetical, literary or historical—so long as they gain attention in a meaningful manner. In the following example, Holger Kluge, president of Personal and Commercial Bank, CIBC, opens his speech to the Diversity Network, Alberta, Canada, with this illustration:

> I'd like to begin my remarks with a little story. A number of years ago we hired an employee as a teller in one of our branches. A few weeks after this individual began work, he was called into the branch manager's office for a discussion.
>
> The manager was a good boss and a good mentor; and he wanted to tell the employee the facts of life about working for the bank.
>
> He told him not to expect to rise too far in the organization.
>
> When the young man asked why, the manager replied:
>
> "You've got an accent. You weren't born in Canada. And you're not Anglo-Saxon. Basically, you've got the wrong name and the wrong background for advancement." He went on to say that the best the employee could hope for was to some day become a branch manager.
>
> I was that young employee.
>
> The irony is, that at the time, I was considered an example of the bank's progressive hiring practices.
>
> Somehow, the significance of this honor eluded me. In the space of a few moments, I had been banished to a wilderness of diminished expectations all because of my name, the way I spoke, and my country of origin.
>
> That was my first encounter with what today we call "organizational culture"—that unconscious, unspoken, unexamined set of assumptions and beliefs that shape the life of an institution.[7]

A final way to introduce a speech in an interesting and creative way is to *use several different attention-getting devices in some appropriate combination.* Gary Trudeau, cartoonist and satirist, delivered some clever introductory remarks when he spoke at Wake Forest University's commencement. To understand the context for this speech, delivered in 1986, it is important to recall that Trudeau is the husband of Jane Pauley, then of NBC's *Today Show,* and that the speech was delivered during the Reagan presidency. In his introduction, Trudeau shared some intriguing statistics, used humor (and satire), and referred directly to the occasion:

> Ladies and gentlemen of Wake Forest: My wife, who works in television, told me recently that a typical interview on her show used to run ten minutes. It now runs only five minutes, which is still triple the length of the average television news story. The average pop recording these days lasts around three minutes, or, about the time it takes to read a story in *People* magazine. The stories in *USA Today* take so little time to read that they're known in the business as "News McNuggets."
>
> Now, the average comic strip only takes about 10 seconds to digest, but if you read every strip published in the *Washington Post,* as the President of the United States claims to, it takes roughly eight minutes a day, which means, a quick computation reveals, that the Leader of the Free World has spent a total of 11 days, 3 hours and 40 minutes of his presidency reading the comics. This fact, along with nuclear meltdown, are easily two of the most frightening thoughts of our time.

There's one exception to this relentless compression of time in modern life. That's right—the graduation speech. When it comes to graduation speeches, it is generally conceded that time—a generous dollop of time—is of the essence.

This is because the chief function of the graduation speaker has always been to prevent graduating seniors from being released into the real world before they've been properly sedated.

Like all anesthetics, graduation speeches take time to kick in, so I'm going to ask you to bear with me for about a quarter of an hour. It will go faster if you think of it as the equivalent of four videos.[8]

**Providing for Audience Orientation** In addition to gaining the audience's attention, the other major function of the introduction is *orienting the audience to the speech's subject.* Although a speaker can choose to do many different things during this time of orientation (such as providing background or defining difficult or ambiguous terms), the speech's orientation phase should include four basic components: advancing the speech's thesis, justifying the topic's importance and relevance to the audience, establishing credibility, and providing a preview. Taken together, the attention getter and the orientation prepare the audience for listening to the speech, while engaging their interest.

- *Articulating the thesis.* One key function of the orientation phase is to *articulate the speech's thesis.* As you prepare your speech, you will prepare both a purpose statement (to help you focus on the response you are seeking from your listeners) and a thesis statement, which states, in a nutshell, the central idea of your speech. Rather than using your purpose statement in your introduction, by saying, for instance, "I want my listeners to start using e-mail more regularly to improve their on-the-job efficiency," you might advance as your thesis, "Using e-mail on the job is an excellent way to improve your efficiency and productivity." By articulating your thesis as part of your introduction, you let the audience see the big picture. They will understand what your central theme, overarching point, or principal argument will be.

- *Offering justification.* In Chapter 4, we stressed the importance of choosing a topic of mutual interest to both you and your listeners. Even so, during your introduction, it is critical to *justify your topic* by showing the listeners its significance—telling them why they should care. You, after all, have been preparing your speech for some time and are well aware of its importance to you. The audience, however, may not focus on the topic until they begin to listen to your speech. So, those early moments are a crucial time to explain to them why the subject of your speech is relevant to them and their concerns.

  For instance, a student speaker highlighted the importance of her topic in this way: "You may be wondering why you should be concerned about colon cancer. Most of us do not associate it with people our age. I know that was my attitude until my 20-year-old cousin was diagnosed with colon cancer earlier this year. When I started to do research, I learned that over 15% of those suffering from colon cancer are diagnosed before the age of 25. And another 20% will be afflicted before the age of 40. I also learned that this potentially deadly disease has stricken more and more teenagers every year since 1990." By showing her classroom audience the relevance of her topic to them, she helped motivate them to want to listen to and learn from her speech.

- *Establishing credibility.*   Another part of orienting the audience involves *establishing your credibility.* In a sense, credibility is an ongoing issue throughout any speech, but for every speaker, the introduction represents an especially critical time to establish her or his credentials. For established professionals, this may be a less daunting task. We expect doctors to know about medicine, attorneys to know about the law, and accountants to be able to answer questions about taxes. For student speakers, however, the issue of establishing credibility is somewhat more challenging. You might establish your credibility by referring to a personal experience (for example, studying in Paris or learning CPR and saving someone's life), by referring to the experiences of those close to you or about whom you care deeply (such as speaking of a friend who was injured by a drunken driver), or by demonstrating your extensive knowledge or education in a particular field or with a special subject (for example, your 10 years of experience as a jazz musician or your knowledge of the author Kurt Vonnegut based on having read all his books). By addressing the issue of your credibility, you are answering the audience's question: "Why should we listen to or believe you?" We will further elaborate on speaker credibility in the next chapter.

**Giving a Preview**   Finally, before moving into the body of your speech, you should complete your orientation phase by *enumerating a preview.* The preview introduces your major points and gives your audience a clear idea of what to expect from the remainder of your speech. In previewing, you are also signaling what it is that you feel is most important, those things you want the audience to remember and to reflect on long after you have finished speaking. If, after enumerating your preview, you follow through with your plan, you will have further enhanced your credibility by demonstrating your careful organization and preparation.

The length of the introduction varies with the needs of the speech situation. Some formal speech occasions demand extensive introductory reference to the events at hand, as well as to significant persons present. Some audiences are already basically attentive; others need considerable coaxing. In general, introductions should not be too extensive, particularly in the classroom context. The introduction does, however, create an important initial impression and should be constructed with care and creativity.

The Body: Common Patterns of Organization

That part of the speech in which you present and elaborate on your major ideas is the body. Most of your speaking time (80 to 90 percent) will be spent here. It is in the body of your speech that you will develop your line of thinking, elaborate on your main points, and develop your arguments.

**Chronological Order**   One commonly used pattern of arrangement is *chronological order.* You begin with a specific point in time and then move forward, or backward, depending on the nature of the subject. Chronological order may be useful with a variety of topics, so long as you are dealing with a subject involving chronological relationships. Thus, the life of Albert

Schweitzer, the development of the labor movement in the United States, the evolution of the Christian Coalition as a force influencing the national political agenda, and changing perspectives on management theory are all appropriate subjects for chronological arrangement.

**Spatial Order**   A second common pattern is *spatial arrangement*. With this pattern, you use space as your ordering principle. A speech explaining the architectural plans for a new library, a presentation describing major tourist attractions of a big city (as one travels from north to south), or a speech describing the best jazz clubs in the United States (moving from the east to the west coast)—all seem like appropriate candidates for spatial organization.

Moreover, you could use spatial order to discuss any of the topics mentioned in the previous section on chronological organization simply by talking of them in terms of locations rather than in terms of their development over time. For example, you might discuss Schweitzer's contributions in several specific geographical locations without regard to the order in which those contributions occurred. Or you might talk of the growth of the Christian Coalition in the South and its spread to the Midwest, the West, and the East. These examples illustrate an important idea: *Most topics can be approached from a variety of ordering perspectives.* Your task is to make a judicious decision in choosing the most appropriate one for the particular situation in which you are speaking.

*Categorical Order*   One of the most common organizational patterns is *categorical order*. When you arrange your ideas categorically, you deal with types, forms, qualities, or aspects of the speech subject. You might discuss higher education by looking at vocational and technical institutes, community or junior colleges, four-year colleges, and universities. Similarly, you might speak about dogs according to breed; people according to religious beliefs or socioeconomic status; or the writings of Shakespeare in terms of type, including sonnets, histories, comedies, and tragedies.

It is often possible to look at the same subject from several categorical perspectives. You might discuss Shakespeare as we just suggested; but you might also rank Shakespeare's work qualitatively and speak about the lesser, the average, and the best of Shakespeare. Moreover, you might discuss the major social issues brought forth in his works or interesting male or female characters. Some topics clearly lend themselves well to varied categorical arrangements.

*Cause-and-Effect Order*   Whenever you choose to make an analytical speech, you may wish to consider using a *cause-and-effect arrangement*. This pattern can move from effect to cause or from cause to effect. For instance, you might use cause-and-effect order to discuss a topic such as the causes of homelessness in the United States, the effects of gang activity on communities, economic factors that lead to recession, or the causes of spousal abuse.

When using causal arrangement, keep in mind that a chronological relationship does not necessarily equal a causal relationship. One event following another may represent chance as easily as cause. You may want to review our discussion of faulty causal reasoning in Chapter 4. In addition, whenever you look at a given effect to seek its causes, you must continually guard against oversimplification. The quest for the single cause is often doomed to failure. Finally, sometimes cause-and-effect order is incorporated as part of an overall problem-solution pattern. Within the structure of a problem-solution speech, you will analyze the problem (effect) in terms of contributing causes.

*Problem-Solution Order*   The *problem-solution pattern* is one of the most frequently used by public speakers. You might propose solutions to such problems as credit card fraud, parking problems on campus, the underrepresentation of minority students among students at your college, or regulating drugs obtained via the Internet.

Depending upon the problem and your assumptions about the audience's prior knowledge, you might spend more or less time discussing the nature of the problem and its contributing causes. In situations where the audience is well versed on the problem, you might only briefly describe it and spend most of your speaking time exploring viable solutions.

*A Special Problem-Solution Pattern: The Motivated Sequence*   One potentially effective approach to organizing a problem-solution speech is the *motivated sequence.*[9] This pattern is organized around five steps: (1) arouse, (2) dissatisfy, (3) gratify, (4) picture, and (5) move. Using this pattern, you first concern yourself with capturing the audience's attention. The next task is to demonstrate the nature of the problem, depicting the difficulties, tensions, or tragedy of a specific situation of immediate concern. Next, you link your recommended solution with the problem so that the audience can understand and accept the proposal as a viable, appealing solution to the problem. The accepting audience is more than one who *understands* how the solution can work. They must, instead, be able to *visualize* the results. Finally, you conclude your speech with appeals and challenges that reflect an understanding of the audience's needs and values and that are designed to move them to accept the solution you have advanced with enthusiasm and commitment.

The motivated sequence encourages a detailed consideration of a proposed solution. It is best suited to those topics that combine emotional with logical appeals. So, if you were addressing the problem of HMO abuses, the motivated sequence might work quite well, but it would likely be less effective if you were proposing a solution to the problem of inadequate recreational facilities in the community.

*Alternative Patterns of Organization*   In addition to the traditional organizational patterns examined above, other options exist. Due to cultural backgrounds or personal preference, *some may prefer less direct and more organic patterns of organization.*[10] For instance, a speech may be organized around telling one or more stories, using a *narrative pattern.* The speaker may begin by introducing a theme, such as the idea that the best business leaders are highly ethical. Then, various stories would be shared to illustrate and reinforce the speaker's thesis. Or, a speaker might pay tribute to a single person by sharing an extended narrative of the person's life. The speech is a continuous narrative with various internal stories drawn out and emphasized. Each would relate to an overarching theme, perhaps by demonstrating how the person being honored lived a life of courage.

## THE EXEMPLUM AS AN ALTERNATIVE ORGANIZATIONAL PATTERN

For hundreds of years, communication educators have used a narrative pattern of organization called the **exemplum.** Five elements are included:

1. State a quotation or a proverb.
2. Identify and explain the author or source of the proverb or quotation.
3. Rephrase the proverb in your own words.
4. Share a story that illustrates the quotation.
5. Apply the quotation or proverb to the audience.

In short, the speaker using this pattern builds the speech around a quotation that is developed through a narrative. This pattern can be especially useful for inspirational or motivational speeches that elaborate on a shared value, such as integrity.

Source: J. R. McNally, "Opening Assignments: A Symposium," *Speech Teacher* 18 (1969): 18–20.

If the speaker wants to build in a sense of drama or climax within a narrative pattern, he or she may choose to use a *spiraling narrative.* For instance, the speaker might give the speech of tribute described by sharing stories that build in intensity. The person's simple acts of courage might be shared first, moving to more unusual acts, and perhaps culminating with uncommon acts of valor. Again, each would be united by the general theme. When delivered effectively, narrative patterns can contribute to a powerful, engaging presentation. See Highlighting Diversity for an extended illustration of another common narrative pattern.

**General Guidelines for Organizing the Speech**   Given the wide variety of organizational patterns from which you can choose, a few general principles should be kept in mind. First, select your organizational pattern carefully. *The way you present your ideas and information should be strategic,* designed to enhance the chance that you will elicit the audience response you are seeking. If you are talking to an audience about a technical area in which they have little background and experience, you have to devote a good portion of your speech to educating them—giving them information they need so that they can understand what you want them to do.

Second, *give some thought to symmetry and balance.* Normally, you would develop each of your main points so that each idea is given equal emphasis. But, if you decide that one idea is clearly more controversial, complex, or important than the others, you may consciously decide to devote more time to that idea. Again, what is important is that the decision be strategic.

Finally, *be aware of primacy and recency effects.* Although researchers have not been able to agree on whether arguments are more memorable and persuasive if they are placed first (primacy) or last (recency), they do agree that those two positions are the most powerful—and that information or arguments embedded in the middle of a message are less likely to have the same impact.[11]

### Transitions as Bridges

A final vital aspect of organization is the *transition*, the bridge connecting one idea with another. Good transitions are critical to the coherence and continuity of the speech. Each major idea needs to be rounded off and related to that which follows. Too many speakers believe that they can move magically from one main point to another. Thus, they concentrate on remembering the main concepts in the speech while paying little attention to the problem of moving smoothly from point to point. Many basically well-structured speeches have been seriously hindered by poor transitions.

Sometimes transitions can be relatively brief. For example, "Now that we've considered the basic dimensions of the problem, let's attempt to analyze its causes." On other occasions, an entire paragraph may be needed to maintain the flow of thought or demonstrate the nature of the relationships involved.

Speakers can sometimes employ *rhetorical questions* as transitional devices. Some examples are: "But what do we really mean by the word 'democratic'?" "How do you think a well-educated person would approach this kind of complex problem?" "What, then, are the ways we can best prepare our children for responsible adulthood?"

If a preview is used at the beginning of the speech, it may be necessary only to use *signposts* subsequently, saying "first, second, and finally," in moving from point to point. No speaker should rely exclusively on this manner of transition.

*Internal summaries* can also be useful as transitions. With the internal summary, you usually review the points already covered, and you may even preview the ideas or approaches to follow; for example, "Now that we've looked at some of the major dimensions of our economic plight, let's move on to consider some ways of improving the situation."

Unfortunately, transitions are often ignored by speakers. Without the skillful use of transitions, speeches seem incoherent. One of the best ways of ensuring that audiences perceive the unity and interrelatedness of your ideas is to make these relationships clear through good transitions. In sum, transitions can create bonds by revealing the speech's main ideas as integral parts of a coherent whole.

## The Conclusion

We've all heard speakers who pause slightly near the end of their speech and then mumble, "Well, I guess that's all I have to say. I sure appreciate your attention. [Further pause.] Thank you." Some might call this a conclusion, but we would contend that the speaker did not conclude; he or she simply stopped. The specific purpose of a conclusion will vary from speech to speech, but the general purpose is to *bring the speech to a strategic close—thus creating a final impact*. We turn now to a consideration of some specific concluding devices.

### Challenging Your Listeners

One common method of concluding persuasive speeches is with a *challenge*. You may challenge the audience to act, to believe, to meet the need, to demonstrate concern, or even to live a different kind of life. At the 1992 Democratic National Convention in New York City, Presidential candidate Bill Clinton concluded his acceptance speech with this compelling challenge:

Somewhere at this very moment, another child is born in America. Let it be our cause to give that child a happy home, a healthy family, a hopeful future. Let it be our cause to see that child reach the fullest of her God-given abilities. Let it be our cause that she grow up strong and secure, braced by her challenges, but never, never struggling alone; with family and friends and a faith that in America, no one is left out; no one is left behind.

Let it be our cause that when she is able, she gives something back to her children, her community and her country. And let it be our cause to give her a country that's coming together and moving ahead, a country of boundless hopes and endless dreams, a country that once again lifts up its people and inspires the world.

Let that be our cause and our commitment and our new Covenant.

I end tonight where it all began for me: I still believe in a place called Hope.[12]

### Summarizing Your Ideas

A second concluding device useful with informative as well as persuasive discourse is the *summary*. In summarizing, you may repeat the main points in a straightforward, almost literal fashion; or you may choose to restate the major ideas in different, and often more concise, phraseology. Summaries are often used in conjunction with another concluding device. A student used the following summary, followed by a rhetorical question, to conclude his speech on the Liberal Arts and Management Program (LAMP), a new interdisciplinary curriculum at Indiana University:

In short, the Liberal Arts and Management Program is an excellent alternative to a traditional college degree. Indiana is one of only a few schools offering this interdisciplinary degree (so, it's a unique opportunity). It combines a broad education in the liberal arts and sciences with a substantial cluster of business courses (giving you the best of both worlds). And, you have a lot of contact with your professors because LAMP is small, with several courses team-taught by faculty from the liberal arts and business. At a time when business leaders are calling for more liberally educated employees, why not look into LAMP?

### Ending with a Quotation

Yet another concluding device is the *quotation*. Quoted material can take the form of expert testimony, poems, songs, or striking, memorable slogans. Quotations should be pertinent and meaningful; they *must* be brief. In a speech from which we quoted earlier, President Carter concluded with a striking quotation:

The struggle for peace—the long, hard struggle to bring weapons of mass destruction under the control of human reason and human law—is the central drama of our age.

At another time of challenge in our nation's history, President Abraham Lincoln told the American people: "We shall nobly save, or meanly lose, the last best hope of earth."

We acted wisely then, and preserved the union. Let us act wisely now, and preserve the world.[13]

### Visualizing the Future

A good way to demonstrate the effects of an advocated plan is to conclude by *visualizing the future*. This device (which is built into the motivated sequence) allows you to picture concretely the projected results of your ideas in an appealing way. One of the most famous examples of an entire speech that visualizes the future is Martin Luther King, Jr.'s speech, "I Have a Dream." In his conclusion, he offers this picture of the future:

> And when this happens, and when we allow freedom to ring, when we let it ring from every village and hamlet, from every state and city, we will be able to speed up that day when all of God's children—black men and white men, Jews and Gentiles, Catholics and Protestants—will be able to join hands and to sing in the words of the old Negro spiritual, "Free at last, free at last; thank God Almighty, we are free at last."[14]

**Referring to the Introduction**   A final concluding device involves *referring to narratives, quotations, or other materials used in the introduction.* Because this device unites the conclusion and the introduction, it has great potential for giving the speech a sense of unity. Consider the following example in which Robert C. Purcell, executive director of General Motors Advanced Technology Vehicles spoke at the 1998 MBA Recognition Ceremony at the Kelly School of Business, Indiana University. He had introduced his speech with a riveting story from May 1961, in which a group of black and white students, riding on a bus together, were attacked by an angry white mob. One young black seminary student, John Lewis, was nearly killed. His life was saved only because a white Alabama public safety officer, Floyd Mann, chased off the crowd by firing shots into the air. Purcell concludes his speech like this:

> There's a postscript to the story I shared with you when I began today.
> Not long ago, John Lewis, that young seminary student, returned to Montgomery, Alabama, to the site of that historic attack 37 years ago, for the dedication of a civil rights memorial. He was one of the honored guests.
> By that time, Lewis had a long and distinguished career. He was now a U.S. Congressman from the state of Georgia.
> As we waited for the ceremony to begin, an older gentleman, who seemed vaguely familiar, came over to him.
> "You're John Lewis, aren't you?" the man said. "I remember you from the Freedom Rides."
> It was Floyd Mann—the same Floyd Mann who had waded into that mob with his revolver, more than 35 years before.
> Lewis was overcome with emotion.
> "You saved my life," he said. And then he embraced Floyd Mann. Not sure as he did so, if even then, black men and white men hugged each other in contemporary Alabama.
> But Mann hugged him back, and John Lewis began to cry.
> And as the two men released each other, Floyd Mann looked at Lewis and said, "You know . . . I'm right proud of your career."
> And if there is one hope that I hold for each of you today—it's that 10 or 20 or 30 years from now, when you look back on your careers, you'll be just as proud.[15]

Like introductions, conclusions should be tailored to the needs of the specific speech situation. As a general rule, they should be brief. Probably the most irritating thing a speaker can do is to say, "In conclusion, . . ." and then drone on and on. Once again, conclusions are used to create a final impact, to remind, to reinforce, and to round out the speech's strategy.

Each part of your speech must be structured carefully. Key parts are shown below.

• • *The speech's introduction—*

Must gain the attention of the audience by doing such things as:

- Establishing common ground with listeners
- Praising the audience
- Acknowledging the significance of the occasion
- Using a rhetorical question
- Using humor
- Using a narrative or an illustration
- Using a combination of these devices

Must orient the audience by:

- Advancing the speech's thesis
- Justifying the topic's significance or relevance
- Establishing the speaker's credibility
- Providing a preview of the speech's main points

• • *The speech's body—*

Must be well organized.
Must use such organizational patterns as:

- Chronological
- Spatial
- Categorical
- Cause-to-effect
- Problem/solution
- Narrative

Must follow other key organizational principles, such as:

- Choose the organizational pattern strategically.
- Consider principles of balance and symmetry.
- Consider primacy and recency effects.

Must use strong transitions throughout, including:

- Initial previews
- Rhetorical questions
- Signposts
- Internal summaries

• • *The speech's conclusion—*

Must create a final impact
Must be brief
Must employ appropriate concluding devices, such as:

- A challenge or an appeal to action
- A summary
- A quotation
- A vision of the future
- A reference to the introduction
- A combination of devices

## OUTLINING THE SPEECH

Although we have chosen to discuss outlining at this point in the chapter, the outline is, in fact, something that develops as you prepare the speech. Most speakers construct a rough outline quite early, representing their initial thinking and ideas they would like to explore. Later, as they read widely and begin to choose some strategy of organization, the outline will grow, change, and be refined. The outline, then, evolves as your ideas emerge. Sometimes it is rearranged; often it is expanded to include more detail or support. The final formal outline will reflect your total speech preparation process.

Types of
Outlines

Although we have spoken of "the" outline, the reality is that you will use several different kinds of outlines as you prepare to speak. First, there is the *formative outline*. This is the outline that you develop as you conduct research, investigate your topic, and reflect on your emerging views. You will change the formative outline many times, inserting new information and rearranging supporting points. By examining your formative outline, you can see if you have given each main point the emphasis you had intended. You can also note whether you have developed your arguments properly, that is, with adequate supporting material. In short, this outline is a kind of diagnostic tool that helps you see where you've been and where you are going. It is for you to use as you see fit.

When you have completed your research and are moving toward the delivery of your speech, your instructor will ask you to prepare a *formal outline*. This outline represents the final written product. Usually, you will develop your outline in full sentences, and you will include a bibliography of the sources you consulted while preparing your speech. By examining this outline, your instructor can see what you have planned and can make some initial assessment of whether you have chosen an effective organizational strategy, whether you have consulted sufficient sources, and whether you have developed your main ideas well. This formal outline is a blueprint of the speech you will give. The sample outline in Figure 5.1 illustrates the kind of formal outline you will develop.

Finally, you will use a *keyword outline* when you deliver your speech. You will transfer your outline onto notecards, using as few words as possible to represent your ideas and remind you of the main points you want to make. You may write out a few things, such as transitions, statistics, and quotations—to make sure you quote accurately. The keyword outline is used to guide your extemporaneous delivery. If you use too many words, you may read from your cards and lose contact with your audience. Practicing with your keyword outline will help you relax and will contribute to a smooth, conversational style of delivery. An example of a keyword outline follows:

I. Reasons for time management:
   A. Efficiency
   B. Productivity
   C. Organization
   D. Credibility
   E. Relationship enhancement
   F. Improved quality of sleep
II. Ways to manage time:
   A. Create a plan.
   B. Devise specific strategies:
      1. Using partners.
      2. Double timing.

FIGURE 5.1     Sample outline of an informative speech

**McDonaldization in Society**

By an Indiana University Undergraduate Student

**Specific Purpose:** I want my audience to understand the meaning of McDonaldization, how and why it developed, advantages and disadvantages of McDonaldization, and some alternatives to this phenomenon.

### Introduction

I. **Attention-Getting Device:** When I was in the first grade, my idea of a good time on Saturday was to get my older brother to take me to McDonalds for lunch. I loved the playland, the Happy Meals, and the ice cream cones. How about you? Did you used to frequent McDonalds when you were a child? Do you still like it?

II. **Orientation Phase:** Of course, McDonalds is only one example of the global fast-food industry. Yet, because it's the first and the largest, McDonalds tends to symbolize the others and their pervasive impact on the world.

   **Credibility:** I have studied business here at IU for three years. I have had summer jobs working at McDonalds and Wendys. Last year I read an intriguing book by the noted economist, Ritzer, *The McDonaldization of Society,* which caused me to see my business knowledge and experiences in a new light.

   **Justification:** Ritzer (1996) points out that the principles of the fast-food restaurant are coming to dominate more and more sectors of our society. The success of McDonaldization is apparent as McDonalds' sales reached $23.6 billion in 1993. Ritzer argues (1994) that no one escapes the influence of McDonalization, even those who do not eat fast food.

   **Thesis:** Because McDonaldization is so much a part of our lives, it is important to understand its meaning, why it developed and its relative advantages and disadvantages.

   **Enumerated Preview:** I'd like to begin today by sharing some of the history of McDonalds. Then I'll go on to discuss the basic principles of McDonaldization. I'll conclude by examining the pros and cons of this phenomenon and looking at possible alternatives.

**Transition:** First, let's look briefly at McDonalds' history.

### Body

III. McDonalds is the first U.S. fast-food chain to gain real international prominence.
   A. Ray Kroc began franchising McDonalds in 1955 and there are now over 14,000 outlets.
   B. You can find McDonalds all over the world: in France, China, Russia, and Japan.

**Transition:** But "McDonaldization" extends far beyond one fast-food chain. What are the underlying principles?

IV. The basic principles of McDonaldization are efficiency, calculability, predictability, and control, based on turn-of-the-century rules of bureaucracy (Taylor, 1911; Weber, 1947).
   A. Efficiency is at the heart of McDonaldization.
      1. All foods are extremely basic and take very little time to prepare.
      2. Most fast-food businesses subtly put the customers to work by having them fill their own drinks, pick up their own condiments, and throw away their own trash.
      3. Seating arrangements in fast-food restaurants are uncomfortable which encourages faster turnovers.

FIGURE 5.1     Sample Outline—*Continued*

**Transition:** How do we see the principle of efficiency playing out in other kinds of organizations?

B. The efficiency principle influences many other areas of society.
    1. Higher education has increasingly become more efficient.
        a. "McUniversities" are dominated by multiple choice examinations which are machine graded.
        b. Note taking services provide typed notes for students which can help them either listen more intently to the lecture, or not go to class at all.
    2. Many businesses increase efficiency by putting customers to work.
        a. NBD, one of the more popular banks on campus, now has teller fees for transactions which could otherwise be performed at an ATM machine.
        b. Computerized answering services force callers to reach their desired person through a series of messages.
    3. TV dinners, microwaves, and frozen foods now dominate home cooking.
    4. Computers, of course, have been the greatest influence towards greater efficiency.
        a. Computers solve complicated problems that once took days in a matter of minutes.
        b. E-mail is much more efficient than sending a letter.

C. The second major principle of McDonaldization is calculability, an emphasis on things which can be quantified.
    1. There are many examples of quick service businesses stressing quantity: McDonalds "Big Mac" and supersized fries, Wendy's "Biggie" menu, Burger King's "Whopper" and a "Big Gulp" from Seven-Eleven.
    2. Food chains create illusions of quantity with fluffy buns and patties which intentionally extend outside of these buns.

**Transition:** Do we see the principle of calculability in other kinds of organizations?

D. The concept of calculability has spread over many other areas of society.
    1. Higher education provides an excellent illustration. Gaining entrance into colleges heavily relies on such factors as test scores, grade point average, and class rank.
        a. Students are beginning to choose colleges largely by their rankings.
        b. Recruiters often save time by only interviewing those college graduates with minimum test scores and/or minimum grade point averages.
    2. Sports have been heavily affected by calculability.
        a. An increase in attention towards total revenue has led to more TV timeouts for advertising.
        b. Much to the dismay of our beloved Bobby Knight, a shot clock has been imposed to increase the scoring in basketball. The three-point line has also been established to increase scoring.
    3. The computer helps increase calculability across several aspects of life.
        a. The computer allows for registration of masses of students at large state universities and grade processing which has dramatically increased the size of such institutions.
        b. The development of the credit card has strongly increased the number of consumer transactions.

**Transition:** Beyond calculability and efficiency, McDonaldization aims for a tightly controlled environment with relatively little ambiguity.

E. Not surprisingly, then, the third principle of McDonaldization is predictability.
   1. Every McDonalds burger weighs exactly 1.6 ounces with a 3.875-inch diameter.
   2. The appearance of different sites are uniform throughout the world. Employees follow guidelines on hair length, dress code, facial hair, etc.

**Transition:** As with the other McDonaldization principles, predictability shows up in other arenas of life.

F. Predictability is the norm in many different kinds of organizations.
   1. Multiple choice exams provide predictability in higher education. Students can often determine what will be on the test and study the most limited amount of information possible.
   2. The popularity of travel agencies has led to vacations becoming much more predictable. Events are often fully planned for the week, leaving little room for spontaneity or exploration.
   3. The popularity of places such as Disney Land indicate society's enjoyment of predictability. Everything about this tourist attraction leads to predictability. People visit year after year to wait in the same long lines for the same old rides.
F. The final element of McDonaldization is control.
   1. Fast-food restaurants have done away with cooks, rather employing step by step instruction on how to prepare rudimentary food items.
   2. Most of fast food comes pre-formed, precut, pre-sliced, and pre-pared often by non-human technologies.

**Transition:** Control is also pervasive throughout American society.

G. All kinds of organizations seek to control employees and customers.
   1. With the rise of HMOs, insurance companies often decide what physicians or medical clinics a family is allowed to visit, rather than the choice being left to the individual.
   2. Shopping malls exert control over their stores by determining universal guidelines such as hours of operations or what can and cannot be sold.

**Transition:** So far, I've described and illustrated the underlying principles of McDonaldization. Let's look now at some of its strengths and weaknesses.

V. There are some clear advantages to the system of McDonaldization.
   A. There are greater varieties of products and greater availability of these varieties.
   B. Goods and services are of far more uniform quality.
   C. Quantification allows for easy price comparison.
   D. When people work in bureaucratic organizations like McDonalds, they usually understand what is expected of them and how they will be evaluated (Jaques, 1990).
VI. On the other hand, there are also many disadvantages to the system of McDonaldization.
   A. A major disadvantage of the McDonaldization system is the increasing gap between rich and poor—a gap that is growing at an alarming rate.
   B. People have shown such a great desire for efficiency that they are willing to ignore the fact that they are eating food that is extremely unhealthy or that products they're buying are made in sweatshops under extremely poor working conditions.
   C. The dehumanizing effect of McDonaldization is evident as more and more jobs are increasingly monotonous routines which require little thinking or creativity. Such jobs are often incredibly unfulfilling and boring (Herzberg, 1987).

FIGURE 5.1          Sample Outline—*Concluded*

**Transition:** It almost seems that McDonaldization is so pervasive, especially in our society, that other ways of creating organizations might be difficult to imagine. Yet, some have surfaced.

VII. There are some alternatives to such a McDonaldized way of life, as Barber points out in a recent article in the *Atlantic Monthly.*
   A. Companies such as Southwest Airlines have bucked the trend of predictability by having spontaneous and creative pilots and service attendants who play games, joke with passengers, and create an overall unique atmosphere where several surprises may arise.
   B. Ben and Jerry's ice cream has taken several measures to avoid becoming McDonaldized. They use an abundance of ingredients in each flavor and they had a standing policy until 1995 that no executive could earn more than five times the lowest paid employee. Additionally, employees do not wear uniforms and are encouraged to be spontaneous.
   C. The recent popularity of bed and breakfast operations indicates a desire by many Americans to try something new and receive personal attention.

### Conclusion

VII. **Summary:** The process of McDonaldization can perhaps best be summarized by considering two contrasting theories. "In a rapidly changing, unfamiliar, and seemingly hostile world, there is comfort in the comparatively stable, familiar, and safe environment of a McDonaldized system" (Ritzer, 12). The opposite point of view argues that a McDonaldized environment offers a dehumanizing setting which increases the gap between rich and poor, and creates fewer jobs involving creativity, rather more monotonous tasks.
**Concluding Device:** Perhaps most of us want the best of both worlds: creativity with some predictability, quantitative as well as qualitative measures of success, and some measure of control in a larger context of individual empowerment. Understanding McDonaldization is one step toward thinking through what we really value.

### Bibliography

Albright, M. "Inside Job: Fast-Food Chains Serve a Captive Audience," *St. Petersburg Times* (January 15, 1995), p. 1H.

Barber, B. "Jihad vs. McWorld." *Atlantic Monthly* (March 1992), pp. 53–63.

Herzberg, F. "One More Time: How Do You Motivate Employees?" *Harvard Business Review 65* (1987), 109–17.

Jaques, E. "In Praise of Hierarchy," *Harvard Business Review 68* (1990), 127–33.

Peters, T. *Thriving on Chaos.* New York: Harper & Row, 1987.

Ritzer, G. *Expressing America: A Critique of the Global Credit Card Society.* Thousand Oaks, Calif.: Pine Forge Press, 1995.

———. *The McDonaldization of Society.* San Diego, Calif.: New Delhi, 1996.

Taylor, F. *Principles of Scientific Management.* New York: Harper & Row, 1911.

Weber, M. *The Theory of Social and Economic Organization.* New York: Oxford University Press, 1947.

C. Assess your progress.

D. Reward yourself.

As is typical of keyword outlines, this one's development is much sketchier than its full-sentence equivalent would be. That is appropriate and should assist with an extemporaneous style of delivery.

A well-constructed outline is of great help during the delivery of a speech. Equally important, it stands as a tangible symbol of the time, effort, and thought you have put into your speech.

| KEY CONCEPTS 5.2 | Outlining the Speech |
|---|---|
| • • *Several different kinds of outlines exist and should be used:* | Formative outlines<br>Formal outlines<br>Keyword outlines |

# DELIVERING THE SPEECH

However well organized you are, the actual delivery of the speech is of paramount importance. Many an intelligent, well-intentioned, and well-prepared speaker has failed to move his or her listeners simply because of an inability to present the speech directly, spontaneously, and emphatically. To deliver any speech effectively, the speaker must approach the situation with some measure of confidence; yet stage fright remains a nearly universal phenomenon.

## Developing Confidence

The term *stage fright* originated in the theater, but most people do not have to participate in a dramatic production to experience this unfortunate malady. Quaking limbs, quivering voices, and dry mouths are only a few of the dreaded symptoms. It is a paradox of human nature that most of us desire attention; but when we receive attention in the form of an audience, we respond with some measure of fear. Essentially, it is a fear of personal failure, for we expose a good deal of ourselves through our public expression of attitudes and ideas.

Even so, many speakers lack confidence because they hold a number of erroneous notions about stage fright. Among these fallacious assumptions are: (1) the speaker is virtually alone in experiencing anxiety in public speaking; (2) only beginners experience apprehension; (3) everyone in the audience can tell exactly how frightened a speaker is; and (4) stage fright is always debilitating for the speaker. Let us consider each in turn.

*Anxiety in public speaking is not an uncommon occurrence.* In fact, only rarely do public speakers experience no anxiety before or during the actual delivery of their speeches. One study demonstrated that 77 percent of all experienced speakers admitted to some communication apprehension on each speaking occasion.[16] Of course, "experienced" speakers are not necessarily synonymous with "great" speakers. Yet, historically, some of the most eloquent orators of all time were besieged by stage fright, including Cicero, Abraham Lincoln, and Winston Churchill. Clearly then, anxiety is not infrequent; nor is it experienced by only the small and insignificant. Business Brief 5.1 dramatizes this point.

## STAGE FRIGHT IN THE BUSINESS WORLD

The *Wall Street Journal* recently published an interesting article focusing on the fear of public speaking in the business world. The article reported that

In this garrulous, smooth-talking world, many executives and professionals are afflicted with what specialists call presentation phobia, or stage fright. A far cry from butterflies in the stomach, it's sometimes severe enough to slow careers to a stop.

The fear can strike not only the chief executive facing a hall of shareholders but also the manager asked to "say something about yourself" at a staff meeting. Bert Decker of Decker Communications, a San Francisco consulting firm, estimates that "roughly half the business population" labors under (some) form of the anxiety and tries to avoid speaking in public.

But as treatment becomes more effective and widely available, more people are getting help. "Of the full range of anxiety disorders," says Charles Melville, an Atlanta psychiatrist, "people can most predictably overcome a fear of public speaking."

Source: Jolie Solomon, "Executives Who Dread Public Speaking Learn to Keep Their Cool in the Spotlight," *Wall Street Journal* (May 4, 1990): B3.

Although exceptions exist, normally stage fright decreases as individuals gain experience as public speakers.[17] It is not uncommon for students in basic public speaking courses to experience fairly intense anxiety during their first speech performance. As public speaking becomes a part of their normal classroom activities, however, they meet future assignments with greater confidence.

Speakers frequently overrate the accuracy with which listeners can judge the extent of their nervousness. Even if there are no physical reactions to anxiety, we often assume that the audience can see through our smiles and calm appearance to the turmoil and uncertainty lurking beneath. Once again, studies do not support this assumption. *Listeners,* including college speech teachers, *are notoriously poor judges of the amount of anxiety speakers experience.*[18] The typical tendency is to underrate stage fright, attributing greater confidence to the speaker than he or she claims to feel. In fact, it is not uncommon for speakers to believe they "acted nervous," while audience members will comment on the degree to which the speakers seemed completely in control and self-assured!

Earlier in this section we referred to stage fright as an "unfortunate malady." While this represents a commonly held view, in truth, anxiety is a hindrance to your performance only if it is severe or uncontrolled. A number of psychological studies have demonstrated that *moderate anxiety can be an asset in performance,* whether you are taking an examination or giving a speech.[19] You should welcome some anxiety as a possible stimulus for a better presentation. Whenever you become anxious before giving a speech, your flow of adrenaline is increased. Unfortunately, this increased source of energy often manifests itself in shaking hands and other signs of nervousness. Yet that same energy can be channeled into positive behaviors that may enhance the effectiveness of your presentation. Moderate tension can provide a creative edge, a more dynamic style of delivery, a more animated presentation. When viewed from this perspective, stage fright becomes a tool for creating a more involving presentation.

Finally, there is perhaps no better way to control anxiety than to *know that you are well prepared* for the speech event.[20] When you have carefully analyzed your audience, engaged in thorough research, strategically structured the organizational pattern of the speech, and practiced the delivery of the speech, and when you are committed to the ideas therein, you are in an excellent position to control your anxiety. Without such diligent preparation, however, some apprehension may be well founded.

## Considering Different Styles of Delivery

There are three major styles of speech delivery: impromptu, manuscript, and extemporaneous. We will discuss each one briefly.

**Impromptu Speaking**    Impromptu speeches are essentially off-the-cuff; they are delivered without preparation, other than perhaps a few minutes to organize your thoughts. As you function in professional and social groups and organizations, you are often called upon to articulate a point of view, make a brief report, or explain a procedure. More often than not, requests for these speeches arise directly within the meeting when someone needs information.

While impromptu speaking is a common occurrence in daily organizational life, you should never elect to give an impromptu speech when you are asked in advance to make a speech. By definition, impromptu speaking excludes the opportunity for research, audience analysis, arranging a strategic plan, and practicing delivery. As a result, you have minimal control over most crucial speech variables.

**Speaking from a Manuscript**    In manuscript speaking, you write the speech out word for word and read the manuscript to the audience. The use of the manuscript is not infrequent among business and professional speakers. In fact, manuscripts are sometimes required when the speaking occasion is an especially important one. In the political world, manuscript speaking is widespread. Nearly all major presidential addresses are delivered with the assistance of a manuscript. If poorly handled, however, the manuscript can become a most deadly form of delivery.

Common problems associated with manuscript speaking are limited eye contact, poor oral style, difficulties associated with reading, and inflexibility. Unless speakers practice frequently before delivering the manuscript, they are apt to become bogged down in the manuscript itself during the presentation. We have all seen speakers who are glued to their manuscripts, looking up only sporadically or failing to look up at all. Without eye contact, a sense of directness and involvement cannot be effectively communicated.

When properly used, the manuscript speech provides the opportunity for maximum speaker control. Time limitations are important and often overlooked by public speakers. By using a manuscript, you can plan precisely with regard to time, again leaving some room for "during delivery" alterations. The potential for excellence in language usage is also great with the use of the manuscript. Descriptive passages can be created with attention to color, precision, simplicity, and figurative elements. Precise verbs can be chosen and incorporated throughout the speech. The manuscript speech can become a work of art so long as you are constantly aware of the need for keeping a conversational quality. Finally, because the manuscript is ordinarily rehearsed with approximate similarity to the speech as actually presented, you should find it possible to practice the delivery with relative precision. This, in turn, makes it possible to face the speaking occasion with an increased sense of confidence.

**Extemporaneous Speaking**    The final style of delivery is *extemporaneous*. Many individuals confuse impromptu and extemporaneous speaking, believing that one does little to prepare for an extemporaneous speech. On the contrary, extemporaneous delivery requires a great deal of preparation. The extemporaneous speech is carefully prepared, thoroughly outlined, practiced but not memorized, and delivered from notes (using a keyword outline). When speaking extemporaneously, you commit key ideas to memory, but precise words, specific phrases, and particular examples vary during practice sessions as well as during the actual presentation of the speech.

When you speak extemporaneously, you can place your outline either on full sheets of paper or on four- by-six-inch note cards, depending upon the particulars of the speech situation. If you plan a great deal of bodily movement, including perhaps the use of a chalkboard, it is probably best to use note cards rather than carrying sheets of paper around the room. On the other hand, papers are entirely appropriate if they are placed on the podium and left there; in fact, they allow you to visualize a greater portion of the speech in one glance. When used properly, with plenty of practice, the notes used for extemporaneous speaking have the potential for allowing maximum flexibility, directness, and spontaneity. Your notes serve as a reminder of strategies planned and ideas developed; but you should feel able to deviate from them whenever the situation demands it. As an extemporaneous speaker, you can make structural alterations, clarify or elaborate with additional examples or illustrations, and omit unnecessary passages because you are creating the speech as you deliver it.

This is not to imply that extemporaneous speakers can do no wrong. There are times when they flounder, groping for the precise words they need (and times when they never find them); they may ramble or use too many examples, especially of a personal nature. With appropriate criticism and guidance, however, these problems usually decrease as the speaker gains experience. Perhaps the greatest advantage of extemporaneous delivery is that it requires total involvement on the part of the speaker.

Characteristics of Effective Delivery

In discussing the three major styles of delivery, we have alluded to the qualities of effective delivery. In general, effective delivery in public speaking is characterized by spontaneity, directness, flexibility, and involvement.

**Spontaneity**    *Spontaneity* is particularly important in the use of gestures and bodily movement. Neither should be planned in advance; they should emerge naturally from the speech, the enlarged conversation. Both gestures and bodily movement should reinforce the spoken words so that movement does not involve aimless wandering around the room. As a general rule, you ought to gesture whenever you feel like it, making some attempt to adjust the size of the gesture to the size of the room (the small classroom versus the 5,000-seat auditorium).

### Directness

*Directness* is another critical quality of effective delivery. Probably the best way to communicate directly with others is to look directly into their eyes while articulating your ideas. We recognize this fact at an interpersonal level, but the importance of eye contact often escapes us when we communicate as public speakers. Whenever possible, you should strive to establish eye contact with everyone in the audience as often as possible.

Directness can also be demonstrated through appropriate vocal qualities. You should speak loudly enough to be heard—but not so loudly that you blast listeners from the room. Some speakers talk with an overly projected, artificial vocal quality, leaving the impression of a dramatic production rather than a speaking occasion. On the other hand, no one cares to listen to a monotone. Ideas are best communicated directly to audiences by speakers who employ vocal variety and expressiveness.

### Flexibility

*Flexibility* is a third quality of effective delivery. To be a flexible speaker, you must be alert to information, responses, and other stimuli that might indicate a need for change in your planned strategy and choice of words. Speakers who insist on delivering the speech precisely as they have practiced it often fail to meet important needs of audience members. They are not responsive to boredom, confusion, or hostility. Thus, they say what they want to say, but the listeners cannot, will not, or do not receive the message. Once again, the most effective public speakers are usually those who are especially responsive to audience feedback.

### Involvement

The final important delivery characteristic is *involvement*. It is imperative that you appear concerned about your communicated message. Involvement is a total delivery concept, including eye contact, movement, word choice, and facial expression. The audience will believe that you are committed to your ideas when you reinforce your words with appropriate nonverbal and inflectional emphasis. The speaker who says, "I couldn't believe in this more" in a deadpan manner without communicating an image of total commitment might as well say, "I couldn't care less about this"; certainly the latter is more likely the meaning the audience will perceive.

## Responding to Questions

Every public speaker should be prepared to answer audience questions, usually following the presentation. There are situations in which the speaker encourages listeners to interrupt him or her during the speech whenever they have a question, when something is unclear, or when they simply wish to relate a personal view. The typical procedure, however, is for the speaker to present her or his ideas without interruption, and then to entertain questions during a forum period following the speech.

No speaker should underestimate the importance of responding meaningfully to listeners' questions. In a sense, the *question-and-answer* or *forum period* is simply an extension of the more formally structured presentation, for the skill with which questions are answered will be a major determinant of listeners' overall response to the speech. The forum period represents yet another

*Following their presentations, most speakers take questions from the audience. The question-and-answer period can be a critical time for speakers to clarify issues, offer additional information, and further build their credibility.*

opportunity to reinforce important ideas, build credibility, provide additional interesting information, and even deal with aspects of the topic untouched by the speech itself.

In handling the question-and-answer period procedurally, it is important that each listener hear and understand the question being answered. Sometimes it is helpful to have the questioning audience member rise and state his or her question; or if the room is especially large, you may simply repeat the question before answering it. If several persons have questions, deal with as many as time permits.

No one questioner should be allowed to dominate the forum period, nor should you pursue irrelevant questions for long. If an irrelevant issue is raised or a question is so technical that you suspect only a few listeners are interested in hearing the response, you might ask the person who raised the inquiry to talk with you following the forum period. You should never attempt to fake your way through a difficult question. It is best to admit that you do not have that kind of experience or perhaps never uncovered that kind of data during your research. While continual responses of "I don't know" damage your credibility, a single admission of ignorance tends to humanize you and give you a positive mark for openness. And just as you should know how long you are expected to speak, it is equally important to learn how much time is available for answering questions. Time limits vary greatly, but whatever they are, they should be respected.

- • *Develop confidence and manage communication apprehension.*

- • *Consider different styles of delivery:*

    Impromptu
    Manuscript
    Extemporaneous

- • *Strive for effective delivery that is:*

    Spontaneous
    Direct
    Flexible
    Involved

- • *Conduct the question-and-answer period skillfully.*

# LANGUAGE: STRIVING FOR GOOD ORAL STYLE

When we speak of good *oral* style, we are really stressing the fact that speaking and writing are not the same. Speakers who read from a written text often sound stuffy or overly formal. In listening to them, we may feel that their remarks really do not speak to us directly.

## Differences between Oral and Written Style

Generally speaking, in contrast to written prose style, good oral style uses:

1. *More personal pronouns* (we, ours, I, mine, you, yours).
2. *More simple sentences* (with some variety).
3. *Shorter sentences* (assisting with audience comprehension).
4. *More rhetorical questions* (gaining and sustaining the audience's attention by challenging them to think).
5. *More repetition of words, phrases, and sentences* (recognizing that listeners, unlike readers, cannot can go back and reread something they have missed, good speakers often intentionally repeat key ideas, colorful phrases, or slogans that they want the audience to remember and ponder after the speech is over).
6. *More simple, familiar words* (knowing that good speeches must be instantly intelligible).
7. *More contractions* (giving the speech a natural, conversational quality).
8. *More figurative language* (using words and phrases that are pleasing to the ear and stimulating the audience's imagination; also making abstract ideas concrete, adding color and life to the speech, and reinforcing key ideas).[21]

## Choosing Words

One of your main goals as a public speaker is to be clear. One way of achieving clarity is to choose your words with great care, paying attention to their concreteness, simplicity, and preciseness.

**Concrete Words**   First, concrete words are usually preferable to abstract words for effective speaking. Concrete words point to real events or objects that the audience can associate with objective experience. As your words become more and more concrete, the pictures you paint in the minds of your audience tend to become clearer and clearer.

Concrete words appeal to the senses. They point to something the listeners can hear, touch, see, taste, or feel: lemon, motorcycle, boots, tea, roses, picnic table, the howl of a wolf, the smell of freshly perked coffee. Whenever you must deal with a relatively abstract concept in your speaking, you can make it clearer and more concrete by providing specific illustrations and examples.

### Simple Words

Besides being concrete, your words should also be simple. Simplicity is related to clarity. When you use simple words, you avoid being vague, pretentious, or verbose. But simplicity is not the same as simple-mindedness. In fact, many great speakers of the past, including Winston Churchill and Franklin Roosevelt, were masters of simplicity.

Although simple words are usually familiar ones as well, there are some phrases that have become clichéd by overuse. Thus, in striving for simplicity and familiarity, you should avoid using clichés. Among the *clichés that should be avoided are*

| | |
|---|---|
| It goes without saying | In the final analysis |
| Few and far between | Tired but happy |
| Easier said than done | All in all |
| Last but not least | Drastic action |
| Method in his madness | Reigns supreme |
| More than meets the eye | Worked like a horse |
| Ignorance is bliss | Clear as a crystal |
| After all is said and done | |

These are only a few examples of expressions that were probably amusing and interesting at one time but are now stale from overuse.

### Precise Words

Concreteness and simplicity in word choice work in tandem with precision. Although we often speak of synonyms, rarely do we find any two words that have *exactly* the same meaning. If you looked up the following five words, you would soon discover that while each has to do with being poor, they still represent subtly different shades of meaning: *destitute, impoverished, bankrupt, impecunious,* and *needy.*

Precise words are accurate. Rather than using the verb *walked,* for instance, you might describe the *way* a person walked by using such verbs as *staggered, ambled, strutted, sauntered, waddled,* or *raced.* By selecting the best word in each case, you also eliminate unnecessary modifiers, such as, "walked *slowly*" or "walked *drunkenly.*" Thus, precise language is usually compact.

## Constructing Sentences

As you choose your words carefully and begin to place them into sentences, some additional guiding principles are useful.

### Keep Subjects and Verbs Close Together

First, construct each sentence so that the subject and the verb are close together. This increases the intelligibility of the sentence. It is also a practical characteristic of daily conversation; therefore, it sounds more natural.

Consider the following sentence, in which subject and verb have been separated:

> This plan, which has been tested in other companies like our own and has resulted in enormous profits, is worthy of your support.

To place the subject and the verb together and thus increase the sentence's intelligibility, you might create two separate sentences, as follows:

> This plan is worthy of your support. It has been tested in companies like our own and has resulted in enormous profits.

**Keep Sentences Short**   Another important guideline is to use short, active sentences. Short sentences are easier for audiences to follow and comprehend. Supposedly, a "standard" sentence is made up of seventeen words.[22] Even so, some variety is essential. Longer sentences can be clear when they are properly constructed. In writing sentences, you should avoid needless repetition, unnecessary modifiers, and circumlocutions, such as *"The reason why* I think this plan will work is because. . . ."

- *Using the active voice.*   One of the best ways to delete unnecessary words is to *use the active voice* whenever possible. Compare the following:

  Much dissatisfaction with this new rotation schedule has been expressed by line workers. (passive voice)

  Line workers have expressed much dissatisfaction with this new rotation schedule. (active voice)

Sometimes the passive voice is unclear because it is wordy, but often it is intrinsically unclear. For example, "This product was chosen because it met governmental standards. . . ." What this sentence does not tell us is who did the choosing. Depending upon the issue being discussed, that might be very important information.

- *Using only necessary modifiers.*   Also related to the issue of sentence length is the use of modifiers. Specifically, *use only those modifiers that are needed.* There are two kinds of modifiers in the English language, those that comment and those that define. Commenting modifiers include *very, most,* and *definitely.* These modifiers tell us nothing new; instead, they try to boost the meaning of the word they modify. Yet if your words are selected carefully, with a concern for precision, they should be able to stand alone without the assistance of modifiers that simply try to make their meaning more emphatic. Of course, some modifiers are essential; they tell us something we need to know. Depending upon whether a plan is described as "innovative," "costly," "sensible," or "outdated," we will and should respond differently. Defining modifiers provide information that the noun standing alone cannot convey.

Good oral style, then, is the kind of style you will use as you deliver your speech extemporaneously. By doing so, you will sound natural and conversational. Because listeners will respond positively to language they find understandable and memorable, you enhance the chances of communicating effectively when you use good oral style.

## USING PRESENTATIONAL AIDS

In every speaking situation, communicating information clearly, concretely, and concisely is an overarching goal. One way of doing this is through the use of presentational aids. When chosen wisely and prepared with care, presentational aids can go a long way toward enhancing the speech and making ideas and information more accessible to listeners.

**Presentational Aid Options**

When you use presentational aids, you reinforce your ideas by letting your audience see them as well as hear about them. If you design and use your aids well, you also enhance your credibility and make your ideas and information more memorable and compelling. A number of options exist.

### The Chalkboard

Probably the simplest and most basic aid is the *chalkboard*. This allows you to put diagrams and sketches on the board as an explanation unfolds. If you are counting on using a chalkboard, however, you had better check in advance to make sure the room has one. The chalkboard is a convenient and potentially effective means of depicting important data. Moreover, physical activity may help you to manage any speech anxiety you are experiencing.

Of course, the chalkboard has its limitations. Because it is so familiar to most audiences, it tends to be less interesting or less impressive than other forms of presentational aids. But if your handwriting is legible, if you are working on a clean board, and if you can practice so that you do not lose contact with the audience while you write, then the chalkboard may be a sensible choice of visual support. If possible, prepare the board in advance and cover it with a screen, to be lifted at the appropriate moment.

### Posterboards and Flipcharts

Other visual aids can be prepared in advance and brought with you to the speaking event. For example, if you want to use color or a sophisticated design, you may elect *posterboard drawings* as a presentational aid. These can be prepared in advance and can be as professional and impressive as budget and talent will allow.

Since posterboards can be somewhat clumsy to handle, especially if two or more are used during the presentation, you may want to use a *flipchart*. With this method, you place the drawings on a rather large tablet and display them on a convenient frame that facilitates movement from one drawing to the next.

**Handouts**   On occasion, you may decide to prepare copies of a *handout* to aid the audience's comprehension. Handouts are especially useful when you are referring to extensive lists of figures, such as budgetary statements in the context of a technical report. You can also use handouts to outline essential information to which the audience can refer during subsequent decision-making sessions. By using handouts, you reduce the need for the audience to take notes. Thus, listeners can devote greater attention to your ideas. The handout also serves as an outline for you, potentially assisting you in your organization and delivery. When using handouts, you should pass them out at the moment you plan to discuss them (not in advance) and make sure that copies are available for everyone.

**Models**   Another kind of frequently used presentational aid is the *model*. Models may be either *one-dimensional* or *three-dimensional*, depending on the subject of the presentation. In Chapter 1, we presented a one-dimensional model depicting the role that communication plays in organizational life. These models are typically rather simple and straightforward.

Three-dimensional models, on the other hand, are miniatures of the real, often larger, object. Suppose an architect has been asked to make a presentation in which he is to discuss his concept of a new museum. He may elect to construct a three-dimensional model of the proposed building so that the audience will have a precise picture of the structure he envisions. One major advantage of these models is the clarity and precision with which they allow you to demonstrate your ideas.

**Objects**   You can also use actual *objects* as presentational aids. Assume that a speaker is proposing the adoption of a new line of toys aimed at fostering creativity and teaching certain critical concepts, such as numbers and spatial relationships. Assume further that samples of these toys exist. What better way to persuade the audience of the uniqueness and value of the toys than by displaying and demonstrating them?

**Transparencies and Overhead Projectors**   *Overhead projectors* are useful for displaying detailed or complex information on a large screen. However, certain principles should be observed when using an overhead projector. The *transparencies* should be as simple and readable as possible. In addition, be sure you do not stand between audience members and the projected image. When using a pointer, do not hold it over the platform of the machine (thereby magnifying by a thousand times any shakiness of the hands you are experiencing); instead, point directly to the screen.

When changing transparencies, try to accomplish the switch quickly and smoothly so that the audience is not blinded by a bath of hot, white light between every slide. Try to avoid "lightheads," or a skewed positioning of the overheads, by placing each transparency squarely on the machine.

FIGURE 5.2    Line graph of gross income

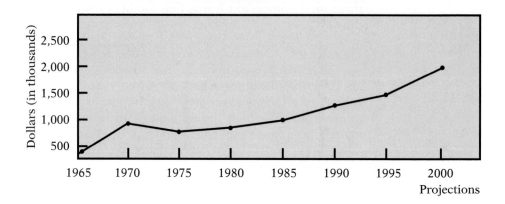

**Slides**    *Slides* are particularly useful for showing pictures or delivering presentations that must be repeated in the future. For maximum effectiveness, slide presentations should be planned in advance to maintain a relatively steady pace. As each new slide is shown, allow a moment of silence so the audience has an opportunity to grasp its contents, then describe and discuss what they are viewing. In addition, avoid turning your back to the audience and talking to the screen; glance at the screen to determine what slide is showing, and then speak directly to the audience as you provide added information.

Depicting
Statistics

In most speaking situations, you will find yourself using statistics as support from time to time. Presentational aids can often help you to present statistical information clearly and concisely.

**Graphs**    Another common method for presenting statistical summaries is by a *graph*. A graph is a representation of numbers by geometric figures drawn to scale. Speakers often use graphs to make statistical information more vivid and to depict relationships. Three of the more familiar and useful kinds of graphs are line, bar, and pie graphs. *Line graphs* are especially useful for depicting comparative relationships through time. Many business and professional presentations focus on information relating to time-based trends—for example, comparing gross or net profits, production, or wages. As a result, the line graph is one of the more useful tools of the presentational speaker. Figure 5.2 presents an example of a line graph depicting gross income.

It is possible to place more than one curve on a single graph, but it may be at the expense of clarity. Moreover, you should recognize that a trend can be distorted simply by compressing or elongating the space allotted to time periods, while keeping the other dimension of the graph constant. The ethical speaker will not knowingly distort a trend simply to dramatize a particular point.

**FIGURE 5.3** | Bar graph of worker productivity

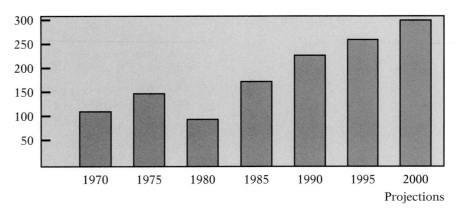

Another kind of commonly used graph is the *bar graph*. These graphs usually depict quantity. Thus, a simple bar graph literally uses bars to indicate amounts and is well suited to presenting comparative statistics. Figure 5.3 depicts comparisons of worker productivity, focusing on five known time periods and one projected one.

Bar graphs are particularly useful as visual aids in that they can be made large enough for the audience to see and easily understand the point being made. As with the line graph, it is possible to depict a number of different statistical comparisons simultaneously on the same bar graph, often through the use of different colors or shadings. Once again, however, simplicity should be sought to avoid confusion.

The final graph that is commonly used to depict statistics is the *pie graph*. The pie graph is useful for showing numerical distribution patterns. In particular, you may want to depict how a total figure breaks down into different parts. For instance, if you wanted to depict the student population at your university according to race or ethnicity, you might use a pie graph, such as the one shown in Figure 5.4.

## Presentational Aids in the Computer Age

Audiences are becoming increasingly accustomed to speakers using professional and polished presentational aids. This expectation is especially salient in the business and professional world. It is hard to imagine a businesswoman rushing to make an important speech with a pile of posterboard drawings under one arm! More realistically, speakers in professional contexts will use transparencies, models, and perhaps flipcharts (especially in workshop settings). Moreover, speakers are increasingly using presentational software and electronic presentation systems to make sophisticated and professional-looking presentational aids.

There are two major ways that computers can assist you in preparing presentational aids. Ideally, you will use a computer to create *and* present

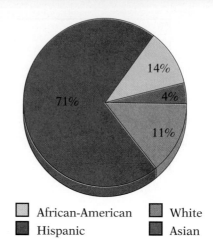

| | | | |
|---|---|---|---|
| ☐ African-American | | ☐ White | |
| ◼ Hispanic | | ◼ Asian | |

Source: ESU Daily News, February 4, 1999, p. 3.

your graphics. If you have used a laptop to prepare your graphics, you will then take it to the meeting where you are speaking and use it, together with a portable screen, to display your visuals. Highlighting Technology demonstrates the ease with which PowerPoint presentations can be prepared. Or, using computers that may not be portable, you can still use a software package (such as PowerPoint, Persuasion, ClarisWorks, or Astound) to create slides and to incorporate images, sound, and even video clips into your presentation. You then save your presentation on a disk and take it with you to a room equipped with a computer and large screen, to be used during your presentation.

Obviously, not everyone will have access to this sort of equipment. Nevertheless, you can still use your computer to generate presentational aids—to construct a graph, table, or other visual display that you want to print out and use as a black-and-white or full-color transparency with an overhead projector. Certainly, in a classroom setting, these sorts of aids will be very well received and will give your presentation a professional air.

### Some Tips for Preparing and Using Computer-Generated Graphics

Once you have learned to prepare and present computer-generated presentational aids, you will probably rarely use more traditional aids. But you will first need to learn how to use the new technologies. Some guidelines follow:

**1.** *Seek out workshops to help you master the software.* You can probably pick up a lot on your own by simply experimenting, but if you can take a short course or workshop, you may learn more quickly and be more likely to discover a wider array of options available to you. Check on whether your campus offers workshops, and make the time to attend one.

## USING POWERPOINT: EIGHT EASY STEPS

*Step 1:* Open PowerPoint.

*Step 2:* Choose "Template."

*Step 3:* Browse templates until you find a design you like.

*Step 4:* Select a format for presenting your information.

*Step 5:* Click on the box of your choice to add text, a graph, or a picture.

*Step 6:* To move to a new slide, go to "Insert" and click on "New Slide."

*Step 7:* To alter the look of slides, go to "Insert" and click on "New Slide."

*Step 8:* To add animation, click on the "Shooting Star" icon.

**What could be easier?**

Source: Holly Baxter, Associate Instructor, Indiana University, Bloomington (Fall 1998).

**2.** *Master the basics.* A good place to begin is by creating graphics that can be used on the overhead projector. You might start by generating a list of main ideas to be discussed in your speech, or you might construct a simple graph or chart. Remember that fonts should be at least 18 point to be visually accessible to listeners. To further enhance their visibility, use bold letters and fonts that are plain and easy to read.

**3.** *Simplicity is the rule.* Your graphics should be designed so that they are simple, uncluttered, and consistent. Most software will allow you to add all sorts of peripheral elements, such as shading and background patterns, as well as movement and highlighting. Even so, you will want to avoid anything that is distracting. Avoid the temptation to have a new main point come flying or spinning onto the screen. Stay away from backgrounds that are glitzy. Remember, computer-generated graphics, like other presentational aids, should support your speech, not distract from it or take undue attention away from you, the speaker.

**4.** *Use the technology to full advantage.* Once you have mastered the basics and have had some experience using computer-generated graphics, you may want to become more creative. If your topic lends itself to such options, you might download images from the Internet—to be made into slides to accompany your presentation. In displaying a bar graph, show the audience one bar at a time, to simplify the statistics and focus the audience's attention on the point you are making. And, of course, experiment with color—choosing color schemes that are vivid, tasteful, and professional.

**5.** *Always have multiple backups!* If you have your graphics on your laptop, save a backup file onto a floppy disk. Always make overheads that could be used in case the screen or computer you've been promised isn't there. As a final backup, prepare handouts in case there are electrical problems or other kinds of equipment failure. The more sophisticated our presentational aids, the greater our tendency to count on them for our effectiveness. This is a mistake. No matter how wonderful your computer-generated graphics may be, you should be able to make your presentation with more traditional means of presentational support and still communicate effectively.

## Practical Considerations in Preparing and Using Presentational Aids

Regardless of the type of presentational aid you choose to use, whether you are using a simple, low-tech chalkboard or PowerPoint presented via your laptop computer, here are some general guidelines you should follow:

**1.** *Use presentational aids only when they are justified.* Some speakers try to jazz up their presentations by using presentational aids. But unnecessary visuals can annoy or distract an audience as easily as persuade them. Presentational aids should be used to clarify, to make more concrete, or to demonstrate something that is difficult to describe without them.

**2.** *Don't hesitate to use presentational aids that are needed.* You cannot tell an audience what a proposed budget is "like." To be clear and complete, you must present it in detail visually, usually by providing a handout. Similarly, it would be foolish to describe a building plan, a surgical procedure, or an automobile design without the aid of presentational aids.

**3.** *Your presentational aids should be large enough so that each member of the audience can see and decipher them with ease.* Any presentational aid that cannot be seen is actually a hindrance and would best be omitted entirely.

**4.** *Your presentational aids should be clear and, if possible, colorful.* Your writing or printing should be neat and clear. Whatever color scheme you choose, your presentational aid should enhance clarity and be pleasing to the eye.

**5.** *Keep your presentational aids simple.* The inclusion of many complicated details will serve only to distract the audience and obscure the point being made. In general, it is best to illustrate only the essentials, with one concept featured with each diagram, overhead, or chart. Remember: graphics software packages can lead you astray. Don't let your graphics upstage you.

**6.** *Consider the needs of each audience member in presenting your presentational aids.* Position presentational aids high enough so that those in the front of the room do not obstruct the view of those in the back. If you are showing an object, for example, and if the speaking context permits, you might want to walk into the audience, showing the object to listeners as you talk about it.

**7.** *Do not inadvertently obscure the view of your presentational aid by standing in front of it.* Speakers often project their own images onto screens, blocking the transparencies they are projecting. Speakers who use chalkboards may do the same thing—partially hiding what they are writing on the board—and, at the same time, talking to the board rather than to their listeners.

**8.** *Direct the audience's attention to the relevant portion of your presentational aid by pointing to it as you discuss it.* In this way, you can help the audience follow your remarks. You can point by using your finger or, with large visual aids, a pointer. Speakers using PowerPoint can direct the audience's attention to each point by having each one appear at the crucial moment.

**9.** *Usually, presentational aids should be displayed only when they are being discussed in the presentation.* When you are finished with them, remove them from view. When presentational aids are randomly displayed at the beginning of the presentation or left in view after they have functioned as aids, you are inviting the audience to continue to look at the visual while ignoring you and your message.

**10.** *Practice with presentational aids prior to the presentation.* Make sure you are comfortable with the equipment. Equally important, be sure you can move smoothly from your notes at the podium to the visual aid and back again without losing either your composure or your sense of directness with the audience.

Presentational aids are potentially useful and compelling supporting devices. Not every speaker should use them, but most presentations would benefit from their skillful use. The careful preparation of presentational aids is simply one way for the speaker to demonstrate a concern for clarity, precision, and audience interest. When properly prepared, presentational aids should, as the name suggests, *aid* audience comprehension. Furthermore, by using them, you are communicating the message that you have cared enough to prepare carefully and to consider the welfare of your audience.

# SUMMARY

There are many reasons public speakers fail to communicate effectively. Chief among them is the speaker's being perceived by the audience as disorganized. Organizing your speech into a form well suited to the audience's needs and your specific purpose is a step crucial to your success as a public speaker. Your task is to choose a pattern of organization that makes sense in terms of your overall speaking strategy. One useful tool for accomplishing this is the outline. By creating a formative outline, you put your ideas down on paper and examine the way your speech is developing. Later, you will develop a formal outline to reflect your final speech plan and to give your instructor insights into your organizational strategy. Finally, you will use a keyword outline to assist you in delivering your speech extemporaneously.

For most public speaking contexts, the extemporaneous style of delivery is best (although you may, on occasion, speak impromptu or from manuscript). Extemporaneous delivery allows you to be direct with your audience, as well as flexible and spontaneous. In general, these qualities will serve you well as you speak within your organization or as a representative of your organization addressing the general public. Through extemporaneous delivery, you are also more likely to use conversational language, so that your sentences are not stilted and your word choice is simple and appropriate. As you speak with increasing frequency and as you work to improve over time, your oral style will continue to improve.

Finally, using carefully prepared presentational aids is an excellent way to enhance your speech. With presentational aids, you can highlight your main ideas, depict statistics, picture things that otherwise have to be imagined, and show the audience that you prepared well for your presentation. Almost any speech can benefit from the use of at least one presentational aid. As with other aspects of your speech, presentational aids will be more effective if they are prepared well in advance (using the criteria discussed in this chapter) and if you practice using them before you deliver your speech. Modern technologies allow for the creation and use of computer-generated graphics, and listeners are increasingly accustomed to seeing them used. Exploring the potential of such technologies is important for public speakers as we approach the beginning of the twenty-first century.

# QUESTIONS FOR DISCUSSION

1. What are some of the elements of an effective speech introduction? Be specific. What are some methods of gaining the audience's attention? Cite examples whenever possible.

2. What are some speech topics that would be well suited to each of the following patterns of organization? Provide at least three examples for each pattern.
   a. Chronological order
   b. Spatial order
   c. Categorical order
   d. Cause-and-effect order
   e. Problem-solution order
   f. The motivated sequence
   g. Narrative pattern

3. Discuss the basic characteristics of good speech conclusions. What are some specific devices that might be used to conclude speeches? Examples?

4. Compare and contrast the formative, the formal, and the keyword outline. How is each useful to a speaker?

5. Refute or defend the following: "Stage fright is a nearly universal phenomenon." Cite evidence to support your position. What are some strategies for developing confidence as a public speaker?

6. Compare and contrast impromptu and extemporaneous speaking. What are the conditions under which each is appropriately used?

7. If given the choice, would you elect to speak extemporaneously or from a manuscript? Why? How would you prepare for the mode of delivery you have chosen?

8. What are some problems you might anticipate with regard to answering questions after a speech? How might you cope with each? Again, be specific.

9. List some of the differences between oral and written style. What happens when a public speaker violates the "rules" of good oral style?

10. What are some of the characteristics of good word choice and sound sentence structure? Cite examples of each quality you name.

11. List several guidelines for the effective use of presentational aids.

12. What are some ways in which computer-generated graphics might be especially helpful in supporting a speech? What are some pitfalls to avoid?

# EXERCISES

1. Choose *one* of the following topics. Assume that you have been assigned to speak on this chosen topic to your classroom audience. What would your specific purpose be? Your thesis? Compose a good introduction and a good conclusion. Choose a tentative strategy of organization for the body, and sketch out an outline. Explain the reasoning behind your choices.
   a. Grade inflation
   b. The job market
   c. Affirmative action
   d. The Peace Corps
   e. HMOs
   f. United Way
   g. Ethics in advertising
   h. Cholesterol
   i. Sugar in the diet
   j. Postretirement years

2. Select a topic of your choice and deliver it to the classroom audience using extemporaneous delivery. Try to capitalize on the qualities of effective delivery outlined in this chapter. Ask your instructor to make a videotape of your speech, if possible, so that you can later watch yourself and gain from self-analysis. At the very least, ask the audience to focus specifically on your delivery and tell you how it might be improved.

3. Choose another speech topic and develop it into a manuscript speech. Be sure to guard against composing it like an essay rather than a speech, and practice it several times

so that you can overcome some of the problems associated with manuscript speaking. Then follow the same procedure in delivering the speech outlined above. Which mode of delivery do you prefer? Or would your preference depend on the context, the topic, and so forth?

4. After each of your speeches, allow the audience to ask you questions. In answering, make every effort to follow the guidelines established in this chapter. After the question-and-answer period, ask the class to evaluate that part of your presentation as well. To what extent, for example, did your responses to questions contribute to your clarity, credibility, and perceived responsiveness?

5. Go to the library and look up *Vital Speeches of the Day*. Select any speech delivered during the past two years, and make a copy of it. Then study it to determine to what extent the speaker used good oral style. Mark specific instances where either word choice or sentence structure is especially good or bad. Then write a brief speech analysis in which you discuss the extent to which the speaker developed her or his speech using good oral style. Be sure to define the criteria you use to assess oral style.

On August 17, 1998, President Bill Clinton ended his silence on the Monica Lewinsky affair and delivered a speech to the nation. Earlier in the day, Clinton had been forced to testify before the grand jury. His testimony was videotaped, and, months later, it was nationally televised. Known for his ability to relate to the American people, Clinton likely viewed the following speech as an attempt to control damage and also as an opportunity to offer some justification for his actions and to shape public opinion.

Following is the text of Clinton's address, as transcribed by the Federal Document Clearing House:

Good evening.

This afternoon in this room, from this chair, I testified before the Office of Independent Counsel and the grand jury.

I answered their questions truthfully, including questions about my private life, questions no American citizen would ever want to answer.

Still, I must take complete responsibility for all my actions, both public and private. And that is why I am speaking to you tonight.

As you know, in a deposition in January, I was asked questions about my relationship with Monica Lewinsky. While my answers were legally accurate, I did not volunteer information.

Indeed, I did have a relationship with Ms. Lewinsky that was not appropriate. In fact, it was wrong. It constituted a critical lapse in judgment and a personal failure on my part for which I am solely and completely responsible.

But I told the grand jury today and I say to you now that at no time did I ask anyone to lie, to hide or destroy evidence or to take any other unlawful action.

I know that my public comments and my silence about this matter gave a false impression. I misled people, including even my wife. I deeply regret that.

I can only tell you I was motivated by many factors. First, by a desire to protect myself from the embarrassment of my own conduct.

I was also very concerned about protecting my family. The fact that these questions were being asked in a politically inspired lawsuit, which has since been dismissed, was a consideration, too.

In addition, I had real and serious concerns about an independent counsel investigation that began with private business dealings 20 years ago, dealings, I might add, about which an independent federal agency found no evidence of any wrongdoing by me or my wife over two years ago.

The independent counsel investigation moved on to my staff and friends, then into my private life. And now the investigation itself is under investigation.

This has gone on too long, cost too much and hurt too many innocent people.

Now, this matter is between me, the two people I love most—my wife and our daughter—and our God. I must put it right, and I am prepared to do whatever it takes to do so.

Nothing is more important to me personally. But it is private, and I intend to reclaim my family life for my family. It's nobody's business but ours.

Even presidents have private lives. It is time to stop the pursuit of personal destruction and the prying into private lives and get on with our national life.

Our country has been distracted by this matter for too long, and I take my responsibility for my part in all of this. That is all I can do.

Now it is time—in fact, it is past time—to move on.

We have important work to do—real opportunities to seize, real problems to solve, real security matters to face.

And so tonight, I ask you to turn away from the spectacle of the past seven months, to repair the fabric of our national discourse, and to return our attention to all the challenges and all the promise of the next American century.

Thank you for watching. And good night.

## Questions

1. What is your overall impression of the President's speech?
2. How did Clinton organize his address? (Discuss his introductory and concluding devices as well as his pattern of organization.) How effective was the pattern he chose?
3. What did you think of Clinton's oral style (word choice, sentence structure, etc.)?
4. How would you evaluate the President's address in terms of ethics? That is, apart from his organization and style, how would you judge his speech in terms of your view of ethical communication? Refer to the ethical perspectives discussed in Chapter 3 to frame your analysis.

# CHAPTER six

*After reading this chapter, you should be able to:*

1 Comprehend the diversity of special presentations you might be asked to make in business and professional settings.

2 Understand the basic principles of persuasive speaking.

3 Develop and present a proposal presentation to a small group audience.

4 Prepare and deliver a sales presentation to a group of prospective clients.

# Special Persuasive Speaking Applications

A few years ago, a group of professionals from a prominent Eastern manufacturing firm approached us, asking us to teach them how to make good oral presentations. The group was quite diverse, composed of, among others, a 21-year-old college intern working in sales as part of his field experience for a degree in marketing, a 30-year-old woman who had just moved into a supervisory position, and a 50-year-old upper-level manager who had been with the company for more than 25 years. Besides their differences in age and status within the firm, their speaking needs also varied. The young man wanted to know how to make better persuasive presentations to customers; the woman was interested in learning how to present concise, informative reports to her newly acquired staff; and the senior manager needed to learn how to make high-quality public presentations to promote the company at conferences around the world. In spite of the differences in their speaking needs, they all had two things in common: Not a single person in the group (nine in all) had ever studied public speaking, nor had they anticipated doing any public speaking when they started their careers.

In many ways, these individuals are typical. Most people assume they will rarely, if ever, make oral presentations after they graduate from college. Yet, public speaking *is* common in the business and professional world. Professionals will speak to diverse groups in highly varied settings—each one presenting special demands and challenges.

## PREVIEW

In this chapter, we turn our attention to two special kinds of public presentations commonly encountered in business and professional life: the proposal presentation and the sales presentation. Both represent particular kinds of persuasive speeches. Thus, we also emphasize key principles of effective persuasive speaking.

## PERSUASIVE SPEAKING: BASIC PRINCIPLES

Without the ability to communicate persuasively, most organizations could not survive, and most professionals would find their ability to solve problems and achieve upward mobility severely hampered. Managers must communicate persuasively whenever they talk to the public about the excellence of their firm or product. Every supervisor toils daily to convince his or her employees that their jobs are important and that they should continue to strive for excellence. Any worker who has a bright idea is immediately confronted with the problem of selling it to others. And all employees involved with sales and promotion are regularly required to approach customers or potential clients and persuade them to make a purchase or an investment.

Persuasive speaking is a common communication activity in contemporary organizations. Persuasion can take place in all kinds of communication contexts—during a private conference, in a small decision-making group, or in front of audiences of varied sizes. Here, we will address general principles of persuasion before going on to examine some specific applications of persuasive speaking that are commonly encountered in professional life.

In our discussion of speech purposes in Chapter 4, we suggested that accomplishing a persuasive purpose can be challenging. The persuasive speaker typically sets out to convince an audience to work harder, consider a product innovation, vote for some new policy or procedure, or invest their time or money in some endeavor. Most listeners can absorb information without feeling threatened, but they often squirm when asked to think creatively, spend money, cast a vote, or invest their valuable time in some specific way. To be a successful persuasive speaker, then, you must begin by thoroughly acquainting yourself with the audience and their needs and values.

## Analyzing the Audience

Every audience can be described and analyzed according to basic demographic characteristics, as we discussed in Chapter 4. Some audiences are mostly male; others are basically youthful, mostly well educated, or rather well-to-do. Thus, you will want to consider the basic listener characteristics of age, gender, socioeconomic status, culture, and educational level, as well as religious and political beliefs. If you wanted, for instance, to convince a group of supervisors in your organization that sexual harassment was a problem, you would need to consider both your gender and your listeners' genders before formulating a persuasive plan. If you were a woman addressing a group of male supervisors on this subject, your approach should be designed to minimize defensiveness.

### Acknowledging Diversity—Seeking a Common Focus

Of course, since audiences are increasingly diverse, assessing their interests, predispositions, and values can be a complex undertaking. In making the persuasive speech on sexual harassment mentioned above, for instance, you would likely be talking to female as well as male supervisors. Moreover, your listeners might possess different sexual orientations. One way of approaching this subject with this particular audience might be to argue that sexual harassment represents (more than anything else) an abuse of power. Whoever is in the more powerful position must carefully scrutinize his or her own behavior. Moreover, same-sex and opposite-sex harassment are treated identically under the law. What you are doing with this kind of strategy is helping listeners to focus on the one thing they all have in common: they are in positions of authority. What is important is not their ages, their political leanings, or their sex, but that they all hold positions of power within the organization. If you can help the audience to focus on this common concern, you will likely connect with them and make an effective persuasive presentation.

### Understanding Listener Motivation

Once you have made a preliminary assessment of audience characteristics, you are then ready to ask some questions about what is likely to motivate your listeners. *Motives* are variable energy sources. Coming from within, they tend to guide the options we choose to pursue. The options we select depend on many factors, including our background experiences, the state of our present needs, and our general philosophies of life and human behavior.

Some human motivation theorists, including psychologist Abraham Maslow, contend that individuals are motivated by unfulfilled personal needs, some of which are more basic to existence than others. Maslow argues that audience members must be physically comfortable and secure before you can appeal to their higher needs for love, esteem, and belonging.[1] Anyone who has been forced to attend a lecture before lunch without the benefit of breakfast is well aware of the learning distraction created by hunger pains! While it is difficult to help people learn when their basic needs are unsatisfied or poorly understood, it is virtually impossible to stimulate their thinking, change their beliefs, or move them to act under such circumstances.

*Habits as Motives*    Although there are many sources of human motivation, for many audience members *habits* serve as motives. They will prefer, now and in the future, what they have known and felt comfortable with in the past. But individuals vary greatly in the rigidity of their response patterns. At one extreme are the persons who are comfortable only with the status quo. They are cautious, conservative, and low in risk-taking in nearly all circumstances. These individuals are invariably opposed to any idea that involves risk. They may not think the present system perfect, but they take considerable consolation in the knowledge that they are accustomed to it. "Creative," "innovative," and "new" are words that automatically elicit negative responses from these persons. At the opposite end of the habit continuum are those who are consistently flexible, open-minded, and ever responsive to change. These individuals may be instantly attracted to an idea or moved to purchase a product simply because it carries the label "new" or "improved."

When you look at your audience, then, you might consider their habits. Are your listeners a traditional group who seem inclined to let things drift along, without taking risks or initiating change? Or, are they a bunch of eager beavers who want to move forward, rise to the challenge, and live life on the "cutting edge"? More likely than not, they will be diverse in their habits (yet another dimension of audience diversity), and your task will be to calm the nerves of the reluctant without boring those who are eager to throw caution to the wind.

*Personal Needs as Motives*    Habits are only one perspective from which to consider human motivation. Every individual has needs that must be satisfied for the person to live and function happily and productively in society. When personal needs go unfulfilled, they create voids, distress, weakness, and other kinds of physical and psychological discomfort. Earlier we referred to the human motivation research of Maslow that identified a hierarchy of human needs. Beginning at the bottom of the needs hierarchy, they are: (1) physiological needs (health and well-being), (2) safety (personal security, fear of the unknown), (3) love and belonging (the social need of knowing that one is regarded warmly and belongs comfortably to groups that are significant to him or her), (4) esteem (moves beyond being accepted to being respected and held in high regard), and (5) self-actualization (striving for ultimate personal fulfillment).[2] Figure 6.1 presents Maslow's hierarchy.

Some audience members will listen to a persuasive speech with the aim of endorsing the best solution or making the best decision for the welfare of the organization. But while organizational representatives, executives, and managers are "organization men and women" in one sense, they are at the

FIGURE 6.1     Maslow's hierarchy of personal needs

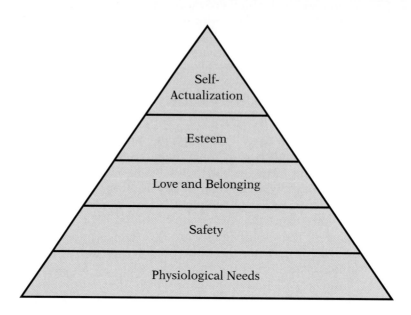

same time human beings with personal needs and motives. Thus, it is critical to consider the diversity of needs. An audience member who is insecure about his own capabilities, is uncertain of his acceptance within his department, and believes that he is held in low esteem presents a different type of persuasive problem than a listener who is completely confident, affectionately regarded by all, and respected as a talented, innovative leader.

Not all writers believe that the needs identified by Maslow are the most telling. McClelland argues, for instance, that all needs are socially acquired. He identifies three major sets of personal needs: (1) *the need for achievement*—being driven to succeed, extremely hardworking, and desiring feedback; (2) *the need for power*—having the ability to make subordinates feel inspired to excel; and (3) *the need for affiliation*—having the desire to be with others, to belong, and to interact socially.[3] The audience member with strong achievement needs may be listening to your speech from the perspective of "What's in it for me?" She may wonder whether the change you are proposing would give her an opportunity to use her abilities and to excel. Her motivation is very different from that of someone who is more affiliative and, hence, concerned with how the proposed change might affect the organization's social environment. As you construct your persuasive strategy, you need to consider the motivational bent of each audience member so that you can make your presentation as compelling as possible.

*The Need to Contribute as a Motive for Action*     The final set of important motivating factors is externally directed. Many professional people have genuine concern for the welfare of the organization as a whole. Ideas they perceive as enhancing the position of the organization will receive their hearty support. Secure in their personal and professional positions within the or-

## THE BOSS WHO MADE A LASTING CONTRIBUTION

Aaron Feuerstein, chief executive officer (CEO) of Malden Mills, a textile company located in Lawrence, Massachusetts, is considered a hero by most of his employees. Always known as demanding but fair, Feuerstein found that his leadership was put to the test in December 1995 when a catastrophic fire nearly destroyed the company's manufacturing plant. Employees were convinced that their jobs were gone. That was before Feuerstein announced that he would keep all his 3,000 employees on the payroll for a month while he started rebuilding the 90-year-old family business. In January, he announced that he would pay them for a second month. In February, he said he would pay them for a third month. By March, most of the employees had returned to work full-time. In the meantime, Feuerstein had paid out several million dollars to give his employees a chance.

What sets this CEO apart? His own words are revealing. When asked how he differed from his fellow CEOs, he said, "The fundamental difference is that I consider our workers an asset, not an expense." He believes that his job goes beyond just making money for shareholders, even though the only shareholders of Malden Mills are Feuerstein and his family.

His philosophy is clear. Feuerstein asserts, "I have a responsibility to the workers, both blue-collar and white-collar. I have an equal responsibility to the community. It would have been unconscionable to put 3,000 people on the streets and deliver a death blow to the cities of Lawrence and Methuen. Maybe on paper our company is worth less to Wall Street, but I can tell you it's worth more. We're doing fine." Before the fire, the plant produced 130,000 yards a week. A few weeks after the fire, it was up to 230,000 yards. Feuerstein notes, "Our people became very creative. They were willing to work 25 hours a day."

A deeply religious man whose command of biblical Hebrew is impeccable, Feuerstein often quotes Hillel, the first-century Talmudic scholar; for example, "In a situation where there is not a righteous person, try to be a righteous person." And again, "Not all who increase their wealth are wise."

Malden Mills stands out in the Lawrence area, once a thriving center for the textile industry. Business after business left Lawrence in search of lower labor costs. Those companies that stayed downsized, laying off hundreds of workers in attempts to stay profitable.

"That goes straight against the American Dream," Feuerstein said. "You work hard and should make a good living and have a good retirement. I could get rid of all the workers who earn $15 an hour and bring in a contract house that will pay their laborers $7 an hour. But that breaks the spirit and trust of the employees. If you close a factory because you can get work done for $2 an hour elsewhere, you break the American Dream."

Source: Michael Ryan, "They Call Their Boss a Hero," *Parade Magazine* (September 8, 1996): 4–5.

ganization, they are committed to advancing the goals of the institution, usually including maximizing profit and rendering some public service. Drucker deals with this last notion in his book, *The Effective Executive,* in which he points to "commitment to contribution" as a characteristic of many successful high-level managers.[4] See Business Brief 6.1 for an illustration of a leader whose desire or need to contribute is clear and compelling. In this instance, the person is motivated by a desire to contribute substantively to society. Such sentiments often involve a widening of the listener's perspective to

FIGURE 6.2    Factors influencing human motivation

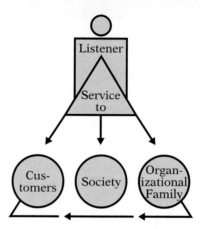

include not only his or her own specialty or department, but the processes, purposes, and goals of the entire organizational family.

This, then, is yet another dimension of human motivation that you need to consider as a persuasive speaker. A proposal for organizational change that aims to improve the quality of a specific company product, ensure a safer environment for its public, or create, in general, a better, more harmonious society would have great intrinsic appeal to a group of employees who are motivated by external, other-oriented concerns. Figure 6.2 illustrates the need to contribute as a factor influencing listener motivation.

Often the key to gaining support for an idea or plan resides not in a rational justification of the idea or solution, but in one's ability to comprehend the forces within the audience that predispose them to believe and behave in predictable ways. Such knowledge makes it possible to create a persuasive strategy that will relate the virtues of the plan to the motives already present within the listeners.

## Building Credibility

Think of the last time someone tried to sell you something and failed. Why didn't you buy? Perhaps you simply didn't have the money, but beyond that, the would-be persuader may have "turned you off" in some way. Maybe he seemed deceptive and you worried that the product wasn't as great as he claimed. Or perhaps you asked him some questions he couldn't answer, and so you grew to doubt whether he knew what he was talking about. Possibly his personal style was offensive. Maybe he came on too strong, or at the other extreme, seemed to be more interested in going to lunch than in making the sale. In short, he may have done something that caused you to view him as lacking credibility. He might have been selling a marvelous product, perhaps the exact kind of self-cleaning microwave oven you have always wanted. But because you were unimpressed with him as a person and a communicator, you decided to keep on looking.

**Factors Contributing to Your Credibility**   What is true for the salesman in this case is true for any public speaker with a persuasive purpose. Thousands of years ago, Aristotle pointed out that the speaker's *ethos* or *credibility* is her or his most powerful source of influence. Even the most carefully constructed and soundly supported speech will fail if the speaker is viewed as low in credibility. Most researchers agree that several factors combine to influence listener perceptions of speaker credibility.[5] In general, if audiences perceive speakers to be *competent, trustworthy, objective,* and *enthusiastic,* they will view them as highly credible. Of course, these dimensions are interrelated. Listeners have little regard for the sincere speaker who is not terribly well versed. Nor will they tolerate the bright but deceptive speaker. Objectivity is important in that listeners, while recognizing that a persuasive speaker has taken a stand, still want to believe that he or she has given fair consideration to more than one point of view. Listeners also prefer to feel that the speaker would still be willing to hear opposing views. Finally, most listeners find it easier to be convinced by a persuasive speaker who is genuinely enthusiastic and dynamic than by one who is either too pushy or too bland.

What can you do to enhance your credibility as a public speaker? First, you must recognize that *even before you begin to speak, your listeners will likely have some impression of your credibility.* If, for example, you are known within your organization as an expert on nutrition and you are speaking on the need for a balanced diet, the audience's perception of your credibility should be quite positive. Even if the audience knows nothing about you, however, they will begin to assess your credibility as soon as they see you. Your appearance counts. The way you dress is important, as is the way you walk, sit, smile, and shake hands. Looking professional, suiting your attire to the occasion, and appearing neatly groomed are also essential.

If you are in a rather formal public speaking situation, *your listeners will also gain some impression of your credibility from the remarks of the person who introduces you.* If you know you are to be introduced, you might send your introducer pertinent information several days beforehand—information geared, in part, toward enhancing your credibility. Avoid sending a long, detailed résumé. Introducers often have trouble picking out the really crucial information.

**Guidelines for Establishing Your Credibility**   You can also do things during your speech to alter your perceived credibility. *Credibility building is a process that unfolds as you share your thoughts with the audience.* Here are some techniques you might try:

**1.** *Establish common ground with the audience.*   In general, audiences enjoy listening to speakers with whom they believe they have something in common. If you once worked in a department like theirs, say so. Whenever you can demonstrate values, concerns, or aspirations that you and your audience hold in common, you help your credibility.

**2.** *Build trust.*   Normally, trust building is a process that evolves only over time. Even so, you can often establish yourself as a trustworthy source of information on a particular subject by techniques such as self-disclosure (admitting that you were terribly out of shape before joining the company's fitness program) or by establishing your individuality (speaking as an executive who once viewed most administrators as incompetent).

**3.** If appropriate, *reinforce your status.* If your introducer does the job well, you may not have to do this. If not, however, *tasteful* references to your experience, education, or position are entirely appropriate. Mention your experience with supervision, student government, sales, and so forth as you address each of these subjects. Obvious name-dropping and repeated references to a prestigious award or position must be avoided.

**4.** *Support your views with evidence.* We have already discussed the importance of using evidence. In general, the better your evidence, the more the audience will perceive you as credible. In the next section, we will discuss specific ways to use evidence that are designed to enhance your persuasiveness.

**5.** *Strive for good delivery.* We have already discussed principles of effective delivery in detail. Here let us simply note that persuasive speakers who deliver their speeches fluently and with apparent confidence, who sound sincere and committed to their ideas, will go a long way toward establishing themselves as trustworthy, competent, and enthusiastic communicators.

**6.** If appropriate, *use presentational aids.* Such aids are not necessary for every speech. If they make sense and if you want to take the time to prepare them, however, they can add color and interest to your presentation. Using handouts or computer-generated graphics highlighting your main points and key statistics will influence the audience to perceive you as well organized. The presence of any carefully prepared presentational aid suggests that you went to some pains to prepare for the presentation and implies you took the task seriously.

There is no standard way to build your credibility. Each topic, audience, and speech situation presents its own set of obstacles to be overcome. No speaker is equally credible on every topic he or she addresses. In some instances, your credibility may be almost automatic. In others, you may want to consider using all the credibility-building devices listed above. In most speaking situations, even highly credible speakers attempt to nurture their images by establishing common ground, using evidence, and striving for excellent delivery. To be an effective and persuasive speaker, your credibility can never be too high.

## Appealing to Audience Emotions

As a persuasive speaker, you often want to get your audience excited about some cause, move them to action, or help them to become less complacent. You will have difficulty achieving those goals on the basis of logical appeals alone. You may decide then to use some *emotional appeals* (or what the Greeks called *pathos*) designed to make your listeners feel sad, happy, angry, sympathetic, compassionate, or proud. To get people to act, to move them to change some policy, you often have to move their hearts as well as their heads.

**Appealing to Emotions with a Concern for Ethics** If your persuasive goal is to move your listeners to action, be sure to use emotional appeals in ways that are ethical (see Highlighting Ethics). You should always build your persuasive speech on a firm foundation of strong evidence and

## ELEVEN COMMANDMENTS OF ETHICAL COMMUNICATION

- Do not use false, fabricated, misrepresented, distorted, or irrelevant evidence to support arguments or claims.
- Do not intentionally use unsupported, misleading, or illogical reasoning.
- Do not represent yourself as informed or as an "expert" on a subject when you are not.
- Do not use irrelevant appeals to divert attention or scrutiny from the issue at hand. Avoid, for instance, "smear" attacks on an opponent's character or appeals to hatred or bigotry.
- Do not ask your audience to link your idea or proposal to emotion-laden values, motives, or goals to which it is actually not related.
- Do not deceive your audience by concealing your real purpose, by concealing self-interest, by concealing the group you represent, or by concealing your position as an advocate of a viewpoint.
- Do not distort, hide, or misrepresent the number, scope, intensity, or undesirable features of consequences or effects.
- Do not use "emotional appeals" that lack a supporting basis of evidence or reasoning, or that would not be accepted if the audience had time and opportunity to examine the subject themselves.
- Do not oversimplify complex, gradation-laden situations into simplistic, two-valued, either-or, polar views or choices.
- Do not pretend certainty where tentativeness and degrees of probability would be more accurate.
- Do not advocate something in which you do not believe yourself.

Source: Richard L. Johannesen, *Ethics in Human Communication,* 4th ed. (Prospect Heights, Ill.: Waveland Press, 1996), p. 34.

sound reasoning. Any attempt to get listeners to act in hasty, unthinking ways is clearly unethical. Discerning listeners will not be moved by a speaker's emotional appeals in the absence of substantiating evidence.

Once you have presented convincing arguments, you can use emotional appeals to kindle your audience's feelings, engage their beliefs, and move them to action. Keep in mind, however, that ethical speaking demands that we treat our listeners as we ourselves would like to be treated when we are audience members.

**Specific Ways to Appeal to Listener Emotions**   Speakers can appeal to audience emotions in a number of ways:

- One of the most common ways of appealing to listeners' emotions is through the use of an *emotionally moving story or illustration.* Discussing basic facts about pay inequity, crowded student housing, or alcoholism among workers is not enough. You need to use specific examples. In this way, the emotional appeal grows from the content of the speech itself.

- Sometimes *your language can* also *evoke emotional responses.* You might describe a competitor, for instance as "profit-driven," "dishonest," or "power-hungry." Or you might describe the philosophy of your own company as "fair-minded," "consumer-oriented," or "loyal to the American tradition of progress." You must be careful if you choose to move your audience in this way, however. Sometimes this technique is simply too obvious. This is especially true if the moving phrases are not developed or supported later in the speech. Thus, stirring words, phrases, and slogans must be used tastefully, ethically, and with restraint.

- Perhaps *the most powerful source of emotional appeal is your sincerity, commitment, and conviction as a persuasive speaker.* You cannot move an audience simply by using the right words and plugging in colorful examples. Audiences are amazingly good at detecting insincerity or apathy. If you are feeling the emotions you wish to arouse in your audience, then everything you say and the way you say it will reinforce your commitment and hopefully convey a compelling message.

Developing
Persuasive
Strategies
for Using
Evidence
We suggested earlier that persuasive speakers are more likely to be successful if they support their views with evidence. Together with pathos and ethos, *logos,* or logical appeals made through the use of sound evidence and reasoning, are a critical part of effective persuasive speaking. In this section, we want to elaborate on the relationship between persuasiveness, the organization of evidence, and credibility.

### Use Sufficient Evidence
First, you need to assess your own credibility in the eyes of the audience. If you are not well known to your audience, or if audience members are hostile to your position or in any way question your authority or motives, you should plan to use abundant evidence. Only those speakers with the highest credibility can make unsubstantiated assertions and still be persuasive.

Equally important, no one has high credibility with all audiences. When you present a proposal, your credibility may be extremely high with those who know you well or those who would benefit from the plan you are advocating. However, for those audience members who perceive themselves to be in competition with you, the ones who have never worked with you or even heard of you, or those who are hostile toward anyone who advocates change, your credibility may be less clearly established. Since most of us are rarely in speaking situations where our credibility is uniformly high with all audience members, the safest strategy is to use evidence to enhance our persuasiveness.

### Use Evidence That Is "News"
Another factor you might want to consider in gathering evidence is whether the audience has heard it before. Using evidence with which the audience is familiar does little to enhance your persuasive impact. If the audience already knows that "professors at this university are paid about $5,000 a year less than those at other Big Ten institutions," they have probably either accepted this evidence as true or rejected it as false. In either case, you have persuaded no one. In short, evidence with which the audience is not familiar is more persuasive than evidence to which they have already been exposed.[6]

### Use Evidence to Promote Future Attitude Change and Make Listeners Resistant to Counterinfluence
Using evidence also plays an important part in long-term attitude change. That is, whenever you are in a position of arguing for some principle of enduring value, something that you want the audience to think about over an extended period of time, or

something about which they do not have to act immediately, you will be more persuasive if you substantiate your ideas with supporting evidence.

In addition, if you know that listeners will be exposed to opposing arguments after listening to you, you can make them more resistant to counterinfluence by using evidence.[7] Suppose, for instance, that you were participating in a public forum on the drug problem in your community, and the event has been organized as a debate. You might speak first, arguing that more money should be devoted to drug education in the elementary and secondary schools. Following your presentation, others might argue that a better way to use resources is to create a drug patrol squad to patrol the schools and to hire more police. In this situation, and others like it, you will have a better chance of being persuasive as you compete with other speakers if your ideas are supported with first-rate evidence.

**Acknowledge Both Sides of the Argument**   Another issue you need to consider is whether you should acknowledge opposing points of view. That is, should you simply present arguments to support your ideas, or should you devote some time to discussing opposing arguments? Most plans, however well conceived, have both advantages and disadvantages. A brilliant idea is expensive. Creating a new division may cause some established departments to be trimmed. Most innovations are accompanied by some risk. Obviously, it is more pleasurable and easier to discuss the strengths of your ideas than to address potential risks or weaknesses. Even so, in most situations, you will be more persuasive if you set forth your own arguments and acknowledge opposing points of view.[8] The only exception might be when you are speaking to an audience that already agrees with you. But when you talk with those who are opposed or ambivalent, those who are bright and well educated, or those who have already heard opposing arguments, you should present both sides. Since most audiences fall into at least one of these categories, the latter is the preferred route.

**Present Evidence Supporting Your Position First**   Once you have decided to present both supporting and opposing arguments, the next concern is how best to arrange them. Should you begin by attacking the opposition or by presenting arguments supporting your own point of view? Usually, the latter course of action is preferable.[9] When listeners are exposed to a speaker's case, they often move in the direction of the speaker's arguments. Once this has happened, they are more likely to stick with the speaker and listen to his or her reasons for opposing other positions. If, by contrast, the speaker begins by pointing to flaws in the opposing arguments (and especially if those arguments are appealing to some audience members), listeners may react defensively by moving even closer to the opposition and becoming more resistant or more closed to the speaker's arguments even before they hear them.

**Establish Common Ground with Listeners before Disagreeing with Them**   Whenever you have to argue against an audience's beliefs, the best approach is to begin by establishing some substantive common ground. Talk about some things both you and the audience hold dear. Suppose you are arguing in favor of increasing property taxes to gain funding for education in your community, and you know that your audience has opposed such increases in the past. You might begin by acknowledging your *mutual* commitment to the welfare of the children of the community and the quality of education within the school corporation. Then you can begin to develop your arguments. Not only is establishing common ground an attention-getting device, but an early affirmation of commonly held values tends to increase the audience's assessment of your credibility as a speaker and makes them more open to hearing your claims.[10]

---

**KEY CONCEPTS 6.1** | **Basic Principles of Persuasive Speaking**

• • *Analyze your audience.*

Acknowledge diversity while identifying common concerns

Understand listener motivation in terms of:
- Habits
- Personal needs
- The need to contribute

• • *Build your credibility*

Establish your competence, trustworthiness, fair-mindedness, and enthusiasm

Use specific techniques, including:
- Establishing common ground
- Building trust
- Reinforcing your status
- Supporting your views with evidence
- Striving for good delivery
- Using presentational aids

• • *Appeal to audience emotions.*

Be mindful of ethics when appealing to listener emotions

Use specific strategies, such as:
- Telling moving stories
- Using emotionally evocative language
- Showing your sincerity and commitment

• • *Develop persuasive strategies for using evidence.*

Use sufficient evidence

Use fresh evidence

Use evidence to promote long-term attitude change

Use evidence to make listeners resistant to counterinfluence

Acknowledge both sides of the argument

Present your side first

Establish common ground with listeners

---

## PROPOSAL PRESENTATIONS

Assume for a moment that you have worked in an organization for several years. Throughout your professional experience, you have learned to communicate effectively, articulating your ideas while listening respectfully to the views of others. Your experience, competence, and interpersonal skills have led you into important group experiences within the organization; you presently belong to several influential committees. But now you find yourself in a slightly different position: You have been asked to present one of your creative marketing concepts to the board of directors, and you must develop a proposal for the board's consideration.

In a sense, you are functioning as a kind of "public" speaker in that you will face an audience and defend a course of action. But the small interacting group is not a typical audience; you are not facing the general public, but a group of organizational members with considerable status and decision-making power. Your success in this kind of situation depends as much on your understanding of the dynamics of this small group audience as it does on the quality of the proposal you put forth.

## Defining the Proposal Presentation

*Proposal presentations* are developed by some member of the organization, often at a superior's request, and delivered to a small group of decision makers. Sometimes presentations are made to small groups of peers, but more often they are delivered to superiors. On occasion, the speaker is not personally acquainted with most members of the audience; he may know them only by reputation. At other times, the speaker may be asked to present a proposal to a small group of high-level executives with whom she consults nearly every day. In either case, proposal presentations require special preparation and practice since those listening are organizational representatives with great demands on their time and energies.

## Preparing for the Presentation

Those who present proposals usually convey a lot of information. They may explain, for example, the meaning of consumer trends or report on matters such as end-of-the-year financial statements. Explaining and reporting are often crucial speaker functions in this context, but the presentational speaker acts largely as a *persuader* in that he or she supports a specific proposal in the presence of decision makers who have the power to accept or reject it.

To be persuasive, proposal presentations must be solution-focused and audience-centered. Presentational speakers are almost invariably proponents of change, agents of innovation. Successful presentational speaking begins with a proposal worth presenting; but it is equally critical that the speaker engage in painstaking preparation, focusing on an analysis of the audience as members of the organizational structure, as individuals, and especially as decision makers within a small group.

**Know the Organization**   As you approach the creation of a proposal presentation, you should recognize that the organization offers a highly structured environment for communication interaction. To varying degrees, all of the formal and informal channels and constraints discussed in Chapter 1 will be operant. For example, presenting a proposal is typically an experience in upward communication. Those to whom you communicate in this context possess both power and status; they are successful executives who can hire and fire and, most significant in this case, accept or reject your proposal. Thus, when you function as a presentational speaker, it is important for you to guard against the tendency to distort information, a common upward communication problem.[11]

Another important aspect of the organizational context is the increasing trend toward specialization. Concomitant with the knowledge explosion came the organizational tendency to seek individuals with increasing depths of expertise.[12] Such depth, however, is often accompanied by considerable narrowness of focus. As a result, the expert who is called upon to make a presentation to a small group of decision makers faces the task of relating her or his expert knowledge to the understanding and needs of the group members. While the problem of audience adaptation is not unique to presentational speakers, the often critical nature of the proposal being presented and the complexities associated with upward communication heighten its importance.

### Know the Immediate Audience

It is only on rare occasions that public speakers know their audiences personally. In this sense, you usually have an advantage in a presentational speaking situation. Often, particularly in smaller organizations, you will know all of the decision makers on a daily working basis. Even if you lack firsthand knowledge, belonging to the organization is an asset; for this allows you access to the information needed to analyze your audience judiciously.

### Understand the Dynamics of the Group

Small group audiences are different from the audiences faced by most public speakers. They have a dynamic quality, possessing psychological bonds, goals, and norms for interacting and decision making. Refer to Chapters 11, 12, 13, and 14 for an extensive consideration of small group communication.

A general understanding of group dynamics allows you to focus on a more specific, in-depth knowledge of the particular group in question. For instance, it is important to discover which members of the group function as leaders. Many assume that the appointed leader is the person to whom arguments should be directed. However, small group research has shown us that appointed leaders may or may not lead the group in a significant sense.[13] What we need to know is which group members *consistently* influence the group. Appeals should be aimed at the most influential individuals.

Equally important is an understanding of how power and status are distributed within the group. Most decision-making groups consist of persons with rather high status within the organization. We might be tempted to assume automatically that a vice president would have more power than a floor supervisor. But, it is more important to identify the *functionally powerful* figures within the group, since high status and power are not invariably associated. Once you have engaged in careful audience analysis, you are ready to plan a fruitful strategy of organization.

### Organize the Proposal

Whenever you make a speech, it is important that your remarks be clearly organized. Like other speeches, the elements of the proposal should be arranged in such a way that they reveal some purposive design. Although different proposals will use different persuasive strategies, several general principles of arrangement take on particular significance because of the organizational context in which proposals are presented. In this sense, then, all proposals should be arranged in accordance with the principles of *unity, coherence, emphasis, completeness,* and *conciseness.*

The principles of unity and coherence are closely related. We usually say that a speech is unified when we can discover a central theme to which each element of the message logically relates. In the context of a proposal presentation, the central purpose is to get the decision-making group to accept and support a given course of action. In a unified presentation, every major subdivision relates to and supports that basic action-oriented theme. This unity is strengthened by the coherence of the arguments as well. Coherence here means that the parts of the message are logically interrelated.

Another basic quality of a well-arranged presentation is emphasis. It is not possible for audiences, even highly skilled decision makers, to digest and remember everything a speaker says. Thus, it is critical that presentations be constructed so that the most important ideas and data are stressed. There are many strategies for emphasizing information. Audiences tend to pay more attention to those arguments they hear first and last.[14] One strategy, then, is to place the strongest arguments early and late in the speech, with less essential ideas in the middle. You can employ a certain amount of repetition as a means of emphasis, although not at the expense of conciseness. Finally, using presentational aids is an effective method of visualizing and stressing critical ideas and statistics.

The fourth characteristic of a well-organized presentation is completeness. Complete presentations are comprehensive—they address the important issues relating to the central theme. The notion of completeness does not imply that you say everything there is to say about a given topic. Rather, it suggests that you present the proposal as completely as possible given the constraints of time and the needs, understanding, and interests of the audience.

Of course, the need to address issues completely and comprehensively must be weighed against the final organizational goal of conciseness. Organizational decision makers need complete information on which to base their decisions. Because of the demands on their time, it is crucial that a complete picture be created in the most concise manner possible. Effective presentations are filled with pertinent information and compelling arguments, but they are never wastefully wordy or unduly repetitious.

## Patterns of Arrangement for Presentational Speaking

As we pointed out in the previous chapter, every effective public presentation should have an introduction, a body, and a conclusion. But there are some special patterns of organization that work particularly well with proposal presentations: the scientific problem-solving pattern, the state-the-case-and-prove-it pattern, and the motivated sequence. We discussed the motivated sequence in Chapter 5; you may want to reread it to refresh your memory. Like the motivated sequence, the patterns presented here could be used with any speech whose goal is to get the audience to take some concrete action.

**Scientific Problem-Solving Pattern**  The first pattern, *scientific problem-solving,* is based on John Dewey's reflective-thinking system.[15] This pattern of organization is most often effective in discussing a relatively complicated problem—especially if the audience is largely ignorant of the facts or if audience hostility is anticipated. Through the scientific approach to problem solving, you lead the audience through a systematic series of steps involving: (1) an introductory definition of the problem (including an understanding of current policies, if any), (2) an exploration of the problem (examining causes and effects), (3) an articulation of criteria to be used in judging the quality of any proposed course of action, (4) an enumeration and evaluation of representative solutions, and (5) the selection of the best solution.

There are a number of advantages to this pattern of organization. When handled effectively, this strategy contributes to your image as an open, fair-minded communicator. You encourage the audience to examine the problem along with you and to consider a variety of possible solutions—not just the particular one you are advocating. With such an approach, members of the audience may feel that they have participated in selecting the best alternative. It is difficult to maintain hostility in the face of such a disarmingly open approach to problem solving.

When the audience is poorly informed, this inductive development of the topic provides a natural framework for the communication of essential information. As a speaker, you do not assume that the audience is already familiar with the problem, its causes, and potential remedies. Rather, you assume that you possess important information which, when shared with the audience, will allow you, together, to discover the best alternative. In this sense, then, the scientific pattern of problem solving creates a feeling of audience participation and has potential for bringing speaker and listeners closer together. Educating the audience has become the vehicle of persuasion.

**State-the-Case-and-Prove-It Pattern**   Another pattern of organization useful for presentational speaking is the *state-the-case-and-prove-it* pattern. This is a relatively simple arrangement entailing the straightforward development of a central thesis with supporting arguments. Normally, each supporting element begins with a contention or topic sentence, followed immediately by substantiating material. Typically, the pattern consists of: (1) an introduction (in which a known problem is briefly acknowledged), (2) a thesis statement, (3) the advancement of a series of contentions (with appropriate elaboration and support), and (4) a concluding summary that repeats the proposition and calls for action.

Whereas the scientific problem-solving pattern is an inductive approach to organization, the state-the-case-and-prove-it pattern is deductive. You begin with a general conclusion and, through the use of specific arguments, attempt to show that it is justified. The speech, then, is one of proof and reinforcement.

The state-the-case-and-prove-it pattern is useful in situations that differ considerably from those that call for the scientific problem-solving approach. Specifically, the state-the-case-and-prove-it pattern is appropriate for organizing the discussion of familiar, much argued, topics of controversy. When the audience is familiar with a particular problem and has perhaps heard it discussed many times before, there is no need for the speaker to explore it gradually and comprehensively. The appropriate strategy is to state one's position clearly, and to systematically support it.

During the introduction of a state-the-case-and-prove-it presentation, you usually acknowledge that the audience is familiar with the problem. Then you explain your reason for reopening a discussion of the issue. It may be that new information has been accumulated or that recent events have modified a previously satisfactory or stable situation. Thus, the controversy needs to be considered from this new perspective. This kind of introduction should leave the audience eager to learn the effects of the new information or situation relating to the old problem.

**Scientific Problem-Solving**

Define the problem.

Explain the problem.

Causes & Effects

Articulate criteria for assessing the solutions.

Examine possible solutions.

Select the best solution.

**State-the-Case-and-Prove-It**

*Briefly* acknowledge the problem.

Advance a thesis.

Advance contentions with supporting evidence.

Offer a concluding summary.

**Motivated Sequence**

Arouse.

Dissatisfy.

Gratify.

Picture.

Move.

Throughout the presentation, you must clearly state the relevance of each supporting element to the general thesis you are advocating. In the conclusion, highlight the significance and value of your arguments, encouraging the audience to reflect on the quality of the proof presented. Then, ask them to support your proposal.

The state-the-case-and-prove-it pattern is solution-heavy. The speaker's goal is to persuade the audience to support his or her particular solution. The challenge, then, is to help listeners realize that the proposed course of action is the one they want to pursue. (See Figure 6.3.)

## Delivering Your Proposal

Because of the relatively intimate communication environment in which proposals are presented, effective delivery is crucial. Here are some guidelines to follow:

- *Use extemporaneous delivery.* You will likely be delivering your presentation in a boardroom environment, perhaps standing (or even seated) at the end of a conference table. You must be direct, flexible, and spontaneous. Your eye contact should include everyone in the room, and you should move and gesture as naturally as possible.

- *Use presentational aids.* When presenting proposals, visuals help the audience follow you, remember your arguments, and picture your plan. Make sure your aids look professional and that you can use them with ease. Check out the room in advance to make sure that the equipment you need is there. Consider using computer-generated graphics (see Chapter 5).

- *Respect time limits.* This group is probably meeting for some time, and you are only a part of their agenda. If your presentation takes more time than they anticipated, listeners may resent being put off their schedule. Leave ample time for questions.

- *Know the group's culture.* Your presentational style should fit in with the group's culture and norms as much as possible. They may prefer a presentation that is highly interactive, allowing for questions along the

*Proposal presentations are usually delivered in a small group setting. When advancing a proposal for consideration and possible approval, speakers often use visual reinforcement to enhance their persuasive appeal.*

way, or they may want a brief presentation, followed by an extensive question-and-answer period. The more you know about their expectations and preferences, the more easily you will be able to connect with them and deliver your proposal presentation effectively.

---

**KEY CONCEPTS 6.2** | **Proposal Presentations**

When preparing and presenting a proposal presentation, remember to:

- • Understand the organization as a communicative context.

- • Undertake a detailed analysis of the small group audience.

- • Understand listeners as members of a dynamic small group.

- • Organize your proposal according to principles of:
  Unity
  Coherence
  Emphasis
  Completeness
  Conciseness

- • Choose an appropriate organizational pattern:
  Scientific problem-solving
  State-the-case-and-prove-it pattern
  Motivated sequence

- • Deliver your proposal effectively by:
  Being extemporaneous
  Using presentational aids
  Respecting time limits
  Adapting to the group's culture

---

## PERSUASION: SALES PRESENTATIONS

The key to success for any organization is sales: Unless someone can sell the organization's services or products to someone else, that organization simply will not survive. Unlike proposal presentations, sales presentations occur between an organization and its environment (such as an individual customer or another organization) rather than within the organization. The speaker acts as a representative for himself or herself, his or her organization, and that organization's products or services.

Like the proposal presentation, the sales presentation typically is given before a small group. Groups to which sales presentations are made may take many forms, depending on the product or service being sold and the organization of which the group is a part. As consultants, for example, the authors have found themselves trying to sell their consulting services to groups of top-level university administrators; members of the personnel department of a major airline; a nursing task force consisting of staff nurses and first-level nursing supervisors; a vice president of engineering and his immediate staff; the vice president of human resources, director of training, director of labor relations, and training manager of a major insurance company; and the entire middle management group (approximately 10 people) of a small manufacturing firm. In situations like these, success depends on several things:

knowledge of your own product or service, an understanding of the organization to which you are selling, and a sensitivity to the characteristics, needs, and biases of the group to which you are speaking directly.

Preparing for
the Sales
Presentation As in any speaking situation, the most important work occurs before the actual presentation takes place. Careful preparation significantly enhances your chances for success; poor preparation virtually guarantees failure.

In preparing your sales presentation, you need to do several things. First, gain information about your audience and the speaking situation. Second, use that information to outline your presentation. Finally, prepare supporting materials (such as visual aids) to use during the presentation.

**Gaining Information**   Typically, you will not be acquainted with the group to whom you are selling. However, you will probably have some contact with at least one member of that group, if only to schedule your presentation. During that initial contact, try to learn as much of the following information as you can:

**1.** *Who will make the decision concerning purchase of the service or product?*
**2.** *Who will be attending the meeting?* Learn how many people are coming (so you know what to expect and how many copies of handout materials you need to bring) and what positions these people hold.
**3.** *If the decision maker is not scheduled to be part of that meeting, why not?* Typically, meetings that do not include the decision maker are not very productive for the sales presenter.
**4.** *How long is the meeting to last?* Obviously, you will need to tailor your presentation to fit the time limitations.
**5.** *Why is this organization considering purchasing this service or product?* In other words, what are the needs? Some needs-analysis questions can be extremely helpful, enabling you to show specifically how your service or product will help this organization.
**6.** *What criteria will be used to make the decision?* Occasionally, this information is not known by the person making the arrangements with you, but if you can get it, you will know what things to emphasize in your remarks.
**7.** *What physical arrangements or equipment are or can be available?* Be sure to ask for any room arrangement you prefer and for any equipment (such as an overhead projector or a videotape player) you need.

Obtaining this sort of information and then using it to shape your presentation will enable you to provide an efficient, effective view of your service or product.

**Organizing the Presentation**   In the preceding section, we considered several organizational patterns for proposal presentations. Any of these patterns might be appropriate for a sales presentation as well. However, there is another pattern that we find equally effective and that parallels the procedures followed during a sales interview: the *Introduction–Need–Presentation–Close (INPC) model.*

Following this model, the *introduction* phase should do several things. First, it should identify who you are and what organization you represent. In a brief statement, give your name and title in your organization, your organization's name, how long your organization has been in this business (if appropriate), your organization's specialties or notable achievements, and some customers who use your products or services. This information helps the group to feel that they are dealing with an experienced, reputable organization and sales representative.

Next, briefly state the purpose of your presentation: to ask some questions of the group (if you have a need and desire to do so), to describe your product or service, and then answer any questions they might have.

Finally, establish the climate for the presentation. Experience shows that informal, extemporaneous presentations are more effective in sales situations. To create such a climate, you might make a statement like "I intend to be fairly informal in my remarks, so please feel free to ask questions whenever you like. And I'll ask you any questions that I have as well." This statement encourages two-way communication between you and the group, and it provides a more relaxed atmosphere for everyone.

The *need* portion of the presentation is important as well. Obviously, some need must exist; otherwise it is unlikely that you would have been asked to make this presentation in the first place. To establish the need, you might simply address a question to the group as a whole, such as "Why are you considering this service or product now?" The group spokesperson or leader probably would provide an answer, looking to other group members for support. However, since this approach might make you seem unprepared, it probably would be better simply to describe the organization's needs as you see them, based on your preparatory conversations. Finally, you could describe typical needs you have found in other similar organizations. By watching audience reactions to the typical needs you describe, you probably will be able to determine which needs are present here.

*Presentation* of your product or service occurs once the needs have been established. Typically, this presentation will consist of three steps: provide an overview of what the product is and how it works or of how the service is performed (taking the group through a step-by-step sequence); describe particularly important features of your product or service as they respond to the group's needs; and explain the benefits of your product or service to the group or their organization.

The *close* in a sales presentation is a bit complicated. Typically, the group will need to meet after you have left to make their decision. Indeed, they may also have met with other sales representatives or have such meetings scheduled in the near future, so that they need to consider the competitors' services or products as well. In short, it is highly unlikely that the group will be able or willing to make a decision while you are there. Therefore, asking for their decision would be inappropriate and potentially embarrassing.

Instead, the close of a sales presentation should do two things. First, it should summarize the benefits you illustrated when you tied the features of your product or service to the organization or group's needs. Again, it is these benefits that should cause the group to select your product or service, and you must make sure they are understood and remembered. Second, you might summarize why the group should choose you and your organization. Refer to the information you provided during the introduction about your organization's experience and reputation. Many products and services are very similar; the unique qualifications of your organization may be the determining factor that gets you the sale.

Finally, ask for *questions*. If the group has asked questions during your presentation, there may be few or none at this point. Our experience, however, has been that many questions are asked and that this is one of the most important elements of the sales presentation. The questions you are asked reveal those things that the group found most important (or most difficult to understand) and thus those things that you need to stress again. The questions may also reveal the individual biases or preferences of the members, allowing you to direct your remarks even more specifically to their concerns. By handling questions effectively, you not only maintain the positive impression you have created up to this point but advance your cause significantly. When preparing for the presentation, try to anticipate questions the group might ask and have answers ready. Figure 6.4 depicts the INPC model.

**Preparing Supporting Materials**   The presentation phase of the presentation often benefits significantly from the use of presentational aids. As discussed in Chapter 5, aids such as chalkboards, flipcharts, overhead transparencies, models, and varied computer-generated graphics add clarity and interest to the presentation. As a rule, every sales presentation should be accompanied by some form of presentational aid (and usually, more than one). In preparing for the presentation, develop aids that are professional in appearance, neat, and communicative, and that add to the credibility of your organization and your product or service.

## Delivering the Sales Presentation

We have already noted some elements involved in delivering the sales presentation:

It should be delivered extemporaneously.

It should be somewhat informal in tone.

It should involve the use of presentational aids.

It should allow for questions and answers.

In addition, we should note that the characteristics of effective delivery presented in Chapter 5 apply here as well. An effective sales presentation is characterized by a delivery that is spontaneous, direct, flexible, and involving.

Particularly important in a sales presentation are the elements of spontaneity and flexibility. As you present your introduction, need, presentation, and close, you must be sensitive to feedback (verbal and nonverbal) from the audience and must adjust to that feedback appropriately. Sometimes the feedback and adjustment are obvious: Someone interrupts your presentation to ask a question, and you adjust by giving an answer. More often, however, feedback and adjustment are subtle, requiring extreme sensitivity and flexibility on the part of the speaker. In this section, we will consider briefly how to read reactions, interpret them, and adjust to them.

**Reading and Reacting to Listeners' Reactions: Highlighting Nonverbal Behaviors**   While knowledge of your product is important, perhaps even more important is knowledge of people. You need to understand the people to whom you talk. You need to know how to read their feelings and reactions accurately and what to do about the things you perceive. With this ability, you are almost certain to be successful. Without it, success will be very difficult to achieve.

FIGURE 6.4    The INPC sales presentation

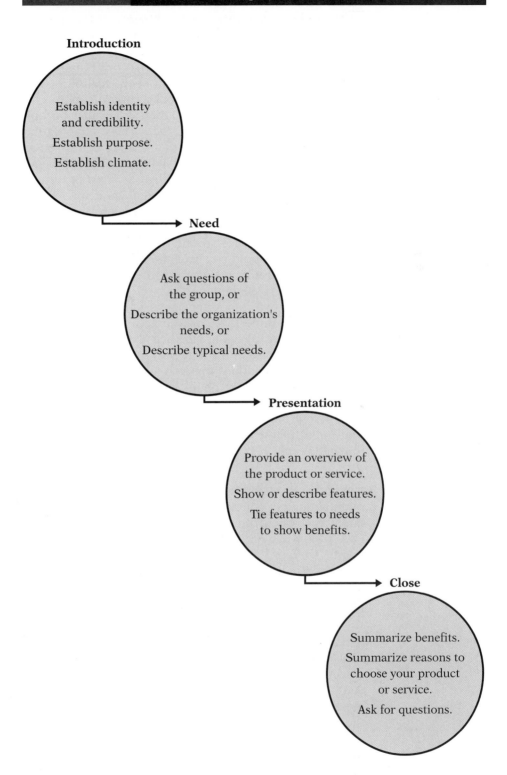

**Introduction**

Establish identity
and credibility.

Establish purpose.

Establish climate.

**Need**

Ask questions of
the group, or

Describe the organization's
needs, or

Describe typical needs.

**Presentation**

Provide an overview of
the product or service.

Show or describe features.

Tie features to needs
to show benefits.

**Close**

Summarize benefits.

Summarize reasons to
choose your product
or service.

Ask for questions.

At the outset, you must remember one important fact: words often tell very little about how a person feels. We express most of our feelings with our eyes, gestures, and voice. Research suggests that only about 7 percent of the feelings we convey are expressed through our words. Another 38 percent (roughly) are expressed through the tone of voice we use—rate of speech, voice inflection, pitch, volume, and so on. Finally, our face, eyes, and gestures account for about 55 percent of the feeling we convey.[16] See Chapter 8 for further discussion of nonverbal communication.

To read people accurately, then, you must become skillful at noticing quick changes in the eyes and face. These changes may be incredibly fast, lasting only a half to a quarter of a second. But if you are observant, you can perceive changes as specific as enlargement of someone's pupils (often a sign of interest), as well as general changes in body posture.

While you speak, the group members are constantly sending messages about their feelings and reactions. Most informative are the eyes: if someone likes you or is interested in your presentation, her or his eyes will seem to brighten as the muscles around the eyes tense. On the other hand, if the person wishes you would go away, the muscles around the eyes may be relaxed, with the face drooping slightly. More than any other factor, the eyes reveal what the mind is thinking.

There are two important dangers in trying to read body language. First, you cannot assume that specific actions have particular meanings. Folded arms may mean rejection, but they also may mean that the individual is cold or is just comfortable in that position. Second, you should not try to keep track of so many actions that you lose your concentration. But if you are able to focus on some general body language groupings, then you might be able to use nonverbal cues to your advantage.

There are five basic groups of nonverbal (and occasionally, verbal) cues that indicate how a person is feeling, together with our suggestions for how to handle each:

*Group 1: Approval*   Nonverbal cues may indicate positive acceptance of you and your claims. Signs of approval include leaning forward toward you, maintaining eye contact, changes in vocal inflection (an animated voice), frequent gestures, a pleasant, smiling expression, frequent head nods, raised eyebrows, willing responses to your questions, and vocal indications of agreement ("Uh-huh," "Yeah," and so on). Sometimes a customer will express approval verbally as well, using approval statements such as "That sounds good" or "I really like that." Such verbal and nonverbal expressions should indicate to you that the customer likes what you are saying and accepts the feature, benefit, or proof you have offered.

*Handling Approval*   When you see signs of approval, what do you do? First, consider closing. If the meeting has gone on for some time, with the group agreeing with or showing interest in the features and benefits you described, you may ask for questions at this point. However, if it is still very early in the meeting, you may decide closing is premature. Instead, you might reinforce the approval.

Sales usually are the result of a series of agreements. If the group seems to be approving, try to get the members to make an open commitment, saying that they agree with a benefit you have described. For example, you might ask the entire group, "You seem to feel that the cases in this book are particularly good. Is that right?" Such reinforcement makes these small battles you have won more memorable and more influential when you try to win the entire war later on. Finally, move on to another point. Once agreement has been obtained or interest shown, it is tempting to continue to "beat the point to death." After all, agreement and interest are pleasant for you, and you are likely to do what you can to get them to continue. However, when agreement has been obtained, note the point of agreement in your mind and then move on to the next point.

*Group 2: Confusion*   While describing features or benefits, you may perceive signs of puzzlement. These signs are important: many people will choose not to ask questions, either because they do not wish to appear uninformed or stupid or because they do not want to prolong the meeting. It is important that you be sensitive to these signs and respond to them appropriately. Nonverbal signs of confusion or lack of understanding include a slight scowl or frown, narrowing of the eyes, tilting the head to one side, raising the eyebrows, or pursing the lips. Verbally, a confused person might ask to have a point repeated, give a response that is "off the wall," ask for an explanation, or give vocal cues such as "Huh?" or "What?" It is important to pick up such signs. Understanding must be achieved if the group is to be convinced to buy what you are selling.

*Handling Confusion*   When you perceive confusion, first review what you just said but in a different way. Say something like, "Let me go over that again, because it's important." Give the group another chance to follow your thinking. If that seems ineffective, blame yourself and ask for a reaction. Noting continued puzzlement, you might say, "I'm really not explaining this very well. Is this making any sense at all?" Alternatively, you might note that others often find this point confusing and again ask for a reaction. For example: "It seems like a lot of people have trouble understanding this. Am I explaining it all right?" Finally, you might simply respond to the reaction. If someone is reluctant to indicate confusion or lack of understanding, your question may prompt the person to admit confusion and tell you what specifically is unclear. However, if the person's reluctance to indicate confusion stems from a desire to get the conversation over with, he or she may insist that everything is perfectly clear, even though he or she is genuinely confused. Therefore, you might review the point one more time, still watching for nonverbal signs of confusion, and then move on to your next point. If you are not convinced that the person understands, look for an opportunity later in the meeting to return to the source of confusion and review it one last time.

*Group 3: Skepticism*   Sometimes listeners find it difficult to believe what you are saying. After all, they may have been subjected to dozens of sales calls from representatives and may have heard the same claims repeated by each. It is only natural for them to be a little suspicious of the things you (and all the other reps) say. Common nonverbal signs of skepticism including raising one eyebrow, tilting the head backward, tilting the head forward and peering out from under the eyebrows, shifting from an open posture to one that is more closed (perhaps by folding the arms or crossing legs), frowning or scowling, narrowing the eyes, looking away from you, or shaking the head.

Some verbal signs of skepticism include "Do you really expect me to believe that . . . ?" and "Well, I rather doubt that . . . ." Each of these statements suggests that your points are not being accepted and that you will need to take some action to convince the group.

*Handling Skepticism* When you perceive skepticism, you first might ask about the behaviors you have observed: "You seem skeptical about this. Do you have some reservations about what I'm saying?" This question invites the group members to state openly any concerns they might have—concerns that otherwise might go unspoken and unanswered. Then respond appropriately to stated reservations and invite the group to raise any other reservations in their minds. Finally, to handle persistent skepticism, you must offer some sort of proof for what you have claimed. Continue to provide proof until the group accepts the validity of your point or it becomes clear that someone is expressing a personal objection rather than skepticism about a particular feature. When such an objection emerges, handle it as you would any other objection.

*Group 4: Indifference* When customers see sales representatives frequently, it becomes easy for them to adopt an attitude of indifference. They have sat through countless presentations, each of which makes the same claims and uses the same buzz words. They have become jaded, adopting an unspoken attitude of "All right, so tell me how *your* product or service is better than all the others." The more experienced they are, the more likely they are to adopt such an indifferent attitude.

Several nonverbal cues convey indifference, including "hanging" facial muscles, a slumped or overly relaxed posture, an expressionless face, a posture that leans away from you, a tapping or wiggling foot, heavy sighs, frequent changes of posture (squirming), drumming the fingers or tapping with some object, and providing very little response to your questions. In addition, the group may simply agree with everything you say, giving no direct expression of indifference but at the same time giving you nothing to go on. To get a sale, you have to motivate them before they will have any interest in the features and benefits you describe.

*Handling Indifference* When you see indifference, stop selling and ask questions designed to uncover needs. The specific question you ask to identify needs is determined by the reason for the group's indifference. If the group sees no need for your product, ask questions for background information. For example:

"Tell me about your work."

"What things need to be improved?"

If the organization has a self-developed procedure, ask about the procedure to see if there might be any problems. For example:

"What have you liked best about that procedure?"

"What things would you improve if you could?"

"What problems have you had?"

"Tell me more about how your system works."

If the client is satisfied with a competitor, ask about the competing product or service, to identify possible problems. For example:

"What do you like most about . . . ?"

"What things might be improved . . . ?"

"What problems have you had . . . ?"

"What complaints have employees offered?"

Often, customers do not want to express their lack of interest. They know you will try to give answers, and rather than taking the time to hear your answers, they decide to suffer through the presentation in silence, ask for a brochure, and let you leave. You cannot afford this type of treatment; you have invested time to put yourself in front of this group, and a meaningful conversation is important. By forcing them to talk to you, you are more likely to uncover some needs that can be met or some problems that can be answered, and in so doing increase the chances of getting a sale.

*Group 5: Objections*   Several nonverbal cues, when shown in combination, often indicate objections to you and your product or service: folded arms, crossed legs, clenched fists or tense hands, posture turned away from you (with shoulders at an angle), frowns, tight lips or facial grimace, avoidance of eye contact, flat voice with very little variance in volume or pitch, and very short answers to your questions. Verbal objections generally show clear disagreement with your arguments or focus on perceived disadvantages of your product.

During your presentation, people are likely to raise complaints, objections, questions, and other roadblocks to a potential sale. Much of your effectiveness throughout the sales call will be determined by how well you deal with the objections that come up. While each client and each situation is different, there are some common reasons why objections are raised and, in some cases, why a particular client seems to be more resistant than others.

Some clients raise objections because they simply want more information or because they don't know what they want or need. Rather than resisting your sales effort, they are expressing an objection to receive assurance on some doubtful point or because they have not properly understood your presentation. For example, they might object because not enough benefits are yet apparent. Indeed, this is the reason for most objections, and once a client sees enough benefits, there is no longer a reason to object.

On the other hand, some clients raise objections based on hidden motives: to show you that they are intelligent, clever, and not an easy sale; because they are tired of seeing the parade of sales representatives knocking at their door; as a stalling tactic to avoid making a decision at this time; because they already have made up their minds but do not want to say no to your face; or because they are resistant to change.

There are many other reasons, of course, why clients raise objections to your claims. Most objections reflect legitimate concern or curiosity about the content and features of your product or service. And each objection gives you an opportunity to exercise your skills as a sales representative.

*Handling Objections*   There are four basic strategies for dealing with objections a client raises. First, you could *meet the objection directly*. This sort of approach handles the objection in an assertive manner, supported by specific evidence. It requires that you be well organized and thoroughly familiar with the features of your product or service. It can be an extremely effective way of dealing with objections as they arise.

Second, you could *sidestep the objection*. If an objection does not seem to be a major concern in the client's mind, you can simply avoid it. But be careful; while sidestepping an objection avoids wasting time discussing trivial matters, you must judge carefully whether the objection is trivial or not. If you sidestep an objection that really is important to the client, you may lose the sale.

*Minimizing the objection* is a third approach, which strives to reduce the impact of objections. You can implement this approach verbally (through the things you say in response) and nonverbally (through your physical reactions). To minimize an objection verbally, you first might remind the client of benefits he or she already has accepted—benefits that might outweigh the objection that has been raised. In reviewing those benefits, first begin with some introductory phrase, such as

"Let's look again at your overall needs."

"Remember some of the things we have talked about."

"Look at the big picture for a second."

Then summarize the benefits already agreed to. However, if there are no benefits to review or if the list does not seem to outweigh the objection, then you need to question to uncover needs. In other words, you start the need and presentation steps over again, in an effort to build a case for your product. Eventually, you hope to compile a list of agreed-to benefits that will outweigh this objection.

Nonverbal reactions can be used to minimize objections, although they must be used carefully. Raising your eyebrows in surprise, for example, indicates your amazement that such an objection would even be raised. Similarly, frowning or shaking your head indicates that, in your opinion, a minor point has been raised. A heavy sigh, shrugging your shoulders, and turning your head away are other signals that you do not view this matter to be important. The client then may simply drop the objection, realizing that it is not a major issue, and you can proceed to more important matters. However, the client also may press the point, which lets you know that the objection is not minor in her or his mind, necessitating a discussion of why the objection can be overcome or is of secondary importance.

The biggest danger in using nonverbal cues to minimize objections is that you may anger the client. The issue may indeed be very important in the client's mind, and your sigh or shrug may offend the client. For that reason, minimizing objections nonverbally should be used very carefully.

*Giving in to an objection* is appropriate when you just cannot win the point. For example:

**You:** I really think this book would meet your needs.

**Client:** Well, that may be. But I have already decided to adopt another text.

**You:** Which one?

**Client:** The one I just wrote.

Another example:

**You:** This new edition is far more attractive visually than the second edition was.

**Client:** Actually, I don't think so. All the illustrations are blue, and there is scientific evidence that blue is more difficult for the eye to distinguish. I absolutely refuse to use a book with all blue illustrations.

When there is no way of overcoming an objection or the objection shows a legitimate preference for a competitor, you may have to give in. But there still may be other ways to get a sale. For example, you might suggest the client use one of your other products or services, admit this one problem but try to counter with other more important advantages, or simply move to other needs the client has. Giving in on an objection does not mean giving up.

By watching for, interpreting, and responding to feedback from the client group, you add significantly to the effectiveness of your sales presentation.

Certainly, there may be other groups of nonverbal and verbal cues that indicate specific reactions or feelings. For our purposes, however, the groups listed above are most relevant, and it is these you should look for and try to read and treat effectively when making a presentation.

## SUMMARY

This concluding chapter has introduced you to two of the specific kinds of persuasive speaking contexts you are likely to encounter as you move into jobs requiring professional training and perhaps involving some managerial responsibility. Often, these presentations are delivered to very important people—board members, upper-level managers, potential customers—in short, people who can make the difference in your professional opportunities and the success of your organization.

Because both sales and proposal presentations are specific kinds of persuasive speeches, it is important to understand the basic nature of persuasion. Among other things, you must consider audience members' sources of motivation, as well as their needs and values. Equally crucial is being seen as credible (that is, as trustworthy, competent, fair-minded, and dynamic) in the eyes of the audience. Knowing how to appeal to audience emotions (within an ethical framework) and how to use evidence in ways that advance arguments and make listeners resistant to counterinfluence attempts is also critical to effective persuasive speaking.

Although we have suggested specific concerns and techniques that may be useful in special public communication contexts, we also want to emphasize that *the underlying principles of effective public speaking are quite similar across situations.* That is, in every speech situation, you must prepare carefully, know your material or product, carefully analyze the audience, clearly and strategically organize your remarks, and present your ideas or information using effective (usually extemporaneous) delivery. And *each* time you prepare to give a speech, you must not lose sight of the transactional nature of communication. When you deliver public speeches, you still exchange roles of sender and receiver. You hope to influence others' ideas and decisions, but as you watch and hear others react to your thinking and arguments, you, too, are often influenced.

That is, in public speaking, as in other communication contexts, you participate in a dynamic process in which all participants share control.

# QUESTIONS FOR DISCUSSION

1. Discuss some of the basic elements influencing human motivation. How significant do you consider each of these elements? Can you think of other motivational factors to add to the factors considered in the book?

2. What are some of the ways in which organizations (and their leaders) demonstrate their "commitment to contribution"? Cite specific examples.

3. What are some things you can do as a speaker to establish your credibility with listeners?

4. How important are emotional appeals in persuasive speaking? What are some specific ways of appealing to audience emotions?

5. How can you use evidence most persuasively? Be specific.

6. In what ways might a small group audience differ from a traditional public speaking audience? How might the differences affect your preparation as a speaker?

7. Explain the following: unity, coherence, emphasis, completeness, and conciseness.

In what ways might these qualities of organization be particularly relevant for speakers who are preparing proposal presentations?

8. Under what circumstances (topic, audience, personal point of view) would you elect to use the following patterns of organization? Why?
   a. Scientific problem solving.
   b. State-the-case-and-prove-it pattern.
   c. Motivated sequence.

9. You are talking to the person who has invited you to make a sales presentation. What kinds of questions should you ask to gain information you need?

10. Briefly describe the INPC model of organization. How does it differ from (and how is it similar to) the patterns of organization referred to in question 9?

11. Reading and reacting to listener reactions when giving a sales presentation are crucial. Name at least two reactions you might look for and describe how you might handle each.

# EXERCISES

1. In a 250-word typewritten essay, respond to the following: Choose an organization to which you have belonged for at least one year (for instance, a sorority, a church, a volunteer organization, or a speech or accounting club). Now assume that you have been asked to present a proposal to this group's executive board. You have come up with a proposal—presenting a plan or course of action for this group to endorse. For example, you might want your fraternity to sponsor a dance marathon to raise money for cancer research.

   With a specific group in mind, analyze your "audience." Consider your small group audience both as individuals and as a dynamic, interacting whole. Be specific in terms of their habits, needs, and other motives. What are their similarities? In what ways are they diverse? Which listeners are most powerful or most respected?

   Based on your analysis, what specific things will you do to enhance the chances that they will accept your proposal (in terms of preparation, organization, and presentation)? Justify your choices.

2. Select a product or service with which you have had some experience and which impresses you very much. Prepare and deliver a four- to five-minute sales presentation to your classmates in which you attempt to sell them the product. Prepare at least three visual aids, and follow the INPC model of organization. As you deliver your presentation, pay particular attention to listener reactions.

   Following your presentation, respond to listener questions, following the guidelines for handling confusion, skepticism, and so on, as discussed in the text.

   When you are finished, ask your classmates to complete the following form:

Name of speaker: _____

Product or service: _____

Indicate below how likely you are to buy this product or service:

Extremely likely _____
Somewhat likely _____
Undecided _____
Somewhat unlikely _____
Extremely unlikely _____

Briefly explain the bases for your reactions:

_____

_____

Collect the forms, read through them, and decide what changes you would make if you were to give this sales presentation a second time to the same or a very similar audience.

# CASE application 6.1

*Making Strategic Choices in Preparing and Presenting a Proposal*

James Goodman is a computer analyst in an automobile manufacturing organization. His boss has asked him to present a proposal advocating the purchase of a new, expensive, and fairly controversial computer for the organization. The small group to which Goodman is to make the presentation is composed of: (1) the vice president for research and development (young, innovative, flexible, liberal); (2) the director of finance (middle-aged, rigid, conservative, in favor of the status quo); (3) the supportive boss who made the request; (4) the director of data analysis (young, brilliant, cautious, conservative); and (5) the president (near retirement, moderate on most issues, listens mostly to the advice of the vice presidents in the organization).

## Questions

1. Given the expense of the computer, the controversiality concerning its worth, and the nature of the audience, what strategy should Goodman adopt?
2. What assumptions might he make about the dynamics of this particular small group?
3. What pattern of arrangement would be most appropriate? Why?
4. What are some lines of argument that might be especially effective?
5. How should Goodman use evidence to be most persuasive?

# CASE application 6.2

*Selling Good Food*

Susan West works for Healthy Options, a food service organization that provides healthy food alternatives to more traditional foods. The organization emphasizes low-fat, low-cholesterol, high-fiber diets and promotes vegetarianism (although some of the products contain poultry and fish).

Susan's job is to try to sell this food service to colleges and universities throughout the United States. Currently, she is scheduled to make a sales presentation to the director of food services and his administrative staff at a large public university located in the South. She has studied the food services this university currently offers students and has found numerous fast-food options, along with dorm menus that feature the influence of Southern cooking (including fried chicken, biscuits and gravy, and heavy desserts).

Susan's persuasive challenge appears substantial.

## Questions

1. What additional information should Susan obtain before planning her presentation?
2. What are some of the biggest objections that Susan will have to be prepared to address? How can she best present her evidence and ideas to deal with those objections?
3. How might she organize her presentation? Why would this pattern likely be effective?
4. Should Susan use emotional appeals? If so, what kinds would be most moving? If not, why not?
5. How might Susan deliver her sales presentation so that her listeners are most likely to be receptive, or at least open to considering Healthy Options alternatives?

# PART three

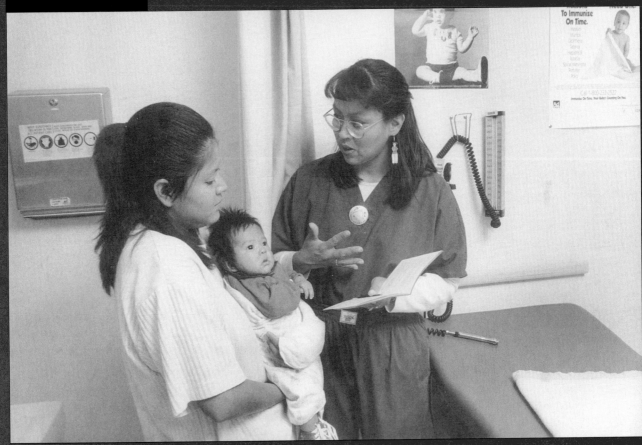

# Dyadic Communication

**WHETHER I'M SELLING OR BUYING,** whether I'm hiring or being hired, whether I'm negotiating a contract or responding to someone else's demands, I want to know where the other person is coming from. I want to know the other person's real self.

—*Mark H. McCormack*, **What They Don't Teach You at Harvard Business School**

# Interpersonal Communication within Organizations: Fundamental Concepts

As organizations become more technologically sophisticated, one might expect human relationships to take on decreasing importance. Quite the contrary, argues John Naisbitt in his best-seller, *Megatrends: Ten New Directions Transforming Our Lives.* He contends that people have a need to be together. Even when most work is done by computer and people have the choice of working in their own homes, he says, "very few people will be willing to stay home all of the time and tap out messages to the office. People want to go to the office. People want to be with people, and the more technology we pump into the society, the more people will want to be with people."[1] To be successful in tomorrow's organization, you will need to establish and maintain good relationships with others.

In many respects, this chapter will serve as a basis for all the chapters that follow. We will consider human relationships and the communication behaviors that compose them. After examining the components of relationships, we will discuss the specific communication elements that bring those relationships about: receiving and sending. Then we will offer some communication strategies whereby relationships in all settings—dyadic, group, and organizational—might be improved.

## THE DIMENSIONS OF HUMAN RELATIONSHIPS IN ORGANIZATIONS

Several theorists have tried to identify the dimensions that make up our relationships. Timothy Leary and his associates concluded from their studies of therapists and patients that relationships have two dimensions: dominance (that is, the extent to which each person makes decisions the other follows) and affection (the extent to which each person likes the other).[2] Later research by Schutz suggested three dimensions: control (or dominance), affection, and inclusion (or the extent to which people identify and interact with each other).[3] Bales observed relationships in groups and found them to consist of positiveness-negativeness (or attraction), power (or dominance), and movement toward the group goal (a group task–related dimension).[4]

If you think about your relationship with someone at work, you probably will see the validity of these dimensions. You have feelings toward that person, just as he or she has feelings (likes and dislikes) toward you. One of you probably has higher status and/or greater influence over the relationship than the other. Certainly, you interact and identify with each other to some degree. Thus, research and our own experiences point to three relationship dimensions: *attraction,* an index of liking or affection; *dominance,* a measure of power or control; and *involvement,* an index of identification with the other person, of unity, and of active inclusiveness. To these should be added a fourth dimension, *situation*, which considers the physical, social, and task environment of the encounter, for all three have some impact upon relationship development.

Attraction

The first dimension considers the degree to which the participants feel positively or negatively about one another. Many factors influence the extent to which we are attracted to someone else. The first of these is *physical proximity*—the sheer accident of physical location determines to a large degree those to whom we will be attracted. Employees working in the same department, for example, see one another relatively often, and relationships between them are likely to form as a result. But we need to emphasize that while contact produces feelings about others, those feelings are not necessarily positive. That is, to dislike someone intensely, we would need to see that person frequently as well. Thus, physical proximity simply causes us to come into contact with others, giving us an opportunity to form opinions about them and develop attraction toward (or repulsion from) them.

Although society tells us that we should not judge a book by its cover or judge people by their appearance, research indicates that we do exactly that. Indeed, *physical attractiveness* seems to be the second major determinant of our attraction to someone else. People who find one another physically attractive, regardless of sex, are more likely to talk with one another and form

*When people work together collaboratively in organizational settings, they need to have a good relationship. Working in close proximity and dressing professionally usually contribute to a positive interpersonal relationship and an enhanced ability to interact effectively.*

friendships. Conversely, people who are extremely unattractive have fewer social contacts and, as a result, fewer friendships.

Third, attraction is influenced by *interpersonal similarity*.[5] A substantial body of research demonstrates that we prefer the company of people who are like ourselves. Similarity in attitudes, values, socioeconomic status, and background determines to some extent the degree to which people are mutually attracted.[6] In organizations, this tendency has been shown to be related to satisfaction with supervisors—employees who were similar in important respects to their immediate supervisors were more satisfied with supervision than were employees who were significantly different from their supervisors.[7] In employment interviews, the interviewers gave more positive evaluations to applicants who were similar biographically to themselves.[8] Clearly, we are more attracted to people like ourselves.

Two final determinants of attraction are *status* and *personal rewards*. People holding status higher than our own are more attractive to us, while people of lesser status tend to be less attractive. People who provide us (or potentially can provide us) with personal rewards are more attractive, while those who will not or cannot reward us are less attractive. Not surprisingly, we are more attracted to people who evaluate us positively or give us praise and less attracted to people who criticize us.[9]

## Dominance

The ability of one person to exert some control or influence over another seems to be a product of three things: the characteristics of the person trying to exert influence, the characteristics of the person receiving the influence attempts, and the influence strategies employed by the person trying to dominate.[10] A person is more influential if he or she wants to exert influence in the first place, if he or she is perceived as an expert in the topic area under discussion, if he or she is skillful in exerting influence, and if he or she has higher status than the people being influenced. On the other hand, the recipient of the influence attempt is more likely to be influenced if he or she wants to obtain rewards or avoid punishments controlled by the source, if he or she likes the source, or if he or she can be convinced that the source's recommendation is the right thing to do. All these characteristics of sources and recipients come into play in the organizational setting.

## Involvement

A third dimension considers the degree to which we are involved with someone else, or the breadth and depth of our relationship with him or her. Some relationships are rich and intense; others are quite superficial. Social psychologists Altman and Taylor suggest that relationships develop in increments, moving from superficial to more intimate levels.

> As two individuals learn more about each other, largely through observing each other's behavior and through self-disclosure, their relationship grows in importance. The number of topics discussed (breadth) and the depth of information shared suggest whether the relationship can be defined as casual or intimate. With casual relationships breadth is often high, but depth is low. The most intimate relationships have high breadth and depth. As individuals disclose information that is central to the relationship, depth increases.[11]

Altman and Taylor's model is useful in understanding the dimensions of involvement and the communication elements that contribute to intimate relationships. Many individuals function effectively in professional settings by maintaining mostly casual relationships. But when greater intimacy is desired, increasing both depth and breadth of interaction can be helpful.[12]

**Situation**   The fourth human relationship dimension existing between people is the situation, which considers environments in which communication occurs. Three aspects of the situation seem particularly influential in interpersonal relationships. First, as the next chapter describes, the *physical environment* influences interaction among the individuals.[13] Such things as office furniture arrangement can influence the dominance dimension of interpersonal relationships, while the attractiveness of the surroundings may influence interpersonal attraction. Second, the *social environment* affects interaction.[14] The number of persons present, the role behaviors expected of the interactants, and the social hierarchy have some impact upon relationships. Finally, the *tasks and purposes present* in the encounter affect relationship development. This aspect of the situation takes into account both the observable goals of the individuals and the motivations underlying their behaviors.

From the preceding description of situation, it would seem that all relationships are situationally determined. However, the distinction must be made between long- and short-term situations. In the long term, the president of an organization is higher in dominance than the manager of employee relations. When discussing actions that should be taken during an employee strike, however, the manager is dominant by virtue of his or her expertise. Employees presenting their recommendations to top management are dominant during that particular meeting, although their long-term status is much lower than that of the people to whom they are speaking. Finally, while everyone attending a meeting may hold the same job in the organization, the person who, by luck or design, is seated at the head of the long conference table often will exert the most dominance during that meeting. Thus, while the organization itself might be considered a situation that influences attraction, dominance, and involvement, our intent here is to call attention to short-term influences that affect relationships in organizations.

**Interactions** Last, it is important to realize that the four dimensions do not operate independently. They interact so that changes in one of them often produce changes in others. For example, attraction and dominance interact to make high-status individuals more attractive than low-status individuals.[15] And this interaction makes people of low status have more desire to communicate with individuals of high status than vice versa. Attraction and involvement also are related. Mutually attracted people are more likely to share personal (involving) information about themselves, and this sharing, in turn, seems to increase attraction.[16] We have already seen that situations produce changes in both attraction and dominance, and that physical and social surroundings influence people's tendencies to become involved with one another.[17] Thus, human relationships represent a complex network of mutually influential dimensions.[18]

---

**KEY CONCEPTS 7.1**  **Dimensions of Interpersonal Relationships**

Interpersonal relationships within organizations are composed of several basic factors:

- • *Attraction—The extent to which people feel positively toward one another.*

- • *Dominance—The extent to which people exert some control or influence over one another.*

- • *Involvement—The depth and breadth of the relationships between people.*

- • *Situation—The impact of the physical, social, and task environment upon the three dimensions.*

- • *Interactions—The impact of the three dimensions upon one another.*

---

# FUNDAMENTALS OF INTERPERSONAL RELATIONSHIPS: PERCEPTION

Basic to the formation of our relationships with others are the conclusions we draw from our encounters with them—our perceptions. Haney defines perception as "the process of making sense out of experience."[19] That is, we encounter environments, experience them through our senses, and then try to sort out experiences so that they become meaningful to us. While all our experiences necessarily involve perception, the most important ones are those that demand perception of people. Therefore, the process of person perception will occupy most of our attention in this section.

**Stages of Perception** Although complex, the perception process seems to involve three successive stages: selecting, sorting, and interpreting. The first, *selecting*, involves both involuntary and voluntary choices. The world presents an infinite array of message stimuli, so that to attend to all of them is utterly impossible. We must make some choices concerning which stimuli we will attend to and which we will ignore. Actually, to some degree, these choices are made for us.

## RUDENESS IN THE WORKPLACE

A study conducted by Christine Pearson, management professor in the University of North Carolina–Chapel Hill business school, illustrated the impact of rudeness in the workplace. In her study of business professionals, 12 percent said rudeness from a colleague has caused them to decrease the quality of their work, 22 percent said their work effort declined, 28 percent lost time at work trying to avoid the rude person, 52 percent lost time from worry about the situation, 26 percent thought about changing jobs, and 12 percent actually took new jobs to escape a rude person.

Source: "The Cost of Rudeness," *Motivational Manager* (November, 1998): 9.

Our *physical location* is one factor determining our perceptions. By making certain stimuli available to us, our location limits the experiences we can have and hence the things that we can perceive. But even within our location, we are further limited as our *physiological capacities* make some stimuli imperceptible to us. For example, we cannot hear sounds below 20 or above 20,000 cycles per second, even though many sounds fall outside that relatively narrow range. We cannot hear a dog trainer's whistle to which a dog will respond immediately. Our eyes are able to see only about one-seventieth of the light spectrum. Of the things that our eyes can see, our brain can assimilate only about one-ten-thousandth. Before we ever begin deliberate selection of available stimuli, then, a great deal of selection already has occurred.

When we finally enter the realm of things our location and senses allow us to receive, another set of factors enters into the perceptual selection process. Particularly important is *psychological comfort*. Just as we seek to be comfortable physically, so too we select information that makes us psychologically comfortable. To a lesser degree, we avoid information that creates psychological discomfort. We tend to seek information that reinforces views we hold and to avoid information that fails to do so. The reason for this behavior seems to lie in our need for self-esteem, or the need to think well of ourselves. Agreeable information implicitly tells us that we are right or that our ideas are good ones. Disagreeable information tells us that somehow our ideas or beliefs are defective and that we are in need of change. Clearly, reinforcing information makes us comfortable about ourselves; conflicting information may make us uncomfortable.

A second factor is *interest*. We tend to select those things that are interesting to us, and to ignore things that are not. Perhaps *"importance"* might be a better term, for the reason something is interesting to us in the first place is that it holds some importance for us. For example, if you are at a party where groups of people are standing around talking, try saying softly the name of one of the people in an adjacent group. Even though that person probably has not heard anything you said before that point, he almost certainly will hear his name. The reason is simple: a person's name is the single most interesting (important) word in the world to that person.

FIGURE 7.1          An exercise in perception

Perception occurs according to a third factor, *past experience*. To a large degree, we perceive what we expect to perceive. Consider the triangles presented in Figure 7.1. Quickly read each of them aloud. Usually, these figures are read as "Dumb as an ox," "Bird in the hand," "Busy as a beaver," and "Paris in the spring." If you saw them that way, look again—you missed something. Unfortunately, this phenomenon of seeing what we expect to see also occurs when we observe people. If we expect them to be obnoxious, they often become that way, regardless of what they normally do. In essence, our prophecies become self-fulfilling.

In addition to molding our expectations, *past experience* influences perception by creating habitual ways of seeing the world. Figure 7.2 presents another example. There you will find a square consisting of three rows having three dots each. Your task is to connect all nine dots using only four lines and never lifting your pencil from the page. Simple, right? Try it a few times. Unless you have seen this before, you probably will have some difficulty figuring it out. Blame it on past experience. We are used to seeing the world in certain ways, and in this instance, we tend to perceive the figure as a square. Thus, we operate within the limits of the square, trying to find some way to draw four lines. As long as you let perceptual habit confine you to the square, you will be unable to solve the problem. You have to go beyond the square to solve it successfully. This principle also applies to people. If you let past habits of perception limit your observations of the people you meet, you probably will not perceive new people accurately.

A final set of variables influencing our selection choices consists of the *characteristics of the stimuli* we encounter. First, we tend to select, often involuntarily, stimuli that are very *intense*. Loud noises, bright lights, and strong smells all attract our attention. To be certain of getting someone's attention,

FIGURE 7.2          The influence of experience on perception

● ● ●

● ● ●

● ● ●

*Interpersonal Communication within Organizations: Fundamental Concepts*      **231**

FIGURE 7.3    Physical proximity and closure

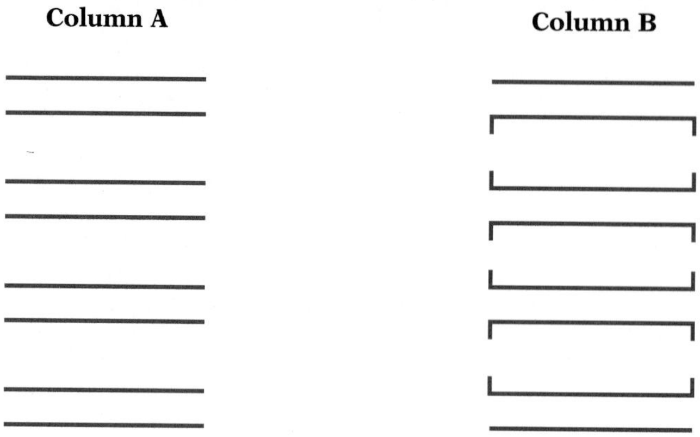

Column A                    Column B

you need only scream. But if you continue screaming, the effect wears off. Hence, you need to use another stimulus characteristic, *change*. Our attention is attracted if a stationary object suddenly moves, a moving object stops, or a loud noise becomes soft. While intense stimuli initially gain our attention, variations in the stimuli are needed to maintain attention. *Novel* stimuli also get attention. In communicating, novel behaviors include humor, unbelievable (but true) statements, profanity, and sometimes silence. Finally, *repetition* adds emphasis and, in so doing, draws attention. As we shall see later, each of these stimulus characteristics can be used in transmitting messages to ensure that the receivers are listening. For now, simply be aware that you heed, often unintentionally, stimuli that have the preceding characteristics.

After we have completed the selection stage of perception, determining which stimuli we will and will not attend to, we move to the second stage, *sorting*. We do not perceive things to be random, unrelated occurrences. Rather, we tend to organize our perceptions into coherent patterns. Generally, this process of organization moves through two phases. First, we give things structure. Several laws seem to govern this. For example, we tend to group together things that are located in close proximity. In Figure 7.3, column A presents eight lines. Although no special relationship exists between any of them, we tend to group them into four pairs simply because of their physical location. Column B adds a second law, closure. We tend to fill in incomplete figures, perceiving the entire figure as though the complete object were there. Thus, in column B, we group the lines differently, tending to see three rectangles with single brackets at the top and bottom of the column. In addition, resemblance affects structure: we group together things that look alike. Finally, we structure our world according to "common fate," relating things that seem to be acting in the same way or moving in a common direction.

When we have selected and sorted stimuli into some coherent pattern, we move to the third stage of perception, *interpretation*. Here, we finally make sense of the things we have experienced. Again, several principles seem to govern the interpretations we form. We interpret people and things in terms of their *context*. For instance, our perceptions of people may change from one context to the next. Someone drinking at a party usually is judged a "social drinker." The same person performing that same behavior in a different context, such as a back alley or a gutter, would be judged a "derelict" or "wino." Yet, only the context has changed.

When we encounter people, we also tend to interpret them in terms of our perception of their *intent*. Unless the behaviors we observe are clearly unintentional, we typically assume that they are done deliberately and for a specific purpose. We seek to determine what that purpose or intent is. To a large degree judgments of intent are based on our perceptions of our own behavior, since we operate on the assumption that other people are like ourselves.

Related to the second principle is a third, *projection*. Essentially, we tend to project onto other people our own characteristics. Classical projection involves two processes: attributing our undesirable characteristics to people we dislike and refusing to acknowledge that we possess those characteristics in the first place. On the other hand, attributive projection occurs when we attribute our own favorable characteristics to people we like. Rationalized projection occurs when we attribute thoughts, intentions, or characteristics to other people without knowing why we do so. An incompetent worker would find it discomforting to confront his own incompetence, so instead he attributes his failures to his supervisor, perhaps claiming, "She's always out to get me." While the supervisor may, in fact, have no such motivation, this sort of projection is a handy device with which to rationalize away things that would trouble the worker if he confronted them directly.

Another determinant of interpretation is the *label* we attach to the thing we are perceiving. People really are ambiguous objects. We can see that they are people, but not much more. Any information we can obtain about them helps us to determine what they are about. One such bit of information is the labels other people provide. Before meeting someone, we might be told, "He's a creep" or "She's a genius." When interpreting this person's behavior, these labels may serve as a sort of filter through which our judgments would pass. Thus, we would have developed a kind of individualized stereotype whereby we judged the person in terms of the label attached to him or her, rather than on the basis of the behaviors we actually observed. Clearly, these sorts of judgments are highly unreliable. We would be well advised to rely on our own observations, ignoring as much as possible the labels with which other people provide us.

The final source of interpretation is *familiarity*—the one saving grace in the perceptual process. While context, intent, projection, and labels all tend to lead us astray because they all are based upon something other than the object being perceived, familiarity considers the extent to which we have developed an acquaintance with the object. As a rule, the more familiar we are with something, the more accurately we are able to perceive it.

The perception process involves three successive stages:

1. *Selecting*—Voluntarily and involuntarily choosing those things to which we pay attention, typically on the basis of:

   Psychological comfort
   Interest importance
   Past experience
   Stimulus characteristics

2. *Sorting*—Organizing our perceptions into coherent patterns.

3. *Interpretation*—Making sense of the things we have experienced, typically on the basis of:

   Context
   Intent
   Projection
   Labels
   Familiarity

To this point, we have explored the process through which we proceed when perceiving anything we encounter in the environment. When we must deal specifically with people, however, as we do in organizations, additional factors become important. In the next section, we shall examine several unique elements composing our perceptions of people.

**Person Perception**   In this section, we will discuss two aspects of our perceptions of other people: the *kinds of information* we use to make judgments about them and the *process by which our perceptual judgments form.* An understanding of each aspect is crucial to the development of our abilities to perceive other people accurately.

The judgments we make about people are derived from some rather specific bits of information. One obvious source of information about people we meet is their *verbal behavior*—the words they speak. However, encounters occur where no words are exchanged or where the words are used to deceive. While we tend to rely heavily upon verbal behavior for information about the person speaking, this source of information can prove unreliable. We therefore look to the person's *nonverbal behavior* as well. The cues that accompany the words the individual speaks (or that operate in the place of words) provide us with a great deal of information about that person. Nonverbal cues may be divided into "static" and "dynamic" characteristics. Static cues include facial features, physique, vocal qualities, clothing, or other elements of the person (such as jewelry, makeup, or hairstyle) that change slowly. Dynamic cues are bodily orientation (the direction in which the person is facing), physical location, posture, gestures, facial expressions, eye contact and direction of gaze, tone of voice, and rate or fluency of speech. These cues help us to form more accurate judgments about people we encounter.

The *context* in which we meet people similarly influences our perceptions of them. Research suggests, for example, that when we meet someone in a pleasant, attractive room, we will react more favorably to that individual than if we were to meet that person in a disagreeable setting.[20]

The *reputation* of the people we meet also has an impact on perception. As we already have seen, we use labels to interpret things that otherwise

### PERCEPTION OF CULTURE AND PERSON

As American corporations hire increasing numbers of immigrants, cross-cultural misunderstandings will occur with greater frequency. For example:

- In the United States, calling attention to oneself (particularly to professional achievements) is considered a sign of self-respect. For many Asians, however, calling inordinate attention to oneself may be rude and unprofessional. In an employment interview, this cultural clash could result in a Vietnamese applicant being viewed as "lacking self-esteem."
- While direct eye contact is valued in the United States, other cultures avoid eye contact as a sign of respect or deference. An applicant from such a culture probably would be viewed as "unassertive" or "untrustworthy."
- Rather than risk losing face or ridicule for misusing an English word, some foreign-speaking workers will simply remain silent. Their American managers often assume they simply have no suggestions or ideas to contribute.
- In parts of Asia, the Hispanic countries, and much of Europe, to initiate even the simplest task without being told specifically to do so is considered a defiance of authority. From the American viewpoint, this "lack of initiative" may be interpreted as laziness or a lack of self-confidence.

As the American workplace becomes increasingly multicultural, we must improve our skills in perceiving people. Rather than interpret others' behaviors in terms of our own cultural norms, we must communicate more carefully and thoroughly to ensure that we understand what others do.

Source: Sondra Thiederman, "Communication: Overcoming Cultural and Language Barriers," *Personnel Journal* 67 (December 1988): 34–40.

---

would be ambiguous. So it is with people. When we form judgments of people whom we have encountered recently, we rely rather heavily—too heavily perhaps—on the labels supplied by people whose opinions we respect. Certainly, other people's observations may be useful to us. However, our own observations should take precedence when we judge others.

Having seen the sorts of judgments we make about others and the pieces of information we use to make them, we turn finally to the process by which perceptual judgments occur. At the beginning of the process lies the object or person to be perceived. Available to us is some, but by no means all, information about that individual: information provided by actions of the person, information about the person provided by other people, and information from the context that influences our perceptions of the person. This information consists of a myriad of cues that vary in intensity, change, novelty, and repetitiveness. Consequently, some of these cues attract our attention while others do not.

Our attention also is directed by psychological factors: comfort, interest, and experience. Parents often overlook faults in their children that are all too obvious to others; supervisors looking for laziness in workers usually are able to perceive it; and psychiatrists experienced in diagnosing psychological disorders are able to perceive and interpret behavioral cues unobservable to

## COMMUNICATING FOR SUCCESS

John R. Graham, president of Graham Communications, suggests that if you want to be considered a "star" performer, you should never say the following things:

- "They didn't get back to me," or "They are getting back to me." Expecting someone to get back to you stops the action. Take the initiative.
- "I thought someone else was taking care of that." Excuses indicate a roadblock to action. Always ask questions to keep things moving.
- "No one ever told me." This statement suggests to others that you operate in a tunnel of your own, oblivious to everything that is going on around you. Go get the information you need.

- "I didn't have time" or "I was too busy." Neither of these statements suggests competence or effective time management skills.
- "I didn't think to ask about that." An inability to see down the road may indicate that you lack the ability to understand and grasp relationships.

The message in business today is clear. The only measure for success is performance. Whatever the roadblocks, it is your job to take the initiative to remove them. If not, you'll be perceived as one of them.

Source: "Never Say These Things," *Communication Briefings*, XV: (1998): 1.

most of us. The attended cues, then, are placed into some coherent pattern according to the organizational rules of proximity, closure, resemblance, and common fate. Subsequent interpretation of this pattern is carried out according to perceived intent, projection, and familiarity. But before the final judgment is rendered, one last element enters the perceptual process: inferences.

Within each of us rests a set of presumptions or rules by which we classify and respond to other people. These rules seem to be of two sorts: *association rules*, which hold that particular characteristics are associated ("People who lack ambition are unlikely to succeed" or "Intelligent people are influential"); and *identification rules*, which provide keys for identifying people who have a particular characteristic ("People who refuse to lend money are stingy" or "People who call other people obscene names in public are impolite and insensitive").

Basically, there are four different approaches to or sources of rules.[21] First, *induction* provides us with rules that are based on our own experiences. We may, for example, interact with several people who have an Ivy League education and find them to be quite arrogant. Based on these unpleasant encounters, we may infer that all people with Ivy League degrees are aloof and arrogant. From that point on, we will expect to encounter an arrogant attitude whenever we are introduced to someone with a degree from Harvard or Yale. On the other hand, *construction* occurs when we invent our own rules. For example, people who have decided that "women are too emotional to be good managers" have likely constructed this rule without any direct experience or information to support it. Indeed, most instances of prejudice or stereotyping involve self-constructed rules.

The third source of rules is through analogy. When we draw an *analogy*, we reason that when one person acts in a particular way, everyone else who is like that person will act in the same way. If an elderly woman hires a young teenager to mow her lawn and the boy proves to be irresponsible, she may conclude that all teenagers are irresponsible. Finally, other people may supply rules to us, so that we obtain them through *authority*. Parents, friends, colleagues, and others with whom we identify may tell us that "People who _____ are _____." The blanks can be completed in endless ways. For example, "People who use drugs are no good," "People who come to work late are lazy," "People who hang around bars are asking for trouble," and so on. Of course, we may accept or reject these rules. One powerful authority, incidentally, is television. We know that people obtain information about what types of people do what types of things from the television shows they watch and that, ultimately, they begin to react to others in ways they have observed on television.

We use these approaches to rules to form impressions of others and to make inferences about their attitudes, aptitudes, and likely actions. In these ways, we use our own inferential processes to make judgments about all kinds of people in all kinds of contexts.

In view of the complexity of the process of person perception, you might expect perceptual problems to be common in everyday work settings. And you would be right. Perceptual disagreements have repeatedly been shown to affect the climate of organizations adversely. Several studies have demonstrated that a lack of congruity in role perceptions between two people is associated with higher interpersonal tension and lower evaluations by each of the other person's job performance.[22] Moreover, this tension is often related to decreases in interpersonal attraction.

Numerous investigators have reported that pairs agreeing on appropriate role behaviors tend to be more mutually attracted than pairs holding incongruent role expectations, and some have noted that violations of interpersonal role expectations produce strain and stress.[23]

This lack of congruence also seems to have an impact on job satisfaction. Investigators have found that perceptual ambiguity between superiors and subordinates concerning the latter's role responsibilities is associated with subordinates' dissatisfaction, anxiety, and lack of job interest. These harmful effects of perceptual breakdowns demand that care be taken to ensure accurate perceptions between organizational members.

How can we improve the accuracy with which we perceive people we encounter? Although there is no simple method, we can suggest four techniques that may prove helpful.

First is the method termed *consensual validation*, which involves seeking the agreement or consensus of other people concerning the nature of "reality." In essence, you simply ask others what they think. There are some dangers here, such as the chance of asking people whose perceptions are as strange as our own or the danger of making ourselves vulnerable to manipulation by those whom we consult. But for the most part, consensual validation is a useful means of determining whether or not we perceive others accurately.

Second, we can use *repetitive validation*, observing the person several times, to determine whether our first impressions were correct. This method may not solve the problems posed by stable stereotypes and prejudices, but it may aid us in the selection and organization stages of perception.

Third, *multisensory validation* involves the use of other senses to confirm what one sense has received. A desert mirage seems real only as long as we look at it. When we try to touch it, it disappears. Or people may present themselves in a certain way, causing us to derive a perceptual conclusion about them; but if we listen to them, we may discover that they are not the way they look at all. Thus, we ought not to rely on just one sense when perceiving others.

Last, with *comparative validation,* we get some indication of perceptual validity by comparing this new perception with experiences of the past. Using this technique, we might ask ourselves, "Does the behavior I am now seeing fit with the behaviors I have seen from this person in the past?" The answer to this question has important implications for our judgments of this person. If the behavior is consistent, perhaps we are in a position to make a judgment about his or her traits; if the behavior is inconsistent, we may need to find out why.

Although any of these four methods may prove useful in increasing perceptual accuracy, our main point is this: Rather than accepting the things we perceive at face value (instead of forming judgments immediately on the basis of what we perceive at the moment), we need to check our perceptions before we judge and act. If we take care in forming perceptions, or if we resolve that we are going to suspend judgment until we have made all the observations we can, we will have done much to improve our perceptions of the people we encounter.

| KEY CONCEPTS 7.3 | Making and Improving Judgments about Others |
|---|---|
| When we perceive other people, the kinds of information we use to form judgments are:<br><br>• • *Verbal behaviors*<br><br>• • *Nonverbal behaviors*<br><br>• • *Context*<br><br>• • *Reputation* | We can improve our perceptions through:<br><br>• • *Consensual validation*<br><br>• • *Repetitive validation*<br><br>• • *Multisensory validation*<br><br>• • *Comparative validation* |

## COMMUNICATION SKILLS FOR IMPROVING RELATIONSHIPS

To this point, we have reviewed the dimensions of human relationships and the elements of perception that allow those relationships to exist. In this final section, we turn to some strategies for improving relationships in the organizational setting.

Listening    Steven Covey, in his best-selling book *The Seven Habits of Highly Effective People,* suggests that one habit effective people develop is to "seek first to understand, then to be understood."[24] The cornerstone to understanding others

## AVOIDING MALPRACTICE SUITS THROUGH COMMUNICATION

Doctors have more control over malpractice suits than they think: A good bedside manner may mean the difference between being repeatedly hauled into court and never getting sued in the first place. In a University of Chicago study, researchers audiotaped routine office visits with patients of 124 family practitioners and surgeons in Oregon and Colorado. They found that doctors who had never been sued tended to laugh and joke more with their patients, to have longer office visits, and to tell their patients what to expect—when the exam would take place, when tests would occur, and so on. They were also good listeners and encouraged patients to talk.

The researchers concluded that handling patients in this fashion is effective because doctors who carefully explain what will happen during the visit make the patient feel less awkward. In addition, they may be less likely to sue a doctor with whom they enjoy two-way communication, thus creating an atmosphere where the patient feels engaged and involved.

A good way for doctors to sharpen communication techniques, the researchers offered, might be to tape office visits and listen to them afterward—or even team up with a colleague to critique one another.

Source: Sue Ellen White, "Best Defense Is No Offense," *Hospitals & Health Networks* 71: 11 (November 5, 1997): 70.

is effective listening. In organizations, *listening is crucial for several reasons*. First, it provides us with information. To do an effective job at work, there are things we must know: what our job is, how it interacts with other jobs, what our superiors expect of us, and what is going on throughout the company. In business, this sort of information is rarely published. Usually, it is given to us orally, either in formal meetings or informal conversations or interviews. If we listen well, we will assimilate the information we need to succeed. If we do not, we probably will find ourselves in trouble. In addition, listening allows us to think critically. By comparing and analyzing what we hear, we can arrive at conclusions that are more likely to be correct. From these two benefits comes another: good listening makes us better senders. If we correctly interpret what people say to us, we are more likely to respond to them in appropriate ways. To a significant extent, then, our success in organizations depends upon our ability to listen well to the things others say to us.

Unfortunately, there are *several barriers to listening* that *affect all of us*. A recent study of perceived listening needs of managers of training in over 100 Fortune 500 industrial organizations revealed that poor listening was one of the most important problems they faced, leading to ineffective performance and low productivity.[25] These training managers pointed out that listening was particularly problematic during meetings, performance appraisals, and in any context involving superior-subordinate communication. Campbell has discovered several sources of systematic error that seem to inhibit listeners' understanding. These include:

**1.** *Length of the message.* Listeners tend to shorten, simplify, and eliminate detail from the messages they receive, thus losing information and accuracy. The longer the message, the greater the loss.

**2.** *Middle of the message.* Dispute continues among communication scholars over whether listeners best remember the first or the last things they hear. But everyone agrees on one thing: listeners tend to forget the middle of the message.

**3.** *Rounding off the message.* Listeners tend to tailor messages to suit their own needs or beliefs, thus distorting the messages' actual content. For instance, an eager employee proposes some bright idea to his boss, who responds with, "That's an interesting idea. Let me give it some thought." Because of his need to feel that the boss responded with affirmation and enthusiasm, the employee may round off her message and "hear" that the boss has endorsed the idea.

**4.** *Expectations.* In some situations, we are confident we know what the source is going to say. As a result, no matter what that person says, we hear what we expect.

**5.** *False agreement.* When confronted with a source we respect or admire, we often modify her message so that it more closely coincides with our own attitudes and beliefs. Knowing that someone with high credibility possesses views that differ significantly from our own can produce tension. One way of avoiding this tension is to simply "hear" a higher level of agreement than actually exists.

**6.** *Dichotomous listening.* We have a tendency to polarize the world, to create dichotomies in which things are either one way or the other—right or wrong, good or bad, beautiful or ugly. Most speakers express ideas falling somewhere between these extremes; but we are inclined to assign those ideas to one category or the other.[26]

As Campbell's list suggests, listening problems present themselves in varied forms. Other factors can lead to what Goffman calls "alienation" in communicative interactions. Each interferes with listening accuracy:

**1.** *External preoccupation.* Whenever we give our attention to something or someone other than the person speaking to us, we are allowing external preoccupation to become a problem. Preoccupations can take many forms— suddenly becoming aware of how long someone is talking (and perhaps glancing at our watches), thinking about a dreaded meeting we have to attend later in the day, or becoming aware of how cold it is in the room.

**2.** *Self-consciousness.* Occasionally, we become overly focused on ourselves—perhaps preoccupied with our appearance, our grammar, or how we are coming across. For instance, in a job interview, we may become so preoccupied with the sort of impression we are making that we have to ask the interviewer to repeat a question. We simply did not hear it.

**3.** *Interaction consciousness.* At times, we may become too preoccupied with the progress of the interaction, neglecting the messages and concentrating only on keeping talk going. Hosts and hostesses suffer from this type of alienation. They don't care what people say, as long as they say something.

**4.** *Other consciousness.* Another source of distraction may be the speaker him or herself. We can become so involved with the speaker emotionally that

## LISTENING EXERCISES

Once you learn how to listen to others, you'll get better feedback, communicate better, and solve more problems. Here are some exercises that will improve your listening skills and help you get the most out of each meeting with a colleague:

- *Clean off your desk.* If there are loose papers on your desk, you'll unconsciously start to fiddle with them—and may even start to glance over them. Clear your desk for every conversation with a colleague so you can focus your attention on what he or she is saying.
- *What is the color of the person's eyes?* Train yourself to notice eye color at the start of every conversation. It ensures that you'll make significant eye contact—which leads to more productive conversations. However, don't focus so much on eye color that you don't listen to what is being said.
- *Train yourself to ask questions rather than make statements.* Don't say, "Joan, don't forget that the Anderson report needs to be in by Monday morning." Rather, ask, "How is the Anderson report coming along, Joan?

Any problems with making the deadline?" By asking questions you'll start a dialogue and you never know what you might learn.
- *Learn to "lubricate" conversations.* Phrases such as, "Yes, I see" and "I understand" do two things: (1) they show that you're listening, and encourage the other person to keep talking; and (2) they keep your attention focused.
- *Don't blurt out questions as soon as the other person is finished speaking.* It looks as if you were formulating your reply rather than listening. Before you ask a question, paraphrase the person's words. For example, "So what you're saying is . . ." Then ask your question: "Well, let me ask you this . . . ." This cuts down on miscommunications.
- *Don't smile the whole time.* Some people do this because they think it sends a friendly message. It can, but people also often mistake it for mental absence or a sign that you're not taking them seriously. Save smiles for humorous remarks.

Source: "Train Yourself in the Art of Listening," *Positive Leadership* (July 1998): 10.

---

we are unable to deal objectively with what he or she is saying. Or the speaker's physical appearance may be distracting. In either case, we become too preoccupied with the speaker to really listen to what he or she is saying.[27]

Still more potential barriers to listening are suggested by other writers:

**1.** *Wasting thought power.* We listen and absorb ideas at a rate much faster than people talk. On the average, most of us can talk at a rate of 125 words per minute, while we can think at 400 to 500 words per minute. Unfortunately, this difference in thought and word speed is responsible for many mental tangents; that is, instead of concentrating on what the speaker is saying, our minds wander off onto other things.

**2.** *Listening only for specific facts or details.* Too often we concentrate only on details or facts and lose sight of the overall message and feelings of the other person. Effective listening occurs only when the big picture is kept in mind; you have to maintain a focus on the overall structure and purpose of the conversation.

**3.** *"Throw-in-the-towel" listening.* When the going gets tough or when it becomes clear that the other person simply is not totally supportive of what we are saying, some of us simply give up and mentally check out. Instead, we should listen even more intently, trying to discover from the other person's words things we can use to further the conversation.

**4.** *Focusing on the speaker's personal characteristics.* Often we are distracted by the speaker's mannerisms, appearance, delivery, and so on. When this occurs, we are not listening to the message, but are concentrating on the messenger. We must focus on the message content, not the peculiar appearance or behavior of the speaker.

**5.** *Faking attention.* Many listeners become skilled at pretending to pay attention. They mutter "uh-huh" while the speaker speaks, they sit with glazed eyes and fixed smiles during conversations, and they generally ignore everything going on around them. In effect, they just go through the motions of listening and do not really communicate.

**6.** *Tolerating or creating distractions.* Poor listeners are easily distracted by other things, or they may even create distractions themselves. For example, the sales representative who attempts to listen while flipping through product information sheets provides a distraction for the customer and, in so doing, probably discourages further communication.

Given the lengthy list of things that can go wrong in listening, it is hardly surprising to discover that listening errors are both common and expensive. Chicago consultant Bridget Maile, head of Innovative Management Technologies, contends the average listening mistake costs a company about $15 in lost time, materials, and deadlines.[28] All told, the listening errors made each day by each employee probably cost organizations millions of dollars in lost efficiency or wasted effort.

There are several techniques you may find useful in improving listening. One is called the HEAR formula. HEAR is an acronym formed by the first letter of the four words you should remember when trying to listen to someone: helpful, empathic, attentive, and responsive.

To be *helpful* when you listen to someone, you should make it easy for her to talk with you. One way to do this is to minimize the waiting time and maximize the meeting time for that person. In other words, when someone comes to talk with you, you should not keep that person waiting, cooling her heels, while you do something else, because this communicates to her that you have more important things to do and that listening to her is not among your priorities.

Similarly, while meeting with another person, you should try to convey the impression that you have all the time in the world—that nothing could be more important than that meeting with that person. This means avoiding glances at your watch or the clock on the wall, not fidgeting, and not giving the impression that you need to get this meeting over as quickly as possible. Even if you are pressed for time, you must always try to convey to the other person the feeling that the time you do have is all his.

Helpfulness also is improved by making the environment as attractive and informal as possible because attractive and informal settings encourage interaction. Similarly, you should eliminate potential distractions (take the phone off the hook or move to a private location), and when the meeting is

## EFFECTIVE LISTENING: THE HEAR FORMULA

| To be helpful: | Minimize waiting time. | To be attentive: | Suspend your reactions. |
| | Act unhurried. | | Show understanding before |
| | Make the environment | | disagreeing. |
| | attractive. | | Paraphrase and summarize. |
| | Eliminate potential | To be responsive: | Maintain eye contact. |
| | distractions. | | Use nonverbal |
| | Invite future interactions. | | reinforcement. |
| To be empathic: | Show that the other's | | Ask questions. |
| | feelings are understood. | | Let the other person talk. |
| | Show that the other person | | |
| | is cared about. | | |
| | Use active listening | | |
| | techniques. | | |

over, you should thank the person for talking with you and invite him to meet with you again some time soon. All of these things help people to talk with you—an important element of being an effective listener.

To be *empathic*, you need to show the other person that you truly understand how she feels and that you care about those feelings. This is very different from sympathy, in which you simply feel sorry for the other person. Most people want empathy; they may resent sympathy. To improve the empathy dimension, you first should ask about the person's well-being; show you care about her as a person, regardless of the topic under question. Then, when she is talking to you, you should occasionally use some of the "active listening" techniques we discuss in the next chapter, such as paraphrasing the things she has just said or reflecting back to the person the feelings she seems to be experiencing.

*Attentiveness* means demonstrating to the other person that you are indeed listening to his or her point of view. To improve the attention you show, first suspend your reactions; do not react until you have heard everything the other person has to say. To the greatest extent possible, withhold judgment and emotions; when you react, do so as logically and calmly as possible. When you disagree, show you understand the other's points before you begin to present your own. Paraphrase or summarize the person's ideas and let him or her know that you did, indeed, understand what was being said. Then present your ideas. Finally, you might periodically summarize the points the other person has just covered ("Let me see. You said that Bill first went to . . . and that he then . . . Is that right?"). You should always avoid distractions or directing your attention somewhere else when someone is talking to you.

Finally, you should listen *responsively*, showing that you not only are paying attention, but that you are actively interested in the person and the topic. Maintain eye contact by looking at people most of the time they are talking to you. Use nonverbal reinforcement (such as nodding your head occasionally and sitting up straight, leaning slightly toward the speaker) to show responsiveness, or use vocal prompts such as "uh-huh," "um-hmm," and "OK." When appropriate, ask questions to display your interest and to get useful information. Avoid giving advice unless you are explicitly asked to do so. And above all, let the other person do the talking.

A key to improving your listening efforts is using some of the techniques of active listening.[29] *Active listening* consists of responding, verbally and nonverbally, to the person who is talking to you. These responses should encourage the other person to tell you more, show that you understand the person's words, and indicate that you empathize with her or his feelings. When you listen actively, you may respond to the content of the other person's words, to your perception of her or his feelings, or to important nonverbal cues.

As a listener, when you respond to something the speaker has said (that is, to the message content), one goal you may have is *to demonstrate your attention and understanding.* You might do this by *paraphrasing*, where you state in your own words what you think the speaker just said; by prodding, where you give short vocal and nonverbal cues that signal you are listening and encourage the speaker to continue talking; or by accepting, where you state your approval or acceptance of the speaker's expressed views.

Another way of responding to the speaker's remarks is to *request further input.* You might do this by *encouraging*, that is, requesting that the speaker give you more information about what happened, what caused a particular problem ("Could you give me a little more background on what happened right before George became department head?"); by *delegating*, where you place responsibility for solutions or ideas back on the speaker, thus involving him or her in the solution ("What ideas do you have that I might pass along?" or "How do you think we might solve that problem?"); by *reconstructing*, where you ask the person to recall or imagine the events that led to the topic you are discussing ("How was that decision originally made?"); or by *reversing*, where you ask for an opposite point of view ("You've discussed a number of problems with the new word processing software. Have you found any advantages to it?").

Yet another goal you may have as you listen actively to a speaker's verbal messages is *to cause him or her to think critically.* You might, for instance, try *testing*, where you ask the speaker to consider the possible results of a problem, solution, or proposed course of action ("How do you think our regular customers would react if we switched to a cheaper vendor?"); or you might try *confronting*, where you challenge the validity of what has been said ("You say that we are charging too much for those microcomputers, but sales have never been better!"). These techniques, of course, will be effective only if they are used with sensitivity and tact.

A final goal you may have in responding to a speaker's ideas and suggestions is *to demonstrate interest and offer help or guidance.* You might do this by *offering*, where you suggest possible alternatives or solutions to a problem; or by *elaborating*, where you build on to what the speaker has just said, communicating understanding, involvement, and approval ("You're right about the importance of the company getting involved with community service projects. I like the ones you've mentioned, especially the blood drive. We might also consider working with the group that's trying to solve the PCB problem").

Perhaps more difficult than responding to the speaker's expressed view is responding to your perceptions of his or her feelings. To do this, you observe reactions that seem to indicate that emotions are present and then tell the speaker what you have noticed and what you tentatively interpret your observations to mean.

As a general rule, *you should respond only to fairly obvious feelings.* Your goal is not to "psych out" the speaker, but to grow to understand that person's emotions and build a better relationship with him or her. By being responsive to another's feelings, you not only show concern for the individual but promote rational discussion by minimizing emotional problems that can get in the way. Therefore, when strong emotions seem evident, you might ask such questions as "I get the feeling you are really upset about something. Would you like to talk about it?" "You seem really sad today. Is anything wrong?" or "You sound pretty depressed. What has got you down?" By taking the time to encourage the speaker to share his or her feelings, you show your concern and begin to build a better understanding, which should lead, ultimately, to improved communication.

Finally, as an active listener, you may need to *respond to the speaker's nonverbal cues.* In some instances, these cues will reinforce the verbal message. On other occasions, they will contradict what is being said. Often, the nonverbal cues will give you insight into the speaker's true feelings. In Chapter 8 we will discuss nonverbal behavior in considerable detail, but a few examples of the kinds of nonverbal cues that you might see while listening may be useful here. For instance, a frown in response to a comment you make may indicate confusion or disagreement; folded arms and sitting back after a comment may suggest anger or withdrawal; rapid hand movements or shifting on the chair may indicate anxiety or nervousness; a smirk on the face may denote an attitude of superiority or disgust; and a variety of other facial expressions may reveal confusion, anger, distrust, or resistance.

Whenever you observe a speaker's nonverbal behavior that seems unclear, or appears to contradict what is being said, you might ask about it, with such questions as "I know you said yes, but you look kind of puzzled. Are there some questions you still have on your mind?" When you make observations about a speaker's nonverbal cues, make your evaluations as tentative as possible. Nonverbal cues can be ambiguous. They may reveal underlying feelings that the speaker is unaware of or not yet ready to acknowledge or discuss. But if you can approach the subject tactfully and patiently, you may be able to help the speaker become aware of how she is coming across to others and help clarify her own reactions. But let the speaker do the interpretation.

Taken together, the ability to ask good questions and the skill and willingness to listen actively will do much to help you become an effective listener in a wide variety of communication contexts.

Common barriers to effective listening include:

- The length of the message
- Middle of the message
- Rounding off the message
- Expectations
- False agreement
- Dichotomous listening
- External preoccupation
- Self-consciousness
- Interaction consciousness
- Other consciousness

## Improving Relationship Dimensions

As we saw earlier, relationships consist of three basic dimensions: attraction, dominance, and involvement. These three vary according to the situations in which the interactants find themselves, and these dimensions influence one another. Nevertheless, we will consider each of them again briefly, noting some ways in which each might be strengthened in the organizational setting.

**Attraction**   It would be foolish for us to try to present "10 ways to make people like you." There simply is no surefire formula for making oneself attractive to everyone, despite the many paperback books that claim there is. We can, however, point to some behaviors that, in the view of several authors, drive people away and thus impair the attraction dimension of relationships. Obviously, our recommendation will be to avoid these behaviors.

Hegarty claims that certain verbal behaviors prevent the development of good relationships in organizations.[30] One such behavior is complaining. While occasional complaining may bring people together for periodic gripe sessions, constant complaining becomes irritating to everyone—particularly one's superiors in the organization. An occasional complaint among friends may promote group cohesiveness; continual complaining, Hegarty argues, brings about social isolation. *Avoidance of complaining* and maintenance of a generally positive attitude will enhance your success on the attraction dimension.

Yet another method for improving the attraction element of organizational relationships is *"showing the right attitude."* This consists of such specific behaviors as speaking as if you like your work; taking a cooperative ("What can we do to solve this problem?") rather than an authoritative ("What are you going to do to solve this problem?") approach to problem solving; taking the attitude that your subordinates work with you, not for you; attacking issues and problems rather than personalities; treating others as equals; and using many of the listening techniques we discussed earlier in this chapter. All of these things demonstrate your liking for others and increase the likelihood they will regard you positively in return.

**Dominance**   In an organization, the dominance dimension is determined both by organizational rank and by situational variables dictating who is in control for the moment. There are several methods for influencing others' behaviors. First is use of *simple force*—threats or physical actions—to gain compliance. Since this method tends to produce resistance, hostility, or resentment and is unjustifiable from most ethical perspectives, it is the least desirable influence method.

Rudeness in the workplace is becoming increasingly common. Academics and industrial psychologists use a number of terms to describe the phenomenon: workplace incivility, counterproductive behavior, workplace aggression, personality conflict, workplace mistreatment, interpersonal deviance, bullying, mobbing. "There are so many terms, I'm keeping a running list," said social psychologist Loraleigh Keashly, an associate professor of urban and labor studies at Wayne State University. Joel H. Neuman, director of the Center for Applied Management at the State University of New York at New Paltz, said research he has conducted during the past four years indicates that workplace aggression rises when budgets are reduced, when workforces become more diverse, when management changes, when computers are used to monitor worker productivity, when pay cuts are planned, and when companies hire more part-time workers and fewer full-time workers.

Some experts attribute the problem, on occasion, to interpersonal conflict. Behavior one person may perceive as cold or brusque, another may view as a no-nonsense, competent, or efficient manner. Workers of different cultures or backgrounds may react very differently to the same behavior. Thus, as the workplace becomes more diverse, the potential for misunderstandings or unintended offenses may multiply.

Source: Kirstin Downey Grimsley, "Rudeness on Job Can Bruise Profits as well as Feelings," *The Sunday Times* (July 19, 1998): H1.

We can also *control rewards and punishments.* We know that people want to satisfy their needs. Thus, we can suggest to them that by doing what we recommend, they can satisfy needs presently unsatisfied, satisfy needs that now are only minimally satisfied, or continue satisfaction of needs now threatened. Conservationists employ the threatened-needs strategy, telling us, "Sure, everything is fine now. But watch out for the future. Unless we conserve fuel, land resources, and clean air, we will be in serious trouble soon." In other words, needs are satisfied now; but unless we make some change, the satisfaction will stop in the near future.

Still another influence strategy involves *obligation.* In our society, there exists a norm of "reciprocity," which tells us that we ought to respond in kind to behaviors we receive. If someone rewards us, perhaps by doing us a favor, then we feel obligated to reward him or her in return. As communicators, we may use an obligation strategy by reminding others of benefits they have accrued or rewards they have experienced and by suggesting that they now have a chance to show their appreciation by, for example, making a financial pledge or voting for a particular issue.

*Controlling the environment* is yet another influence strategy. Instances of this sort of influence are rather common. Confronted by several rowdy students, a teacher may put them all in the front row of the classroom so that they may more easily be intimidated, or may scatter them throughout the classroom so that they are removed from one another's influence. Similarly, upon perceiving a group of troublemakers, the foreman of a production line may place them on different shifts or scatter them throughout the assembly line.

Some individuals point to the positions they hold as a strategy for getting others to comply. Thus, *legitimate power* lets an individual exert influence simply because the recipient believes he or she has the right to do so.[31] The father who answers his child's "Why?" with "Because I told you to" exerts power of this sort. He has only to tell his child what to do. His position as parent gives him the authority to exert influence without question. Similarly, an organization's hierarchy confers legitimate power to people of high status. They command and their positional power causes their subordinates to obey.

We can also exert influence through *reason.* If we can convince someone that our point of view is correct, then he or she will willingly accept our influence. In our view, this influence strategy is most desirable, producing compliance for the best possible reason—because it is believed to be right.

As we repeatedly have indicated throughout this text, managerial effectiveness in today's rapidly changing environment depends on influence, the ability to get things done through people over whom one has no formal control. Jane Carroll Jackson, vice president of the Forum Corporation, outlined the results and implications of research by her company on influence as a process and as a management tool.[32] Based on data obtained from 4,000 individuals, Jackson defined a three-part model of effective influence behavior.

Part one is *building influence.* This involves a core practice of being supportive and helpful to others. In effect, you first must develop good personal relationships with other people (relationships with high degrees of attraction and involvement), and then you can exert influence without giving orders or relying on your positional authority. Part two is termed *using influence.* Jackson claims that sharing power is the core practice that allows for trying new ideas and working through alternatives. While the manager remains the dominant person in the situation, he or she asks for input from the subordinate individual and involves him or her in making the decision. *Sustaining influence* is the third part. In this element, trust forms a basis for gaining consensus and demonstrating openness. Even when the decision has been made, the dominant individual remains open to suggestions and criticisms, and subordinates feel enough trust in their superior to speak their minds without fear of reprisal.

Involvement    Obviously, frequent interaction with someone else is likely to produce an increasingly involved relationship. As Josefowitz notes, however, in many organizations there are people who are unreachable, stubborn, and impossible to convince and with whom it is difficult to maintain a conversation.[33] These people "switch to automatic and become immune to input from the outside"; they are "unwilling or unable to see the possibility of another way of looking at an issue." They demonstrate their unreachability through lack of eye contact, fidgeting or rigid body posture, apparent interest in other activities or frequent interruptions, yawning, looking at their watches repeatedly, giving "yes, but . . ." responses, or not responding to the topic under discussion.

Josefowitz suggests several strategies for getting through to the unreachable person. First is the *direct approach,* in which one confronts nonresponsiveness directly, saying such things as "It upsets me when you don't pay attention to me" or "I don't feel you hear me, and I don't know what else to do." Usually, this will alert the person to his or her own behavior (and to the speaker's awareness of that behavior), and it will cause the unreachable person to let his or her defenses down, at least for the moment.

Next is the *preventive approach*, which can be taken at the beginning of a conversation. The speaker might say, "I know you have had trouble listening to me in the past, but would you please try to hear a different point of view?" Again, the person's behavioral pattern may be broken.

The *therapeutic approach*, the third alternative, encourages the person to examine both his or her own behavior and the reactions it produces. The speaker might say, "You seem to have difficulty focusing on the discussion and often retreat behind a wall. This really frustrates me because I feel I can't reach you. What can we do to solve this problem?"

During conversations, another method for increasing involvement is *leveling* with the other person—communicating with him or her openly, candidly, and honestly. As Stagnaro reports, some organizations have adopted leveling as a corporate practice.[34] The ROLM Corporation has adopted communication norms designed to promote leveling. One is the use of tactful phrasing, such as "You might consider this," "This might be helpful," or "We have a problem," to show employees the manager is on their side and that he or she is willing to listen to their viewpoint. Another is the use of the "I perceive" technique, in which managers report to employees how they are coming across to them: "This is how I see you," stated honestly and specifically. Such statements provide employees with important feedback on how others in the organization see them. Note, however, that leveling can have unpleasant results. Occasionally, people are unable to take criticism constructively, and conflict or hurt feelings can result. Before adopting leveling as a general practice, then, an organization and an individual must consider the risks involved.

Rossiter and Pearce discuss at length the concept of *"honest" communication*, in which one person reveals his or her true and innermost feelings to another.[35] Culbert terms this strategy *"self-disclosure,"* which he defines as "an individual's explicitly communicating to one or more others some personal information that he believes these others would be unlikely to acquire unless he himself discloses it"—that is, the disclosure of personal information, or of hidden secrets, to someone else.[36] According to Luft, people possess four types of information about themselves: things unknown to both themselves and others; things known to them but hidden from others; things known to both themselves and others; and things known to others to which they themselves are blind.[37] In self-disclosing, the individual reveals things once hidden, to self, to others, or to both.

Two important characteristics of self-disclosure deserve consideration. First, it is risky. Since the information is personal, we make ourselves vulnerable to several undesirable consequences by presenting it to others. We risk rejection—a devastating experience. When we are presenting a front or playing some social role, we can always rationalize away rejections when they occur. After all, it was not we they rejected, just our front. But if we present our true selves and are rejected, there is no place to which to retreat—our very essence has been deemed unacceptable. Fortunately, this sort of rejection occurs infrequently. People are usually accepting and understanding when we open ourselves up to them. Nevertheless, the risk of rejection is a real problem that we must consider when deciding whether or not to disclose our true feelings to someone else.

**Ways of Improving Human Relationships**

Techniques for improving relationships with others include:

| Dimension | Methods for Improvement |
|---|---|
| Attraction | Avoid complaining |
| | Take a cooperative approach |
| | Speak as if you like your work |
| | Treat others as equals |
| | Demonstrate liking for others |
| | Use active listening techniques |
| Dominance | Control rewards or punishments |
| | Create obligations |
| | Control the environment |
| | Exert legitimate power |
| | Use reason |
| | Use organizational influence |
| Involvement | Try to reach "unreachable" people |
| | Use leveling |
| | Use self-disclosure |

A second source of risk is the possibility that the information we disclose might be used against us. Chester Burger, a management consultant in New York, tells of a corporate vice president who disclosed his job anxieties to a colleague at lunch one day.[38] In so doing, he destroyed his image of invulnerability and self-confidence, and encouraged the other man to try to take his job—as he soon did. This negative experience reinforces an important point: Self-disclosure must be based on trust to minimize the risk of having information you reveal used against you.

Another risky aspect of self-disclosure is that it may force us to confront our own weaknesses, thus discovering things about ourselves we may not like very much. Discovering that we are inadequate in some way is painful. Finding that we are not all we could have become is disappointing. Thus, self-disclosure poses the danger of revealing characteristics we might rather ignore.

If self-disclosure is so risky, why should we try it? The answer is the second characteristic of self-disclosure: it produces better, more involved, more satisfying relationships. Studies have repeatedly shown that we need relationships based upon self-disclosure if we are to be happy and fulfilled.[39] Despite its risks, then, self-disclosure is an important means for establishing more involved personal relationships with others.

Having seen the benefits of self-disclosure, our next concern is how it might be accomplished. In general, there are five rules to observe when we express our personal feelings to other people:

**1.** *Self-disclosure should be as immediate as possible.* We should report our feelings as they occur rather than waiting until some later time to discuss them.

**2.** *Self-disclosure should be voluntary and natural.*   We should not reveal personal information because we feel compelled to do so. Rather, revelation should naturally grow out of a relationship that has developed some degree of trust and supportiveness.

**3.** *Self-disclosure should be self-descriptive.*   Good self-disclosure is purely descriptive, noting one's emotions and how they relate to the other person's behaviors. For example, we might describe our feelings by saying, "When you yell at me, I feel angry and resentful."

**4.** *Self-disclosure should strive to improve the relationship.*   If the relationship is likely to be harmed in the long run, perhaps because our true feelings might make the other person feel defensive or hurt, then we probably should not disclose. If, on the other hand, we think disclosure will help the relationship, then it probably is appropriate. It is crucial here to make a distinction between immediate and long-range effects. It may be painful for the other person to discover that he or she has made us feel hurt or angry, but if, through our self-disclosure, he or she can grow to understand how that feeling resulted, perhaps a better relationship can evolve.

**5.** *Self-disclosure should be as specific as possible.*   When reporting our feelings to someone else, we should try to avoid generalizations and speak as specifically as we can about how we feel and why. What incidents have made us feel upset? Are there patterns we can perceive? Why do we react as we do?

While self-disclosure is one useful method of increasing involvement, we still face the problem of encouraging disclosure by the other person. To do so, we must find some means of minimizing the risk that disclosure poses to him or her. One useful method of accomplishing this is through supportiveness. That is, our responses should create a climate of support and trust so that the other person feels secure enough to self-disclose to us.

## SUMMARY

Our purpose in this chapter has been to consider a fundamental element of the organization's social system: human relationships. In examining the nature of human relationships, we concluded that they consist of four basic dimensions: attraction, dominance, involvement, and the situations in which persons interact. We can develop communication practices that allow us to deal effectively with each of these dimensions. Fundamental to our effective communication skills is learning to listen to others so that we both learn from them and are perceived as good listeners. The basics of effective communication are important in every organizational setting—from the interview to the public presentation.

## QUESTIONS FOR DISCUSSION

1. If, as many futurists project, more people will begin to work at home using computers, what effect will it have on organizational relationships?

2. What aspects of an organization with which you are very familiar serve to shape the dominance dimension? Be specific.

3. What are some important factors influencing perception in organizational settings?

4. What are some ways in which we can be helpful as listeners? How can we be attentive? Empathic? Responsive?

5. What are some possible dangers of open, honest communication?

## EXERCISES

1. Select an organization with which you are very familiar. Describe how the attraction factor is shaped within that organization; that is, how do proximity, attractiveness, and so on play a role in interpersonal attraction there?

2. Choose an organization you know well. How does that organization's physical environment show status differences? How does it control who talks to whom?

3. Think of someone who has some control over your life. Then think of one example of each kind of influence (force, rewards, punishments, and so on) that person uses.

4. Suggest principles related to the dominance dimension of human relationships that you might use to be a better supervisor. How would you use them, generally, if you were supervising the work of 10 engineers?

# CASE application 7.1

In parts of corporate America, private offices are becoming as scarce as typewriters and cubicles are shrinking as companies increasingly rethink the traditional workspace. Gone are floor-to-ceiling walls, windows for executives and even elevators. Now workers—including CEOs—ride escalators to "neighborhoods" of small workspaces and meet in "teamwork" rooms and even kitchens. The changes are aimed at dragging old offices into a new world of work—where rank has few privileges, teamwork rules and privacy is a rare commodity. Yet taking down the walls is both liberating and painful. Communication between co-workers rises, but so do distractions. To limit distractions, companies ban speakerphones except in meeting rooms, pipe in special white noise, and issue "protocols" on keeping voices low in public spaces. The savings can be significant: Xerox expects to save $10 million annually by going to smaller individual workspaces, where some

managers now sit in small glass-walled windowless offices (often half the size of their old domains) and other managers work in brightly colored cubicles surrounded by their staff. Meetings occur in "teaming" rooms or kitchenlike "commons areas," and phone booths are available for personal calls.

In Pittsburgh, Alcoa will abolish all private offices—even for its chief executive officer—in its new $60 million headquarters building.

Source: Maggie Jackson, "Thinking Outside the Box," *Chicago Tribune* (June 14, 1998): sec. 6, p. 1.

## Questions

1. What effect do you think this approach to improving organizational communication would have on each dimension of interpersonal relationships?
2. Would you want to work in an organization having this philosophy? Why, or why not?

# CASE application 7.2

People care deeply about their titles. "Your self-concept depends on what you do and what you're called, and even if you simply change the title it affects your ego. It affects your personality," said Patrick Lennahan, director of the Career Center at Roger Williams University in Bristol, R.I. Many people would rather have a prestigious title than money, probably because a title boosts job satisfaction, he found. Much of the reason is how coworkers react to the person with the higher

title. People defer more readily to a vice president—no matter how incompetent—than a manager, and so on down the line. "How long somebody will wait for you, whether you can be put on hold on the telephone or not—those are things that people aren't always thinking about but something people do without thinking," Lennahan said.

Some progressive companies experiment with new "organic" structures and have shed the title system as a holdover from the "hierarchical" days, said Frank Shipper, professor of management at Salisbury State University in Maryland. One such company is Newark, Delaware–based W. L. Gore and Associates, makers of Gore-Tex fiber for activewear, which calls its top two executives president and secretary-treasurer. The other 5,000 or so employees all answer to "associate," a title meant to make them feel like members, not just replaceable employees. The founder, William Gore, believed that titles get in the way of communication. "If people need to talk to somebody, they should talk to them as people with expertise rather than people with a certain title," Shipper said. In the future, corporations will not organize permanent departments but temporary task forces, he predicted. "The title you have today is obsolete tomorrow, just like your product is," Shipper said.

Source: Claudia Coates, "Take My Desk, My Raise, Not My Title," *The Sunday Times* (July 19, 1998): H1.

## Questions

1. How do you feel about this effort to eliminate traditional corporate "labels"?
2. What effect would this approach have on the dimensions of interpersonal relationships?

# CHAPTER eight

# Interpersonal Communication within Organizations: Verbal and Nonverbal Messages

In the previous chapter, we talked about the nature of interpersonal relationships within organizations and the processes of perceiving and listening to other people. Now, we move to the other end of the communication process, sending messages.

We must again emphasize the importance of skill in sending messages to other people. Just as listening and perceptual skills are vital to the establishment of desirable relationships in organizations, so too is skill in the use of verbal and nonverbal symbols. For example, Sullivan reported the results of research comparing successful company presidents with average college graduates.[1] The findings showed that presidents excelled in several areas, including (in order): verbal skills, mathematical reasoning, logical thinking, personality (presidents were more dynamic and assertive, with more positive attitudes toward other people), energy and drive, ascendance (presidents had more leadership confidence and assertiveness), personal relations (presidents had greater ability to get along with others and, perhaps surprisingly, were kinder and more sympathetic, understanding, tolerant, and warm-hearted), and values (most presidents placed high value on gaining power and responsibility and on attaining the financial rewards that go with those objectives). The importance of verbal skill is therefore obvious; what is less obvious is that each of these other qualities manifests itself in various communication behaviors. As we have said repeatedly, your ability to succeed is directly tied to your ability to communicate.

## PREVIEW

The cues we transmit to other people traditionally have been divided into two general categories: verbal messages (those that involve spoken, written, or electronically transmitted words) and nonverbal messages (cues that convey meaning without the use of words or that modify the meaning of the words that are used). Although the adage "Actions speak louder than words" is one we endorse, we'll begin with a discussion of verbal messages and then move to a consideration of nonverbal cues. Through our discussion of the impact of words and non-verbal cues upon communication within organizations, we hope to enable you to improve your use of these fundamental tools.

## VERBAL MESSAGES

Most of this book is about words. In various chapters, we discuss what to say to influence the thoughts and actions of others, what to ask to solicit information during interviews, how to structure words so they make sense in conveying information, and how to use words to lead groups effectively. But in this section, we want to take a more microscopic view of words and the impact they have on communication within organizations.

Semantics    Often we hear people say something like "It's just a question of semantics" or "We're having problems with semantics." What they mean is that they are concerned with words. And well they should be—perhaps the most imperfect part of the imperfect process we call communication is the words people send one another. Seeking to improve our understanding of language, an entire field called *general semantics* developed several decades ago to investigate the effects words have on our everyday lives.

**Problems of Semantics**    Through the efforts of Johnson, Korzybski, and others, several problems common to the words we use have been brought to light.[2]

*Bypassing*    This problem stems from the nature of "meaning." Often meaning is assumed to be a characteristic of words—something they contain permanently, naturally, and obviously. Following this assumption, we use words with confidence, certain that everyone shares our meaning. In fact, we often are wrong; words have no meaning in and of themselves. Rather, we have agreed that certain words symbolize certain ideas or things, and it is through this shared agreement that words have utility. We have agreed, for example, that the thing you are holding in front of you is called a "book"; we might just have easily agreed that it be called a "wombat." The meaning ("a thing having pages with words on them") remains the same.

*Allness*    Another problem with words springs from the word "is." Often we apply this word to people, noting that "She is a manager," "He is a secretary," and so on. Labels like "manager" and "secretary" pose no terrible problems; labels like "lazy," "disgruntled," and "chauvinist" are another matter. Essentially, the "allness" principle holds that when we apply a label to someone by using the word "is," we are saying, "She or he is that, and nothing more." Thus when a manager concludes that a certain worker is "lazy," the manager tends to see that individual only as a lazy person. As a result, he continually watches over the employee, often creating resentment within the worker that in turn makes him or her less inclined to work hard. Thus, the term "lazy" becomes a self-fulfilling prophesy. Since people are complex and constantly changing, our treatment of that person is likely to be inappropriate.

*Stereotyping*    Related to the allness principle is the tendency to infer a variety of characteristics on the basis of the one we observe. We may infer that all students take drugs, all blue-collar workers are eager to avoid work, all executives are greedy, and so on. Our stereotypical conceptions of students, workers, or executives lead to a variety of inferences, any or all of which may be wrong. In addition, stereotypes cause us to see the same characteristics in everyone to whom a label is applied. Managers often see all line workers as being alike; professors see no difference between students (nor students differences among professors); racists cannot distinguish among members of minority groups. They may therefore treat all members of those groups in the same way, attributing to each of them the characteristics they have inferred.

*Time-Fixing*   Still another problem attributable to language is our failure to recognize that people change over time. When we apply a label such as "lazy" to someone, we tend to fix that person in time; that is, we assume that the person always will possess that characteristic. But the behaviors we observed may have occurred purely as a function of the situation, so we may have misperceived them in the first place. Since we know that people change continually, time-fixing may lead us to incorrect conclusions about them.

*Polarization*   The words we use often cause us to think in dichotomous or polarized terms. As Haney points out, "polarization occurs when one treats contraries as if they were contradictories; when one deals with a situation involving gradations and middle ground in strict, either-or, contradictory terms."[3] That is, while people and things typically occur in gradations ("shades of gray"), we often see them as being one thing or another ("black or white"). In addition, we tend to attach evaluations to these labels. A worker may feel that workers are good and management is bad; a manager may believe that supervisors are hardworking and employees lazy. Language thus encourages us to see things as opposites, both in their characteristics and in their values.

*Signal Responses*   When we deal with words, we can respond signally or we can respond symbolically. Signal responses are immediate and automatic: We jump when we hear an unexpected noise, we stop the car when the traffic light turns red. A symbolic response requires interpretation and thought and thus occurs more slowly. While our responses to words ought to be symbolic, involving careful and rational thought, too often they are a signal. When we hear an emotion-charged word like "communist," "reactionary," or "racist," our response typically is immediate and unthinking. When we make such quick responses to words, we have fallen into yet another trap posed by language.

## Avoiding Problems of Semantics

How then can we avoid these pitfalls of language? In fact, we cannot. But we can minimize the probability of being misled by words through the use of certain techniques.

*"E-Prime" Language*   Semanticists have sought to alleviate the problems attendant with the word "is" through the use of what Bourland terms "E-Prime" language, or "standard English with the exclusion of the influential forms of the verb 'to be.'"[4] Writing and speaking without using any form of "to be" obviously is difficult and probably would preoccupy our efforts to a degree that we could think of nothing else. Yet the purpose of E-Prime language is laudable: to be sensitive to the difficulties inherent in "is." If we avoid using "is," substituting "seems" or describing behaviors rather than attaching labels ("He doesn't seem to devote much effort to his job" rather than "He is lazy"), we can avoid some of the problems "is" causes; if we are sensitive to others' usages of "is," we may avoid jumping to erroneous conclusions.

*"Etc."*   To avoid the "allness" error, we can mentally add "etc." to statements we make. Rather than simply noting, "She is an executive" (thus limiting her

to one specific role or identity), we should think, "She is an executive, etc." We thus recognize that we can never say everything about people or things and that our labels consider only small parts of those referents.

*"Indexing"*    The problem of stereotyping, or perceiving as identical everyone falling into a particular category, can be minimized by mentally applying a numerical index to each person about whom we speak. Rather than saying "worker," we should say "worker1," thus distinguishing her from "worker2," "worker3," and all other workers. In this way, we recognize the uniqueness of each individual within the category. Perhaps the best way to deal with the "allness" trap, however, is to avoid categories altogether and speak only of individuals (such as "Professor Hill," "Professor Peters," etc.).

*"Dating"*    By mentally attaching a date to our words, we can recognize the changing nature of reality and people. "He was obnoxious (January 1, 1999)" demonstrates that the behavior was situational and not an unchanging characteristic of the person. Similarly, "love (2001)" is different from "love (1991)," and "anger (January)" is different from "anger (March)." By mentally attaching dates, we recognize that things continuously change and that responses that previously were appropriate now may be destructive.

*Clarifying Strategies*    To avoid misunderstandings, we can employ any of several strategies that promote clear communication:

**1.** *Succinctness.*    Use only necessary words, speaking as simply as possible.
**2.** *Definition.*    Define terms and explain meaning. We must try to anticipate potential misunderstandings and explain or define clearly our meaning.
**3.** *Singularity.*    Consider only one topic at a time, taking things step by step.
**4.** *Repetition.*    Repeat key issues, difficult points, and ideas that may be confusing to the receiver. Such repetition should not be a simple restatement of the idea but a rephrasing in which different terms are employed to make the same point.
**5.** *Analogy.*    Draw parallels between this and other situations, using one instance to clarify another.
**6.** *Structure.*    Carefully organize the message into a clear, coherent pattern. Generally, the topic under consideration dictates the structural pattern we would use. Some topics require a chronological sequence ("First this happened, then this, and then this"); some require a spatial pattern ("You take the first right you come to, then go two blocks and make a left"); others a procedural sequence ("First you jack up the car, then you unscrew the lug nuts, . . ."). In any case, it is important that some logical structure be followed so the listener can use that structure to more accurately understand the information.

The language we use is riddled with imperfections and inadequacies, and semantic breakdowns occur all too often. By recognizing the traps language poses and using some of the techniques suggested above, however, we can minimize this barrier to communication and improve the flow of messages throughout the organization.

## Verbal Strategies

Closely related to semantic barriers are the problems created by the verbal strategies we employ. Research has demonstrated that certain verbal behaviors tend to produce worsened communication and relationships. We shall consider several such behaviors, noting the effects they produce and some alternative behavioral strategies that seem preferable.

### Defensiveness-Producing Behaviors

As described many years ago by Gibb and more recently by Ellison, defensive behavior occurs when an individual perceives or anticipates a threat or an attack from someone else.[5] One feels that one's well-being is in danger, that one is likely to lose status, that one may be rejected by the other, or that some other undesirable event will occur. Thus one takes steps to protect oneself—one behaves defensively. There are, Gibb claims, certain behaviors that cause people to feel threatened to a degree that they act defensively. Those defensiveness-producing behaviors include:

**1.** *Evaluative behavior.*   If we seem to be passing judgment on the other person, evaluating her worth or characteristics, she naturally will tend to become defensive. There always is a chance that our judgment will be unfavorable to her, in which case her self-esteem may be damaged. Rather than take that risk, she may withdraw from us or, worse yet, launch a counterattack.

**2.** *Control-oriented behavior.*   Speech that attempts to control the other person usually provokes resistance. In essence, control-oriented statements imply superiority on our part, inferiority on the other's. We, through our vast wisdom, know what is best for him; he is incapable of making judgments for himself. Therefore, our statement implies, we will do him the favor of telling him how to direct his behavior. Again, by threatening his self-esteem, we cause him to become defensive.

**3.** *Strategic behavior.*   If the other person perceives that we have something sneaky in mind, or that we are pursuing a covert strategy, one naturally will defend oneself. No one likes to have others "put something over" on one or to be tricked. Hence whenever one perceives that someone has hidden motives or is following some preplanned strategy, one engages in defensive maneuvers.

**4.** *Neutral behavior.*   If we appear unconcerned about the other person's welfare, dealing with her as an object rather than a person, she probably will become defensive. Since we do not care about her, she assumes, we probably would harm her without a second thought. This potential threat in turn causes her to take protective measures.

**5.** *Superioristic behaviors.*   When we communicate to another that we feel superior in ability, position, morality, power, or some other characteristic, we arouse defensiveness (even though, in our hearts, we know we're right). No one wants to feel inferior to another, and usually people will protect themselves when they confront others behaving in superioristic ways.

**6.** *Dogmatic behaviors.*   If we make it clear to the other person that our point of view is right and all others are wrong, he probably will become defensive. He knows that to express his thoughts is to invite attack from us, so he simply withdraws from the interaction.

Through these verbal behaviors we usually cause others to feel threatened. This is particularly true in situations involving persons of unequal status. Since the high-power person controls to some degree the fate of the lower-power person, the subordinate probably will feel in some danger and will engage in defensive maneuvers.

What are these defensive maneuvers? Goffman lists several defensive behaviors: *physical avoidance,* where individuals completely avoid interacting with others who might pose a threat; *physical retreat,* in which the individual makes a gracious withdrawal before a threat materializes; *verbal avoidance,* or changing the topic to something less threatening; *verbal retreat,* where the individual simply does not mention information that might evoke a threatening response; *information control,* or engaging in ambiguous or deceptive verbal behaviors; *interaction control,* in which the potential threat is neutralized through the use of humor or some other distracter; *aggression,* or attacking the threatening person; *tactful blindness,* where the threat is ignored; *projection,* in which feelings of inadequacy are transferred to the other so he becomes the one who, in the view of the defensive person, is afraid; and *verbal rationalization,* where a presumably "rational" explanation is used to rationalize the threat away.[6] Each of these behaviors creates a barrier to communication. The receiver is so concerned with protecting his or her well-being that she or he fails to understand truly the transmitted message. It is important, then, that defensiveness-producing behaviors be avoided.

**Aggressive Behaviors**   A second set of communication behaviors that are detrimental to communication and interpersonal relationships within organizations is behaviors that release (and in turn often provoke) aggression. While these behaviors provide temporary benefit to the performer, allowing him to vent his aggressions and hostilities, in the long run they usually are detrimental to one's relationships with others. Some of these behaviors, many years ago labeled "verbalizers" by Palmer, include[7]:

**1.** *Arguing.*   Like each of Palmer's verbalizers, arguing is a socially acceptable method of releasing aggressions. The person simply waits for someone else to state an opinion and then argues with that person. On a short-term basis this strategy is extremely effective. The arguer releases hostilities while at the same time appearing knowledgeable and intellectually active to others. In the long run, however, this strategy is disastrous: others eventually get fed up with the continual argument and simply avoid the arguer altogether.

**2.** *Complaining.*   Another method of releasing hostility is to complain. Used occasionally, this strategy is not detrimental to relationships and may provide entertainment for one's coworkers. When employees gather in a break area and gripe about their boss, their pay, their parking facilities, and everything else, they are performing a mutually useful function by giving each other a chance to express hostilities harmlessly. The person who complains constantly, however, will find it difficult to establish good relations with others—particularly his or her boss.

**3.** *Gossiping.*   While virtually everyone enjoys a good gossip session occasionally, people who habitually spread gossip usually find their relationships breaking down. When others perceive that an individual tells everything he or she knows, they probably will have little trust in that person and will avoid communicating anything important or confidential to him or her lest those things be spread around the organization.

**4.** *Martyrdom.*   This strategy involves seeking sympathy from others by constantly portraying oneself as a victim. Indeed, highly skilled users of martyrdom can make people feel vaguely uneasy even when they are doing the person a favor. The strategy usually begins with the phrase, "That's OK, I'll . . ." For example, a martyr might tell us that his car isn't working. Trying to be of help, we offer him a ride to work the next day. He responds, "That's OK, I can walk, even though my old football injury is acting up again." We repeat the offer; he still replies, "That's OK, I don't want to be any bother." Finally, after a long and bitter struggle, he lets us give him a ride. Thus he uses this strategy to vent his aggressions by making us feel uneasy, and at the same time he reaps the benefits of our generosity (unless, of course, we conveniently "forget" to pick him up the next morning, thereby making him late for work). Not surprisingly, this strategy soon wears thin; people stop communicating with the martyr altogether.

In addition to Palmer's verbalizers, Fleishman suggests other forms of verbal aggression[8]:

**5.** *Interrupting.*   By repeatedly interrupting the statements of others, we can both vent our hostilities and control the flow of the interaction. In so doing, however, we irritate other people and may ruin our relationships with them.

**6.** *Name calling.*   This strategy involves attaching labels to people directly ("You're crazy!") or indirectly ("Only an idiot would think that!"). While this is an effective method for releasing aggression, it typically is not appreciated by the crazy idiot to whom you are speaking.

**7.** *Challenging integrity.* Hostilities can be expressed by questioning the other person's motives, character, or behavior. Although no direct charges of dishonesty are made, such questions as "What's in this for you?" and "What are you trying to hide?" carry clear implications and place the person in a defensive posture. Not surprisingly, the other person will not find the conversation particularly enjoyable.

**8.** *The "brush-off."* This technique involves simply ignoring the other person. When she disagrees with you or tries to explain her point of view, you simply keep talking or occupy yourself with something else—rearranging the contents of your briefcase, picking dirt from under your fingernails, looking out the window, or studying the acoustical tiles on the ceiling. A useful release of aggression, this behavior nevertheless tends to frustrate others and produce a quick end to the communication.

The remedy for aggressive behaviors is simple: Avoid them. Carrying out this remedy can be more difficult, however, as it often requires changing habitual verbal behaviors. Yet the effort is worthwhile, for only by avoiding these verbal behaviors can we build good relationships with others.

| KEY CONCEPTS 8.2 | Defensiveness-producing **Verbal Behaviors** |
|---|---|
| Verbal behaviors that often produce defensive reactions include: | Verbal behaviors that release (and provoke) aggression include: |
| • • Evaluative behaviors<br>• • Control-oriented behaviors<br>• • Strategic behaviors<br>• • Neutral behaviors<br>• • Superioristic behaviors<br>• • Dogmatic behaviors | • • Arguing<br>• • Complaining<br>• • Gossiping<br>• • Martyrdom<br>• • Interrupting<br>• • Name calling<br>• • Challenging integrity<br>• • The "brush-off" |

## Supportive Behaviors

To improve interpersonal communications with others, suggests Gibb, we should establish a "supportive" climate.[9] Rather than appearing to be a threat to the listener or releasing our own feelings of aggression, we instead should demonstrate our support for that person's well-being. Just as some verbal behaviors create defensiveness or display aggression, then, others seem to produce this supportive climate. Among them:

**1.** *Descriptive behavior.* Rather than passing judgment on the other's behavior, we should simply describe the behavior and our reaction to it. Instead of saying "You're disgusting," it would be more supportive to say, "When you put your bare feet on the dinner table while we are eating, it makes me uncomfortable." Thus the focus of the interaction is not the worth of the person but the behaviors in which that person is engaged.

**2.** *Problem-oriented behavior.* Trying to control the other person creates defensiveness; suggesting that you work cooperatively to solve a problem avoids the implicit superiority that control-oriented statements contain and instead makes the person more willing to interact. The focus on the interaction is shifted from the person to an objective problem, thus reducing the possibility of a perceived threat.

**3.** *Spontaneous behavior.* Behaviors that are spontaneous, growing from the immediate situation, tend to avoid the defensive reactions produced by strategic behaviors. Rather than planning strategy ahead of time, it usually is preferable to let the situation dictate appropriate behaviors. Obviously, there are exceptions to this rule. Speeches and interviews must involve some planning. In everyday conversation, however, spontaneous reactions rather than strategically motivated behaviors produce better relationships.

**4.** *Empathic behavior.* Rather than appearing neutral or unconcerned, we should demonstrate to the other person that we do indeed care about him and his well-being. Empathy involves a genuine concern for the other, which we communicate in our interaction.

**5.** *Equalistic behavior.* Superiority produces defensiveness; we therefore should stress equality in our interactions. Even conversations between superiors and subordinates may contain elements of this technique, as the superior stresses commonalties of the relationship (for example, organizational goals toward which both are working) rather than emphasizing the differences in status.

**6.** *Provisional behavior.* Since a dogmatic "my way or the highway" attitude produces defensiveness, it generally is preferable to take a provisional attitude. Our communication should indicate that our attitudes are tentative, not cast in concrete, and that we are willing to listen to other viewpoints. By minimizing the threat of attack upon the other, we make her more willing to communicate her true feelings.

On a more specific level, Hegarty suggests some verbal habits to avoid if words are to be used to your greatest advantage.[10] There are, he claims, some verbal behaviors that either annoy other people or cause them to draw unfavorable conclusions about the speaker. Among them are the following:

**1.** Repeated use of the same conversational closing, such as "Take care" or "Take it easy." These are impersonal and indicate a lack of creativity and thoughtfulness.

**2.** Repeated use of the same designation (referring to everyone as "you guys"), the same modifier (calling everything "cool," "awesome," or "bogus"), the same expression ("Wow," "Good grief!" or "No kidding!"), the same cliché ("a stitch in time" or "strike while the iron is hot"), or conversational fillers such as "you know" and "like." These become annoying and show sloppy mental habits.

**3.** Mistakes in usage, such as the double negative ("They can't hardly expect us to do that!"; "Irregardless"; "He never did nothing"); misuse of "do" and "did," "don't," and "doesn't" ("He don't have any right to do that" "She admitted she done it"); misuse of "knew," "know," and "known" ("He knowed we couldn't do it"); misuse of "gone" and "went" ("I wish I had went"); misuse of personal pronouns ("They fired him and I," "They did it to her and myself"); misuse of "was" and "were" ("They was going"); use of "dem" and "dose" ("I don't like dose guys").

Mistakes in grammar and pronunciation call undesired attention to you. It makes no difference whether you grew up in the hills of West Virginia or on the streets of Chicago's South Side; improper use of the language will hurt your credibility in an organization and probably limit your ability to rise in the hierarchy. Be sure your English is good.

The final recommendation we can offer in the effective use of language concerns courtesy. Too often, people in organizations are under pressure and, as a result, begin treating one another discourteously. Barton discusses the use of "put-downs and vulgarity" in business, claiming that "managers who use vulgarity often feel it adds an extra bit of shock and sophistication to their interchanges with employees.[11] In most cases, however, it alienates employees and places them on the defensive. Using put-downs, snappy replies, and vulgarity destroys the speaker's credibility." The person who can remain courteous even in a crisis impresses everyone else with his or her coolness under fire and professionalism in dealing with others.

Today, many organizations are recognizing and responding to the problematic aspects of language. "In big organizations with massive, complex operations, there's a tendency to think in terms of labels," remarked A. W. Clausen, who headed Bank of America during the 1970s. "Those people over there are tellers, those are managers, these are officers. These are grade 20s, grade 15s, grade 30s, and so on. The names are forgotten along with sensitivities, anxieties, frustrations. The tendency is to dehumanize."[12] Such dehumanization can be avoided only if we use words carefully.

With all these principles and recommendations in mind, then, we move to the nonverbal elements of communication in human relationships.

| KEY CONCEPTS 8.3 | Verbal Behaviors that Enhance Relationships |
| --- | --- |
| Desirable verbal behaviors include: <br> • • Descriptive behaviors <br> • • Problem-oriented behaviors <br> • • Spontaneous behaviors <br> • • Empathic behaviors <br> • • Equalistic behaviors | • • Provisional behaviors <br> • • Varied conversational closings <br> • • Varied phrases <br> • • Proper verbal usage, grammar, and pronunciation <br> • • Courtesy |

## NONVERBAL MESSAGES

Verbal messages are of undeniable importance, forming the basic unit of our communications with others. But of at least equal importance are the myriad of unspoken, nonverbal cues that accompany spoken messages. Indeed, Birdwhistell argues that these cues are even more important than words.[13]

**Roles of Nonverbal Cues**

To understand nonverbal cues as they operate in human communication, we need to consider the roles they play or the things they do when people interact. These roles become most apparent when we consider nonverbal cues as they relate to verbal messages. To see nonverbal messages in action, consider this hypothetical situation. You walk into the company president's luxurious office to ask him to give you a raise. During the encounter, the nonverbal cues you receive perform the following roles:

1. *Repeating.* "Sit *down*," the president says, pointing to a chair in front of his huge desk. His nonverbal cue, a hand gesture, serves to repeat the message he has spoken. "Would you care for a cigarette?" he asks, holding a box out toward you (in violation of the company's smokefree environment policy). Again, his gesture repeats his words and illustrates his apparent feeling that he is "above the law" in his own organization.

2. *Contradicting.* "You know," he begins as you use his diamond-encrusted lighter to light your cigarette, "I'm a simple man. I've always been satisfied with little things." His office, with its wood paneling, leather-upholstered furniture, deep-pile carpet, and teak desk, contradicts his words, and his $2,000 Armani suit suggests expensive tastes. "Now, I've always been happy to talk to people who are eager to improve their lot in life." But he kept you waiting for nearly an hour in his outer office, and now speaks to you with a scowl on his face while staring at the wall behind you. His nonverbal cues thus suggest that he is anything but happy to see you.

3. *Substituting.* "And I wish the company had enough money to give everyone who deserves it a raise. But . . ." His voice trails off, and he shrugs and shakes his head. These gestures substitute for words. He does not have to say, "The company's broke, and there's nothing I can do about it." His nonverbal gestures have said it for him.

4. *Elaborating.* Suddenly, the president bursts into tears. Between sobs, he manages to stammer, "I hate having to turn down an ambitious, valuable employee like you. You can't imagine how bad I feel about not being able to give you a raise. Sometimes this job is absolute hell!" His words express his feelings, but his actions elaborate on them, showing us just how much he means what he says.

5. *Accenting.* Slowly, the president rises from his chair, struggling to regain his composure. "Darn it!" he explodes, pounding his fist on the desk. "Darn it, I may not have any money, but I'm going to give you something anyway, even though we can't afford it." From beneath his desk, he pulls a T-shirt with the company logo on the front and his picture on the back. "I know that someone as loyal and supportive of this company as you will be proud to wear this shirt—heck, it's probably better than money." His fist pounding serves to accent his "Darn it!" and his rising out of his seat likewise accents both his dominance and his generosity.

6. *Regulating.* "I'm glad you came in here," he concludes, extending a clammy hand. "We need to talk like this more often." He then sits down, turns away, and begins reading the *Wall Street Journal*. The role of these last behaviors is to regulate or control the interaction. In essence, he is saying, "Our conversation is now over. No further communication is desired. Please leave." As you exit through his outer office, you notice that his secretary, too, is wearing a T-shirt.

Thus, the roles of nonverbal cues can be defined by their relationships to spoken messages. Nonverbal behaviors may produce or change meaning by repeating the verbal message, contradicting it, substituting for it, elaborating on it, accenting parts of it, or regulating it. Each of these functions is important, as our example demonstrates, and each of them shows the crucial nature of nonverbal communication in our everyday interactions.

| KEY CONCEPTS 8.4 | Roles of Nonverbal Cues |
|---|---|
| The roles of non-verbal cues include:<br><br> • • Repeating<br> • • Contradicting | • • Substituting<br> • • Elaborating<br> • • Accenting<br> • • Regulating |

## The Impact of Nonverbal Cues

Although nonverbal cues can be divided into any number of categories, researchers typically have placed them into six. We will consider each category individually, noting how the behaviors and cues in each seem to influence human communication.

**Environment**    The physical setting in which communication occurs constitutes the environmental element of nonverbal communication. As you might suspect, the work environment is important, particularly from the viewpoint of those within that environment. A study by the Buffalo Organization for Social and Technical Innovation showed that satisfaction with work space created an extra $1,600 of productivity annually in a white-collar worker.[14]

According to Steele, the dimensions and functions that immediate physical settings have for people include the following[15]:

**1.** *Security and shelter.*   Such protection can include both physical and psychological security; privacy, for example, may be provided or prevented by the physical surroundings.

**2.** *Social contact.*   Arrangements that permit or promote social interaction, such as the water cooler around which people come into face-to-face contact, take into account the arrangement of facilities, the locations of people in relation to one another, and the amount of mobility allowed by the setting. The presence or absence of central gathering places (such as break areas or coffee machines) also is influential in promoting or discouraging communication.

**3.** *Symbolic identification.*   The messages sent by settings that tell someone what a person, group, or organization is like or what his, her, or their position in the organization is. Companies will select arrangements, furniture, and so on to project a certain image or corporate culture both to their employees and visitors. For example, at Systek Corporation in Oak Brook, Illinois, Rick Wargo, director of national sales, selected teak furniture for all his sales staff. The reason for his choice was that "Systek is a people-oriented company and the wood has a warmth much greater than steel."[16]

The Herman Miller Company in Zeeland, Michigan, has developed a computer program designed to match workers to an office space tailored to their personality types:

- "Visionaries" are long-term planners who tend to be scholarly and work through new ideas logically. Their offices need ample storage space and various surfaces for working on several projects at once.
- "Catalysts" tend to make decisions based on personal values rather than logic, to work in spurts of energy, and to need interaction with others. Their offices should include a table and chairs for meetings or a conference room nearby and lots of work surfaces to handle their clutter.

- "Cooperators" thrive on personal communication, and they value comfort over privacy. Their offices should have low panels and counter space to provide easy contact, a table and chairs for meetings, and plenty of in and out boxes.
- "Stabilizers" do everything by the book and believe organizations run best when everyone follows written policy. Their offices should have high walls and doors for privacy, they should have plenty of storage space, and they should have a cockpit-like work area with telephone and computer in easy reach.

Source: Jose Martinez, "Can You Be Categorized as Visionary or Stabilizer?" *Chicago Tribune* (March 15, 1992): sec. 7, p. 7.

*The environment in which communication occurs may have a dramatic impact on the quality of the interactions that take place. Here, the White House Communications office in Washington, D.C. creates an interesting setting for critical organizational communication.*

In traditionally managed organizations, the physical arrangement has clear implications for the dominance dimension of organizational relationships. The relative status of individuals, groups, and entire departments is communicated by the arrangement of the physical environment. For example, in large buildings, individual floors often express the dominance implicit in the hierarchy. The corner offices on upper floors are occupied by senior executives or department heads. Middle offices are occupied by executives of lesser status. The most powerful executive has the largest office with the most windows and best view. Middle management personnel have one-window offices. Employees on the lowest rungs—clerks, secretaries, typists—work together in a large, open room.

Similarly, accessibility is inversely related to status in traditionally led organizations. Presidents often have two or three secretaries and two or three waiting rooms a visitor must go through to get to them. Lower-level managers have one secretary and no waiting room. In short, the more important you are, the more difficult it is to see and communicate with you.

This odd characteristic of organizations, incidentally, is one communication-related problem with severe implications. The people who must be involved in organizational communication are the executives. The more important an executive is, the more crucial it is that he or she be in the communication network. Yet organizational arrangements work to produce the opposite effect. Important executives are inaccessible, while clerk-typists are a part of virtually everything. It is small wonder, then, that studies of organizations repeatedly have found that executives know far less about organizational matters than do secretaries and clerks.[17]

Furniture arrangement is another important element of the environment. Michael Korda, a publishing house executive, describes how placement of a desk and chairs in an office can influence the dominance the occupants exert over their visitors.[18] Figure 8.1 illustrates three office arrangements, each exerting a different level of dominance. In the first arrangement, power is minimized. The visitor sits next to the desk, making him or her virtually equal to the occupant and forcing the occupant to assume a relatively uncomfortable position to talk to him or her. In the second arrangement, the

| FIGURE 8.1 | Furniture arrangement as part of environment |

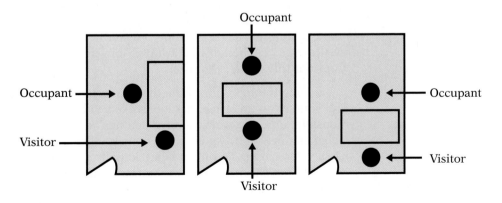

occupant is more powerful. He sits regally behind his desk, which is interposed between him and his visitor. But the third arrangement is most dominant of all. The visitor sits with his or her back to the wall, occupying minimal space, while the occupant has the remainder of the office in which to move about. This, coupled with the interposed desk, makes the situation the most domineering.

Finally, things within the environment can communicate information about the individual occupant. One study found, for example, that the presence of aesthetic objects (such as paintings, a color calendar, and a potted fern) in a faculty member's office significantly increased perceptions of his or her authoritativeness and trustworthiness. The same study also discovered that the presence of profession-related objects (including award plaques and a professional-looking library) in a faculty member's office produced a similar effect.[19]

**4.** *Task instrumentality.* The appropriateness of facilities for carrying out tasks is determined by a consideration of specific settings and tasks, such as the soundproof room needed for taping records, the locations of groups that work together, the presence of equipment, and sensory conditions. While physical environments affect interaction, perceptions of status, and the like, it is important to remember that they are constructed to get work done. Industrial engineers and architects have traditionally concerned themselves only with the task instrumentality of the environments they design. Only recently have they begun to focus on the impact of environments on the relationships among the people working within them.

**5.** *Pleasure.* The gratification the place gives to those who use it, such as the views employees enjoy from the sixtieth floor of the Sears Tower in Chicago, includes the absence of unpleasant stimuli (noise, smells, temperature) and the presence of pleasant stimuli (music, colors, and other visual stimuli). However, it is important to remember that pleasure is an individual thing; conflicts over what stimuli are pleasurable sometimes occur among organizational members.

In recent years, some organizations have come to the realization that design of offices, factories, warehouses, stores, and shops can contribute to company outcomes in a number of ways.[20] Good design either helps or hurts productivity by creating a workspace that contributes to efficiency and boosts morale. Good design promotes or frustrates creativity by offering workers informal places they can gather to trade ideas and share insights. And perhaps most importantly, good design expresses or suppresses the company's own character, which is of critical importance in competing for talent, as smart, ambitious workers scope out the way a workplace looks and feels before they decide whether they want to join the company.

Consider three real examples:

- If you go to the top floor of the third-tallest building in Dallas, you will find yourself in an office that looks like a video game. Demons and monsters lurk atop walls; slanted ceilings and multilevel floors all suggest a challenging, slightly gory game come to life. Why an office that looks like a video game? To reflect what actually goes on there. These are the offices of Ion Storm, one of the country's fastest-growing computer-gaming companies.

A telecommuting program adopted in February 1997 by the General Counsel's Office of the Internal Revenue Service and the National Treasury Employees Union has been deemed a success by both employees and managers. The program allows employees to work at an alternate site, such as at home or at another government office closer to their home, for up to 40 hours per month. Managers base approval of employee requests to telecommute on several factors, such as the nature of the work to be performed (it must be portable, definable, and specific), ability to verify progress on work projects, adequacy of staff coverage in the employee's home office, and availability of equipment at the alternate work site. A one-year study of the effectiveness of the program found that it enhances productivity by improving concentration, reduces commuting costs, and improves flexibility.

Source: "Telecommuting Given Thumbs Up," *BNA's Collective Bargaining Bulletin* (December 3, 1998): 169.

- If you go to Brampton, Ontario (a Toronto suburb), you can stroll through a massive factory that resembles a city laid on its side. There are two main arteries—Main Street and the Colonnade—seven indoor parks, a Zen garden, a dry cleaner and a bank, basketball and volleyball courts, and a wide array of cafes and restaurants. This is the headquarters of Nortel, a global telecommunications giant, which transformed a 600,000-square-foot factory into a citylike environment. Why a city? To win over its headquarters employees who were reluctant to move from Toronto to the suburbs.

- If you go to Freeport, Maine, you could get lost in a 650,000-square-foot warehouse, equipped with 3.5 miles of conveyor belts, storage for 4 million items, 25 shipping docks, and its own built-in Federal Express package-handling center. But it's not just a warehouse. It's the new L. L. Bean order fulfillment center, a facility that handles 12 million packages a year. What's so special about a warehouse? The employees of L. L. Bean helped to design it.

Progressive organizations have learned some important lessons concerning the design of their workplaces. First, good design considers how people really work. There's a reason the best offices look like coffee shops: that's a design for a workplace in which people can talk, compare notes, share ideas, and develop innovations. It's the same reason factories look more like offices, with separate "pods" where teams can meet to solve problems and offer suggestions. Even the language of design has changed from isolated workspaces to "caves and commons": caves are private spaces where people can write, think, talk on the telephone, and focus on individual tasks; commons are flexible meeting spaces where teams can quickly huddle to design new approaches to doing their work.

Second, companies have learned to involve employees in the design process. In the case of L. L. Bean, the company involved hundreds of workers on a number of teams, each of which researched the best way to design their part of the warehouse. Nortel created two committees: a 200-person group that worked full time on the design of the new headquarters, and a 20-person group that linked various departments. This approach is vastly different from the historical design process, where executives and architects decided what sort of environment would be best for their workers.

Third, organizations have come to the realization that design communicates the company's very essence—its mission and values. According to David Dunn, Nortel's director of global workplace planning, "This project was about more than consolidating bricks and mortar. We understood that we could align the factory's reinvention with the company's reinvention—and with our core values." One reason Ion Storm has gone to such lengths in the design of its video-game office space is to send a message to the people who work there—and to those the company hopes to attract as employees in the future. The design is a way of saying that you won't find a more cutting-edge game company—and that counts in the competition to attract and keep talent.

There may also be a lesson for employees and would-be employees: Do not go to work in an office or factory that looks like it's out of the past. In fact, even before you sit down for an interview, you might ask for a tour of the workplace. If it looks like the maze of cubicles found in Dilbert cartoons, you might know all you need to know about that company.

**Proxemics** Proxemics is the placement of individuals relative to other individuals—their physical closeness—as well as the way they communicate through interpersonal space and distance. In general, people tend to sit close together when they are involved in a group and working on a common problem. But if the same group members are given individual tasks to work on for a few minutes, they will tend to move farther apart. Overall, groups perform better, more persuasively, and more cooperatively at close, face-to-face distances (18 inches versus 36 inches). But if the group describes itself as "crowded," these positive characteristics begin to disappear.[21]

Gender differences have been found in reactions to group density. American women tend to sit closer together in groups than do men. All-male groups sit farthest apart, mixed-sex groups at an intermediate distance, and all-female groups closest together. It has been argued that women in groups are more likely to develop warm, close, affiliative relationships than are men. In general, males have been found to prefer meeting in large rooms and to give each other higher ratings in that setting, while women prefer smaller meeting rooms. Several studies have concluded that dense environments have a more adverse effect on males than on females.[22]

The *seating arrangement* of a group of people is particularly important in proxemics. A great deal of evidence suggests that seating has a significant impact on patterns of communication. Research indicates that people seated directly across a table from one another communicate most often and that people seated at the end of the table communicate more with the entire group than do people seated in any other position. These effects on interaction in turn have an effect on group leadership; people seated at the ends almost always emerge as group leaders by virtue of their easy access to all the other members.[23] Our physical proximity to other group members, then, influences our ability to influence them.

*The way employees dress, whether they wear uniforms or suits, influences the way they are perceived by others, in terms of status, power, and competence.*

**Artifacts**   The things with which we decorate our bodies also are important in communication. In most organizations and in society as a whole, clothing seems to be a strong indicator of status. The implications of this clothing-status relationship become apparent when we consider a study conducted by Lefkowitz, Blake, and Mouton, who observed the conformity behavior of pedestrians in a large city.[24] An accomplice wandered about the city violating the "Don't Walk" sign at street corners, while the experimenters watched the behavior of other pedestrians to determine whether they followed his example. This was done on two consecutive days. On the first day, the accomplice wore a high-status outfit—a suit—and carried an attaché case. On the second day, he was dressed in a low-status janitor's outfit. The results were startling. When the accomplice was well dressed, several people followed him across the street; but when he was poorly dressed, no one followed him. The researchers concluded that status, as shown by one's clothing, has an impact upon one's ability to influence other people.

A variety of books have been published dealing with the impact of clothing upon success in the organization. *Dress for Success* probably is the most widely read, although many others also are on the market.[25] Our own observations, however, indicate that the rules suggested by *Dress for Success* and other such works do not hold in today's organization. Rather, a variety of factors determine which "uniform" is most appropriate in a particular company. Many organizations have a dress code for their employees, and many require (and often provide) uniforms.

Still other differences are found in different industries: financial institutions (for example, banks and insurance companies) seem to value conservative, dressy outfits (such as blue three-piece suits for men and suits in conservative colors for women). Newer high-tech companies (such as Apple Computer) encourage employees to dress more casually, and a three-piece suit worn in their manufacturing plants would be regarded as strange. Interestingly, however, the father of high-tech, IBM, traditionally has had an unspoken rule that everyone wears blue suits and white shirts or blouses, and only recently has that norm been relaxed to allow colored shirts and less conservative suits. Small manufacturing concerns almost always are shirtsleeves organizations; supervisors and managers wear slacks and open-collared shirts rather than blue jeans and T-shirts, but rarely do people wear suits.

In any event, what is important is that every organization has its norms for appearance. By adhering to those norms, and perhaps developing an appearance just slightly "better" than that expected by the organization, you can enhance your own credibility to some degree. However, by violating the norms and dressing to either extreme (too casual or too dressy), you may harm your image in the organization and even be subject to disciplinary action. It is also important to dress in a way that makes you feel good about yourself. Research has shown that those who feel inappropriately dressed often exhibit hostility, withdrawal, or aggression. However, those who feel positively about the way they are dressed tend to be more outgoing, friendly, happy, and relaxed, and they report feeling more confident.[26]

**Kinesics**   The category of kinesics includes general body movements—postures, gestures, facial expressions, and eye behavior. Each of these has been found influential in communication. In studies of body posture, Mehrabian found a close relationship between *posture* and liking for the other person.[27] For example, when confronting someone they intensely dislike, women tend to look away from the other person as much as possible. If they like the other person, they vary their direction of face, sometimes looking squarely at that person and sometimes looking away. When dealing with a total stranger, they tend to look directly at that person. No consistent results were obtained for males. For both sexes, however, leaning forward seemed to indicate liking for the other, while leaning backward seemed to convey negative feelings. Experts on nonverbal communication agree that our posture communicates much about our moods and emotions. We judge whether others are happy, sad, confident, or determined based on the way they carry themselves. In general, wider, more open body postures result in more perceived credibility and persuasive power, whereas narrower postures (legs and arms held close together) reduce status.

While the effects of *gestures* upon others remain somewhat a mystery, we do know something about the factors underlying a person's gestural behavior. Mehrabian and Williams observed that people trying to be persuasive show more gestures and head nods and fewer postural shifts than others.[28] When gestures are tied to the rhythm of our speech, they appear to help listeners follow our remarks. People who are relaxed as they communicate tend to use more gestures and to use gestures that are more natural and conversational. Highly nervous speakers may use no gestures at all, too many repetitive gestures, or touch themselves (for example, by playing with hair or jewelry)—all of which are perceived as signs of nervousness or discomfort.[29]

## DIFFERENT GROOMING STANDARDS FOR MEN AND WOMEN?

The U.S. Supreme Court let stand an appeals court decision on employee grooming. In the case, three employees of Blockbuster Entertainment Corp. challenged the company policy that prohibited men, but not women, from wearing long hair. The U.S. Court of Appeals for the Eleventh Circuit upheld the right of a company to set such rules, even though they create different standards for males and females.

Source: "Supreme Court Lets Stand Decisions on Grooming Policy, Light-Duty Transfers," *Labor Relations Week* (November 25, 1998): 1279.

We may also use kinesic communication to control or regulate interpersonal communication. One example is *turn-taking*. We may signal the end of our turn by stopping or by relaxing our hand movements. We may shift our heads or eye position, or change our posture. Most important, we can signal our desire to talk by leaning forward and/or using gestures prior to speaking. In group settings, dominant persons are often seen leaning forward and using gestures to maintain the floor, preventing interruptions from other group members. Some scholars believe that it is largely kinesic behavior that determines who talks when and for how long. Listeners' kinesic movements are also important to observe since they provide clues to who really is being listened to and whose opinions are valued. Listeners typically turn their bodies toward someone they want to hear. By not turning toward someone who is speaking, they communicate the opposite attitude.[30]

*Facial expressions* and *eye contact* are other areas of kinesics that seem important in communication. Rosenfeld noted that people seeking approval seem to smile more frequently, and Mehrabian and Williams observed that people trying to persuade others also showed an increase in facial activity.[31] Several studies have shown that, unlike other aspects of nonverbal communication, basic facial expressions are rather universal, carrying the same fundamental meaning throughout the world.[32] Because we all feel that we are pretty good at reading others' facial expressions, we sometimes believe that we can accurately assess others' reactions to what we or others are saying. But often we are inaccurate because most people mask or conceal their facial expressions with "public faces." Studies of eye contact in human communication have identified the situations in which we seek or avoid eye contact with others. Generally, we will seek eye contact with others when we want to communicate with them, when we are physically distant from them, when we like them, when we are extremely hostile toward them (as when two bitter enemies try to stare each other down), or when we desire feedback from them. Given the positiveness of eye contact, we should find that it improves communication—and indeed it does. Some investigators have found that messages accompanied by eye contact were more favorably interpreted by observers than were messages sent without eye contact.[33] Indeed, aversion to eye contact in a group setting is sometimes perceived by others as an indication of disinterest, apathy, rudeness, shyness, nervousness, or even dishonesty or deceit!

**Touch**    The fifth aspect of nonverbal behavior, touching, is perhaps the most primitive. Even in the womb, the child can be stimulated by touch.[34] As a form of communication, touching is very important. Montagu argues that a person's social and psychological development is hampered if that person receives too little touching from others early in life.[35]

One of the most common forms of touching in the American workplace is the *handshake*—an action that is used for meeting others, greeting others, and saying goodbye. While it is a seemingly minor act, the handshake can convey a variety of meanings and create many different initial or final impressions. For example, according to career salesman J. T. Auer, handshakes fall into ten categories[36]:

1. *The flabby handshake.*    A limp, soft paw used by pessimists.
2. *The hesitant handshake.*    Extended by people who want you to make the first move.
3. *The squeezing handshake.*    Usually used by men wanting to show their strength and power.
4. *The next-to-the-body handshake.*    The arm and elbow are bent while the right hand stays close by the side—favored by politicians and those who hesitate to take risks.
5. *The impelling handshake.*    Used by people eager to shake hands; this involves quick and vigorous shaking.
6. *The nongripping handshake.*    The hand is thrust forward, but the fingers do not move; says "I really don't want to get involved."
7. *The robot.*    The hand is offered automatically and indifferently, without feeling.
8. *The jackhammer.*    The shake of a hand pumper with a lot of willpower and determination.
9. *The prison handshake.*    The person holds your hand too long and gives it back reluctantly.
10. *The normal handshake.*    Firm, brief, open, and honest. This is the most effective of the handshake styles.

A firm, brief handshake conveys confidence and professionalism in most North American and European countries, while handshakes of a different sort often create a variety of undesirable impressions in the mind of the other person. Thus, this is an important element of nonverbal communication.

Although touching can serve many different functions, from an organizational perspective, two are especially important: *expressing supportiveness and communicating power or dominance.* Touching in a supportive way can take many forms—putting our arms around other people, patting them on the arm or hand, holding their hands in our own. Generally, we do not touch people we dislike (unless we are fighting with them), so the act of touching someone communicates a general message of liking and support. In general, in casual encounters, we keep touching at a minimum. As relationships develop, the nature and frequency of touching change dramatically.

Some management theorists have warned about appropriate uses of touching. Blanchard and Johnson, in their popular book, *The One Minute*

As American corporations hire increasing numbers of immigrants, cross-cultural misunderstandings will occur with greater frequency. For example:

- In the United States, calling attention to oneself (particularly one's professional achievements) is considered a sign of self-respect. Many Asians, however, think that calling inordinate attention to oneself is rude and unprofessional. In an employment interview, this cultural clash could result in a Vietnamese applicant's being viewed as "lacking self-esteem."
- While direct eye contact is valued in the United States, other cultures avoid eye contact as a sign of respect or deference. An applicant from such a culture probably would be viewed as "unassertive" or "untrustworthy."
- Rather than risk losing face or ridicule for misusing an English word, some foreign-speaking workers will simply remain silent. Their American managers often assume they simply have no suggestions or ideas to contribute.
- In parts of Asia, the Hispanic countries, and much of Europe, to initiate even the simplest task without being told specifically to do so is considered a defiance of authority. From the American viewpoint, this "lack of initiative" may be interpreted as laziness or a lack of self-confidence.

As the American workplace becomes increasingly multicultural, we must improve our skills in perceiving people. Rather than interpret others' behaviors in terms of our own cultural norms, we must communicate more carefully and more thoroughly to ensure that we understand what others do.

Source: Sondra Thiederman, "Communication: Overcoming Cultural and Language Barriers," *Personnel Journal* 67 (December 1988): 34–40.

*Manager,* point out that managers should touch others only when they are communicating something positive, such as encouragement, reassurance, or support.[37] They view negative touching, associated with criticizing, admonishing, or disciplining, as quite inappropriate.

One of the reasons that Blanchard and Johnson offer this advice to managers is the power, or dominance, function of touching. That is, it is the high-status person who has the power to touch. It is the police officer who touches the accused, the teacher who touches the student, the doctor who touches the patient, and the manager who touches the employee. As Nancy Henley points out in *Body Politics,* it would be a breach of etiquette for the lower-status person to touch the person of higher status.[38] Henley further argues that in addition to indicating relative status, touching also demonstrates the assertion of male power and dominance over women.

Whether or not Henley's assertion is true, much research has examined gender differences in touching. Mothers have been found to touch children of both sexes and of all ages a great deal more than fathers do.[39] Women touch their fathers more than men do. Female babies are touched more than male babies. And women reportedly have a greater desire to be held than do men.[40] In general, more touching reportedly occurs among opposite-sex friends than among same-sex friends. However, since our culture tends to frown on same-sex touching, many people may not feel comfortable acknowledging the extent to which they touch those of the same sex.

Whatever gender differences exist, cross-cultural differences are more apparent. In one study, for example, students from the United States reported being touched twice as much as did students from Japan.[41] In Japan, there is a strong taboo against strangers touching, and the Japanese are especially careful to maintain adequate distance. Another obvious cross-cultural difference is found in the Middle East, where same-sex touching in public is extremely common. Men walk with their arms on each other's shoulders, a practice that would not be comfortably received in the United States, except in specific situations, such as locker-room celebrations.

These cross-cultural nonverbal differences can cause real problems when people from different countries and cultures attempt to interact effectively. The Japanese, for instance, may be perceived as distant or aloof, while southern Europeans may be viewed as pushy or aggressive. An awareness of and sensitivity to cultural differences in touching behavior are crucial as people from different cultural backgrounds try to work together in organizations.

**Vocalics**    Aspects of the voice—pitch, volume, quality, and rate—that accompany spoken words make up the final category of nonverbal cues: vocalics. Apparently, people make several sorts of judgments about others on the basis of vocal cues. As Addington discovered, we judge personality characteristics on the basis of voice. Among the responses he found to various types of voices were:

**1.** *Breathy voices.*    Males were rated young and artistic. Females were rated pretty, petite, effervescent, and high-strung.
**2.** *Nasal voices.*    Both males and females were given a wide variety of negative characteristics.
**3.** *Throaty voices.*    Males were rated older, realistic, mature, sophisticated, and well-adjusted. Females were termed masculine, unintelligent, lazy, ugly, sickly, careless, naive, and neurotic, and were assigned a variety of other undesirable characteristics.
**4.** *Flat voices.*    Males were rated masculine, sluggish, cold, and withdrawn. Females received identical characterizations.[42]

Another judgment that is based on vocal cues is *speaker recognition*. On the basis of vocal cues alone, we can accurately recognize the identity of the person to whom we are listening (provided, of course, we already are acquainted with that person and his or her voice).[43] On the basis of voice we also may be able to recognize personal characteristics of the speaker, such as age, sex, or race.[44] Vocal cues give us hints about the emotional state of the speaker—whether he or she is happy, sad, angry, or pleased.[45]

Perhaps the most important function of vocalics is *modifying our verbal messages*. For instance, researchers have identified at least two dozen ways of saying yes.[46] There is the definite yes and the wishy-washy yes, the happy yes and the sad yes, the seductive yes, the confused yes, and the assured yes. When we interact with others, they will tend to believe our vocal meaning whenever our verbal and vocal messages are at odds.

Key dimensions of nonverbal cues in organizations include:

- • The physical environment
- • Proxemics
- • Artifacts
- • Kinesics
- • Touch
- • Vocalics

Not long ago, it was enough for an executive to "dress for success"—to wear power ties, navy suits, and other clothing conveying and contributing to the success the executive sought. Now, however, there is a growing recognition that the ingredients for success go beyond clothing and include such nonverbal communication factors as animated gestures, well-timed smiles, and careful use of vocal pitch.

John Ransford Watts, dean of the School of Theatre at De Paul University, reports seeing a rise in the number of business executives and other professionals seeking the help of drama, voice, and acting coaches to improve their communication skills. "There's an enormous number of people in high levels that have skills and knowledge that sit between their ears but they don't know how to transmit that knowledge in a personal way," he observes. "To seek coaching is a good idea, and many executives are coming to this realization."[47]

While executives today are seeking training in the effective use of nonverbal cues, however, our intent in this section has been primarily descriptive. We have sought to sensitize you to the nonverbal cues encountered in communicating with others in almost any setting. By putting this knowledge into practice, you should be able to communicate effectively in your daily encounters with other people.[48]

# SUMMARY

Our purpose in this chapter has been to consider two fundamental building blocks of communication and relationships within the organization's social system: verbal messages and nonverbal cues. To communicate effectively with others, we must understand the nature of language and perception, and must be able to speak clearly, articulately, and influentially. The way we speak is important, as is our ability to use every nonverbal communication element to our advantage, including our attire, our office decorations, our eye contact, and our posture. The basics of effective communication are important in every organizational setting—from the interview to the public presentation.

# QUESTIONS FOR DISCUSSION

1. How do the principles of the general semanticists relate to the attraction dimension described in the previous chapter? The involvement dimension?

2. Choose an organization with which you are familiar. How does its physical environment communicate what that organization is like? How does the

environment promote or inhibit the personal growth of its occupants?

## EXERCISES

1. Think of the most obnoxious, unpleasant person you know. Then list all the verbal habits that person has that you find offensive. How should these habits be overcome?

3. What dress code seems to apply to people working in any organization with which you are familiar?

2. Choose an organization you know well. How does that organization's physical environment show status differences? How does it control who talks to whom?

On Chicago's far South Side, George Pullman built not only a factory in which his employees would work to build luxury train cars, but a town in which they would live. When "Pullman Town" opened in 1881, it was saluted as the epitome of modern town planning. The homes reflected the standing of the occupants within the company: on the corners, big substantial homes were built for executives and managers; in the middle of the block, the smaller row houses and apartments were for ordinary workers. Only one church was provided for the community, however. Pullman reasoned that, if industry could use standardized, interchangeable parts, so too could the various religious denominations. He allowed no taverns in Pullman, although visiting dignitaries could drink in the Florence Hotel, the centerpiece of the town.

Not everyone was happy with the arrangement, however. Some argued that, since every last stick within the town was owned by Pullman, his employees could never realize the American dream of home ownership. "We were born in a Pullman house," one worker told a newspaper reporter, "fed from a Pullman shop, catechized in the Pullman church, and when we die we shall be buried in the Pullman cemetery and go to a Pullman hell."

When a depression drained the company's business, Pullman cut his workers' wages. He insisted, though, that the same rents be subtracted from their paychecks, which often meant they had only a few pennies left with which to feed their families. As a result, 3,000 workers went on strike. While the strikers eventually were forced back to work, the company's victory was short-lived: The Illinois Supreme Court ruled in 1898 that Pullman Village should be sold off because a company town was "incompatible with the theory and practice of our institutions." George Pullman died three years after the strike, his name synonymous with management hostility toward workers. Marking his passing, a Chicago newspaper noted that he had built a fatal flaw into his model city: He could not understand how deeply the ordinary worker wanted to become a homeowner.

Much of Pullman Village still stands and can be toured by visitors.

Source: Ron Grossman, "Pullman Village Was No Utopia for Its Working Inhabitants," *Chicago Tribune* (December 9, 1998), sec: 5, p. 1.

# CHAPTER nine

# Fundamentals
# of Interviewing

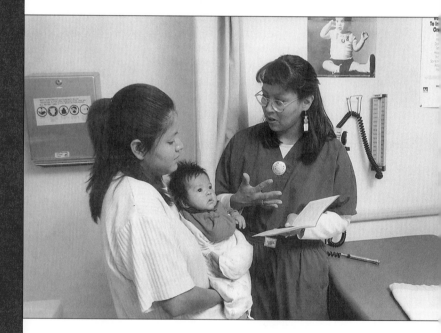

While dyadic encounters are frequent in all human interactions, both personal and professional, in organizational settings no form of dyadic communication is more significant or more frequent than the interview. It is in the employment interview that we often are initially accepted or rejected by the organization. Subsequent interviews will inform us of our progress, promise, and problems in our daily work activities. In the context of the interview, we will likewise complain and be counseled, provide and receive information, and be praised and disciplined. We will participate in problem solving and persuasion; and often before we retire from or leave the organization, we will reflect on our accomplishments, disappointments, defeats, and triumphs in final exit interviews. Clearly, interviewing pervades all organizational activity—serving a multiplicity of functions, operating at numerous levels within the organizational hierarchy, and continuing throughout the lives of each organizational employee.

Interviewing, like all interpersonal communication, normally involves face-to-face interaction (although telephone interviews do occur on occasion) between two parties (interviewer and interviewee) who take turns acting as sender and receiver. However, some other characteristics make interviewing a unique form of dyadic communication. First, interviews are *purposive*, conducted to achieve some specific objective. Informal interactions may have underlying purposes as well, but in an interview, the purpose is more clearly stated and understood by the participants. Second, interviews are more *structured* than informal conversations: The interviewer usually has some preestablished agenda that is followed during the conversation. Implicit in this characteristic is a third: Interviews are more carefully *prepared* than are informal conversations. Typically, the interviewer prepares carefully for the interview before it is conducted. Often, the interviewee prepares just as carefully (as before an employment interview). Finally, the *sequence* of the interview is more predictable: The interviewer selects topic areas and asks questions, for the most part, while the interviewee provides responses and answers. In summary, then, interviews are prepared, structured interactions between two or more parties in which questions and answers are used to achieve relatively specific and mutually understood purposes.

Knowledge of interviewing is important, both for short-term and long-term reasons. In the short term, it is likely you will experience these interviews as an interviewee. To participate effectively, you need some knowledge of how interviews function and what the interviewer has (or should have) in mind. In the long term, you may achieve supervisory or management status in an organization. As a supervisor or manager, your success may be determined to a significant extent by your competence in conducting various types of interviews. Your immediate and long-term professional success, therefore, rests to some degree on your understanding of and skill in various forms of interviews.

I n this chapter, we will examine the unique nature of interviews as communicative events. Taking the perspective of the interviewer, we will consider the nature of interviews in general and some specific purposes for which interviews are used in organizational settings. Then we will examine some types of interview questions and suggest sequences by which those questions might be organized. Finally, we will turn our attention to several of the most commonly encountered kinds of interviews in organizational settings: appraisal, corrective, and complaint-resolution interviews.

## BASIC CONCEPTS OF INTERVIEWING

Although interviewing is a common organizational activity, it is not necessarily an easy one. Perhaps Stewart and Cash put it best in their introductory chapter on interviewing:

> If you . . . tend to believe that interviewing comes naturally—like swimming to a dog—think of your recent experiences: the inept company recruiter who kept answering her own questions; the car sales representative who was determined to sell you a large sedan when you wanted a small economy car; the counselor who told you all of his problems instead of listening to your problems; the public opinion interviewer who asked biased questions; the encyclopedia sales representative with a canned pitch.[1]

To avoid the kinds of problems mentioned by Stewart and Cash, we will examine some interviewing techniques and strategies that apply to all interviewing situations. More precisely, we will discuss the preliminary planning that interviews require, some strategies and questions for interviewing, using probes, coping with inadequate responses, acting as listener and respondent, and closing the interview.

**Preliminary Planning**

While there is no certain way to create a climate for ideal interviews, careful preliminary planning can assist you in establishing a potentially constructive interviewing setting. It is to be hoped that, as an organizational member functioning as an interviewer, you will receive some training in the interviewing process. Through training the interviewer learns methods for structuring interviews. Too many untrained interviewers approach each interview without a specific strategy. This is not to imply that you should employ totally canned procedures without sensitivity to the demands of the situation and the needs of each particular interviewee. But interviews that are systematic, structured, and guided are more valid than those that are unguided, unstructured, and without design or system.

Most interviews are conducted on the premises of the organization. Many are carried out in the interviewer's own office. When this is the case, the interviewer is responsible for creating the best possible environment in which the interview can occur. First, each interview should be conducted under circumstances that promote comfort and privacy. Comfort involves such physical considerations as room temperature and seating comfort, as well as matters related to psychological comfort. The physical distance between you and the interviewee (proxemics) is important, as is the arrangement of the furniture in the room. In the American culture, physical distances of two to five feet seem to be the most psychologically comfortable for conversation. Other potential barriers to communication include chair arrangement, the presence or absence of a desk, note taking, and tape recording. If you plan to take notes or record the conversation, mention the fact directly and indicate the reasons for the practice. In each instance, you should give careful consideration to the kind of climate you wish to create and attempt to use space, distance, and other verbal and nonverbal factors to enhance the interview setting.

The interviewee's psychological comfort will also be enhanced if you do all you can to ensure that the interview remains a private exchange. Although privacy is absolutely mandatory in the context of counseling and corrective interviews, nearly all interviews benefit from a private communication environment. Your secretary should not dash in with urgent messages or put calls through to you. If you must interrupt the interview to deal with some critical issue, apologize to the interviewee.

Depending upon the kind of interview you are conducting, you will probably need to plan the general approach you want to take, the kinds of questions you want to ask, and the kind of information you need to share. If you are conducting an employment interview, you should plan a core of basic questions, read the applicant's résumé in advance, and bring information about the job's critical requirements. With a corrective interview, you must decide how to describe your perception of the problem and how and when to encourage the interviewee to respond. In the context of a work appraisal interview, you should study your written comments, prepare to make positive comments as well as suggestions for future improvements, and decide how to encourage the interviewee to join you in setting future goals. The kind of planning you do will depend upon the purpose of your interview.

| KEY CONCEPTS 9.1 | Key Considerations in Planning an Interview |
|---|---|
| Effective planning for an interview includes consideration of:<br><br>• • *Comfort.*<br><br>• • *Potential barriers to communication.* | • • *Privacy.*<br><br>• • *Approach to be taken.*<br><br>• • *Objectives of the interview.* |

## Opening the Interview

The opening of the interview sets the tone for the remainder of the communication encounter. Although individual interviewers vary in their interpersonal styles, a generally desirable opening approach is one of warmth (seasoned with professional restraint), interest, and genuine personal concern for the interviewee. This may include a handshake, a smile, and a word of thanks for the interviewee's presence at the interview. The goal is to *establish rapport* by creating a climate of trust and goodwill. One traditional approach to putting the interviewee at ease is to engage in initial small talk. Some brief exchanges concerning sports, weather, families, and so forth may enhance rapport. But excessive small talk may backfire and cause the interviewee to be anxious and eager to settle down to the serious business of participating in the interview.

Soon after the initial greeting, you should make some *orientation statement.* In some types of interviews, both parties know essentially why they are there. Even so, it is often helpful to state your perception of the purpose of the interview. In many interviews, the interviewees are tense, uncertain, and perhaps overly aware of the status and power of the interviewer. This is especially so in appraisal, employment, corrective, and grievance contexts. To assist in overcoming this problem, you might make some early statement expressing your view that the purpose of this interview is for both you and the interviewee to exchange information so that both of you might make a wise decision concerning employment, performance, and other factors. This kind of orienting remark not only clarifies the purpose of the interview but also may serve to relax the interviewee.

At this point, you may wish to *preview* the kinds of topics you hope to discuss. While a preview is not necessary for selection interviews, previewing can provide some sense of direction for the interviewee, increase interpersonal trust, and improve the overall efficiency of the interviewing process. Once again, it is extremely important to be sensitive to the needs of the person being interviewed. An extended orientation phase is especially helpful with highly anxious interviewees.

## Basic Interviewing Strategies

Each interview must have a goal, and the interviewer usually formulates an overall design that will theoretically lead to that goal. Many interviewees will have their own strategies and goals, some of which will complement and others of which will conflict with your goals as an interviewer. In an employment interview, each of you may have as a mutual goal the discovery of whether or not you should become professionally associated. To achieve that goal, however, both of you may hope to spend a maximum amount of time during the interview gaining information from the other. Clearly, these goals are not compatible, given the time constraints that are usually present. Thus, both interviewer and interviewee must be prepared to adjust to the unanticipated demands of the communication situation.

From your perspective as an interviewer, there are two basic strategies you can adopt. The first is *directive.* Using a directive strategy, you establish the purpose of the interview and strive to control the pacing of the interview and the subjects covered during it.[2] This approach is highly structured. It is particularly applicable when you believe you know the desired interview goal and the precise steps for getting there. The directive strategy takes the form of probing specific topics in a particular sequence with considerable flexibility in follow-up questions and overall structure. It is especially efficient for acquiring large quantities of information.

As we mentioned earlier, highly structured interviews tend to have high validity. Nevertheless, the directive strategy has some potential weaknesses. Using a structured, familiar interview format is somewhat akin to playing the same role in a play over and over again: You must labor to make each appearance seem fresh, original, and interesting. No interviewee should leave the interview feeling that he or she has just been exposed to the organization's assembly line!

The second basic interviewing strategy is *nondirective*. When you choose a nondirective strategy, you allow the interviewee to control the purpose, the topics to be covered, and the pacing of the interview.[3] Nondirective interviewing was developed by therapist Carl Rogers and is most commonly used in counseling situations. Even though this approach allows the interviewee to explore whatever areas he or she wishes with only minimal structural constraints, it is not without some interviewer control. Your role is one of empathic, nonjudgmental listening, while permitting the interviewee to structure his or her own thinking with flexible and subtle guidance.

The obvious advantages of the nondirective approach are flexibility and the opportunity to explore interesting subjects in depth. By using this method, interviewer and interviewee can begin to establish an ongoing relationship. Moreover, with this approach, the interviewee has every opportunity for self-expression. Nondirective interviews are not without their disadvantages, however. They are less efficient than directive interviews and can be very time consuming. Because the interviewees choose most of the content to be pursued, each interview is likely to cover entirely different ground. Thus, as an interviewer, you cannot really compare interviewee responses across several interviews. Nondirective interviews require considerable interviewer sensitivity and excellent listening skills.

While the typical approach to most interviews remains the directive strategy, many interviewers plan several major questions, allowing a great deal of flexibility in the ways in which these questions are pursued by interviewees and providing considerable time for interviewee questions, comments, and insights. This combined approach is practical and allows the interview to be a shared communicative experience.

---

| KEY CONCEPTS 9.2 | Fundamental Interviewing Strategies |
|---|---|

Basic interviewing strategies are:

- • *Directive, where you establish the purpose of the interview and work to control the topics the interview covers; the interviewer is in charge.*

- • *Nondirective, where you allow the interviewee to determine some aspects of the interview, such as the purpose of the interview, the topics to be covered, or the pacing of the interview.*

## Questions

A key communication tool used by interviewers is the question. Whatever your overall design, you will ask many questions as a primary means of collecting the data you need to plan and make decisions. You may choose to use one of two basic types of questions: open or closed. *Open questions* are broad in nature and basically unstructured. Often they indicate only the topic to be considered and allow the interviewee considerable freedom in determining the amount and kind of information he or she will provide. Open questions let the interviewee know that you are interested in his or her perspectives, attitudes, and value system.

Some questions are extremely open ended, with virtually no restrictions, such as: (1) "Tell me about yourself." (2) "What do you know about General Motors?" (3) "How do you think this organization can be improved?" Other questions are more moderately open: (1) "Why did you major in marketing?" (2) "What can be done to improve this organization's productivity?" (3) "What do you know about General Motors' new design plants?"

Open questions allow the interviewee to talk with relative freedom. Because there are so many different ways to respond to them, they are not very threatening and they tend to reduce interviewee anxiety. Open questions give the interviewer insights into the interviewee's prejudices, values, and commitments. Of course, open questions are not without their disadvantages. They take a good deal of time, collect much irrelevant information, often require several follow-up questions, demand excellent listening skills on the part of the interviewer, and can be difficult to evaluate following the interview.

On the opposite end are *closed questions*. These are structured and restricted, and they often include several possible answers from which to choose. Thus, potential responses are limited. On occasion, a closed question will probe for a brief bit of specific information, such as: (1) "When did you first notice that you were drinking excessively?" (2) "How many years did you consult?" (3) "What starting salary would you anticipate with this job?" Others are even more closed, requiring the interviewee to select the appropriate response from among those you provide, such as: (1) "What brand of toothpaste do you presently use: _____ Crest, _____ Colgate, _____ Aim, _____ Aquafresh, _____ or Gleem?" (2) "Where would you prefer being located with our company: _____ New Orleans, _____ New York, _____ San Francisco, or _____ Chicago?"

The most extreme form of the closed question is the *yes-no bipolar question*. Usually the interviewee is allowed to respond only with yes or no, or possibly "don't know." For example: (1) "Do you smoke?" (2) "Do you agree with this church's stand on women in the clergy?" (3) "Are you familiar with our new drug abuse program?" Inexperienced, unskilled interviewers have a tendency to rely heavily on this type of questioning in spite of the fact that it requires maximum questioning effort and generates only small amounts of information per question. Occasionally a yes-no question is appropriate, but long series of such questions should be avoided.

In general, closed questions save time, increase the probability of obtaining relevant responses, are efficient, and are relatively easy to tabulate following the interview. By using closed questions, the interviewer maintains substantial control over the flow of the interview. On the other hand, closed questions generate limited information and often cause interviewees to respond less accurately (since their views may not fit precisely into any one of

Tom S. owns a small public relations consulting firm headquartered in Chicago. When his office receptionist resigned to take a job with another firm, he began recruiting for her replacement. Several applicants "looked good on paper," and he called each of them in for separate interviews.

One of his interviews was particularly interesting. After asking the interviewee about her qualifications and describing the job requirements and company environment, Tom concluded the interview by asking, "Do you have any other questions you would like to ask me?" "Yes," said the interviewee, "I have one more question. Do you think O. J. Simpson was guilty?"

If you were Tom, how would you interpret and respond to that question? Would the characteristics of the interviewee affect your interpretation or response?

the offered alternatives). They decrease interviewee talking time and increase the number of questions the interviewer must generate. Finally, they fail to explore the reasons behind attitudes and opinions and stifle the offering of valuable, but unanticipated, information.

### Probing: A Special Kind of Questioning

Sometimes an interviewee will respond only partially to a question, answer it inadequately, or make a provocative point that causes you to desire additional information. When this occurs, you may attempt to stimulate discussion by probing for further information. *Probes* may request exploration, elaboration, or justification. Some examples are (1) "What do you mean by that?" (2) "Why did you feel that way?" (3) "Could you give me an example?" Research by Tengler and Jablin suggests that probes are frequently used and needed by employment interviewers to obtain substantive responses to open questions.[4]

There are several kinds of specialized probes. Two commonly used in employment interviews are hypothetical and reactive probes. The *hypothetical probe* places the interviewee in a situation, not unlike one he or she might encounter on the job, and asks how he or she would handle the situation. You might say, "Suppose you had been working here for a few months and one day you heard a rumor that drastic layoffs were impending. How do you think you'd react to that?" Hypothetical probes can be useful for determining basic attitudes or approaches to problem solving, but they also encourage a certain amount of second guessing, where the interviewee gives the ideal response (that is, the one she or he thinks you want to hear) rather than an honest response.

You may also choose to use *reactive probes* in which you make a statement simply to get the reaction of the interviewee. Perhaps you ask the interviewee to agree or disagree with a stated position or issue. For example, a high school principal used a reactive probe in interviewing a young woman for a teaching position when he asked the following question: "There are many teachers who believe that most major corrective problems should be brought to the attention of the principal, while others prefer to handle these matters without administrative assistance, except in the most severe instances. How do you feel about dealing with discipline?"

In a sense, hypothetical and reactive probes are similar in that they provide a frame of reference and set the stage for the interviewee's response. But the reactive probe focuses on real rather than hypothetical cases. By using such probes, you can gain some insights into applicants' views on pertinent real-life issues without in any way challenging their ideas.

Another method for obtaining follow-up information is the use of *restatement* (sometimes referred to as the "mirror" technique). With this technique, you do not directly request that the interviewee provide additional information. Rather, you restate part or all of the person's comments in such a way that it encourages him or her to continue. In this manner, you can communicate genuine interest, indicating that you are "with" the other person. Restatement does not demand additional information; it simply provides the opportunity for elaboration and deeper examination. Compare the following interviewer responses, one using a probe and the other restatement:

**Interviewee:** I left my job at the small accounting firm because I found it unchallenging. It was dull.

**Interviewer (using a probe):** How was it dull and unchallenging?

**Interviewer (using restatement):** You felt it was dull and unchallenging?

Restatement is a technique particularly useful for allowing people to clarify their ideas and listen to their own language without in any way commenting on or evaluating them.

**Question Bias**   Still another method by which types of questions can be distinguished is based upon the extent to which the question reveals the attitudes of the questioner or suggests the sort of answer that the respondent is supposed to give. For example, "How do you feel about labor unions?" suggests little about the thinking of the questioner. "You don't like labor unions, do you?" suggests quite a bit more. "You wouldn't join one of those pinko-commie anti-American labor unions, would you?" clearly indicates the feelings of the questioner. When biased questions are used accidentally, they place the interviewee in a difficult position; when used carefully, however, they can reveal much about the respondent.

As with other types of questions, unbiased and biased inquiries range along a continuum from very biased to completely neutral. Most of the examples we have offered in this section have been unbiased. For example, "How well do you feel you performed this past year?" says nothing about the feelings of the interviewer and leaves interviewees free to answer as they please without fear of being trapped by the question. Somewhat more biased or leading is the question, "You like working with machinery, don't you?" At the most biased end of the scale is, "Are you going to improve your output next month, or should I start a search for your replacement?" Because these three questions vary in their revelations of the interviewer's feelings, they exert different degrees of pressure upon the interviewee to respond in a particular fashion.

In deciding whether to use biased, moderately biased, or completely neutral questions during the interview, you first must take into account your purpose. If you are seeking the interviewee's true feelings or attitudes, you probably should avoid biased questions. If, however, you are trying to persuade the interviewee, biased questions may be useful. Research on attitude change suggests that if we can encourage an individual to state a certain opinion, he or she is likely to adopt that opinion as his or her own. Thus, if an interviewee initially had no intention of changing the behaviors for which you were disciplining him, you might persuade him through a sequence of questions, such as:

"You understand that we have to have people here at work in order to maintain our responsiveness to customers, don't you?"

"You know that absenteeism hurts our ability to get the product to customers when they need it, don't you?"

"You realize that when someone is late for work, we have to move everyone around to cover for him?"

"You know that just as we promise to provide you with pay and benefits, so you promise to come to work regularly and on time?"

"So what are you going to do to improve your attendance record?"

The yes answers produced by the first four questions probably will lead to a constructive plan of action in response to the fifth, while at the same time leading the interviewee to an understanding of the necessity of good attendance. Thus, biased questions produce the same effect that a lecture or series of commands would achieve, but in a more palatable manner.

Finally, biased questions also can serve to test an interviewee. We can use them to determine how independent workers are or how likely workers are to provide socially acceptable responses. For example, if we asked, "Are you biased against moving women into managerial positions?" most male executives would say no. However, if we asked, "Do you think that women are often too emotional to take the daily stresses of management positions?" a "closet sexist" would be much more likely to reveal his true feelings. However, we must use biased questions with care. At times, their use is deceptive and unethical. Their implications may make the interviewee suspicious, angry, or skeptical of our own opinions or judgment. For the most part, then, we are much safer in using neutral questions and relying on the openness created by other interviewing skills to elicit honest answers from the interviewee.

---

**KEY CONCEPTS 9.3**  |  **Types of Questions Used in Interviews**

Types of questions used during interviews include:

- • *Open questions, which allow the respondent to talk with relative freedom.*

- • *Closed questions, which restrict the nature and content of the respondent's answer.*

- • *Probes, which encourage the respondent to provide additional information.*

- • *Biased questions, which imply the answer the interviewer would like to hear.*

- • *Unbiased questions, which are neutral and give no indication of the interviewer's preferences.*

---

### LISTENING: THE KEY TO EFFECTIVE INTERVIEWING

Key to effective interviewing is effective listening. Chapter 7 discussed some techniques for effective listening. Here are more tips for listening effectively during interviews:

- Realize that you could do better: Some experts claim that 50 percent or more improvement in listening can come about simply from realizing that you have bad listening habits and can do better.
- Practice: Catch yourself not listening and try not to let it happen again, making a conscious effort to use good listening techniques.
- Rephrase what you're hearing: Adopting the practice of periodically restating what you just heard is an important "reality check" to ensure you understand—emotionally and intellectually—what the other person is saying, forces you to pay attention, and is a good test for your listening effectiveness.
- Conquer fear of silence: While the urge to fill silence can be almost irresistible, the practice of letting some silence occur after the other person has stopped talking and before you begin your reply allows you time to give a more thoughtful response and may encourage the other person to add more information.
- Take notes: This shows the other person that you care so much that you are going to write down what he or she says; it keeps you occupied so you can't talk so much; and it allows you to conclude by saying, "Now, let me review my notes to be sure I have accurately captured what you said."

Source: David Stauffer, "Yo, Listen Up: A Brief Hearing on the Most Neglected Communication Skill," *Harvard Management Update* (July 1998): 10–11.

## Coping with Inadequate Responses

Unfortunately, not all questions asked in interviews elicit the kinds of responses sought. Interviewee answers may be inadequate in many ways and for many reasons. Sometimes the interviewer's question is not clearly understood because of content, language, or structure. On occasion, an interviewee may not know how to respond appropriately because of inadequate knowledge or a misunderstanding of the interviewer's expectations (that is, he or she is uncertain how much detail and elaboration is expected). Finally, the interviewee may be naturally reticent or may feel that the interviewer is asking for irrelevant or overly personal information.

Whatever the reason, as an interviewer you will encounter many inadequate responses from interviewees. Each will challenge your wits and require you to respond creatively to the interpersonal communication difficulties posed by such interviews. Some responses, for example, are *oververbalized*. They are often the product of compulsive talkers who go on and on, seemingly indefinitely. As we have pointed out, the use of open questions encourages more elaborated responses. When you perceive that you are dealing with a compulsive talker, you would do well to alter your strategy to a more directive one, using closed questions to limit the response range.

Interviewers quite often encounter *partial* responses or even *nonresponses*. Both are inadequate because they provide little or no information. Interviewees who consistently respond "Yes," "No," "I don't know," or "I don't think so," or who only partially and superficially answer questions, provide a great challenge for interviewers. If the interviewee's response is incomplete or hesitant, you might nudge him or her by saying, "I see," "And then?" "Yes?" or "What happened next?" Superficial responses might be followed by, "Why do you think you felt that way?" "Tell me more about your reasons for doing that," or "How did you react when that happened?" Vague answers could be greeted with, "What do you mean when you use the word 'liberal'?" "How are you using the term 'participation'?" or "I'm not sure I understand."

In general, a useful strategy with any reticent interviewee is to phrase all questions in an open manner so that it becomes impossible to answer them sensibly with one-word responses. Nontalkers often lack confidence or are highly anxious about the interview. Thus, the best initial approach is one of extended rapport building and orientation. It is also imperative that the first question or two be easy. If highly anxious persons are asked a difficult question initially, they may never be able to relax and communicate fully and effectively.

## Question Sequences

Another important element of effective interviewing is the order in which questions are asked. While a virtually infinite number of sequences could be identified, we shall consider five types, distinguishable by their use of open and closed questions.

The first type of sequence, the *funnel*, begins with open questions and builds upon them with questions of increasing specificity. The funnel sequence is particularly appropriate when interviewees are quite familiar with the topic and feel free to discuss it or when they are emotionally charged and need a chance to express feelings. We might begin by asking a general question about the interviewee's attitudes toward work and then become increasingly specific by focusing on particular aspects of the interviewee's position. If, for example, the interviewee formerly was an effective worker but recently has let her performance slip, we might begin the interview with general questions about the interviewee's morale and overall job satisfaction. Then we would move to her performance over the past several years and become even more specific, considering her most recent performance level. Finally, we could deal with precise elements of her job, such as attendance or amount of work produced, and try to determine those factors that may have caused these elements to go downhill. Of the question sequences used in all types of interviews, the funnel sequence (illustrated in Figure 9.1) is one of the most common.

The second sequence, the *inverted funnel*, is the reverse of the preceding. As demonstrated in Figure 9.1, the interviewer begins with specific, closed questions and gradually moves to more general, open questions. This approach may be useful if the interviewee is reluctant to talk at all. While open questions might get no response, specific questions (such as, "Did it take you long to find this place?" or "How long have you been working here?") may be an effective way to motivate the interviewee to respond freely. Once he or she is talking, the interviewee may be encouraged to deal with more open questions, demanding greater depth of response. One recent study of employment interviewing suggested that most interviewers use the inverted funnel sequence.[5]

FIGURE 9.1     A comparison of two basic questioning sequences

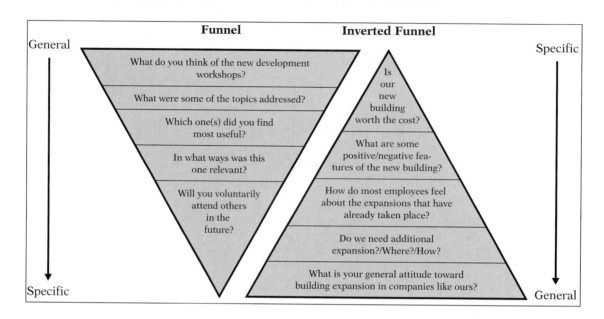

**Funnel**

**Inverted Funnel**

General

Specific

What do you think of the new development workshops?

What were some of the topics addressed?

Which one(s) did you find most useful?

In what ways was this one relevant?

Will you voluntarily attend others in the future?

Is our new building worth the cost?

What are some positive/negative features of the new building?

How do most employees feel about the expansions that have already taken place?

Do we need additional expansion?/Where?/How?

What is your general attitude toward building expansion in companies like ours?

Specific

General

The third and fourth sequences involve combinations of the first two. The *diamond sequence* begins with closed questions; moves to open ones; and then narrows again to specific, closed inquiries. When counseling an employee who seems to have a drug or an alcohol problem, we might begin with specific questions about similar situations, then move to more open questions about the employee's own life and work performance, and then center again upon his own problems and concerns. We begin with a relatively easy topic of discussion (someone else's problems), move to something a little more personal but still not too difficult to discuss (his life in general), and then arrive at the most difficult and the most specific portion of the interview—his own problems and what to do about them. This questioning sequence is often useful in dealing with potentially painful topics or difficult problems.

The *hourglass sequence* begins with open questions, moves to closed questions, and then becomes open once again. When conducting a performance review with a supervisor who has been steadily criticized by her own workers, for example, we might begin with a discussion of people and how motivated they are in very general terms, then move to specific questions about her situation, and encourage her to develop her own supervisory action plan by asking increasingly open-ended questions toward the end of the interview. Such a sequence of questions might include:

"What do you think makes people want to work?"

"How do you think they get these things from work?"

"Does the supervisor play a role in providing these things?"

"Does this apply to your staff as well?"

"Do you provide the things they want or need?"

"What are some things you might do more of as a supervisor?"

"What will you try to accomplish during the next year?"

This sequence is much shorter than the entire interview would be, but it illustrates the open-to-closed-to-open procedure found in the hourglass sequence. This sequence is especially useful if you want to begin by establishing some general principles, then move to a specific application (closer to home), and finally go on to examine some action strategies for the future.

Finally, the *tunnel sequence* uses questions that are all of the same degree of openness. Interviews conducted in shopping centers by market researchers who stop shoppers at random and ask them a series of questions typically follow this pattern. Very specific, factual questions are asked in a rapid sequence to gain maximum information in a minimum amount of time. In contrast, some psychotherapists use exclusively open questions in their counseling interviews with patients. Their goal is to cause the patients to talk and so arrive at solutions to their own problems.

Your selection of a question sequence, then, is based largely on your purpose in the interview and your knowledge of the interviewee's state of mind. A reluctant respondent may require use of an inverted funnel. A disagreeable interviewee may be persuaded through a diamond sequence. An uninformed or uneducated interviewee may be taught to apply general principles to his or her own situation through an hourglass sequence. Interviewers must carefully assess their purpose and the nature of the interviewee and then carefully plan their overall questioning strategy.

---

### KEY CONCEPTS 9.4  Common Questioning Sequences

Common question sequences include:

- • *Funnel, which begins with open questions and then narrows to questions of increasing specificity.*

- • *Inverted funnel, which begins with specific questions and then becomes increasingly open-ended.*

- • *Diamond, which moves from specific questions to general ones, and then back to specific questions again.*

- • *Hourglass, which moves from general questions to specific ones, and then back to general questions again.*

- • *Tunnel, which uses questions that are all of the same degree of openness.*

---

## Closing the Interview

Perhaps the interviews you conduct will be subject to external time constraints; there may be only 20 or 30 minutes available. Usually you will be in a more flexible situation that allows you to decide when prolonging the interview would not be profitable. One interviewing researcher points out that in every communication encounter, there are *"crucial junctures—those* moments in an interview when the next response . . . will determine whether its continuance will be productive or not, whether vital data will be elicited or if tangential information will be forthcoming."[6] Your ability to recognize critical junctures will improve with experience. What is important to remember is that you should terminate an interview whenever you feel that your mutual goals have been accomplished.

The end of the interview is as important as the beginning, and failure to attend to it may result in undermining earlier accomplishments. To thank an interviewee for his or her participation in an interview and to mumble something about "being in touch" is not an adequate conclusion. In general, the tone of the closing should be similar to that of the rest of the interview—appreciative of the interviewee's participation and showing interest in him or her as a person. You should encourage the interviewee to ask questions and devote the remainder of the interview to exploring the procedure to be used next. In other words, there must be some *orientation toward the next step.* If the interview has been a selection situation, you should tell applicants what will happen next: who will contact them and when the contact will be made. Or you may make the decision to hire or not to hire right then and inform each applicant accordingly. At the end of an appraisal interview, you and the interviewee should agree on what the interviewee will strive to accomplish during the next few months and discuss how you will keep track of his or her achievements. To close a counseling interview, you might discuss when your next appointment will be. To close a sales interview, you should ask for the sale. In each case, the closing should reflect the purpose of the meeting and should emphasize the things you want to happen as a result of the discussion. And above all, this closing should be prepared every bit as carefully as the rest of the interview. You should not simply assume that the momentum of the interview will carry you automatically into an effective closing.

## TYPES OF INTERVIEWS IN ORGANIZATIONS

As one of the most common and important types of communication that occurs daily within every organization, interviews can take many forms. Among them:

- **Information-giving interviews** often occur during periods of orientation and training in organizations. In the context of information-giving interviews, employees are trained, instructed, and coached in particular behaviors. Orientation interviews assist new employees in adjusting to an unfamiliar work environment. Early interviews in organizations provide a structured opportunity for managers to explain job requirements, explicate procedures, and answer questions.

- **Information-seeking interviews** can take many forms—for example, judicial settings in which a lawyer interviews a client in an attempt to obtain a clear account of the client's view of the case; medical settings where doctors or nurses seek patients' medical histories and descriptions of current disorders; business or government settings in which an executive calls in a staff assistant to be briefed on a particular subject about which the assistant is especially knowledgeable; and journalistic research settings where press conferences and private interviews provide the context for interviewers to elicit facts and opinions from a person of special interest or expertise, often a celebrity.

- **Persuasive interviews** occur informally among organizational members all the time, but some employees function primarily in the specific context of persuasive interviews. The most common example of this type of interview is the sales transaction, in which a salesperson attempts to sell a specific product to a prospective customer.

- **Counseling interviews** usually are directed toward personal considerations. Organizations are increasingly recognizing the impossibility of disassociating an employee's personal and professional life. Personal problems can, and often do, create and intensify problems at work. While counseling interviews are seldom appropriate for rehabilitating employees suffering from such problems as alcoholism, depression, marital problems and the like, they are often used to obtain valuable preliminary information and to encourage workers to obtain professional assistance.

- **Exit interviews** occur at a time of change in an employee's organizational affiliation. Finding good employees is never easy, and the expense of training new ones increases every year. Thus, many organizations conduct exit interviews to learn why employees leave their jobs.

*Interviews occur frequently in organizations. None is more frequent or important than the sales interview. Successfully persuading someone to invest in a service or product, such as insurance, requires a clear understanding of "audience" needs and interests and the ability to clearly connect the product with those needs.*

Much of the information discussed earlier in this chapter applies to information-seeking interviews, and later chapters will discuss techniques for giving information. Thus, in the sections that follow, we will review techniques necessary for effectively conducting three other common interview types: corrective, appraisal, and complaint-resolution.

## Corrective Interviews

Corrective interviews are a necessity in every organization. Organizations must have behavioral expectations for their members, and often those expectations are stated in the form of rules, policies, and procedures. In turn, people occasionally may violate these expectations. When such a violation occurs, it becomes the responsibility of the interviewer (often a supervisor or manager) to determine why it occurred and to motivate the violator not to do it again. All of this should be achieved via corrective interviews. In this section, we will consider the pitfalls surrounding corrective interviews and suggest procedures whereby such interviews can be used to improve performance while respecting others' rights.

**Purposes**   The corrective interview achieves a number of necessary things. First, it corrects behaviors that violate the expectations of the organization. The key word is "corrects." The goal of discipline in an organization is not punishment; it is correction.

Corrective interviews also serve as a notice to other employees that rules are enforced and that violations of those rules are simply not ignored. When it becomes clear that violations of rules, policies, and procedures are confronted and corrected, employees will take greater care to conform to the rules.

Protection of employees is another purpose of corrective interviews. Many organizational rules relate directly to employee safety. Rules against horseplay, drinking on the job, using drugs, theft, sabotage, and failing to follow established work procedures are all designed to protect employees from other employees or even from themselves.

Corrective interviews should preserve justice and fairness. They should ensure that everyone is treated equally and that the rights of all employees are respected and preserved. This is perhaps the most important purpose of corrective actions.

**Problems**   A virtually limitless number of problems occur during corrective proceedings. For example, as Alpander notes, supervisors generally are reluctant to criticize or discipline in the first place.[7] Lacking the knowledge they need to discipline constructively and desiring popularity with their people, they simply avoid taking action against employees at all. The opposite problem is overcriticism—angrily bawling out the employee in front of others. In such situations, the employee usually is taken by surprise, is embarrassed in front of others, and is given no opportunity to respond or react.

Still other problems stem from procedural matters—failure to document corrective action so that appropriate records are retained and the supervisor is protected against charges of bias or discrimination, failure to take action promptly, failure to learn all the facts before taking action, failure to follow written policies concerning corrective proceedings, failure to discipline in privacy, failure to develop a positive plan of action. Many of these failures are similar to the problems encountered in appraisal interviews; indeed, there are many parallels between these two interview types.

### ONE APPROACH TO DISCIPLINE

While formalized procedures for taking disciplinary action with hourly employees are relatively common, corrective action for salaried professionals tends to be done much more haphazardly. One company, HR Textron, Inc. in Valencia, California, has attempted to implement a four-step policy specifically designed for salaried employees. These steps include:

1. A formal, documented discussion between the employee and his or her supervisor, with the supervisor keeping the paperwork generated by this discussion.
2. Another formal, documented discussion, with the paperwork being placed in the employee's personnel file along with the write-up from the first step.
3. A third documented discussion that may involve a probationary period or some time off from work, along with a warning that continued behavioral problems will lead to termination.
4. Termination.

All supervisors and managers were trained to implement this procedure effectively, and legal changes associated with discipline of professional staff dropped dramatically.

Source: Martin Levy, "Discipline for Professional Employees," *Personnel Journal* 69 (December 1990): 27–28.

Unfortunately, there is one important way in which corrective interviews and appraisal interviews differ. When appraisal interviews are done badly, they adversely affect the performance of the employee, but they do not typically lead to spectacular consequences. Not so with corrective proceedings. If an employee feels he has been wronged through corrective action, he may file a grievance. In unionized situations, this grievance may be accompanied by union demands for redress or management action against the offending supervisor. If such action is not forthcoming, strikes or work slowdowns could result. In nonunion settings, the employee may take her grievance to an outside arbitrator, who may rule against the organization. In cases of dismissal, for example, this may result in the employee being reinstated and given back pay. Either way, the supervisor is caught up in a swirl of controversy and often is sorry he or she took the action in the first place. Fear of such consequences only makes other supervisors more hesitant to discipline their employees.

Briefly put, corrective procedures can be dangerous to the supervisors who invoke them. Nevertheless, discipline must be invoked on occasion, and if the supervisors know what they are doing, the corrective interview can be an effective way of correcting behavior and improving performance. Our purpose in the following sections is to suggest ways to minimize the risks of disciplining and to maximize the utility of those encounters.

Preparation    Corrective interviews depend heavily on thorough preparation for their success. Before initiating a corrective meeting, you should do a number of things.

First, identify and analyze the problem. Identify specifically what has been happening and determine why it has happened. Be sure a problem exists that calls for corrective action before you confront the interviewee.

## OFFERING CRITICISM WITH TACT AND SENSITIVITY

Here are 12 guidelines to remember the next time you have to tell someone that he or she has done something wrong.

1. Identify the behavior that you want to criticize. Direct your criticism at the action, not the person.
2. Make criticisms specific. Not "You always miss deadlines," but "You missed the March 15 deadline for your report."
3. Be sure the behavior you're criticizing can be changed. Foreign accents, baldness, and other things tangentially related to some business dealings cannot always be changed.
4. Use "we" and "us" to stress that you want to work out the problem together, rather than making threats.
5. Make sure the other person understands the reason for your criticism.
6. Don't belabor the point. Short and sweet; no lectures.
7. Offer incentives for changed behavior. Offer to help the person correct the problem.
8. Don't set a tone of anger or sarcasm. Both are counterproductive.
9. Show the person you understand his or her feelings.
10. If you're putting your criticism in writing, cool off before writing the critical letter or memo. Be sure only the person it is intended for sees it.
11. Start off by saying something good.
12. At the end, reaffirm your support for and confidence in the person.

Source: Blue Cross and Blue Shield of Michigan, *Highlights,* reprinted in *The Working Communicator* (October 1998): 2–3.

Second, check the interviewee's work record. Determine whether she has been corrected before and, if so, for what. Determine whether she has been a good, dependable worker in the past and whether the present situation represents a continuation of bad behaviors or a sudden change in behavior. While you must be consistent in the way you administer the organization's rules, you also must adapt your own behavior to the individual case.

Third, review the organization's corrective rules. In most organizations, work rules have been developed that specify the types of punishable infractions and perhaps the severity of the action to be taken in each case. Repeated lateness, for example, is typically handled by an oral warning, while theft and sabotage are handled by immediate suspension or dismissal. You need to know what the appropriate action is.

Finally, examine your own attitudes and motives. The relationship that exists between you and the employee has a significant impact on the corrective interview that is about to take place. You must be certain that your actions are based on objective facts and behaviors and not on your personal biases or feelings about the employee.

Procedures    The first step is to notify the interviewee that you want to meet with him. Obviously, you should not confront the employee in front of his peers and publicly embarrass the employee by yelling at him. The interview should be held privately and after any emotions or anger have cooled down, and it should be done as soon after the infraction as possible (again allowing time for the preparation described above).

When the employee arrives (and the door is closed), get directly to the point. Engaging in small talk to relax the interviewee would probably be counterproductive. The way in which you state the point, however, is crucial. Under no circumstances should you begin by condemning or accusing the employee. The most certain way to make the employee defensive and to stop two-way communication is to begin with statements like:

"Karen, what are you trying to do to this department (or me)?"

"Ralph, I'm fed up with you always being late to work."

"You've goofed off for the last time, Maria. I'm writing you up."

Generally, corrective interviews should be treated as problem-solving sessions. You and the interviewee have a mutual problem, and the two of you need to arrive at a solution. The best way to begin the interview is to define that problem by stating two things: (1) the behavioral expectation (such as the applicable rule or job requirement) and (2) the information you have about the person's behavior. For example:

"Jim, you know that shop rules prohibit drinking on the job. When people drink, their own work suffers, and they become dangerous to everyone else. Now, I've been told by three different people that you've been seen drinking during break periods. I'm concerned about that, and that's why I asked you to come in. What can you tell me about this?"

Through this statement, you have posed the problem, and you have asked the person for input. You have not said, "What do you have to say for yourself?" which would create a trial-like atmosphere. Instead, you've simply indicated a desire for information from the interviewee.

Your next task is to listen. By letting the person talk, and by asking questions when necessary, you should determine what, in the interviewee's view, actually took place. You should also obtain her explanation of why it happened, and you should ask her to explain the appropriate rules to you.

Having heard these things, you then face two tasks. First, you must tell the person what corrective action is to be taken against him. This action may range from a written warning placed in his file, to a suspension from work, to outright termination. Then, if termination is not the action, you should work with the interviewee to determine how he will improve in the future. Through two-way, cooperative communication, the two of you decide what the person is to do, how he is to achieve that, and what you might do to help. Then you set some sort of follow-up schedule whereby you meet again to determine what progress, if any, has occurred.

When the interview has been completed and a behavioral action plan has been agreed to, the proper documentation must also be completed. Most organizations have forms for this purpose, and the supervisor is required to indicate the actions taken, reasons for discipline, and plans for future improvement. The supervisor then signs the form, as does the employee, and the completed paperwork is sent to the supervisor's immediate superior or to the personnel department. Since most organizations have corrective policies that

## AVOIDING LAWSUITS THROUGH HONESTY

How well employees are treated when being fired or laid off may determine whether they sue their ex-bosses, Ohio State University (OSU) researchers found. The school also found in a study of nearly 1,000 fired Ohio workers that they were more likely to sue if they weren't given a full explanation of why they were being let go. Jerald Greenberg, a professor of management and human resources at OSU's Fisher College of Business, estimated companies could save at least $13,200 per termination by being honest with fired workers.

Source: "When Firing Workers, Courtesy Pays Off," *San Francisco Examiner* (July 19, 1998): sec. J, p. 1.

---

say that subsequent offenses receive more severe punishment, this record will guide future corrective actions for this employee.

### Tips for When You Are Disciplined
It is hoped that you never will be on the receiving end of a corrective interview. Still, if you find yourself being disciplined, there are some things you should do both to protect your rights as an employee and to ensure that you avoid similar corrective actions in the future.

**1.** *Be sure you know what the work rules and policies are.* Often, corrective actions come about because employees unknowingly broke some rule or policy. Whenever you go to work for a new boss, ask him or her to discuss the rules and policies for your department.

**2.** In a corrective interview, *listen calmly to everything your boss has to say.* Hear him or her out before you react. Often, quick and angry reactions from employees being disciplined cause these situations to escalate out of hand.

**3.** *Encourage your boss to focus on specific behaviors.* Statements like "You're always breaking the rules" and "You're always late" are too general to tell you what specifically happened. Ask your boss to report what you did, when and where it happened, and so on.

**4.** *If there are circumstances that need to be explained, give them.* Do not offer excuses, however; simply explain any factors that might cause your boss to take a different view of what happened.

**5.** *Express your desire to avoid this kind of thing in the future.* Ask your boss to help you develop some sort of action plan that will improve your performance or work-related behaviors. Also ask for frequent feedback from your boss that will help you do better.

**6.** *Be sure you understand the corrective action being taken.* Determine whether this conversation counts as an oral warning or a written warning and what the next step in the corrective process is if this happens again.

**7.** *If you feel the action is unfair,* say *so calmly and in a matter-of-fact way.* Give your reasons. Then ask your boss what additional steps or channels are available to you. Typically, there is a grievance procedure through which corrective actions can be protested.

Above all, you should try to maintain a problem-solving attitude throughout the proceedings. Obviously, your boss must think there is a problem; otherwise, you would not be having this conversation. Your task is to determine why your boss feels a problem exists, and then to lay out a personal action plan whereby similar problems can be avoided in the future. By asking for the most complete information you can get and for assistance in improving your behavior, you encourage your boss to be helpful rather than punishing.

---

**KEY CONCEPTS 9.5    The Corrective Interview: Keys to Success**

Keys to conducting effective corrective interviews include:

• • *Establishing a clear purpose for the interview, including correcting behaviors, setting an example, protecting employees, and preserving justice and fairness.*

• • *Preparing for the interview by identifying and analyzing the problem, identifying the person's past record, reviewing the rules and regulations, and analyzing your own motives and attitudes.*

• • *Conducting the interview by getting right to the point, defining the problem, listening to the interviewee's perspective, announcing the disciplinary action (if any) to be taken, and developing a plan for improvement.*

---

**Appraisal Interviews**

The director of the Medical Records Department at St. Luke's Hospital, Nancy Walserbock, had a reputation for being one of the toughest managers in the hospital. She disapproved of socializing among the Medical Records employees, constantly emphasized that they should get as much work as possible done as quickly as possible, and closely watched everyone's activities at work. Productivity in the department was extremely high, and very few errors were made by the employees. On the other hand, morale among employees was not particularly good, and conflicts between Medical Records personnel and the physicians and nurses working in the hospital were common.

Mary Straton had worked in Medical Records for eight years, making her the second-longest-term employee in the 24-person department. She did not particularly like working for Nancy but needed the job and, in fact, took some pride in the quality of her work. Her annual appraisal interview was scheduled soon, and she expected to receive good ratings and a substantial raise.

The date for Mary's appraisal came and went. In fact, four weeks passed and she had heard nothing. One day, however, Nancy walked up to Mary's desk and said, "Mary, I'd like to see you for a minute." "Sure," Mary replied. Nancy handed her three sheets of paper. "Here are three copies of your performance review. I've already filled them out, so read them and sign them, and then give them back to me. I didn't give you much of a raise; your attitude hasn't been good lately, and you were late coming to work last week. Try to improve." Nancy walked off before Mary could reply.

This appraisal interview, such as it is, illustrates almost everything that commonly is done wrong in interviews of this type. The interview was late. No notification was given to the employee. No review of job requirements occurred. No review of performance standards or measures happened. The "recency" effect prevailed. No strengths were noted and no plans for improvement made. Small wonder that Mary filed a grievance that same afternoon and that Nancy eventually was removed from the directorship of the department.

Few situations create more discomfort for both managers and employees than performance appraisals. McGregor undoubtedly was correct when he observed that "managers are uncomfortable when they are put in the position of 'playing God.'"[8] He probably could have added that employees are equally uncomfortable about having their bosses enact that role. Yet performance appraisals are a necessity if employee performance is to be evaluated and rewarded.

**Purposes**   While there is no substitute for good day-to-day communication between supervisor and employee, the formal yearly (or semiyearly) performance appraisal serves some specific functions.[9] Ideally, such an appraisal should:

**1.** Tell the employee where she stands—how the supervisor judges that employee's performance to have been during the review period.
**2.** Give the employee guidance for doing a better job in the future by clarifying what is expected of him.
**3.** Plan developmental and growth opportunities for the employee and identify specific areas in which the employee needs to improve her knowledge and skills.
**4.** Give the employee an opportunity to express his feelings about performance-related matters.

**Problems**   Research has revealed a number of common failings in performance interviews. Lahiff found that appraisal interviews often tend to *dwell upon the individual's negative characteristics.* This is a highly destructive approach, as is indicated by Kay, Meyer, and French's discovery that the more weaknesses the manager mentions during the interview, the poorer the worker's performance becomes, and the lower he or she rates the organization's appraisal system.[10]

A second common fault is the *halo effect,* a term first used in 1920 to describe the tendency people have to see one positive trait in someone and then to attribute to that person a variety of other positive traits. Thus, we mentally place a halo around the head of that person. If an employee arrives early and leaves late every day, we probably will be impressed. However, if this causes us to overlook the poor quality and quantity of his work or his inability to get along with his peers, then we have fallen victims to the halo effect.

The *central tendency effect* is yet another common problem. We may tend to classify others as "average" and not do the hard work necessary for spotting gradations. If we assign the same average rating to everyone, then we do not have to think very much about the characteristics that distinguish their performance levels. Similarly, the *leniency effect* occurs when everyone is given an equally high rating. The *critical effect* takes place when no employee can measure up to the supervisor's standards, so that all of them are judged deficient. The *recency effect* occurs when we allow more recent events to outweigh past history. A recent mistake by an employee may, psychologically, cause us to erase from the record the many previous occasions on which the employee did well. The question thus arises: How can we avoid all these problems and use appraisal interviews in ways that maximize their effectiveness as analytic and motivational tools? Our own experience suggests that effective appraisal interviewing is a result of two things: careful preparation and skillful procedures. We will consider each of these in turn.

**Preparation**   You should do three things as you prepare for an appraisal session. First, you should review the requirements of the employee's job. Much evidence suggests that supervisors and subordinates have quite different perceptions of the employee's job and that supervisors rarely are able to provide accurate descriptions of their employees' written job duties as expressed in job descriptions.[11] It is vital that you review the tasks that the employee ought to have performed and that you decide in your own mind which of them is more important than the others. If you have conducted past appraisals for this employee, you should also review those to remind yourself of any plans for performance improvement that the two of you developed in previous meetings.

Second, you should obtain input from the employee concerning his level of performance. Using a written questionnaire (perhaps similar to the preappraisal form in Table 9.1), the employee should describe for you those objectives he felt he was to achieve, the behaviors he was to perform, the strengths and weaknesses of his performance, and his short- and long-range career

## TABLE 9.1
**Employees' Preappraisal Summary**

| Instructions: In the space provided below, answer the questions posed. |
| --- |
| 1.  Since your last interview, how well do you think you have performed? Give specific examples, details, information, and so on that indicate why you feel as you do. |
| 2.  Looking toward the future, in what ways do you think your performance can be improved, and how can your supervisor help you to achieve those improvements? |
| 3.  What long-term goals for personal development or achievement do you have? How can your supervisor help you achieve them? |
| 4.  What long-term objectives for personal and professional development do you have? How can your supervisor help you to achieve them? |
| 5.  What additional comments, if any, do you have concerning your performance during the past year, your future objectives, or your upcoming performance appraisal? |

objectives. Remember, superiors and subordinates typically have different perceptions. By obtaining this sort of information, you are able to review the employee's perceptions before your interview begins.

Third, you should complete the performance review form, if any, that your organization requires. These forms are important, for they provide a written record of the decisions you and your employee make about his or her performance.[12] As such, they may serve as the basis for future personnel decisions (such as promotions, transfers, or discharge), or they may protect you from action taken against you by an employee.

When completing the review form before the interview, you must make one final decision: Will the ratings you provide serve as the final appraisal of the employee, or will they simply be a worksheet that you will use to guide the interview, which you will revise when the interview is over? Strong arguments can be offered for each alternative. If your ratings stand, then you will not be persuaded by employees who are not good workers but who are good salespersons. More than once we have seen good workers suffer because they are not very skilled interviewees and poorer workers come out well because they are good at "slinging the bull." If your rating is to be final, then the principle of cooperative problem solving is violated. Thus, you may want to take a compromise approach: Use the rating forms to provide your final rating of the employee's performance (perhaps taking into account the self-perception information you have obtained in advance), and use the interview to communicate those ratings to the employee and then to cooperatively develop a plan for future improvements in his or her performance.

**Procedures**   While a number of approaches to the appraisal interview are available, one of the most reasonable systems is that suggested by Brett and Fredian.[13] They suggest a seven-step model for performance appraisal. The first step is to get to the point of the interview. The appraisal should begin with a statement of the purpose of the meeting and a brief overview of the structure that the interview will follow.

The supervisor next should describe specifically the important elements of the employee's past performance. She should talk about criteria that both of them understand (amount of work, quality of work) and should give both good and bad examples of the employee's performance. These specifics are important. The employee learns nothing if he is simply told, "You are doing a good job." The discussion should focus on work-related matters and should deal only with performance areas that are really important. Perhaps the best way to ensure these things is to state the specific job requirement and then provide specific indications of performance. For example:

"Pat, part of your job is to write monthly summary reports of employee relations activities in each production plant and to have those to all members of top management by the fifteenth of the next month. In 5 of your 12 reports, you were more than one week late in getting those reports out. I want to discuss this with you."

This statement indicates the job requirement, provides specific information, tells Pat what is important to the supervisor, and indicates that he will have a chance to discuss the matter before any final decisions are reached. This is far superior to simply saying, "Pat, your ER reports are often late."

## KEY QUESTIONS FOR PERFORMANCE APPRAISAL

Performance evaluations can help people to reach their potential when they include such questions as:

- What are five key projects or goals you have here, and how can I help to support them?
- Does our company need you? What do you want to do here? What are you planning to do to reach your goals?

- What will you do in the coming year to develop the three highest-potential people who work for you?
- What are your personal plans for continuing education and development for the coming year?

Source: "Performance-Review Questions," *Communication Briefings* (February 1993): 6.

Third, the supervisor should provide employees with a chance to give their own observations. As you invite them to describe their performance, you perform step 4 in the appraisal process: listen. Using the techniques reviewed in earlier chapters, actively and attentively listen to the employees, both encouraging them to talk and retaining the information for use in the last portions of the interview.

When we have analyzed past performance, the fifth step is to lay out future plans and goals. Here, we need to take the problem-solving approach to two things—improving performance weaknesses from the past and assessing new objectives or goals to be accomplished in the future. What does the employee feel he should do to achieve his goals, and how does he feel you should evaluate the quality of his performance in doing them? Naturally, you have your own ideas about his goals and objectives, so you will need to work together to arrive at an action plan for next year's performance. Finally, just as the employee commits to achieving certain things, so too must the supervisor commit to providing any assistance he might need. Part of the performance action plan, therefore, should include the assistance and resources that the supervisor is to provide.

The last two steps of the procedure make up the interview's closing. First, to make sure that both parties understand what decisions have been reached, the employee should be asked to summarize the discussion. Second, supervisor and subordinate should agree on some follow-up procedure. Rather than waiting until the next annual review, they should schedule meetings for progress reports and feedback, enabling both of them to adjust their behaviors as necessary. If performance problems arise, they can correct them quickly rather than waiting for the entire year to elapse.

Typically, all these things are put in writing, signed by both parties, and placed in the employee's permanent file. Again, this sort of record keeping is important to the employee, the supervisor, and the entire organization.[14]

### Tips for the Appraisee
When you are being appraised, you should communicate in ways that help your boss to appraise you more effectively

and that protect your rights as an employee. Briefly, you always have a right to know the standards by which you are evaluated, to discuss points that are unclear to you, to dispute things you feel are unfair or untrue, to have some input in determining your future goals and performance objectives, and to know what the final outcome of the appraisal will be. With these rights in mind, you should do the following:

**1.** *Keep track of your own performance.* Be sure to maintain your own performance file by keeping copies of memos, letters, achievements, shortcomings, comments from other people, and so on that help provide a clear picture of how you have performed.

**2.** *Know what the performance standards are.* If your company has a performance evaluation form, be sure you get a copy of it (ask for one from your supervisor). If there is no such form, ask your supervisor to spend some time with you outlining his or her priorities and expectations. This information should be obtained whenever you go to work for a new boss.

**3.** *Encourage your boss to talk about behaviors, not personalities.* Statements like "You are lazy," "You are irresponsible," or even "You are very pleasant with others" tell you little about what you did or should do. Always ask for specific examples of behaviors to be sure you know what your boss means.

**4.** *Ask your boss to suggest methods of improvement,* both in your short-term performance and in your long-term professional growth. Part of the plan coming out of your evaluation should deal with things you will do to improve yourself over time and possibly ways in which your boss will help that improvement.

**5.** *Ask for a copy of the appraisal in writing,* just to keep for your own records. If the appraisal has an effect on your raise, ask what that will be.

**6.** *If you disagree, do so in a way that stresses the facts and is not argumentative.* Give examples to support your opinions, but recognize that, in the end, your boss probably will be "right."

**7.** *If you feel the appraisal is unfair, say so* (in a matter-of-fact, nonaccusatory way) to your boss and ask what your next step should be: Most companies have a grievance procedure through which unfair evaluations can be protested.

**8.** *Between evaluations, ask your boss for feedback.* If you do not know how you are doing during the year, it is too late to correct performance problems when the time for performance evaluation arrives.

---

**KEY CONCEPTS 9.6**  **The Appraisal Interview: Critical Considerations**

Keys to conducting effective appraisal interviews include:

• • *Careful preparation by reviewing the requirements of the interviewee's job,*

*obtaining the person's input concerning his or her level of performance, and then completing a performance review form.*

***Continued***

---

## Complaint Resolution Interviews

Occasionally, interviews will be initiated not by the interviewer, but by an interviewee who has a particular issue in mind—a complaint, a problem needing resolution, or even a formal grievance. While these situations often allow little or no preparation by the interviewer, taking a systematic approach to complaint-resolution interviews helps to turn these potentially inflammatory conversations into positive, constructive experiences.

**Purposes**    Since the interviewee initiates this type of interview, it is important to consider first some purposes he or she may have in mind, such as:

- "Blowing off steam" by getting a problem off his or her chest.

- Reporting misbehavior on the part of another person.

- Conveying information to the interviewer just to keep him or her informed.

- Bringing a problem or concern for discussion and resolution.

Before deciding how to proceed with the interview, the interviewer often must first determine why the interviewee has come and what his or her expectations are. Trying to engage in constructive problem-solving when the interviewee just wants to blow off steam, for example, is likely to be unproductive and could even create greater frustration.

From the interviewer's perspective, several purposes might be achieved:

- Demonstrating to the interviewee a genuine interest in his or her concerns.

- Determining what the interviewee would like to see done with regard to his or her issue.

- If appropriate, developing an acceptable solution and plan for action that resolves the interviewee's concern.

- Establishing clear expectations for follow-up after the interview.

By achieving these objectives, the interviewer can both resolve the issue at hand and, long-term, build a better relationship with the interviewee.

**Problems**    When a complaint is brought to us, our reaction determines to a large extent how successful this interview will be and how likely it is the interviewee will bring another problem to us at some later time. Unfortunately, there are many common reactions that make complaint-resolution interviews less than successful. For example, reacting defensively serves to stifle conversation rather than enhance problem solving. Yet if we perceive the complaint to be a potential attack on our competence, character, or intent, we are likely to respond by surrendering, retreating, or counterattacking, as described in a previous chapter. On the other hand, jumping to a solution may appear positive (since the interviewer evidently is attempting to resolve the interviewee's issue), but may be unsuccessful because the solution does not adequately consider the actual nature of the problem. And finally, taking responsibility for the other person's issue allows the interviewee to delegate the burden of problem solving to the interviewer, and may even allow the interviewee to play "critic" and shoot down every potential solution the interviewer suggests. Generally, it is far better for the interviewer to put responsibility for developing potential solutions squarely where it belongs: on the shoulders of the person raising the issue in the first place.

How can we avoid these inappropriate reactions and react in ways that maximize the problem-solving and relationship-building effectiveness of complaint-resolution interviews? Research and experience suggest that effective complaint resolution comes about through the systematic application of information-gathering and problem-solving skills.

**Procedures**   An effective approach to handling complaints or problems brought to you by others is to proceed through the following interviewing steps:

1. *Listen.*   Hearing both the intellectual and the emotional content of the interviewee's concern is a crucial first step toward arriving at a workable solution. Moreover, in many instances the interviewee simply wants to blow off steam, and wants nothing more than an attentive hearing.
2. *Ask exploratory questions.*   To develop a thorough understanding of the issue (and to help the interviewee fully express his or her concerns), ask questions that encourage further elaboration of the issue: What happened? Where did it happen? When did it happen? Why did it happen? Who was involved? By asking these questions, you both gain a more thorough understanding of the problem and you demonstrate to the interviewee your interest in his or her concern.
3. *Summarize what you think you have heard.*   To be sure you have understood the interviewee correctly (and to illustrate your desire to understand), state for the interviewee what you think you have heard and observed. You should report in summary form what the situation seems to be, of course, but you also might report your observations concerning how the person is feeling: "You seem to be really angry about this," or "I can see this really has you concerned."
4. *Ask for the interviewee's suggested solutions.*   Often, the interviewee already has in mind what he or she would like to have done in response to his or her concern. Rather than attempting to guess the interviewee's preferred solution, it often is most effective to ask, "What do you think ought to be done about this?" If the interviewee cannot or will not suggest a possible

solution, discontinue the interview until some specified later time and date and ask the interviewee to think about possible solutions and bring them to the next session.

**5.** *Evaluate suggested solutions.* Once some approaches to resolving the issue have been listed, the next step is to evaluate each in terms of its desirability. Will the suggested solution actually solve the problem? Will it have any undesirable side effects? Could it create any new problems?

**6.** *Develop a plan for action.* When a solution acceptable to both has been devised, a specific plan of action should be developed that answers the questions "Who will do what, when, where, and how?" Obviously, the more specific this plan, the more likely it is the actions will be taken and the better able both parties will be to track the success of their solution.

**7.** *Develop a schedule for follow-up.* An appointment should be made for another interview, one in which discussion will focus on how successful the agreed-upon action has been in resolving the interviewee's concerns. This follow-up conversation will allow both parties to evaluate how pleased they are with the progress that has been made, and to make whatever adjustments are necessary in the initial action plan.

**8.** *Thank the interviewee.* Although it can be uncomfortable (at least initially) to have a complaint brought to you, such interviews are important. Problems cannot be resolved if they remain hidden, and trust cannot be built if risks are not taken. Therefore, the interviewer should express sincere appreciation to the interviewee for having raised the issue, and should encourage him or her to bring similar issues to the fore in the future.

By making a habit of this sort of systematic approach to handling problems and complaints, we can overcome the lack of preparation time such interviews typically allow and use to maximum advantage these communication opportunities.

---

**KEY CONCEPTS 9.7** | **The Complaint Resolution Interview: Key Components**

Keys to conducting effective complaint resolution interviews include:

• • *Identifying the other person's reasons for bringing you the complaint.*

• • *Carefully conducting the interview by:*

1. Listening.
2. Asking exploratory questions.
3. Summarizing what you think you have heard.
4. Asking for the interviewee's suggested solutions.
5. Evaluating suggested solutions.
6. Developing a plan for action.
7. Developing a schedule for follow-up.
8. Thanking the interviewee.

Why must performance evaluations be conducted appropriately and ethically? Consider these cases:

- A marketing manager received excellent ratings but was demoted because she refused to stop dating a salesman from a competitor. She resigned, then sued her employer, claiming that she had in effect been fired. The court reviewed her evaluation records and concluded that the employer was guilty of wrongful discharge. The company was fined $300,000.
- Appraisals of an engineering department manager showed steadily declining performance and indicated he had become increasingly sarcastic and disruptive in meetings. But when he was fired, he sued, claiming that after 23 years on the job, he did not believe the warnings he had been given could lead to discharge. The court found that since his evaluations did not indicate he could be fired, the manager should be reinstated and paid more than $60,000 by the company.

Careful communication and documentation during performance evaluations are becoming increasingly important as employees show greater willingness to take former employers to court.

Source: James M. Jenks, "Do Your Performance Appraisals Boost Productivity?" *Management Review* (June 1991): 46.

## THE ETHICS OF INTERVIEWING

In a sense, conducting an interview is no different from engaging in other forms of organizational communicative interaction, in that ethical behavior is important. But being an interviewer places a special emphasis on the need for ethics. Almost by definition, interviewers are individuals with authority. In most cases, the interviewer has the ability to make some decision affecting the fate or well-being of the interviewee. In employment interviews, the interviewer can eliminate the applicant from further consideration. In corrective interviews, the interviewer can choose the terms of the punishment or the nature of the contract employees must fulfill if they wish to remain with the company.

In any interview, the interviewer officially represents the organization, and his or her conduct reflects on the standards, values, and ethics of the organization. The interviewer who asks offensive or illegal questions, who speaks rudely or condescendingly to a fellow employee, or who refuses to listen to the interviewee's explanations or ideas not only reveals him or herself as insensitive or unethical; he or she also suggests that the company condones such behavior. One of our former students was interviewed by a personnel manager who represented a major U.S. manufacturing company. This woman was initially quite pleased when she received the opportunity to interview with this company. During the interview, however, the interviewer asked her several personal (and illegal) questions, focusing in particular on her fiancé's attitude toward the prospect of her traveling all over the country. Not only did this woman leave the interview with a feeling of disgust, she decided that she wanted no further dealings with this organization. Even when she received a letter inviting her to visit the company for a second interview, she declined.

Illegal interviewing practices are always unethical. But unethical interviewing occurs whenever interviewers treat interviewees with disrespect, use their authority to make employees feel powerless or threatened, or refuse to listen or even to give an interviewee the chance to speak. By contrast, the ethical interviewer

- Shows concern for the interviewee and his or her feelings.

- Is interested in finding out what the interviewee thinks.

- Genuinely listens.

- Demonstrates respect for the interviewee by the way he or she communicates.

- Plans the interview time so that information exchange can, in fact, occur.

- Is familiar with the law and other organizational rules to be sure that he or she is operating within a legal framework.

- Is knowledgeable concerning the organization's code of ethics, either formal or informal.

- Is sensitive to power and authority differences in the interview setting and seeks to minimize their potentially negative effects.

Behaving ethically as an interviewer is a matter of knowledge, common sense, goodwill, and hard work.

## SUMMARY

In this chapter, we have acquainted you with the types and functions of interviews in organizations. We have pointed out the pervasiveness of interviewing activities, as well as the critical communication functions served by interviews, such as information giving and seeking, persuading, and problem solving. In the interviewing context, we hire people, evaluate them, counsel them, discipline them, sell things to them, solve problems with them, gain information from them, and occasionally fire them. Certainly, we also find ourselves on the receiving end of these interview functions. Our ability to function effectively in each of these contexts will contribute to our success in organizational life.

More than any other single factor, the key to successful interviewing is preparation. As we saw in this chapter, whether the interview is aimed at appraisal, corrective, or complaint resolution, we must first analyze our own purposes, and we must consider the attitudes, knowledge, behaviors, and characteristics of our interviewee. Then we must carefully plan the opening of the interview, the types of questions we will ask and the order in which we will ask them, and the way in which we will close the encounter. Moreover, we must take care to listen and react to the interviewee, so that modifications in our interview game plan can be made when needed. Above all, we must resolve to treat the interview as a problem-solving situation, one in which both we and the interviewee each have our own needs and in which we work together to develop action plans whereby each of our needs can be met. By taking this sort of approach, we significantly enhance our chances for success as an interviewer.

# QUESTIONS FOR DISCUSSION

1. How would you distinguish an interview from other kinds of dyadic encounters?
2. What are some of the types of interviews commonly encountered within organizations? What are some of the characteristics and potential problems associated with each?
3. From the interviewer's perspective, describe the planning necessary for conducting effective interviews.
4. Compare and contrast the following, giving examples of each:
   a. Directive versus nondirective strategy.
   b. Open versus closed questions.
   c. Probing versus restatement.
   d. Hypothetical versus reactive probes.
5. Discuss the concept of question bias. How can biased questions be used effectively? Are they ever unethical? How?
6. Compare and contrast the following questioning sequences: funnel, inverted funnel, diamond, hourglass, and tunnel.
7. What are the goals of a corrective interview?
8. What are some common problems associated with corrective interviews?
9. What should be done to prepare for a corrective interview?
10. How does the "shared problem-solving" concept apply to discipline?
11. What are some common problems associated with appraisal interviews?
12. What objectives should an appraisal interview achieve?
13. What should be done to prepare for an appraisal interview?
14. How does the "shared problem-solving" concept apply to performance appraisal?

# EXERCISES

1. Check with several local organizations to see what kinds of performance evaluations they use. What are the strengths of their systems? What are the weaknesses? How would you improve their systems?
2. Obtain a copy of a nearby organization's corrective policy or work rules. Using the skills described in this book, how would a supervisor in that organization deal with an employee who was repeatedly late to work? Be specific.
3. Select a current topic of interest and controversy, and choose an interviewee who feels differently from the way you do. Conduct a thorough analysis of that person; then plan an overall persuasive interviewing strategy. Indicate specifically what your closing question would be.

A medium-sized business recently hired a new manager, Frederick Vine. Although Fred viewed his new position as a definite step up, in that this company was more prestigious than the one for which he had previously worked, he was extremely unhappy with his new secretary, Harry. Harry preferred to think of himself as an "administrative assistant" rather than a secretary. He was quite active in the clerical union and spent many hours (during the workday) discussing union-related activities on the telephone. Harry also had a bad back and severe allergies, and often called in sick. Fred perceived him as lazy, irresponsible, and uncooperative.

When Fred first arrived, he simply tried to go with the flow and adjust to his new secretary's habits. This proved difficult, however, because he found Harry's habits very offensive. At his previous company, in contrast, he had had an ideal female secretary who was sharp, motivated, and hard-working. After a short time, Fred decided he had to do something.

Fred began by summoning Harry to his office and sharing with him a lengthy document he had written on office procedures. He explained to Harry why they were important. He noted that although his predecessor had not articulated such procedures, he simply could not operate without them. The procedures specified a number of work rules that affected all members of the staff—with a particular emphasis on the secretaries. Fred asked if Harry had any questions, and Harry responded negatively. Fred assumed, therefore, that he had made himself clear and that things would improve.

Fred was soon proved wrong. Harry's behavior did not change. In fact, about a week after he received the new set of rules, he e-mailed Fred that his back was really in bad shape and therefore he couldn't come to work

that day. The next day he had a close friend call another secretary in the department and leave Fred a note indicating that Harry's back was so bad that he would probably not be in for the rest of the week.

Fred was furious. He decided to take additional, more aggressive action. He began by interviewing several members of his department to discover their perceptions of the situation. He was informed of several specific examples involving instances of what he considered to be unprofessional behavior on Harry's part (like playing computer games nearly every day from 4:00–5:00 P.M.). Upon Harry's return, Fred began to keep a careful log of all Harry's peculiarities, noting how they deviated from the new office procedures. Predictably, he accumulated quite a list. After several weeks, he consulted with the director of personnel to make sure he wasn't violating any company rules. Then, he wrote Harry a stern three-page letter in which he listed all his deficiencies in specific detail. He left this letter on Harry's desk so that he encountered it the first thing on a Monday morning, and then busied himself with other tasks.

Later in the day, Fred called Harry in to ask if he had made himself clear. He asked if Harry understood the changes he needed to make if he were to remain gainfully employed. With teeth gritted, Harry said he did. He offered a few comments on how difficult it was to adjust to Fred's style of leadership—a style that stood in stark contrast to his previous boss's. Harry mentioned the fact that he was 45 years old and had legitimate health problems. During the conversation, Fred interrupted him several times to inquire about other sorts of issues, such as how soon Harry thought he would be able to master some newly acquired software, a mail merge program. As Harry attempted to respond to his questions, Fred tipped back in his chair and quietly watched him. Harry couldn't help noticing that Fred occasionally tapped his fingers on his chair arms with a subtle air of impatience.

## Questions

1. Using the information about corrective interviews and performance appraisals presented in this chapter, how would you evaluate Fred's communication behavior?

2. How might Fred have communicated with Harry more effectively?

3. What role (if any) did the choice of communication modes (face-to-face, written [the procedures and the letter], the telephone, and e-mail) play in affecting this situation? How might the varied modes have been used more effectively?

# The Employment Interview

Every year, in colleges and universities across the nation, seniors work through their campus placement agencies as they prepare to meet prospective employers. They prepare résumés, write letters of application, and sign up for interviews. Most participate in a number of interviews—preliminary screenings that will determine who will be invited to the company for more in-depth interviews. These are exciting and potentially anxiety-producing moments for most. They know that how well they perform in their 20-minute, or longer, interview will determine what doors are opened to them, where they will live, with whom they will work, and how smoothly they make the transition from college to professional life.

The employment interview is a culminating experience. The applicant must find a way to prepare—to pull together his or her years of study, of cognitive and social development, of life and work experiences, and to communicate about them effectively and persuasively. For the employer, the interview is also critical. How discerning he or she is in screening prospective recruits determines the future of the organization. So, careful preparation and effective performance during the interview are important for both parties.

## PREVIEW

In this chapter, we focus on the employment interview, from the perspective of the employer and the applicant. Understanding both roles is important to effective performance in each. We trace the preparatory steps for the interviewer-employer. We also look at the process of initiating the job hunt from the perspective of the applicant-interviewee. For both roles, we focus on how to perform effectively during the interview itself. When both parties know what they are doing and do it well, the interview's outcome is more likely to be satisfying for everyone concerned.

## THE FUNCTION AND IMPORTANCE OF THE EMPLOYMENT INTERVIEW

In the preceding chapter, we discussed the fundamental principles of interviews and examined a few special interviewing applications, such as the appraisal interview. By definition, formal interviews are important. Yet, of the many functions interviews can serve, none is more important than the employment interview. For the supervisor or manager, this interview determines the quality of his or her people, and this in turn determines how successful he or she will be as a manager.

For the interviewee seeking employment, the interview is equally important. In beginning a career, selecting the right job is of particular importance.

Raelin claims that "the characteristics of a person's first job are important in explaining their later employment success."[1] His research suggests that jobs that provide challenge, opportunities for growth, and independence improve one's attitudes toward and aptitudes in work, thus enhancing chances for success in the future. Therefore, first-time job seekers should choose very carefully what positions they accept: their future could depend on making the right choice.

As we noted above, we will examine the employment interview from two perspectives: that of the interviewee seeking a position and that of the interviewer looking for qualified candidates. Only when both parties are skilled in their own roles and each has an understanding of the other's role can the employment interview be maximally effective.

# THE ROLE OF THE INTERVIEWER

As the person seeking a new employee, the interviewer must be involved in a number of processes. These include understanding the interview's legal environment, defining the job, recruiting, prescreening applicants, and interviewing. We will consider each of these processes in turn. First, however, it's important to be aware of some common mistakes that interviewers have made in the past, so that they can be avoided.

**Common Problems to Avoid**

Everyone expects the novice interviewer to make some mistakes, but often even those with years of interviewing experience may go awry. Interviewers may believe that when they sit down and look applicants in the eye, they will instinctively "know" which ones are best qualified. But, without adequate preparation for the interview and vigilance during the interviewing, many things can go wrong.[2]

Here are some things to guard against:

- *Failing to know what the job requires.* If those who are interviewing applicants do not understand (and agree on) the job's critical requirements, they will be hard pressed to make a good decision, or even to be able to agree on whom to hire.

- *Neglecting to read the applicant's materials before the interview.* Some interviewers only look over the résumé, references, and other materials a few seconds prior to the interview (or even during the interview). When this happens, chances are they will ask for information they already have and fail to pursue more interesting and fruitful lines of questioning.

- *Failing to formulate key questions before the interview.* Sometimes interviewers rely on the inspiration of the moment to think of a good question. When that happens, some questions may be poorly worded, some may be illegal, and critical applicant experiences may be ignored.

- *Making a hasty decision.* Research has shown that interviewers often make accept or reject decisions very early in the interview—often within the first four or five minutes![3] When this happens, the rest of the interview is wasted time, and applicants are evaluated during the precise time when they are most likely to be nervous.

- *Treating applicants you like differently from those with whom you are less impressed.* Interviewers may inadvertently show more enthusiasm, ask more animated questions, or simply "look" more interested when they are interviewing a promising applicant. Yet, everyone must be given an equal opportunity throughout the interview. Verbally *and* nonverbally, the interviewer must treat all applicants the same.

- *Discriminating against applicants for any reason.* Historically, applicants have been discriminated against because of their sex, sexual orientation, ethnicity, age, race, and physical attractiveness. It is critically important that the interviewer knows the laws that prohibit such discrimination and follows them faithfully.

Fortunately, these and other problems can be avoided or minimized through conscientious preparation. The foundation for an effective interview is doing your homework, knowing what you're talking about, and being committed to treating all applicants fairly. Let's begin by considering the laws that govern interviewing.

## Knowing the Employment Law

Equal Employment Opportunity (EEO) laws have been on the books for decades; yet, some employers who are involved with interviewing either ignore them or are ignorant of them. Even if an employer is innocent in asking an illegal question, he or she can still be held accountable. *The courts are not interested in interviewers' intentions—only in their behavior.* If an applicant can show that he or she has been asked an illegal question, or has been discriminated against in any way, then he or she can take the employer to court. Failure to comply with the law can be costly.

Nearly all organizations must comply with EEO laws. These federal laws pertain to all organizations that deal with the federal government, have more than $50,000 in government contracts, have more than 15 employees, and engage in interstate commerce.[4] See Highlighting Ethics for a list of key EEO laws. In addition, there are state laws and these may be more stringent than federal laws.

Although the laws may look abundant and somewhat intimidating, complying with them is not that difficult. In general, there are three rules to follow:

1. *Avoid asking questions out of general interest or curiosity.* It may seem natural to ask some personal questions about, for example, an applicant's spouse—not because one intends to discriminate, but simply because one is genuinely interested. Whatever the intention, however, such curiosity-driven questions are usually illegal.

2. *Ask the same questions of all applicants.* Of course, you will ask some résumé-specific questions of each applicant, but in general, the major questions planned and posed should be asked of everyone.

Those who ask certain questions only of female, disabled, older, or minority applicants are undoubtedly asking unlawful questions.

3. *Ask only questions that pertain to the job's critical requirements.* These critical requirements are called *bona fide occupational qualifications (BFOQs)*—the knowledge, skill, ability, talent, and so on that are essential for performing a particular job. BFOQs usually include work experience,

**Staying within the Law: Key EEO Laws to Remember**

- *The Civil Rights Acts of 1866, 1870, and 1871.* Generally prohibit discrimination against minorities.
- *The Equal Pay Act of 1963.* Requires equal pay for men and women who are performing similar work (requiring similar levels of skill, etc.).
- *The Civil Rights Act of 1964.* Prohibits the selection of employees based on race, color, sex, religion, or national origin, and requires employers to be proactive in discovering discriminatory practices and eliminating them.
- *The Age Discrimination in Employment Act of 1967.* Bars discrimination against people because of age.
- *The Equal Employment Opportunity Act of 1972.* Extends the 1964 Civil Rights Act to public and private educational institutions, labor organizations, and employment agencies.

- *The Americans with Disabilities Act of 1990.* Prohibits discrimination against individuals with mental or physical impairments which limit or restrict the condition, manner, or duration under which they can perform one or more major life activities and requires reasonable accommodation by employers.
- *The Civil Rights Act of 1991.* Caps compensation and punitive damages for employers, provides for jury trial, and created a commission to investigate the "glass ceiling" for women and minorities and to reward organizations who offer opportunities for minorities and women.
- *The Family Medical Leave Act of 1993.* Provides an extended time (12 weeks within any 12-month period) for the birth of a child; the care of a sick child; or the care of a seriously ill spouse, child, or parent that prevents the employee from performing the functions of the job.

training, skills, education, or personality characteristics that have a direct bearing on ability to perform the job effectively. BFOQs usually exclude sex, sexual orientation, age, race, religion, marital status, physical appearance, ethnicity, disabilities that are irrelevant to the job, citizenship, family ties, and arrest records.

To ensure that your interviewing practices are consistent with legal requirements, you should become familiar with the American Psychological Association's Principles for the Validation and Use of Personnel Selection Procedures and with the Uniform Guidelines on Employee Selection of the Equal Employment Opportunity Commission (EEOC).[5]

Under current regulations, it is *unlawful* to ask an applicant:

**1.** If he or she has *ever worked under another name,* unless the applicant previously worked for your organization under another name. However, if the applicant is female, you can usually request that she indicate her maiden name.

**2.** For his *birthplace or the birthplace of his parents, spouse, or other close relatives.* This could reveal the national origin or race of the applicant.

**3.** For her *birthdate or age.* However, you may ask if the applicant is over 65 or under 18.

**4.** For his *religious affiliation, church, or the religious holidays he observes.*

**5.** If she is a *naturalized citizen.* This could easily establish race or national origin.

**6.** *How he acquired the ability to read, write, or speak a foreign language.* This could easily determine ethnic background. If the ability to speak French is a BFOQ, however, asking about the applicant's ability to speak it is quite acceptable.

**7.** To *provide names of relatives other than father, mother, husband, wife, or minor-age dependent children.* This may reveal national origin, race, creed, or ethnic background of the applicant or spouse.

**8.** For the *names of all clubs, societies, and lodges to which she belongs.* This could reveal the individual's ethnic background and color. However, the applicant can be asked to indicate membership in organizations that are not based on ethnic origins or religious membership practices.

**9.** To *include a photograph* with the application for employment.

**10.** To reveal *the number of his dependents.*

**11.** To *indicate whether she has ever been treated for a mental disorder.* This would reveal past mental health problems and the applicant is protected by the Americans with Disabilities Act (ADA).

**12.** *If he will need a braille keyboard due to his limited vision.* Under the ADA, the employer must be willing to make "reasonable accommodations," which would include such a keyboard.

**13.** *How a woman's husband would feel about her having to travel so much.* The question reveals a gender bias, and would rarely be asked of males.

**14.** *If he has ever been arrested.* Many innocent people are arrested. So long as one has not been convicted, an arrest has no bearing on qualifications for the job.

Although some questions can be identified as clearly illegal, keep in mind that the legality of many questions can be judged only in relationship to an understanding of the job's critical requirements. Those who apply for modeling jobs should expect to have their appearance judged. And again, many questions regarding weekend travel, and child and elder care are often asked only of women. They are unlawful primarily because they are not asked of all applicants.

## Knowing the Job's Requirements: Developing an Applicant Profile

Once you feel comfortable in your understanding of the laws governing the selection process, you must next determine the nature of the position to be filled and the corresponding qualifications that a potential applicant must possess. This information should be the basis for recruiting and selecting people for the available position. Among the qualifications you should consider are education, experience, knowledge and skills, physical demands of the job, integrity or trustworthiness, contact with other people, and any other special requirements (such as odd working hours or unusual working conditions).

By identifying these requirements and creating an *applicant profile,* you achieve a number of things. First and foremost, you identify the BFOQs that *must* serve as the basis for your selection decisions. As noted above, EEO laws state that such personal factors as age, sex, race, religion, ethnic origin, and veteran's status cannot be involved in hiring decisions *unless* a BFOQ necessitates incorporation of that factor. For example, if the job is "men's room attendant" in a hotel, sex becomes a BFOQ, and you are allowed to exclude women from consideration. In most instances, however, you must give equal consideration to all applicants without regard to their demographic characteristics, and you must base your hiring decisions in every instance on the requirements of the position itself.

Constructing an applicant profile also points to the sorts of applicants you need, the places in which you should recruit for applicants, the information you should look for when reviewing résumés or application forms, and the information you should seek during the selection interview.

You can construct an applicant profile in several ways. You may talk with managers and human resources personnel, you may observe skilled employees doing the job for which you will be recruiting, and you can talk with coworkers to see what traits they most value in their fellow employees. Whatever approach you use, make sure you check your perceptions against others'—and especially those others who will be interviewing applicants along with you. If you and your fellow interviewers can agree on the job's critical characteristics, you will find yourselves far more likely to agree on which applicants are most qualified following your interviews.

The applicant profile, then, is what you and others will use to guide you as you prepare for and conduct each interview. You will use the profile to plan questions, to examine résumés and cover letters, and to assess each applicant after the interview is over.

## Recruiting

When looking for potential applicants, you should consider a number of sources. First, look at *sources in your own organization*. In almost every organization, it should be a policy to promote from within whenever possible. This policy shows employees that they have a chance to grow within the organization and that the quality of their performance will be rewarded by upward movement.

When additional candidates are desired, *employee referrals* should be solicited. Often, employees know people who might be qualified, and they know the organization well enough to have an idea of the type of candidate who would fit the organization.

*Advertising in newspapers, on radio, and occasionally on television* is another common recruiting technique. Professional journals, trade association newsletters, and other written media sent to specific types of employees are also commonly used. These sources must be used carefully, for the law prohibits advertisements that may discriminate on the basis of age, sex, veteran's status, or some other characteristic not related to the job.

*Public and private employment agencies* can provide job applicants. Headhunters have become the most common source for recruiting executive-level applicants, and many recruitment firms handle lower-level positions as well. Most trade schools, business schools, junior or community colleges, high schools, and colleges and universities have placement offices and counselors who refer students or graduates. Some schools have internship or work-study programs that are excellent sources for part-time employees and, ultimately, experienced help.

*Former employees* who left the organization on good terms may refer potential applicants, or they may even fill in as temporary help. In some cases,

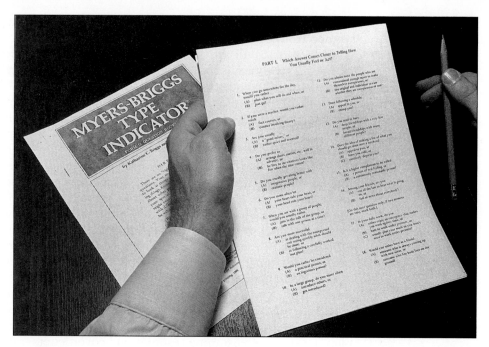

Some employers use pre-employment testing as a way of screening job applicants for such personal qualities as honesty, values, and personality traits. The results of such tests are used in the broader context of other information obtained from references, cover letters, résumés, and interviews.

changed family situations (for example, a child now old enough to be cared for by someone else) may make a former employee available for work again.

*Electronic sourcing* can also be used to locate skilled applicants. Most major newspapers can be accessed through the computer, but there are many databases available as well. Here are a few examples: Employers' Job Net Electronic Bulletin Board (609-683-9191), Skill Search (800-252-5665), Ki Nexus Employer and Student Listing (800-828-0422), and Job Bank U.S.A. Pre-Qualified Résumés (800-296-1 USA). The Internet is also a potential source, but résumé accuracy can be a problem.

Screening
When the recruiting sources have produced a group of applicants, the next task is to sort out those who clearly are unsuited for the job. Typically, several pieces of information are used to screen out unqualified candidates—a résumé (or application form), references, and often a cover letter. In some instances, you will also have the results of preemployment testing.

*Cover letters* typically accompany résumés. By reading them, you can get a sense of the applicants' writing quality and style and the sorts of skills or qualification they emphasize. You may get a sense of why they are applying for this particular job. No two cover letters look alike, and sometimes comparisons are difficult. But, if a letter is poorly written, if the applicant doesn't appear to have a realistic sense of the job, and/or if the skills highlighted are less than impressive, the wisest course may be eliminating him or her from further consideration.

For every applicant, you will obtain *a résumé or application form*, which will present basic information about educational and work history, personal references, and short- and long-term goals. Review the information that the applicant has provided and assess the implications of this information. The things you should look for include:

1. *Time gaps.* Are there any time periods unaccounted for? Might these gaps be important? Why?
2. *Education.* Imagine this individual is applying for a position in sales. How would you evaluate his or her educational background? How would you verify it?
3. *Incomplete information.* Are there any instances where more information should have been given? Could the omissions be important? Why?
4. *Employment history.* Does this record show success? Stability? What can you infer from the information given?
5. *Salary.* Is consistent progress shown? What can you infer about the applicant, based upon her or his salary history?
6. *References.* Are the right people listed as references? Do important people seem to be missing? What can you infer?
7. *Appearance of the application.* Is it neat and easy to read? Grammatically correct? Professional looking? As Arthur points out, the care with which application forms or résumés are prepared often provides insight into the care with which the applicant would do his or her work.[6]

*The references provided by the applicant* provide the other source of information you should use during the screening procedure. Typically, you would contact references only for those applicants whose written materials have kept them in contention. The purpose of such reference checks is to get more in-depth information about the applicant and to verify the accuracy of the information provided on the application form or résumé. When properly done, a reference check may provide information about the employee's motivation level, attitudes and personality, relations with others, judgment and common sense, resourcefulness, integrity, energy level, ability to handle pressure and meet deadlines, and leadership and responsibility levels. Obviously, this information goes far beyond that provided on the application form, and it allows you to make a far more accurate judgment concerning the suitability of a candidate.

As a rule, you should *seek several* such *references.* Work-related references are best, although personal references may be appropriate, particularly for younger applicants who have little work experience. Consider the total information accumulated during your reference checks when you decide whether or not to pursue the candidate further. That is, one slightly unfavorable reference should not outweigh two or three favorable ones. However, a single, strongly unfavorable reference may be a signal that you should investigate the applicant more thoroughly.

In some cases and for certain kinds of searches, you will have letters of recommendation as part of the applicant's application package. Some are skeptical of letters of recommendation—assuming that the applicant will

An unusually exhaustive hiring process is used by Toyota Motor Manufacturing U.S.A. in Georgetown, Kentucky:

Step 1: The Kentucky Department of Employment Services has applicants complete application forms and view a one-hour videotape describing Toyota's work environment and selection system.

Step 2: Applicants take the Situation Judgment Inventory, which tests their interpersonal skills and ability to work in a team environment. The test is administered and scored by the Kentucky Department of Employment Services.

Step 3: Applicants participate in four hours of group and individual problem-solving and discussion activities conducted at Toyota's assessment center. In addition, applicants for assembly-line jobs participate in a five-hour assembly simulation, with other candidates playing the role of manager.

Step 4: A one-hour group interview is conducted by Toyota with several candidates, allowing their group communication skills to be assessed.

Step 5: Applicants undergo 2 1/2 hours of physical and drug and alcohol tests at an area hospital.

Step 6: New hires are closely monitored and coached on the job for their first six months at work; those unable to perform acceptably are immediately discharged.

Source: Gary Dessler, "Value-Based Hiring Builds Commitment," *Personnel Journal* 72 (November 1993): 98–102.

only ask those to write who will offer praise and further, that no one will write a "bad" letter. While those perceptions are usually true, it is still possible to glean some valuable insights from letters of recommendation. For instance, a discerning reader can usually tell how well the letter writer knows the applicant and whether the writer is *extremely* impressed by the applicant or simply happy with his or her work. Detailed letters that provide specific examples of the applicant's accomplishments, work habits, and exhibited attitudes can really help the employer get a picture of the applicant as a person.

Sometimes you will also have the results of *preemployment tests* to guide your screening (although in some cases, such tests will be administered only *after* applicants have passed through an initial screening). In the 1970s and 1980s, for example, polygraph tests (lie detectors) were commonly used to screen applicants. Later, most states outlawed the use of such tests because of problems with their accuracy and potential misuse. More recently, however, organizations use *honesty tests* to help assess the honesty of applicants, especially those applying for positions that involve handling large sums of money. While some of these tests are believed to yield valuable insights into the honesty of those tested,[7] their results ought to be considered in a broader context (including other relevant performance and attitudinal qualities, reference checks, and performance during the interview itself).

*Job skills testing* of applicants for non-white-collar positions (such as clerical or secretarial jobs or work on production lines) is also increasing. Of the companies surveyed in an American Management Association study, 22.5 percent tested applicants for nonmanagement jobs.[8] Tests of applicants for management positions were far less frequent. Skills testing is more common in some kinds of organizations than others. For instance, insurance companies often give tests to assess sales skills and believe them to be accurate. Again, skill test results should be taken in context; and if they are to be useful, they should be validated on a cross-section of the population and meet EEO guidelines.

As an interviewer, it is important that you be fully aware of your organization's testing policies and practices. In addition, you should be sure that all applicants for a position take the same tests: selective application of tests has been found to be evidence of discrimination. Of course, organizations vary in the nature and extent of their screening practices. Business Brief 10.1 provides an unusual illustration of one organization's approach to screening and hiring.

Upon completion of the preliminaries, you will have concluded the screening portion of the employment process. At this point, you should have eliminated applicants who clearly are unsuited for the position. Now you are ready to undertake the interviewing process.

## The Interviewing Process: Goals

Despite the many refinements that have been developed in recruiting and screening methods, the interview is still considered the most vital part of the selection process. The interview offers the prospective employee and the employer the opportunity to obtain information, form impressions, and make observations that would not be possible otherwise. Normally, the objectives of the employment interview are:

**1.** To allow the interviewer to obtain enough knowledge about the applicant to determine whether she or he is suitable for employment in a particular position.

**2.** To provide sufficient information about the organization and the particular job to enable the applicant to decide whether to accept or reject the job, if offered.

**3.** To treat the applicant in a manner that will create and maintain goodwill toward the organization.[9]

Achievement of these objectives requires careful planning.

## Preparing for the Interview

The first step is to *prepare.* Like good speeches, the foundation of a good interview is preparation. Here are some guidelines:

- *Review again the applicant profile* (detailing the job's critical requirements).

- *Carefully examine the information about each applicant* that you have obtained through written materials and reference checks.

- *Plan a core of questions that you will ask of each applicant,* following the guidelines for question construction discussed in Chapter 9.

- *Prepare some questions for each applicant that are résumé-specific,* allowing you to probe each one's particular qualifications. In planning all questions, work within the framework of BFOQs and plan with time constraints in mind.

- *Assemble information about the organization and the position to share with the applicant.* The interview is, after all, an opportunity for you to share as well as gather information.

- *Take care to eliminate potential distractions* (such as telephone calls or unexpected visitors) *and to make the surroundings as comfortable as possible.*

Having done all these things, you are ready to meet the applicant.

Conducting the Interview

The hours of planning finally culminate in the actual interview—where a great deal must be accomplished in a relatively short period of time.

**Opening the Interview: Setting the Stage**   *Gaining rapport* is an important first step in the interview. As interviewer, you should be courteous, show sincerity, express interest, and give complete attention to the interviewee's remarks. First impressions are particularly important in an employment interview from both perspectives, and your appearance, conduct, and attitude will influence the applicant just as much as his or her appearance and conduct will influence you.

*Greet the applicant by name, shaking his or her hand.* Engage in a little small talk, but don't get carried away. The interview time is precious. The applicant will appreciate knowing how you intend to proceed with the interview. *Providing an orientation to the interview* is helpful. Simply tell the applicant what you will do first, let him or her know that you'll be glad to provide information and respond to questions a bit later, and mention the time available for the interview. Then you are ready to move to the first question.

**Questioning: The Key to Effective Interviewing**   As you question each applicant, your continuing concern should be to use the time wisely, to ask good, substantive questions, and to avoid poor questioning practices often associated with interviews. To be avoided, then, are: (1) asking questions that can be answered with a simple yes or no (and thus reveal little about the interviewee's abilities in self-expression); (2) asking a series of run-of-the-mill questions for which the astute applicant has long since prepared ready-made answers; (3) using leading questions that suggest the "proper" answer to the applicant or asking questions already answered by the résumé; (4) asking questions not related to the task at hand; and, of course, (5) asking unlawful questions.

What kinds of questions *should* you ask? What substantive areas should you probe? You, of course, will want to frame your own questions, but there are certain question areas on which you will likely want to focus your attention. These include:

*The Applicant's Work Experience*   A person's work experience is important and is a natural and easy place to start the interview. Some key questions might include:

**1.** One of the things we want to talk about today is your work experience. Would you tell me about your present job?
**2.** What are some of the things on your job you feel you have done particularly well or in which you have achieved the greatest success? Why do you feel this way?
**3.** What are some of the things about your job that you found difficult to do? Why do you feel they were difficult for you?

**4.** Most jobs have pluses and minuses. What were some of the minuses in your last job?

*How the Applicant Feels about People*   The way the applicant feels about people—her or his co-workers and supervisors—has an important part in determining job success. Here are the kinds of questions that will help you explore this important area:

**1.** What do you feel were your supervisor's greatest strengths?
**2.** In what areas do you feel your supervisor could have done an even better job?
**3.** What kind of people do you like working with? What kind of people do you find most difficult to work with?

*The Applicant's Job Objectives*   The interviewer needs to know what the applicant's job objectives are in a job or career—what he or she is looking for or wishing to avoid. Here, again, proper questions can be of great help in obtaining such information. For example:

**1.** What are some of the things in a job that are important to you?
**2.** What are some of the things you would like to avoid in a job, and why?
**3.** What is your overall career objective? What are some of the things, outside of your job, that you have done or that you plan to do that will assist you in reaching this objective?
**4.** What kind of position would you expect to progress to in five years? Ten years?

Besides the kinds of core questions we have just suggested, *you will want to use many of the other questioning techniques we discussed in Chapter 9.* Whenever your initial question does not elicit the kind of information you had hoped to obtain, you probably should follow it up with some kind of probe.

### The Interviewer as Information Source: Responding to Questions   When you have obtained all the information you need, *be sure that the applicant has a chance to ask questions.* The quality of questions applicants ask may tell you a great deal about their thinking, the extent to which they investigated the organization or position ahead of time, and their familiarity with the field of work. Your purpose is to provide complete, accurate information so applicants can make informed, correct decisions about you and your organization. You will want to present a positive impression of your organization, without exaggerating. Applicants are usually interested in the company's reputation and stability, what a typical workday is like, and avenues for advancement.

If there is a particular philosophy that distinguishes your organization from others, you might want to share that—such as an emphasis on self-management, teamwork, or diversity. In fact, a number of forward-looking organizations are striving for a more diverse workforce, and this philosophy influences their hiring practices and organizational culture in a variety of ways. See Highlighting Diversity for a review of some of the reasons that many organizations are promoting workforce diversity.

## ARGUMENTS FOR CULTURAL DIVERSITY IN ORGANIZATIONS

### Cost Argument

As organizations become more diverse, costs of poor integration will increase. Companies that are able to integrate a culturally diverse workforce will realize considerable cost savings over those companies that cannot or choose not to do so.

### Resource-Acquisition Argument

Companies develop reputations as good places for women and minorities to work. Those with the best reputations will be able to attract the best people. As the labor pool shrinks and changes in composition, this advantage will become more important.

### Marketing Argument

For multinational organizations, the insight and cultural sensitivity that employees with roots in other countries bring to marketing efforts should improve the effectiveness of such efforts. This reasoning also applies to ethnic groups within the United States.

### Creativity Argument

Diversity of perspectives and less emphasis on conformity and adherence to past practices should improve the level of innovation and creativity among employees.

### Problem-Solving Argument

Heterogeneous decision-making and problem-solving groups are likely to produce better solutions because they allow critical analysis from multiple perspectives.

### System-Flexibility Argument

Organizations that are able to manage multicultural diversity effectively will necessarily become less standardized, more open, and more fluid within. This fluidity should create greater flexibility to react to environmental changes.

### Empowerment Argument

Individuals who work in organizational environments characterized by sensitivity and respect for diverse talents and perspectives grow to feel more valued and empowered, to relate better to co-workers, and to gain greater satisfaction from their jobs.

Source: T. Cox and S. Blake, "Managing Cultural Diversity: Implications for Organizational Competitiveness," *Academy of Management Executive, 5* (1991): 45–56.

**Concluding the Interview and Following Through**   After all the applicant's questions have been answered, your final task is to *outline the next steps, if any.* If you have reached a decision and have the power to extend an offer at that time, you may choose to do so. Similarly, if you have decided that the employee is not suited to the job, you may also inform him or her of that decision. If you are not in a position to make a decision at that point, tell the applicant what will happen next: when the decision will be made and how it will be communicated. Then follow through.

After the applicant has departed, take a few minutes to note your impressions of the applicant. It is imperative that you *not* mark on the résumé, application form, or any other materials that are part of the applicant's file. Instead, make your own notes. Better still, use an evaluation form to quickly record your impressions before going on to interview other applicants. See Figure 10.1 for a sample interview evaluation form.

FIGURE 10.1

## INTERVIEW EVALUATION FORM

**Applicant:** _____   **Position:** _____

**Interviewer:** _____   **Date:** _____

Scales should be interpreted as follows: 1 = poor; 2 = fair; 3 = average; 4 = good; 5 = excellent

| | | | | | |
|---|---|---|---|---|---|
| Interest in the Position | 1 | 2 | 3 | 4 | 5 |
| Knowledge of the Company | 1 | 2 | 3 | 4 | 5 |
| Education/Training | 1 | 2 | 3 | 4 | 5 |
| Work & Life Experiences | 1 | 2 | 3 | 4 | 5 |
| Communication Skills | 1 | 2 | 3 | 4 | 5 |
| Ability/Intelligence/Readiness to Learn | 1 | 2 | 3 | 4 | 5 |
| Motivation to Work | 1 | 2 | 3 | 4 | 5 |
| Maturity | 1 | 2 | 3 | 4 | 5 |
| Character | 1 | 2 | 3 | 4 | 5 |

*Comments:*

1. What are the applicant's greatest strengths?



2. What are his/her weaknesses?



Overall Assessment:     Negative     1     2     3     4     5     Positive

---

**KEY CONCEPTS 10.1**   **The Interviewer's Role**

As you prepare to interview applicants, remember to:

•   • *Avoid common problems. Problems to avoid include inadequate preparation, the tendency to make hasty decisions, and treating some applicants differently from others.*

•   • *Know the laws that govern the employment process. Identify and use BFOQs to guide your behavior.*

***Continued***

*Concluded*

- • • *Develop an applicant profile, based on BFOQs.*

- • • *As you recruit, seek varied sources to identify prospective applicants.*

- • • *Screen applicants by examining cover letters, résumés, and/or application forms, references, and results of preemployment tests.*

- • • *Plan a core of questions to be asked of all applicants and résumé-specific questions for each applicant.*

- • • *Prepare to respond to applicant questions about*

*the job and the organization.*

- • • *Prepare the interview room for comfort and privacy.*

- • • *Greet each applicant, gain rapport, and provide an orientation to the interview.*

- • • *Ask good questions, focused on work, education and training, attitudes toward people, and job objectives.*

- • • *Give the applicant a chance to ask questions of you.*

- • • *Conclude the interview by telling the applicant what will happen next.*

- • • *Record your impressions of the applicant.*

# THE ROLE OF THE INTERVIEWEE

Much of the preceding section is also of interest to the job applicant. When seeking a job, you should be aware of the needs and strategies of employers; and you should use that awareness to prepare for your interviews. In this section, we will consider the specific principles that employment interviewees should follow—principles that significantly enhance the likelihood that you will obtain the position of your choice (provided, of course, that you possess the qualifications that the position demands).

Initiating the Quest for Employment: The Self-Inventory and Job Assessment

Many people assume that when they think they are ready to look for a job, they should begin by going to a placement service. However, before seeking *external* assistance with employment, you must begin with an *internal assessment* by thinking about who you are, what you know, what skills you possess, and what you value, in a job and in life.

The first step then, in initiating any employment quest is to make a thorough *self-inventory.* Your college major is important, as are work experiences and other kinds of experiences you have had. They are important especially because they indicate something about your values, interests, attitudes, ambitions, and skills. Often we take stock only of our obvious and relatively superficial aspects. We assume, for example, that without a college degree in a specific field, we should never seek employment in that area of specialty. Yet consider the example of the man who, as vice president for development, saved a small private college from financial disaster. His educational background was in counseling, speech communication, academic affairs, and the ministry. He had never studied development, fund raising, or grant solicitation. His formal knowledge of annual giving programs, capital campaigns, and deferred giving was minimal. Even so, he succeeded in his position because he possessed the skills that allowed him to understand people and their needs and interests, to have compassion for them, and to move them persuasively to support causes in which they believed. Thus, his skills were transferable from his academic background and professional experiences to the business of fund raising. It is important that you *identify and list those skills and personal attributes you possess that might be attractive to a prospective employer.*

Once you have conducted your self-inventory, you should move on to a thoughtful consideration of the kind of job you would be most comfortable in and the sort of organization you would really like to work for. Some jobs pay well, but are accompanied by high stress levels. Some require extensive travel. Others require the ability to work alone, without much human contact, in contrast to still others that necessitate teamwork for most major projects and extensive human interaction. There is nothing necessarily "good" or "bad" about any of these kinds of jobs. What is critical is knowing what *you* want, what you would find appealing and motivating, and then trying to match your skills, values, and interests to the job and the organization. *Taking some time to consider the things that you most value in a job is the second step in initiating the employment quest.*

## The Employment Quest: Where to Look for Jobs

Once you are satisfied with your self- and job-assessments, you are ready to start looking for specific jobs that are available. A detailed study of job hunting in the United States revealed that the greater the number of auxiliary avenues used by the job seeker, the greater his or her success in finding a job.[10]

The traditional routes include, first, *friends, relatives, and former employers.* These individuals can provide the names of people to contact in the organization. You can then address letters of inquiry to specific individuals, avoiding the impersonal "Dear Sir." Positive internship experiences can lead to employment opportunities. In this situation, you know the company, the company knows you, and you know exactly whom to contact.

*Placement agencies* are a second common starting place. College and university placement services are often free or involve a nominal fee, and they provide students with job contacts and interview opportunities. Some colleges have a course associated with their placement services; in this course, you learn how to prepare a job portfolio, assess your skills, develop a résumé, and interview. You may also have the chance to hear prospective employers give job talks, or informational presentations about the organizations they represent. Based on what you hear at these talks, you can better decide which jobs and organizations you want to pursue.

Other placement agencies demand fees and are often affiliated with professional organizations for management, communication, accounting, and teaching. General placement agencies find jobs for individuals for a specific fee, often a certain percentage of the first month's or year's salary. In general, these services should be approached with caution.

You may also want to consult various *publications*. Don't overlook newspaper classified advertisements. Consult the *Wall Street Journal*, an excellent source of openings around the country. Visit the library or campus placement service for other useful sources. For instance, *Jobs 95* is published annually and provides addresses, toll-free numbers, and industry groupings. In addition, Career Communication Incorporated publishes a number of useful sources, including *Job Hunters Yellow Pages*, which lists more than 15,000 employment agencies and services.

Finally, you might want to explore the *Internet*. Many organizations are beginning to advertise positions through the World Wide Web. Among the Internet sources you might consult are: Careermosaic (http://www.careermosaic.com/), On Line Career Center (http://www.occ.com/occ/), and Career WEB (http:/www.cweb.com/).[11]

## Researching the Organization and the Field

Once you have identified some potential jobs, it's time to look seriously at the organizations in which those jobs are embedded. Bolles, an expert on job hunting, believes that *organizational research* should be a major focus of each person's preliminary employment strategy.[12] At the very least, you should learn the location of the organization's plants, branches, and offices; the age of the company; the kinds of services it offers; and its growth and future potential. Other question might include:

1. How does the organization rank within its field?
2. Is the organization family-owned? If so, does this influence promotions?
3. How innovative is the organization?
4. What kind of image does the organization have in the mind of the public?
5. What kind of staff turnover does it have?
6. What is the attitude of current employees?
7. Does the organization encourage its employees to further their education?
8. Is there evidence that the organization is "family-friendly" (through child and elder care policies, etc.)?
9. To what extent is the organization committed to diversity and to the support of women and minorities?
10. In general, how does communication flow within the organization? Is decision making highly centralized, or is it spread throughout the organization?

Sources of information on organizations are numerous and include the following: Better Business Bureau reports on the organization, chambers of commerce, college libraries, and the organization's annual reports. Other sources include:

*Business Week*

*The Career Guide: Dun's Employment Opportunities Directory*

*Dictionary of Occupational Titles*

*Dun and Bradstreet's Middle Market & Million Dollar Directories*

*Fortune Magazine*

*Fortune's Plant and Product Directory*

*Guide for Occupational Exploration*

*Moody's Industrial Manual*

*Standard and Poor's Industrial Surveys*

*Standard and Poor's Register of Corporations, Directors, and Executives*

*The One Hundred Best Companies to Work for in America*

*Thomas's Register of American Manufacturers*

*The Wall Street Journal*

As with other areas of research, there are a growing number of databases about organizations. Many are on CD-ROM, such as American Business Disc, Company ProFile, and Dun's Electronic Business Directory.

*Never overlook or minimize the value of people sources.* Talk with anyone affiliated with the organization—college alumni, friends, brokers, and certainly employees—who can provide helpful insights. It's always good to talk to employees whose positions are similar to the one you are interested in. If possible, chat with those in lower-level positions, such as clerical workers. Learning that they are happy in their jobs bodes well for the entire organizational climate. Ask your sources to describe their best and worst experiences; urge them to be specific. The more stories you gather about the organization, the better able you will be to interpret the more statistical and factual information you gain through other sources.

Finally, as you do research on the organizations you are interested in, *learn as much as you can about your chosen field*—its trends, history, leaders, challenges, current and future problems, and employment opportunities. Try to think about a typical workday in accounting, sales, marketing, or public relations. Develop realistic expectations. Those who interview you will be interested in discovering how much you know about your field and how mature and realistic you are about what will be expected of you. Doing internships, visiting and observing, or volunteering for short stints can provide further insights.

Learn everything you can. This will help you narrow and focus your interests and will assist you in developing your cover letter and résumé and presenting yourself well during the interview.

Presentation
of Self
in Writing

For many job seekers, the initial contact with the organization is through writing. Dozens of books exist that provide comprehensive guidelines for writing cover letters and résumés.[13] The following discussion focuses on only the essentials of both forms of written communication.

### The Cover Letter: The Power of the First Impression

Most of the time when we think of first impressions, we think of the interview itself. But it's important to recognize that the employer's first impression of you will come from the letter and the résumé you prepare. If these documents are not favorably received, there may never be an interview. Typically, your *cover letter* will be the first thing the employer sees—accompanied by your résumé. The cover letter *is* important. One study reported that this letter may have even more impact than the résumé in affecting hiring decisions.[14]

Following are some guidelines for writing the letter of application:

- *Send each prospective employer an original cover letter.* Each letter should be specifically adapted to the organization and position you are seeking.

- *Follow proper business letter writing format.*

- *Address your letter to the specific person who will be actively involved in the recruiting process.* Avoid the impersonal: "To Whom It May Concern," "Dear Recruiter," or "Dear Sir."

- *Keep it short*—usually no more than one page.

- *Make sure that your letter is neat, well written, and checked for spelling.* The employer will look at your letter as a writing sample. If your cover letter is well written, the employer may infer that you will also approach your job responsibly and with care.

- *Immediately state the position you are interested in, and how you found out about it.*

- *Briefly describe your areas of interest, special skills, knowledge and experience.* Do *not* simply reiterate information contained in the résumé, but creatively amplify it.

- *State your reason or reasons for selecting this particular position and organization.* Show the employer that you have done your homework, and help him or her to see that you and the organization are a good match.

- *In the final paragraph, indicate your times of availability for interviewing, and how you can be reached to arrange for an interview.*

Figure 10.2 presents a sample cover letter.

The cover letter is typically accompanied by a *résumé* (also referred to as a personal fact or data sheet). According to one extensive survey, 98 percent of all organizations prefer to receive both as part of the initial contact.[15]

Like the cover letter, résumés should be *reasonably brief* (one to two pages)[16] and should include the following basic information:

- *Personal information.* Work and home phone numbers and addresses, and e-mail address.

- *Professional goal or job objective.* The goal or objective should recognize the employer's needs, as well as those of the applicant; for example, "salesperson with an innovative firm where self-motivation and discipline are encouraged."

- *Educational background.* Majors and minors in college, knowledge acquired, degrees received, and dates associated with each.

- *Work experience.* Jobs held, responsibilities associated with and skills developed in each, and dates and places of employment.

- *Awards and honors.*

- *Activities.* Memberships in organizations and offices held in college, community, and volunteer organizations.

FIGURE 10.2     Sample cover letter

February 15, 1999

208A Clark House–Read Center
Indiana University
Bloomington, IN 47405

Mr. Phillip Johnson, Director of Recruitment
Ameritech
1633 N. Meridian Street
Indianapolis, IN 46208

Dear Mr. Johnson:

Earlier this month, I met with Tim Schick, your regional Ameritech representative who works here in Bloomington. He told me that you were looking for a college graduate who is interested in working in public relations and encouraged me to write to you. I have always admired your organization and I am very excited about the prospects of doing public relations work for Ameritech.

As you can see from my résumé, I am about to graduate from Indiana University with a double major in public relations and organizational behavior. The public relations major at Indiana is competitive and rigorous, and I performed quite well. Besides my formal education, I also have worked in a variety of organizations, doing public relations and advertising. I have designed company brochures, written news releases, and made speeches at social and business functions. I consider myself an excellent writer and speaker—and have won awards for both. I love a challenge. I consider myself to be a good team player, but I'm also very happy working on my own.

My interest in your organization grew from last summer's internship. I worked at Ameritech's Bloomington branch. It was a wonderful experience! I reported directly to Tim Schick, and he gave me many opportunities to further develop my skills and expand my knowledge of public relations. During the summer, I wrote several news releases that were published throughout the state, and I helped design an ad campaign (the "Ameritech for the Year 2000" series) that aired on Channel 4 this past September. Even as an intern, I was sent to two training programs. This commitment to continuing education, together with ongoing opportunities to show initiative and creativity, are very attractive to me!

Would it be possible for us to meet for an interview? I am available every day after noon. You can reach me at (812) 337-4697, at the above address, or by e-mail at echenson.indiana.edu. I'd be delighted to travel to Indianapolis at any time that is convenient for you. Thank you so much for your consideration.

Sincerely,

*Emily Henson*

Emily Henson

- *Special skills or talents.* Computer skills or fluency in a foreign language.

- *References.* Reference may be listed as "available upon request" or may be listed with specific names, positions, and contact information.

Grades may be listed as part of educational accomplishments, or referred to indirectly under "Honors," such as, "Dean's List every semester of college." Many employers will ask for a copy of your college transcript, to be attached to the résumé, or provided following the interview.

Your résumé should be thoughtfully developed and designed with your particular credentials and the employer's interests in mind. No two résumés should look alike. If you are applying for more than one kind of job, you may want to develop a different résumé for each—emphasizing the things that will make you most attractive for each.

There are many different ways of organizing and presenting résumé information. For instance, you may prefer a more standard, *chronological approach,* as is illustrated in the résumé appearing in Figure 10.3. The advantage of the chronological résumé is that it presents your credentials in a straightforward, step-by-step manner. The categories are fairly standard, and the employer can easily see what you have been at each step of your educational and work experience. *Present information in reversed chronological order,* so that you emphasize your *most recent* activities and accomplishments.

You can also organize your résumé using a *functional approach.* Some functional résumés include few dates, so that the reader gets little sense of chronology. Emphasized, however, are skills, talents, and relevant learning and work experiences. Most functional résumés combine some dates and traditional categories with categories that highlight skills. In the Mary Kelly résumé shown in Figure 10.4, for example, you will see that the objective and education categories are fairly traditional. Next comes a "qualifications summary," followed by four sections that emphasize Kelly's skills and experiences: training, organizational, recruiting, and technical. Other skills often emphasized on functional résumés include: communication, computer, leadership, teamwork, problem solving, and so forth. Some believe the functional résumé encourages more creativity and allows the applicant to better present himself or herself as an individual. Others worry that the functional résumé may be perceived as less complete than the chronological résumé—and perhaps more difficult for employers to compare to the résumés of other applicants. What's critical is to choose wisely, making a decision based on your objective, the job, the employer, and the information you plan to present. For your first job you may choose a chronological résumé; later, when you have held several positions, you may want to switch to a more functional format. Over many years and many positions, chronological résumés can become very long.

Whatever structure you choose, each résumé should be carefully planned, checked for spelling, and presented in an attractive way. Some bulleting and highlighting is desirable. Make sure your résumé is easy to read and error-free. It should look professional, and should be printed on off-white or light beige bond paper. In short, your résumé should create a first impression of you as an interesting individual—with unique skills and contributions to offer.

In addition to preparing a traditional résumé, you may also want to prepare a résumé that can be read by computer, a so-called *scannable résumé.* This is a résumé from which a computer can extract information. Recruiters and managers access résumé databases; they can search for your résumé in particular, or more likely, they will search for applicants with specific experiences using key words to guide their search. See Highlighting Technology for some tips for preparing a scannable résumé.

FIGURE 10.3    Sample chronological résumé

## EMILY C. HENSON

**Present Address:**
208A Clark House-Read Center
Bloomington, IN 47405
e-mail: echenson.indiana.edu
(812) 337-4697

**Permanent Address:**
1706 Maple Avenue
Elkhart, IN 46207
(317) 695-7422

**Professional Goal:** To obtain a public relations position in a corporate setting where creativity and motivation are stressed.

**Education:** *B.A. in Public Relations and Organizational Behavior,* Indiana University, May, 1999.

- G.P.A.: 3.5; G.P.A. in public relations major: 3.8
- Completed minors in communication and Spanish

**Work Experience:**

Sept. 1997–present    *Editorial staff of Indiana Daily Student*

- researched and wrote over 50 news stories
- assisted in design of IU's *Alumni Magazine*

Summer, 1998    *Public Relations Internship, Ameritech, Bloomington branch*

- wrote news releases
- designed brochures
- helped design TV advertising campaign

Sept. 1996–May 1997    *Part-time Assistant to the IU Director of Alumni Affairs*

- organized and conducted alumni telethons
- made speeches to alumni groups

Summers, 1996 & 1997    *Staff Writer for the Elkhart Tribune*

- wrote articles focusing on women's issues

**Awards and Honors:**
Outstanding Intern, Ameritech, 1998
Outstanding Journalist, *Indiana Daily Student,* 1998
First Place, Rotary's State Public Speaking Contest, 1997
Dean's List, Indiana University, 1996–present
Outstanding Young Women of America, 1996

**Activities:**
Alpha Chi Omega, vice president, 1998–99; member, 1996–97
Women in Business, chair, public relations committee, 1997–99
Student Speaker's Bureau, IU, 1997–99
Big Brother's and Big Sister's Program, Bloomington, 1997–99
IU Foundation, chair, telethon, 1998–99; member, 1996–97

**References:** Furnished upon Request

FIGURE 10.4     Sample functional résumé

**MARY E. KELLY**

409 S. Ramble Road
Cincinnati, OH 45201
(513) 794–6308; kellym@sprynet.com

### Objective

**Human Resource Specialist.** To use my graduate education, knowledge of training, recruitment, and performance appraisal to develop highly trained, motivated, and productive employees for a progressive organization.

### Education

**Indiana University Graduate School,** Bloomington, M.A. Organizational Communication, 1998
  • M.A. Thesis: Conflict Management and Performance Appraisal, GPA 3.9/4.0
  • Awarded Indiana University Arts and Sciences Full Fee Scholarship

**Indiana University,** Bloomington, B.A. Telecommunications, 1995, GPA 3.4/4.0
  • Kappa Alpha Theta Women's Fraternity: Panhellenic Representative and Rush Counselor

**Boston University,** London (England) Journalism Internship Program, August–December 1993

### Summary of Qualifications

• Developed and taught courses for the Indiana University Department of Speech Communication and School of Business. Topics included EEO policies, management theory, interviewing, and group decision making.
• Developed and presented workshops on conflict management, briefing techniques, and diversity.
• Recruiting experience in both academic and business environments.

### Skills

**Training**

**Trainer,** <u>Atlanta Executive Services Corps</u>, *Present*. <u>U.S. Defense Intelligence Agency</u> *July* 1998 <u>Bloomington (IN) Department of Human Resources</u> *May 1997–May 1998*. Design, develop and facilitate training on diversity, briefing techniques, and conflict management.

**Associate Instructor,** <u>Indiana University</u>, Bloomington, *August 1996–June 1998.* Designed and presented lectures, activities, and examinations to teach the fundamentals of business and professional communication. Received 1997 Arts & Science Excellence in Teaching Award. Selected to teach a course previously reserved for Ph.D. level instructors.

**Entertainment Supervisor,** <u>Kings Island Theme Park</u>, Cincinnati, OH *Summers 1990–1992*
Trained and supervised crew of forty people, managed entertainment facilities.

**Organizational**

**Account Executive,** <u>WBWB FM Radio Station</u>, Bloomington, IN *May 1995–June 1996.* Consulted with clients regarding advertising needs, budget, development of advertising campaign, and production of commercials. Managed over eighty accounts, recognized by corporate president for having tripled productivity of accounts within first six months.

**Guest Relations Manager,** <u>Kings Island Theme Park</u>, Cincinnati, OH *April–August 1993*
Addressed needs of park guests through problem solving and advising park management.

**Recruiting**

**Masters Faculty Representative,** <u>Indiana University</u>, Bloomingotn, IN *August 1996–May 1997.*
Interviewed candidates applying for faculty positions. Gathered information on candidates' qualifications and graduate students' impressions and reported findings to department faculty.

**Recruiting Assistant,** <u>Management Recruiters</u>, Cincinnati, OH *June–August 1996*
Matched human resource needs of client organizations with suitable applicants.

**Recruiter,** <u>Indiana University Admissions Office</u>, Bloomington, IN *April 1994–May 1995*
Traveled with admissions staff, made presentations to prospective I.U. students and parents.

**Technical**

**Computer,** proficient in Wordperfect, Microsoft Word, and Vax Mail System
**Audio/Visual,** experience in audio and video production.

References available upon request.

## PREPARING A SCANNABLE RÉSUMÉ

New technologies are providing new ways of presenting your credentials to prospective employers. One of the newest is called "electronic applicant tracking," and many leading organizations are beginning to use it to locate qualified applicants.

If you use the latest technology, your résumé can be scanned into a computer system and kept active for years. The computer can search for all sorts of things in your résumé. You may discover that you are qualified for all kinds of jobs that you never even knew existed.

When you prepare a résumé for the computer to read, it must be "scannable." That means it's clean so that the scanner can get a clean image.

### Formatting Tips

- Use white or light-colored 8 1/2 × 11 paper.
- Provide a laser-printed original if possible.
- Do not fold or staple.
- Use standard typefaces, such as Courier, Times, Universe, Optima, and Futura.
- Use a font size of 10 to 14 points.
- Don't condense spacing between letters.
- Use boldface and/or all-capital letters for section headings.
- Avoid fancy features, such as underlining, italicizing, and shadowing.

- Avoid two-column format, as well as horizontal and vertical lines.
- Place your name on the top of the page on its own line.
- Use standard address format below your name.
- List each phone number on its own line.

### Content Tips

- Use enough specific words to define your skills, experience, education, etc. (maximizing the number of "hits").
- Describe your experience, using concrete words (for instance, "supervised a sales force of 15" versus "responsible for supervising sales staff").
- Be concise and truthful (as on any résumé).
- Use as many pages as you need; the computer can handle it.
- Use jargon and acronyms specific to your business or field.
- Increase your key word list by including specifics (e.g., list the specific languages you speak).
- Use common headings, such as "education," "honors," and "experience."
- Describe your interpersonal skills, traits, and attitudes.

Source: Based on information provided by Texas Instruments; see http://www.ti.com/recruit/docs/resume_tips.html.

## Planning for the Interview

In a sense, everything you have done so far—assessing yourself, researching the position and the organization, preparing your cover letter and résumé—all have prepared you for the interview. Only a few more things remain. First, *try to anticipate the kinds of questions the employer is likely to ask you* and think about how you will respond to them. Nearly every interviewer will ask you to describe your strengths and weaknesses, for example. Think also about how you will elaborate on your assertions. For instance, if you say you have good teamwork skills, you'll have to explain what you mean, what your experiences and successes have been. Practice responding to key questions aloud.

You should also *plan questions that you will ask the interviewer.* Nearly every interviewer will give you some time to pose questions near the end of the interview. It's important to have good questions to ask, to show that you are knowledgeable about the company but still interested in learning more. As you listen throughout the interview, other questions may occur to you, but you'll want to have tentative questions planned in advance.

*Read widely about current events.* Knowing what's going on in the nation and the world is always important. Employers are increasingly looking for employees who are good citizens, interested in their community and country, and committed to solving world problems. Subscribe to a good newspaper, such as the *Wall Street Journal* or the *New York Times,* and read it regularly as part of your interview preparation.

Finally, *anticipate what you will do if you are asked an inappropriate question.* Reread the section on the laws governing the employment interview. Know that some interviewers, regardless of the law, will ask unlawful questions. If you are a woman or a minority, you will want to be especially vigilant. If you are uncomfortable in the interview, you might not be comfortable working in the organization either. *The interview is a two-way street in terms of decision making;* each of you (interviewer and interviewee) must decide whether you want to work together in the future.

## Behavior during the Interview

Just as it is important for the interviewer to establish rapport early in the interview, it is also critical for you as interviewee to make a favorable initial impression.

### The Initial Impression

As we noted earlier, too many interviewers make their decisions during the first four or five minutes of the interview. Thus, what you do and say during that time is crucial.

Arrive on time for the interview. In our culture, *punctuality* is indicative of good manners and interest in the forthcoming interaction. Secure the name of the interviewer and use it as you greet him or her. Walk confidently over to shake his or her hand. Look *pleasant, yet professional.*

An important part of the initial impression will be determined by your *appearance.* Dress professionally—in a way that is consistent with the kind of attire commonly worn by those in the position for which you are interviewing. Each interview should be approached with intelligence and common sense regarding the sort of image you wish to convey (casual versus formal), the sort of job for which you are interviewing, and the kind of organization represented by the interviewer (industrial firm, elementary school, or artistic organization). In general, you'll want to dress "up" a bit; avoid clothing, jewelry, and other artifacts that call attention to themselves and serve as a distraction. If there is some doubt regarding the most appropriate attire, it is best to err on the conservative side.

### Communicating Effectively: Nonverbal and Verbal Strategies

Throughout the interview, you will communicate both verbally and nonverbally. Through the use of body, voice, and language, you will articulate ideas and, perhaps more subtly, express attitudes and reveal values. Many aspects of *nonverbal communication* that apply to any communication encounter were discussed in Chapter 8. In the interview context, you will be evaluated by the manner in which you:

- *Walk.* Slovenly, aimlessly, purposefully?

- *Shake hands.* Limply, warmly, vigorously?

- *Sit.* Slumped, rigid, comfortable?

- *Express yourself facially.* Darting eyes, full open-eye contact, animated, or expressionless?

- *Move.* Animated, inert, tense, or relaxed?[17]

The *use of your voice is also important.* Vocal quality, pitch, audibility, intelligibility, and expressiveness all count, and so does language usage—especially vocabulary and grammar. It is usually best, for example, to avoid slang, and to speak clearly, fluently, and grammatically. It is also vital that you articulate your views persuasively. Avoid speaking in a monotone; sound interested and enthusiastic throughout the interview.

Several studies have revealed that the applicant's communication effectiveness has a profound impact on how she or he is rated by the interviewer and on whether or not she or he receives a job offer.[18] Research has shown that various *verbal communication strategies* are commonly associated with successful interviewing.[19] Here are some guidelines that grow from that research.

- *Show how you and the position are a good fit.* In discussing your skills and abilities, try to relate them to the specific position for which you are interviewing. Specify how and why you think you are well suited to *this* job. By so doing, you demonstrate your knowledge of the position and match the demands of the job with your talents.

- *Compliment the organization.* Tell the interviewer why you want to work for this particular organization—what attracted you to this particular job. This goes beyond knowing the job's requirements: Here you are showing that you know a lot about the company and you are impressed with what you've learned.

- *Substantiate your self-assertions with evidence.* Whatever claims you make about your positive qualities, abilities, or skills, always provide support. It is not enough to say, "I'm really motivated." You need to support that assertion with examples of situations in which you demonstrated motivation or quote the testimony of others who have endorsed your abilities.

- *Accentuate the positive; don't dwell on the negative.* The interview is, among other things, an opportunity for you to present yourself in the best possible light. Don't hesitate to show what you know, to stress what you have accomplished and what you can do. You needn't sound boastful, but you must sound confident and convinced that you can do the job. If you are confronted with some negative aspect of your record, *briefly* explain it (e.g., low grades during your first year of college); take responsibility for the problem (not blaming circumstances or others); and quickly move to the present and the future, stressing learning and improvement.

- *Develop your responses adequately.* Some interviewees give terse, underdeveloped responses, forcing the interviewer to probe endlessly. Research shows that successful applicants talk more than do those who are interviewing them—not the reverse.[20]

- *Speak fluently.* Many applicants do not convey clear messages because their sentences are punctuated by vocalized pauses (uh), verbal fillers (you know), and other disfluencies. This is where "what is said" and the "how it is said" begin to interact. Practicing aloud before the interview can help you communicate more articulately.

- *Communicate honestly.* We have emphasized positive self-presentation during the interview. However, the interview, if it is to be successful, *must* be based on a candid exchange of information. Neither interviewer nor interviewee should exaggerate the truth, make unjustified claims, or intentionally mislead the other in any way. No one wants a job for which he or she is not really well qualified. No one wants to work for an organization in which he or she feels out of place. Honesty is a must in the interview, for the good of all concerned.

## Attitudes to Reveal during the Interview

As we saw in Chapter 1, there are many qualities interviewers look for during an employment interview: oral communication skills, motivation, initiative, and so on. Your behavior during the interview must exhibit these characteristics. During the interview, you should reveal the qualities and behavioral characteristics that are indicative of these desirable traits.

One behavior that is desirable during an interview is *directness*. Directness is revealed, in part, through appropriate eye contact, posture, and other mannerisms. An applicant who is withdrawn will often shrink back into her chair, will seldom gesture, and usually avoids eye contact with the interviewer. Equally important, however, is verbal directness. As an interviewee, you should never evade questions but respond to them thoroughly and directly. Avoid starting your statements with such phrases as, "Well, I could be wrong, but . . ." or "I guess I think this would work. . . ." Instead, phrase your ideas decisively and clearly.

Closely related to directness is *responsiveness*. The interviewer should not feel that he is "prying" information from you. After all, an important purpose of the interview is for the employer to gain additional information from you. Thus, you should approach the interview with an expectation of participating actively.

---

### KEY CONCEPTS 10.2 The Interviewee's Role

As you prepare to initiate your search for employment and participate in interviews, remember to:

- • Conduct a thorough self-inventory and consider job factors of importance to you.

- • Identify available jobs by using placement services, seeking out advertisements,

talking to people, and exploring the Internet.

- • Do thorough research on organizations of interest to you.

- • Learn as much as you can about your chosen field.

- • Prepare a carefully developed and well-written cover letter and résumé,

*Continued*

---

**Concluded**

*making strategic decisions concerning the best way to present your credentials for each kind of job.*

• • *Prepare for the interview by anticipating questions, planning questions to ask the interviewer, and reading about current events.*

• • *Create a favorable initial impression; communicate pleasantly and professionally.*

• • *Communicate effectively during the interview, both verbally and nonverbally.*

• • *Communicate with directness, responsiveness, and alertness, showing emotional control and honesty.*

• • *At the end of the interview, make sure you understand what will happen next.*

• • *Consider writing a thank-you note to the interviewer.*

Interviewers also expect interviewees to be *mentally alert.* This, of course, is not synonymous with brilliance but is related to one's comprehension of questions and one's articulateness in responding to them. Preparing carefully for the interview and getting a good night's rest the night before can also contribute to mental alertness.

Alertness should be matched by general *emotional control.* Occasionally, interviewers will ask a question that is designed to put the applicant on the spot and to see how he or she reacts to stress. Remember: there's nothing wrong with an interviewer's doing that, so long as the ability to handle stress (or think quickly under pressure) is a crucial part of the job—and so long as the question is asked of all applicants.

Certainly not the least important of the qualities to be demonstrated during the interview is your *character.* Ethical judgments are never easy to make. Sometimes information regarding personal integrity and responsibility can be gleaned from your credentials. For example, any existing history of financial responsibility or testimony provided in letters of recommendation may serve as evidence. For the most part, however, character will be judged on the basis of the personal behavior you exhibit during the interview—particularly in relationship to openness, honesty, and balanced self-assessment.

The
Interview:
Closing and
Follow-Up

At the conclusion of the interview, you should *pose any questions you have not yet had an opportunity to ask.* It is imperative that you *know what to expect next.* The interviewer should provide this information. In the event that he or she does not, you need to find out where you stand and when and how the next communication is to occur.

Immediately *following the interview, you might send a note to the interviewer, thanking the person for her time* and reiterating the fact that you will be pleased to hear from the organization soon. It is also appropriate to offer to send any additional information the interviewer might desire. A sample thank-you letter follows in Figure 10.5.

FIGURE 10.5     Sample "thank-you" letter

March 15, 1999

208A Clark House—Read Center
Indiana University
Bloomington, IN 47405

Mr. Philip Johnson
Director of Recruitment
Ameritech
1633 North Meridian Street
Indianapolis, IN 46208

Dear Mr. Johnson:

Thanks again for taking the time to meet with me last Tuesday. I really enjoyed the time I spent with you, and I left the interview even more convinced that I could make a positive contribution to Ameritech.

During the interview, you indicated that you are looking for two things: practical experience and an ability to be flexible. In both areas, I feel I have a great deal to offer. My work on the editorial staff of the *Indiana Daily Student,* with the Ameritech public relations office, and in the Director of Alumni Affairs office at I.U., all have given me the firsthand experience that is so important to success in any organization. And in each of these positions, changing deadlines, priorities, and events in the community taught me flexibility. No one could have survvied in those positions without being able to adapt almost instantaneously!

You asked me to provide some references. May I suggest you contact the following:

| | | |
|---|---|---|
| Mr. Robert Jordan | Richard L. Enos, Editor | Mr. Timothy A. Hill |
| Faculty Advisor, *Indiana Daily Student* | *Terre Haute Tribune* | Director, Public Relations |
| Indiana University | 12 Terre Haute Ave. | Ameritech |
| Bloomington, IN 43703 | Terre Haute, IN 42802 | Bloomington, IN 43703 |
| (812) 855–8713 | (817) 695–7751 | (812) 339–8487 |

Each of these individuals would be able to give you their perceptions of my work performance and my ability to adapt to changing priorities.

Again, I appreciate your having taken the time to meet with me. Please feel free to contact me if you need any additional information.

Sincerely,

*Emily C. Henson*

Emily C. Henson

Concluding
Perspective:
The Interview
as a
Problem-
Solving
Session

There is one overriding problem that, more than anything else, contributes to poor employment interviewing: the natural desire on the part of each participant to be wanted by the other. As a result, each participant tries to sell the organization or self to the other. Neither participant provides the other with complete, accurate information; and each participant concentrates too much upon making a good impression on the other.

To avoid this pitfall, *both parties must take a problem-solving approach to the interview*. As an applicant, you have a problem: finding a compatible, interesting, rewarding job. As an interviewer, you also have a problem: finding a qualified, productive, and—it is hoped—satisfied new employee. Really, these two problems are one and the same. Rather than trying to sell each other a product, the interviewer and the applicant should work toward the resolution of a common problem: determining whether the position's requirements and the applicant's qualities are compatible.

The problem-solving perspective is the key to success in employment interviewing, both as an applicant and as an interviewer. Only by exchanging information can each of you educate the other to the extent that both of you can make the best possible decision. So be prepared, make a good impression, ask good questions, and follow up after the interview. Above all, be open and honest as you communicate with representatives of the organizations with whom you interview.

## SUMMARY

This chapter has focused on the employment interview, from the perspective of both interviewer (employer) and interviewee (applicant). Those who participate in interviews should understand both roles.

For the interviewer, knowing the laws that govern the employment interview is essential. Asking unlawful questions is not only unethical; it can lead to costly lawsuits and to the loss of one's job.

The interviewer should also prepare for the interview by studying all written materials provided by applicants (cover letters, résumés, letters of recommendation, etc.). The primary communication tool of the interviewer is the question. Good questions must be prepared in advance—with a core of questions to be asked of all applicants and some résumé-specific questions to be asked of each applicant. The interviewer should welcome the applicant and set the stage for the interview by providing a brief overview of how the interview will be conducted. As the interviewer poses questions, he or she must be ready to listen very carefully

(taking notes to assist in accuracy) and to probe when the applicant's responses are inadequate in some way. At the conclusion of the interview, the interviewer must specify what will happen next and record impressions of the applicant as soon as he or she departs.

For the applicant, careful preparation for the interview is equally vital. The first step in any employment quest is self-assessment. The applicant then considers what is really important to him or her in a job and an organization. Once jobs have been identified, the applicant's next task is to study the organizations where the attractive jobs are located—learning everything possible about each organization's history, practices, stability, and values. The next step is to prepare a résumé and write a letter of application. Both should be carefully developed and adapted to the specific job and organization. Many options exist for arranging and developing résumés; the choice of résumé structure is a strategic one. Before the interview, the applicant should anticipate questions, practice responding aloud, and plan questions for the employer. During the interview, the applicant must present himself or herself well, both verbally and nonverbally.

The employment interview is always an important communicative encounter for both parties. Its outcome determines whether applicants gain employment and whether companies make good decisions in selecting those who will thrive, or rejecting those who will be less successful. Careful preparation, skillful communication, and judicious decision making by both applicant and employer are essential if the interview is to be a success.

## QUESTIONS FOR DISCUSSION

1. Why is the employment interview important, yet complicated?
2. What is a BFOQ? How are BFOQs related to your preparation, as employer, for interviewing a pool of applicants?
3. Why are there so many laws to govern the interviewing process? What are some laws of special importance? Why are they important?
4. How would you initially screen out the clearly unqualified candidates, leaving only those who seem better suited for the job?
5. How will you plan the questions you will ask of each applicant?
6. What are major question areas on which you should focus your attention during an employment interview? Why are these appropriate areas to probe?
7. What other responsibilities do you have as you conduct the interview?
8. As applicant, how will you go about assessing your skills, knowledge, and so on, as you plan for your first interview? Why is such self-assessment important?
9. What are some things that you will look for as you do research on jobs and organizations?
10. What are some guidelines you will attempt to follow in communicating verbally and nonverbally during the interview?
11. What are some important attitudes and personal characteristics that an interviewee should possess? How, as an interviewee, might you demonstrate these qualities to an interviewer?

## EXERCISES

1. Select a specific job that interests you. Then, as precisely as you can, list all sources you would consult if you were a personnel manager, a recruiter, or an employer seeking someone to fill that job. In addition, list all the qualifications you would look for as you sought potential candidates. How would you go about determining those qualifications?

   When you have completed your research, construct a one-page applicant profile that could be used during an interview.

2. Imagine you are interviewing for a job and the interviewer asks you your age, your religion, whether you have ever been arrested, or how your spouse feels about your traveling on weekends.

   Then, assume first that, regardless of the interviewer's behavior, you really want this job. In a brief paragraph, sketch out your response to one of these questions.

   Now assume that you have other options and you are less concerned about landing this particular job. Now sketch out your response to the same question.

3. Create a résumé and a cover letter that you might use if you were applying for the job you researched in exercise 1.

4. Now, place yourself in the role of interviewer and develop an evaluation form that you would use if you were interviewing applicants for that same job.

*Applying for a Dream Job*

For most of her life, Holly has been fascinated by Disney. Now, as she is about to graduate from Indiana University with her Ph.D. in hand, she discovers an opportunity to work at Disney University! She immediately does careful research on the organization, considers her skills and knowledge, and decides that the fit is perfect.

Following are the cover letter and résumé that Holly sends to Disney University. Read them carefully and respond to the questions that follow.

14 December 1998

3061 East Amy Lane
Bloomington, IN 47408

Disneyland Resort
Professional Staffing
P.O. Box 3232
Anaheim, CA 92803-3232

To whom it may concern,

From my earliest memories to my current taste in art, Disney and its characters have been a part of my life. Every time I go to a mall or drive by a Disney store, my friends and family instinctively know that they will be asked, pleaded, and politely encouraged; well, perhaps threatened is a better word, to stop and browse. I was browsing the Disney web page and decided to look at career opportunities and was thrilled to learn of an opening as the Director of Disney University WOW.

While I may not have current hospitality experience, I do have an extensive knowledge of Disney's business, resorts, and practices. In addition, my life-long love of Disney, my proven ability to learn new concepts quickly, and my enthusiasm for taking on challenges would more than compensate for this. While it may appear initially from my enclosed resume and application that I only have experience teaching, this is certainly not the case. While I do have a passion for university-level teaching, what I have taught shows my diversity and flexibility. I have taught business management majors the essentials of interviewing, public and professional speaking, diversity and conflict management, and how to create and present professional proposals using the newest technology available. In addition, teaching has perfected my interpersonal and organizational skills, and made me an expert in conflict resolution. My educational background and advanced degrees in Communication and Human Resource Management have honed my skills in analytical and strategic problem solving, quantitative research methods, and developing appropriate communication strategies to deal with every situation imaginable. Finally, my dissertation research strengthened my skills in managing focus groups, designing training and development programs, and effectively dealing with the stress of producing high-quality work under tight deadlines. In addition, working for a company such as Disney would be tremendously exciting and would offer me constant challenges to grow and improve my skills in the aforementioned areas.

While my resume can illustrate my qualifications, it cannot show the sheer enthusiasm, motivation, and dedication with which I approach every aspect of my life. I hope you will give me the opportunity to demonstrate these qualities in an interview, as I feel my exceptional communication skills, creativity, and energy would be an asset to Disney. I can be reached at (812) 339-6965 or at hcbaxter@indiana.edu. I look forward to meeting with you in the near future to discuss the possibility of becoming a member of the Disney team.

Sincerely,

*Holly Carolyn Baxter*

Holly Carolyn Baxter

# Holly Carolyn Baxter

3061 East Amy Lane
Bloomington, IN 47408
(812) 339-6965
hcbaxter@indiana.edu

## CAREER OBJECTIVE

Seeking a position that would allow me to utilize my exceptional communication skills, passion for teaching, and in-depth knowledge of diversity issues and human resource management, while allowing me to continue to broaden my knowledge in each of these areas.

## EDUCATION

Indiana University, May 1999, Ph.D. (Major: Organizational Communication; Minors: Organizational Behavior and Human Resource Management) Dissertation Title: "A Comparison of Diversity Training Methods on Perceptions of Individuals with Physical Disabilities in the Workplace."

Indiana University, June 1997, M.A. (Major: Organizational and Interpersonal Communication)

University of Dayton, Dayton, OH; May 1993, B.A. summa cum laude, departmental honors, (Major: Communication with a concentration in Public Relations; Minors: Political Science and Criminal Justice)

## PROFESSIONAL EXPERIENCE

Course Director, Business anad Professional Communication, Department of Speech Communication, Indiana University. January 1999–present.

- Manage staff of six instructors.
- Responsible for all administrative duties, including scheduling of classes, developing syllabus, and refining course requirements.
- Use skills gained as a mediator to resolve conflict-related issues and settle disputes to the satisfaction of all parties involved.

Internship in Human Resource Management (Training and Development); Deloitte & Touche, Indianapolis, IN; Spring 1998.

- Designed an instrument for evaluating the effectiveness of a leadershipi-training program.
- Refined quantitative research skills in SPSS and Excel.

Internship in Human Resource Management (Selection Systems); Otis Elevator, Bloomington, IN; Fall 1997.

- Helped to develop a competency model for First-line Supervisors.
- Polished interviewing and evaluation skills.

## TEACHING EXPERIENCE

Managing Workforce Diversity (V452), School of Public and Environmental Affairs, Indiana University, January 1999–present (1 section, 20 students) Will prepare students majoring in management to deal with diversity issues in the workplace. Focus on legal and ethical issues as they relate to selection topics, training and development, issues between co-workers, and termination decisions.

Business and Professional Communication (S223), Department of Speech Communication, Indiana University; 1997–present (Six sections taught, 24 students per section) Prepare students for professional communication, such as resume and cover letter writing, interviewing, small group theory and communication, and development of professional proposals.

Representative Americans: People with Disabilities (A201a), Division of Extended Studies, Indiana University; July 1998 (Correspondence course) Responded to questions and evaluated assignments while appointed instructor was on a leave of absence.

Interpersonal Communication (S122), Department of Speech Communication, Indiana University; 1995–1998 (ten sections taught, 35 students per section) Taught fundamentals of interpersonal communication theory and basic conversational analysis skills.

Public Speaking (S121), Department of Speech Communication, Indiana University, 1993–1994 (seven sections taught, 26 students per section) Taught basic fundamentals of Public Speaking; helped students deal with and overcome fear of public speaking.

## AWARDS AND HONORS

- Nominee, Indiana Speech Tradition Award for Excellence in Teaching, Indiana University (to be awarded in February 1999).
- Faculty Award for Academic Excellence in Communication, University of Dayton, 1993 (Awarded to the graduating senior with the highest overall and major grade point average.)
- Golden Key National Honor Society; Inducted 1993.
- Deans List; University of Dayton; Every semester 1990–1993.
- University of Dayton Leadership Award, University of Dayton, 1990–1993 (Awarded fo outstanding academic achievement and leadership skills.)
- Beavercreek Jaycee's Scholarship, Dayton, OH; 1990 (Awarded for academic excellence and community service.)

## SERVICE ACTIVITIES

- Departrment of Speech Communication, Peer Mentor for new Associate Instructors, Indiana University; 1995–present.
- Disabled Student Services, Volunteer, Indiana University; 1996–present.
- Dayton Mediation Center, Certified Mediator, Dayton, OH; 1992–present.
- Faculty and Staff for Student Excellence (FASE), Mentor for first generation college freshmen, Indiana University, 1996–1998.

## PROFESSIONAL PRESENTATIONS

- Designed and presented; "Workshop for Associate Instructors on using electronic media in teaching," Indiana University, October 1998.
- Presented and facilitated group discussion; "Workshop on interpersonal communication and listening skills for high school Mentors for Children," Monroe County Library, Bloomington, IN, September 1998.
- Designed and presented; "Legal ramifications and diversity issues in the workplace as related to the American's with Disabilities Act of 1990," Department of Business Law, Indiana University, May 1998.

## REFERENCES

Available upon request.

## Questions

1. What are some of the ways that Holly presents herself positively in her letter of application?
2. How effectively does she compliment Disney and show the match between her, the organization, and the position?
3. What criticisms do you have? How might she further improve her letter?
4. Describe how Holly organizes her credentials on her résumé. Does her chosen structure seem effective? What are some other options she might consider?
5. What are the greatest strengths of Holly's résumé?
6. How might her résumé be further strengthened? Be specific.

# PART four

# Small Group Communication

**GROUPS, LIKE INDIVIDUALS,** have shortcomings. Groups can bring out
the worst as well as the best in man. Nietzsche went so far as to say
that madness is the exception in individuals but the rule in groups.

**—*Irving Janis,* Groupthink**

# CHAPTER eleven

*After reading this chapter, you should be able to:*

1 Understand the importance and multiple roles of small groups in organizational settings.

2 Understand how socio-emotional variables impact small group interaction and performance.

3 Discuss the ways that pressure for uniformity, role structure, status and power, and cohesiveness affect group functioning and effectiveness.

# Group Functions and Socio-Emotional Variables

As professionals or business persons, all of us will function in numerous small groups throughout our productive lives. We will put in hundreds of hours attending staff meetings, departmental meetings, subcommittee meetings, and unit gatherings. As we participate in groups, we will learn, form friendships, and contribute knowledge and skills vital to the task of solving the organization's problems. Participating in a group is not the same kind of experience as dealing individually with one other person or solving a problem alone. A group is both dynamic and complex. These qualities can inspire innovative decision making or, by contrast, create the conditions for groupthink.

The frequency with which you will participate in groups is in itself reason enough to make the next four chapters important ones. We must also emphasize one other point: Your success in any organization will be influenced significantly by your performance in group settings. Every meeting represents an opportunity for you to impress your superiors, have your ideas adopted, assert positive influence over others, and demonstrate your capabilities for greater responsibility. On the other hand, we have seen careers stalled because of group participation. Employees who frequently arrive late or unprepared, fail to talk during meetings, behave disagreeably or discourteously, or otherwise perform poorly in the group setting rapidly develop a bad reputation among their peers and superiors—one that is virtually impossible to overcome. Finally, organizations are increasingly placing emphasis on participative problem solving at the lowest levels of the hierarchy, so the opportunities for you to perform well or poorly in a group are increasing. In some countries, such as the Scandinavian nations, workers are required by law to participate in industrial decision making. In American organizations, labor and management groups come together to attempt to keep companies open, to increase productivity, and to fight competition from foreign producers. For all these reasons, then, developing skill in group participation is vital to you and your organization's short- and long-term well-being.

## PREVIEW

In this chapter, we discuss the reasons small groups are such an important part of contemporary organizational functioning. We begin by overviewing the basic functions and types of groups, highlighting teams and quality circles. Then we briefly discuss group meetings that occur in public settings. Finally, we focus on critical socioemotional variables—pressure for uniformity, role structure, status and power, and cohesiveness—that profoundly influence the experience of working together in groups.

Before going further, it is important to examine the concept of a small group. It is quite possible for several individuals to be together for some period of time, yet not really be considered a group. Patients waiting in a dentist's office, students sitting in a classroom on the first day of the semester, or a dozen travelers snoozing in the TWA departure area waiting to catch a midnight flight are all examples of small groups of people, but not in the sense we are using the term here.

## Defining the Small Group

For small groups to exist, it is essential that group members perceive themselves as something other than a collection of independent individuals. Bales was among the first to point to the importance of group members developing a *psychological relationship*, a sense of a mutual awareness and interdependence.[1] The creation of this mutual psychological awareness rarely occurs all at once. Rather, it develops over some period of face-to-face interaction. Members' relationships are furthered by repeated encounters, normally accomplished through communicative exchanges.

*Communication facilitates interaction* and, by doing so, helps to define the psychological relationship that develops within the small group. Small group members also have some degree of shared interest. Often this interest is expressed as *a goal upon which there is mutual agreement.*[2] When small groups form to meet the personal needs of group members (such as the coffee break group), the goal may grow naturally from the group itself. Group members may meet to provide mutual support, listen to one another's complaints, or provide some diversion from routine work. Other small groups form in response to a formal organizational assignment. These groups are largely task-oriented and are often asked to make decisions or solve problems.

The size of the "small" group can vary, usually ranging from as few as 3 to as many as 20.[3] In general, the larger the group, the more complex the patterns of interaction and the more formalized the procedures necessary to handle the group's functioning. Studies of committees have revealed the most common group sizes are five, seven, and nine.[4] For the most part, however, *most experts agree that face-to-face interaction, the presence of a bond or psychological relationship, and some significant degree of common interest or goal are the critical characteristics of the small group*, rather than the specific number of group members.

Groups in organizations do not exist as isolated units. They are, instead embedded within the larger organizational system. Their members are part of, as Jablin has noted, "an interlocking network of organizational roles."[5] Moreover, each individual typically belongs to multiple groups and is often subjected to conflicting pressures. Finally, organizational groups operate within formal hierarchies and normally function with appointed leaders.[6] In professional settings, teams and quality circles are two of the most prominent kinds of groups.

## Teams

We have already discussed the teamwork philosophy of organization theory, as well as the use of self-managing teams as a current application of human resources management. The Center for Effective Organizations at the University of Southern California recently conducted a survey of Fortune 1,000

**TEAMWORK IN ACTION**

In an effort to improve quality and productivity, many companies are attempting to shift from classical organizational thinking (specialized jobs and narrowly defined tasks improve performance) toward a broader team-oriented approach (a more flexible, multiskilled workforce performs best).

- Even traditionally unionized companies, such as General Motors and National Steel, have improved morale, speed, and efficiency by loosening job classifications and developing a more flexible workforce through intensive cross-training and job rotation. For example:
- Motorola dissolved six pay categories at its Arlington Heights, Illinois, cellular phone factory. Now all workers are in the same category, and their pay increases are based on learning new skills while maintaining high work quality.
- Lechmere, Inc., a 27-store retail chain, bases pay raises on the number of jobs employees learn: cashiers are encouraged to also sell products, salespeople are taught to drive forklifts, and so on.
- AT&T created nearly a dozen cross-functional teams to participate in developing a new cordless phone and through cross-training and employee involvement was able to cut development in half.

Source: D. Keith Denton, "Multi-Skilled Teams Replace Old Work Systems," *HR Magazine* 37 (September 1992): 48–56.

companies. The finding was that 68 percent of these companies use self-managing teams.[7] As small groups within organizations, teams generally consist of either project or work teams.

*Project teams* have existed for many years in organizational settings. Typically consisting of employees representing an array of specialties (such as marketing, sales, and engineering), they coordinate the successful completion of a particular project, product, or service. Project teams have been part of the space program for many years and are common in electronic, computer, and other research-based industries. These teams typically work quickly to clarify goals, roles, and responsibilities. They often possess little history, are likely pressured by deadlines, and may have difficulty establishing mutually satisfying working relationships. Nevertheless, cross-functional project teams are potentially valuable in that they keep individuals from different organizational divisions communicating with and educating each other, while reminding them of the importance of customer needs and satisfaction.

The other, and most innovative, kind of team is the *work team*. Wellins, Byham, and Wilson define the work team as "an intact group of employees who are responsible for a 'whole' work process or segment that delivers a product or service to an internal or external customer."[8] Work teams have become increasingly popular and are used in such diverse organizations as 3M, General Electric, AT&T, and Corning. Each of the companies that has won the Malcolm Baldrige National Quality Award (such as Millikin, Motorola, Westinghouse, and Xerox) fostered teamwork among employees as a crucial component of its improvement efforts.[9]

*Regardless of the kind of organization, nearly every employee works in groups. Teams and quality circles meet in both formal and informal settings. Many manage their own projects and move at their own pace.*

Katzenbach and Smith studied 50 different teams in over 30 organizations.[10] Based on their observations, they believe that the critical factor in establishing successful teams is to assemble a small number of people with complementary skills who share a commitment to a common purpose and who adopt a set of performance goals for which they hold themselves mutually accountable. They argue that teams develop direction, momentum, and commitment by working to shape a meaningful purpose. Team members then translate their common purpose into specific performance goals, such as reducing the rejection rate from suppliers by 40 percent or increasing the math scores of graduates from the 60th to the 80th percentile. Moreover, when team members work together toward common objectives, trust and commitment follow.

Can teams be empowering? Indeed they can, under the right circumstances. Dumaine argues that the best teams "are truly empowered to organize their work and make decisions".[11] And mutual accountability is also a key ingredient. As Katzenbach and Smith put it:

> This sense of mutual accountability . . . produces the rich rewards of mutual achievement in which all members share. What we heard over and over from members of effective teams is that they found the experience energizing and motivating in ways their "normal" jobs never could match.[12]

There is an important distinction between being held accountable by one's boss and being accountable to oneself and one's team.

There are, however, no guarantees. Sometimes teams are "set up" to fail. They may get launched in a vacuum, with little or no training or support, no changes in the design of their work, and no new technologies like e-mail to foster communication within and between teams. Managers must make a commitment to empowerment by demonstrating a willingness to give teams the actual authority to get the job done. This means providing access to resources, information, and technical assistance while allowing the teams to make decisions about how to proceed, how to delegate responsibility, and so forth.

Whether or not a team is effective, then, depends upon members' skills, mutual trust, sense of purpose, and commitment to objectives—as well as factors external to the group. When managers are truly committed to empowerment through teamwork, however, and are willing to put aside constraints associated with the traditional hierarchy and to think in fresh, creative ways, work teams can serve as true vehicles of empowerment. In its Statement of Aspirations, Levi Strauss & Company defines empowering leadership as that which "increases the authority and responsibility of those closest to our products and customers. By actively pushing responsibility, trust, and recognition into the organization, we can harness and release the capabilities of all our people."[13] Not surprisingly, work teams are an intrinsic component of the Levi Strauss culture.

## Quality Circles

One of the most contemporary approaches to organizational problem solving and employee participation is the use of *quality circles*. These are small groups of people who meet voluntarily to define, analyze, and solve work-related problems.[14] Typically these people come from the same department or work group, or at least perform similar job functions, so that the problems they discuss are familiar to all of them, and each member can contribute to the development of solutions.

At a general level, quality circles meet to analyze and solve the organization's problems. More specifically, however, their functions are often detailed and diversified. Among the things quality circles do are:

- Improve the quality of services or products.

- Reduce the number of work-related errors.

- Promote cost reduction.

- Develop better work methods.

- Improve efficiency in the organization.

- Improve relations between management and employees.

- Promote participants' leadership skills.

- Enhance employees' career and personal development.

- Improve communication throughout the organization.

Although the concept of quality circles originally developed in Japan, they are increasingly common in the United States. Ninety percent of Fortune 500 companies reportedly use quality circles.[15]

## SELF-DIRECTION THROUGH TEAMWORK

Many employees dread Monday mornings, the start of another work week. Not so for Al Reynolds and Amanda Dunston, employees at Northern Telecom's Morrisville, North Carolina, repair facility. "I now look forward to coming to work. I don't *have* to go to work, I *get* to work," claims Reynolds. Dunston adds, "I enjoy the challenge. Every day, I'm learning something new."

Both are part of a set of self-directed work teams recently formed by their company. As team members, they are involved in ordering materials, tracking and scheduling overtime work, calculating and monitoring productivity, reviewing budgets, and interviewing prospective team members. Soon, they will also be conducting peer performance reviews and taking corrective action when their peers do not perform adequately.

The key to successful implementation of self-directed teams at Northern Telecom was top-level management involvement. All members of supervision and management participated in intensive workshops designed to change how they think about worker-management relations and how they manage on a day-to-day basis. But not all managers were able to make the transition: company statistics indicate that about 25 percent of its first-line supervisors left after the team approach was adopted.

Source: Jana Schilder, "Work Teams Boost Productivity," *Personnel Journal* 71 (February 1992): 67–71.

Quality circles have been used with reported success in many organizations; even so, QC groups may experience problems. Case studies by Meyer and Scott suggest that quality circles may be no different from other committee meetings in some organizations in that supervisors may dominate them; the groups may lack a sense of clearly defined purpose, stray from problem solving, and get bogged down in never-ending problem analysis; and group members may be unequally committed to the group tasks.[16] Equally critical is the fact that for many organizational members, there are simply no tangible rewards associated with participating in quality circles, and supervisors themselves may send mixed messages, inviting criticism and open discussion during quality circle meetings, but rarely asking for suggestions or criticisms in other contexts.[17]

In spite of potential problems, quality circles continue to thrive in many organizations when participation in them is voluntary. By helping build employee problem-solving and communication skills, as well as management leadership and communication skills, and by creating a formal structure for ongoing communication throughout the organization, the quality circles system has the potential for developing a more goal-oriented and team-centered management climate. With an effective quality circle program, many positive outcomes are possible.[18]

## Group Discussions in Public Settings

Most of the time, communication taking place in small groups in organizations occurs in private settings. On occasion, however, we will be called upon as professionals to participate in a small group discussion for the benefit of an audience. These public discussions are important, for they provide the opportunity for organizational representatives to interact directly with a portion of the organization's relevant environment. Most public discussions are planned for the enlightenment of an audience. Public discussions often bring together representatives from several different organizations, all of whom share some expertise on the discussion topic, but each of whom possesses a different perspective.

Public discussions can occur in several different formats or patterns of discussant interaction. A *panel discussion* is a format in which the participants interact directly and spontaneously with the guidance of a moderator. No participant has a planned speech. Instead, each speaks briefly, rather frequently, and within the realm of courtesy, whenever he or she desires. A more formal mode of public discussion is the *symposium,* in which discussants prepare brief speeches representing their viewpoints. Each group member speaks in turn without interruption or interaction. As the panel moderator, the symposium leader usually introduces the group members and provides a summary at the end of the discussion. During the actual discussion, however, there is no need for moderator intervention or guidance— except for providing transitions between speakers. Both the panel discussion and the symposium may be followed by a *forum* period during which members of the audience are encouraged to ask questions and express opinions. The forum is generally guided by the moderator, and questions may be directed to individual members or to the group as a whole.

Public discussions in organizations take a similar variety of forms and are conducted for a variety of "publics." As the need for a consumer-oriented corporate culture grows, an increasing number of organizations are holding symposia, panels, and forums for community groups, stockholders, customer groups, and others. One large manufacturer of hospital supplies, for example, has begun conducting seminars on "Managing Hospital Resources" across the country for hospital executives. During the seminars, those attending listen to short speeches by experts in many areas of management, watch as these experts discuss with one another, and then ask questions related to their own concerns. Similarly, many companies have started conducting such meetings for their own employees, to increase the visibility of their executive group and to promote interaction among employees and management. Our own observations indicate that public meetings, both inside and outside the organization, will become increasingly common.

| KEY CONCEPTS 11.1 | Defining and Understanding the Scope of Small Groups |

To understand the nature and importance of group work, keep in mind that:

- • *Groups consist of individuals who have developed a bond, who interact over time, and who have a mutual goal.*

- • *Groups vary in size and function.*

- • *Groups are embedded in some formal organizational structure.*

- • *Some of the most important groups in*

**Continued**

**Concluded**

organizations that are aiming for a participatory, empowering climate are teams and quality circles.

• • Some group discussions take place in public settings and include symposia and panels, followed by a forum period.

## KEY SOCIO-EMOTIONAL VARIABLES IN GROUPS

At the beginning of this chapter, we pointed to the existence of a bond or psychological relationship among members as one of the group's defining characteristics. The development of this relationship may be influenced by the kind of task the group is confronted with and the cognitive functionings of group members in relation to that task. But it is largely socio-emotional factors that contribute to the development of interpersonal bonds within the group. Chief among these are pressure for uniformity, role structure, status and power, and cohesiveness.

### Pressure for Uniformity

The phenomenon of social influence has long fascinated scholars in a variety of disciplines. In the field of organization theory, researchers of the human relations school were the first to recognize the potent influence of small informal work groups on the behavior of individuals. As early as 1911, however, Taylor noted the presence of group norms that appeared to affect industrial productivity.[19] Over the past half-century, the collective efforts of social scientists have identified the small group as one of the major contexts in which social influence or pressure for uniformity may be most potent.

The classic social influence investigation was conducted by Asch, who performed a series of experiments involving simple line discrimination tasks.[20] In fact, the perceptual task of matching one of three comparison lines with a test line was so easy (as illustrated in Figure 11.1), that Asch discovered any individual with normal vision could make the correct match nearly

**FIGURE 11.1** | A line discrimination task typical of Asch's research

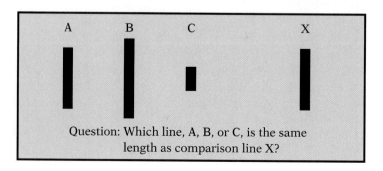

Question: Which line, A, B, or C, is the same length as comparison line X?

100 percent of the time. Asch subsequently coached a group of confederates to make deliberately erroneous judgments on the same perceptual tasks. When a naive individual was placed among Asch's group of confederates and asked to listen to the judgments of others before stating his or her own estimates, the results were radically skewed in the direction of the majority. Approximately one-third of all estimates made by the subjects were identical with or in the direction of the distorted majority estimates. *Only one-fourth of the naive subjects remained completely independent* over a series of trials.

What is especially provocative about these findings is that the individuals were not acquainted with one another before their brief encounter. Moreover, the confederates made *no overt attempts* to influence the behavior of the naive individual. Finally, the line discrimination tasks had no real intrinsic importance to the subjects, to their future relations with others, or to the fate of anyone in the room.

We have mentioned *norms* several times in the preceding discussion. Schein defines a norm as "a set of assumptions or expectations held by the members of a group or organization concerning what kind of behavior is right or wrong, good or bad, appropriate or inappropriate, allowed or not allowed."[21] Those who conform are acting in ways they perceive as consistent with those group norms. Norms may be either *implicit* (not actually articulated, but known and understood) or *explicit* (formally stated either orally, in writing, or both). Organizations often provide explicit norms in the form of rules, regulations, and other codes or conduct. These norms may include such varied items as personal appearance (hair length, cleanliness, appropriate attire), language usage, length of lunch and coffee breaks, and strategies and procedures to be used in committee meetings. Implicit norms are even more potentially diverse, dealing, for example, with one's political views, the make of car one drives, or even the kind and quantity of dinner parties one gives.

Whether or not we adhere to the norms of our group or organization depends upon a variety of factors. Chief among them is the *degree to which we value our membership and identify strongly with the group or organization*.[22] In addition, people possess different motives for conforming. In some instances they may listen to other group members' arguments and actually become convinced that the group is right. By contrast, others may simply find it easier, less stressful, or more politically astute to mouth their agreement, even though they privately disagree.

By interviewing his subjects after the experiment, Asch discovered that only a small percentage of the yielding subjects really believed the majority estimates were correct. In most cases, the group's judgment had been accepted publicly while private views remained the same.[23] In actual organizational settings, *compliance may be ingratiating*, strategically aimed at increasing the worker's attractiveness in the eyes of his or her boss, or *it may reveal the subordinate's fear of open discussion*.

*Failure to conform to the group can be psychologically uncomfortable. Or, conformity can be viewed as strategic.* One organizational leader recently disclosed that he always "cooperated" with others on issues which he saw as insignificant in the grand scheme. He laughingly noted that when he voted with others, he always made them aware of it, sometimes by joking that they "owed him." However, he actually viewed the situation as demanding that others would reciprocate. He had scratched their backs, and he fully expected

*The classic film, Twelve Angry Men, vividly portray the methods used by groups to attempt to pressure a "deviant" group member to support the majority's views. In this case, Henry Fonda, the deviate, was able to turn the tables and persuade the majority to follow him.*

others to extend the same courtesy to him. Implicit in this approach to conformity is the idea that individuals might conform when an issue is not of central importance to them, while remaining quite independent on issues about which they care deeply.[24]

For years, scholars debated whether the tendency to conform should be viewed as a personality characteristic. For the most part, however, situational factors seem to most influence the individual's tendency to conform.[25] In general, *individuals appear to be more likely to conform when they are in situations:*

1. That are ambiguous or confusing.
2. Where the members of the group are unanimous.
3. Where the group contains those of higher rank.
4. Where the group is highly cohesive.
5. When a state of crisis or emergency exists that seems to demand uniformity (e.g., jury deliberations).

*Groups exert pressure for uniformity in a variety of ways.* Human Relations researchers noted the verbal and nonverbal methods informal work groups used to get deviates "back in line." Tactics such as *teasing, ridiculing, punching, and shoving* were not uncommon in factory settings. Schachter's laboratory research pointed to *increases in the quantity of communication* as a major pressuring tactic.[26] Subsequent research by Taylor found that the verbal behavior of majority group members was characterized by *reasonable-*

## GROUP PRESSURE THAT STIFLES CREATIVITY

The impact of group pressure is especially potent when the group's majority is composed of those in power. John Z. De Lorean's account of committee meetings inside General Motors dramatizes this point:

Original ideas were often sacrificed in deference to what the boss wanted. Committee meetings no longer were famous for open discourse, but rather either soliloquies by the top man, or conversations between a few top men with the rest of the meeting looking on. In . . .

meetings, often only three people . . . would have anything substantial to say, even though there were fourteen or fifteen executives present. The rest of the team would remain silent, speaking only when spoken to. When they did offer comment, in many cases it was just to paraphrase what had already been said by one of the top guys.

Clearly, this kind of pervasive conformity is detrimental to good decision making.

Source: J. Patrick Wright, *On A Clear Day You Can See General Motors* (New York: Avon Books, 1979): p. 47.

---

*ness, dominance, and hostility.*[27] More recently, Thameling and Andrews described the communication behavior of majority group members as being *cooperative, opinionated, and emotional.*[28] Finally, Wenburg and Wilmot have identified *five sequential steps taken by most groups* as they attempt to influence opinion deviates. These are:

1. *Delaying action*—Doing little overtly and hoping the deviate will conform without pressure.
2. *Chatting among themselves*—Perhaps involving joking with the deviate.
3. *Ridiculing the deviate*—Overtly recognizing his or her behavior as different and unacceptable.
4. *Engaging in severe criticism*—Possibly including threats.
5. *Rejecting the deviate*—Ignoring and isolating him or her, and prohibiting future interaction with the group.[29]

This is only a rough model, and does not take into account unique group characteristics (e.g., level of cohesiveness) or the relationship between the deviate and the group.

One of the most critical variables affecting a deviate's treatment is his or her *position or status within the group.* In general, groups tolerate more deviant behavior from those of high status.[30] There are, however, exceptions. The high-status person may be treated more harshly by other group members if he or she commits an act perceived as extremely serious or damaging. In general, however, high status permits greater freedom.[31]

*How does one respond to group pressure? Both individual and situational variables play a role.* For instance, some tend to "go with the flow" in most situations, preferring to fit in with the group rather than to be perceived as "making waves." Others may change their minds and begin to agree with the group's perceptions—either because, in fact, they are genuinely persuaded, or because they have forced themselves to deny the validity of their own views or senses. Of course, some respond to group pressure by refusing to yield. Challenging the group's authority in this way may result in a variety of outcomes. For instance, if the group or organization is threatened by the deviate's act, they may punish him or her severely. Tompkins recounts the story of Roger Boisjoly, one of the engineers who unsuccessfully argued against launching the space shuttle Challenger. Boisjoly subsequently "deviated" further by going against the advice of management and reporting his reservations to the Rogers Commission, which was investigating the disaster. Tompkins notes:

> He [Boisjoly] then lost his job at Thiokol. Residents of the town he lived in, who had once elected him mayor, now began to shun him and his wife . . . and many members of his own church refused to speak to him. A dead rabbit was placed in his mailbox. On several occasions while taking long walks near his home, he said, vehicles swerved as if to hit him.[32]

Boisjoly's situation was complicated in that his unwillingness to conform also served to blow the whistle on a group of very important people with a very great deal to lose.

More *common instances of deviation can also lead to unpleasant consequences, especially under circumstances in which those in positions of power are intolerant of dissent.* One woman recently challenged her boss during a departmental meeting. She had just learned that he had withheld important information from the group and had also misrepresented the truth with regard to some important recruiting in which the department was engaged. When she challenged his version of affirmative action at the meeting, he told her (in a loud and forceful voice) that she was "out of order." Then, giving her a cold, sharklike stare, he told her that he would not forget what she had said during the meeting. The next day, she found a note on her desk informing her that she had been removed from two important committees (one of which she had founded) and reassigned to a task force whose mission was largely to plan social events. Although many of her co-workers were sympathetic (and sent her e-mail messages, cards, and flowers in support), none stood with her in opposing this department head. Apparently, they feared retaliation. Behind the boss's back, however, they began to refer to him as "Hitler," and some exchanged cartoons making fun of tyrants.

*In a healthier organizational climate, expressions of disagreement or dissent may be more positively received.* One study demonstrated, for instance, that an intelligent, articulate deviate might exert considerable influence on the views of the majority, particularly on topics about which the deviate knows much and the other group members know little.[33] However, when it is the group members composing the majority who are better informed, the deviate's influence is lessened.

Considered by themselves, pressure for uniformity and conformity behavior are neither good nor bad. They are simply facts of group and organizational life. Every group has norms—some of which are quite constructive and empowering, such as tolerating and encouraging the exploration of diverse points of view, being supportive of others, and so forth. Groups must examine their norms with vigilance. Whenever majority members attempt to pressure opinion deviates into publicly complying, they run the risk of suffering depleted morale and impaired decision making.

## Group Role Structure

The norms that develop in groups typically suggest (or require) appropriate modes of conduct for all group members. At the same time, however, groups need considerable role diversity among their membership to function effectively. Group members perform different, although often interdependent, functions as they work together on varied tasks.

Conceptually, roles include behaviors and how those behaviors *function* within the group. For instance, a group member may use humor during a meeting. Her humor, however, may function in diverse ways—to relieve tension, to diminish someone else's ego (especially if the humor is sarcastic), to get the group off track by distracting members from the task at hand, or to build group cohesiveness. Clearly, some of these are more functionally related to group goal accomplishment and maintenance than others. Similarly, asking a question can function as a simple request for information ("Do we have projected trends for next month yet?"); as a strategy for changing the subject; as a vehicle for introducing a new topic; or as a put-down or challenge ("What would *you* know about working in a factory?"). Thus, *roles are behaviors that perform some function in a specific group context.* The individual's enactment of a role will depend upon his or her interpretations of a given situation.

Various classification schemes have been developed to describe the roles or behavioral functions that group members enact. Typically, these roles fall into one of two main categories: (1) group task roles and (2) group building and maintenance roles.

*Task roles* involve the communication functions necessary for a group to accomplish its task, which often involves problem solving, decision making, information exchange, or conflict resolution. Based on the classic work of Benne and Sheats, these roles include:

**1.** *Initiator.* Proposes new ideas, procedures, goals, and solutions; gets the group started.

**2.** *Information giver.* Supplies evidence, opinions, and related personal experiences relevant to the task.

**3.** *Information seeker.* Asks for information from other members, seeks clarification when necessary, and makes sure that relevant evidence is not overlooked.

**4.** *Opinion giver.* States her or his own beliefs, attitudes, and judgment; is willing to take a position, although not without sensitivity to others' views.

**5.** *Opinion seeker.* Solicits the opinions and feelings of others and asks for clarification of positions. Ideally, those who give opinions will be equally willing to seek opinions.

**6.** *Elaborator.* Clarifies and expands the ideas of others through examples, illustrations, and explanations. This role is valuable so long as elaborations are task-relevant.

**7.** *Integrator.* Clarifies the relationship between various facts, opinions, and suggestions, and integrates the ideas of other members.

**8.** *Orienter.* Keeps the group directed toward its goal, summarizes what has taken place, and clarifies the positions of the group.

**9.** *Evaluator.* Expresses judgments about the relative worth of information or ideas; proposes or applies criteria for weighing the quality of information or alternative courses of action.

**10.** *Procedural specialist.*   Organizes the group's work; suggests an agenda, an outline, or a problem-solving sequence.
**11.** *Consensus tester.*   Asks whether the group has reached a decision acceptable to all; suggests, when appropriate, that agreement may have been reached.

Although early discussions of group task roles treated them as being part of a single dimension of group behavior, the contemporary view suggests that *two different task dimensions may be represented by those roles: those that focus on the substance or content* of the issue being discussed (such as giving information) and *those that deal with procedural matters* (such as orienting and organizing the group). These two dimensions may function in tandem, if, for example, someone initiates the discussion (a procedural act) by tossing out an idea (a substantive move).

The second major category of group roles is *group building and maintenance roles.* These roles build and sustain the group's interpersonal relationships. Discussants playing these roles help the group to feel positive about the task and to interact harmoniously. By reducing the competition between individual group members and their ideas, these behaviors nurture an enhanced sense of cooperation. These roles include:

**1.** *Supporter.*   Praises and agrees with others, providing a warm, supportive interpersonal climate.
**2.** *Harmonizer.*   Attempts to mediate differences, introduce compromises, and reconcile differences.
**3.** *Tension reliever.*   Encourages a relaxed atmosphere by reducing formality and interjecting appropriate humor.
**4.** *Gatekeeper.*   Exerts some control over communication channels, encouraging reticent discussants, discouraging those who tend to monopolize the discussion, and seeking diversity of opinion.
**5.** *Norm creator.*   Suggests rules of behavior for group members and challenges unproductive ways of behaving; gives a negative response when someone violates an important group norm.
**6.** *Solidarity builder.*   Expresses positive feelings toward other group members; reinforces sense of group unity and cohesiveness.
**7.** *Dramatist.*   Evokes fantasies about persons and places other than the present group and time; may test a tentative value or norm through hypothetical example or story; dreams, shows creativity, and articulates vision.

Although these roles are presented as largely desirable and constructive, they must be evaluated as they are enacted in a specific group context. For instance, establishing and maintaining norms is quite valuable so long as the norms are sound. If the group is committed to encouraging dissent, for instance, and someone attempts to stifle a minority view, reminding the group of its norm (tolerance for diversity) would clearly have a positive function. However, helping the group maintain an attitude of intolerance would, by maintaining that norm, be counterproductive. Moreover, stereotypically, roles in the building and maintenance category are associated with pleasant, harmonious social interaction. However, enacting some of them could readily produce tension and conflict, such as discouraging those who are domi-

FIGURE 11.2        Group role clusters

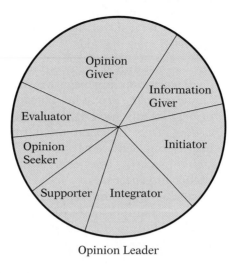

Opinion Leader

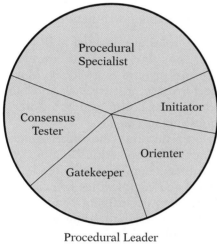

Procedural Leader

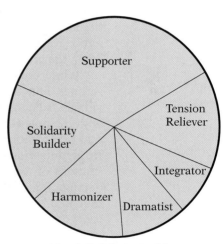

Morale/Solidarity Builder

nating the discussion or challenging someone who is behaving unproductively. This suggests that if groups are to maintain themselves over time, they will of necessity go through moments of conflict and norm testing.

As noted earlier, most group members will perform diverse roles, and often the roles can be grouped together to form broader role clusters (see Figure 11.2). Thus, those who function largely as opinion leaders, for instance, likely give their opinions rather frequently—but they also seek the views of others, evaluate everyone's views, support ideas they like, and occasionally offer procedural guidance. Similarly, the supportive role cluster might involve everything from supporting others to relieving tension to showing solidarity, while also offering information and opinions as task behaviors.

Finally, not all roles function constructively in groups. To be avoided are those roles that tend to further self-interests over group interests and goals. The *self-centered roles* include:

**1.** *Blocker.*   Constantly objects to others' ideas and suggestions, insists that nothing will work, is totally negative; may also repeatedly bring up the same topic or issue after the group has considered and rejected it.
**2.** *Aggressor.*   Insults and criticizes others, shows jealousy and ill will.
**3.** *Storyteller.*   Tells irrelevant, often time-consuming stories, enjoys discussing personal experiences.
**4.** *Recognition seeker.*   Interjects comments that call attention to his or her achievements and successes.
**5.** *Dominator.*   Tries to monopolize group interaction.
**6.** *Confessor.*   Attempts to use the group as a therapeutic session, asks the group to listen to his or her personal problems.
**7.** *Special-interest pleader.*   Represents the interests of a different group and pleads on its behalf.
**8.** *Noncontributor.*   Is reticent and uncommunicative; refuses to cope with conflict or take a stand; fails to respond to others' comments.[34]

In general, when positive roles are enacted and shared in groups (with negative roles minimized), positive group outcomes, such as enhanced morale and sound decision making, are more likely. Moreover, from a functional view, those who perform the positive task and building and maintenance roles are actually serving as group leaders insofar as their behaviors assist the group in accomplishing its goals.

While much research on group roles has been conducted in laboratory settings, enacting roles in actual organizations is more complex. When individuals participate in committee, team, or quality circle meetings, they do so with the potential constraints and complexities associated with whatever formal organizational role they play (department head, secretary, new recruit). In organizational groups then, individuals bring with them *role perceptions* (notions of what their role should consist of) and *role expectations* (their understanding of what others expect of them). Weighing and balancing those, individuals choose how to enact their roles, a process to be negotiated and renegotiated over time. Highlighting Diversity points to some ways in which traditional sex roles and the expectations associated with them can affect role diversity.

## Status and Power

So long as the concept of hierarchy prevails in organizations, issues of status and power will remain potent variables affecting small group and organizational behavior. Most of the time, persons who occupy positions of high status in the organizational hierarchy also possess considerable power. Thus, the two concepts are practically associated but conceptually quite distinct. Specifically, *status* is the value, importance, or prestige associated with a given role or position. *Power,* on the other hand, focuses on the opportunity to influence or control others. Throughout organizations of all kinds, individuals occupy positions that are highly valued by others (that is, high-status

### TRADITIONAL SEX ROLE EXPECTATIONS

- Women will ask many questions.
- Women will talk less than men.
- Women will listen attentively and supportively.
- Women will mostly perform group building and maintenance roles.
- When offering their opinions, women will express an air of tentativeness ("I'm not an expert in this area, but I think we might. . . .").
- Men will play mostly task roles in groups.
- Men will dominate the conversation by talking frequently and at length.
- Men will interrupt everyone, but especially women.

### NEGATIVE IMPLICATIONS OF THESE EXPECTATIONS

- Those who violate traditional expectations may be viewed as "deviant"—and may even be punished.
- The group as a whole suffers because individuals are not encouraged to make the unique contributions they are capable of making.
- Turn-taking norms are violated; dominance by a few is likely.
- Women are less likely to be allowed to function as group leaders, even if they are highly qualified.

positions); yet, in fact, they have little opportunity to influence the behavior of others (that is, they possess little power). The vice presidency of the United States is a classic example of a position of considerable importance and prestige that carries minimal power.

Just as the concepts of power and status differ, the type of power varies from situation to situation. French and Raven distinguish seven types of social power, or power base, and designate them as: (1) reward, (2) coercive, (3) referent, (4) legitimate, (5) expert, (6) informational, and (7) connectional.[35] *Reward power* refers to the ability to elicit a desired response from another by providing the other with positive reinforcement. A realtor may show houses to prospective clients each evening, working long after traditional hours are over in hopes of gaining a large sales commission when a house is finally sold. Besides hoping for this monetary reward, however, she may also toil for fear that her employer will fire her if she doesn't make a significant sale soon. The latter thinking represents an example of *coercive power,* or, in this case, the ability of her employer to elicit a desired response (hard work leading to sales) by means of potential punishment (firing).

The third type of social power is *referent,* and it functions most potently when a person strongly identifies with another, holding him or her in high esteem and respecting the individual's judgment on appropriate behavioral standards. Small, informal work groups within organizations are often potent sources of referent power. Individual workers within these groups may increase or decrease their productivity, not in accordance with the formal reward and punishment system of the organization, but simply because other members of their small informal work group are doing it (and, in this manner, indicating it to be the appropriate way to behave).

The next power base discussed by French and Raven, *legitimate power*, focuses on recognized authority. Individuals responding to this type of power do so, not because they anticipate a specific reward or fear some punishment, but simply because they believe that the person requesting the response is fully authorized to make the request. People holding organizational status higher than our own are often accorded this sort of power. The manager of some other department, for example, probably does not have direct power to discipline or fire us; yet when he makes a request that we provide his staff with some information, we probably will comply simply because we believe he has the right to make such a request.

When we follow the directions or take the advice of another because of that person's recognized competence, we are behaving in response to *expert power*. An intelligent supervisor or manager, in fact, makes much use of this sort of power, not by exerting it but by being influenced by it. The most effective executives surround themselves with expert advisers, frequently ask those people for advice, and use the advice when making decisions. They recognize that their advisers know more than they themselves do about marketing, engineering, sales, the law, and so on, and they allow the advisers to exert expert power by acting on the adviser's advice. Of course, by increasing your own expertise in a specific topic or area, you increase your own ability to exert expert power over others.

*Informational power* refers to the power to control the availability and accuracy of necessary information. If we can control the flow of information someone receives, we can control his or her behavior to some degree (again, consider the powerful secretaries who significantly influence organizational functioning by determining what information their bosses receive). Similarly, we all want to do the correct thing; thus, we are influenced by information we perceive to be accurate. People who can supply such information are likely to be influential for us. Figure 11.3 depicts these bases of power.

The final power source is *connectional power*. Of all the power bases, this is the most political, based on social psychologists' notion that every exercise of power involves some form of social exchange. Connectional power is the influence that leaders have as a result of who they know and the support they have from others in the organization. In general, connectional power is asso-

| FIGURE 11.3 | The bases of power |

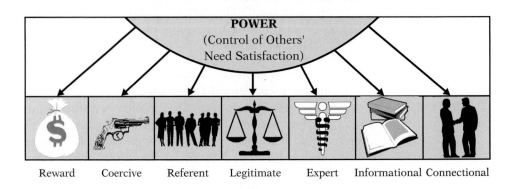

| Reward | Coercive | Referent | Legitimate | Expert | Informational | Connectional |

ciated with a person's general connections with others whose knowledge, ideas, support, cooperation, and resources are needed for effective leadership. More than the other power bases, connectional power is based on a norm of reciprocity. Anyone who wields power from this base should be prepared to cooperate with and support others.

In comparing the effects of different types of power, it is important to remember that these categories are not mutually exclusive. The same persons can have, and often do have, several sources of power, particularly in organizational settings.

Individuals in organizations often belong to small groups composed of members with varying power and status. In these groups, persons do not communicate as equals, a fact that is often an obstacle to effective interaction and decision making.[36] Several studies have shown that those possessing high status are treated with more deference by fellow group members than are those of low status. High-status members are also less likely to be held personally responsible for behaving in ways normally viewed as inappropriate by others.[37] Communication directed to those possessing high status is also distorted in certain important ways.

A number of studies have investigated the nature of *upward-directed communication distortions.*[38] In general, in communicating with someone of higher status, one is likely to communicate supportively and cautiously, to attempt to seek approval, to downplay "bad" news, and to act deferentially. Of course, *much depends on the nature of the relationship between the parties.* If the boss is someone who truly values accurate feedback and insists on hearing the bad news along with the good, subordinates are better able to communicate openly and accurately. When trusting and supportive communication climates exist within groups and organizations, the distortions often associated with upward communication may virtually disappear.

In every organization, there are many persons who possess considerable status and power. Not all of them use their positions and influence in the same manner, however. A powerful organizational executive can stifle opinions contrary to his or her own and encourage superficial analysis of problems and explorations of solutions. But the same person can wisely recognize the difficulties that attach to speaking with one's superiors, reward accurate, honest expressions of opinion, and elicit the articulation of divergent points of view.

In the film *Effective Decisions,* Peter Drucker tells the story of Alfred P. Sloan, who for years was the brilliant chief executive of General Motors (GM). On this particular occasion, the executive board of GM was considering a proposal that sounded innovative, interesting, and financially sound. Not one member of the board raised an objection. Sloan asked each one, "Do you see anything wrong with this proposal?" Each one responded negatively. Sloan wisely commented, "Well, I don't see anything wrong with it either. For that reason, I move that we postpone its consideration for one month to give ourselves some time to think." Drucker reports that the proposal was soundly defeated one month later. A poor proposal was appropriately rejected in this instance because a wise manager believed that those in power had the obligation to ensure that dissenting views were voiced, and he insisted on hearing conflicting views before he would act.[39]

*All* group members must be concerned with the effectiveness of the group's problem-solving ability. By virtue of their power or status, some group members are in strategic positions for greatly influencing the quality of the groups's decision-making process. The judicious use of authority to encourage the free expression of ideas and to reward initiative and innovative thinking can go far in eliminating the doubts and skepticism of less powerful group members.

## Cohesiveness

A final significant socioemotional variable affecting group interaction is *cohesiveness*. As a small group characteristic, cohesiveness is related to solidarity, the group's "stick-togetherness," and its ability to maintain itself over time and through crisis.[40] Not surprisingly, cohesiveness and conformity are related in that the highly cohesive group usually clings to its norms, attitudes, and values. Those who are part of such groups feel a strong sense of belonging, are proud of their group affiliation, and develop close friendships with other group members.

As a socioemotional variable, cohesiveness often has a positive effect on group functioning. The sense of "we-ness" in cohesive groups often transcends individual differences and motives.[41] High cohesiveness and high group member morale are often closely associated. Studies of decision-making conferences reported a close relationship between high cohesiveness and groups members' satisfaction with the meeting experience.[42] In addition, members of cohesive groups like each other. They rate each other highly with respect to attractiveness, motivation, and performance.[43]

While it is clear that the atmosphere in highly cohesive groups is pleasant, we often erroneously assume that these groups will therefore make superior decisions or be extremely productive. Yet, research has demonstrated that cohesiveness neither increases nor decreases group productivity.[44] Instead, it serves to heighten the susceptibility of group members to mutual influence. Thus, if a highly cohesive group establishes a standard of low productivity, group members are likely to conform to the norm and produce little.

Sometimes cohesiveness can have an even darker side. Consider psychologist Irving Janis's account of events occurring a few days before disaster struck the small mining town of Pitcher, Oklahoma, in 1950. Janis reports that the local mining engineer had warned the town's citizens to leave immediately because the land the town sat on had been accidentally undermined and was in danger of caving in at any moment. But the day after the warning was issued, at a meeting of leading citizens belonging to the Lions Club, the members joked about the warning and "laughed uproariously when someone arrived wearing a parachute."[45] Complacency, born of cohesiveness, caused these men to reason that disasters of this sort just couldn't happen to fine folks like them in a nice little town like theirs. Within a few days, this flawed reasoning cost several of these men and their families their lives.

Although this incident occurred nearly 50 years ago, it is scarcely an isolated event. Groups and organizations often make poor decisions—in part because their cohesiveness contributes to a mindset that discourages dissent and the rational examination of alternative courses of action. The tragic decision to launch the Challenger was clearly influenced by the inability of those near the bottom of the organization to freely and fully express their skepticism to their superiors about the wisdom of launching the shuttle in extremely cold temperatures.[46]

As noted earlier, pressure for uniformity often occurs in groups characterized by high cohesiveness. This pressure serves to reduce the range and quality of information and opinions presented and diminishes the advantages of having groups rather than individuals make decisions. We have already discussed some of the general problems associated with pressure for uniformity. In cohesive groups, group pressure can also gradually shift the group toward the position taken by the majority or by its most vocal members. Since such shifts depend more on intragroup pressures than on the quality of argument and information available, the group may end up making "extreme" decisions—ones that mindlessly continue existing policies, or are inordinately risky.[47]

One of the most extensive investigations of the potentially negative impact of cohesiveness on a group's ability to make intelligent decisions was conducted by Irving Janis.[48] Janis examined the decision-making processes leading to several historic military and political fiascoes, including the decision to cross the 38th parallel in Korea, and the decision to invade the Bay of Pigs, the choice to escalate the war in Vietnam, and the decisions surrounding the Watergate cover-up. To explain how poor decisions were made in each of these instances, Janis introduces the concept of *groupthink,* which he originally defined as "a model of thinking that people engage in when they are deeply involved in a cohesive in-group, when the members' striving for unanimity overrides their motivation to realistically appraise alternative courses of action. . . ."[49] Later, Janis modified the groupthink construct to focus on "premature concurrence seeking," stressing the notion that although most groups strive for agreement over time, those who are caught up in "groupthink" seek consensus so swiftly and relentlessly that full and free discussion of alternative courses of action simply never occurs.[50]

Janis goes on to identify eight negative qualities that commonly lead to groupthink:

**1.** An *illusion of invulnerability,* which creates excessive optimism and encourages excessive risk taking.
**2.** *Collective rationalization* to discount warnings that might lead members to reconsider their assumptions.
**3.** An *unquestioned belief in the group's inherent morality,* causing members to ignore the ethical consequences of their decisions.
**4.** *Stereotyped views of opposition leaders* as either too evil to warrant genuine attempts to negotiate or too weak or stupid to be a viable threat.
**5.** *Direct pressure exerted on any member who expresses dissenting views,* making clear that such dissent is unacceptable.
**6.** *Self-censorship* by group members, attempting to minimize the importance of any doubts they might have.
**7.** A *shared illusion of unanimity* concerning opinions conforming to the majority view.
**8.** The *emergence of self-appointed "mindguards,"* members who protect the group from conflicting information that might shatter their shared complacency.[51]

Janis does not argue that all highly cohesive groups fall prey to group-think. Rather, he points out that strategies exist for counteracting it. Janis believes that the group's leader is in a position to insist on the open-minded pursuit of alternative courses of action. Specifically, he suggests that the group's leader should:

- Assign to everyone the role of critical evaluator.

- Avoid stating personal views, particularly at the outset.

- Bring in outsiders representing diverse interests to talk with and listen to the group.

- Play and ask specific others to take turns playing the devil's advocate.

- Let the group deliberate without the leader from time to time.

- After a tentative decision has been made, hold a "second-chance" meeting, at which each member is required to express as strongly as possible any residual doubts.[52]

When leaders insist on and groups endorse these kinds of norms, cohesive groups should function extremely effectively. Cohesiveness need not doom a group. On the contrary, with appropriate vigilance, cohesiveness can contribute to constructive, satisfying group communication and outcomes.

---

**KEY CONCEPTS 11.2    Critical Group Variables**

Understanding the socioemotional variables that influence group effectiveness is important. Some of the most important of these are listed below.

- • *Group pressure for uniformity:*
  Implicit and explicit norms
  Situational factors influencing conformity
  Personal factors affecting conformity
  How groups exert pressure
  How deviates respond to pressure and attempt to exert influence

- • *Group role structure:*
  Task roles—substantive and procedural

Group building and maintenance roles
Self-serving roles

- • *Status and power:*
  Varied power bases: reward, coercive, referent, legitimate, expert, informational, and connectional
  Status and power differences can affect communication

- • *Cohesiveness:*
  Cohesiveness can affect groups either positively or negatively
  Groupthink can be a problem
  The leader plays a key role in avoiding groupthink

---

# SUMMARY

As members of organizations, we spend considerable time interacting in small groups. Some groups are informal and exist primarily to satisfy personal needs. Others are more formally structured and focus on the accomplishment of specific tasks, often involving decision making and problem solving. Group discussions occur in both private and public settings, and involve all levels of the organizational hierarchy.

Many socioemotional variables affect the functioning of small groups, including pressure for uniformity, role structure, status, power, and cohesiveness. For instance, groups often insist that their norms be upheld. Sometimes, an individual group member may not agree with the norm or may not accept the majority viewpoint. Groups exert pressure in varied ways, and individuals respond to this pressure in different ways, depending upon the situation, the issue, and the personalities of those involved. In some situations, deviant group members can influence the majority, but doing so requires considerable communication skill.

Healthy groups are structured so that members play multiple and diverse roles. There are various ways of making constructive contributions to the group's effort. Some individuals perform task roles while others help the group feel positive and appreciate each other's efforts. Self-serving roles should be avoided—those that advance individual interests over those of the group.

In organizational settings in which groups are embedded, power and status differences are common. Those differences can lead to distorted communication, but they need not impede the group's ability to interact effectively—especially if the members with greater power encourage others to share ideas openly and honestly. Power can grow from many sources, including one's position, the ability to reward or punish others, one's level of information or expertise, and the ability to provide political connections for others.

Finally, groups vary in their levels of cohesiveness. When group members are strongly bonded, they may function very productively; or they may fall prey to "groupthink," which leads to impaired decision making. The leader of a cohesive group can set the tone for the group's interactions by insisting that diverse opinions be expressed and by not allowing the group to make a hasty decision.

Taken together, these socioemotional variables play powerful roles in determining the climate in which group members interact, make decisions, and carry out their other responsibilities.

# QUESTIONS FOR DISCUSSION

1. How would you distinguish a collection of individuals from an interacting small group?
2. Compare and contrast organizational teams with quality circles. Describe their relative advantages and disadvantages.
3. Compare and contrast a panel discussion and a symposium.
4. Discuss your understanding of norms. What are some examples of established norms in specific organizations with which you have had experience?
5. What are some of the personal, group, and situational variables contributing to conformity behavior? How do groups exert pressure for uniformity? How do deviates respond to social influence?
6. What types of roles do individuals play in small groups? What, in your view, is the relative significance of each role?
7. Why is it important for groups to be characterized by role diversity?
8. What is the difference between status and power? Provide an example from your own group experience that illustrates the difference.
9. Discuss the seven bases of power, providing examples of each. What combinations of power are most common in your experience? Most effective? Least effective?

10. What are some of the positive and negative factors associated with highly cohesive groups?

11. What are the defining characteristics of groupthink?

12. What can leaders and other group members do to discourage groupthink?

# EXERCISES

1. Think of an organization to which you now belong or to which you belonged for some length of time in the past. Make a list of several norms (both implicit and explicit) operating within this organization. Then think of a time when some member (possibly you) deviated from one of those norms. How did the group treat the deviate? What was the deviate's response?

2. Break into groups of five to seven members and discuss a controversial question of the group's choice. After 20 minutes, terminate the discussion and analyze the role behavior of each group discussant. Some, for example, serve as information givers or seekers, others as clarifiers, others as facilitators, and still others as blockers. Which roles seemed most useful to your particular group? Why?

3. Suzanne Martin has been hired recently as a sales representative of a prestigious women's clothing store in New York. The job is extremely important to Suzanne, as she hopes to rise first to the position of assistant buyer and ultimately to the position of buyer. In this particular organizational setting, there is great potential for advancement, and Suzanne is thrilled with her new job. There is, however, one problem. Every Friday at the close of the workday, all seven of the sales personnel in Suzanne's division visit a nearby cocktail lounge and chat informally for some time. The chatting invariably involves organizational gossip, rumor transmission, and speculation. Suzanne finds the custom distasteful, but has been warned that those who fail to "be sociable" often have trouble getting along with co-workers on the job, and that upward mobility becomes difficult for them.

In a well-developed 250-word essay, respond to the following questions:
   a. What norm (or norms) are operating in this situation?
   b. Are these norms implicit or explicit?
   c. What are the advantages of conforming?
   d. What are the disadvantages?
   e. What would you advise Suzanne to do in this situation? Why?

4. Consider the following brief description of an organization and some of its members:

Michael Carr is a lower-level manager in Organization ABC. He is young, assertive, extremely bright, and particularly innovative in his approach to problem solving. Among his subordinates, he is known as "the brain."

Richard Walls is vice president in charge of sales in the same organization. In terms of the organization's chart, he is two levels above Carr. Walls is an autocrat who rewards liberally and punishes only occasionally. When he does punish, he often does so by firing.

Peter Arden is president of Organization ABC. Near retirement, he has an impressive record with the company, but lately, he has grown relatively out of touch with the cutting edge of the organization.

In a well-developed 150-word essay, respond to the following questions:
   a. Discuss the relative status of each of these individuals.
   b. What kind of power base is each operating from?
   c. If the three gave conflicting orders, which one would most workers obey? Which would you obey? Why?

# CASE application 11.1

*Self-Managing Teams: Hope or Hoax?*

When Pete became head of a major department in a large bank holding company, he thought he had arrived. He was proud of his title and rank, and his department was responsible for determining policy for hundreds of bank branches and those who managed them (viewed by Pete as "superclerks"). Pete was in charge of hiring his own staff, and he sought the brightest and the best—mostly MBAs from prestigious schools. He offered them excellent salaries and the chance for quick promotions.

Then the world began to fall apart. For the first time in recent memory, the bank lost market position and decided to emphasize direct customer service at each of its branches. The people Pete considered clerks began to depart from Pete's standard policies and to tailor their services to local market conditions. The branches moved to the team concept, with self-managed teams working together to come up with ideas for improving customer service. As these teams considered their options and went about collecting data, they actually demanded services and responses from Pete's staff, and the results of these requests began to figure into performance reviews of Pete's department. In an attempt to cooperate with the branches, Pete's people began spending more and more time in the field with the branch managers and clerks, and with their self-managed teams.

To further complicate matters, the bank's strategy included a growing role for technology. Pete felt that because he had no direct control over the information systems department, he should not be held accountable for every facet of product design and implementation. But fully accountable he was.

He had to deploy people to learn the new technology and figure out how to work with it. In addition, the bank was asking product departments like Pete's to find ways to link existing products or develop new ones that crossed traditional categories. Pete's staff soon became involved in their own self-managing teams and were often away working with one of these cross-departmental teams just when he wanted them for an important internal assignment.

Caught between upper management's high expectations and the turbulence and uncertainty of the chaotic environment over which he supposedly presided, Pete felt confused and resentful. His superior said that what was important was "leading, not managing," but Pete wasn't sure what that meant—especially since he seemed to have lost control over his subordinate's assignments, activities, reward, and careers. Pete felt as if he had lost both power and status, both of which were very important to him.

## Questions

1. What are some of the potential problems with self-managing teams revealed in this case?
2. What are the implications of Pete's boss's comment about "leading, not managing?"
3. If you were in Pete's position, what constructive moves might you make to improve the situation, both for yourself and for your subordinates?

Source: Based on an illustration given in Rosabeth Moss Kanter, "The New Managerial Work," *Harvard Business Review* 67 (1989): 85–92.

## CHAPTER twelve

# The Process of Group Decision Making

*After reading this chapter, you should be able to:*

1 Describe the positive and negative aspects of working in groups.

2 Understand the steps involved in preparing for participating in a decision-making-problem-solving meeting.

3 List and distinguish among the different kinds of discussion questions that organizational groups typically address.

4 Be familiar with key research on group problem-solving patterns.

5 Distinguish the characteristics of effective from ineffective decision-making groups.

6 Understand different ways of organizing a meeting agenda.

7 Comprehend the role that technology can play in assisting group decision making, together with strengths and weaknesses.

8 Describe the characteristics of effective group participation and practice them in a group meeting.

Committee work abounds in organizations. Yet anyone who has spent more than a few minutes in a committee meeting knows that being in a small group can be a frustrating experience. Groups often get off the track, bicker among themselves, and consume seemingly endless hours. Managers who decide to share problem-solving and decision-making responsibilities with their employees need to begin by considering both the assets and the liabilities associated with group work.

## PREVIEW

I n this chapter, we examine the process of group decision making. Every group participant must understand how to prepare for group meetings in terms of both content and attitude. Groups address diverse issues, and identifying the underlying discussion question being considered in those meetings is an important preliminary step. Equally vital is knowing how groups do structure their deliberations and understanding options for organizing group meeting agendas. Technology, and especially group support systems, too can play a role in facilitating group deliberations. When group members bring such qualities as open-mindedness, excellent preparation, careful listening, and ethics to the meetings they attend, those meetings are likely to have positive outcomes. However, there are clearly liabilities as well as assets associated with group work, and we begin by considering those.

## PROS AND CONS OF GROUP WORK

First, let's consider the possible negatives. At the top of the list is the simple fact that *groups take time.* The individual decision maker doesn't have to take the time to listen to others or deal with interruptions or group morale. As a result, he or she is usually able to reach a solution fairly efficiently. In organizations, time and money are interdependent. When an executive who makes $80 an hour takes four hours to consider a problem and make a decision, that decision costs the company a little over $300. But if five executives making $80 an hour meet to make a decision about the same problem, even if they take only the same amount of time, that decision costs the organization $1,600.

Besides the time-cost factor, *many people lack training in group discussion skills.* As a result, group meetings are often poorly organized, and members come unprepared, expecting others to carry the major burden. *Some group members are overly talkative* and dominate the discussion, *while others remain mute.* As we discussed in Chapter 11, *cohesive groups may fall prey to group-*

*think,* resulting in impaired decision making. Finally, *some leaders do not really allow groups to make decisions.* Instead, they use the meeting as an arena to sell their own ideas. Still others listen (or pretend to listen) to the group and then go off and quietly make the decision alone.

## Making the Case for Groups

Given these potential liabilities, the obvious question is: *Why bother with groups?* Researchers who have pursued this question have found some rather encouraging results. There is some evidence to suggest that *groups who reach decisions through a process of cooperative deliberation do,* in fact, *generate more ideas and produce better-quality decisions than do individuals who work on problems alone.*[1] Certain discussion techniques, such as brainstorming, nominal grouping, and the use of idea-generating agendas, *can also stimulate creativity.*[2] *Group members often possess considerable knowledge and information,* typically more than any one member working alone would possess. Certainly, there is *a greater diversity of perspectives,* and this diversity can serve to discourage the thinking ruts that often characterize the problem-solving attempts of individuals.[3]

Besides the quality of the decision itself, *people who help make decisions understand how and why they were made.* Participating in decision making *increases group members' commitment to decisions* and generally improves their morale.[4] We may give our time to committee work grudgingly on occasion, but in the long run, *most of us feel more useful, more productive, and more valued as professionals when we have a chance to share in making significant decisions.* Most of the so-called liabilities we discussed are not inherent to small group deliberations. They tend to occur, rather, when group members are ignorant of group processes and are poorly informed regarding sound decision-making procedures.

Group decision making offers significant advantages to organizations. It is important to remember, however, that *skill in decision making is equally important to individual group members.* As management becomes more participative, more team-oriented, employees are becoming more involved in making decisions that affect them and the organization directly. *Good decisions improve the employee's own working life and the success of the organization as a whole;* poor decisions adversely affect both. And, as we have seen, *those who are skilled in group decision making are much more likely to rise both in the esteem of their peers and superiors and in the organizational hierarchy.*

As you approach working with others in small groups or teams, you might want to think of decision making as a *process* rather than a procedure. As with other processes, the operative elements are interdependent and delicately balanced. A personality clash among members not only disrupts interpersonal relations but also affects the problem-solving ability of the group. Besides, groups are far from static. As you interact with others in your group, you will be affected by them and they by you. The mood, balance, and focus of the group may shift from moment to moment. It is impossible, therefore, to point to a given procedure that ought to be followed in all decision-making groups. Rather, being aware of critical group variables, knowing how best to prepare for group meetings, and understanding the ways groups develop over time can help you adapt appropriately to each new group context.

## PREPARING FOR GROUP PARTICIPATION

In organizational settings, you will find yourself working in decision-making groups for three basic reasons. First, *you will acquire some group memberships* simply by joining the organization. You will participate in department or unit meetings, for example, and you will attend companywide meetings, employee training sessions, and other meetings directly related to your responsibilities. Second, *you will be assigned other group memberships.* Your boss may ask you to work with a task force comprising people from several departments, or your turn to be your department's representative on a fundraising committee may come up. Finally, *you will be appointed to groups whose membership you seek.* Quality circles, for example, consist only of employees who volunteer to participate. If you are one of the volunteers chosen, you have been appointed to membership.

However you obtain group membership, your initial responsibility to the group will be to prepare carefully. Often, your assignment or appointment to group membership is based on expertise you happen to have; however, even in those situations, you will gather and organize information that you can contribute to the group's functioning. As we have already suggested, failure to prepare adequately for a group meeting is one of the most common causes of poor performance.

*Group members who are able to show that they are well prepared for meetings, who help keep the group organized, and who assist in leading the group usually have considerable impact on such group outcomes as productivity and group decision quality.*

## Taking a Personal Inventory, and Collecting and Analyzing Information

The first step in preparing for a group meeting is to take a *personal inventory* of the ideas, information, and other relevant data already in your possession. As we noted earlier, most decision makers in organizations would not belong to the group exploring a particular problem unless they were believed to possess some useful information, perspectives, or insights. In the classroom setting, discussion groups are usually free to select the subjects they wish to consider, with only reasonable restrictions. Thus, choosing a topic for group exploration is probably based on some shared interest in topics, such as the parking problem on campus, how the community should dispose of PCBs, the most recent tax law, or academic dishonesty. In actual organizations, topics or tasks are more likely to be assigned.

*Initially, then, group members should take stock of their existing attitudes, opinions, and knowledge.* In fact, it is often useful for some members of the group to meet prior to the actual meeting to assess the nature and quality of the members' collective knowledge. The deficiencies that are found in this store of existing information suggest guidelines for subsequent research. If you know how you feel about a problem but recognize that these feelings are based largely on some specific personal experiences, then perhaps the most productive strategy for you is to read widely regarding the issue or problem, attempting to be as open-minded as possible.

Once you have completed your self-inventory, you will identify your information gaps. At that point, you will go through a *research process* that follows the steps you would take if you were giving a speech on the problem or issue to be discussed. Refer to Chapter 4 for a thorough discussion of where to go for information. As part of your research, you may need to interview individuals, go to the library, read local or national newspapers, and explore the Internet. *Approach your research with a spirit of open-mindedness and a desire to be as knowledgeable as possible prior to the group's meeting.*

*Just as important as collecting information is assessing it to determine its quality.* Several criteria should prove useful in evaluating the quality of the information you have assembled: accuracy, recency, completeness, and the reliability of the source.[5] Not all these criteria need be applied to every piece of information, but in most cases, using one or more of them will allow you to make judicious decisions about the basic quality of your evidence. Refer to Chapter 4 for a detailed discussion of how to evaluate evidence and information.

## Keeping an Open Mind

A final critical factor concerning preparation is that you approach the decision-making discussion with an attitude of *open-mindedness.* There is a strong tendency for group members to reach definite conclusions about the best solution to the group's problem *before* the discussion. They then enter the discussion as advocates of a given position. This prohibits the group from exploring the problem together; it creates a situation in which a number of adversaries attempt to convince each other of the superiority of their points of view. Obviously, such a confrontation is more like a debate than a decision-making discussion.

To discourage this confrontational sort of situation from developing, it is important to recognize that the *group* has been asked to reach a decision. While each person's contributions are both solicited and appreciated, no one individual should attempt to dominate the group's effort. Only when diverse perspectives are explored open-mindedly can any small group hope to reach a judicious decision, one that demonstrates the value of collective decision making.

---

**KEY CONCEPTS 12.2    How to Prepare for Group Participation**

Conscientious preparation for any group meeting involves:

- • *Taking a personal inventory of what you already know, have read, and have experienced*

- • *Collecting information from multiple sources, including interviews, library research, and the Internet*

- • *Assessing information for its accuracy, recency, completeness, and source reliability*

- • *Approaching the group's deliberations with an attitude of open-mindedness, and with a desire to share decision making with fellow group members*

---

Meetings are notorious time wasters in most organizations. To conduct meetings more effectively, G. Laborde Associates, a communication consulting firm in Mountain View, California, recommends use of the "Pegasus" procedure:

P—present desired outcomes for meetings—make the goal of the meeting crystal clear.
E—explain evidence so that anyone can hear, see, or feel proof that the meeting accomplished its goals (that is, what should people experience if the meeting is successful?).
G—gain agreement from each person concerning the goal of the meeting.

A—activate sensory acuity—be perceptive to others' nonverbal cues.
S—summarize each decision after all decisions have been reached.
U—use a relevancy challenge—ensure that all points brought up during the meeting fit the meeting's objective.
S—summarize the next step and report back on it—make sure any required follow-up is clear.

Source: Gary M. Stern, "Here's a Way to Stop Wasting Time at Meetings," *Communication Briefings* (April 1991): 8a–8b.

## DISCUSSION QUESTIONS: TYPES, CHARACTERISTICS, AND EXAMPLES

Although several patterns of organization may be used to structure the communication activities of decision-making groups, these patterns should be approached with flexibility and open-mindedness. One important determinant of an appropriate organizational strategy is the kind of question the group is addressing. *Underlying each discussion topic or issue is a fundamental question of fact, conjecture, value, or policy.* Knowing which question is at the heart of the issue you are discussing helps you and the group know how to plan and organize the discussion.

### Questions of Fact

*Factual questions* concern matters of truth or falsity. They can be answered affirmatively or negatively without consulting the beliefs or attitudes of group members. The correct answer to the question of fact is a matter of actual events, particular properties, or specific states of affair, not simply *perceived* truth. Here are some examples of questions of fact relevant to decision making in organizations: "Is this organization meeting the antipollution standards established by the federal government?" "Is this hospital meeting the health care standards recently established by the AMA?" and "Is this company equipped with facilities to accommodate the needs of disabled employees?"

Of course, agreeing on the response to a factual question does not necessarily make it true. But, the group's assessment of the question is more likely to be sound if critical terms are defined and understood by all participants. In the question about disabled employees, for instance, your group would need to reach a common understanding of such terms as *equipped, facilities,* and *disabled.* The group defining a disability primarily in relation to employees confined to wheelchairs might reach quite different conclusions from a group that conceives of it as involving blindness, deafness, and certain learning disabilities.

## Questions of Conjecture

Similar to the question of fact is the *question of conjecture*. However, instead of dealing with the present, this question focuses on the future. Organizations must live with (and perhaps learn from) mistakes made in the past. The only events they can influence, however, are those that lie ahead. Since questions of conjecture focus on events as yet unseen, in discussing them, *your group must base its conclusions on probabilities*. Even so, it is often possible to base an intelligent prediction of the future on a substantial knowledge of the past.

In essence, the discussion of a question of conjecture demands the same knowledge and intelligent analysis as the question of fact. Examples of questions of conjecture include: "Will the demand for product X increase in the coming months?" "Will the demand for mathematics teachers increase in the years ahead?" and "Are large numbers of people likely to withdraw their funds from financial institutions as we approach the year 2000?"

## Questions of Value

Not unlike questions of fact or conjecture, the *question of value* can usually be answered affirmatively or negatively. But value questions deal with neither truth nor probability. Rather, the beliefs, attitudes, values, and motives of the members of your group are sought in discussing value questions.

Values are formed in various ways, and, once established, they tend to endure. Because values cannot be "proved," questions of value should never be treated like questions of fact. When your group discusses value questions, you must recognize that it is simply *approving* the conclusions reached, not demonstrating them irrevocably. Examples of questions of value are: "Is living together before marriage a good idea?" "Is teaching the most important mission of this university?" "Is training our employees in communication skills worth the cost?" and "Is ordaining women consistent with our church's doctrine?" Value-related issues underlie many contemporary problems confronting organizations.

## Questions of Policy

The kind of question most frequently discussed in organizational settings is the *question of policy*. In discussing this, your group will be involved in determining the most appropriate course of action to be taken or encouraged. Underlying almost every question of policy are one or more questions of fact, conjecture, and value. As your group makes judgments about the most suitable course of action to be taken in a specific situation, it will be continually confronted with factual and conjectural questions, as well as issues related to the opinions, attitudes, and motives of individuals within the group. Thus, the policy question is the most complex. Examples of questions of policy include: "Which presidential candidate should this newspaper support?" "What should be the stand of this church regarding the acceptance of homosexuals as members?" and "Should this organization appropriate additional funds to support research and development?"

Notice the diversity of subsidiary questions that might logically arise within these discussions. The policy question relating to homosexuality might include the discussion of factual questions, such as "What is the present stand of the church regarding homosexuals?" and "What is the attitude of the church leaders regarding this question?" Conjectural issues might also be raised, including, "What will be the reaction of the average church member if this church grants membership to homosexuals?" Finally, questions of value include "Is homosexuality immoral?" and "What are our personal reactions to this issue?"

## Characteristics of Good Discussion Questions

Regardless of the specific kind of question discussed, your group should make every effort to phrase the question appropriately. The three most important criteria for determining the quality of any discussion question are simplicity, objectivity, and controversiality.[6] A simple question is one that is clearly worded and that avoids unnecessary ambiguity or complication. *Simplicity* should not be confused with simple-mindedness. Rather, through careful wording and the avoidance of unnecessary jargon, simple questions avoid the pretentiousness and confusion associated with more ambiguous questions.

Discussion questions should also be phrased objectively. While complete *objectivity* is never possible, your group should make every attempt to remove highly subjective language and phrasing from the discussion question. Objective questions are free of loaded language and implied premises. Consider, for example, the question, "What should be done in this community to stop the spread of drug abuse?" The subjectivity in this question resides in its assumption that drugs are being abused in the community and that the abuse is *spreading*. Further, it is assumed that the correct solution must involve halting such drug usage. A more objective way of phrasing the question would be, "To what extent are drugs used in this community?" This kind of phrasing does not preclude the discussion of drug abuse, but it does not begin with the assumption that abuse exists.

Finally, discussion questions should be characterized by *controversiality*. This is not to imply that all discussions should be full of argumentativeness and emotional confrontations. There should be, however, at least *two* points of view for which support can be gathered. The discussion of a question lacking in controversiality is really not a discussion but a simple meeting to confirm previously existing and agreed upon beliefs. When a question *is* controversial, however, group members can then explore their differing views and share in finding common ground, exploring conflicting information, and reaching for a consensus that reflects their diversity.

| KEY CONCEPTS 12.3 | Identifying and Testing Questions for Discussion |
|---|---|
| Each issue or problem addressed by a group reflects an underlying question. The four types of discussion questions are: <br><br> • • *Questions of fact* <br><br> • • *Questions of conjecture* <br><br> • • *Questions of value* <br><br> • • *Questions of policy* | Regardless of question type, a good discussion question will be characterized by: <br><br> • • *Simplicity* <br><br> • • *Objectivity* <br><br> • • *Controversiality* |

*Small Group Communication*

# ORGANIZING DECISION-MAKING DISCUSSIONS

There are many different ways of organizing a discussion. Depending upon the kind of question being addressed, the amount of time available for the meeting, and the goals of the participants, different approaches may be more or less appropriate. Before we explore some of these approaches, it may be helpful here to review what is known about the ways groups typically go about making decisions and solving problems.

The manner in which a group discusses a problem is definitely related to the group's success.[7] A linear model of task group development was proposed by Tuckman and Jensen.[8] Their group stages include:

**1.** *Forming.*   Group members seek to establish their relationships, to get to know one another, and to form some sense of group spirit.

**2.** *Storming.*   Group members begin to react to the demands of the situation. They may question the group's charge and the authority of others in the group, articulating some assertions of differences and independence.

**3.** *Norming.*   The group agrees on rules of behavior, criteria for decision making, and ways of doing things.

**4.** *Performing.*   The group really examines the task or problem; information is shared; ideas are explored; questions are raised (in contrast to phases 1–3, which focused more on relationship development).

**5.** *Adjourning.*   As group members' time together draws to a close, they strive for closure on both task and relationship issues, moving toward adjournment.

## Process Models of Decision Making

As early as the 1960s, some small group researchers challenged the linear view of group decision making. Scheidel and Crowell, for instance, proposed a *spiraling model* in which group members bounced ideas back and forth as they moved toward consensus.[9] Far from being a linear progression, their decision-making model focused on group members' testing ideas, circling back, and then retesting.

More recently, studies by Poole suggest that groups develop according to a *multiple sequence model*.[10] That is, the groups he studied tried to implement logical, orderly problem-solving sequences, but frequently other factors, such as lack of information, task difficulty, and conflict, interfered. Moreover, periods of idea development and exploration were often broken by periods of integrating activity, such as joke telling, sharing personal stories, and mutual compliment passing. Taken as a whole, Poole's research suggests that *group development may not be as orderly as earlier models proposed.*[11]

## Distinguishing Effective from Ineffective Groups

There is nothing magic about making decisions in groups. Some groups work quite effectively and consistently make pretty good decisions, while others flounder. For years, researchers have attempted to compare effective and ineffective groups, trying to distinguish their behaviors and communicative activities.

Based on a number of studies spanning more than two decades, Hirokawa argued that *effective groups* can be distinguished by:

**1.** *The way in which group members attempt to evaluate the validity of opinions and assumptions advanced by fellow discussants.* Evaluations tend to be more rigorous in effective groups.

**2.** *The careful, rigorous manner in which groups try to evaluate alternatives, measuring them against established criteria.*

**3.** *The kind of premises on which decisions are made.* Effective groups are more likely to use high-quality facts and inferences, whereas ineffective groups rely more on questionable facts and assumptions.

**4.** *The sort of influence exerted by prominent group members.* In highly effective groups, leaders are more supportive and facilitating and less inhibiting. They ask appropriate questions, challenge invalid assumptions, clarify information, and keep the group from going off on irrelevant tangents.[12]

**5.** *Whether the group begins the meeting by seeking to understand the problem.* Successful groups tend to begin their discussion by attempting to analyze the problem *before* trying to search for a viable solution; unsuccessful groups tend to begin the discussion by immediately trying to search for a viable solution.[13]

**6.** *The attitudes group members bring to their deliberations.* When group members take the task seriously, when they are vigilant in their critical thinking, and when they weigh different alternatives carefully and judiciously, they are far more likely to make sound decisions. Thus, *the spirit with which the problem is tackled significantly influences the quality of the group's work.*[14]

## Problem-Solving Patterns: Some Pragmatic Considerations

Some writers are skeptical of any approach to decision making that is based on the premise of rationality.[15] For instance, in Cohen, March, and Olson's *garbage can model*, decision making is seen as a garbage pail in which people, problems, alternatives, and solutions slush around until there is sufficient contact among these elements for a decision to emerge. According to these theorists, groups will attempt to make their decisions *seem* rational retroactively through rationalization, but the decisions are really due to chance. They argue that the effectiveness of a decision should be judged according to group members' abilities to implement it and make it work rather than on the intrinsic effectiveness of the decision itself.[16]

While acknowledging that decision making is scarcely a completely rational process, most experts believe that groups can benefit from discovering and adopting procedures that minimize the widely acknowledged weaknesses associated with group interaction, such as looking at solutions before understanding the problem.[17] For example, Nutt reviewed 76 cases of organizational decision making and reported that in 84 percent of them, a solution-centered process was used.[18] An initial focus on solutions may lead to a cursory consideration of alternatives. Even more serious, real problems may go unidentified in favor of problems that fit existing solutions. When this happens, the group actually formulates and attempts to solve the wrong problem.

**The Reflective Thinking Sequence** In an attempt to address some of these problems and to encourage groups to examine problems more thoroughly and systematically, several writers and researchers have offered problem-solving patterns for groups to use. One of the most popular of these is John Dewey's *reflective-thinking sequence*. Particularly useful with questions of policy, this pattern consists of several questions:

1. How shall we define and limit the problem?
2. What are the causes and extent of the problem?
3. What are the criteria by which solutions should be judged?
4. What are the alternatives, and the strengths and weaknesses of each?
5. What solution can be agreed upon?
6. How can we put the solution into effect?[19]

The value of the reflective-thinking sequence is its emphasis on careful problem assessment, a thoughtful consideration of the criteria to be used in evaluating the competing solutions, and its insistence on asking the group to grapple with the particulars of solution implementation.

**Question-Agenda Model**   Earlier in this chapter, we discussed the kinds of questions appropriate for decision-making groups. We suggested that different kinds of questions should be approached from different perspectives for a maximally productive discussion to occur. Gouran has outlined several different agendas that he believes are conducive to structured and yet reasonably spontaneous interaction among discussants.[20] The agenda selected depends upon the kind of question being discussed, as follows:

## Agenda for Discussions on Questions of Fact and Conjecture
1. What evidence do we have to support an affirmative position?
2. What weaknesses, if any, exist in this body of evidence?
3. What evidence do we have to support a negative position?
4. What weaknesses, if any, exist in this body of evidence?
5. Have we accumulated enough information to reach a decision?
6. In light of the evidence examined, what position on the question appears to be most defensible?

## Agenda for Discussions on Questions of Value
1. What are our individual positions on the question?
2. On what bases have we arrived at these positions?
3. Which of these bases for our respective positions are sound, and which are questionable?
4. Are there positions other than those represented in the group that we should explore?
5. Which of the bases for additional positions are sound, and which are unsound?
6. Has our evaluation led to any changes in position?
7. Is there one position we can all endorse?

## Agenda for Discussions on Questions of Policy
1. What problems, if any, exist under the status quo?
2. What are the alternatives among policies that we could endorse?
3. What are the relative strengths and weaknesses of each of the alternatives?
4. On the basis of our analysis, which policy shall we endorse? (Note, the policy agenda is similar to Dewey's reflective thinking sequence.)

These suggested agendas are proposed only as tentative models, as potentially fruitful structures for the discussion of each kind of question. The advantage of using a different agenda for each type of question is that it is virtually impossible to neglect the nature of the question under consideration. Using these agendas, for example, your group is more likely to treat value questions as ones involving attitudes and motives and factual questions as ones necessitating the collection of considerable evidence before the discussion.

## Problem-Solving Strategies Emphasizing Idea Generation

Groups are notorious for making judgments about the quality or feasibility of members' ideas too early in the discussion. As a result, some researchers have proposed problem-solving strategies that encourage the generation of a maximum number of ideas without premature interpretation or analysis. For instance, some have advocated *brainstorming*, where ideas are proposed and listed without any type of judgment or criticism. This procedure has been shown to produce fresher, better-quality ideas than more ordinary problem-solving procedures.[21] A related approach, the *nominal group procedure*, gives each group member an opportunity to brainstorm privately on paper. An appointed clerk then collects the lists of ideas and compiles a master list. Ultimately, group members vote on the items they consider most important.[22]

Research comparing brainstorming groups with nominal groups has found that the nominal group procedure is more effective than brainstorming for groups composed of highly apprehensive members; it also appears better than brainstorming in terms of idea generation.[23] Its disadvantage (other than logistics) is that since the brainstorming is private, group members cannot be stimulated by hearing the ideas of others. Of course, Group Support Systems (GSS) allow groups to function as nominal groups by allowing members to brainstorm, organize, and evaluate their ideas anonymously using computers.[24]

---

**KEY CONCEPTS 12.4**  **The Structure and Organization of Groups**

In structuring a decision-making group's meeting, remember that

• • *Traditional research contends that groups go through several steps or phrases in their problem-solving efforts*

• • *Most recent research suggests that group development and problem solving may be less orderly than earlier models proposed*

• • *Effective groups may be distinguished from less effective groups according to:*
  Their rigor and vigilance
  Their use of high-quality information
  The quality of their leaders
  Their ability to understand and focus on the problem
  The spirit with which they approach their task

• • *Group decision making may not be an entirely rational process*

• • *Some problem-solving patterns, such as the reflective thinking sequence and the question-agenda model, are helpful in organizing decision-making meetings*

• • *Other techniques, such as brainstorming and nominal grouping, can assist groups in idea generation*

---

Scholar Harold Leavitt argues that companies sometimes need groups that managers can't control. He calls these groups "hot groups," lively, high-achievement, dedicated groups, usually small, whose members are turned on to exciting and challenging tasks.

The defining characteristics of hot groups are:

- Total preoccupation with the task at hand
- Intellectual intensity, integrity, and exchange
- Emotional intensity
- Fluid role structure
- Usually small size

Hot groups are most likely to pop up under these conditions:

- When organizations permit openness and flexibility
- When leaders encourage independence and autonomy
- When organizations put people first—hiring great talent and then giving individuals plenty of elbow room

- When the organizational culture is committed to truth seeking
- When a state of crisis or keen competition with other groups exists

Members of hot groups may be described as:

- Connective individualists, independent individuals who are also team players

Three key roles are prominent:

- *Conductors,* who lead the orchestra—obvious movers and shakers
- *Patrons,* who support it—working behind the scenes to protect, coach, listen, offer suggestions
- *Keepers of the flame,* who sustain the group through time—nourishing new ideas, new solutions, and new partners in a long chain of hot groups

Source: Harold J. Leavitt and Jean Lipman-Blumen, "Hot Groups," *Harvard Business Review* 73 (1995): 109–116.

## USING TECHNOLOGY TO FACILITATE GROUPS: GROUP SUPPORT SYSTEMS

Group support systems, interactive, computer-based systems, are rapidly being adopted and used by more corporations. GSS meeting rooms (see Figure 12.1) incorporate the use of a local-area network, individual personal computer (PC) workstations, and GSS software to support such traditional meeting activities as idea generation, idea consolidation, the evaluation of alternatives, and decision making.

GSS Features
Originally, GSS were designed with several specific features intended to enhance group interaction.[25] First, GSS enable *parallel communication*. Because group participants brainstorm, consolidate ideas, and vote using their networked PCs, *GSS allow each participant to contribute simultaneously;* therefore, no group member need wait for another to finish "speaking."

In addition, GSS support *group memory* by recording all typed comments electronically, allowing participants to withdraw from the group process to think or type comments and then rejoin the group discussion. At the same

FIGURE 12.1     A GSS meeting environment

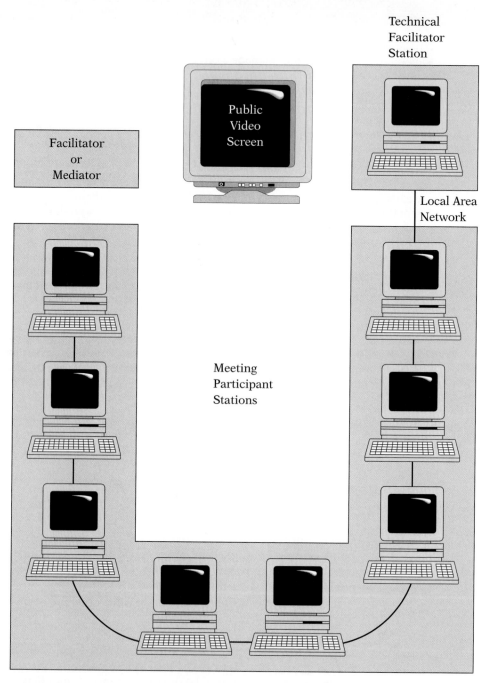

time, these systems enable participants to contribute to the group *anony-mously*, thus reducing the pressure to conform and diminishing both communication and evaluation apprehension.[26] Since ideas typed into the computer do not reveal the identity of the contributor, participants can evaluate their merits on the basis of their content rather than their contributor.

Finally, GSS can be used to *provide structure and channel group behavior* to maintain the group's focus on the task.[27] Ventana Corporation, maker of GroupSystems™, argues that these features help meeting participants contribute more fully, keep meetings on track, complete projects more rapidly, and develop consensus.

## Pros and Cons of Groupware

Although there are clearly advantages associated with the use of technology like group support systems, some losses are also possible. Advantages and disadvantages must be thoughtfully weighed.[28] For instance, typing comments into GSS PCs takes more time than speaking, thus potentially reducing the amount of information available to the group. On the other hand, the group benefits in that reading is faster than listening.

Because GSS anonymity separates the identity of the participants from their comments and votes, individuals are depersonalized—and thus presumably better able to express their true opinions. At the same time, however, this condition may also promote "deindividuation," that is, a loss of self- and group-awareness, which is associated with "flaming," in which feelings (especially negative sentiments) are expressed quickly and without reflection. Moreover, keyboarding may actually inhibit socializing, resulting in reduced group cohesiveness and satisfaction.

One important GSS feature, group memory, allows participants to pause and think during the group keyboarding activity without missing information being submitted by other group members. The GSS capacity to record information can also reduce memory and attention losses, attention blocking, and the incomplete use of information.[29] However, voiced comments and important nonverbal cues may go unnoticed and are, in any event, not documented.

Anonymity is widely heralded as a GSS feature that can reduce status consciousness, pressures to conform, and evaluation apprehension. However, it may also increase free riding because it is more difficult to determine who is not doing his or her fair share.[30]

The final notable GSS capability, parallel communication, reduces interruptions and increases air time—providing equality in both access and voice. No one need wait for someone else to stop talking. However, this feature can also generate information overload and increase redundancies since, at times, no one is electronically listening to what others are electronically saying.

GSS may also improve the rationality of decision making by providing group members with step-by-step procedures that substitute for or supplement their own (possibly deficient) approaches to problem solving. Several studies have shown that GSS-driven procedures can lead to improvements in defining problems, generating alternative solutions, and improving the quality of the group's decisions.[31]

## The GSS Environment: Beyond Technology

It's important to note that there are also nontechnology elements of the GSS meeting environment that may affect the nature of the group interaction process. Because GSS meetings do not take place in anyone's office, no participant is disadvantaged by having to travel to someone else's office for the meeting, perhaps finding himself or herself on something less than neutral turf. GSS facilities suggest by their very design and layout a concern for equality and a commitment to task. For instance, a number of meeting rooms are organized (as depicted in Figure 12.1) so that participants are seated at

## CREATIVE TRAINING IN THE USE OF NEW TECHNOLOGIES

An innovative use of group dynamics was attempted by Lutheran Brotherhood, a Minneapolis-based financial services company. When it learned that the laptop computers used by members of the sales force had become outdated and virtually useless, management decided that new laptop technology and new sales force computer skills were desperately needed.

Rather then employing traditional training methods, Lutheran Brotherhood decided to use direct sales force participation in developing a training program and to require interdepartmental involvement by employees throughout the company. A 21-member task force was formed and spent six months researching available laptops before making a final selection. It then initiated an organizationwide communication effort to announce the new system and upcoming training—including news articles in company publications and a music video featuring Lutheran Brotherhood executives in ponytails and spiked hair.

The task force received training in use of the new technology and in turn trained a 110-member deployment team consisting of employees from all functional areas of the organization. Training sessions then were conducted by the task force and deployment team members, each of whom had walkie-talkies with which to contact technical experts when difficult questions arose during the sessions. In just five weeks, almost all of the 1,500 salespeople learned how to use the new technology.

Source: Victoria Obenshain, "Peer Training Yields Speedy Results," *Personnel Journal* 71 (April 1992): 107–110.

equal distances around a U-shaped table. All can see a large screen that is prominently situated at the front of the room. At times, a meeting facilitator may stand in front of the group to provide instructions or assist the group process. What is important, however, is that this kind of meeting environment promotes equitable interactions.

In traditional meeting rooms, those with higher rank or status are often advantaged, while those with lower rank, confidence, or skill are disadvantaged. For instance, a group member with higher status, often the group's leader, typically elects to sit at the head of the table, giving him or her greater visual access to others (while being the focus of everyone's attention), as well as the potential for greater influence. Studies have shown that those seated in key positions will, in fact, talk more than others and will also be perceived as more influential. At the other extreme, those with high communication apprehension will invariably choose the most obscure seats, allowing them to withdraw from communication more easily and to avoid being the focus of attention. Interestingly, the GSS meeting environment neither promotes the would-be star nor provides hideouts for the apprehensive.[32]

The adoption and use of GSS and other such "groupware" products are increasing rapidly. Many organizations have chosen to downsize, and they want to make the time spent by managers and professional staff in meetings (30 to 70 percent of their time) as productive as possible. Corporations now employ GSS to support a wide range of purposes (such as team building, strategic planning, quality control, joint applications design, and project management), and productivity gains as high as 90 percent have been reported by firms using this technology.[33]

## The Role of Organizational Culture

Just as there is nothing magical about working in groups, using technology to facilitate group work may or may not be successful. Group members must be willing to experiment with the technology and to use it in constructive ways.[34]

Groupware can facilitate collaborative communication, but it can't be used effectively so long as people view possessing information as a personal competitive advantage within an organization. If the corporate culture emphasizes and reinforces individual effort and ability and does not promote cooperation and information sharing, the underlying premise, or spirit, of the groupware technology is undermined.

Regardless of the kind of question being discussed or the organizational or technological approach chosen by your group, there are certain kinds of behaviors that group members should display throughout the discussion. We will now focus on these behaviors and suggest appropriate guidelines.

---

### KEY CONCEPTS 12.5 — The Use of Technology to Support Group Work

**Group Support Systems possess several *advantages*, including:**

- • *Providing for parallel communication, resulting in more air time for everyone and reduced interruptions.*

- • *Supporting the group's memory—reducing memory and attention losses and providing an accurate account of what transpired.*

- • *Enabling group members to maintain anonymity—allowing for the open sharing of views and possibly reducing communication apprehension.*

- • *Providing structure and channeling behavior—contributing to improved problem definition, generation of alternatives, and a high-quality decision.*

**Possible disadvantages sometimes associated with groupware include:**

- • *Typing in comments can be more time-consuming than speaking.*

- • *Verbal and nonverbal communication cues are lessened as a source of meaning and understanding.*

- • *Deindividuation may lead to feelings being expressed strongly and without reflection.*

- • *Keyboarding may reduce socializing, leading to reduced group cohesiveness.*

- • *Restricted presentation of text may lead to the incomplete use of information.*

*Continued*

## BEHAVIORAL GUIDELINES FOR DISCUSSION PARTICIPANTS

A discussion is only as good as its participants. Informed, participative members bring about an effective discussion. Uninformed, uninvolved, or unskilled interactants virtually guarantee the group's failure. In this section, we will lay out some behaviors we have found effective in promoting both your own success as a group member and the overall success of the group.

### Participate Actively

To begin with, *every group member must take an active part in the discussion and activities of the group.* If you sit back silently during group meetings, you contribute nothing to the group or to your own credibility in the group or the organization. On the other hand, if you participate actively and make positive contributions to the group, you will help the group achieve its goals, improve your own standing within the group, and build an organizationwide reputation as someone who is valuable to have in group situations. Such a reputation will do much to enhance your long-term success.

### Be Knowledgeable

*Every group member needs to be as knowledgeable as possible regarding the subject of discussion.* It is probably inevitable that some members of your group will be better informed on certain aspects of the discussion subject than you are. But it is still vital that you explore all facets of the question as thoroughly as possible, given the constraints of time.

### Approach the Discussion with a Group Orientation

We previously noted the importance of approaching the discussion with a desire to be a part of the *group's decision-making effort.* You should not make irrevocable judgments in advance. Rather, *each person should be group-oriented* throughout. The point of participation in the discussion is not to satisfy your need for social approval or to gain acceptance for a personal prejudice or point of view. Each person shares some responsibility for the success or failure of the entire group. Whenever anyone allows personal ambitions to replace commitment to the objectives of the group, he or she is functioning in a manner detrimental to the group's success.

### Maintain an Attitude of Open-Mindedness

Closely related to a group-oriented attitude is one of open-mindedness. *Group members should enter the discussion as open-mindedly as possible and strive to maintain an attitude of open-mindedness throughout the decision-making process.* Encourage the expression of all points of view. State your own views with some degree of tentativeness, and do not hesitate to change your mind if others persuade you.

In addition to the other behavioral guidelines offered in this chapter, *every group member should strive to interact ethically.* This means showing concern for others' ideas, respect for their feelings, and willingness to give them time to reflect on new information. The ethical discussant is less interested in winning an argument than in achieving a consensus based on mutual understanding and respect. He or she does not use the group as an arena for promoting special interests or ruthlessly advancing his or her own status at the expense of others.

The ethical discussant is as eager to learn and listen as he is to offer opinions and sage advice. He insists on accuracy in information and is willing to take extra time and put up with extra meetings for the sake of a better, more fully informed decision. Ethics involves developing a sense of responsibility for the good of the group as a whole, while not losing a feeling for the relationship between the group and the rest of the organization. The ethical discussant is mature enough to realize that other groups have different priorities and that no matter how hard this group works or how excellently it performs, others work hard as well and have legitimate needs to be fulfilled. Thus, the ethical discussant is a good thinker, a good listener, a hard worker, and a responsible member of the organizational community.

## Listen Carefully

Throughout every phase of the discussion, *all discussants should carefully listen.* Attentiveness to the ideas of other group members is, of course, common courtesy. Careful listening has important implications for the effective functioning of your group as well. If you listen carefully, you are less apt to introduce irrelevant or redundant ideas and information. You are also better able to legitimately challenge the opinions of others whenever those ideas seem to lack supporting evidence. Unsupported and unchallenged statements pose a threat to the validity of the group's conclusions.

## Seek Understanding

Closely related to challenging unsupported assertions is the important function of *asking for clarification of ideas, evidence, or opinions* that are unclear to the listener. Most of us are only too skilled at pretending to understand things we do not, in part because we fear revealing our ignorance and, occasionally, because we are too lazy or uninterested to seek further understanding. The responsible, intelligent discussant will recognize when someone uses an unfamiliar or ambiguous word or expresses an idea in an obscure fashion, will realize that the other group members also probably don't understand, and will see that the statement is clarified before the group continues.

## Focus on Matters of Substance

*Every group member should strive to concentrate on substantive concerns.* Every decision-making group has a task before it; the individuals composing the group, however, are human beings who possess personalities that occasionally conflict. Severe personality clashes can destroy the socioemotional climate of the group and render the accomplishment of the group's task an impossibility.

As a mature group member, you should realize that it is impossible to be equally attracted to every other member. It stands to reason that some of your fellow discussants will seem insensitive, uninformed or unintelligent, domineering, or rude from time to time. Even so, the important consideration from the viewpoint of the group's welfare is to assist all members, regardless of personality peculiarities or irritations, to contribute their best effort to the group's task. Table 12.1 provides one example of an evaluation form that can be used in reacting to any group member's contribution, as well as assessing the group as a whole.

## TABLE 12.1
### Group Discussion Evaluation

**Group Member's Name:** _____

**Instructor's Name:** _____

Ratings should be interpreted as follows: 1 = Excellent; 2 = Good;
3 = Average; 4 = Somewhat Lacking; 5 = Poor.

**Individual Evaluation:**

| | | | | | |
|---|---|---|---|---|---|
| Was well prepared and knowledgeable. | 1 | 2 | 3 | 4 | 5 |
| Made specific references to information sources. | 1 | 2 | 3 | 4 | 5 |
| Contributions were concise and clear. | 1 | 2 | 3 | 4 | 5 |
| Comments were relevant to the issue being discussed. | 1 | 2 | 3 | 4 | 5 |
| Contributions were made readily and voluntarily. | 1 | 2 | 3 | 4 | 5 |
| Frequency of participation was appropriate. | 1 | 2 | 3 | 4 | 5 |
| Nonverbal communication was effective. | 1 | 2 | 3 | 4 | 5 |
| Listened carefully to fellow group members. | 1 | 2 | 3 | 4 | 5 |
| Seemed open-minded, willing to consider others' views. | 1 | 2 | 3 | 4 | 5 |
| Was cooperative and constructive. | 1 | 2 | 3 | 4 | 5 |
| Helped keep the discussion organized. | 1 | 2 | 3 | 4 | 5 |
| Contributed to the critical evaluation of ideas and information. | 1 | 2 | 3 | 4 | 5 |
| Was respectful and tactful in responding to others. | 1 | 2 | 3 | 4 | 5 |
| Encouraged everyone to participate. | 1 | 2 | 3 | 4 | 5 |
| Encouraged the expression of diverse points of view. | 1 | 2 | 3 | 4 | 5 |
| Assisted in leadership functions, if appropriate. | 1 | 2 | 3 | 4 | 5 |

**Group Evaluation:**

| | | | | | |
|---|---|---|---|---|---|
| Chose a substantive question of policy, characterized by simplicity, objectivity, and controversiality. | 1 | 2 | 3 | 4 | 5 |
| Demonstrated a grasp of important issues pertaining to the discussion question. | 1 | 2 | 3 | 4 | 5 |
| Created and flexibly followed an appropriate agenda. | 1 | 2 | 3 | 4 | 5 |
| Showed evidence of having conducted good research. | 1 | 2 | 3 | 4 | 5 |
| Interacted spontaneously. | 1 | 2 | 3 | 4 | 5 |
| Interacted cooperatively and considerately. | 1 | 2 | 3 | 4 | 5 |
| Made reasonable progress toward reaching consensus. | 1 | 2 | 3 | 4 | 5 |
| Handled conflict openly and constructively. | 1 | 2 | 3 | 4 | 5 |
| Encouraged everyone to participate. | 1 | 2 | 3 | 4 | 5 |

**Comments:**

# SUMMARY

Working in groups to make decisions can be satisfying when the organizational culture supports collaboration; when participants are eager to work with others; and when group members know how to plan, organize, and conduct an effective meeting. Although "participatory management" has been a buzzword for many years, getting employees involved in committee meetings can be challenging.

A small group can function effectively only under conditions where its members know something about group process and are interested in and willing to try to work together to share information and make good decisions. Understanding decision-making processes is an important first step. Groups are not always orderly and organized, and do not always proceed in a step-by-step fashion. Some groups may go through distinct phases, but most are likely to proceed in less orderly ways. Being organized in a particular way may be less important than the qualities of mind, and the work ethic, and the spirit with which the group approaches its task.

Underlying problems that groups address are discussion questions of fact, conjecture, value, or policy. These questions should be articulated with simplicity and objectivity—and should possess some degree of controversiality. Creating an agenda that is consistent with the kind of question being addressed is very helpful in organizing the group's interactions.

Technology in the form of group support systems also has the capacity to assist groups by increasing each member's "talking" time, by allowing for anonymity, by providing for a collective memory or record of the meeting, and by giving the meeting structure. Using groupware does not ensure a successful group effort; members may suffer from a sense of isolation, nonverbal cues may be missed, and group members may flame. But with good intentions, training, and a collaborative culture, GSS has the potential to truly facilitate group efforts.

As with other communication skills, we assume that any organization member can *learn* to interact effectively in a small group setting. But effective group membership does require knowledge, the right kinds of attitudes, and a willingness to work at it. Every group is different. Each will present special challenges. By following the principles advanced in this chapter, it is hoped, you will be well equipped to deal with difficult committee assignments and to help other group members move toward satisfying and productive outcomes.

# QUESTIONS FOR DISCUSSION

1. In what sense is group decision making a process rather than a procedure?
2. What are some ways (methods) of preparing for participation in a group discussion? Which seem to you to be most useful? Why?
3. What is meant by "having a group orientation"?
4. Identify each of the following discussion questions in terms of *fact, conjecture, value, or policy*. Then evaluate the merit of each as a potential discussion question in terms of *simplicity, objectivity,* and *controversiality*.

   a. What should be the policy of the United States concerning gun control?
   b. What is the value of a college education?
   c. Is there a positive correlation between violence on television and the crime rate?
   d. Is having sex before marriage desirable or morally problematic?
   e. Is teenage alcoholism a serious problem in our society today?
   f. What should be our attitude toward gay rights?

5. Compare and contrast the reflective-thinking sequence, the nominal group procedure, and the question-agenda model. What are the strengths and weaknesses of each? Can you think of other potential approaches? Elaborate.

6. What are some of the advantages and disadvantages of group support systems?

7. Discuss some of the behavioral characteristics of effective discussion participants. Refer to examples from your own experiences.

## EXERCISES

1. Take any two of the following topics and phrase them into all four types of discussion questions (fact, conjecture, value, and policy). Check each question carefully to make sure it meets the criteria of simplicity, objectivity, and controversiality.
   a. Euthanasia.
   b. Pass-fail grading.
   c. The Christian coalition.
   d. Antidepressants.
   e. Internet pornography.
   f. Homelessness in our community.
   g. Social Security.
   h. HMOs.
   i. Animal rights.
   j. Public versus private schools.

2. Break into groups of five to seven members each. Choose a topic of mutual interest and some controversiality, and phrase it into a question for a decision-making discussion. After appropriate time for individual preparation, meet again as a group and discuss the question, attempting to reach consensus.

3. Following the above discussion, critically consider the quality of the group's decision-making efforts in terms of the problem-solving pattern used, the quality and quantity of the contributions of individual group members, and the socioemotional variables operating within the group. Use the group evaluation form provided in Table 12.1, or generate a critique sheet of your own.

*Reynolds and Reynolds Co.*

Like many companies, Reynolds and Reynolds Co., in Moraine, Ohio, was looking for ways to improve productivity without increasing costs. Its discovery: that the best results come from asking workers who actually do the jobs how those jobs can be done more efficiently.

One key Reynolds and Reynolds plant, the Moraine plant, repairs computer and peripheral components, such as printers and monitors, for the company's automotive-dealer information system. While this plant is relatively small, employing 45 people, it plays a large role in the company's success. Specifically, repairing each of its own components costs Reynolds and Reynolds, on average, $35, while sending the same part outside for repairs would cost $185. Thus, with a large volume of components to be repaired, the Moraine plant saves the company nearly $8 million every year.

In spite of their substantial savings, managers believed that the Moraine plant could operate even more efficiently. Among the 45 employees, performance varied a great deal. Tension was in the air.

An initial investigation of barriers to effective performance revealed conflict between the repair functions of the Moraine plant, which worked on a quota system, and the distribution function, which tried to be responsive to the needs of customers (people at other company locations). Since each function blamed the other for any problems, a five-person task force composed of people from both areas and one from internal engineering was formed and named "ACT"— Accomplishing Communications Team. This group then conducted a 2 1/2 hour plantwide meeting of all employees, with no supervisors or managers present. While some employees expressed skepticism during the meeting about management's true intentions in launching this effort, all eventually agreed to give the new system a try.

The ACT members funneled employees' ideas to management over the next several months, including proposed revisions in the weekly work schedules (which would be drawn up by employees themselves), a plan for cross-training repair technicians, and an improved method for labeling repair parts. All these measures, and many others, were implemented, with significant cost savings to the company.

Ultimately, the approach has increased productivity by nearly 40 percent, reduced the time parts wait for repairs from two weeks to 24 hours, and eliminated the need to recheck returned parts.

## Questions

1. What aspects of group process probably helped the Reynolds and Reynolds performance improvement effort to succeed? What factors probably impeded the effort's success?
2. What were the dangers of undertaking the effort described in this case; that is, what might have gone wrong?
3. Are there situations in which this sort of process probably should not be attempted? As a manager, what things would you consider when deciding whether or not to institute a process similar to that used by Reynolds and Reynolds?

Source: Based on information provided by Raju Narisetti, "Bottom-Up Approach Pushes Plant's Performance to the Top," *Chicago Tribune* (November 29, 1992): sec. 7, p. 13.

# CHAPTER thirteen

## Conducting Group Meetings

*After reading this chapter, you should be able to:*

1. Identify situations in which meetings should and should not be called.

2. List and explain factors to consider in preparing to conduct meetings.

3. Develop an effective announcement for a meeting.

4. List and explain four types of meetings and the situations in which each is most appropriate.

5. List problem participants in groups and how they might be handled.

6. Comprehend the underlying principles of parliamentary procedure.

7. List and describe types and precedence of motions made in formal meetings.

One of the most common complaints we hear from supervisors, managers, and executives is that "there are too many meetings." Indeed, the higher one goes in an organization's hierarchy, the more time one is going to spend conducting or participating in meetings. It seems likely that the use of meetings in organizations is going to increase rather than decrease in the future. In his book *Megatrends: Ten New Directions Transforming Our Lives*, John Naisbitt claims that "people whose lives are affected by a decision must be part of the process of arriving at that decision."[1] He goes on to argue that "whether or not we agree with the notion or abide by it, participatory democracy has seeped into the core of our value system. Its greatest impact will be in government and corporations." Already this trend is clear in the business setting. In response to a survey of management practices conducted nationwide, only 15.3 percent of all top executives and 12.3 percent of all managers said they make major decisions without consulting all their direct subordinates in meetings; all the rest used participative decision making to some extent.[2]

With this increasing emphasis on participative decision making has come an increased need for two other things: skills among employees and supervisors in participating in meetings and skills among supervisors, managers, and executives in conducting meetings. James O'Toole of the Center for Future Research at the University of Southern California claims that "what America will require is workers who are humane individuals, with analytical and entrepreneurial skills, who know how to work in groups, and who know how to solve problems."[3]

## PREVIEW

I n keeping with this growing need, previous chapters discussed the factors of group participation. In this chapter, we will consider techniques for leading group meetings. Specifically, we will discuss the times at which meetings should and should not be called; how to prepare for meetings; how to announce meetings; general approaches to leading meetings; specific formats by which certain types of meetings can be run; things to do as a follow-up to a meeting; and strategies for dealing with problem participants in groups. We will conclude with a section on conducting large meetings, briefly introducing the principles of parliamentary procedure. All this should help you develop your skills in conducting group interactions in the organizational setting.

## BEFORE THE MEETING: PREPARATORY STEPS

Deciding
When to Call
Meetings

Many of the complaints or "bad press" that meetings receive are due to their inappropriate usage. Too many meetings are held when no meeting really is needed. Conversely, too many decisions are made without a meeting when, in fact, a meeting should have occurred. As a first step in knowing when and when not to have a meeting, Auger suggests you keep in mind the following principles:[4]

You *should* call a meeting when you need to:

1. Reach a group judgment as the basis for a decision.
2. Discover, analyze, or solve a problem.
3. Gain acceptance from the group for an idea, program, or decision.
4. Achieve a training objective.
5. Reconcile conflicting views.
6. Provide essential information for work guidance or for the relief of insecurities or tensions.
7. Ensure equal understanding of company policy, methods, or decisions.
8. Obtain immediate reactions to a problem that requires a speedy response.

On the other hand, you *should not* call a meeting when:

1. Other communications, such as telephone, telegram, letter, e-mail, or memo, will produce the desired result.
2. There is not sufficient time for adequate preparation by participants or the meeting leader.
3. One or more key participants cannot attend.
4. The meeting is not likely to produce satisfactory results because of personality conflicts or conflicts with overall management strategy.
5. Expected results do not warrant spending the money it will cost to hold the meeting.

When deciding whether to call a meeting, always remember the old saying "Time is money." Meetings consume a lot of both, and you must be sure the investment is worthwhile before convening any meeting. Indeed, the safest philosophy may be to call meetings only as a last resort, when no other communication mechanism will do.

### Preparing to Conduct Meetings

Much of the effort that goes into making a meeting successful occurs before the meeting happens. Only through careful planning can you be sure that the meeting will be as successful as possible. Yet research conducted by Frank suggests that preparation often is lacking: When asked, "How frequently are group meetings well planned?" 40.6 percent of the respondents in his survey of 416 organizations responded "almost never" or "sometimes."[5]

To ensure thorough preparation, you should ask yourself several questions, such as:

1. Have I clearly defined the purpose or purposes of the meeting?
2. What are the outcomes that should emerge from this meeting? (Information? Plans to gather information? Possible courses of action? A solution to a problem? A policy statement?)
3. Who should participate? As a rule, invite to the meeting people who are expected to carry out a decision to be reached at the meeting, people who possess unique information that they can contribute to the meeting, people whose approval may be needed, people who have official responsibility for the matter under discussion, and people who have a personal contribution to make from a strategic standpoint (that is, whose support you want or whose opposition you want to avoid politically).
4. How should people be notified of the meeting? We will talk further about methods of announcing meetings in the next section.
5. How much time will the meeting probably take?
6. What information, if any, do members need before the meeting?
7. What follow-up, if any, will be needed after the meeting?
8. What agenda will the meeting follow?
9. What is the best time and place for the meeting?
10. What physical arrangements need to be made for the meeting?

Answering these questions will probably provide adequate preparation for a meeting.

The facility or setting in which the meeting is to be held should be given careful consideration as part of the planning process. The physical location of a meeting and the equipment to be used during that meeting have a powerful impact on the meeting's success. As a result, you must plan carefully the physical facilities to be used during the session.

Generally, you should consider five basic elements: task, comfort, acoustics, visibility, and interference.

- *Task* is a consideration of the work to be done in the meeting and of the equipment necessary to do that work. If a presentation is to be given, for example, an overhead projector, a slide projector, or laptop computer, and a screen may be needed. If participants' comments are to be solicited and discussed, a "flip pad" or easel pad of large sheets of paper will be needed. A blackboard also may be needed. Occasionally, videotaping equipment, such as cameras, playback units, and monitors, is used. The leader should ensure that all such equipment is at the meeting site, that spare bulbs for projectors are on hand, that electrical outlets have been located and the necessary extension cords procured, and that there are markers or chalk for use on the flip pad or blackboard.

- *Comfort* involves several aspects of the environment. Temperature and ventilation are important. You need to determine how to control the room's temperature and ventilation, should the room become too cold, hot, or stuffy during the meeting. In all instances, speed of change is the primary concern. Any room can have its temperature or ventilation changed; the issue during a meeting is whether the change can be achieved quickly enough.

Another aspect of comfort is the chairs: Are they padded enough or flexible enough to provide comfort for a long meeting? Are they too comfortable (creating the possibility of people's dozing off during the meeting)? Are they moveable so that people can face each other if necessary? Will desks or tables be needed? Any equipment that participants may need, such as writing tablets, pencils, or erasers, should also be set out at each person's seating place before the meeting begins.

- *Acoustics,* or the ability of people to hear one another, is also an important consideration. You should be sure that sound carries well even when the room is full of people (sound always carries better in an empty room) and that the room is not overly large so that people will sit too far from one another. If necessary, obtain microphones and loudspeakers so everyone can be heard.

- *Visibility* is also important. People should be able to see anyone who is talking, whether that person is the meeting leader or another group member. If charts, graphs, slides, movies, or other visuals are to be used, everyone must be able to see these as well. Consider the impact of any seating arrangement on group interaction. Be sure that everyone has equal access to everyone else if group discussion is to be an important part of the meeting (sitting around a circular table might be helpful in this regard) or that committee members who need to work together are seated next to one another.

- *Interference* is one final concern. Interruptions should be prevented and background noise eliminated if at all possible. You need to investigate what things, if any, will be happening in adjoining rooms during your meeting. You also need to select a meeting location that is away from the normal work area, unless the meeting is to be very brief and informal. A "Do not disturb" notice on the door may be helpful, and participants should be told ahead of time to have messages taken for them during the meeting so interruptions will not occur.

## Announcing Meetings

Too often meetings fail because they are poorly announced. The wrong people show up, participants arrive unprepared, or members have to leave before the end of the meeting because no one knew how long the meeting would take. To avoid such problems, you should send a written announcement at least one week in advance to everyone involved in the meeting. Do not rely on telephone calls, face-to-face interactions, or even e-mail (since some people don't check their e-mail regularly).

The written announcement of the meeting should say:

- *Why* the meeting is being held. Members should know what the purpose of the meeting is and what their role is to be. This gives them a chance to prepare for the meeting if necessary, and it lets them know what matters will not be part of the meeting's contents.

- *When* the meeting starts and ends. Most announcements indicate the starting time; too few say how long the meeting is expected to last. To

## AVOIDING MEETING PITFALLS

An important element of preparing to conduct a meeting is anticipating and avoiding common meeting pitfalls. Here are seven of the most common meeting pitfalls, along with some suggestions on how to avoid them.

- *Lack of clarity about the meeting's purpose:* Many meetings suffer from "mission creep," whereby the goal of the meeting becomes lost over time and the meeting becomes simply a regular activity (such as the weekly staff meeting that occurs once a week whether it is needed or not). At Motorola, the opening minutes of every meeting are spent discussing its purpose, and the meeting is disbanded if the purpose cannot be clearly stated. As a first step, always ask, "What are the results this meeting should produce?"
- *Goals that could better be accomplished by means other than a meeting:* Sometimes the best solution is to avoid meeting in the first place. To test this, write down what change a meeting is supposed to accomplish, and then assess whether a meeting is the best way to reach that goal. Meetings held for the purpose of sharing information and project updates, for example, should be canceled in favor of e-mails and information-sharing software, such as Lotus Notes.
- *Inadequate preparation:* For a meeting to function effectively, as much as possible should be decided ahead of time: the purpose, who is coming, what is to be decided, how long the meeting will last, the best meeting space, what problem-solving procedures will be used, what the agenda will be, and so on.

- *A haphazard decision-making process:* Meetings are the forum in which team-based organizations reach many of their decisions. Yet very often there is no sense of how decisions are to be made within a group. A decision-making agenda should be selected and used as the basis for the meeting's procedures.
- *Jumping to conclusions:* In reaching a decision, groups rarely establish criteria or standards by which solutions will be evaluated. Instead, they ignore systematic analysis in favor of the most current, dramatic, or controversial aspects of a problem. This emotional approach to selecting a solution can result in flawed meeting results and unsatisfactory problem solving.
- *Overdeveloped egos:* Some meetings end up being not about problem solving at all. Issues may be decided not on their merits, but on the competing interests of people at the table. The meeting leader must anticipate conflicts that have little to do with the goal of the meeting and must look to create norms that curb headstrong, ego-driven acts.
- *Insufficient follow-up:* Meetings typically end with people being assigned to carry out the conclusions. But the meeting process does not end until someone is assigned to do follow-up. Without some means of checking back and ensuring that assignments are completed, there is no way of knowing whether a meeting has been effective.

Source: Edward Prewitt, "Pitfalls in Meetings and How to Avoid Them," *Harvard Management Update* (June 1998): pp. 9–10.

avoid people leaving early due to other commitments, state in the announcement how long the meeting is expected to go or when it will adjourn.

- *Where* the meeting is to be held. If attendees are likely to be unfamiliar with the location, a map or some description of how to find it should be included.

**SAMPLE MEETING ANNOUNCEMENT**

To:     All Training Department Members
From: H. K. Thompson, Director of Training &
        Development
Re:     Upcoming Department Meeting
Date: November 10, 1994

On Friday, November 21, we will have a meeting of the Training Department, to be held in Training Room C in the Training Center, Building C. It will begin at 12 noon and be over by 1:30 P.M.

Mr. Don Johnson, Vice-President of Personnel, will be present to talk about his objectives for the training function next year, and Mr. Gary Howard, Director of Employee Relations, will attend to discuss the role of Corporate Training support for in-plant locations.

The purposes of the meeting are (1) to discuss plans for the department and to choose specific programs to offer next year, (2) to review participant responses to this year's programs, and (3) to discuss any matters of concern to you. *Please bring all of your participant rating sheets to the meeting; you will be asked to present the average ratings received for each of your programs to the rest of the group.*

Our agenda is as follows:

1. Plans for next year
   a. Objectives of the Vice-President—Mr. Johnson.
   b. The Role of Corporate Training for In-Plant Location—Mr. Howard.
   c. Specific programs we should offer at Corporate facility (group suggestions).
   d. Specific programs we should offer at individual plant sites (group suggestions).
2. Program evaluations
3. Training staff's matters of concern

- *Who* is going to attend. The complete list of attendees should be provided for everyone to see. The list need not give everyone by name ("the entire training force" would be sufficient), but each attendee should know who else is coming.

- *What* is going to be considered in the meeting. An agenda or outline of the meeting's proceedings should be included. If attendees are allowed to suggest items for inclusion in the agenda, this fact also should be stated, and attendees should be told to whom their items should be sent and by what date those items should be received.

Business Brief 13.2 presents a sample announcement letter. While the contents of such a letter will change from one meeting and group to the next, the basic types of information contained in this announcement should be included in every meeting notification.

## SELECTING A LEADERSHIP STYLE: APPROACHES TO CONDUCTING MEETINGS

An important element of group leadership is the extent to which the leader shares power with the group members. Some leaders, for example, take total control of the meeting and decision making, simply telling everyone else what is going to happen, who is going to do what to whom, and so on. Other leaders are just the opposite: they allow a great deal of participation by the group members, both in interacting and in making decisions. How a meeting is to be conducted is something the leader must decide.

Regarding the concept of shared or conserved power, we can identify four basic approaches to conducting meetings:

## Autocratic Meetings

Autocratic (highly directive) leadership occurs when the leader does virtually all the talking and decides everything (or virtually everything) the group will do. Meetings led by such leaders consist primarily of announcements the leader makes to the attendees, followed by any questions the attendees have for the leader. In other words, communication is almost exclusively downward and decision making is virtually nonexistent.

Generally, autocratic meetings are not really meetings but rather presentations by the group leader to the group. As we already have seen, some situations demand this sort of meeting. Time may be of the essence, the group may not know enough about the topic to participate, the group may have no control over the topic so that participation would be meaningless, and so on. Whatever the case, the leader chooses to use the one-to-group setting to communicate information to the participants.

The autocratic meeting is really an exercise in public presentation. Therefore, the principles described in previous chapters will be of help in conducting this type of meeting. At this point, however, we can offer an agenda and some principles to follow when conducting the autocratic meeting:

I. Introduction
   A. Call the group to order.
   B. Announce the purpose of the meeting.
   C. If appropriate, explain why the meeting is being handled this way and why the group is not participating in making the decision or formulating plans.
   D. Preview the meeting agenda. List the order in which the topics will be covered, when breaks (if any) will be taken, when questions should be asked (any time; at the end of each announcement; at the end of the meeting), and when the meeting will probably end. The agenda might be written on a blackboard or flip pad at the front of the room to help keep participants oriented to the topic.

II. Presentation
   A. Announce the first topic; where appropriate, give the background of the topic, current actions or decisions, and future implications for this group.
   B. Announce the second topic; handle in the same way.
   C. Announce the third; continue through announcements.
   D. As much as possible, use visual aids: handouts, charts, graphs, overhead transparencies, and the like. Accompanying visual stimuli help participants both to understand and to remember the announcements.

III. Conclusion
   A. Ask for and answer any questions.
   B. State again any future implications the announcements have for the group.

C.  Tell the group what follow-up will occur. ("I'll send each of you a memo saying in writing what I've announced today. If you have any questions or concerns later, give me a call.")

D.  Dismiss the meeting.

The keys to successful autocratic meetings are clarity, completeness, and comprehension. The information you provide must be as clear as possible to the members. (Watch their feedback carefully for signs of puzzlement or confusion, and let them ask questions.) It must be complete, particularly if the members are to have a role in implementing the decision or if it will affect them. Finally, they must comprehend the reasoning behind the decision or the implications of the information.

## Consultative Meetings

Consultative leadership encourages input from group members, although the leader still makes the final decisions. In effect, the leader "consults" with the members, asking for their thoughts and ideas concerning problems, decisions, actions, and so on. They participate in the interaction, and they have some influence over the leader's thinking. However, they have power only to the extent that they can persuade the leader to adopt their suggestions or proposals.

In consultative meetings, the leader maintains decision-making authority but asks the group to suggest alternatives, ideas, causes, and so on. At the beginning of the meeting, it is important to make this situation clear to the participants. The leader should state the problem, decision, or situation she is facing, and should tell the group that their ideas or suggestions are desired, but make it clear that the leader ultimately will have responsibility for the decision. Thus, while the leader promises to listen, she does not promise to do everything (or anything) the group suggests.

As an agenda for the meeting, the leader might choose to use one of those outlined in Chapter 12: the reflective-thinking sequence, the nominal group procedure, or a questions-agenda model. Regardless of the agenda he suggests, however, the leader will have to solicit participation from the group. Several strategies may be useful here.

*Presidents of the United States most frequently use a consultative leadership style. Franklin Roosevelt was a master of such a style. By consulting with members of the Cabinet and other experts, the President makes decisions based on maximum information and input. When the President speaks, his views are usually informed by such input.*

First, the leader might use an *overhead question*—one asked of the group as a whole. Such a question might be "What do you think of this?" or "What ideas do you have concerning solutions to this problem?" The problem with overhead questions, however, is that they may go over everyone's head; no one has responsibility for answering the question, so often no one answers. The silence that follows an overhead question is often deafening. If the overhead question does not produce participation or discussion, a more specific approach might prove useful.

One way to encourage participation is to use the *directed question*. That is, call on someone for an answer. Make an effort to call on someone you know to have information, whose nonverbal cues indicate he has an opinion (for example, a member who shakes his head negatively when you introduce the topic), or with whom you have spoken prior to the meeting to let her know she will be called upon at the beginning of the meeting.

Directed questions should also be sufficiently open, requiring more than a yes or no response. Asking "Bill, do you agree with that?" and having Bill grunt "Uh-huh" hardly produces stimulating interaction. Ask, "What are some things you think we should do, Bill?" or "Bill, how do you feel about this issue?" Directed questions also should be passed around the group. There is a temptation to call again and again on the same member, either because he is such a good answer-giver or because you are personally acquainted with that member and feel comfortable calling on him. You must make a deliberate effort to call on different members at different times.

Finally, encourage participation by asking redirected questions. That is, when a group member asks you a question, redirect the question back to the group, rather than immediately providing a response. For example, you might make it an overhead question: "What do all of you think of that?" Or you might direct it to another member: "Diane, how would you answer Bill's question?" Again, your purpose is to stimulate interaction among the members; conducting a question-and-answer session with individual members does not achieve active group discussion.

In larger groups (more than 10 people), another participation-producing device is to subdivide the group into smaller groups, give them a topic to discuss, and have them report back a few minutes later. For example, you might divide your group of 10 into two groups of 5 members each and instruct them: "Now I want each of your groups to come up with the longest list possible of things we might do to improve the courtesy we show patients in the hospital. After about 10 minutes, I'll stop you and have you report your answers for everyone." The small group setting and specific assignment of topics are very effective in getting people to talk with one another, and this interaction will continue when the larger group is reformed later on.

At the end of a consultative meeting, one of two things should occur. First, if you have the ability and inclination to make decisions on the spot, you should do so. Tell the group which of their recommendations you will accept and which will you reject (along with reasons why you choose not to do those things) or which suggestions you will pass along to upper management and which seem not to be feasible (again offering explanations). While some members may be disappointed that their ideas are not used, they nevertheless feel that some action will be taken based on their input, and this feeling is far

## VISION ENGINEERING

A process called "vision engineering" has been used by such companies as Bridgestone/Firestone, Norsk Hydro, Sears, and U.S. Cellular to develop an organizational vision statement that is truly meaningful. Developed by Gemeni Consulting, the process begins with an executive team entering a room and finding a long table bearing about 100 stacks of cards at one end. Printed on the cards in each stack is a single fact or a demographic, social, technological or economic trend—such as "Baby-boomers are reaching 50," "Work schedules are more flexible," or "The power of microprocessors will continue to increase." Some cards are industry specific: A beverage maker's executives found a card stating that store brands are becoming more important. All the cards hold true statements developed on the basis of the consultants' research, advice from outside experts, and industry trends the executives themselves have identified. All the executives walk around the table studying the cards. Their objective is to string sets of cards together and put "headlines" on the strings. For example, cards stating "Increased use of credit cards," "Growing value of brand equity," "Rising number of Internet users," and "Ability to use technology to do specific market segmentation" might be strung together and headlined, "It's possible to bypass retailers to sell branded merchandise on the Web."

When everyone has taped a few strings and headlines to the wall, small groups debate, edit, and perhaps combine them. The groups then report to the team as a whole for another round of debate. When this phase is done, the team should have 6 to 12 headlines, each telling a story about something happening in their business world, and each a factor that should drive change.

The next phase of the exercise is for the team to figure out how each headline affects each link of their organizational chain, from research and development to customer service, for every line of business. The headlines are made into lists of threats and opportunities and lead to the final phase: a look at the capabilities and assets the company has or must develop if it is to meet the threats, take advantage of the opportunities, and ride the waves of change the future is going to bring. Thus, rather than producing a high-flown statement of vision, this process produces a cluster of opportunities, supported by a set of existing and to-be-developed assets, and bounded by a realistic view of how the world is changing. As such, it avoids the "groupthink" pitfall described by one CEO, who observed, "There is a fine line between vision and hallucination."

Source: Thomas A. Stewart, "A Refreshing Change: Vision Statements That Make Sense," *Fortune*, 134:6. (September 30, 1996): 195–96.

---

more satisfying than being told "I'll get back to you with my decision" (particularly if the leader never gets back to them).

In some situations, however, you may not have the ability or desire to make an on-the-spot commitment. Then you must use the "I'll get back to you" statement, but you also should tell them when and how you'll get back to them: "I'll send you all a memo next week telling you what I have decided" or "We'll meet again next Tuesday at this same time so I can present my decisions to you and answer any questions." Do not, under any circumstances, leave the group hanging without any feedback or follow-up.

Democratic leadership adheres to the principle of "one person, one vote." The leader simply facilitates the meeting while group members interact, make decisions, and solve problems. In democratic meetings, decision-making power and group interaction are shared among all members. The leader has no more power in making the decision than does any other group member. However, he or she does control the methods used by the group, setting the agenda they will follow, controlling interaction among them, and even deciding how decisions will be made.

In democratic groups, decisions can be made in several ways:

- *Consensus.* Consensus is probably the ideal method of decision making. The group simply discusses the topic until everyone agrees. In Japan and among some religious sects (such as the Quakers), decision making by consensus is rigidly followed; nothing is decided until everyone agrees. Such decision making is desirable in that everyone supports the decision arrived at by the group, but it is also disadvantageous if there are time limits. As an extreme example, the Quakers debated the issue of slavery during the nineteenth century for nearly 50 years; they finally concluded their debates (without reaching consensus) long after the Civil War was over. If your group cannot reach consensus within a reasonable time period, you should move to some other technique for making a decision.[6]

- *Group ratings or rankings.* There are mathematical techniques for arriving at compromise solutions. If, for example, two alternatives remain and the group cannot choose between them, hand everyone a sheet of paper and ask them to rate each alternative on a scale from 0 to 10 (with 0 meaning it is a totally unacceptable solution, 5 meaning the solution is largely neutral, and 10 meaning it is the perfect solution to the problem). Then collect the ratings, calculate the average rating for each alternative. If several alternatives remain, you might ask the group members individually to rank-order them (a ranking of 1 for their favorite, 2 for their second favorite, and so on). Collect the rankings, calculate the average ranking for each alternative, and select the one with the lowest number. Either ratings or rankings can help the group make a decision without there being any "winners" or "losers;" everyone's ratings or rankings had an impact on the decision.

- *Process of elimination.* Sometimes no alternative emerges as clearly the best. The strategy then might be to eliminate the worst. One technique for achieving this is called the "murder board." An alternative is written on a large sheet of paper or blackboard at the front of the room, and the group then tries to "kill" the idea by listing everything that could possibly be wrong with it. When they have run out of ideas, the next alternative is put up and subjected to the same treatment. The alternative that receives the fewest objections or has the fewest serious problems is chosen. Sometimes, however, all the alternatives are "killed;" then the group must generate new solutions to the problem or new decisions they can make.

- *Majority vote.* In small groups, the majority vote method generally should be avoided. Whenever there is a vote, someone loses. This minority may be embarrassed, resentful, angry, frustrated, and so on, and they are not

*Some organizational groups work without much formal leadership. Even in this informal context, group members need to agree on goals and procedures and divide roles and responsibilities. When teams can do this, even without formal structure, they often accomplish a great deal.*

likely to support the group's decision. Granted, there are times (such as when parliamentary procedure is used) when majority votes are called for, but in most meetings, some other method of decision making should be employed whenever possible.

## Laissez-Faire Meetings

Laissez-faire leadership occurs when the leader has virtually no role in the meeting. If, for example, a supervisor asks an employee to conduct the meeting while the supervisor sits at the back of the room or if the boss announces in advance that he or she will not attend a particular meeting so that a less inhibited discussion might occur, he or she is practicing laissez-faire leadership. If this leadership style is to be effective, it ought to be occasional and strategic. Since the laissez-faire leader gives away power, the group takes on both control and responsibility for its actions.

In a sense, any meeting can be a laissez-faire meeting; the leader has only to appoint a substitute leader, sit in back, and let things happen as they may, or for strategic reasons (like discouraging groupthink) not attend the meeting at all. In one type of laissez-faire meeting, facilitation by a leader is required, but decision making and interaction are almost entirely within the control of the group. This type is the team-building meeting.

While different authors suggest different team-building strategies, they generally agree on the goals team building should achieve. First, it should cause the group members to agree on their common goals and objectives. Second, it should sort out the roles each member will play in working toward the goals and objectives. Third, it should cause the group to decide on the procedures they will follow when working together. Fourth, it should help them arrive at mutually satisfactory relationships with one another. All four of these might be achieved in a single meeting lasting as long as three or four days, or they might be accomplished one at a time through a series of meetings.

Littlejohn describes one common approach to team building that requires two one-day sessions.[7] The first day is devoted to a discussion of members' perceptions of the organization and of the team members themselves. They exchange opinions and ideas about the organization as a place in which to work, and they exchange knowledge about themselves. The second day focuses on planning and goal setting. Members deal with such issues as mission (Why do we as a team exist?), situation (Where are we now?), and strategies (How are we going to reach our goals?). Procedures such as these ultimately achieve the goals of team building.

Several specific techniques can be used to encourage interaction and achieve team-building objectives. For instance, you might have participants individually (or in small groups) develop a list of habits or practices they think the team should develop, modify, or improve. You might have them address the question "Why do we exist as a functioning team?" Have them report their answers. Then, from the composite list produced by all groups, have the groups meet again and rank the answers according to their importance. Another interesting question members might discuss in small groups is "What would we be like if we were the 'ideal' team?" Have each group report its answers and write them on a blackboard or flip pad. Then have the groups meet again and, taking each characteristic one at a time, answer the question "Is this us?" That is, does the overall team have that characteristic? Again, have the groups report their answers. Finally, for those characteristics where the consensus of the group is no, ask everyone, "Is this characteristic important?" If the consensus is yes, an area needing change has been identified.

The next step is to move the group toward analyzing and solving the problem. To begin, you might put the members into small groups and then assign each group one or more of the characteristics needing change. For each characteristic, have the group answer the question, "Why are we not like this now?" Have them report their answers. In doing so, they will have identified the causes of the problems confronting the team. Then, assign each small group one or more of the characteristics identified as needing change. Ask the groups to develop the longest possible list of ways the group might achieve each characteristic. Practicality should not be a concern; wild and crazy ideas should be encouraged. Have the groups report their lists of possible solutions. For each possible solution reported by a small group, ask the entire group, "Will you do this?" If the general feeling seems affirmative, ask, "How?" Record the answers as the team's action plan.

Finally, to improve relationships among group members, give each individual member enough sheets of paper so that he or she can write a message to every other individual member. Then instruct the participants to write their own name and the name of the participant to whom they are writing at the top of each page. Finally, ask them to provide information related to three statements:

"If you were to do more of the following, it would help me to do my job better."

"If you were to do less of or stop doing the following, it would help me to do my job better."

"If you would continue to do the following, it would help me to do my job better."

When everyone has finished writing, have them exchange messages so that everyone has one message from every other member. Then have each member write his or her own personal action plan, listing commitments for the following statements:

"I will keep doing the following."

"I will do less of or stop doing the following."

"I will continue doing the following."

These statements of personal commitment should be taped to the walls of the meeting room for everyone to see, and members should be allowed to walk around the room and read everyone else's sheet. Copies of the sheets also are kept after the meeting to serve as reminders of the pledges each member made.

In a sense, the team-building meeting is not really a laissez-faire meeting in the stereotypic sense, because the leader actively participates by asking questions, recording answers, and assigning tasks to individuals or small groups. However, all decisions are made by the group with no input from the leader or facilitator, so that all authority is delegated by the leader to them. Indeed, some executives hire consultants specializing in team building to come to the organization and conduct these meetings. In those situations, the executive exerts true laissez-faire leadership.

## SELECTING A LEADERSHIP STYLE: CRITERIA

No one approach to leading a group is always best. Each situation must be examined to determine which style of leadership will be most effective. Several factors should be considered when selecting a style (and corresponding meeting agenda). First, *group expectations* are important. What sort of leadership does the group expect you to provide? *Group purposes* should also be taken into account. What is the group trying to achieve? Learning, socializing, or team building require minimum leader control, while communicating specific information to the group is much more directive. *Group methods* are another consideration. Some group processes, such as brainstorming or rating problem priorities, require strict procedural control, while others, such as discussing a problem's underlying causes, can be done with virtually no leadership. *Time* is also a consideration. Participation takes time, while announcements can be given quickly. If a decision must be made at once, autocratic leadership may be required.

In choosing a leadership style, *group members' skills and maturity* should also be considered. Experienced, mature group members require less guidance and control than do new, inexperienced members. Moreover, the more people participate, the better they become at participation. Thus, gradually giving more and more participation to group members is one way of increasing the skills and maturity of the group. *The leader's own skill and confidence* are also factors to be considered. In general, directive leadership is easier to exert than consultative or democratic leadership. The latter two require skill in listening, handling conflict, controlling group interaction, and so on. Thus, as leaders become more skilled, they tend to become more participative over time.

Finally, the kind of leadership style most appropriate in a given situation will depend, in part, upon the *need for group support* and the *group's interest and involvement* in the issues under discussion. Some decisions need the active endorsement of the group. In addition, participation in decision making increases the commitment of those making the decision. Simply being told what to do or how to do it minimizes commitment and motivation. And, of course, the more controversial, involving, and interesting the issue being discussed, the more the members of the group will want, and should be encouraged, to participate.

---

### KEY CONCEPTS 13.1    Different Ways of Leading Meetings

- Autocratic meetings take place when the leader does all the talking and makes all the decisions.
- Consultative meetings occur when the leader encourages group input but keeps the final decision for himself or herself.
- Democratic meetings share power so that the group leader has the same amount of decision-making power as everyone else.

- Laissez-faire meetings have no formal leader and are governed by leadership functions played by each member spontaneously.
- The determination of which approach to use should be driven by group expectations, purposes and methods, time available, group and leader skill and maturity levels, and the need for group support for the decisions made.

---

## CONDUCTING GROUP MEETINGS: HANDLING PROBLEM PARTICIPANTS

As group leader, you will frequently encounter group members whose behavior is not helpful to the group. And as group leader, it will become your responsibility to deal with these people. On occasion, group pressure or some assertive group member will bring the problem participant back into line, but as a rule, the group will look to you, literally and figuratively, to take some action.

While it is impossible to anticipate every bizarre behavior that can occur in a group, we have compiled some common problem behaviors and some techniques whereby a leader can address them. Problem behaviors fall into two types: members who talk too much and prevent others from participating and members who don't talk or participate enough. Specific problem types in each category are listed next, along with some strategies you might use to deal with them.

*Show-offs* know a great deal about the topic and are eager to prove it. They dominate the interaction out of a desire to exhibit their in-depth knowledge, and in so doing, they prevent everyone else from talking. To deal with a show-off, you might politely interrupt with a summarizing statement and ask someone else a direct question or interrupt with an observation: "Ken, you've made some interesting points, but I want everyone to have a chance. Let's hear what Tanya thinks about this." In addition, you could assign the member some specific project, such as gathering information or developing recommendations, and then have him present these to the group for their discussion.

*Quick and helpful* members know all the right answers, but in providing them, they keep other members from participating. Unlike the show-off, their motive is not to exhibit skill and win approval but simply to help the group. You might manage such members by tactfully interrupting them and asking direct questions of other members, by talking about the interaction ("Juan, I really appreciate your ideas. Now let's see what someone else might contribute.") or by assigning the member a communication role, such as "idea evaluator." Before a meeting or during a break, for example, you might approach the member and say, "You really know a lot about this. Would you mind helping me evaluate the ideas that the other members contribute? We'll get their ideas, and then you indicate which seems best." Generally, the member will appreciate having such a clear and important function.

*Ramblers* babble incessantly during meetings, and invariably take the group away from the topic and onto something else. Other group members are quick to recognize and react to this sort of person: As soon as she begins to speak, they look at each other or cast their eyes heavenward out of frustration. The leader must step in. For example, when the rambler stops for a breath, thank her, rephrase one of her statements to make it relevant to the topic, and move back to that topic with a question to the group. Alternatively, you might interrupt and ask a direct question of someone else. Finally, you could refer to the agenda or, if the topic is written on the blackboard or an easel pad, point to the board or pad and ask the member which topic she is discussing. This method is potentially embarrassing to the member, however, and could cause anger or resentment.

*Arguers* constantly disagree with others, try to make trouble, and seem generally hostile. Such behavior disrupts the group, and it may be motivated by any number of things: frustration at not being the leader, dislike for the other group members, general crankiness, and so on. To prevent this behavior from upsetting and frustrating the other members, the leader must deal with it relatively quickly. You could seat the disruptive member next to you, making it easier for you to control him and to break in when arguments begin. You also might talk with the member privately and describe the behaviors you have observed. Ask the member to tell you what problems or concerns he has. Finally, if all else fails, you might privately ask the member to leave the group.

*Side conversationalists* insist on conducting private meetings of their own. Usually, a group will have two such problem members, who will be seen whispering or muttering to each other during the meeting. Such behavior is disruptive to other members and distracts these two participants from the group proceedings. To deal with this situation, you could direct a question to one of the conversationalists: "Kim, what do you think of that?" Kim either will have to answer, which automatically brings her back into the discussion, or she will have no idea what you are talking about, and her embarrassment will keep her involved in the discussion, at least for a while. In addition, you could talk privately to the conversationalists and express your concern about their behavior. Finally, if the same two people continually converse during meetings, assign seats for the next meeting with these two members at opposite sides of the group.

*Complainers* blame the group's problems on things not under the control of the group: management, company policy, the economy, and so on. They would rather gripe about the evils of these things than deal with the problem the group faces. In addition, they adopt a "what's the use" attitude that may cause apathy among other group members. To manage a complainer, you might address her directly and point out that some things cannot be changed by the group. Rather, the goal of the group is to operate as best it can under the present system. Alternatively, you might ask the member for a solution to her problem: "Well, Carol, what do you think we should do about the economy?" When she answers, "We can't do anything about it," ask, "Then should we just give up and go home?" She and other members will say no, enabling you to say, "Then what should we do?" In so doing, you will bring the group back to the topic and illustrate the futility of the member's complaints.

*Selfish* members have a problem of their own that they want to discuss. They continually bring the group back to that problem, thus moving the group away from the topic at hand. To handle a selfish member, you could have the group discuss the member's problem. Get their opinions and recommendations; than return to the original topic. In addition, you might talk about the behavior and suggest that the member's problem be considered when the group has completed its current task: "John, you keep raising this problem. How about if we hold off on it for a while and talk about it when we have finished what we're doing?" Then deal with the member's problem when the group finishes the topic at hand. Finally, you could talk privately with the member about his problem and see if a solution can be developed outside the group.

*Poor speakers* lack communication skills: they speak too softly, do not speak clearly, express ideas poorly, and so on. The ideas may be good, but no one can tell because the member is inaudible or incomprehensible. To assist this sort of group member, repeat her ideas in your own words: "In other words, you're suggesting that. . . ." In addition, you may need to repeat the member's comments for everyone to hear, or ask the member to repeat her comments while she stands, faces the group, and speaks loudly. However, do not use this strategy if it is likely to embarrass the member.

*Squabblers* are two or more members who simply dislike one another and argue frequently as a result. You must be careful to distinguish between personality conflicts, which are disruptive to the group, and topic-based conflicts, which are based on real disagreements over the topic. When two members argue over several different conflicts and give off nonverbal cues indicating real dislike for each other, the leader needs to step in. For example, interrupt their argument with a direct question to one of them. This

The movement by many organizations to teams has been particularly troublesome from a diversity perspective, according to Leigh Thompson, an organizational behavior professor at Northwestern University's J. L. Kellogg Graduate School of Management. "The research suggests women are viewed more harshly than men," she said. "Even people who say out loud they don't carry prejudices will revert to classic sex-role thinking in a group dynamic. In any team situation, there is an early natural status competition based on gender, age and race."

Source: Janet Kidd Stewart, "Teams Don't Always Work," *Chicago Tribune* (July 5, 1998): sec. 13, p. 7.

forces that member to talk to you, enabling you then to get other members involved in the interaction. Or you could summarize the comments each has made and then move on to another topic. Third, you might seat the two so that it is difficult for them to see one another. Finally, if other strategies fail, you might meet privately with the two of them, describe how their behaviors are affecting the group, and involve them in solving their own conflict.

A recent article in *Communication Briefings* identified a few more types of difficult group members, along with some suggested methods you might use to handle such people when they try to seize control of a meeting.[8]

- *Monopolizers* interrupt often, ramble, and repeat themselves because they enjoy hearing themselves talk. To manage them, don't argue but don't hesitate to confront them. Wait for them to take a breath and interrupt them by name. Note that they have made their point and immediately invite someone else to comment on the topic.

- *Distracters* also seek attention, and to get it they may bring up irrelevant topics that waste time. To handle such distractions, firmly halt the distracter, restate the meeting purpose, and ask the members to answer a specific question that gets them refocused on the main topic.

- *Skeptics* continually find fault with what everyone else says. To manage them, have a friendly talk with them before the meeting and firmly say what behaviors you expect. If that fails, firmly cut them off during the meeting by repeating that you want solutions, not criticisms, and then asking them to contribute.

- *Snipers* use snide comments and quips, often in quiet stage whispers, to undercut others. It may be effective to shine the spotlight on them by asking them to share their comments with everyone. Often they will decline to do so out of embarrassment and discontinue their sniping.

Certainly, there are other types of members who talk too much. However, the basic strategies described above can be applied to any member who prevents others from talking. The key is to determine the motives underlying the member's behaviors and then take action appropriate to those motives.

*Uninterested* members simply do not care about the group or its topic. As a result, they sit silently, perhaps looking out the window or doing something of their own (like writing notes or reading a book). To deal with this situation, you might direct a question to the member; ask for experiences as they relate to the topic. Be careful, however, to ask something the member can answer; otherwise, you add embarrassment to the apathy he is already feeling. In addition, you could assign the member specific responsibility. Have him collect information, list possible solutions, and so on. Be careful of giving that person some task vital to the group, however; the member might not come through on the task he is assigned. Other approaches are to meet privately with the member to discuss what the problem might be, form groups only on a voluntary basis (allowing uninterested members to leave), or seat the member in the middle of the group so that all interaction occurs around him (apathetic members usually try to sit at the back or on the fringes of the group, where they go largely unnoticed). Finally, you could play the devil's advocate: Ask the member for his opinion, and when it is given, disagree. By starting an argument with the member, you draw him into the group, and you may stir his interest.

*Listeners* are interested in the topic but prefer to listen rather than speak. They do nothing disruptive and may even provide helpful nonverbal reinforcement (head nods, attentive posture) to those who talk. But they do not contribute any ideas. To build a listener's participation, you might ask her to give an opinion whenever the member shows either agreement or disagreement nonverbally: "Susan, you seem to agree with Nancy's point. Why do you feel that way?" This sort of question is useful because you know Susan has an answer (she has been showing agreement nonverbally) and because your question draws her into the discussion. You also could direct questions to the member or, if you know something about the member, try to bring the topic around to an area in which the member has some experience. Then ask the member to recount those experiences. Or finally, you could simply accept her preference to listen.

*Shy* group members simply are not very assertive. Nonverbal cues help you to identify them: They occasionally seem about to speak, but then some other member begins talking and they remain quiet. Directing a question to the member (be sure it is a question he can answer) can be helpful, or you might frequently ask the member for his agreement. By turning to him for approval, you increase the member's standing in the eyes of the other group members, making them more likely to involve the member as well. In addition, when the member seems to want to talk, call on him, even if it means cutting off a more assertive member who has just begun to speak.

*Fearful* members suffer stage fright in group situations. They are afraid of ridicule or failure, or of seeming stupid in the group's eyes. Rather than risk rejection or disapproval, they simply sit quietly. To gain a fearful member's participation, you could ask her a question that you know she can answer and then praise the answer given. In addition, you might turn frequently to the member for agreement or approval, thus building her status in the eyes of other members. Finally, you might seat the member next to you in an effort to build an association between the two of you. Your status in the group will reflect well on her.

Again, there are many other reasons why members choose not to participate. However, by controlling the overly talkative members and drawing out the nonparticipants, you can equalize members' contributions to the group interaction.

| KEY CONCEPTS 13.2 | Types of Problem Participants |
|---|---|

| Members who talk too much: | Members who talk too little: |
|---|---|
| The show-off | The uninterested person |
| The quick and helpful person | The listener |
| The rambler | The shy person |
| The arguer | The fearful person |
| The side conversationalist | |
| The complainer | |
| The selfish person | |
| The poor speaker | |
| The squabblers | |

## CONDUCTING LARGE GROUP MEETINGS: PARLIAMENTARY PROCEDURE

Generally speaking, the larger the group, the more difficult it is for the group leader to control the meeting. In very large group meetings, such as stockholders' meetings or meetings of legislative bodies, the leader frequently chooses to use a very structured format to ensure orderly communication. Perhaps the most commonly used large group format is parliamentary procedure.

The rules of parliamentary procedure were not developed by any single person or group of people. Rather, they evolved over hundreds of years through the experiences of thousands of self-governing assemblies. They have become somewhat complicated over time, but their basic principles have rarely changed. If you understand the principles, the rules make more sense and are easier to apply. These principles include:

*The majority rules.* Obviously, this is a democratic approach to group communication. Rarely can total agreement be reached on any issue. To have some basis for action in cases where disagreement occurs, the principle is followed that the preferences of the majority are carried out.

*The rights of the minority are protected.* The majority cannot be granted unlimited power. Every member of the assembly has individual rights, regardless of whether he or she happens to agree with the majority. These rights include the right to a secret ballot, the right to nominate for office, and the protection of the constitution and bylaws of the organization. As leader you must ensure that these rights are protected and that no one is steamrollered by the majority.

*Business must be accomplished.* Meetings are held to bring about some action. The group welcomes free presentation of all the facts and opinions on any problem under discussion, but the discussion cannot consume an entire meeting, nor should it get in the way of getting things done.

*Feelings must be respected.* We must be careful not to lose sight of individual feelings as we conduct the group's business and control its interaction. Just as courtesy is important in all our social relationships, so too must it be maintained in large group meetings.

Obviously, these four principles will contradict one another at times; for example, the rights of a minority may interfere with the rapid accomplishment of the group's business or with the rule of the majority. As group leader or chairperson, you must do all you can to maintain a balance among these principles. The rules of parliamentary law have been developed to help you achieve such a balance.

The order of business used by a large group will vary somewhat. However, a typical group agenda includes the following elements:

1. *Call to order.*   After determining that a quorum (the minimum number needed to transact business, usually a simple majority of the total membership) is present, the chairperson gets the attention of the group (often by rapping a gavel on the podium) and says, "The meeting will please come to order."

2. *Opening ceremonies.*   Many groups open their meetings with a prayer, pledge of allegiance, song, and so on. If such a ceremony is used by this group, the chairperson next would say, "Let us open our meeting by . . ."

3. *Roll call.*   If a roll call is desired to determine who is in attendance, the chairperson says, "The secretary will please call the roll." Occasionally, she might add, "Members will answer to their names by . . . ," stating the way in which members should respond to their names.

4. *Reading of the minutes.*   The chairperson next says, "The secretary will read the minutes of the last meeting." When the minutes have been read, he or she then asks, "Are there any corrections or additions to the minutes?" If none is offered, the chairperson states, "The minutes stand approved as read." If corrections are offered (and agreed to by the chairperson and the assembly), the secretary is instructed to make the necessary changes. Then the chairperson states, "The minutes stand approved as corrected."

5. *Reports.*   After the reading of the minutes, the chairperson typically calls on the chairpersons of standing and special committees to make reports to the group. If there are no objections, the report is accepted by the group (not endorsed but filed for future reference). If any proposed action grows from a committee report, it is introduced later under "new business."

6. *Unfinished business.*   The chairperson says, "We now will consider any unfinished business." Anything left over or postponed from the previous meeting may be discussed and voted on at this time.

7. *New business.*   The chairperson says, "We will now consider any new business." As a rule, this portion of the meeting consumes most of the time spent by the group.

8. *Program.*   Occasionally, the group has some program (such as a speaker, film, or presentation) planned as part of the meeting. When no more new business is forthcoming, the chairperson asks, "Is there any further new business to come before this meeting? If not, will the chairperson of the

program committee (or other member in charge of the program) please take charge of the program planned for this meeting." The chairperson and secretary may then sit in the audience for the program.

9. *Miscellaneous, announcements, and so on.*    Before adjourning, the chairperson may ask if there are any announcements to be made, notes to be read, or other routine matters not requiring group action. Some groups do this earlier in the meeting, following the reading of the minutes.

10. *Adjournment.*    One of two procedures may be used to adjourn a meeting. If the meeting always adjourns at a fixed time and that time arrives, the chairperson may say, "The meeting is adjourned." If not, the chairperson may ask, "Is there a motion to adjourn?" In the latter case, some member of the group says, "I move we adjourn." This motion must be seconded by another group member, and it cannot be discussed. The motion is put to a vote, and the result announced: "The motion is adopted; the meeting is adjourned." In the highly unlikely event that the motion to adjourn is defeated, the chairperson would announce the vote and call for any additional new business on the assumption that the majority had something else they want to do before closing the meeting.

In large group settings where parliamentary procedure is used, the purpose of the meeting generally is to decide on various courses of action. Possible courses of action are suggested by the group members, who do so in the form of *motions* for discussion by the group. One such motion, as we already have seen, is the motion to adjourn—a suggestion that the meeting be terminated and everyone leave. Almost all decisions made by the group are handled in a similar fashion: A member suggests a course of action (that is, she states a motion), the group considers it, and ultimately a decision to adopt or reject that motion is made. The real "work" involved in leading a large group meeting is handling the members' motions and ensuing discussion while preserving the four principles we stated earlier.

Several steps are followed in handling motions offered by members. First, the member obtains the floor. The member rises, calling out, "Mr. (or Madam) Chairperson." In smaller or more informal groups, the member might remain seated and address the chair. The member should not rise without addressing the chair if he wants to obtain the floor. The chairperson then recognizes the member by saying the member's name, nodding in the member's direction, or in some other way referring to the member. The member should not speak until receiving recognition from the chair.

The member states the motion by saying, "I move that we . . . ," thus suggesting the action she wants the group to take. The motion should be as complete as possible so that no unnecessary amendments need be made but it should not be overly long and complicated. Long motions should be submitted in writing.

For a motion to be considered, it usually must be supported by at least one other group member. Thus, the next step is that the motion is seconded. The person giving the second need not rise; he only needs to call out, "Second" or "I second the motion." If no one seconds the motion, the chairperson may ask, "Is the motion seconded?" If still no one seconds the motion, the chairperson states, "The motion is lost for lack of a second." If a second is given, the chairperson then states the motion to the group by saying, "It has been moved and seconded that we. . . ." Then the chair calls for discussion: "Is there any discussion on the motion?"

The next step in the process is that members discuss the motion. Several points should be kept in mind here. Each member who wants to speak must first obtain the floor (be recognized by the chairperson), just as if a new motion were being offered. Discussion must be confined to the motion at hand, and the one who offered the motion usually is given first opportunity to discuss it. Usually, people are recognized as they stand and address the chair; however, if someone rises and interrupts the previous speaker, she is ruled out of order and not given the floor. If many people desire to speak, the chair tries to "alternate the floor," first recognizing someone in favor of the motion and then recognizing someone against it, giving each position a turn to speak. Any member who has already spoken once is not recognized until all members wanting to express themselves for the first time have done so. Finally, the chair does not offer her or his opinions on the motion; his or her job is simply to keep order.

Ultimately, the chair determines that the discussion is finished. When members stop rising to request recognition, the chairperson asks, "Is there any further discussion?" If some is offered, the chair repeats the question later. When no further discussion is offered, she or he proceeds to the next step, restating the motion. He or she might say, "If there is no further discussion, we are ready to vote. The question is on the motion to. . . ."

Next, the members vote on the motion. This can occur in several ways. Frequently, the group uses a voice vote, where the chairperson says, "As many as are in favor of the motion say aye; those opposed no." If the number of ayes (pronounced "I") clearly is larger than the number of nos, or vice versa, the decision is announced. The group also can vote by raising hands or by standing to show support for or opposition to the motion. If the motion requires a two-thirds majority, standing or hand-raising votes should be taken to enable the chairperson to count the votes. Members can request this type of vote by calling, "Division," or by saying, "I call for a division of the house." Then the chairperson must request that a standing vote be taken. Finally, a group can vote by secret ballot or by general consent. In the latter case, the chairperson says, "If there is no objection, we will . . ." (stating the action that the motion requires). The chairperson then pauses to allow members to object. If no one does, the motion is considered to be passed by unanimous approval; if an objection is offered, a vote is taken by voice, show of hands, standing, or ballot.

The chairperson has a right to vote whenever her or his vote will change the outcome. However, the chairperson may not want to reveal her or his opinions and thus may choose not to vote except in the case of a secret ballot. However, if the chairperson's vote will either create or break a tie, he or she may want to vote openly. A tie vote defeats a motion (majority rule means that half of those voting plus one must support the motion). By creating a tie with her or his vote, the chairperson would defeat a motion; by breaking a tie, the chairperson would carry the motion.

When the vote is taken, the chairperson announces the result of the vote. If there is no doubt of the result, the chairperson says, "The ayes have it; the motion is carried" or "The nos have it; the motion is defeated." Then the chairperson indicates the effect of this vote. He or she says, "We will therefore . . ." (stating the action that the motion requires the group to take). Finally, the chairperson moves to the next piece of business. If a main motion was voted on, the chairperson asks, "Is there any further business to come before us?"

There are different types of motions that group members can offer, and these must be handled in different ways. So far, we have primarily discussed main motions, motions that bring a subject before the group for consideration and action. However, other types of special motions require unusual handling. To be effective, the chairperson must be able to answer several questions in his or her own mind whenever a motion is offered and to then take appropriate action. These questions include:

What type of motion is it?

What motions may it displace in receiving the attention of the group, and which motions may displace it?

Does it require a second?

May it be discussed?

What vote does it require: majority or two-thirds?

To help you understand the types of motions you or other group members might make, we will consider some special motions that commonly occur. The first group are all considered *main motions*.

**1.** *The motion to take a matter "off the table."*   When some motion has been tabled or "placed on the table," discussion of that motion has been suspended temporarily. A member can bring the matter to the attention of the group again by moving that the original motion be taken off the table and considered by the group.

**2.** *The motion to reconsider action previously taken.*   This motion can be offered only by someone who voted in favor of the original motion, and its effect is to place the original motion before the group again as though a vote never had been taken. It is important to note, however, that a motion to reconsider is appropriate only for matters the group can undo; things that now cannot be changed should not be reconsidered. This motion is also appropriate only during the same meeting in which the original motion was passed or during the next meeting the group holds.

**3.** *The motion to repeal or rescind an action previously taken.*   This motion is similar to the preceding but is used in later meetings when the motion to reconsider is no longer appropriate. It can be offered by any member, and its effect is to reverse the action previously taken.

A second group of motions are *subsidiary motions,* which are applied to main motions to get them in proper shape so the group can take action on them. They include:

**1.** *The motion to amend.*   When the group does not like the wording of the main motion, they may change that wording by amending the motion. The group may add words, remove words, or substitute words; however, they can do only one of these things at a time (that is, they cannot simultaneously add some words, remove others, and substitute for still others). The maker of the main motion does not need to approve these changes; the majority vote of the group determines whether the main motion is amended. To amend a motion, a member rises, addresses the chair, and says, "I move we amend the motion by adding (removing, substituting) the words . . . after the words . . . so that the motion will read. . . ." This motion requires a second before it can be considered. The group may also want to amend the amendment, and this is moved in the same way. The process cannot be carried any further, however (that is, you cannot amend an amendment to an amendment). The voting order is (a) amendment to the amendment, (b) amendment, and (c) motion.

**2.** *The motion to refer to a committee.* The group may want to have some committee handle a matter rather than devoting time to the matter in this meeting. Thus, a member might rise, address the chair, and say, "I move we refer this motion to . . ." or "I move that a . . . committee be created to handle this matter."

**3.** *The motion to postpone to a particular time.* A member might rise, gain recognition, and say, "I move that we postpone consideration of this matter until our next meeting" or "I move that we postpone consideration of this matter for 10 minutes." A specific time must be stated, and it may not be beyond the next regular meeting of the group.

**4.** *The motion to put an end to discussion and vote at once.* If this motion is made and passed by two-thirds of the group, it immediately stops discussion and brings about an immediate vote on the matter before the group. To make such a motion, a member rises, is recognized, and says, "I move that we put an end to discussion on this matter." An alternative way of stating this motion is "I move the previous question."

**5.** *The motion to lay a matter on the table.* Like the motion to postpone consideration, this motion delays consideration of the matter at hand; however, it does not state any time limit. The person offering the motion simply says, "I move that this matter be laid on the table." If the motion is seconded and supported by a majority vote, discussion of the matter stops until the matter is taken off the table at some future time. If not seconded or supported by a majority vote, the motion to table is defeated, and discussion on the original matter continues.

*Incidental motions* make up the third motion group. They are offered during the course of a meeting when an unusual situation arises that needs immediate action by the group. These may be offered at virtually any time, and they must be decided upon before discussion returns to the matter at hand. Some common incidental motions are:

**1.** *A point of order.* When anyone makes a mistake in parliamentary law, any member may rise without being recognized and say, "Mr. (or Madam) Chairman, I rise to a point of order." The chairperson then will say, "State your point of order." The member then explains the error that was made. Usually, the chair will rule on the matter by stating, "Your point of order is well taken" (then making the necessary changes ) or "Your point of order is not well taken" (with no changes being made).

**2.** *An appeal from the decision of the chair.* Whenever the chairperson makes a decision that a member believes is wrong (including a decision on a point of order), the member may rise and say, "I appeal from the decision of the chair." If this motion is seconded, the member has a right to explain her position, the chair may defend himself or herself, and other members may speak on the matter. A vote is then taken, and the decision of the majority is followed no matter what the chairperson may think. A tie vote serves to uphold the chairperson's decision since it is assumed the chairperson would vote for himself or herself.

**3.** *A motion to suspend the rules.* This is done so that some procedure or motion normally out of order can be used or discussed. Rules may be suspended only for a specific purpose and for the limited time necessary to accomplish the proposed action. Many rules cannot be suspended, such as basic rules governing a quorum, voting requirements, or voting methods. For the most part, only procedural rules are suspended. The motion to suspend the rules requires a two-thirds majority for adoption.

**4.** *A motion to object to the consideration of some matter.* This allows the group to avoid the discussion of an issue because it is viewed as embarrassing, unnecessarily contentious, frivolous, or inopportune. This motion also requires a two-thirds majority for adoption. The only time the motion to object is in order is immediately after the objectionable motion has been stated by the presiding officer. If discussion of the motion has begun, it is too late to object to its consideration.

**5.** *A parliamentary inquiry.* This motion's purpose is simply to seek advice from the chairperson. This advice usually focuses on issues such as the appropriate parliamentary procedure to follow in making a particular motion. Whenever a group member is uncertain about how to refer some matter to a committee, how to word a motion properly, or how to nominate a candidate for office, she might conduct a parliamentary inquiry. Like other special motions designed to maintain the rules, the parliamentary inquiry may interrupt a speaker, although the chairperson may choose to hold her or his reply until the person who has the floor has concluded.

The final group of motions, *privileged motions,* are of such importance that they can be made at almost any time. They include:

**1.** *The motion to adjourn.* This motion is for closing the meeting or sometimes, strategically, for terminating the discussion of a particular question. This motion may not interrupt a speaker, but it is in order at any time. As we pointed out earlier, it is neither amendable nor debatable, and it must be put to an immediate vote.

**2.** *The motion to recess the group.* Unlike the motion to adjourn, the motion to recess the group is intended to temporarily disband the meeting. Recesses are occasionally needed to obtain additional information, to discuss voting procedures, to rest, or to count votes. The motion to recess may interrupt any business other than the process of voting. It may not interrupt a speaker.

**3.** *The question of privilege.* This motion requires that the presiding officer deal with some situation affecting the welfare of the organization's members, such as fire, offensive remarks, or poor acoustics. The question of privilege is unusual in that it needs no second, and it can interrupt both business and speaker. The presiding officer may decide the matter or may submit it to a vote of the group.

This list is not intended to be exhaustive but to highlight major motions that are often used in formal business meetings.

# TABLE 13.1
## Order of Precedence of Motions

| Types of Motions[a] | Requires Second? | May Be Discussed? | May Be Amended? | Vote Needed |
|---|---|---|---|---|
| *Privileged:* | | | | |
| To fix the time of the next meeting | Yes | No | Yes | Majority |
| To adjourn | Yes | No | No | Majority |
| To recess | Yes | No | Yes | Majority |
| Question of privilege | No | No | No | Chair [e] |
| *Incidental:* | | | | |
| An appeal from the decision of the chair | Yes | Yes [b] | No | Majority |
| A point of order | No | No | No | Chair [e] |
| To suspend the rules | Yes | No | No | Two-thirds |
| To object to consideration | No | No | No | Two-thirds |
| Parliamentary inquiry | No | No | No | Chair [d] |
| *Subsidiary:* | | | | |
| To lay on the table | Yes | No | No | Majority |
| To put an end to discussion (to call the previous question) | Yes | No | No | Two-thirds |
| To limit debate | Yes | No | Yes | Two-thirds |
| To postpone to a certain time | Yes | Yes | Yes | Majority |
| To refer to a committee | Yes | Yes | Yes | Majority |
| To amend a motion | Yes | Yes [b] | Yes | Majority |
| To postpone indefinitely | Yes | Yes | No | Majority |
| *Main:* | | | | |
| An ordinary main motion | Yes | Yes | Yes | Majority |
| To take a matter off the table | Yes | No | No | Majority |
| To reconsider action previously taken | Yes [c] | Yes [b] | No | Majority |
| To repeal or rescind action previously taken | Yes [c] | Yes | Yes | Majority [d] |

[a]Listed in order of precedence from highest to lowest; a second motion cannot be considered unless it has higher precedence than the motion already before the group.
[b]May be discussed, unless it applies to an undebatable question.
[c]Opens the main motion to discussion as well.
[d]If prior notice is given that such a motion is forthcoming, a majority is needed; if no such notice is given, a two-thirds vote is needed.
[e]Requires only chairperson's decision; a majority vote is needed if appealed from chair.

As we said earlier, the chairperson must know not only the types of motions, but their *precedence*—that is, what motions may displace other motions. One motion may replace another already before the house if the new motion has sufficient power or precedence to do so. It is important that you know which motions have which levels of precedence. If one motion is under consideration and another is made, you must decide whether the new motion is appropriate for consideration or whether consideration of the new motion should be denied until discussion of the original motion is completed.

To help you keep track of precedence, the chart in Table 13.1 lists types of motions in order of precedence. It also indicates whether each motion requires a second from another group member, whether discussion of the motion is allowed, whether the motion can be amended, and what level of voting support (simple majority or two-thirds) is needed.

Again, parliamentary procedure is complicated, and our purpose here is simply to acquaint you with basic decisions you will have to make when conducting large group meetings under these rules. For a more detailed and complete understanding of parliamentary procedure, you should consult one of the many excellent books devoted to that topic.[9]

## CONDUCTING MEETINGS VIA TECHNOLOGY

With the advent of new technology for communicating within organizations, it is not surprising to find that meetings, too, are taking place through technological channels. Telephone conference calls have been commonplace for years, of course, and videoconferences are growing in popularity as well. In addition, a new technology called "spontaneous area networking" enables participants to connect their PCs instantly with others in the room and with people who are off site. This technology allows anyone to make and record notes on "whiteboards" projected on a screen, then download them to individual computers.[10]

"Cybermeetings" are meetings involving participants in scattered locations linked by videoconferencing equipment or e-mail. Because of decentralization, a projected increase in the number of meetings, and the incidence of crash projects that require people to interact intensely (sometimes for weeks or months), cybermeetings probably will see increasing usage. Videoconferencing equipment on desktops will eliminate the need to run to another floor, to another building, or onto a waiting jet. In addition, "groupware" makes it possible for people to work together even if they are scattered all over the world.

This in turn will create new roles, according to Michael Michalko:[11]

- *The wizard.* The primary goal of the wizard should be to help make collaborative technologies easy to use so that meeting participants aren't overwhelmed. The wizard can mastermind the technology so that people weak in technology can concentrate more on the work and less on the machines.

- *The scribe.* Typing into technology may frustrate people who absorb information visually and verbally, and it may stifle creative thought. He recommends using an assigned or paid scribe to keep everyone on track.

- *Express mail carrier.* To encourage feedback, have everyone play express mail carrier by using the anonymous remailer in the intranet (company e-mail system) to send the boss complaints, suggestions, and ideas.

"Teleconferencing" is a useful way to conduct meetings involving participants across the globe. To make the best use of teleconference meetings, Solomon suggests:[12]

- Use the best equipment possible; the quality of sound varies tremendously.

- Allow individual participants ample time to learn to use their technology.

- The group should choose a conference leader and rotate that leadership.

- Written agendas should be distributed to everyone in advance, perhaps via e-mail.

- The group should decide in advance how long the conference will last.

- The conference leader should state the goals of the discussion at the beginning and review any updates since the previous teleconference.

- The leader should encourage everyone to participate, calling on particularly quiet individuals or encouraging them later with a phone call or e-mail.

- The group should be sensitive to time zone differences; since someone will always be inconvenienced, it may be best to rotate the times meetings are held.

- Someone should write and e-mail to the others a brief summary of the main points covered during the conference.

Certainly, new challenges are going to arise as technology becomes more prominent in the conduct of group meetings. Nevertheless, some of the hints listed above may prove useful.

## FOLLOWING UP MEETINGS

Whenever a meeting has been concluded, regardless of the style used to conduct that meeting, some follow-up must occur. At least three things need to be done. First, the group should be asked to examine their own proceedings and evaluate how effective the meeting was. Such evaluation can be done at the end of the meeting (by asking the participants to take a moment to express their thoughts in writing or to discuss briefly how well they thought the meeting went) or some time after the meeting (by distributing questionnaires about the meeting to the members and asking them to return the completed questionnaires to the leader). As a brief, informal approach to evaluating a meeting, we have found it useful to ask the participants to write their answers to three questions:

What part (or parts) of the meeting did you like most?

What part (or parts) of the meeting did you like least?

How might future meetings of this type be improved?

More complicated, but thorough, is the "Meeting Effectiveness Questionnaire" shown in Table 13.2. By having members complete the questionnaire, the leader can get quantitative feedback on each element of the group's proceedings. Regardless of the form and timing of feedback, groups should almost always be asked to evaluate the quality of the meeting in which they participated.

Second, the actions of the meeting should be reported to those who need to be advised. The report need not necessarily be a long set of notes or minutes but should contain enough information that those who could not attend or who will be affected by the results will know what was done and what was planned. In our view, such reports serve as useful reminders to the group participants and as notice of the group's achievements to other groups and individuals throughout the organization. Thus, we recommend that after every important meeting, a report be distributed both to the attendees and to anyone else who might have even a passing interest in the group's actions.

# TABLE 13.2
**Meeting Effectiveness Questionnaire**

Circle the number that best describes how you feel about each statement below.

Key:    1 = Strongly Disagree    2 = Disagree    3 = Neutral    4 = Agree    5 = Strongly Agree

| | | | | | | |
|---|---|---|---|---|---|
| 1. I understood the propose of the meeting clearly. | 1 | 2 | 3 | 4 | 5 |
| 2. The persons most directly involved with the purpose of the meeting were present. | 1 | 2 | 3 | 4 | 5 |
| 3. All members had the opportunity to participate by expressing their views and opinions. | 1 | 2 | 3 | 4 | 5 |
| 4. I had sufficient time and information to prepare for the meeting. | 1 | 2 | 3 | 4 | 5 |
| 5. The leader of the meeting kept things on track and minimized time wasted on side issues. | 1 | 2 | 3 | 4 | 5 |
| 6. I understand what the results of the meeting mean for me. | 1 | 2 | 3 | 4 | 5 |
| 7. I support the results of the meeting. | 1 | 2 | 3 | 4 | 5 |
| 8. The leader of the meeting was open to all ideas presented. | 1 | 2 | 3 | 4 | 5 |
| 9. I understood what was expected of me at the meeting. | 1 | 2 | 3 | 4 | 5 |
| 10. Ideas were presented clearly and were easily understood by everyone present. | 1 | 2 | 3 | 4 | 5 |
| 11. The participants seemed to want to work for the good of the group. | 1 | 2 | 3 | 4 | 5 |
| 12. At the conclusion of the meeting, it was obvious to me that everyone knew what was expected of him or her. | 1 | 2 | 3 | 4 | 5 |
| 13. The proper amount of time was allocated to this meeting. | 1 | 2 | 3 | 4 | 5 |
| 14. The agenda or topics of the meeting were clear and easy to follow. | 1 | 2 | 3 | 4 | 5 |
| 15. The meeting facilities were comfortable and appropriate. | 1 | 2 | 3 | 4 | 5 |
| 16. Participation was spread evenly among the members; everyone talked about the same amount. | 1 | 2 | 3 | 4 | 5 |
| 17. Conflicts between group members were resolved quickly and to everyone's satisfaction. | 1 | 2 | 3 | 4 | 5 |
| 18. Decisions were made in ways that were fair to all group members. | 1 | 2 | 3 | 4 | 5 |
| 19. Members dealt courteously with one another. | 1 | 2 | 3 | 4 | 5 |
| 20. Each participant and all visual aids used during the meeting were easily visible to everyone. | 1 | 2 | 3 | 4 | 5 |

In the future, we might improve similar meetings by:

Third, the leader must check to be sure that commitments made during the meeting are carried out. Are people doing what they said they would do? Are they staying on schedule? Have they encountered new or unanticipated problems? Are there things the leader is committed to do for the group (such as get back to them with an answer)? In effect, the leader must monitor herself and the progress of the members as they do the things agreed to. Such monitoring might be achieved by speaking with members individually, asking for written progress reports, making occasional telephone calls to members, or calling another meeting.

Clearly, the work done by a group does not stop when the meeting concludes. Often, in fact, the meeting is only the beginning of the real effort. Effective, thorough follow-up is vital to the continuation of the things the group meeting began.

## SUMMARY

At one time or another, most of us find ourselves in the role of committee chairperson. We may not be managers or administrators in the formal sense, but we are leaders in that we plan and organize meetings, call and arrange for meeting rooms, and conduct the meeting when the other members arrive. Sometimes we chair on a one-shot basis, especially if we are working with an ad hoc group—or, more likely, we chair an ongoing committee, which may continue for months, or even years. Our ability to manage these meetings effectively will influence many important outcomes, such as our own professional well-being. Moreover, when we lead a group to make sound decisions, we make a really important contribution to the organization as a whole.

Most of our opportunities to lead groups occur in the context of small committee meetings, but on certain occasions, we are elected to leadership positions that require us to conduct business meetings involving much larger groups of people. These sorts of meetings necessitate the use of parliamentary procedure. Although the rules of parliamentary procedure may seem complicated at first, most can be learned with relative ease as one uses them over time. The rules of parliamentary procedure are all based on important principles, like the right of all members to have their views aired. That's why, for instance, limiting or restricting discussion requires the support of two-thirds of the organization's members. Other important motions grow from such principles as turn taking, the right of the majority to prevail, and the right of the minority to be protected. Most chairpersons have the support of a parliamentarian, so that parliamentary questions can be resolved as expediently and judiciously as possible. Even so, the more the chairperson knows about parliamentary procedure, the more smoothly each business meeting will proceed.

Whether we are leading small, informal groups or large business meetings, we will function more effectively if we think carefully about the meaning of leadership, prepare carefully, follow a plan or agenda, and understand something about the principles of group dynamics discussed earlier in this book. Through the way we communicate, by asking appropriate sorts of questions, by making timely procedural and organizational suggestions, and by listening carefully to the ideas of other group members, we have an excellent chance of being able to conduct really effective meetings.

# QUESTIONS FOR DISCUSSION

1. Why have meetings gained such a bad reputation in most modern organizations?
2. Why is it important to an organization to have effective meetings?
3. When should you avoid calling a meeting?
4. How do the facilities in which a meeting is held affect the success of that meeting?
5. In what types of situations are autocratic meetings most desirable? Consultative meetings? Democratic meetings? Laissez-faire meetings?
6. Why should majority vote be avoided as a decision-making device?
7. Why are team-building meetings important in an organization?
8. As a leader, how can you judge whether a group member's actions are harmful to the group as a whole?
9. What are the underlying principles of parliamentary procedures?
10. Describe five motions that you feel are critical to upholding these principles.

# EXERCISES

1. Write an announcement for a meeting (create your own purpose, list of attendees, and so on).
2. Conduct a mock meeting using the principles of parliamentary procedure.
3. Conduct a mock meeting using one of these leadership approaches: autocratic, democratic, consultative, or laissez-faire. Then have members complete the "Meeting Effectiveness Questionnaire" table. Have members report and explain their answers for each item on the questionnaire.
4. Conduct a mock meeting, and at the beginning of the meeting, assign some of the problem-member roles to some group participants. Do not announce which member has which role. Assign a leader to conduct the meeting. At the meeting's end, discuss how effectively the leader handled each problem participant.

# CASE application 13.1

For students pursuing a degree in the School of Business at the University of the Southern Pacific (USP), graduation requirements for undergraduates have remained unchanged for 10 years. Now, however, a special committee (composed of both faculty and students) has been established to examine the current requirements and likely initiate some changes.

Committee members are aware of certain widely perceived problems with the current system. Among them are the following:

1. Faculty complain that even seniors cannot write well.
2. Students' oral communication skills are perceived by faculty to be deficient.
3. Students can obtain the business degree without having been introduced to another culture or a foreign language.
4. In spite of faculty complaints about student skill deficits, grade inflation is rampant—the B is considered an average grade.
5. Students complain that the faculty, on the whole, are not very good at teaching. Most are more interested in their research and their graduate students.
6. Students complain that too many graduate students are used as graders, discussion leaders, and even lecturers.

The committee is also working in an organizational environment that includes the following factors:

1. The dean of the School of Business is concerned about dropping enrollments in business. Ten years ago, 55 percent of entering freshmen declared the intention of majoring in business. Now that figure has dropped to 30 percent.
2. With globalization an increasing reality in the business world, faculty agree that business students should be required to complete a foreign language and/or culture studies requirement. However, there are complications. First, many students currently choose business to avoid the foreign language requirement of the School of Liberal Arts and Sciences. Thus, adding that kind of new requirement to the business degree could lead to further enrollment problems.
3. The state legislature (USP is a public, state-supported institution) is pressing the university to create an assessment system. If the university does not develop its own assessment system, then the legislature is threatening to create one—and mandate its use.
4. Both the legislature and the newly elected president of USP's board of trustees are very concerned about the quality of teaching, including such issues as whether graduate students who teach (or help teach) are appropriately trained and supervised, how much teaching faculty do, whether faculty who teach well are rewarded appropriately, and so on.

## Questions

1. Assume that you have been asked to co-chair this committee. What would you do to prepare yourself and others for the first meeting?
2. What approach to conducting meetings would you use and why?
3. How would you organize an agenda for the first meeting?
4. What kinds of problems would you anticipate and how will you handle them?

## CHAPTER fourteen

# Managing Conflict

*After reading this chapter, you should be able to:*

1. Explain the concept of "conflict."

2. List ways in which conflict can benefit and damage an organization.

3. Explain how various organizational philosophies might view the desirability and management of conflict.

4. List at least five common causes of conflict.

5. List the major settings in which conflict occurs.

6. List and explain behaviors that escalate and deescalate conflict.

7. Describe five styles of conflict management.

8. Explain techniques involved in collaborative conflict management.

9. Explain the concepts of "arbitration" and "mediation."

10. Describe how technology is being used to resolve conflicts.

11. Describe how labor-management conflict is changing in philosophy and practice.

Someone once observed that "life is just one damned thing after another." In most organizations, those "damned things" are conflicts of various sorts, for all too often corporate life seems to be one conflict after another. Indeed, organizational conflict seems to be inevitable. Throughout this text, we have stressed the interdependence of organizational members and the continuing need for them to behave cooperatively. Yet this interdependence, this continuing necessity for interaction among people, makes conflict unavoidable. As Bernard points out, stress and conflict will occur in organizations because they are "inherent in the conception of free will in a changing environment."[1]

Berelson and Steiner define social conflict as "the pursuit of incompatible, or at least seemingly incompatible, goals, such that gains to one side come about at the expense of the other."[2] Herbert provides another view of conflict, defining it as occurring "whenever the attainment of a goal is hindered."[3] While these definitions disagree in some minor respects, both imply that conflict involves the simultaneous presence of two or more incompatible elements.

As we shall soon see, conflict is not in and of itself bad. Indeed, in many situations, some conflict is necessary for the organization to function at maximum efficiency. The key is how conflict is managed and how the energy conflict generates is channeled. If some conflicts remain unsolved or if they are managed poorly, the organization as a whole will suffer.

## PREVIEW

In this chapter, we turn our attention to another aspect of communication among groups of people: identifying, analyzing, and managing conflict. Communication to manage conflict comprises a complex set of strategies involving both informative and persuasive elements. In an effort to understand these strategies, we will consider the role of conflict in organizations, noting attitudes toward conflict and the settings, causes, and consequences of organizational disputes. Then we will examine several methods by which each type of organizational conflict may be managed. In so doing, we hope to develop communication strategies by which organizational conflict may be managed for the benefit of the organization as a whole.

# THE ROLE OF CONFLICT IN ORGANIZATIONS

## Philosophies Regarding Conflict

As we saw in Chapter 2, a great number of changes have occurred in the thinking of organizational theorists during the past century—thinking that has important implications for communication within organizations. Some of that thinking concerns the nature and role of conflict within organizations.

Philosophers taking the Theory X view of people, for example, would see conflict as an undesirable thing, particularly since the desires of employees (avoiding work at all costs) conflict with the objectives of the organization. In addition, conflict would suggest disagreement to those taking an S.O.B. or autocratic view of management, and since management's wishes should be followed at all times in such organizations, conflict should be avoided or stamped out.

Other schools of thought concerning organizations would advocate avoiding conflict for a very different reason. Someone adopting a high-relationship, low-achievement style, for example, would feel that the key to organizational functioning is the maintenance of satisfactory social relationships. Since conflict seems to indicate a breakdown in human relationships, such philosophers would feel the success of their organization rests upon management's ability to prevent conflicts from ever occurring. Managers adhering to such philosophies thus spend considerable time and energy making sure everyone is happy and no one is arguing. Workers in such organizations spend an equal amount of time and energy hiding conflicts from their managers lest they be reprimanded for engaging in such antisocial behaviors. As a consequence, conflicts are swept under the rug, not managed, so that while they disappear temporarily, they often reappear some time later, bigger and more difficult to handle than before. By stressing conflict avoidance, "high-relationship" managers, like very autocratic managers, do not succeed in truly avoiding conflict. Rather, they create frustrations and conflicts that are far greater than the original problem.

More recent views of organizational conflict happily have been somewhat more realistic. Evan typifies these views in his characterization of recent attitudes about conflicts[4]:

**1.** Conflicts always occur because of disagreement about expectations or organizational goals.
**2.** Conflicts can be good or bad for both the organization and the individual.
**3.** Conflicts legitimately can be validly minimized in some types of organizations, such as those geared toward crises (armed forces) or those that perform routine tasks (some manufacturers), but in other types of organizations (such as organizations stressing knowledge or technology) conflict should actually be encouraged.

Thus, theorists and practitioners in organizational development all have arrived at the realization that conflict in organizations not only is inevitable but may be beneficial. Some advantages conflict can provide include:

- Clarifying thought and generating better solutions.

- Improving group cohesiveness and performance.

- Clarifying dimensions of organizational relationships—particularly power.

- Defusing more serious conflict.

In fact, some organizational leaders take the view that creating conflict can be a useful strategy for achieving organizational change. Many managers constantly are fighting inertia. If no tensions are felt, the status quo is likely to continue. That's why some leaders create conflict: to demonstrate, for example, how organizational values are not reflected in employee behavior, how advertising is false or misleading, or that supervisors have standards for their employees that are different from the standards they have for themselves. The tension generated by conflict typically leads to some attempts to reduce or eliminate the tension level—and that means that the conflict must be confronted. With effective leadership, it will be confronted and managed in an appropriate way. But to manage conflict effectively, one must know something about the causes, settings, and consequences of conflict. We turn now to these matters.

## Another Day in the Life

In Chapter 1, we briefly observed a day in the life of Debbie, an employee for an insurance company located in Chicago. Debbie survived that day, but now is having another memorable one.

Debbie arrives at work at 8:00 in a foul mood, having slept very little the night before. Two things are on her mind. First, she has serious concerns about the memo she and her co-workers received two days ago from their boss, telling them to "reduce the number of claims we pay so the company can improve its profitability" and announcing a new policy whereby "those failing to reduce claims paid by at least 40 percent will be terminated." Being told to fight paying claims whether or not they are justified bothers Debbie. Being threatened about it hacks her off. Second, yesterday Debbie received a call from a "headhunter" concerning a job at another company in which she might be interested. The job pays slightly less than she currently receives but has long-term potential (provided the small company survives—it is a small start-up firm that has been in existence only nine months). Taking the job also would require moving to a small town in Southern Indiana, a prospect Debbie does not relish.

Naturally, the first people Debbie encounters as she enters the building are her union steward and the director of Human Resources (HR), chatting together in a friendly way. Debbie isn't particularly fond of either. She believes her union steward did a poor job of helping her through the grievance she filed against her boss four months ago. In fact, deep down Debbie suspects that the steward was biased toward the company all along (since negotiations are coming up and he didn't want to "make waves") and didn't really make an effort to represent her point of view. Moreover, she isn't pleased with the support she received from the Human Resources director, who, in her opinion, is a "lackey" for the company and has no interest in employee concerns.

"Good morning, Debbie," the director says cheerily upon seeing her.

"Yeah, yeah," Debbie mutters in response, thinking to herself, "Moronic cheerleader; that's all those HR people are good for—pretending everybody's happy."

The HR director's shocked look causes Debbie to realize that, in her sleepless fog, she has just thought to herself out loud.

Slinking to her desk, Debbie logs onto her computer and checks her e-mail. Ten messages, all from co-workers. She reads each message and finds they all say much the same thing: "We have to do something about our boss." Having learned the dangers of e-mail, Debbie visits each co-worker's cubicle during the next 30 minutes, inviting everyone to meet in the break room at 9:30.

Everyone comes to the meeting. For the next 30 minutes, almost everyone vents anger at the boss's directive.

"We should all walk out," someone suggests.

"We should get the union to fight this thing," another worker argues.

"We should just shoot the little Nazi," suggests Debbie, forgetting for a moment the security cameras placed in the break room.

But one person disagrees: Mary argues strongly that the boss "is doing what is best for all of us by trying to improve the company's profits. After all, that will mean job security for all of us."

No one pays much attention to Mary, since she is widely perceived to be "cozy" with the boss, who appointed her to a "lead" position several others wanted without going through the company's job posting procedure.

Most of the suggestions are shot down. "If we walk out, they'll fire us," someone observes.

The union hasn't done us any good up to now; how would they help?" asks another.

Ultimately, however, someone hits upon a useful approach: "Let's go to the employee ombudsperson."

All agree, and at lunch they meet with Madeline, the company's ombudsperson. Madeline listens to the group's concerns and agrees she will take their issues to the boss in an effort to persuade him to change his thinking.

The conversation between Madeline and Debbie's boss does not go well. During the conversation, some of the boss's comments include: "This is none of your business; I'm the one in charge of this department." "Your job is just to meddle in the business of others; why don't you go do something that actually helps this company?" "You're a bleeding heart, just like all the other women around here." "The only reason you have your job is because you're Black." "If you don't get out of here now, I'm going to the president to get you fired." After a few hours of listening to comments like these, Madeline probably would agree with the suggestion Debbie offered during the group's meeting.

When Debbie and her co-workers leave work that evening, they do so not knowing the outcome of Madeline's conversation with the "little Nazi." They can still hear the voices of the boss and Madeline coming from the boss's office as the two argue loudly.

**Causes of Conflict**

As Debbie's day illustrates, there are many possible causes of conflict. Although it is probably impossible to identify every possible cause of conflict within organizations, in the next section we will discuss some of the more common contributors to organizational conflict.

1. *Competition for rewards or resources.* Every organization offers a limited number or amount of rewards to its members. Individuals compete for promotions, raises, and status symbols; departments compete for budget allocations; organizations compete for a larger share of the market. These situations are called "win-lose" or "zero-sum" conditions. What one competitor wins, another loses, so that if the amount won and the amount lost are summed, they add to zero. Mary's appointment to a lead position coveted by others illustrates competition (however unfair) for a desired reward.

2. *Interlevel incompatibilities.* The organization is composed of many levels of hierarchy. Some research suggests that as we move from one level of the hierarchy to the next, our perceptions of the corporation tend to change. For instance, Likert discovered that top staff, foremen, and line workers all felt that they understood other people's problems but were themselves misunderstood, and in fact discovered that none of them shared congruent perceptions of what the other's problems were.[5] Labor unions for decades have operated under the assumption that what management wants (maximizing profits, in part by keeping employee pay and benefits to a minimum) is inherently in conflict with what employees want (maximizing their pay and benefits). Indeed, some believe that cooperation between union and company representatives is in conflict with the adversarial role unions should have with management, just as Debbie was unhappy with the perceived cooperation between her steward and the director of Human Resources.

3. *Differences in values and goals.* Production and sales units often conflict in this way since sales is more geared toward rapid production for high volume and speedy delivery, while production prefers a slower pace that emphasizes quality. When "speed" as a value and "quality" as a value clash (as they often do when the sales division puts in a rush order or when production slows down), conflict is likely to result. Similarly, individuals may have incompatible personal goals that cause them to come into conflict. The conflict between Debbie's boss's values (maximize profits by withholding payment) and the values of Debbie and her peers (do the right thing) occupied much of Debbie's workday.

4. *Misinformation, misunderstandings, or communication breakdowns.* An important message may not be received; a supervisor's instructions may be misinterpreted; decision makers may arrive at different conclusions because they used different databases. Conflicts based on missing or incomplete information tend to be straightforward in that clarifying previous messages or obtaining additional information generally resolves the disputes. Since value systems are not being challenged, these conflicts tend to be easily addressed by dealing directly with the information deficiency.

5. *Specialists versus generalists.* As jobs have become increasingly complex and science has made technology more intricate, the need for specialists to perform those jobs and use those technological innovations has become more

### WHEN THE BOSS IS WRONG

A particularly ticklish conflict situation arises when you feel your boss is wrong. Submission to authority is expected in most organizations, but thinking employees will ask, "Don't I have a responsibility to speak up if I see something wrong?" Of course, you do. But the key issue is authority: How can you provide your boss with information he or she needs about his or her decision without usurping the boss's decision-making authority?

When you need to disagree with your boss, try to offer alternatives rather than direct opposition. For example:

- If your boss asks you to do something you feel should not be your responsibility, don't say, "But that isn't in my job description." Instead, you might offer to take the work to some other more appropriate person ("Maria does this kind of thing a lot. Do you mind if I ask her to do this?"), or ask your boss what activities you should give up to perform this new task ("I'd be happy to do this, but I need your help in deciding what things I should leave until later.").
- If your boss has an idea you feel won't work, don't say, "That won't work; I have a better idea." Rather, ask the boss, "Help me to understand why we are going to do it this way." After hearing the reasons, you might add, "If that's what you want, I'll do it; but could I suggest a way that might be faster (cheaper, more efficient, and so on)?"
- If your boss gives you a directive that contradicts some other boss's instructions (particularly instructions given you by your boss's boss), you are caught in the middle. But don't say, "That goes against this other boss's directives." Instead, let your boss know of the other instructions you have been given and suggest that the three of you meet to identify what the priorities are.
- If your boss asks you to do something you feel is not right, don't say, "I won't do that; it's unethical." Try to prevent this situation from ever arising by discussing ethical issues with your boss well in advance: What things does the company stand for, and what do you personally believe in? If, nevertheless, you are asked to do something you feel is unethical, explain the conflict between the request and your ethical standards and ask the boss not to ask you to do that.

Source: Presented by Don Michael McDonald, "How to Tell Your Boss He's Wrong," *Management Solutions* 43 (December 1988): 3–9; Fernando Bartolome, "When You Think the Boss is Wrong," *Personal Journal* 69 (August 1990): 66–73.

and more pressing. Yet management functions typically require generalists to perform them. Most organizations are constructed so that a large number of specialists must be governed by a small number of generalists, which creates a host of potential conflicts. The generalist manager often knows less about the job than does the specialist worker, so that the worker may find it frustrating or nonproductive to communicate with his boss. The worker may "short-circuit" the organization's formal lines of communication, often to the dismay of the supervisor. Or there may be conflicting loyalties. Among professionals, loyalty to a discipline often conflicts with loyalty to the organization, as when a researcher feels himself a chemist first and a member of the organization second.

**6.** *Role conflict.* Occasionally, the job behaviors (termed one's organizational "role") expected of an individual provide a source of conflict. Generally, these sorts of conflicts fall into three categories. First, *intrarole* *conflict* occurs when an individual occupying a single role is subjected to stress. Organizational foremen often are subjected to contradictory expectations, as when management expects them to represent management interests during negotiations, while labor expects them to act as representatives of labor. Similarly, Debbie's expectations of her union steward (support her in her grievance) may have conflicted with the union's expectations of that same steward (don't make waves before negotiations).

*Interrole conflict,* on the other hand, occurs when someone is expected to simultaneously perform two different roles. Killian reports an instance of this sort of role conflict in his study of the disastrous Texas City fire.[6] When oil refineries caught fire and the blaze threatened the entire town, police were confronted with competing role demands: to play their "police" role by trying to protect the town's populace or to undertake their "father" role by looking after their families. In every case except one (a policeman whose family was out of town), the policemen chose the role that was more important to them and tended to their families. They experienced role conflict and resolved it by selecting the role they judged most important.

Finally, *interpersonal role conflict* occurs when two or more individuals have overlapping roles that cause them to do the same things in different ways at the same time. Parents disciplining a child in different ways are an example of this role conflict type, as is the conflict between Madeline and Debbie's boss, both of whom have some responsibility for responding to employee concerns.

**7.** *Status conflict.*   An important element of any organization is status, or the ranking of roles in the organization according to importance. Organization members usually seek increases in status, which are achieved through promotions and accompanied by an increased number of status symbols: a bigger office, perhaps with a window; a larger desk; a personal parking space; or a key to the executive washroom. However, an item symbolizing status may be not only a source of motivation but a source of conflict. In past years, new members of an organization have entered at the bottom of the hierarchy and "worked their way up the ladder." With the advent of new technologies and an increased emphasis upon expertise and specialization, highly qualified and trained young specialists now are superseding older organizational members, much to the latter's dismay. Working for someone who is younger and has less seniority has produced a great deal of status conflict among older subordinates in modern organizations.

**8.** *Personal incompatibilities.*   Individuals may simply not like one another and thus conflict with one another regardless of topic, situation, and so on. None of Debbie's co-workers (with the possible exception of Mary) likes "the little Nazi" they work for, making it likely they will resist anything he requests.

**9.** *Environmental stress.*   Things taking place around an individual, a group, or an organization can cause worry or stress among people, leading to increased conflict. Over the past few years, for instance, many large organizations have been downsizing, resulting in many people losing their jobs. In turn, this has caused many workers to worry about their own job security, even if no layoffs have occurred in their organizations. When people

As companies "go global," the frequency and importance of cultural conflict are growing. According to Doug Ready, founder and CEO of the International Consortium for Executive Development Research (an alliance of 30 global companies and 20 leading business schools that swaps information and conducts research on doing business globally), a "global mindset" is the "capacity to appreciate the beliefs, values, behaviors and business practices of individuals and organizations from a variety of regions and cultures." Americans are not particularly good at this: according to the Centre for International Briefing, roughly 25 percent of American managers fail overseas— three to four times higher than the failure rate experienced by managers from European and Asian companies. For example, at a business meeting in Tokyo, business cards were exchanged. The Japanese go through a very elaborate ritual when exchanging business cards, but the American executive simply threw some of her business cards across the table at the stunned Japanese executives. One of them turned his back on her and walked out. Needless to say, no deal went through and the American was called home.

Source: "Don't Be an Ugly-American Manager," *Fortune* 132: 8 (October 16, 1995): 225.

feel their jobs are threatened, and especially if there is much uncertainty about the rules by which the organization is operating, they will likely respond with frustration, hostility, and increased competitiveness. Memos threatening employees with termination if they fail to carry out management's orders (such as the one Debbie and her co-worker received) contribute to this sort of environmental stress.

**10.** *Disagreements.*   Frequently, conflict is simply a matter of disagreement over any number of things, such as facts (What is right or wrong?), methods (What is the best way to do things?), goals (What are we trying to accomplish?), or values (What is the "right" thing to do?). Obviously, there was some disagreement among Debbie's colleagues concerning the best course of action.

**11.** *Cultural differences.*   As workforces become more diverse, the likelihood of "culture clashes" increases. Differences in background, education, socialization, age, and expectations can produce different needs, perceptions, and goals. Employees from the United States, for example, may have a very different set of practices and expectations regarding giving and accepting gifts than employees in Japan; employees from some U.S. cultures (such as Native Americans) may have very different interpretations of eye contact than do the white Anglo-Saxon males running their organizations. These differences in expectations and practices can and often do produce misinterpretations that, in turn, may lead to open conflicts. If those differences stem from different values, the resulting conflicts can be severe. In communicative exchanges involving individuals who are personally incompatible as well, discussions can become highly emotional and take on moral overtones. Debbie's boss obviously has deep-seated biases that shape his reaction to Madeline's intervention.

**Common Causes of Conflict Within Organizations**

- • Competition for rewards or resources
- • Interlevel incompatibilities
- • Differences in values and goals
- • Misinformation, misunderstandings, or communication breakdowns
- • Specialists versus generalists

- • Role conflict
- • Status conflict
- • Personal incompatibilities
- • Environmental stress
- • Disagreements
- • Cultural differences

All these factors can and do cause conflict within organizational settings. In addition, there is evidence that conflict is more likely when:

- Lack of communication promotes separate interests.
- Consensus is necessary (requiring agreement before action).
- There is a history of past conflicts.
- Roles are ambiguous.
- Resources and rewards are scarce.
- People are diverse.

Finally, there are some factors that contribute to the escalation of conflict, making it more difficult to manage or resolve:

**1.** *Competition.*   In conflict, each person's behavior to a large extent is a reaction to the other person's behaviors. When one person begins to compete, the other is likely to respond in the same manner to defend himself or herself.
**2.** *Righteousness.*   Most conflicts begin simply as a disagreement. As conflict continues, one party might begin to feel he or she is completely, morally right while the other is entirely wrong. This may lead him or her to begin making personal attacks on the other's values or morality, moving the conflict from one over an issue to a more personal one.
**3.** *Not listening.*   Communication is needed to arrive at a joint decision. When one party stops listening, the other is likely to become angry or frustrated, seeing that party as unreasonable and uninterested in arriving at a solution.
**4.** *Bickering.*   Haggling over minor issues often comes about as frustrations rise, and in turn makes those frustrations even greater. Emphasis can shift from the original source of the conflict to focus on these minor (and often irrelevant) matters.
**5.** *Threats.*   When one party becomes frustrated with the other's refusal to agree, he or she may resort to threats in order to get compliance. This shifts attention away from the issue to a struggle over who has the most power to hurt whom.
**6.** *Intentional hurt.*   When one person feels sufficiently angry or hurt by the other's behavior, he or she may resort to insults, embarrassing examples, or

other tactics in a deliberate effort to hurt that person's feelings. At this point, the relationship between the conflicting parties may become irreconcilable.

**7.** *Violating social rules.* As hostility increases, concern for proper social behavior may decrease. "Scenes" may be created and other normally "unthinkable" actions initiated or tolerated. Physical assault may be the end result.

Many of these escalators occurred during the meeting between Madeline and Debbie's boss. Certainly, escalators such as these are to be minimized or avoided when conflict situations occur—yet they are seen in organizations every day.

| KEY CONCEPTS 14.2 | Conditions that Contribute to Conflict |
|---|---|
| There is evidence that conflict is more likely when: | Factors that contribute to the escalation of conflict, making it more difficult to manage or resolve: |
| • • *Lack of communication promotes separate interests* | • • *Competition* |
| • • *Consensus is necessary (requiring agreement before action)* | • • *Righteousness* |
| • • *There is a history of past conflicts* | • • *Not listening* |
| • • *Roles are ambiguous* | • • *Bickering* |
| • • *Resources and rewards are scarce* | • • *Threats* |
| • • *People are diverse* | • • *Intentional hurt* |
| | • • *Violating social rules* |

**Settings of Conflict**

The day in Debbie's life also illustrates some common settings in which conflict within organizations commonly occurs:

**Conflict within Individuals** Two conflict forms, frustration and goal conflict, occur commonly within individuals in organizations. *Frustration* is the simpler of the two, occurring when one's ability to attain a goal is hampered by the imposition of some barrier. For example, we may have a strong desire to perform in a superior fashion, yet because of some limitation (limited ability, inadequate education, or a supervisor who does not like us), our performance evaluations consistently are "average." We then might try somehow to improve matters, perhaps by working harder, taking evening courses at a local college, or trying to obtain a transfer to another department. If these measures fail, frustration results and less productive behaviors are likely to follow. Debbie's desire to behave in an ethical manner at work, one might argue, potentially was frustrated by a directive from her boss to avoid paying claims whenever possible.

More complex than frustration is a second sort of conflict within individuals, *goal conflict*, where the attainment of one goal excludes the possibility of attaining another. Three principal types of goal conflict can be identified.

**1.** *Approach-approach conflict.* The individual is caught between trying to decide on one or another of two attractive goals that are mutually exclusive. Debbie likes the people with whom she works and thus would like to stay in her present job, but the prospect of another job offering career advancement is also attractive.

**2.** *Approach-avoidance conflict.* The individual has both positive and negative feelings about trying to attain a goal because the goal possesses both attractive and unattractive characteristics. A job offering advancement potential in a company that may not exist in the future (and, worse yet, is located in Southern Indiana) poses these kinds of mixed advantages and disadvantages.

**3.** *Avoidance-avoidance conflict.* The individual must choose between two mutually exclusive goals, both of which are unattractive. Debbie, for example, has to choose between continuing to work for the "little Nazi" and taking a job in another city.

### Conflict between Individuals

Conflict between organizational members also takes two forms: *individual versus individual* and *individual versus group*. Examples of the first are infinite: two managers competing for the same promotion, two women vying for a tennis championship, two executives advocating a particular solution to a problem they face. Although competition may even be enjoyable to the participants (such as players in a tennis match), uncontrolled conflict of this sort is often destructive to the organization. The conflict between Madeline and Debbie's boss probably was enjoyable to neither.

On occasion, conflict also occurs between an individual and a group. As we pointed out previously, some groups demand absolute conformity by their members, so that a "rugged individualist" who happens to join that group might find himself in conflict with other members. Or an individual who is particularly eager to promote her own interests may do so by breaking group norms. Work groups, for example, typically have informal but rigidly enforced production limits such that anyone outproducing the rest of the group is labeled a "rate buster" and pressured to conform. Mary's disagreement with the group's desire to fight Debbie's boss's decision (and her perceived status as being "cozy" with the boss) certainly put her in conflict with her colleagues.

Conflicts between individuals produce stress within the organization and must be managed correctly if they are to become beneficial rather than detrimental to the organization.

### Conflict between Groups

As we already know, much of our life in organizations is spent in groups: work groups, decision-making groups, social groups. Often these groups come into conflict with one another. Two particular types of intergroup conflict deserve mention. *Functional conflicts* occur when business functions are divided up into departments that often have entirely different perspectives of organizational processes. Manufacturing divisions tend to have short time perspectives and seek to maximize their own goals of long production runs and standardized products to meet unit cost goals. Marketing divisions tend to have long time perspectives, to evaluate products and services from the perspective of the consumer, and to endeavor to customize and provide many options to suit each customer individually. Conflicts between these groups are common, and managers must seek means for their resolution.

*Line and staff conflicts* represent a second type of intergroup conflict, as staff groups are responsible for measuring, monitoring, analyzing, and projecting the work and results of the organization, while line groups are concerned only with the actual execution of the work. Line may see staff as being impractical, overeducated, inexperienced, or abstract; while staff may view line as dull, narrow, inflexible, or unimaginative. Perceptual incongruities such as these are virtually guaranteed to produce conflict between line and staff groups.

### Conflict between Organizations

While individuals and groups within organizations often are embroiled in conflicts, the organizations themselves usually are involved in disputes as well. For example, consider some of the organizations with which an automobile manufacturer comes into contact. General Motors buys automotive parts from Borg-Warner. Although these two corporations are acting cooperatively to build automobiles, they are also in conflict: Borg-Warner wants to get the highest possible prices from General Motors for the parts it supplies, while General Motors wants to pay the lowest possible prices. Similarly, advertising agencies handling the General Motors account want to charge the highest possible prices, while General Motors wants to keep its advertising budget as low as possible. Executive recruiting firms are eager to charge high fees for finding new executives to staff General Motors, while GM wants to keep recruiting costs low. The United Auto Workers want as many union members as possible to be employed by General Motors (since those people must pay dues to the UAW), and they are eager to have their members well paid by General Motors. General Motors wants to keep its labor costs down. The federal government imposes regulations concerning safety and pollution that are supposed to reflect the public interest. General Motors tries to keep manufacturing costs minimal. The automobile-buying public wants quality cars at low prices, while General Motors want to make a profit. In all of these instances, partial conflict (but also a partial sharing of goals) exists between each group. Yet only by overcoming these conflicts can each group have its needs met to some degree.

---

**KEY CONCEPTS 14.3   Settings for Organizational Conflict**

Settings for conflict in organizations commonly include:

• • *Conflict within individuals*

• • *Conflict between individuals*

• • *Conflict between groups*

• • *Conflict between organizations*

---

Conflict is helpful to organizations only if it is managed effectively and the energy it produces is channeled constructively. At the outset, it is clear that conflict management and resolution is more likely when certain conditions exist:

- There is a "we-versus-problem" rather than a "we-they" attitude.
- There is a focus on all gaining rather than win/lose.
- There is an effort among conflicting parties to see others' viewpoints.
- There is an emphasis on goals, values, understanding motives, and building long-term relationships, not just on getting to a quick solution.
- There is open communication that promotes input and feedback.
- There are organizational rewards for cooperation rather than competition.
- There is an effort to achieve a solution that is both acceptable to everyone and of high quality.

Thus, resolving conflict often involves attempting to build on any of these things that already is present, or to create these things if they do not already exist.

## Communicating to Resolve Conflict

Just as some conditions and behaviors serve to escalate conflict, so do other behaviors help to reduce conflict and make it manageable:

1. *Listening and trying to understand.* Most conflicts are resolved not when one side gives in, but when one or both sides begin to reexamine their positions in the light of new information. Trying to understand the other side shows a willingness to consider new information, and interest in cooperation and an effort to establish an atmosphere of reason.

2. *Concern for feelings.* When "sensitive" issues arise, they often can be defused by showing concern for the other's feelings and by being careful to avoid points or phrases that could aggravate him or her. Tact is important in resolving most conflicts.

3. *Appeals to deescalate.* Many times escalation of conflict happens when people do not stop to think about the consequences of their actions. Sometimes this can be reversed by drawing attention to what is going on and pointing out the consequences: "This kind of talk isn't getting us anywhere and is just making us mad. Let's both calm down and get back to the real issues."

4. *Good will gestures.* Trust and good will sometimes can be built by making symbolic gestures—perhaps as concessions or favors to one another. This is most likely to be effective when one person announces his or her intent to rebuild goodwill, encourages the other to reciprocate, and then responds positively to the other's goodwill gestures.

5. *Airing feelings.* When hostility and hurt have become strong factors in a conflict, they probably will have to be aired before the conflict can deescalate. If the people experiencing these feelings have a chance to get them off their chests, the feelings will lose their intensity and both sides may

be better able to focus on the real issues. In order for this to happen, however, the two sides must accept and listen to one another's feelings. If they ignore the feelings or respond defensively, the conflict will continue to escalate.

**6.** *Finding alternatives.* Frequently conflict escalates because neither party can suggest alternative solutions. Without options, they feel boxed in and expend most of their energies on holding their positions. A constructive effort to generate alternative actions or solutions can build cooperation and lead to a position acceptable to everyone.

By initiating communication behaviors such as these, one side may be able to encourage the other to become cooperative, stop escalating the conflict, and move toward cooperation.

Kare Anderson offers a three-step procedure that she terms "triangle talk" as a means of handling conflict effectively. In her view, the tendencies most people have to either fight back or withdraw from conflicts can best be overcome by:

- *Knowing exactly what you want.* By asking yourself "What do I want in this situation?" you can gain greater control and focus.

- *Finding out what the other person wants and making him or her feel heard.* Knowing the other person's objectives provides a basis for negotiations.

- *Proposing action in a way the other person can accept.* This helps create the top of the triangle—the common ground between the two sides.

These three steps are best achieved by asking questions, Anderson contends. Vague, general questions should be used initially (such as "What do you think about this situation?"), but more specific questions should be used as negotiations continue ("Exactly what would make this proposal work better for you?").[7]

Finally, some specific communication skills seem useful in handling conflict among team members:

- *Ask those who disagree to paraphrase one another's comments.* This may help them learn whether they really understand each other.

- *Work out a compromise.* Agree on the underlying source of conflict, then engage in give-and-take, and finally agree on a solution.

- *Ask each member to list what the other side should do.* Exchange lists, select a compromise all are willing to accept, and test the compromise to see if it meshes with team goals.

- *Have the sides each write 10 questions for their opponents.* This will allow them to signal their major concerns about the other side's position. And the answers may lead to a compromise.

- *Convince team members they sometimes have to admit they're wrong.* Help them to save face by convincing them that changing a position may well show strength.

- *Respect the experts on the team.* Give their opinions more weight when the conflict involves their expertise, but don't rule out conflicting opinions.[8]

FIGURE 14.1      Conflict management styles

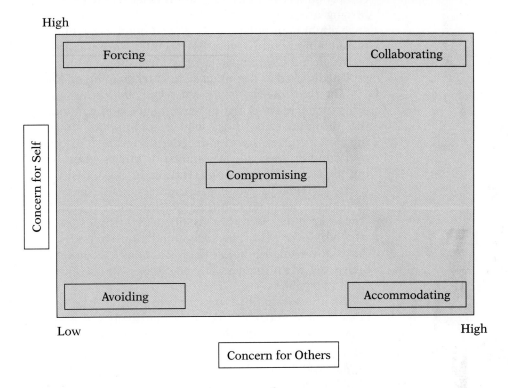

All these communication techniques should be considered in situations where the management and resolution of conflict are needed.

Styles of Conflict Management

Researchers have discussed different conflict management styles since the mid-1960s. Among the first were Blake and Mouton, whose five-category conflict management grid was soon replicated and refined by others.[9] Blake and Mouton conceptualized conflict style as a characteristic mode or a habitual way that a person handles a dispute. Style can also be viewed as an orientation toward conflict or conflict tactics and strategies (either planned or enacted). The styles studied generally emanate from a five-category scheme based on concern for self (or task) and concern for others. The five conflict styles are depicted in Figure 14.1.

The first conflict style is *avoiding*. Although aware of conflict at a cognitive level, the person using this style may withdraw by removing herself (psychologically or physically) from the conflict situation, refraining from arguing, or simply failing to confront. If the conflict is over serious or complex issues, avoidance behaviors may contribute to frustration, deny others' feelings, and generally aggravate the problem. Moreover, at a practical level, in organizational settings where interdependent tasks are commonly addressed, long-term avoidance is probably not an achievable strategy.

At the other extreme of managing conflict is *forcing*. Those who employ this style rely on coercion rather than on persuasion or collaboration. They use assertiveness, verbal dominance, and perseverance. When all else fails, they resort to their position power or formal authority, ordering others to comply simply because they are in charge. Less direct, manipulative forms of forcing are also possible, however. For instance, a manager with a forcing style might manipulate the composition of a committee so that the solution he prefers emerges through a "democratic" process. Although forcing may be effective in some situations (where, for instance, quick action is required), when repeatedly used as a conflict style, it tends to breed hostility and resentment.

The third conflict style is *accommodating,* an approach that glosses over differences, plays down disagreements, and generally trivializes conflict. In the ultimate sense, those who accommodate simply give in, setting aside their own concerns and surrendering to those of others. Those who smooth over conflicts basically accommodate others, often with the goal of maintaining pleasant interpersonal relationships. Occasionally, accommodating is used strategically when someone sets aside her concerns on a particular issue, with the hope that the next time there is conflict, the other person will "owe her one." Whether or not this strategy is effective depends upon whether the terms of the accommodation are understood, as well as the standards governing the other party's actions. Accommodating is most appropriately used when the person who chooses to accommodate truly perceives the issue as trivial.

As an even-handed approach to conflict, the *compromising* style carries considerable appeal. Compromising involves searching for an intermediate position, splitting the difference, and meeting the opponent halfway. Thus, for both parties, partial satisfaction is achieved. Unlike the first three approaches, compromising appears fair and requires considerable effort and interaction (presumably involving both persuading and listening). The difficulty with compromising as a typical conflict style is that it is, above all, expedient. When used consistently, it sends the message that the individual is more interested in resolving the conflict than in actually finding an excellent solution to the problem. Moreover, no one is ever fully satisfied. While there are no real losers, neither are there any real winners. The feeling of accomplishment that can grow from working through a problem to consensus is never realized through compromise.

Finally, the preferred conflict style in many organizational contexts is *collaborating* or *problem solving.* This style calls upon the disputants to face the conflict openly and directly and to seek, by working together, an integrative solution. Collaboration grows from a trust-building process. It encourages everyone to express themselves assertively while reinforcing the value of listening to others and approaching the problem constructively. Consistent with notions of supportive communication behaviors and attitudes discussed earlier in this book, the collaborative approach demands a focus on the problem and its thoughtful analysis rather than on placing blame. It works best in organizational environments that foster openness, directness, and equality. With collaboration, the integrative approach to problem solving (as defined earlier) must prevail, wherein the "pie" is expanded by avoiding fixed, inflexible, incompatible positions. For complex, important issues, the collaborative approach is preferable, both in quality of the outcome achieved and in the feelings of empowerment that grow from people having successfully exercised their problem-solving skills in addressing a significant issue.

While the collaborative approach is consistently hailed as effective in managing conflict, it is not always the most appropriate conflict management style for every situation. For instance, collaboration is not appropriate when the conflict is trivial and quick decisions are required. Avoidance may be quite effective for handling less important and highly volatile issues, and forcing may be appropriate for crisis situations or for moving forward with unpopular courses of action. Problem solving or collaboration generally works well in situations where parties are interdependent, where supporting and implementing the solution is required, and where the conflict stems from ambiguity or inadequate shared information.

The limited or inadequate use of the collaborative style in managing conflicts has resulted in considerable speculation. Some argue that problem solving is not taught by our society as a way of life. Instead, the emphasis is upon obeying authority figures, such as teachers and parents. When children mature and eventually become authority figures, they may expect to be obeyed or to dominate others. This power-oriented view inhibits the individual's ability to choose problem solving or collaboration as a natural conflict management style. Moreover, in comparison with any other style, collaboration requires a greater degree of time, energy, and commitment. Thus, the combined problems—lack of skill in constructive confrontation and an unwillingness or inability to expend the necessary time, energy, or commitment—serve to diminish the extent to which collaboration is used in conflict situations.

Whatever the conflict style or strategy chosen, its effective implementation will depend on the disputants' ability to adapt to the situation, their fairness and objectivity in approaching the conflict, and the way in which they communicate. There are many different ways of forcing, for instance, ranging from soft, persistent argument to unpleasant, loudly projected references to one's power and authority. Others will react differently, depending on the specific verbal and nonverbal communicative behaviors that make up the overall conflict style. Moreover, timing is important. Executives report that early intervention is critically related to effective conflict management—the longer the delay, the more likely it is that the conflict will escalate, perhaps out of control.

## Collaborative Conflict Management

Ideally, individuals, groups, and organizations are able to manage their own conflict through negotiation and bargaining rather than having to call in third parties. Effective outcomes are more likely to be realized when individuals voluntarily solve their own disputes than when leaders or other third parties are asked to intervene. Thus, developing an understanding of productive collaborative approaches to managing conflict is crucial.

All groups experience conflict at one time or another. In decision-making ventures aimed at building consensus, for example, actions taken or decisions made will clearly not meet with everyone's complete approval. Consensus is difficult to reach since most of us find it difficult on occasion to compromise our views. To help us make progress, we may choose to adopt external ground rules or guidelines to structure our group interactions, with the goal of approaching our tasks more positively and productively. For instance, Hall and Watson's guidelines might be used to help minimize conflict.[10] These guidelines instruct group members to:

*When leaders embrace a collaborative approach to conflict management, all participants may hope to have real input and achieve some satisfaction with the outcome. When genuine collaboration occurs, group members must agree on over-arching, superordinate goals and agree to focus on issues rather than personalities.*

**1.** Avoid arguing for your own evaluation. Approach the task on the basis of logic.
**2.** Avoid changing your mind only to avoid conflict. Support only solutions with which you are somewhat able to agree.
**3.** Treat differences of opinion as indicative of an incomplete sharing of relevant information.
**4.** View differences of opinion as both natural and helpful rather than as a hindrance in decision making.

Where it is possible and desirable to approach conflict from a problem-solving perspective, several integrative negotiation strategies have been shown to foster collaboration. First, and perhaps most important, is *establishing superordinate goals*. The parties involved in the conflict should begin by focusing on what they share in common. As individuals become aware of the salience of their shared goals—for example, greater productivity, a safer work environment, lower costs, a fairer evaluation system, or improved working relationships—they tend to become sensitized to the merits of resolving their differences so that these mutual goals will not be jeopardized. When consensus on common goals is achieved, the disputants can begin to examine their specific differences. Once established, superordinate goals must be referred to throughout the deliberations. Some researchers have cautioned, however, that

## NEGOTIATION SKILLS MOVE TO THE FORE

The importance of effective conflict resolution techniques is illustrated by the Harvard Business School's replacement of its traditional course in managerial economics with a course titled "Data, Decision, and Negotiation." This focus on negotiating skills stems from important changes in the workplace, according to Assistant Professor Robert Robinson:

- *The move away from permanent work groups.* Temporary work teams assembled for specific tasks cannot use traditional bureaucratic methods to resolve conflicts and must instead depend on effective communication and negotiations.

- *The increasingly global marketplace.* Negotiations across different cultures and legal systems require greater skill than ever.
- *The increasingly diverse workforce.* Employers now must take into account the often-conflicting interests of the workforce when dealing with such issues as family and medical leave, granting same-sex spousal benefits, or establishing work schedules.
- *The changing nature of information technology.* E-mail, faxes, voice mail, and other electronic technologies all must be used effectively for handling conflicts and can muddy issues by creating information overload.

Source: From Marcie Schoor Hirsch, "New Ways to Negotiate," *Working Woman* (December 1993): 25–26.

superordinate goals are more likely to reduce perceived rather than underlying conflict.[11] Whether or not superordinate goals are helpful depends on the groups developing a culture for mutual understanding and constructive interaction patterns.[12]

Another important collaborative behavior involves *separating the people from the problem.* Having defined the mutual benefits to be gained by successfully resolving the conflict, attention must be directed to the real issue at hand—solving a problem. Negotiations are more likely to result in mutual satisfaction if the parties depersonalize the discussions. The participants might benefit from viewing each other as advocates for differing points of view rather than rivals. They may need to suppress their desire for personal revenge or one-upmanship. From a communicative perspective, a person would refer to "an unreasonable argument" rather than calling her counterpart "an unreasonable person." In general, it is crucial to avoid loaded language, such as labeling others' ideas as stupid, crazy, naive, or "Nazi."

In situations involving conflict, *identifying and using criteria for determining the quality of alternative solutions* to a problem is crucial. No matter how many goals are shared, some interests are bound to be incompatible. Rather than seizing on these as opportunities for testing wills, determining what is fair is far more productive. This requires that both parties agree on how fairness should be judged. As objective criteria are discussed and agreed upon, individuals begin to shift their thinking from "getting what I want" to "deciding what makes most sense"—fostering an attitude of reasonableness and open-mindedness.

Also related to the open-minded pursuit of solutions is *focusing on interests, not positions.* In bargaining and negotiation settings, positions are thought of as bottom-line demands the negotiator makes. By contrast, interests constitute the substructure of the evidence and reasoning underlying the demands. Establishing agreement on interests is easier because they tend to be broader and multifaceted. Achieving agreement, however, even on interests, involves a fair measure of creativity in redefining and broadening the problem to make it more tractable. For instance, once a problem has been defined, there are a variety of ways to enlarge, alter, or replace it. If a problem such as sagging productivity has been defined in a specific way (for example, worker laziness), other contributing causes exist and can be articulated. Thus, one way to proceed is by generating at least two alternative hypotheses for every problem discussed. The strategy is to broaden the problem definition by thinking in plural rather than singular terms. The questions should be phrased, "What are the problems?" "What are the meanings of this?" "What are the results?" Another possibility is to reverse the problem's definition by contradicting the currently accepted definition to expand the number of perspectives considered. For instance, a problem might be that morale is too high instead of too low or that a work environment is characterized by too little rather than too much structure. Opposites and backward looks often enhance creativity. When a variety of interests and problem definitions are examined, individuals are better able to understand each other's points of view and place their own views in perspective. The integrative question is "Can you help me understand why you are advocating that position?"

Another negotiation strategy requiring creativity is *inventing options for mutual gains*. Here, however, the creativity is focused on generating unusual solutions. While some negotiations may necessarily be distributive, negotiators should never begin by adopting a win-lose posture. By focusing both parties' attention on brainstorming alternatives, mutually agreeable solutions, the negotiation dynamics naturally shift from competitive to collaborative. Moreover, the more options and combinations there are to explore, the greater the probability of reaching an integrative solution. Both goodwill and creativity are required as the parties ask, "What can we do that we haven't tried before?"

Several small group techniques discussed in previous chapters might prove useful, both in defining interests and problems and in generating solutions. Brainstorming (where ideas are tossed out without evaluation) is one potential technique. In addition, the nominal group procedure might be used, in which each participant brainstorms on paper, and then the ideas are collected, shared, and discussed. Finally, group support systems allow for computer-assisted brainstorming, encouraging creativity and preserving anonymity. Whatever approach to brainstorming is employed, those who participate in the process are basically asking, "Now that we better understand each other's underlying concerns and objectives, let's brainstorm ways of satisfying both our needs."

It is important to note, however, that during group meetings, conflicts may surface as ideas are generated, explored, consolidated, and evaluated—in other words, throughout the decision-making process. In an idea generation activity, for example, the brainstorming process can create polarization effects since each individual learns, perhaps for the first time, how other group members view the issue being discussed. In some cases, a particular group member may assume, before the meeting, that others support the same job candidate, course of action, or policy that he does. As views are expressed during a meeting, however, he may learn that he is wrong. When brainstorming is used to generate ideas, McGrath recommends that groups adopt techniques designed to[13]:

**1.** Make sure that the creativity of each individual is not stifled by social influence processes that often operate in groups. Fear of social embarrassment, conformity pressures, and status systems that inhibit participation by low-status members should be actively discouraged.
**2.** Take maximum advantage of whatever creativity-enhancing forces may operate in groups. Social support, reenforcement for contributing, and cross-stimulation of group members should be promoted.

Finally, the parties' approach to the notion of "success" is critical. Maintaining a realistic, optimistic attitude means that *success can be defined in terms of gains, not losses.* The employee who seeks a 12 percent raise and receives an 8 percent raise can choose to view that outcome as either an accomplishment (that is, a gain over the present situation) or as a disappointment (in that expectations were not realized). Whichever interpretation, the objective outcome is the same, but the employee's satisfaction is likely to vary significantly. Individual reactions to an outcome are greatly influenced by the standards used to judge it. Thus, the agreed-upon criteria are especially salient and should be called upon to judge the value of the proposed solution or outcome. The question to be asked is "Does this outcome constitute a meaningful improvement over current conditions?"

Perhaps the best summary of the collaborative approach to conflict resolution is provided by participants in the Harvard Negotiation Project, who suggested an alternative to traditional "positional" bargaining between labor and management they called "principled negotiation" or "negotiation on the merits."[14] This problem-solving approach can be summarized in four points:

- *People.* Separate the people from the problem. The participants should see themselves as working side by side, attacking the problem rather than each other.

- *Interests.* Focus on interests, not positions. Rather than focusing on people's stated positions, the object of a negotiation should be to satisfy their underlying interests.

- *Options.* Generate a variety of possibilities before deciding what to do. Searching for one "right" solution inhibits creativity and narrows vision. A designated time should be set aside to develop a range of possible solutions that advance shared interests and creatively reconcile differing interests.

- *Criteria.* Insist that the result be based on some objective standard. Developing a set of criteria whereby possible solutions might be judged (such as market value, expert opinion, custom or law) ultimately will help to arrive at a fair solution.

Certainly, focus on these four factors would help to achieve conflict resolution collaboratively.

Collaborative conflict
management is facilitated by:

- • *Using proper
  communication behaviors*

- • *Setting superordinate goals*

- • *Separating people from the
  problem*

- • *Identifying and using
  criteria for assessing
  alternatives*

- • *Focusing on interests, not
  positions*

- • *Working for mutual gains*

- • *Defining success in terms
  of gains, not losses*

## Third-Party Intervention

When the conflicting parties are unwilling or unable to arrive at a resolution to their situation, they may resort to calling in a neutral third party for assistance. In this way, they extend or elaborate on the negotiation process. The third party could be a supervisor (in conflicts between employees), an upper-level manager (in conflicts between two departments), the chief executive officer (in conflicts between divisions), a government-appointed mediator (in labor-management disputes), or a judge in a courtroom (in conflicts between organizations). Some companies establish a formal position for a person whose job it is to help resolve conflicts. Often this person is called the "employee ombudsperson." Madeline, the employee ombudsperson in Debbie's company, is an example of an employee serving in this kind of formal conflict-resolving position.

A third-party intervener can play one of two roles: an *arbitrator* who, after hearing both sides of the issue, makes a decision that both parties must live by, or a *mediator* who tries to facilitate communication between the parties so that they can work through their problems and arrive at a decision of their own. Debbie's employee ombudsperson does not have the authority to make a decision regarding the conflict between Debbie's co-workers and their boss, and thus must act as a mediator. Although both arbitration and mediation rely on communication to manage information and exert social influence, mediation is a type of facilitation that hinges almost exclusively on communication for its success.[15]

The mediator's task requires sensitivity. Assisting with the logical, decision-making part of the conflict is only a small part of the mediator's role. Because conflicts have usually escalated before the mediator becomes involved, she or he often finds that the parties are no longer particularly logical. Thus, the mediator will have to deal with a number of nonrational postures shaped by hurt feelings, a preoccupation with settling old scores, defensiveness, and distorted perceptions. Mediators, however, also have an advantage in this task. Because they are not as emotionally involved as are the disputants, they are usually much better able to maintain a proper perspective.

In the political world, mediation is often used to diffuse hostilities and establish some common ground. President Bill Clinton functioned as a mediator when he sought to bring world leaders Arafat and Netanyahu together in the quest for peace in the Middle East.

Mediators use varied tactics, including directive, nondirective, procedural, and reflexive techniques. *Directive tactics* allow the mediator to exert substantive control over the negotiation by recommending proposals, giving opinions about positions, assessing the costs associated with demands, and occasionally enforcing compliance. In general, directive tactics are more effective in the latter stages of mediation than in early meetings. *Nondirective tactics* capitalize on the mediator's role in securing information for the disputants and in clarifying misunderstandings. Thus, the mediator may act as a conduit by passing information between the parties or as a clarifier by paraphrasing messages and narrowing topics for discussion. As *procedural tactics,* the mediator may organize separate or joint sessions, establish protocol for the sessions, regulate the agenda, and establish deadlines. Finally, mediators may use *reflexive tactics* by influencing the affective tone of the mediation—developing rapport with participants, using humor, and speaking the language of both sides. Effective mediators use a combination of these tactics, although they report that reflexive tactics are more effective than directive and nondirective ones in facilitating joint collaboration. Clearly, communication is central to the mediation process. As Kolb points out, mediators are like the directors of a drama, who set the scene, manage impressions, orchestrate the script, and maintain dramatic inquiry throughout the process.[16]

In other chapters, we have seen how technology might be used to facilitate communication, team building, leadership, and organizational change. However, technology can also contribute to conflict by depersonalizing individuals or groups and thus making it easier for them to deal with one another in stereotyped, hostile ways. E-mail, for example, removes the sender from the receiver, making it easier for the sender to "flame" the receiver in ways he or she might hesitate to use when in the presence of the other. In addition, it provides only verbal messages with no nonverbal context, making misinterpretations and misunderstandings more likely.

On the other hand, some technological approaches to resolving group conflict are showing some promise. Computer systems, particularly group and negotiation support systems, can act as intervention mechanisms specifically to address issues related to group conflict management.

*Group support systems (GSS)* use software and hardware to promote and enforce these conditions. GSS act as a group process intervention by:

**1.** Imposing process-related structure on the meeting.
**2.** Providing an electronic meeting channel that can improve communication among group members.
**3.** Delivering a structured heuristic to analyze the problem or task.

As we noted in Chapter 12, GSS allow anonymous input and parallel and simultaneous processing, encouraging group member participation since views can be aired without inhibition or constraints. GSS also facilitate the imposition of decision-making heuristics and meeting agendas. These can help keep groups on track while allowing them to systematically work through conflict. And the ability of GSS to provide an electronic record of the meeting can help group members share a common understanding of what has transpired in their meetings.

Researchers Poole, Holmes, and DeSanctis conducted one of the first and the most extensive studies designed to test the impact of GSS on group conflict management.[17] In their study, they compared groups using GSS to groups using only paper and pencils and to groups using no support at all. Discovering mixed results, the researchers concluded that GSS does not necessarily directly determine conflict interaction or outcomes. Rather, they argue, the way groups use the technology is what mediates its impact. They found, for instance, that some GSS groups used the structure better than others.

Despite their mixed findings, Poole, Holmes, and DeSanctis remain confident that GSS can provide a number of benefits for conflict management. Because of the anonymity feature, GSS can, they argue, distance people from ideas, thereby depersonalizing and sometimes defusing difficult conflict situations. GSS make conflict management procedures salient to group members, bringing order to group meetings. In addition, procedures such as voting can surface hidden conflicts.

The impact of GSS on conflict management likely depends on the nature of the GSS and how the group applies it. Poole, Holmes, and DeSanctis note that the GSS used in their study had no specialized conflict management capabilities. Moreover, a facilitator was not used in these GSS sessions. In all likelihood, a facilitator might have been able to help more groups adapt GSS in a manner conducive to productive conflict management. Users of any technology are influenced by expectations. How GSS is explained to users and the level of training they are provided will surely influence how they will use the technology in conflict situations.

Another technology available for groups to use in resolving conflicts is *negotiation support systems*—decision support technologies that specifically focus on providing computerized assistance for situations in which group members strongly disagree on factual or value judgments. Negotiation support systems are interactive, computer-based tools that are specifically intended to support negotiating parties in reaching an agreement. These systems focus on enhancing the prospect of consensus with the intent of making compromise possible.

Negotiation support systems may include decision support software with modeling capabilities, such as decision trees, risk analysis, forecasting methods, and multiattribute functions, as well as software supporting structured group methods, such as electronic brainstorming, nominal grouping, and delphi techniques. Some of these systems even include artificial intelligence to help groups define and solve problems. Many commercial software products are available (including GSS) that encompass some or all of these features.

Ironically, computer systems themselves have been a source of conflict in employee-management relations. Savage points out that many labor unions were once vociferous in their crusade against office automation.[18] They felt, with some justification, that technology threatened a loss of jobs for their members. However, many unions have come full circle and now offer training in computer use to enhance their members' development and advancement opportunities. Instead of simply using technology training to retrain members whose skills are being passed by, Savage notes, many unions have embraced technology to further their goals and to keep members abreast of computer skills. For example, the Air Line Pilots Association, whose pilots are already computer-literate, has established services enabling members to access information about new technologies, as well as services that facilitate communication and negotiations with their employers.

**Labor-Management Conflict**

Perhaps the best illustration of how philosophies concerning the use of communication in managing conflicts are changing is the arena of labor-management bargaining. Traditionally, labor-management relations in the United States have been largely adversarial. However, rising competition from foreign firms has forced labor and management to adopt a more cooperative approach to contract negotiations: *"win-win bargaining."*

Among the earliest users of win-win bargaining were the United Paperworkers International Union Local 264 and the Waldorf Corporation's St. Paul, Minnesota, facility. Both sides also adopted a set of ground rules concerning the contract talks:

- Discussion was to focus on issues, not personalities.

- Everyone was to be permitted to speak, not just the spokespersons for each side.

- Both sides would work at all times to maintain a "positive relationship."

- Agendas would be developed and followed for each bargaining session.

- Notes concerning each meeting would be kept jointly and approved by the participants at the next session.

- Information would be shared and disseminated to employees through a jointly sponsored hot line and bulletin board communications.

The resulting contract was ratified by the membership almost unanimously and with far less turmoil than had been the case three years earlier. Participants in the process also reported much higher levels of satisfaction both with the process itself and with the contract it produced.

More recently, Chrysler Corporation and the United Auto Workers (UAW) have worked cooperatively to develop a more effective, less acrimonious approach to contract negotiations. A key element of that effort has been the development of *modern operating agreements* (or MOAs) for some Chrysler plants.

The MOA concept evolved in 1986–87 as a joint effort between Chrysler management and the UAW to improve quality and productivity on the assembly line. The objective of the MOAs was to create a more democratic work environment. MOAs eliminated superficial labor-management distinctions and inefficient practices; reduced job classifications, supervisory personnel, and union representatives; and established self-directed work teams and a pay system that rewards workers for their job-related knowledge.

Each MOA has a team that participates in daily audits, assists in developing work assignments, corrects minor and reports major tooling and maintenance problems, provides input regarding production standards, assists in planning work methods, monitors and controls performance, coordinates overtime work, arranges vacation schedules, and performs various other tasks.

Generally, MOA plants have reported reduced operating costs, lower turnover, fewer grievances, and lower absenteeism. All of this has been a direct result of the realization that the company and the union share common interests and that working together rather than as adversaries more effectively serves those interests.

Finally, an approach to improving contract negotiations between labor and management that is gaining increasing acceptance is *"interest-based bargaining."* The approach is designed to find the common ground between negotiating parties, to build relationships and to eliminate the adversarial elements of traditional collective bargaining. One dramatic example of such bargaining occurred when the Salt River Project (SRP), a public electric and water utility based in Phoenix, Arizona, faced a growing stalemate with the leadership of the International Brotherhood of Electrical Workers (IBEW), who represented SRP employees. The Federal Mediation and Conciliation Service (FMCS) was invited to assist the union and company management in developing a more effective approach to settling on a contract.

Initially, about a half-dozen representatives from each side participated in a FMCS-conducted seminar titled "Partners in Change." The seminar focused on building participants' brainstorming and consensus-building skills and was designed to improve their effectiveness in working in committees, overcoming individual differences, and working toward a mutually beneficial settlement. A few weeks later, 20 more participants (10 from each side) attended a two-day seminar about interest-based bargaining, again facilitated by the FMCS. Then the bargaining began.

During negotiation sessions, negotiators sat intermingled rather than in segregated groups or on opposite sides of the table. Everyone became involved because the process would fail if only a few strong personalities dominated. In addition, both sides shared information about their interests and concerns. They created a menu of possible solutions to their concerns and worked to achieve a solution that best met everyone's needs. As the talks continued, more people were called in as committees were formed to address various issues. The FMCS commissioners monitored the progress of the talks, but insisted on remaining in the background.

Initially, the progress seemed slow and laborious. Yet the negotiating parties were able to make a tentative agreement nine days before the old contract expired—quite a feat, considering how past negotiations had always extended well beyond expiration of previous contracts. In addition, one participant's comments were particularly telling: "In the past, once we reached a settlement, both sides were eager to get away from each other. This time, after we reached a settlement, a majority of the participants went out for a happy hour."[19]

# SUMMARY

Conflict is a controversial subject. Even among those who herald its virtues, ambivalence persists. In organizations, however, the reality of interdependence, competition for scarce resources, and the necessity of coping with change while working together on all sorts of tasks create conditions where conflict is inevitable. The types and sources of conflict are numerous, perplexing, and often tenacious. Even so, individuals at all organizational levels can learn under the appropriate circumstances to approach conflict cooperatively and collaboratively. On occasion, technology may function as a source of conflict, but it also offers new and ever-changing tools for groups to use in managing conflicts. With conflict comes the opportunity for growth and change, for innovation and empowerment, for problem solving and consensus building. Those who learn to confront their differences openly and honestly, to communicate about their differences with sensitivity and integrity, can contribute to a constructive and satisfying organizational climate.

# QUESTIONS FOR DISCUSSION

1. What are some ways in which conflict can be good for an organization and some ways that it can be bad?
2. In what settings can conflict occur?
3. What are approach-approach, approach-avoidance, and avoidance-avoidance conflict?
4. Explain the idea that "every organization is in partial conflict with every other social agent it deals with."
5. Describe three types of role conflict.
6. When does increased communication fail to reduce conflict?
7. How effective is avoidance in resolving conflict? Why?
8. Compare and contrast the five styles of conflict management.
9. Describe some of the key steps in collaborative conflict management.

10. How can technology be used as a tool in managing conflict?

# EXERCISES

1. Examine Debbie's day and identify every instance of conflict, past and present, it contains.
2. Think of an organization to which you now belong or to which you belonged in the past. List one instance of each conflict setting that occurred in that organization and how it was (or should have been) resolved.
3. Tim Hill is a mediator who has been asked to work with the National Basketball Association (NBA) Player's Association and the NBA Owner's Association to help them resolve their long-standing feud over players' salaries and right not to be traded without the player's consent. What advice would you give Tim before the meetings begin?
4. Think of a time in your life when you experienced some conflict, preferably in a job-related situation. In a brief essay, describe the nature and extent of your conflict, the contexts in which it occurred, and the methods you and others used to manage the conflict. To what extent did you resolve the conflict? What other methods would you have tried if you had it to do over again?
5. Choose an organization and arrange for an interview with someone in a management position. As you interview this individual, address some of these issues.
   a. In what ways has this organization experienced conflict?
   b. What role, if any, has the union played in conflicts that have occurred?
   c. What kinds of groups or departments within the organization experience the most conflict? Why?
   d. What approaches to resolving conflicts have been tried? To what extent have they been successful?
   e. Is conflict beneficial in any way? If so, how? If not, why not?
   f. What are some different techniques of conflict resolution that might yet be tried?

Many contemporary writers have pointed with alarm to the rapid decline of U.S. businesses in an increasingly global environment. On the plus side, globalization brings an expanded market for products and services. The potential threats, however, are numerous. To be competitive, U.S. businesses are increasingly seeking the lowest possible labor costs, often turning to less expensive workers from other countries. These practices are beginning to affect white-collar as well as blue-collar employees. In many instances, U.S. businesses are closing their operations at home and moving abroad. Here is one example:

A plant in northern California makes steel irons used in the home for pressing clothes. It employs approximately 800 production workers whose average wage is $10.50 an hour. This plant is owned by General Electric. Over a year ago, GE announced that it would be closing the plant and moving production to Singapore where, instead of the metal irons, a plastic iron will be manufactured.

The shutdown of the plant will have a serious economic impact on the local community. Jobs at the plant were highly sought after. Workers would wait three to four years in hopes of securing a job at the GE plant because wages and benefits were superior to those elsewhere in the community, and workers believed that job security at the GE plant was quite high.

The plant's closing has outraged the union. Workers are bewildered, feeling they have been cheated. GE management points out that wages in Singapore are $1.10 an hour. Moreover, in Singapore, government policy basically precludes the formation of unions. Management alleges that over the years the California union has been responsible for restrictive work rules that, in addition to decreasing efficiency and increasing costs, have been a continuing source of labor-management strife.

The union reports a willingness to negotiate givebacks, including reduction of wages. But union leaders and many of the workers say that they are unwilling to give up everything they have fought for over these many years. Management, in turn, has pointed out that there is no way the California plant can compete with a plant in Singapore, with its $1.10 an hour wage, or, for that matter, with plants in Mexico where wages are about $2 an hour. The union charges that GE is calloused and is interested only in profit.

## Questions

1. What instances of conflict do you see in this situation?
2. What principles of conflict management might be helpful in dealing with this complicated situation?

*A Cross-Cultural Success Story*

In 1982, the General Motors automobile plant in Fremont, California, was the model of the United States in decline. With an absentee rate that hovered at about 20 percent, wildcat strikes were not uncommon. There were typically about 5,000 grievances outstanding, or about one per employee. GM decided to shut Fremont's doors, and later turned it over to Toyota as part of a joint venture called New United Motor Mfg. Inc. (NUMMI).

Over the next few years the Fremont plant underwent an amazing transformation. NUMMI's Japanese bosses set up a typical Toyota production, with just-in-time delivery and a flexible assembly line run by teams of workers in charge of their own jobs. They hired back most of the former United Auto Workers members who wanted work—even the militant leaders. NUMMI's 2,500 employees assemble 240,000 cars per year, roughly equal to what it took 5,000 or more people to produce under GM. Absenteeism runs under 2 percent and grievances have virtually disappeared.

Analysts who study these Japanese transplants (others exist in Ohio and Tennessee) point to the Japanese managers' adroit handling of U.S. workers. The Japanese approach to production, emphasizing flexible teams and attention to quality, demands extremely high employee loyalty. To cultivate this loyalty in the United States, Japanese management has learned how to translate Japanese methods to fit the U.S. values of equality and individualism. Japanese managers elicit loyalty by presenting themselves as equals. At NUMMI, there are no privileged parking lots for executives. Top executives eat in the employee cafeteria. Employees are called "associates" and help decide how their jobs will be set up—and they often find faster ways to do things. For instance, in the old GM plant at Fremont, the person who installed windows on right front doors had to walk from his toolbox to each car three times as it moved along the assembly line. Now, because of a rearrangement of the equipment, the worker can go to the car just once, and can follow along as it passes. The job now requires 11 steps rather than 23.

## Questions

1. What possible sources of conflict existed in this situation?
2. What methods did the Japanese use to avoid or resolve conflict?

# Notes

## Chapter 1

1. John C. Hafer and C. C. Hoth, "Selection Characteristics: Your Priorities and How Students Perceive Them," *Personnel Administrator* (March 1983): 25–28.
2. "As You Climb the Ladder, Style Counts," *Management Review* 76 (May 1987): 9.
3. W. O. Underwood. "A Hospital Director's Administrative Profile," *Hospital Administration* 9 (1963): 37–39.
4. M. J. Cetron, W. Rocha, and R. Luchins, "Into the 21st Century: Long-Term Trends Affecting the United States," *The Futurist* 17 (1988): 29–40.
5. Everett Rogers and Rehka Agarwala-Rogers, *Communication in Organizations* (New York: Free Press, 1976), p. 6.
6. Peter Drucker, *The Practice of Management* (New York: Harper & Row, 1959), p. 92.
7. Herbert A. Simon, *Administrative Behavior,* 2d ed. (New York: Macmillan, 1958), p. xvi.
8. Linda L. Putnam, "The Interpretive Perspective," in *Communication and Organization: An Interpretive Approach,* eds. L. L. Putnam and M. E. Pacanowsky (Beverly Hills: Sage, 1983), p. 45.
9. Alex Bavelas and Dermot Barrett, "An Experimental Approach to Organizational Communication," *Personnel* 27 (1951): 368.
10. Thomas J. Peters and Robert H. Waterman, Jr., *In Search of Excellence* (New York: Harper & Row, 1982), p. 124.
11. Raymond G. Smith, *Speech Communication: Theory and Models* (New York: Harper & Row, 1970), p. 14.
12. John Wenburg and William Wilmot, *The Personal Communication Process* (New York: John Wiley & Sons, 1973), p. 6.
13. S. Axley, "Managerial and Organizational Communication in Terms of the Conduit Metaphor," *Academy of Management Review* 9 (1984): 428–37.
14. Thomas W. Hourihan, "Help Employees to Understand Their Benefits," *Personnel Administrator* 28 (April 1983): 92–98.
15. John Garnett, "Team Briefings' Improving Communications in U.K. Firms," *AMA Forum* 72 (June 1983): 29–30.
16. "What Employees Want to Know," *Communication Briefings* (December 1993): 3.
17. "How to Keep Good Workers," *Communication Briefings* (July 1993): 5.
18. "Suggestion Systems: An Answer to Personnel Problems," *Personnel Journal* 59 (July 1980): 552–53.
19. Mike Hopkins-Doerr, "Getting More Out of MBWA," *Supervisory Management* (February 1989): 17–20.
20. Catherine Romano, "Fear of Feedback," *Management Review* 82 (December 1993): 38–41.
21. S. L. Yenney, "In Defense of the Grievance Procedure in a Nonunion Setting," *Employee Relations Law Journal* 2 (Spring 1977): 437.
22. Phillip K. Tompkins, "Organizational Communication: A State of the Art Review," in *Conference on Organizational Communication,* ed. G. Richetto (Monograph, NASA, G. C. Marshall Space Flight Center, Huntsville, Alabama, 1967).
23. William H. Read, "Upward Communication in Industrial Hierarchies," *Human Relations* 15 (1962): 3–15.
24. Janet Fulk and Sirish Mani, "Distortion of Communication in Hierarchical Relationships," *Communication Yearbook* 9 (Beverly Hills: Sage, 1986), pp. 483–510.
25. Alan Zaremba, "Communication: The Upward Network," *Personnel Journal* 68 (March 1989): 34–39.
26. Frederic M. Jablin, "Superior-Subordinate Communication: The State of the Art," *Psychological Bulletin* 86 (1979): 1201–22.
27. Christopher Lorenz, "For Epson, 'Rugby Team' Angle Computes." *San Francisco Examiner* (July 12, 1987), p. D-3.
28. "The Horizontal Corporation," *Business Week,* (December 10, 1993): 76–81.
29. Rosabeth Moss Kanter, *The Change Masters: Innovation for Productivity in the American Corporation* (New York: Simon & Schuster, 1983), p. 30.

30. Mary Connors, "Go Online to Locate Tips on Salesmanship," *Crain's Chicago Business* 21 (November 9, 1998): 25.

31. Frank Corrado, *Getting the Word Out* (Homewood, Ill.: Business One Irwin, 1993).

32. Anthony Downs, *Inside Bureaucracy* (Boston: Little, Brown, 1967).

33. Tompkins, "Organizational Communication."

34. K. H. Roberts and C. A. O'Reilly, "Organizations as Communication Structures: An Empirical Approach," *Human Communication Research* 4 (1978): 283–93.

35. Terrence E. Deal and Allen A. Kennedy, *Corporate Cultures* (Reading, Mass.: Addison-Wesley, 1982).

36. Peters and Waterman, *In Search of Excellence*, 4 pp. 121–22.

37. Walter Kiechel III, "Beat the Clock," *Fortune* (June 25, 1984): 148.

38. Keith Davis, "The Care and Cultivation of the Corporate Grapevine," in *Readings in Interpersonal and Organizational Communication*, 3d ed., ed. R. C. Huseman et al. (Boston: Holbrook Press, 1973), pp. 131–36.

39. Gordon Allport and Leo Postman, *The Psychology of Rumor* (New York: Henry Holt, 1947).

40. Davis, "Corporate Grapevine," pp. 131–36.

41. J. K. Sheperd, "The Spread of Rumors," *Indianapolis Star Magazine* (November 21, 1979), p. 4.

42. Davis, "Corporate Grapevine," p. 132.

43. James L. Esposito and Ralph L. Rosnow, "Corporate Rumors: How They Start and How to Stop Them," *Management Review* 72 (April 1983): 44–47.

44. John Eckhouse, "Snapple Fights Rumors That It Supports KKK," *San Francisco Chronicle* (September 12, 1993), p. B1.

45. John Naisbitt, *Megatrends: Ten New Directions Transforming Our Lives* (New York: Warner Books, 1982).

46. Samuel Greengard, "Increase the Value of Your Intranet," *Workforce* 76 (March 1997): 88.

47. Sherwood Ross, "Job Interviews on Video: The Electronic Handshake," *Chicago Tribune* (May 24, 1998), sec. 6, p. 21.

48. Samuel Greengard, "Storing, Shaping and Sharing Collective Wisdom," *Workforce* 77 (October 1998): 82–88.

49. Ibid.

50. "Consider E-Mail as Permanent," *Workforce* 7: 77 (July 1998): 38

51. "Avoid These Common Mistakes When Using E-Mail to Manage People," *Motivational Manager* (July 1998): 2

52. "Your Job," *Chicago Tribune* (March 19, 1998), sec. 6, p. 5

53. Chris Serb, "You Never Call: Health Plans Overlook an Easy Step to Keeping Seniors Satisfied," *Hospitals and Health Networks* 72 (October 22, 1998): 32–33

54. Beverly Davenport Sypher and Theodore E. Zorn, Jr., "Communication Related Abilities and Upward Mobility: A Longitudinal Investigation," *Human Communication Research* 12 (1986): 420–31.

## Chapter 2

1. Terrence E. Deal and Allen A. Kennedy, *Corporate Cultures* (Reading, Mass.: Addison-Wesley, 1982).

2. Frederick Taylor, *Scientific Management* (New York: Harper & Row, 1911).

3. Douglas McGregor, *Professional Manager* (New York: McGraw-Hill, 1967).

4. Marc Ballon, "Extreme Managing," *INC.* 20 (July, 1998): 60–66.

5. Rensis Likert, *New Patterns of Management* (New York: McGraw-Hill, 1961); Rensis Likert, *The Human Organization* (New York: McGraw-Hill, 1967).

6. Robert Blake and Jane Mouton, *The Managerial Grid* (Houston: Gulf Publishing, 1964).

7. Paul Hersey, Kenneth H. Blanchard, and R. K. Hambleton, *Contracting for Leadership Style: A Process and Instrumentation for Building Effective Work Relationships* (Columbus: Ohio State University Center for Leadership Studies, 1977); Paul Hersey and Kenneth H. Blanchard, "Life Cycle Theory of Leadership," *Training and Development Journal* 23 (1969): 26–34; Paul Hersey and Kenneth H. Blanchard, *Management of Organizational Behavior: Utilizing Human Resources*, 3d ed. (Englewood Cliffs, N.J.: Prentice-Hall, 1977).

8. Daniel Katz and Robert L. Kahn, *The Social Psychology of Organizations* (New York: John Wiley & Sons, 1966), pp. 16–17.

9. Richard Tanner Johnson and William G. Ouchi, "Made in America (Under Japanese Management)," *Harvard Business Review* 52 (September–October 1974): 61–69; William G. Ouchi, *Theory Z: How American Business Can*

*Meet the Japanese Challenge* (New York: Addison-Wesley, 1981).

10. See, for example: Charles Heckscher, *White Collar Blues* (New York: Basic Books, 1995); Jennifer Laabs, "The New Loyalty," *Workforce* 77 (November, 1998): 35–39.

11. Edward E. Lawler, *High-Involvement Management: Participative Strategies for Improving Organizational Performance* (San Francisco: Jossey-Bass, 1986), p. 3.

12. David L. Bradford and Allan R. Cohen, *Power Up: Transforming Organizations Through Shared Leadership* (New York: John Wiley and Sons, 1998).

13. Brian Dumaine, "Who Needs a Boss?" *Fortune* (May 7, 1990): 52–60.

14. Janet Kidd Stewart, "Teams Don't Always Work," *Chicago Tribune* (July 5, 1998), sec. 13, p. 7.

15. "Jeans Therapy: Levi's Factory Workers Are Assigned to Teams, and Morale Takes a Hit," *Wall Street Journal* (May 20, 1998), p. 1.

16. Dumaine, "Who Needs a Boss?"

17. Michael E. Pacanowsky and Nick O'Donnell-Trujillo, "Organizational Communication as Cultural Performance," *Communication Monographs* 50 (1983): 146; Nick Trujillo, "Organizational Communication as Cultural Performance: Some Managerial Considerations," *Southern Speech Communication Journal* 50 (1985): 201–24.

18. Stephen R. Covey, *The 7 Habits of Highly Effective People* (New York: Simon and Schuster, 1989).

19. Stephen R. Covey, *Principle-Centered Leadership* (New York: Summit Books, 1990).

20. Ken Blanchard and Michael O'Connor, *Managing by Values* (San Francisco: Berrett-Koehler Publishers, 1997).

21. George Labovitz and Victor Rosansky, *The Power of Alignment* (New York: John Wiley and Sons, 1997).

22. See, for example, James O'Toole, *Leading Change: The Argument for Values-Based Leadership* (New York: Ballentine Books, 1995); Joseph V. Quigley, *Vision: How Leaders Develop It, Share It, and Sustain It* (New York: McGraw-Hill, 1993); Eric Harvey and Alexander Lucia, *Walking the Talk Together* (Dallas: Performance Publishing, 1998).

23. Robert S. Kaplan and David P. Norton, *The Balanced Scorecard* (Boston: Harvard Business School Press, 1996).

24. Thomas J. McCoy, *Creating an "Open Book" Organization* (New York: American Management Association, 1996).

25. John Case, *Open-Book Management* (New York: HarperCollins Publishers, 1995).

26. Richard C. Whiteley, *The Customer Driven Company* (Reading, Mass.: Addison-Wesley, 1991); Richard C. Whiteley and Diane Hessan, *Customer Centered Growth* (Reading, Mass.: Addison-Wesley, 1996).

27. Fred Wiersema, *Customer Intimacy* (Santa Monica, Calif.: Knowledge Exchange, 1996).

28. Peter M. Senge, *The Fifth Discipline* (New York: Doubleday, 1990).

29. William Gifford and Elizabeth Pinchot, *The End of Bureaucracy and the Rise of the Intelligent Organization* (San Francisco: Berrett-Koehler Publishers, 1993).

30. Ben Nagler, "Recasting Employees into Teams," *Workforce* 77 (January, 1998): 101–106.

31. Al Neuharth, *Confessions of an S.O.B.* (New York: Doubleday, 1989).

32. Allan Sloan, "The Hit Men," *Newsweek* (February 26, 1996): 44–48.

33. Ibid.

34. Gary Strauss, Tom Lowry, and David Henry, "Sagging Profits Sink Iron-Fisted Chairman," *USA Today* (June 16, 1998), p. 1A.

35. "Villains? Heck No. We're Like Doctors," *Newsweek* (February 26, 1996), 49.

36. Eileen C. Shapiro, *Fad Surfing in the Boardroom* (Reading, Mass: Addison-Wesley, 1995).

37. Thomas J. Peters and Robert H. Waterman, Jr., *In Search of Excellence* (New York: Harper & Row, 1982).

38. Alan Farnham, "In Search of Suckers," *Fortune* 134: 7, (October 14, 1996): 119–26.

39. John Micklethwait and Adrian Wooldridge, *The Witch Doctors: Making Sense of the Management Gurus* (New York: Time Business Books, 1998).

40. James A. Belasco and Ralph C. Stayer, *Flight of the Buffalo* (New York: Time Warner, 1993).

41. Dudley Lynch and Paul L. Kordis, *Strategy of the Dolphin* (New York: Fawcett Columbine, 1988).

42. Farnham, "In Search of Suckers," 122.

43. Shari Coudron, "Be Cool: Cultivating a Cool Culture Gives HR a Staffing Boost," *Workforce* 77: 4 (April, 1998): 50–61.

44. Ibid.

45. Robert Tannenbaum, I. R. Weschler, and Fred Massarik, *Leadership and Organizations: A Behavioral Science Approach* (New York: McGraw-Hill, 1961), p. 11

46. John Naisbitt, *Megatrends: Ten New Directions Transforming Our Lives* (New York: Warner Books, 1982).

47. Ian Morrison and Greg Schmid, *Future Tense: The Business Realities of the Next Ten Years* (New York: William Morrow, 1994).

48. Gerald Celente, *Trends 2000: How to Prepare for and Profit from the Changes of the 21st Century* (New York: Warner Books, 1997).

49. Warren Bennis and B. Namus, *Leaders: Strategies for Taking Charge* (New York: Harper & Row, 1985).

50. Jay A. Conger, "Leadership: The Art of Empowering Others," *Academy of Management Executive* 3 (1989): 17–24.

51. Michael E. Pacanowsky, "Communication in the Empowering Organization," in *Communication Yearbook 11*, ed. J. Anderson (Beverly Hills: Sage, 1987), pp. 356–79.

52. K. Thomas and B. Velthouse, "Cognitive Elements of Empowerment: An 'Interpretive Model' of Intrinsic Task Motivation," *Academy of Management Review* 19 (1990): 666–81.

53. Kent Hodgson, "Adapting Ethical Decisions to a Global Marketplace," *Management Review* 81 (May 16, 1992): 53–57.

54. Charlene Marmer Solomon, "Transplanting Corporate Cultures Globally," *Personnel Journal* 72 (October 1993): 78–88.

55. Mary A. DeVries, quoted in "Words and Phrases to Avoid," *Communication Briefings* (April 1993): 7.

56. Marcy Huber, quoted in "Dealing with Different Cultures," *Communication Briefings* (June 1993): 5.

57. "The Horizontal Corporation: It's about Managing Across, Not Up and Down," *Business Week* (December 20, 1993): 76–81.

58. Ibid.

59. See, for example, James Champy, *Reengineering Management* (New York: Harper Business, 1995); Michael Treacy and Fred Wiersema, *The Discipline of Market Leaders* (Reading, Mass: Addison-Wesley, 1995); Daniel Morris and Joel Brandon, *Reengineering Your Business* (New York: McGraw-Hill, 1993).

60. Michael Hammer and Steven A. Stanton, *The Reengineering Revolution* (New York: HarperCollins Publishers, 1995).

61. Chris Serb, "Is Remaking the Hospital Making Money?" *Hospitals & Health Networks* 72: 14 (July 20, 1998): 32–33.

62. Vicki Clark, "Employees Drive Diversity Efforts at GE Silicones," *Personnel Journal* 72 (May 1993): 148–53.

63. Karin Price Mueller, "Diversity and the Bottom Line," *Harvard Management Update* (April, 1998): 8–9.

64. Lawrence Otis Graham, *Proversity: Getting Past Face Value and Finding the Soul of People* (New York: John Wiley and Sons, 1997).

65. Kathleen Murray, "Companies Rethink One-Shot Diversity Training as New Problems Are Created," *Chicago Tribune* (September 13, 1993), sec. 4, p. 6.

66. Jim Kennedy and Anna Everest, "Put Diversity in Context," *Personnel Journal* 70 (September 1991): 50–54.

## Chapter 3

1. Bowen H. McCoy, "Applying the Art of Action-Oriented Decision Making to the Knotty Issues of Everyday Business Life," *Management Review* (July 1983): 20–21.

2. Robert C. Solomon and Kristine Hanson, *It's Good Business* (New York: Harper & Row, 1985), p. 5.

3. Samuel Greengard, "50% of Your Employees Are Lying, Cheating & Stealing," *Workforce* 76: 10 (October 1997): 44–53.

4. Ibid.

5. Stephen M. Shortell, Ellen M. Morrison, and Bernard Friedman, *Strategic Choices for America's Hospitals* (San Francisco: Jossey-Bass, 1990).

6. "Hospice Firm Pays Nurses to Recruit Patients," *Chicago Tribune* (August 26, 1990), sec. 2, p. 1.

7. "Health Care in the 1990s: Forecasts by Top Analysts," *Hospitals* (20 July 1989): 34–40.

8. Solomon and Hanson, *It's Good Business*, p. 184.

9. "On Sneaker Battlefield, PUSH Is Just One More Foe for Nike," *Chicago Tribune* (August 26, 1990), sec. 7, p. 1.

10. Judith Crown, "BP Might Soften Amoco's Emissions Stance," *Crain's Chicago Business* (November 16, 1998), p. 9.

11. See Charles J. Stewart and William B. Cash, *Interviewing Principles and Practices*, 3d ed. (Dubuque, Ia.: Wm. C. Brown, 1982), pp. 163–67.

12. Such discrimination is forbidden by Title VII of the Civil Rights Act of 1964. Since 1972, the Equal Employment Opportunity Commission has had the power to take organizations to court. See Ruth G. Schaeffer, *Nondiscrimination in Employment, 1973–1975—A Broadening and deepening National Effect* (New York: Conference Board, 1975).

13. "Age Discrimination Actions Flooding Courts, New BNA Special Report Funds," *Labor Relations Week* 3 (1989): 1109.

14. Lin Farley, *Sexual Shakedown: The Sexual Harassment of Women on the Job* (New York: McGraw-Hill, 1978).

15. *Federal Register* 45: 219 (November 10, 1980), 2.

16. Gary N. Powell, "Sexual Harassment: Confronting the Issue of Definition," *Business Horizons* 26 (1983), 24–28.

17. Donald J. Peterson and Douglas Massengill, "Sexual Harassment—A Growing Problem in the Workplace," *Personnel Administrator* (October 1982): 79.

18. "With Problem More Visible, Firms Crack Down on Sexual Harassment," *Wall Street Journal* (August 8, 1986), p. 12.

19. Jennifer Laabs, "What You're Liable for Now," *Workforce* 77 (October 1998): 34–42.

20. Brenda Paik Sunoo, "After Everything Else—Buy Insurance," *Workforce* 77 (October 1998): 45–50.

21. Carolyn C. Dolecheck and Maynard M. Dolecheck, "Sexual Harassment: A Problem for Small Businesses," *American Journal of Small Business* 7 (1983): 45–50.

22. James C. Renick, "Sexual Harassment at Work: Why It Happens, What to Do about It," *Personnel Journal* (August 1980): 14–17.

23. Dolecheck and Dolecheck, "Sexual Harassment."

24. Peterson and Massengill, "Sexual Harassment."

25. Ibid.

26. Eric Rolfe Greenberg, "Workplace Testing: Results of a New AMA Survey," *Personnel* 65 (April 1988): 36–44.

27. "Phone Monitoring a Fairness, Privacy Call," *Chicago Tribune* (August 27, 1990), sec. 4, p. 1.

28. Ibid.

29. "Bosses Peek at E-Mail," *USA Today* (May 24, 1993), sec. B, p. 1.

30. Anne Fisher, "How Safe Is My E-Mail?" *Fortune* 134: 7 (October 14, 1996): 220.

31. Stephanie Armour, "E-Mail Delivers Legal, Privacy Issues," *USA Today* (November 12, 1998), p. 3B.

32. Samuel Greengard, "Privacy: Entitlement or Illusion?" *Personnel Journal* 75: 5 (May 1996): 74.

33. Richard Lacayo, "Nowhere to Hide," *Time* (November 11, 1991): 34–40.

34. Bruce Horovitz, "Playboy Considers Telling All about Its Catalog Customers," *USA Today* (November 12, 1998), p. 1B.

35. Solomon and Hanson, *It's Good Business,* p. 188.

36. Carol Kleiman, "20 Million Industrial Jobs Hinge on 'Fetal Protection' Court Case," *Chicago Tribune* (August 27, 1990), sec. 4, p. 2.

37. Ibid.

38. Gary M. Wederspahn, "Exporting Corporate Ethics," *Global Workforce* 2: 1 (January 1997): 29.

39. LaRue Tone Hosmer, *The Ethics of Management* (Homewood, Ill.: Richard D. Irwin, 1987), p. 106.

40. John F. McMillan, "Ethics and Advertising," in *Speaking of Advertising,* eds. J. S. Wright and S. S. Warner (New York: McGraw-Hill, 1963), pp. 453–58.

41. Wroe Alderson, "The American Economy and Christian Ethics," in *Advertising's Role in Society,* eds. J. S. Wright and J. E. Mertes (St. Paul: West, 1974), pp. 163–75.

42. Lawrence J. Flynn, "The Aristotelian Basis for the Ethics of Speaking," *Speech Teacher* 6 (1957): 179–87.

43. Kenneth Burke, *The Rhetoric of Motives* (Cleveland: World, 1962); Kenneth Burke, *Language as Symbolic Action* (Berkeley, University of California Press, 1966).

44. Kate Ludeman, *The Worth Ethic* (New York: E. P. Dutton, 1989), p. xv.

45. Milton Rokeach, *Beliefs, Attitudes and Values* (San Francisco: Jossey-Bass, 1968), p. 124.

46. Franklyn Haiman, "Democratic Ethics and the Hidden Persuaders," *Quarterly Journal of Speech* 44 (1958): 385–92.

47. Karl Wallace, "An Ethical Basis of Communication," *Speech Teacher* 4 (1955): 1–9.

48. "Looking to Its Roots," *Time* (May 25, 1987): 27.

49. See Richard L. Johannesen, "The Emerging Concept of Communication as Dialogue," *Quarterly Journal of Speech* 57 (1971): 373–82; Paul W. Keller and Charles T. Brown, "An

Interpersonal Ethic for Communication,"
*Journal of Communication* 18 (1968): 73–81;
David W. Johnson, *Reaching Out: Interpersonal
Effectiveness and Self-Actualization*
(Englewood Cliffs, N.J.: Prentice-Hall, 1972);
John Stewart, "Foundations of Dialogic
Communication," *Quarterly Journal of Speech*
64 (1978): 183–201; Richard L. Johannesen,
"Perspectives on Ethics in Persuasion," in
*Persuasion: Reception and Responsibility*, ed.
Charles U. Larson (Belmont, Calif.:
Wadsworth, 1973).

50. Johannesen, "The Emerging Concept," 373–82.
51. F. G. Bailey, *Humbuggery and Manipulation:
The Art of Leadership* (Ithaca, N.Y.: Cornell
University Press, 1988), p. ix.
52. Jerome H. Want, "Corporate Mission: The
Intangible Contributor to Performance,"
*Management Review* 75 (August 1986): 46–50.
53. Alan Weiss, "The Value System," *Personnel
Administrator* 34 (July 1989): 40–41.
54. Christopher K. Bart, "Sex, Lies and Mission
Statements," *Business Horizons* 40: 6
(November–December 1997): 19–20.
55. Michael Davis, "Working with Your
Company's Code of Ethics," *Management
Solutions* 33 (June 1988): 5–10.
56. Robert Hershey, "Corporate Mottos: What
They Are, What They Do," *Personnel* 64
(February 1987): 52–65.
57. Anthony J. Rutigliano, "Steelcase: Nice Guys
Finish First," *Management Review* 74
(November 1985): 46–51.
58. Samual Greengard, "50% of Your Employees
Are Lying."
59. Kenneth Labich, "Making Diversity Pay,"
*Fortune* 134: 5 (September 9, 1996): 177–80.
60. Greengard, "50% of Your Employees are
Lying," 53.
61. Carolyn B. Alfin, "Work Strife Keeps 9to5 on
the Job 25 Years Later," *Chicago Tribune*
(October 11, 1998), pp. 9–10.
62. Ibid.
63. Maynard M. Dolecheck, "Doing Justice to
Ethics," *Supervisory Management* 10 (July
1989): 35–39.
64. Sally Blank, "Hershey: A Company Driven by
Values," *Management Review* 75 (November
1986): 31–35.
65. "Looking to Its Roots," 29–41.
66. James L. Hayes, *Memos for Management:
Leadership* (New York: American Management
Association, 1983), p. 103.

67. Thomas J. Peters, *Thriving on Chaos* (New
York: Knopf, 1987), p. 519.
68. Schmidt and Posner, "Managerial Values in
Perspective," p. 11.
69. Dale Dauten, "When Business Ethics Are
Profit-Driven," *Chicago Tribune* (July 12,
1998), sec. 5, p. 8.

## Chapter 4

1. Peter Drucker, "How to Be an Employer,"
*Fortune* (May 5, 1952), p. 126.
2. Cal Downs, David Berg, and Wil Linkugel, *The
Organizational Communicator* (New York:
Harper & Row, 1977).
3. Sandy Whiteley, ed., *The American Library
Association Guide to Information Access: A
Complete Research Handbook and Directory*
(New York: Random House, 1994).
4. Sheila Wellington, "Women Are in the Wrong
Conduits: Moving Talented Women Upward,"
*Vital Speeches of the Day* 63 (1997): 149.
5. David D. Ho, "Science as a Candle of Hope:
We Can Change the World," *Vital Speeches of
the Day* 63 (1997): 661.
6. Cesar Chavez, "Pesticides Speech," in
*Contemporary American Speeches*, 8th ed., eds.
Richard L. Johannesen, R. Allen, Wil A.
Linkugel, and Ferald J. Bryan (Dubuque, Ia.:
Kendall/Hunt, 1997), pp. 207–08.
7. This speech extract is based on a presentation
given in a class at Indiana University by Holly
Baxter, a doctoral student in the Department
of Speech Communication.
8. A. Thomas Young, "Ethics in Business," *Vital
Speeches of the Day* 58 (1992): 726–27.
9. Mario Cuomo, "Keynote Address," *Vital
Speeches of the Day* 50 (1984): 644.
10. See James C. McCroskey, *An Introduction to
Rhetorical Communication*, 7th ed. (Boston:
Allyn and Bacon, 1997), pp. 87–104.

## Chapter 5

1. Irwin Edmond, *The Works of Plato* (New York:
Simon & Schuster, 1928), p. 309.
2. Jimmy Carter, "U.S. Response to Soviet
Military Force in Cuba," *Vital Speeches of the
Day* 46 (1979–80): 2.
3. Neal W. O'Connor, "The Freedom to
Communicate: An Advertising Man Re-reads
the First Amendment," *Vital Speeches of the
Day* 42 (1976): 179.

4.  Eric Rubenstein, "Homelessness and Values: A Stopping Point or a Way of Life?" *Vital Speeches of the Day* 58 (1992): 401.

5.  John D. Garwood, "Back to the Basics: A Commitment to Excellence," *Vital Speeches of the Day* 46 (1979–80): 42.

6.  Richard Lamm, "Unexamined Assumptions: Destiny, Political Institutions, Democracy and Population," *Vital Speeches of the Day* 64 (September 15, 1998): 712.

7.  Holger Kluge, "Reflections on Diversity: Cultural Assumptions," *Vital Speeches of the Day* 63 (1996–97): 171.

8.  Gary Trudeau, "The Impertinent Question," *Vital Speeches of the Day* 52 (1985–86): 619.

9.  This pattern was originally introduced by Alan Monroe in *Principles and Types of Speech* (New York: Scott, Foresman, 1935) and has been refined in later editions.

10. See Karen Zediker, *Rediscovering the Tradition: Women's History with a Relational Approach to the Basic Public Speaking Course,* paper presented at the Western States Communication Association, Albuquerque, New Mexico, 1993. This paper reviews the work of Christine Jorgensen-Earp, who argues that these patterns are often used by women and ethnic speakers.

11. See James C. McCroskey, *An Introduction to Rhetorical Communication,* 7th ed. (Boston: Allyn and Bacon, 1997), pp. 205–22.

12. William Jefferson Clinton, "Acceptance Speech," *Vital Speeches of the Day* 52 (1992): 645.

13. Carter, "U.S. Response to Soviet Military Force in Cuba," p. 4.

14. Martin Luther King, Jr., "I Have a Dream," in *Contemporary American Speeches,* 8th ed., eds. R. L. Johannesen, R. R. Allen, W. A. Linkugel, and F. J. Bryan (Dubuque, Ia.: Kendall Hunt Publishing Company, 1997), p. 369.

15. Robert C. Purcell, "Values for Value: Integrity and Stewardship," *Vital Speeches of the Day* 64 (October 1, 1998): 766.

16. E. D. Wrenchley, "A Study of Stage Fright in a Selected Group of Experienced Speakers," M.A. thesis, University of Denver, 1948. Also see James C. McCroskey, "Oral Communication Apprehension: A Summary of Recent Theory and Research," *Human Communication Research* 4 (1977): 79–96.

17. William Hamilton, "A Review of Experimental Studies of Stage Fright," *Pennsylvania Speech Annual* 17 (1960): 44–45.

18. Theodore Clevenger, Jr., "A Synthesis of Experimental Research in Stage Fright," *Quarterly Journal of Speech* 45 (1959): 135–59.

19. See John P. DeCecco and W. R. Crawford, *The Psychology of Learning and Instruction: Educational Psychology* (Englewood Cliffs, N.J.: Prentice-Hall, 1974).

20. Other ways of managing stage fright include systematic desensitization and cognitive restructuring. See James C. McCroskey, "The Implementation of a Large Scale Program of Systematic Desensitization for Communication Apprehension," *Speech Teacher* 21 (1972): 255–65; and Jo Ayres and T. S. Hopf, "Visualization: A Means of Reducing Speech Anxiety," *Communication Education* 34 (1985): 318–23.

21. Jane Blankenship, *A Sense of Style* (Belmont, Calif.: Dickenson, 1968), pp. 112–24.

22. Rudolph Flesch, *The Art of Plain Talk* (New York: Harper & Brothers, 1946), p. 38.

## Chapter 6

1.  Abraham Maslow, *Motivation and Personality* (New York: Harper & Row, 1954).

2.  Ibid.

3.  David C. McClelland and David H. Burnham, "Power is the Great Motivator," *Harvard Business Review* 73 (1995): 126–39.

4.  Peter F. Drucker, *The Effective Executive* (New York: Harper & Row, 1967). Also see Peter G. Northouse, *Leadership: Theory and Practice* (Thousand Oaks, Calif.: Sage Publications, 1997), pp. 130–58, for an extensive discussion of transformational leadership.

5.  Jack L. Whitehead, "Factors of Source Credibility," *Quarterly Journal of Speech* 54 (1968): 59–63.

6.  See James C. McCroskey, *An Introduction to Rhetorical Communication,* 7th ed. (Boston: Allyn and Bacon, 1997), pp. 87–107, for an excellent review of the research of ethos.

7.  James C. McCroskey, "The Effects of Evidence as an Inhibitor of Counter-Persuasion," *Speech Monographs* 37 (1970): 188–94.

8.  James C. McCroskey, "A Summary of Experimental Research on the Effects of Evidence in Persuasive Communication," *Quarterly Journal of Speech* 55 (1969): 169–76.

9.  Michael Burgoon and Judee K. Burgoon, "Message Strategies in Influence Attempts," in *Communication Behavior,* eds. G. J.

Hanneman and W. J. McEwen (Reading, MA: Addison-Wesley, 1975), pp. 149–65.

10. Ibid., p. 158.

11. Janet Fulk and S. Mani, "Distortion of Communication in Hierarchical Relationships," in *Communication Yearbook* 9, ed. M. L. McLaughlin (Newbury Park, Calif.: Sage Publications), pp. 483–510.

12. See, for example, P. G. Clampitt, *Communicating for Managerial Effectiveness* (Newbury Park, Calif.: Sage Publications, 1991); and Alvin Toffler, *Powershift* (New York: Bantam Books, 1990).

13. See Patricia Hayes Andrews and Richard T. Herschel, *Organizational Communication: Empowerment in a Technological Society* (Boston: Houghton Mifflin, 1996), pp. 170–79.

14. See McCroskey, *An Introduction to Rhetorical Communication*, p. 203.

15. John Dewey, *How We Think* (Boston: Heath, 1910).

16. See Virginia P. Richmond and James C. McCroskey, *Nonverbal Behavior in Interpersonal Relations*, 3d ed. (Boston: Allyn & Bacon, 1995); and Edward T. Hall, *The Silent Language* (New York: Fawcett Books Group–CBS Publications, 1959).

## Chapter 7

1. John Naisbitt, *Megatrends: Ten New Directions Transforming Our Lives* (New York: Warner Books, 1982), p. 45.

2. Timothy Leary, *Interpersonal Diagnosis of Personality* (New York: Ronald, 1957).

3. William C. Schutz, *FIRO: A Three-Dimensional Theory of Interpersonal Behavior* (New York: Holt, Rinehart & Winston, 1958); William C. Schutz, *The Interpersonal Underworld* (Palo Alto, Calif.: Science and Behavior Books, 1966).

4. Robert F. Bales, *Personality and Interpersonal Behavior* (New York: Holt, Rinehart & Winston, 1971).

5. See Ronald B. Adler and Neil Towne, *Looking Out/Looking In*, 4th ed. (New York: Holt, Rinehart & Winston, 1984), p. 299.

6. Ellen Berscheid and Elaine H. Walster, *Interpersonal Attraction* (Reading, Mass.: Addison-Wesley, 1969).

7. John Daly, "Homophily-Heterophily and the Prediction of Supervisor Satisfaction" (paper presented at the annual meeting of the International Communication Association, Portland, Oregon, April 1976).

8. Thomas M. Rand and Kenneth N. Wexley, "Demonstration of the Effect: 'Similar to Me,' in Simulated Employment Interviews," *Psychological Reports* 36 (1975): 535–44.

9. David Landy and Elliott Aronson, "Liking for an Evaluator as a Function of His Discernment," *Journal of Personality and Social Psychology* 9 (1968): 133–41.

10. John R. P. French and Bernard Raven, "The Bases of Social Power," in *Group Dynamics*, eds. D. Cartwright and A. Zander (New York: Harper & Row, 1960), pp. 259–68.

11. Irwin Altman and Dalmas Taylor, *Social Penetration: The Development of Interpersonal Relationships* (New York: Holt, Rinehart & Winston, 1973).

12. See, for example, Michael L. Hecht, "Satisfying Communication and Relationship Labels: Intimacy and Length of Relationship as Perceptual Frames of Naturalistic Conversation," *Western Journal of Speech Communication* 48 (1984): 201–16; Donald J. Cagala, Grant T. Savage, Claire C. Brunner, and Anne B. Conrad, "An Elaboration of the Meaning of Interaction Involvement," *Communication Monographs* 49 (1982): 229–48.

13. Albert Mehrabian, *Public Places and Private Spaces* (New York: Basic Books, 1976).

14. W. Barnett Pearce, "The Coordinated Management of Meaning: A Rules Based Theory of Interpersonal Communication," in *Explorations in Interpersonal Communication*, ed. Gerald R. Miller (Beverly Hills: Sage, 1976), pp. 17–35.

15. Marsha Houston Stanback and W. Barnett Pearce, "Talking to 'The Man': Some Communication Strategies Used by Members of 'Subordinate' Social Groups," *Quarterly Journal of Speech* 67 (1981): 21–30.

16. Charles M. Rossiter and W. Barnett Pearce, *Communicating Personally* (New York: Bobbs-Merrill, 1975).

17. Albert Mehrabian, *Silent Messages* (Belmont, Calif.: Wadsworth, 1971).

18. Robert A. Bell, Sheryl W. Tremblay, and Nancy L. Bverkel-Rothfuss, "Interpersonal Attraction as a Communication Accomplishment: Development of a Measure of Affinity-Seeking Competence," *Western Journal of Speech Communication* 51 (1987): 1–18.

19. William Haney, *Communication and Organizational Behavior* (Burr Ridge, Ill.: Richard D. Irwin, 1967), p. 56.

20. Mark L. Knapp, *Nonverbal Communication in Human Interaction*, 2d ed. (New York: Holt, Rinehart & Winston, 1978), pp. 94–95.

21. Theodore R. Sarbin, Ronald Taft, and Daniel E. Bailey, *Clinical Inference and Cognitive Theory* (New York: Holt, Rinehart & Winston, 1960).

22. Eugene Jacobson, W. W. Charters, and Seymour Liberman, "The Use of the Role Concept in the Study of Complex Organizations," *Journal of Social Issues* 7 (1951): 947–99; John E. Haas, *Role Conception and Group Consensus* (Columbus: Bureau of Business Research, Ohio State University, 1964); Bond L. Bible and James D. McComas, "Role Consensus and Teacher Effectiveness," *Social Forces* 42 (1963): 225–32.

23. Henry W. Riecken and George C. Homans, "Psychological Aspects of Social Structure," in *Handbook of Social Psychology,* ed. G. Lindzey (Cambridge, Mass.: Addison-Wesley, 1954), pp. 786–832; A. Paul Hare, *Handbook of Small Group Research* (New York: Free Press, 1962).

24. Stephen R. Covey, *The 7 Habits of Highly Effective People* (New York: Simon & Schuster, 1989).

25. Gary T. Hunt and Louis P. Cusella, "A Field Study of Listening Needs in Organizations," *Communication Education* 32 (1983): 368–78.

26. Donald T. Campbell, "Systematic Effort on the Part of Human Links in Communication Systems," *Information and Control* (1958): 334–69.

27. Erving Goffman, *Interaction Ritual* (New York: Doubleday, 1967).

28. "'Listening' Errors Prove Costly for Firms," *San Jose Mercury News* (March 14, 1984), p. 1F.

29. Andrew D. Wolvin and Carolyn Gwynn Coakley, *Listening*, 2d ed. (Dubuque, Ia.: Wm. C. Brown, 1985).

30. Edward J. Hegarty, *How to Talk Your Way to the Top* (West Nyack, N.Y.: Parker, 1973).

31. French and Raven, *"The Bases of Social Power."*

32. Arlene Yerys, "How to Get What You Want through Influential Communication," *Management Review* 71 (June 1982): 12–18.

33. Natasha Josefowitz, "Getting through to the Unreachable Person," *Management Review* 71 (March 1983): 48–50.

34. Frank Stagnaro, "The Benefits of Leveling with Employees: ROLM's Experience," *Management Review* 71 (July 1982): 16–20.

35. Charles M. Rossiter and W. Barnett Pearce, *Communicating Personally* (New York: Bobbs-Merrill, 1975).

36. Samuel Culbert, *Interpersonal Process of Self-Disclosure: It Takes Two to See One* (Washington, D.C.: NTL Institute for Applied Behavioral Science, 1967).

37. Joseph Luft, *Group Processes: An Introduction to Group Dynamics* (Palo Alto, Calif.: National Press Books, 1970).

38. Rafael Steinberg, *Man and the Organization* (New York: Time-Life Books, 1975).

39. Rossiter and Pearce, *Communicating Personally.*

## Chapter 8

1. William P. Sullivan, "Have You Got What It Takes to Get to the Top?" *Management Review* 72 (April 1983): 7–11.

2. William Johnson, *People in Quandaries* (New York: Harper & Row, 1946); A. Korzybski, *Science and Sanity* (Lancaster, Pa: Science Press, 1951).

3. William Haney, *Communication and Organizational Behavior: Text and Cases* (Homewood, Ill.: Irwin, 1967).

4. D. Bourland, "The Semantics of Non-Aristotelian Language," *General Semantics Bulletin* 35 (1968): 60–63.

5. J. Gibb, "Defensive Communication," *Journal of Communication* 11 (1961): 141–48; Sharon Ellison, *Don't Be So Defensive* (Kansas City: Andrews McMeel, 1998).

6. E. Goffman, *Encounters* (Indianapolis: Bobbs-Merrill, 1961).

7. S. Palmer, *Understanding Other People* (New York: Crowell, 1955).

8. A. Fleishman, "How to Sabotage a Meeting," *ETC.* 24 (1967): 341–44.

9. Gibb, "Defensive Communication."

10. Edward J. Hegarty, *How to Talk Your Way to the Top* (West Nyack, N.Y.: Parker, 1973).

11. G. Michael Barton, "Communication: Manage Words Effectively," *Personnel Journal* 69 (January 1990): 34.

12. Hegarty, *How to Talk Your Way to the Top* p. 25.

13. Ray Birdwhistell, "Background to Kinesics," *ETC* 13 (1955): 10–18.

14. Michael Maas, "In Offices of the Future . . . The Productivity Value of Environment," *Management Review* 72 (March 1983): 16–20.

15. Fred I. Steele, *Physical Settings and Organizational Development* (Reading, Mass.: Addison-Wesley, 1973).

16. Pat Gerlach, "Offices Get Down to the Business of Looking Good," *Chicago Sunday Herald* (26 August 1984), sec. 2, p. 1.

17. Mehrabian, *Public Places and Private Spaces* p. 46.

18. Michael Korda, *Power! How to Get It, How to Use It* (New York: Random House, 1975).

19. Edward W. Miles and Dale G. Leathers, "The Impact of Aesthetic and Professionally Related Objects on Credibility in the Office Setting," *Southern Speech Communication Journal* 49 (1984): 361–79.

20. Alan M. Webber, "When It Comes to Creative Companies, Design Matters," *USA Today* (December 8, 1998), p. 15A.

21. D. W. Stacks and J. K. Burgoon, "The Persuasive Effects of Violating Spacial Distance Expectations in Small Groups" (paper presented at the Southern Speech Communication Association, Biloxi, MS., 1979).

22. Peter A. Andersen, "Nonverbal Communication in the Small Group," in *Small Group Communication: A Reader*, 5th ed., eds. R. Cathcart and L. Samovar (Dubuque, IA.: Brown, 1988), pp. 333–50.

23. Albert Mehrabian, "Inference of Attitude from the Posture, Orientation, and Distance of a Communicator," *Journal of Consulting and Clinical Psychology* 32 (1968): 308.

24. M. Lefkowitz, Robert Blake, and Jane Mouton, "Status Factors in Pedestrian Violation of Traffic Signals," *Journal of Abnormal and Social Psychology* 51 (1955): 704–06.

25. John T. Malloy, *Dress for Success* (New York: Warner Books, 1978).

26. Andersen, "Nonverbal Communication in the Small Group," pp. 334–35.

27. Mehrabian, "Inference of Attitude from the Posture, Orientation and Distance of a Communicator."

28. Albert Mehrabian and M. Williams, "Nonverbal Concomitants of Perceived and Intended Persuasiveness," *Journal of Personality and Social Psychology* 13 (1969): 37–58.

29. Andersen, "Nonverbal Communication in the Small Group," p. 337.

30. A. E. Scheflen, *Body Language and the Social Order* (Englewood Cliffs, N.J.: Prentice-Hall, 1972).

31. Howard M. Rosenfeld, "Instrumental Affiliative Functions of Facial and Gestural Expressions," *Journal of Personality and Social Psychology* 4 (1966): 65–72; Mehrabian and Williams, "Nonverbal Concomitants of Perceived and Intended Persuasiveness."

32. Paul Ekman and W. V. Friesen, *Unmasking the Face* (Englewood Cliffs, N.J.: Prentice-Hall, 1975).

33. R. Exline and C. Eldridge, "Effects of Two Patterns of a Speaker's Visual Behavior upon the Perception of the Authenticity of His Verbal Message" (paper presented to the Eastern Psychological Association, Boston, 1967).

34. Joseph A. DeVito, *The Interpersonal Communication Book*, 4th ed. (New York: Harper & Row, 1986), p. 208.

35. Ashley Montagu, *Touching: The Human Significance of the Skin* (New York: Columbia University Press, 1971).

36. J. T. Auer, *The Joy of Selling* (Toronto: Stoddard Publishing, 1992), pp. 45–51.

37. Kenneth Blanchard and Spencer Johnson, *The One Minute Manager* (New York: Morrow, 1982).

38. Nancy Henley, *Body Politics: Power, Sex, and Nonverbal Communication* (Englewood Cliffs, N.J.: Prentice-Hall, 1977).

39. Sidney M. Jourard, *Disclosing Man to Himself* (New York: Van Nostrand Reinhold, 1968):

40. Ibid.

41. DeVito, *The Interpersonal Communication Book*, pp. 211–13.

42. David W. Addington, "The Relationship of Selected Vocal Characteristics to Personality Perception," *Speech Monographs* 35 (1968): 492–503.

43. M. H. L. Hecker, "Speaker Recognition: An Interpretive Survey of the Literature," *ASHA Monographs*, no. 16 (Washington, D.C.: American Speech and Hearing Association, 1971).

44. Howard Giles and Richard Y. Bourhis, "Voice and Racial Categorization in Britain," *Communication Monographs*, 43 (1976): 108–14; Norman J. Lass, Karen R. Hughes, Melanie D. Bowyer, Lucille T. Waters, and Victoria T. Broune, "Speaker Sex Identification from Voiced, Whispered and Filtered Isolated Vowels," *Journal of the*

*Acoustical Society of America* 59 (1976): 675–78.

45. Joel R. Davitz, *The Communication of Emotional Meaning* (New York: McGraw-Hill, 1964); Mark Snyder, "Self-Monitoring of Expressive Behavior," *Journal of Personality and Social Psychology* 30 (1974): 526–37.

46. Andersen, "Nonverbal Communication in the Small Group," p. 340.

47. Mary Maguire, "Prime-Time Executives: Theatrical Training Lifts Careers," *Chicago Tribune* (October 19, 1992), sec. 4, p. 1.

48. John E. Baird, Jr., and Gretchen K. Wieting, "Nonverbal Communication Can Be a Motivational Tool," *Personnel Journal* 58 (1979): 607–10.

## Chapter 9

1. Charles J. Stewart and William B. Cash, *Interviewing: Principles and Practices*, 3d ed. (Dubuque, IA: Brown, 1982), p. 7.
2. Ibid., p. 14.
3. Ibid., p. 15.
4. Craig D. Tengler and Frederic M. Jablin, "Effects of Question Type, Orientation, and Sequencing in the Employment Screening Interview," *Communication Monographs* 50 (1983): 245–63.
5. Ibid., pp. 262–63.
6. James M. Lahiff, "Interviewing for Results," in *Readings in Interpersonal and Organizational Communication*, eds. R. C. Huseman, C. M. Logue, and D. L. Freshley, 3d ed. (Boston, Holbrook Press, 1973), p. 335.
7. Guvenc G. Alpander, "Training First-Line Supervisors to Criticize Constructively," *Personnel Journal* 59 (1980): 216–21.
8. Douglas McGregor, "An Uneasy Look at Performance Appraisal," *Harvard Business Review* 58 (1957): 66–71.
9. Randall Brett and Alan J. Fredian, "Performance Appraisal: The System Is Not the Solution," *Personnel Administrator* 26 (1981): 61–68.
10. James M. Lahiff, "Interviewing for Results," in *Readings in Interpersonal and Organizational Communication*, eds. R. C. Huseman, C. M. Logue, and D. L. Freshley, 2d ed. (Boston: Holbrook Press, 1973); Emanuel Kay, Herbert H. Meyer, and John R. P. French, "The Effect of Threat in a Performance Appraisal Interview," *Journal of Applied Psychology* 49 (1965): 311–17.

11. Cal W. Downs, G. Paul Smeyak, and Ernest Martin, *Professional Interviewing* (New York: Harper & Row, 1980).
12. J. Key, "Many Employee Evaluation Systems Are Rating Bad Scores," *Chicago Tribune* (January 25, 1982), sec. 8, p. 3.
13. Brett and Fredian, "Performance Appraisal."
14. For a more detailed consideration of employee performance appraisal, see Elaine F. Gruenfeld, *Performance Appraisal: Promise and Peril* (Ithaca, N.Y.: Cornell University Press, 1981); Charles A. Dailey and Ann M. Madsen, *How to Evaluate People in Business* (New York: McGraw-Hill, 1980); and Donald H. Brush and Lyle F. Scheonfeldt, "Performance Appraisal for the '80s," *Personnel Administrator* 27 (December 1982): 76–83.

## Chapter 10

1. Joseph A. Raelin, "First-Job Effects on Career Development," *Personnel Administrator* 28 (August 1983): 71–92.
2. See Renee Ruhnow, Robert M. Noe, Randall Odom, and Stanley Adamson, "Interviews: A Look at Their Reliability and Validity," *HR Focus* (February 1992): 13.
3. Richard D. Arvey and James E. Campion, "The Employment Interview: A Summary and Review of Recent Research," *Personnel Psychology* 35 (1982): 281–321.
4. See Patricia R. Bergeson, *The Americans with Disabilities Act (ADA): Practical Considerations for Employers* (Chicago: Pope, Ballard, Shepard & Fowler, 1991); Phillip M. Perry, "Your Most Dangerous Legal Traps When Interviewing Job Applicants," *Law Practice Management* (March 1994): 50–56.
5. American Psychological Association, *Principles for the Validation and Use of Personnel Selection Procedures*, 1975; Equal Employment Opportunity Commission, *Uniform Guidelines on Employee Selection, Federal Registrar* 25 (August 1978); Fredic M. Jablin, "Use of Discriminatory Questions in Screen Interviews," *Personnel Administrator* 27 (March 1982): 41–44; and Charles J. Stewart and William B. Cash, *Interviewing: Principles and Practices*, 8th ed. (Boston: McGraw-Hill, 1997), pp. 193–223.
6. Diane Arthur, "Preparing for the Interview," *Personnel* 63 (May 1986): 37.

7. Carol Kleiman, "From Genetics to Honesty, Firms Expand Employee Tests, Screening," *Chicago Tribune* (February 9, 1992), 8–1.

8. Eric Rolfe Greenberg, "Workplace Testing: Results of a New AMA Survey," *Personnel* 65 (April 1988): 36–44.

9. See Steven M. Ralston and Robert Brady, "The Relative Influence of Interview Communication Satisfaction on Applicants' Recruitment Decisions," *Journal of Business Communication* 31 (1994): 61–77.

10. H. L. Sheppard and H. Belitsky, *The Job Hunt: Job-Seeking Behavior of Unemployed Workers in a Local Economy* (Baltimore, Md.: Johns Hopkins University Press, 1971).

11. See Martin Yate, *Knock 'Em Dead: The Ultimate Job Seeker's Handbook* (Holbrook, Mass.: Adams, 1996), pp. 295–96, for further details of Internet sources.

12. Richard N. Bolles, *The 1998 What Color Is Your Parachute? A Practical Manual for Job-Hunters and Career-Changers* (Berkeley, Calif.: Ten Speed Press, 1998).

13. See, for example, Lois J. Einhorn, Patricia H. Bradley, and John E. Baird, Jr., *Effective Employment Interviewing: Unlocking Human Potential* Glenview, Ill.: Scott, Foresman, 1982); A. B. Kanter, *The Essential Book of Interviewing: Everything You Need to Know from Both Sides of the Table* (New York: Times Books, 1995); Yate, *Knock 'Em Dead*.

14. Howard M. Sherer, "Effective Entry-Level Organizational Communication as Assessed through a Survey of Personnel Recruiters" (Ph.D. dissertation, Indiana University, 1984).

15. Harold D. Janes, "The Cover Letter and Résumé," *Personnel Journal* 48 (1969): 732–33.

16. It is important to note that the length of the résumé will partly be determined by the employee's background (a mid-career applicant is likely to have a longer résumé); and some employers, including those who hire college professors, expect to see résumés that are quite lengthy. Like everything else, the résumé must be adapted to the context.

17. Rosalia Sears, "Nonverbal Communication in the Employment Interview: A Review of the Literature," *Indiana Speech Journal* 18 (1986): 20–32.

18. Steven M. Ralston, "The Relative Effectiveness of Interviewee Communication Behavior, Job Application and Job Description upon Simulated Personnel Selection Decisions" (Ph.D. dissertation, Indiana University, 1986).

19. See Einhorn, Bradley, and Baird.

20. Lois J. Einhorn, "An Inner View of the Job Interview: An Investigation of Successful Communicative Behaviors," *Communication Education* 30 (1981): 217–28.

## Chapter 11

1. Robert F. Bales, *Interaction Process Analysis: A Method for the Study of Small Groups* (Cambridge, Mass.: Addison-Wesley, 1950).

2. William Scott, *Organization Theory* (Homewood, Ill.: Richard D. Irwin, 1967).

3. Michael S. Olmstead, "Orientation and Role in the Small Group," *American Sociological Review* 19 (1959): 741–51.

4. Clovis R. Shepherd, *Small Groups* (Scrantan, Pa.: Chandler, 1964).

5. Frederic M. Jablin, "Groups within Organizations: Current Issues and Directions for Future Research" (unpublished manuscript, University of Texas at Austin, 1980).

6. See Gay Lumsden and Donald Lumsden, *Communicating in Groups and Teams: Sharing Leadership*, 2d ed. (Belmont, Calif.: Wadsworth, 1997).

7. Brian Dumaine, "The Trouble with Teams," *Fortune* (September 5, 1994): 65–70.

8. R. Wellins, W. Byham, and J. Wilson, *Empowered Teams* (San Francisco: Calif.: Jossey-Bass, 1991), p. 3.

9. See David A. Whetton and Kim S. Cameron, *Developing Management Skills*, 2nd ed. (New York: HarperCollins, 1991).

10. Jon R. Katzenbach and Douglas K. Smith, "The Discipline of Teams," *Harvard Business Review* 71: 111–20.

11. Dumaine, "The Trouble with Teams," p. 67.

12. Katzenbach and Smith, "The Discipline of Teams," p. 116.

13. As quoted in Lumsden and Lumsden, *Communicating in Groups and Teams*.

14. *Quality Circles Participants' Manual* (Prospect Heights, Ill.: Waveland Press, 1982), pp. 5–16.

15. E. E. Lawler and S. A. Mohrman, "Quality Circles after the Fad," *Harvard Business Review* 63 (1985): 65–71.

16. G. W. Meyer and R. G. Stott, "Quality Circles: Panacea or Pandora's Box?" *Organizational Dynamics* 13 (1985), 34–50.

17. Ibid.

18. Cynthia Stohl, "Quality Circles and Changing Patterns of Communication," *Communication*

Yearbook 9 (Beverly Hills, Calif.: Sage, 1986), pp. 483–510.

19. Frederick Taylor, *Scientific Management* (New York: Harper & Row, 1911).

20. Solomon E. Asch, "Studies of Independence and Conformity: A Minority of One against a Unanimous Majority," *Psychological Monographs* 70 (1956).

21. Edgar Schein, *Process Consultation* (Reading, Mass.: Addison-Wesley, 1969), p. 59.

22. George Cheney, "On the Various and Changing Meanings of Organizational Membership: A Field Study of Organizational Identification," *Communication Monographs* 50 (1983): 342–62.

23. Asch, "Studies of Independence and Conformity."

24. Carolyn W. Sherif, Muzafer Sherif, and Roger E. Nebergall, *Attitude and Attitude Change: The Social Judgment-Involvement Approach* (Philadelphia, Pa.: Saunders, 1965).

25. Patricia Hayes Andrews, "Ego-Involvement, Self-Monitoring, and Conformity in Small Groups: A Communicative Analysis," *Central States Speech Journal* 36 (1985): 51–61.

26. Stanley Schachter, "Deviation, Rejection, and Communication," *Journal of Abnormal and Social Psychology* 46 (1951): 190–207.

27. K. Phillip Taylor, "An Investigation of Majority Verbal Behavior toward Opinions of Deviant Group Members in Group Discussions of Policy" (unpublished doctoral dissertation, Indiana University, 1969).

28. Carl L. Thameling and Patricia Hayes Andrews, "Majority Responses to Opinion Deviates: A Communicative Analysis," *Small Group Research* 23 (1992): 475–502.

29. John R. Wenburg and William Wilmot, *The Personal Communication Process* (New York: John Wiley, 1973).

30. Dennis S. Gouran and Patricia Hayes Andrews, "Determinants of Punitive Responses to Socially Proscribed Behavior: Seriousness, Attribution of Responsibility, and Status of Offender," *Small Group Behavior* 15 (1984): 524–44.

31. E. P. Hollander, "Conformity, Status, and Idiosyncrasy Credit," *Psychological Review* 65 (1958): 117–27.

32. Phillip K. Tompkins, *Organizational Communication Imperatives: Lessons of the Space Program* (Los Angeles, Calif.: Roxbury, 1993).

33. Patricia Hayes Bradley, C. Mac Hamon, and Alan M. Harris, "Dissent in Small Groups," *Journal of Communication* 26 (1976): 155–59.

34. Kenneth D. Benne and Paul Sheats, "Functional Roles of Group Members," *Journal of Social Issues* 4 (1948): 41–49.

35. John R. P. French and Bernard Raven, "The Social Bases of Power," in *Studies in Social Power,* ed. D. Cartwright (Ann Arbor, Mich.: Institute for Social Research, 1959), pp. 65–84.

36. Dennis S. Gouran and Randy Y. Hirokawa, "Counteractive Functions of Communication in Effective Group Decision-Making," in *Communication and Group Decision-Making,* eds. R. Y. Hirokawa and M. S. Poole (Beverly Hills: Calif.: Sage, 1986), pp. 81–90.

37. Gouran and Andrews, "Determinants of Punitive Responses to Socially Proscribed Behavior."

38. See Tompkins, *Organizational Communication Imperatives;* Jacob Hurwitz and Alvin Zander, "Some Effects of Power in the Relations among Group Members," in *Group Dynamics,* eds. D. Cartwright and A. Zander (New York: Harper & Row, 1960), pp. 483–92.

39. Peter Drucker, *Effective Decisions* (Effective Executive Series, 1968).

40. Shepherd, *Small Groups,* p. 67.

41. William Foster Owen, "Metaphor Analysis of Cohesiveness in Small Discussion Groups," *Small Group Behavior* 16 (1985): 415–24.

42. D. G. Marquis and Kurt Back, "A Social Psychological Study of the Decision-Making Conference," in *Groups, Leadership, and Men,* ed. H. Guetzkow (Pittsburgh: Carnegie Press, 1951), pp. 55–67.

43. Leonard Berkowitz, "Group Norms among Bomber Crews," *Sociometry* 19 (1956): 141–53.

44. Leonard Berkowitz, "Group Standards, Cohesiveness, and Productivity," *Human Relations* 7 (1954): 509–19.

45. Irving Janis, *Groupthink,* 2d ed. (Boston: Houghton Mifflin, 1982), p. 3.

46. See Larry Browning, "Interpreting the *Challenger* Disaster: Communication under Conditions of Risk and Reliability," *Industrial Crisis Quarterly* 2 (1988): 211–27; Dennis S. Gouran, Randy Y. Hirokawa, and Amy E. Martz, "A Critical Analysis of Factors Related to Decisional Processes Involved in the *Challenger* Disaster," *Central States Speech Journal* 37 (1986): 119–35; and Tompkins, *Organizational Communication Imperatives.*

47. Steve M. Alderton and Larry Frey, "Effects of Reactions to Arguments on Group Outcomes," *Central States Speech Journal* 34 (1983): 88–95; David Seibold and Renee Meyers, "Communication and Influence in Group Decision-Making," in *Communication and Group Decision-Making,* eds. R. Y. Hirokawa and M. S. Poole (Beverly Hills, Calif.: Sage Publications, 1986).

48. Janis, *Groupthink.*

49. Ibid., p. 9.

50. Rebecca Cline, "Detecting Groupthink: Methods for Observing the Illusion of Unanimity," *Communication Quarterly* 38 (1990): 112–26.

51. Janis, *Groupthink,* pp. 197–98.

52. Richard C. Huseman and Russell W. Driver, "Groupthink: Implications for Small Group Decision Making in Business," in *Readings in Organizational Behavior: Dimensions of Management Actions,* eds. R. C. Huseman and A. B. Carroll (Boston: Allyn & Bacon, 1979), pp. 100–10.

## Chapter 12

1. Keith Davis, *Human Behavior at Work* (New York: McGraw-Hill, 1972). Note, however, that the distinction can be made between conjunctive tasks (which requires pooling information), at which groups excel, and disjunctive tasks, at which individuals can work quite well alone.

2. Stephen L. Ross, "Creative Problem Solving," in *Organizational Communication,* 2d ed., eds. S. D. Ferguson and S. Ferguson (New Brunswick, N.J.: Transaction Books, 1988), pp. 481–88.

3. Norman R. F. Maier, "Assets and Liabilities in Group Problem-Solving: The Need for an Integrative Function," *Psychological Review* 74 (1967): 239–49.

4. Ibid.

5. Dennis S. Gouran, *Discussion: The Process of Group Decision-Making* (New York: Harper & Row, 1974).

6. Ibid., pp. 66–80.

7. Robert F. Bales and Fred L. Strodtbeck, "Phases in Group Problem-Solving," *Journal of Abnormal and Social Psychology* 46 (1951): 485–95.

8. B. W. Tuckman and M. A. C. Jenson, "Stages of Small-Group Development," *Group and Organizational Studies* 2 (1977): 419–27.

9. Thomas M. Schiedel and Laura Crowell, "Idea Development in Small Groups," *Quarterly Journal of Speech* 50 (1964): 140–45.

10. Marshall Scott Poole, "Decision Development in Small Groups I: A Comparison of Two Models," *Communication Monographs* 50 (1983): 1–24.

11. Marshall Scott Poole and J. Roth, "Decision Development in Small Groups IV: A Typology of Group Decision Paths," *Human Communication Research* 15 (1988): 323–56; Marshall Scott Poole and Carolyn Baldwin, "Developmental Processes in Group Decision Making," in *Communication and Group Decision Making,* eds. R. Hirokawa and M. S. Poole (Thousand Oaks, Calif.: Sage, 1996).

12. Randy Y. Hirokawa and R. Pace, "A Descriptive Investigation of the Possible Communication-Based Reasons for Effective and Ineffective Group Decision Making," *Communication Monographs* 50 (1983): 363–79.

13. Randy Y. Hirokawa, "Group Communication and Problem-Solving Effectiveness: An Investigation of Group Phases," *Human Communication Research* 9 (1983): 291–305.

14. See Dennis S. Gouran, *Making Decisions in Groups: Choices and Consequences* (Prospect Heights, Ill.: Waveland, 1982); Randy Y. Hirokawa and K. Rost, "Effective Group Decision-Making in Organizations," *Management Communication Quarterly* 5 (1992): 267–88; and Randy Y. Hirokawa, Larry Erbert, and Anthony Hurst, "Communication and Group Decision-Making Effectiveness," in *Communication and Group Decision-Making,* 2d ed., eds. R. Y. Hirokawa and M. S. Poole (Thousand Oaks, Calif.: Sage, 1996), pp. 269–300.

15. See Charles Conrad and Marshall Scott Poole, *Strategic Organizational Communication: Into the Twenty-First Century,* 4th ed. (Fort Worth, Tex.: Harcourt Brace College Publishers, 1998).

16. M. D. Cohen, J. G. March, and J. P. Olson, "A Garbage Can Model of Organizational Choice," *Administrative Science Quarterly* 17 (1972): 1–25.

17. Marshall Scott Poole and J. Roth, "Decision Development in Small Groups V: Test of a Contingency Model," *Human Communication Research* 15 (1988): 549–89.

18. P. C. Nutt, "Types of Organizational Decision Processes," *Administrative Science Quarterly* 29 (1984): 414–50.

19. John Dewey, *How We Think* (Boston: Heath, 1910).

20. Gouran, *Discussion*, pp. 76–77.

21. See Lumsden and Lumsden, *Communicating in Groups and Teams*, pp. 205–10.

22. Donald C. Mosley and Thad B. Green, "Nominal Grouping as an Organization Development Intervention Technique," *Training and Development Journal* (March 1974): 30–37.

23. Frederic M. Jablin, David R. Siebold, and Rich L. Sorenson, "Potential Inhibiting Effects of Group Participation on Brainstorming Performance," *Central States Speech Journal* 28 (1977): 113–21; Frederic M. Jablin, "Cultivating Imagination: Factors That Enhance and Inhibit Creativity in Brainstorming Groups," *Human Communication Research* 7 (1981): 245–58.

24. Jay F. Nunamaker, Alan R. Dennis, Joe Valacich, Doug Vogel, and Joey George, "Electronic Meeting Systems to Support Group Work," *Communications of the ACM* 34 (1991): 40–61; also Conrad and Poole, *Strategic Organizational Communication*, pp. 166–85.

25. B. Gallupe, G. DeSantis, and G. Dickson, "The Impact of Computer-Based Support on the Process and Outcomes of Group Decision Making," *MIS Quarterly* 12 (1988): 277–98; Patricia Hayes Andrews and Richard T. Herschel, *Organizational Communication: Empowerment in a Technological Society* (Boston: Houghton Mifflin, 1996), pp. 223–30.

26. Suzanne Herrick-Walker, "The Effect of Group Decision Support Systems on Decision-Making Groups Containing High Communication Apprehensives: Satisfaction, Participation, and Productivity" (unpublished master's thesis, Indiana University, 1991).

27. See Andrews and Herschel, *Organizational Communication*.

28. Jay Nunamaker, A. Dennis, J. Valacich, D. Vogel, and J. George, "Group Support Systems Research: Experience from the Lab and Field," in *Group Support Systems: New Perspectives*, eds. L. M. Jessup and J. S. Valacich (New York: Macmillan, 1993), pp. 78–96.

29. _____. *Electronic Meeting Systems to Support Group Work: Theory and Practice at Arizona* (Arizona Working Paper, University of Arizona, 1990).

30. Nunamaker et al., pp. 78–96. "Group Support Systems Research."

31. Gallupe, DeSantis, and Dickson, "The Impact of Computer-Based Support."

32. Richard T. Herschel and Patricia Hayes Andrews, "Empowering Employees in Group Work: A Case for Using Group Support Systems," *Information Strategy: The Executive's Journal* 9 (1993): 36–42.

33. David Kirkpatrick, "Here Comes the Payoff from PCs," *Fortune* 23 (March 1992): 93–100.

34. N. Wrenden, "Regrouping for Groupware," *Beyond Computing* 2 (1993): 52–55.

## Chapter 13

1. John Naisbitt, *Megatrends: Ten New Directions Transforming Our Lives* (New York: Warner Books, 1982), p. 159.

2. Allan Cox, *The Cox Report on the American Corporation* (New York: Delacorte, 1982), p. 136.

3. Perry Pascarella, *The New Achievers: Creating a Modern Work Ethic* (New York: Free Press, 1984), p. 106.

4. B. Y. Auger, "Staff Meetings: Energy Waste or Catalyst for High Performance," *Data Management* 20 (May 1980): 39–41.

5. Allan D. Frank, "Trends in Communication: Who Talks to Whom?" *Personnel* 62 (December 1985): 41–47.

6. For example, see William G. Dyer, *Team Building: Issues and Alternatives* (Reading, Mass.: Addison-Wesley, 1977).

7. Robert F. Littlejohn, "Team Management: A How-To Approach to Improved Productivity, Higher Morale, and Longer Lasting Job Satisfaction," *Management Review* 71 (January 1982): 23–28.

8. "Manage Meeting Malcontents," *Communication Briefings* 17: 4 (November 1998), p. 1.

9. For example, see General Henry M. Robert, *Robert's Rules of Order Newly Revised* (Glenview, Ill.: Scott, Foresman, 1970); Alice Sturgis, *Sturgis Standard Code of Parliamentary Procedure*, 2d ed. (New York: McGraw-Hill, 1966); John E. Baird, *A Guide to Conducting Meetings* (New York: Abingdon Press, 1965).

10. Mildred Culp, "Cyber Meetings: Showing Off the Latest Way of Showing Up," *Chicago Tribune* May 24, 1998), sec. 6, p. 21.

11. James Creighton and James Adams, "CyberMeeting: How to Link People and

Technology in Your Organization," AMACOM, 1998.

12. Charlene Marmer Solomon, "Make the Most of Teleconferencing," Global Workforce 3:6 (November 1998), 14.

## Chapter 14

1. Chester Bernard, *The Functions of the Executive* (Cambridge, Mass.: Harvard University Press, 1950), p. 14.

2. Bernard Berelson and Gary A. Steiner, *Human Behavior: An Inventory of Scientific Findings* (New York: Harcourt Brace Jovanovich, 1964), p. 588.

3. Theodore Herbert, *Dimensions of Organizational Behavior* (New York: Macmillan, 1976), p. 347.

4. William Evan, "Conflict and Performance in R&D Organizations," *Industrial Management Review* 7 (1965): 35–46.

5. Rensis Likert, *New Patterns of Management* (New York: McGraw-Hill, 1961).

6. Lewis M. Killian, "the Significance of Multiple-Group Membership in Disaster," *American Journal of Sociology* 57 (1952): 309–14.

7. From Kare Anderson, *Getting What You Want: How to Reach Agreement and Resolve Conflict Every Time* (New York: Penguin Books, 1993).

8. "How to Deal with Conflict," *Communication Briefings* XV: 1 (1998), 1.

9. Robert R. Blake and Jane S. Mouton, *The Managerial Grid* (Houston, Tex.: Gulf, 1964).

10. J. Hall and W. H. Watson, "The Effects of a Normative Intervention on Group Decision-Making Performance," *Human Relations* 23 (1970): 299–317.

11. G. Northcraft and M. Neale, *Organizational Behavior* (Chicago: Dryden Press, 1990).

12. David A. Whetton and Kim S. Cameron, *Developing Management Skills*, 2d ed. (New York: Harper-Collins, 1991).

13. J. E. McGrath, *Groups: Interaction and Performance* (Englewood Cliffs, N.J.: Prentice-Hall, 1984).

14. Roger Fisher and William Ury, "Getting to Yes," *Management Review* 48 (1982): 16–21.

15. A. Douglas, *Industrial Peacemaking* (New York: Columbia University Press, 1962).

16. D. M. Kolb, *The Mediators* (Cambridge, Mass.: MIT Press, 1983).

17. M. S. Poole, M. Holmes, and G. DeSanctis, "Conflict Management in a Computer-Supported Meeting Environment," *Management Science* 8 (1991): 926–53.

18. J. A. Savage, "Unions Cutting Bargain with High-Technology 'Devil'" *Computerworld* 24: 1 (July 23, 1990): 115.

19. Mark Estes, "Adversaries Find Common Ground," *Workforce* 76: 3 (March 1997): 97.

# Photo Credits

# Name Index

# Subject Index